YOUNG SAN FRANCISCAN SANDBOXES
From the Mud Grew Lotuses

YOUNG SAN FRANCISCAN SANDBOXES

From the Mud Grew Lotuses

TERENCE QUINLAN

RICHARD CAÑAS

BARRY SULLIVAN

Book orders: visit www.quinlanbook.com or www.sandbox.com
Information: itfma@sbcoxmail.com

ISBN 978-0-9850047-0-5

Editor: Susan Quinlan

Printed in the United States of America

Table of Content

Age 13: I Am Those Around Me (continued)

High School – The Most Important Sandbox (1954-1958)

Indexes

Names of Places, Attractions and Entertainment Index

Street Addresses Index

Preface

It was a special time in a special place, never before seen and never again to be experienced. It was San Francisco at its best. It was a time that allowed a kid to become all that he could be, with or without the help and guidance from parents and others. This is a story about kids who grew up in the Golden Age of San Francisco in the 1940s and 1950s and three particular "brothers" who came from completely different backgrounds – an immigrant Latino kid from El Salvador who spoke no English, a kid from a low income Irish family in the Mission District with an alcoholic father, and a kid from a middle income family in the Sunset District with an abusive father with excessive expectations. Each of the "brothers" was raised by one strong parent figurehead and blessed with the right attitude, determination, and lady luck in their corner in order for each to overcome their own handicaps and to succeed in their own ways during two of the best decades in San Francisco history.

The times we lived in were exceptional, special and unique in many ways. They were the best of times. If there were negatives, they stemmed from things beyond our control, such as, the inability to choose our parents, cruel classmates, or the innate stupidity from being young. The freedom, independence, opportunities, friendships, schools, teachers, coaches and unique features of San Francisco provided the closest a kid could ever get to Shangri-La or Camelot.

It was an era unlike any other. Many grandparents lived through the hardships of the First World War. Parents lived with the challenges of the Great Depression in the 30s. The same parents and their children survived the sacrifices made in the Second World War. And many of us were children of immigrants to the U.S. who started with nothing. We came from a humble background but tough stock. We adapted to living without things, thought nothing of living in lower class neighborhoods, found our own ways to cope with being a have-not, and overcame challenges to rise to a much higher level. This is the story of those kids' journey through remarkable times in San Francisco history. This is the story of one of those kids, the "brother" he never had, and another "brother" who was the mirror image of his life rising from nothing to someone who came a long way. The journey included their best friends and classmates through grammar school and high school – their critical formative years. The local radio personality Don Sherwood signed off each morning, "Out of the mud grows the lotus," which served as a constant reminder of my humble roots to self-motivate myself throughout my youth. Those roots were nurtured and built upon as I grew to excel in what I put my mind to do.

For 18 years, my generation moved in and out of different "sandboxes" (environments). We were born at the beginning of WWII to parents, many of whom were immigrants, who started with little and worked hard throughout our youth to provide the best for their children. We lived in the aftermath of a war where we developed a patriotism and pride in our country. We learned to appreciate the simple things in life coming out of a period of sacrifice and rationing during the war. San Francisco provided so many interesting experiences, opportunities and dedicated teachers for kids to meet their potential. We were fortunate to experience a life of sacrifices to be motivated to do better than our parents. Opportunities allowed us at an early age to work part-time to be financially independent and lighten the load on our folks. Parents stressed the need for a good education and enrolled us in schools that provided discipline, Christian values, quality education and an environment that surrounded us with kids who had a good influence on us – a pool of good kids for establishing lasting friendships. Most importantly, we felt free as young kids. We had parents who gave us the independence to explore on our own. We could walk and ride our bikes all over. We were allowed to make our own decisions to learn from our successes and failures to build self-confidence.

Our youth was actually spent in three "sandboxes" during the years that shaped and determined the adults that we became. In each sandbox, we learned and adopted different interests, habits, qualities, virtues and values. We also made different mistakes, which we learned not to repeat. The first sandbox was the one at the playground and its surroundings up to age five. The next sandbox was grammar school and the neighborhood to age 14, and the last sandbox was our high school and the City of San Francisco to age 17 or 18. The kids that emerged from those sandboxes are the adults we are today. Along the way, I concluded that "the meaning of life" was that this life is our only chance at heaven, as we envision it. This is the story of my journey along with my "brothers," friends and classmates that shared that journey. Each of us was in the same or similar sandboxes, but we all turned out differently but similar in some respects for the better. We were no angels, but that was not a prerequisite to enter my heaven.

This is a book about kids, for kids. We all faced challenges, albeit different challenges, during our childhood. Some had greater handicaps than others, whether they were physical, racial, mental, social, parental or financial. Some wound up bigger winners than others. But as the cliché goes, "It is not who wins and loses but how you play the game." It was why "C" students could be bigger "winners" than the "A" students – because they started out with bigger handicaps. The fastest kid in the class is always going to win the race, but he seldom improves his time much.

The slower kids can improve their times considerably, so their personal goals are so often exceeded. This book is about kids blessed with growing up in the best possible "sandbox" of a city, which kids today do not have a chance to experience, and about our challenges, joys, sorrows, successes and failures from which today's kids can learn from to "get it right" for themselves and make fewer mistakes than us. Even parents and teachers might benefit from this story. Welcome to my sandboxes!

As I was bouncing head over heals down the front steps of our home at six months of age, I should have known then that there were going to be a lot of bumps along the way of growing up, but let me start from the beginning. Being born was the most unlikely event outside of the unlikelihood of a long life. There were so many coincidences that needed to occur for one to be born and so many things we did that could take our life prematurely. In my case, I owed my life to a devastating fire, the loss of two lives, an unintentional conception, and a wrong career choice by a parent.

Before My Time: Lifetime Shaped by Tragedy (1902-1940)

Mom was born in February 1902 in Tralee, County Kerry, Ireland. Her name was Catherine Frances Collins, but she went by "Frances" all her life. Her friends called her "Francie." Dad was born in May 1901 in Tralee, County Kerry, Ireland. His name was Patrick Joseph Quinlan and everyone called him "Pat." His father, Maurice, was the principal and he taught the 3 R's of reading, writing and arithmetic at O'Brennan Boys School in Tralee. Mom and Dad became friends at age 10, went steady at age 18, and got married at age 29. It was the events during their 11-year courtship that had the greatest effect on the lives of the Quinlan family.

During the 1919-1923 Irish revolutionary period in Ireland in the fight for Irish independence from the British, there were hundreds of houses deliberately burned down, blown up, or otherwise destroyed by the Irish Republican Army (IRA) and pro-British Black and Tans. Most of them were destroyed during the Irish Civil War (1922-1923). [1] Many of the burnings were carried out by the IRA, either to deny the structures as billets to the British forces or as reprisals for the Black and Tans burning of dwellings and other properties of IRA activists and supporters. [2]

Mom's parents had a grocery store on the first floor, and they lived above the store on Upper Castle Street in the town of Tralee. The building caught fire on December 30, 1922. Mom said the Black and Tans possibly set the fire because they suspected a member of the IRA might be sheltered there. Another possibility was that the fire was tied to her dad's (Eugene Collins) scheduled court appearance to testify against a military police lieutenant who on December 8 fired warning shots in a hall at a church bazaar, causing panic and a near stampede, while killing an unarmed

1

young civilian in a struggle for the officer's weapon. [3] Everyone got out of the fire except her dad who was trying to retrieve the money in the store and save the books as some customers still owed him money. Mom's 15-year-old sister Lil (Bridget Elizabeth) went back in to save her dad but both were trapped and died in the fire. He was 60 years old. The tragedy made Mom want to leave Ireland forever to escape the memories.

At the time of the fire, Mom and Dad had been going steady for a couple of years. Mom insisted they move to the United States to get away from all the reminders of the fire and family tragedy. There was a large presence of Irish residents in the U.S. who had arrived from Ireland in the 1920s. Although a lot of the Irish settled in New York and Chicago, most seemed to be settling in San Francisco, which was one of the reasons Mom and Dad chose to move there. Also Dad's sisters had talked about leaving the Old Country and they liked San Francisco too. So nearly four years after the fire, Dad at age 25 left from the cruise port of Cobh in County Cork and arrived in New York City in August 1926 on the ship *RMS Adriatic*. Dad's two sisters Margaret Quinlan (Sullivan) and Hannah Quinlan (Prendiville) came out from Ireland about a year after he arrived in San Francisco. The Irish tended to settled near their relatives in the U.S.

Dad got a job as a salesman in men's wear at O'Connor, Moffat & Co. on lower Stockton Street, which became Macy's in 1945. Later he was a salesman in the linen department at the City of Paris where he became the assistant buyer and in line for a promotion to buyer.

Dad was in San Francisco for four years after he proposed marriage before he sent for Mom. Mom came to the U.S. in 1930 by boat to New York City, and took the train to Oakland, CA where Dad met her. In New York, members of an Irish society met her and helped her with her train connections. She was sick on the boat and train, but as soon as she set foot in San Francisco, she said to herself, "This is where I belong. I will never leave it." She never had any desire to go back to Ireland, she was never homesick, nor did she ever return, "Because the memories were too sad." But Dad was homesick until the day he died. He wanted them to return to Ireland. Mom would have none of it. She told him if he went back, she would move to New York where she had relatives. Dad backed off and never mentioned it again.

2

Mom stayed with Alex and Theresa Cronin in the Richmond District and had a job in a dress store until she got married in San Francisco February 1931 and stopped working. Witnesses were Pat Ahern, who lived on 22nd Avenue off Balboa Street, and Dad's sister Margaret Quinlan, who lived on the corner of Ulloa and Wawona Streets. Initially, Mom and Dad lived in a flat way out in the Richmond District and then moved to the Mission District, which took its name from Mission Dolores that was established under Father Junipero Serra and located on Dolores Street between 16th and 17th Streets. The Mission District was bounded by Dolores Street on the west, Potrero Avenue on the east, Army Street (Cesar Chavez) on the south, and 14th Street on the north. "The Mission District was one of only a few neighborhoods in the City that was not burned to the ground in the 1906 earthquake fires that destroyed so many of the neighborhoods. Those from burned-out areas moved to the Mission and pushed out the middle class families that had occupied the neighborhood, making it into a low-income working class neighborhood and the most heavily Irish populated area of San Francisco. This migration of Irish families extended to Noe Valley, Eureka Valley, Potrero Hill, Bernal Heights and Glen Park. Many Italian immigrants also moved into the Mission after 1906." [4]

Mom and Dad applied for U.S. citizenship in 1932 and became U.S. citizens in 1937. Dad was 36 years old, 159 pounds and 5'8". Mom was 35 years old, 134 pounds and exactly 5'0" tall, the same height (5' 1/2") as actress Mary Pickford – something Mom mentioned with great pride whenever the subject of her height came up. They lived in the Mission District on Folsom Street between 21st and 22nd Streets from 1932 to 1940 when Dad was selling men's clothing.

Mom and Dad only wanted two children. She had given birth to my brother Patrick Joseph Quinlan Jr. in 1932 and to my sister Kathleen in 1934. My brother went by "Joe" so not to be confused with Dad who had the same first name. So when Mom got pregnant in 1940 at the age of 39, life changed a lot for the family. Never could anyone have foreseen how much and how negatively the changes would be. They moved a half a block away to a larger flat on Folsom Street at the corner of 21st Street for extra room to accommodate a family of five. The rent was higher and there would be the added expense of raising a third child, something they had not foreseen. Mom was not working because she was raising two children and men's retail stores did not pay their employees well, so Dad felt pressured to make ends meet.

A good friend of Dad from Ireland, Dan McCarthy, had come to San Francisco to open a bar. Dad knew him when they were growing up in County Kerry. Dan had opened his first bar on Mission Street called McCarthy's Big Glass in 1936. He was an early contributor to creating the eventual reputation of San Francisco having more bars per capita than any other city in the U.S. The bar catered to a working class, with a large Irish clientele and many in the local unions. They served a mug of beer, a large hot dog, and a bowl of beans for 15 cents. Over the years Dan opened other bars at 4th Street and 8th and Market Streets. Years later, Dan's son Leo McCarthy served as Lieutenant Governor of California in 1983-1994 and defeated the notorious Willie Brown for the position of Assembly Speaker. Along the way, Leo got my brother Joe a job as Sergeant of Arms in the State Legislature, where he worked all his life.

Dad frequently stopped by McCarthy's bar for a drink, and one day he was talking to Dan about his need for a better paying job and Dan offered him a job. The money would be better than he was paid at the City of Paris, especially when you add in tips. Dad came home to ask Mom first, and she said, "No. I don't want you to work in a bar because you are not the type of man to work in taverns." He did not listen to her and took the job offer. Years later Mom said that was a huge mistake and tragedy due to the physical and mental effects that life style had on the family and on Dad over the rest of his life. She always said she wished he had stayed in the men's clothing business or anything other than bartending.

I will never know if he took the job mainly due to the financial pressures of raising a third child or if he saw the job as a way of reliving his life in Ireland by surrounding himself with the Irish, "drinking with the boys," meeting those just out from the Old Country with the latest news, and living a life of free drinks from customers. If it was due to financial pressures, it would mean that he did it for a noble cause and he should be commended. That was what I always liked to think was the case. But it also meant that it was my birth and me that led him to accept a job that contributed to a life of alcoholism and mental institutions.

Pre-School Years: The First Sandbox (1940-1945)

On November 15, 1940, I was born at St. Mary's Hospital (Stanyan and Hayes Streets) in San Francisco, the hospital of choice for a lot of Irish Catholics in the City. "Terrance" was the name on my birth certificate, probably because a hospital receptionist guessed at the typical spelling of the name. My mother intended it to be spelled as "Terence." "Terence" was from an Irish name meaning "one who aids or assists." Mom said that I was named after a famous Irish author and Mayor of Cork, Terence MacSwiney. "His hunger strike and death brought worldwide attention to Ireland's freedom struggle against the British Empire." [5] With all of the talk and riots over Terence MacSwiney's hunger strike and his name in the newspapers in 1920 when Mom was nearly 19 years old, it was natural for Mom to still remember his name when years later she was given the chance to name the second son in the family since the first son was named after Dad. Somehow, my name was spelled and appeared as "Terence" all of my life and no one ever challenged the spelling or had a need to compare it to my birth certificate. Mom's stay in the hospital for my birth was only eight hours. Those were the days of getting people in and out as soon as possible. As I learned years later, I was not a planned birth. Mom said she did not want me because they were too old at 39 to raise a third child. Mom was smart enough to wait to tell me this until I was in my mid-twenties so I held no resentment or let it affect my love for both of them. So often during the remainder of my life I thought how grateful I was for being an "accident." I may never have been born and never experienced all the wonderful things in life. Knowing how easily it could have been that I was never born helped motivate me to appreciate life more and to do whatever was necessary to succeed and make my folks proud in return.

My birth was the very beginning of my life and the life of my family, as I would know it. Knowledge of everything prior to that point in time was mostly lost forever. A big regret of mine was that I never made an effort to have Mom and Dad tell me about their lives prior to my birth and the reasons for the many decisions both made along the way. They told us a few stories about the Old Country, but not many. Later in life, I found this true of most people I knew. Children knew nearly nothing about the early lives of their parents and adults knew little about the early lives of their spouses. It was as if when one was born or got married, there was no interest in the parent or spouse prior to their birth or marriage. Unless a child asked their parents about their earlier life, most parents went to their grave without their children knowing anything about their youth as if the parents never lived those earlier years. It was a sad omen about mankind.

We lived in a three-unit set of flats at the corner of 21st and Folsom Streets over a store. Owners of the building were the Saccos, an Italian family that lived in one of the other flats. They never raised the rent on us the entire 12 years we lived there. Mom said they were more interested in keeping good tenants.

Lessons From a Near-Death Experience

When I was six months old, my six-year-old sister Kathy was carrying me down the stairs to the front door on our way to have my first picture taken in front of our house. I guess I got upset at her for waking me up from my nap because I started to make a fuss by kicking and twisting. With 15-20 steps still to descend, Kathy accidentally dropped me and I tumbled to the bottom of the steps. Fortunately, the steps were carpeted and I was no worse for the wear as evident by my smiling face in the picture that was taken shortly afterwards. But over the years, I often thought back how my life could have ended that day. I know that memory made me work harder to make my life worthwhile, and I must have known then that life was going to be filled with surprises and challenges and that I would need a lot of luck and independence by relying less on others and more on myself if I was going to make it in this world.

My earliest recollections and favorite form of play started at age one when Mom played "Rock-a-bye Baby" or sang to me. She put me on her lap and recited, "Rock-a-bye baby on the tree top, when the wind blows, the cradle will rock. When the bow breaks, the cradle will fall. Down will come baby, cradle and all." At that moment, she spread her legs and I fell toward the ground. Of course Mom held on to me, so only my feet hit the floor. She and I would laugh so loud every time, no matter how many times we played this in a row – usually until Mom got tired. What had the greatest impact on me at such an early age was hearing Mom sing Irish songs to me, and listening to Irish music that always gave me a sense of connection with our family history and Irish roots. Mom rested my head on her chest and sang Irish lullabies to me. It was her way of passing on some Irish heritage, and it certainly enforced my pride in being Irish. My favorites were "Danny Boy," "That's an Irish Lullaby" (Too-Ra-Loo-Ra-Loo-Ra), "Galway Bay," "My Wild Irish Rose," and "The Rose of Tralee" (where Mom and Dad grew up).

Mom did not tell her kids many stories about her days in Ireland due to her sad memories about her dad and sister and the fire, but she did tell her kids a few at an early age, especially about four-leaf clovers and the leprechauns. The legend of the four-leaf clover was that if you found one, it would bring you good luck – a belief ingrained in the Irish. She told us

7

leprechauns were very small men who never came out during the day – only at night. They could be seen by moonlight in the ditches along the roadside. She claimed that she saw them too. Her story was so convincing that my brother still believed in them at age 50. When I questioned why all those years he thought leprechauns existed, he said, "Mom never lied to me, so I believed the stories had to be true."

Mom was a woman very set in her ways. It was her way or no way. Mom put me to bed right after dinner at 6:00 p.m. every evening. She never allowed visitors to the house to peek into the bedroom to see me sleeping at night or during my daytime naps. She was as protective when Joe and Kathy also were very young. She always said her children needed a good night's sleep and insisted that no one disturb our sleep. Although Catholics were raised with pictures of children and adults saying their prayers on their knees, Mom never required me to do the same. I slept in a crib, so Mom lifted me up and over the railing to put me to bed. As I lay in the crib on my back, Mom listened until I finished my nightly prayers: "Now I lay me down to sleep. I pray the Lord my soul to keep. If I should die before I wake, I pray to God my soul to take."

Mom was protective of us kids in other ways. She refused to let strangers take care of her children. As a result, she did not attend a lot of the picnics, dances and other social events conducted by the Hibernians (Ancient Order of the Hibernians), which was an Irish Catholic fraternal organization that held social events to bring the Irish together and to provide financial assistance to immigrants from Ireland. The one and only exception was the time Mom and Dad attended an Irish banquet. Dad got a woman who dropped in to McCarthy's occasionally to take care of me that night. Before leaving, Mom saw my babysitter go into the kitchen pantry. Mom knew she was hiding something. She asked Dad if the woman drank, and he said, "She likes a drink, but I wouldn't let that worry you." Mom was worried the whole time and gave Dad quite a bad time about her concern the entire evening. As a result, they came home early and Mom found the woman passed out from drinking from the whiskey bottle Dad kept in the pantry for entertaining guests. Never again did Mom let anyone babysit me.

By age 3, taking a bath was becoming a chore and interfering with my playtime. So as an incentive for me to stop making a fuss about bathing and being scrubbed by Mom, she introduced me to bubble baths. I loved creating towers and buildings made of different sized mounds of foam. Later I brought boats from my toy box along with me so I could run them through the mounds of bubbles as if they were sailing through river passages. My favorite boat was one that ran on vinegar and baking soda. Vinegar was added to baking soda placed in a compartment that created a gas that propelled the boat forward.

One day Mom was starching some white shirts for Dad in a large pan of boiling water and starch on the kitchen counter. She left the room for only a moment, and not knowing what she was doing and what was in the pan, I reached up and grabbed the side of the pan to pull myself up for a better view. The pan tipped over and the boiling content poured over my head and shoulders. My life-long badges of courage were two-inch patch-shaped scars on my right shoulder and right side of my chest.

Growing up while World War II (WWII) was going on and having the war end before I was five years old was probably a blessing and a curse. The Mission District was like an island for me where I was completely unaware of things that were going on around the City. Especially in the early days of WWII, there were some concerns about the Japanese coming across the Pacific Ocean and attacking the West Coast, which resulted in evening blackouts. There was an eerie quiet in the streets and darkness in the houses. Streetcars often ran with their interior lights turned off and the headlights were shielded. I was in bed before the evening blackouts were enforced and the searchlights were turned on in search of enemy planes. There were air raid sirens being tested during the day, but they meant nothing since they were not for real. I did not see the Japanese in the City being uprooted and moved out of state, the movement of military trucks around the Presidio and Fort Mason, the war ships sailing in and out under the Golden Gate and San Francisco-Oakland Bay Bridges, the wounded coming and going at Letterman's Hospital, or the sailors and soldiers on leave along Market Street and in the North Beach area.

When the Germans surrendered in May 1945 and the war was finally over, I was completely unaware of the people out in the streets celebrating and beeping their car horns in the other parts of the City. By not being older, I missed out on the patriotism for the U.S. that one developed when our country was at war, people making sacrifices, soldiers getting killed, and the military winning battles. On the other hand, being raised later on war movies and newsreels at the theaters, and later on television, instilled a strong patriotism in my buddies and me that lasted a lifetime. The movies contributed to a strong respect for the American flag, the military and winning. We always beat the enemy. The U.S. was always the good guys fighting for all the right things – things important to Americans. We fought fairly and had strong bonds between our war buddies – the idea of always bringing back our injured and killed.

Due to the WW II war effort, certain foods were being rationed. It started in 1942, lasted through the war, and it pretty much ended in 1946. Families received ration books that contained different colored stamps good for different rationed goods, such as sugar, meat, and canned goods. Mom had to give the grocer the specific stamp for the item or she could not buy it. Even at age three, I could tell that the family was affected by the war that was going on. I heard Mom and Dad talking about not being able to find certain food on the shelves. I was now at the age of rummage-ing through drawers out of curiosity. I ran across the ration books and was flipping through the pages of colored stamps when Mom said, "Stop playing with them. Those stamps are like money and not to be played with." She stopped leaving the books around for me to find again.

Folsom Park: The Playground Sandbox

Mom insisted all of her children got lots of fresh air. She did not roll us around in a stroller, but we lived across the street from Folsom Park (now Jose Coronado Park), and that was where we went to get fresh air. Mom took me to the kid's section of the playground every day. The kid's section was about 55' x 30' and had a 3-foot-high cement wall that ran along the west and north sides of the area, which contained a sandbox with benches on two sides for parents to watch their kids, a wood slide, metal monkey bars, a set of four or five swings, and a large thick cement table top for playing games. Initially, I just played in the sandbox. It was only later that I was big enough for the slide and tall enough to reach and swing on the bars. I preferred the sandbox to be my own play world and got annoyed if another kid got in with me. I eventually got used to sharing the box, but I continued playing by myself in my world. There were four drain holes – one on each side of the sandbox floor. The challenge was to dig through the sand to find the holes, which was a great achievement, because in the hole was a wet clay that provided an ideal mud when mixed with sand to create things. A 12-inch cement ledge ran around the eight-sided sandbox where I could build my houses, forts and mountains. If the clay was too wet from rain, I learned to sprinkle dry sand on my creation to solidify it. When Mom thought I had played enough, she had me sit and rest on the bench with her to watch other kids play in the sandbox and Park.

The time came when I felt the kid's sandbox was just for little kids. So I spent less time there and more time playing on other contraptions – the slide, metal monkey bars and swings. This was a larger sandbox as the ground was all covered with white sand to help prevent kids from getting hurt. The slide was made of wood, so the surface was not very slick, especially after a rain. I did not care that I did not zip down the slide. It was fast enough. Rather than climb the stairs to get to the top of the slide like the other kids, I preferred climbing up the crisscross support beams of the slide to get to the top. It was different and more challenging. As I got a little older and the slide was too slow for me to descend, I used a piece of cardboard under me to go down much faster. The slide gave me a chance to be different. I could run up from the bottom of the slide and pull myself up the rest of the way to the top. The Park director was always yelling at me to stop it and to climb up the steps like the other kids.

I loved playing on the metal monkey bars, going across one hand at a time or shimmying along as I ran my hands along the two sides. As I got older and my arms got longer, I could skip every other bar to get across twice as fast. When others were not using the bars, I could hang upside down with my legs wrapped over one bar and my feet tucked under another. Looking at the world upside down was different and weird – seemed like a grownup thing to do.

The swings were my favorite. They were rubber baskets with holes in the front and back to slip my legs through so I did not fall off. By rocking myself I could swing as high as possible but never feared that I would do a 360-degree loop, hard as I might try. The older kids sat on the upper rim of the basket because they had gotten too big to stick their legs through the holes. Of course, my buddies and I had to follow suit and do the same so we could act older. The fun from sitting on top of the basket was to see who could swing as high as possible and jump off and land the furthest from the swings. It was a constant competition with different winners most of the time. Again, the Park director was always yelling for us to get off because "You are going to break the swing," but we never listened. So part of playing in the kid's area was to keep an eye open for the director so we could have our fun while breaking the rules, which made us feel like teenagers. Although the Park had a regular director, occasionally there were fill-in replacements that could be spotted by the felt armband they wore with "Director" printed on it. It was their badge of authority and we knew who to go to for help like when the big kids kicked us off the basketball court.

As I got older, my favorite game in the kid's area was playing tag, but we could not touch the ground. We confined ourselves to the kid's area where we could avoid being tagged by climbing along the chain-link fences on the sides of the area, run on top of the sandbox and along the benches surrounding the sandbox, and jumping onto the slide, metal bars, cement game table and swings. The game exercised every part of our body. I always wished all the adults and other kids would get out and let us take over for our game of tag.

Whenever I was sick, I had to stay in bed all day with no exceptions. Meals were served on a tray. I felt so special being waited on hand and foot. Mom brought me hot tea all day. The Irish believed that hot tea was the cure-all for all ailments. The tea had to be boiling hot. Hot Lipton tea was the house brand. Mom felt that Lipton tea was the only tea in the U.S. that tasted like the tea in Ireland. Everyone in the family drank tea with sugar and milk. The only exception was Dad's coffee with sugar and cream in the morning. Hot tea was the medicine for upset stomachs and for curing colds – the more tea during the day, the better. A hot water bottle was used to keep our feet warm to avoid chills. It was a household without drugs and medicines – a habit I lived by my entire life. We relied solely on the remedies used in the Old Country.

Whiskey was also the medicine for lots of ailments in our household – another Irish custom. For earaches, whiskey was applied in the ear with a Q-tip swab of cotton. For a toothache, we swished an ounce of whiskey around the ache, but I was not allowed to swallow it. For cuts, whiskey was used as a disinfectant. For adults, it was used to warm up the body on cold days. Cod liver oil was the "vitamin pill" of our family. Besides the value from the vitamins, Mom said, "It is like oiling all the parts of the body, and it makes them work better." Another word of advice was "Never put anything in your ear deeper than your elbow will go."

Grammar School Years: The Second Sandbox (1945-1954)

Family Peculiarities and Values

Whether or not an obsessive-compulsive disorder ran in the family, we certainly lived with compulsive behaviors involving orderliness and following a strict routine. Mom was compulsively neat and the house was always clean. Dad was compulsive about checking that the doors were locked, chain was on the front door, and all the gas burners on the stove were turned off each evening before going to bed. This went on every night of my childhood. Mom said checking the stove was a carry over from the constant memory of her family members being killed in the 1922 fire, which meant the compulsive action was Mom's idea. After a while, it just became a habit and nightly routine for Dad. I later developed traits to be a perfectionist, in control, counting things encountered each day, and putting things in specific orders, whether they were on a shelf, in drawers or hanging in a closet. I suspect that I got those habits from Mom.

Mom's manner of dress was always immaculate. I suppose it might be considered a compulsive behavior too. Appearances were important to her. She always was well dressed, whether it was going shopping, to work, to church or visiting others. She always wore a dress, one-inch heel dress shoes and a hat wherever she went. She said, "A woman is not completely dressed unless she wears a hat." Buying a new hat seemed to be one of the highlights of the year for her, especially since it was not an annual treat. Like Mom, "Dad was an impeccable and snappy dresser ever since his younger days," according to Mom. He always wore a three-piece suit, tie and felt fedora hat. He nearly always wore long johns, especially at work where the front door of the bar was always letting in cold air with the coming and going of customers.

Mom, Dad and us kids were not known for expressing or showing our emotions. No one ever said, "I love you." No one ever cried in front of the others. Our family was not huggers. That was why I felt so uncomfortable as I was growing up when I found relative strangers or people I saw once a year hugging me when we met. They were always adults. I would not have minded it so much if it was a young, good-looking girl, but that was never the case.

14

Dad was a quiet man who grew quieter with time. A customer at work once said he looked like Humphrey Bogart, which brought a smile and a proud look on his face when he asked me years later if I also thought so too. I told him there was a resemblance, which was true. What was even truer was that Mom looked very much like Queen Elizabeth, the Queen Mother of England, not only in facial features, but Mom was only two inches shorter than the 5'2" Queen Mother and both wore hats everywhere.

Dad mostly worked the night shift during the 35 years he was at McCarthy's. I suspect it was his way of never having left Ireland where drinking and mingling with his cronies was the thing for Irish immigrants to do. I grew up without seeing much of him. He often got home well after 2:00 a.m. and was gone the next day by 3:00 p.m., so he was seldom around in the afternoon or evening when I was home from school. Mom said years later that he should have been a priest. At first I thought she was referring to bedroom issues as she said he never saw her naked in their 40-plus years of marriage because "That is just how things were," meaning that was how she was raised. Later I realized that her reference to Dad being a priest had more to do with his avoidance of the every day tasks expected of a husband and father. He chose a life where he was rarely around for Mom or the kids. He took no responsibility for things that needed to be done around the house. Mom was the rock that held the family together, shouldered all of the responsibilities, raised the kids, and eventually went to work to help pay the bills. He was not the type to take us kids places, probably because he had few interests outside of drinking, horse races and Irish football.

Throughout the 1940s and 1950s, Christmas and Thanksgiving dinner rotated among the houses of our relatives, who all came from Ireland. There were the Quinlan's (our house), Margaret (Dad's sister) and Eugene Sullivan, Hannah (Dad's sister) and Jim Prendiville, and Katherine "Kay" (daughter of Hannah and Jim) and Johnnie Braga. My favorite was Aunt Hannah and Jim Prendiville on Army Street [I was disappointed when the street name was changed to Cesar Chavez Boulevard years later because it took away some of our family history and memories] because their entire family was sure to be there. There were a couple of hours of chips and dip, simple hors d'oeuvres, and drinking before dinner – mostly whiskey and other alcohol for the adults. There was no heavy drinking – maybe a couple of highballs each. Liquor was never served to anyone under 21. Meals were so special because they were so elaborate compared to our day-to-day meals. There was turkey, dressing, cranberry sauce, baked ham, mashed potatoes, gravy, various vegetables (at least one I liked such as peas, carrots, spinach), olives, pickles, and two or three desserts, often brought by the guests. Everyone at the dinner table was Irish Catholics. Before each meal, the person at the head of the table, always the male host, led us in saying grace, which was preceded and followed by the Sign of the Cross. We all bowed our heads and prayed along: "Bless us O Lord and these Thy gifts, which we are about to receive from Thy bounty through Christ our Lord. Amen." It was a prayer we all learned back in kindergarten and it stayed with us all our lives. I kept waiting for someone over the years to recite a different prayer, but it never happened, probably because others would not be able to join in the praying.

Each of our houses had small living rooms, so people sat in an oval. There was always lots of laughing and only one person spoke at a time. There were seldom two conversations going on at the same time. There was no talking over someone else. This way everyone could focus on the speaker, and I being the youngest, could get to know everyone better. Kids were expected to sit with the adults – not go in another room by themselves. This made it possible to get to know their relatives and appreciate them more. They always let the kids join in the conversation. It made us feel like we were part of the family. It also helped the kids get over their shyness around adults. Jim Prendiville was always asked to recite a lengthy Irish verse or two. They lasted 5-10 minutes and they were all done from memory. I was always so impressed that he could recite all of this from memory since he was not an actor or university professor. He actually worked for the San Francisco Municipal Railway (Muni). I always thought he was in the wrong line of business. Years later he left his wife Hannah and moved back to Ireland after 40-50 years of marriage. Supposedly he was homesick for the Old Country the entire time he was in this country, which was pretty common for a lot of the guys including my dad.

Aunt Hannah had seven children over a period of nine years. Mom used to shake her head in sympathy when she mentioned it to us. Mom never mentioned she also came from parents in Ireland who had seven children over 11 years and Dad from parents who had nine children over 14 years. Norah was a daughter who was mentally challenged but the sweetest person. Their son Mossie (short for Maurice) worked his entire life at the U.S. Mint in San Francisco and never got married. He was a big husky guy, probably very strong from pushing around the carts of coins at the Mint, but always extremely soft spoken and a really gentle soul. Just before he retired, he was found under the freeway with a gunshot to the head. No one ever said who had done it or why he may have done it. By age seven, I had a crush on one of their daughters Mary, who was at least 20 years older than me. I thought she was so pretty. She probably sensed it because she teased me about "being so cute," especially when she saw how embarrassed I got and turned red. Their son Tom worked for the U.S. Border Patrol after getting out of the U.S. Army after WWII. He told the story of being on patrol with his partner. They were parked on the side of the road. His partner had his feet out the window with no shoes on, when the guys they were looking out for drove by. His partner scrambled to pull his feet in, get his shoes on and take off after the bad guys, who they eventually caught, but Tom said it was a scene out of a Charlie Chaplin movie. I always tried to sit next to Tom or by his feet while the adults talked throughout the evening, while I sat there quietly. It was a feeling of safety, admiration and being part of the family. Years later I saw so many generations of kids not having the opportunity to be around their relatives, hearing stories from the past, and having no knowledge of their family history. It was a blessed time in my life.

I loved my Aunt Hannah the most of our relatives. When I was five, she was 53, very short, always with a smile but always looked 83. Mom said it that maybe it was the strain of having so many kids in such a short period of time. I knew she loved me too, because whenever we would be leaving and saying goodnight to everyone, she always slipped me a one-dollar bill without my parents seeing what she was doing. A dollar to me was a lot of money. The money was always nice, but knowing someone who was so kind and generous was so special to me. When I was about 10, Mom and Dad took me to see Aunt Hannah in the hospital. All they said was that she was sick, if they even said that. As I entered her room, Mom and Dad were behind me and I felt my face turn to horror. Aunt Hannah was lying in bed and had a hole the size of a half dollar cut out of her left cheek. There was just this large black hole in her face. I could hardly recognize her. I just stopped. Mom kept prodding me to go closer to see her, but I refused. I just wanted to get out of there. I refused to believe she was Aunt Hannah. She kept telling Mom to let me leave and that "It is OK." I did leave. I never saw Aunt Hannah again. She did not live much longer, as the operation had been to remove cancer, but it was one of the two or three things in my entire life that I really regretted doing. She was so special to me, and I let her down when she needed me. Tears come to my eyes every time I think of what I did. I try telling myself that Mom should have warned me. I was only 10 years old, but I have never lost my extreme guilt or forgiven myself.

My cousin Gene Sullivan Jr. was about my brother's age. I could never figure out if he had a brogue that he picked up from his parents, who were both from Ireland, or he had a speech impediment. He always called me "Turns" instead of Terence. I always thought it strange that a kid, even though he was older than me, called another kid, especially a cousin, by their given name rather than by their nickname. Maybe it was because Mom called me "Terence." She loved that name. She never once called me "Terry" my entire life. Whenever we visited the Sullivans, young Gene always was leaving the house. He never came in, sat down and joined the conversation. It was probably a teenager thing to be around adults and little kids as little as possible, so I never had much of a chance to get to know him.

Over the years as my brother, sister and relatives moved away after getting married and getting jobs, the family get-togethers disappeared. That was one of my greatest regrets. Some of the happiest days of my life were no longer available to the future generations of our relatives – so sad not to know our aunts, uncles, nephews and nieces. There was no longer a family heritage or interest in where we came from. We missed out on telling stories of the good old days and how life got better after surviving hardships and working our way up from having nothing. Family history was lost forever – clues to who we were and why, were buried in the sands of time.

Humble Beginnings: Motivation to Succeed

Our flat on Folsom Street consisted of rooms lined up one after another. Our home reflected a humble lifestyle that served as a constant reminder throughout my youth as to the roots I came from and the reason why I was determined to escape to be successful and wealthy some day. It was one of the reasons why I was a pretty humble and insecure kid for so long. In the rear of the flat was an outside porch with five clotheslines for Mom to hang out the wash. Most days she could rely on the sunny, warm weather to dry the wash before dark. An inside porch had a coal shed where things were stored including several burlap sacks of coal.

A horse drawn coal wagon traveled slowly along Folsom Street where Mom would wave down the driver. He was always nice enough to carry the sacks up our backstairs for Mom. The coal was used in our stove to help heat the kitchen on cold days. We also stored empty glass bottles and bundles of old newspapers in the shed. We sold the bottles and paper to the junkman who came along Folsom Street in his horse drawn wagon yelling, "Rags, bottles, sacks." He paid a pittance for the discards, but it saved us space in our one garbage can for more perishable and smelly things. These guys were shrewd bargainers who pretty much dictated how much they paid for things. Sometimes he had a rag boy with him, who was probably no more than eight years old – like a character out of *Oliver Twist*. Although they dressed shabbily in their dirty, ratty clothes to gain the sympathy of the public and to justify how little they paid for your recyclables, some junkmen were known to live in some of the most expensive houses in San Francisco and owned income property. There also were garbage men who came weekly in their open trucks, dumped our garbage can into 75-gallon aluminum containers, emptied the contents into a large sheet of burlap, carried over 100 pounds up seven steps to the top of the truck, dragged the burlap load across the garbage, and emptied it to search for newspapers, cardboard, bottles and rags. I doubt there was a harder, sweatier job.

Across from the coal shed were our icebox and washing machine. The left side of the 4-foot-wide icebox stored one large block of ice, and food was stored in the compartment on the right. There was not a lot of space but enough to hold a bottle of milk, butter, meat and a few other things. With

Jack's grocery store kitty corner (diagonally) across the street, we shopped there every two or three days so there was no need for a lot of cold storage. Each week a small open produce truck with shelves of fruits, vegetables and a scale hanging on the back came on the same day of the week and about the same time. Mom never considered giving him any business because he was a competitor of Jack and his wife across the street – sort of the idea of supporting our local small businessman.

The Union Ice Company used to deliver ice to the houses in the neighborhood and double-parked on the street. We put the "Ice" card in our bedroom window so the iceman knew we needed ice delivered. He chipped away a block of ice, grabbed it in his steel ice tongs, pulled the ice out, flung it on his back, which was protected from the cold and dampness by a black leather cape (semi-jacket), and brought the block of ice up the backstairs to our Leonard Cleanable white ice box with chrome handles on the back porch. He used the ice pick to chip off the sides so the ice block fit into the icebox compartment, with just enough space for the ice. There were always loose chunks of ice in the open bed of the truck that other kids and I snatched when the driver was inside. It was a great free treat for us, especially on hot days. Although I viewed it as stealing due to the strict teachings of the Catholic Church, I doubt the iceman cared, especially since it was going to melt anyway. I eventually had the job of getting down on my hands and knees, lifting the ice box faceplate, pulling out the oval pan of melted ice, and emptying out the water.

Our large single-tub clothes washing machine filled automatically with water, but we had to remove the top lid and pour the detergent in the water along with the clothes. When the wash was done, the water emptied through a rubber hose that rested over the lip of the cement sink. There was no such thing as spin-drying, so Mom loaded the wet clothes into a big pan and hung them on the line outside. If it was an overcast day, it might take two days on the line for the clothes to dry. To dry the clothes quicker, the washer had an 18-inch-wide wringer consisting of two rubber rollers. Mom placed the edge of the clothing between the rollers and turned a crank by hand that pulled the clothes through the wringer to the other side. It got all the water out of the clothes, but they still had to hang on the line outside for a while to dry completely. On overcast days, Mom stuck some of the clothes in the oven to dry them faster.

Next to the inside porch was the kitchen. We ate our meals at a small white table with five uncomfortable wood chairs. The table was covered with a vinyl tablecloth, which was easy to clean off with a damp dishrag. Our family did not have money for things, but Mom made sure that we ate well. For breakfast I sometimes joined Dad and had a soft-boiled egg that sat in a whiskey shot glass. We would crack off the top of the egg with a spoon, but high enough so the runny yolk did not flow out. Running the spoon along the inside edge of the egg, we could scoop out a spoon full of egg white and the liquid yolk. But my daily breakfast was nearly always cereal. Mom let me choose the cereal at Jack's, so I could not say I did not want to eat it for breakfast. I tried various cereals but finally settled on Cheerios. So many cereals had an unpleasant wheat taste, but Cheerios had a flavor I liked best. But the most appealing aspect was the little donut shape of each kernel that felt funny on my tongue and floated around on the surface of the milk. I used my spoon to play with them as if they were little boats or life rafts in the milk. Mom was constantly telling me, "Stop playing with your food. I need to clean up." Later, when I was going to school, it was "You need to get to school."

Mom normally had a cup of hot tea and a piece of buttered toast. She insisted all food had to be served hot and tea had to be "piping hot" made from boiling water. Tea was the only thing I ever saw Mom send back at a restaurant with the message for the cook "It has to be piping hot!" Our toaster had two side doors that were pulled open to toast two pieces of bread at the same time. When one side was done, I opened the sides and flipped around the bread to toast the other side.

Sunday breakfast was everyone's special meal – the one meal we really looked forward to eating. It was the "luxury" in our lives that made us not feel poor and deprived while living a frugal lifestyle. It was the reward for getting through the week's challenges and sacrifices For breakfast we had a traditional "fry," which was all cooked in a frying pan and consisted of calf's liver, beef kidney (or blood sausage), bacon, chopped up fried onions sprinkled over the meat, and fried eggs sunny-side up with a gooey yellow yoke so we could scoop up the runny yolk with a piece of buttered toast. Mom insisted it had to be calf's liver – not beef liver. The calf's liver was the more tender of the two for sure. She would "walk miles" if necessary to find her calf's liver. Nothing was too good when it came to the health of her family. Many a time she told us how many places she had to go to before she found calf's liver. Everyone seemed to carry only beef liver. It sometimes meant that she had to go to three or four different markets to find it, and this was shopping that was all done on foot. She cooked the fry over a low flame. Although it took longer, the liver came out soft and tender – not like liver served at most restaurants where the meat was overcooked and tough. I had a glass of milk, Dad had a cup of freshly brewed coffee, and everyone else had a cup of hot tea with milk and two small spoons of sugar. I drank my tea the same way when the occasion arose. If the tea was too hot, we drank it from a saucer. My brother, sister and I were never allowed to drink coffee at home. It was a grown-up's drink. Another special meal for me was pancakes and lots of maple syrup. Since we did not have sweets around the house, this was as close to a dessert as it got. Not having desserts at home made me learn not to expect things and to do without what other kids might have been given. I appreciated and was thankful for the things I had and never expected more than what Mom and Dad could afford.

Dinner was nearly always meat, potatoes, vegetables and milk. Mom always wanted the best for her children when it came to feeding us. Meat for dinner was often lamb chops, the household favorite. Mom cooked nearly everything for dinner in the oven. When homemade steak fries (never french fries) were served, we sprinkled vinegar over them – an Irish and English thing. But the baked potato was the potato of choice in our household – another Irish thing. Mom said the best and healthiest part of the potato was the exterior potato skin, and I had no reason to doubt her since she came from Ireland where potatoes were such a staple at their meals. So I spread butter on its inside and ate all of the skin first. I was surprised later in life to find so many people just threw away their potato skins. Artichokes were my favorite vegetable, which we did not get that often. I liked dipping each leaf into my spoon full of mayonnaise – a form of playing with my food. Mom spent hours cooking meals involving corned beef, beef roast, Irish stew, and turkey. Crab salad was a specialty of hers. There was never dessert unless we had company or it was one of our birthdays – probably an economic thing in our household. To satisfy my sweet tooth, I experimented with different concoctions from around the kitchen until I found my favorite homemade dessert that was cheap to make. I took a slice of white bread, spread butter all over it, sprinkled it with a thin layer of sugar, folded it in half, and enjoyed every sweet bite.

My favorite birthday cake was a white angel food cake covered with dark chocolate frosting baked by Mom. I also got to lick the chocolate off the mixing spoon. There was a lit candle for each year of my age. I was always able to blow them all out, but my wishes rarely came true. Wishes were always for toys or games and never for clothing. I stopped wishing for a new bike after a few years of not getting one. My folks always said they were too expensive when the subject came up.

Bone marrow was another favorite of mine. Mom once said it was good for me to eat the marrow from bones, so anytime we had beef that had bone marrow, I loved sucking the marrow out of the bone. Some cuts of meat had a bone that had marrow the length of the bone. That was special.

Our gas stove had a trash burner compartment for paper and coal covered with a round metal cover that was used to heat the kitchen in the morning because the house did not have forced air heating. A long metal handle was inserted in a small hole or slot to lift off the cover. Coal was placed on a layer of newspapers and a lit match was thrown in to ignite the paper. A short L-shaped fire poker with a pointed end was used to stoke the fire and embers. At the other end of the house in the dining room, there was a wall gas heater. I turned on the gas and inserted a lit match into the face of the heater and the gas caught fire. A fireproof facing confined the flames. There was no other heat other than this heater, the stove burner and a hot water bottle.

We got a mouse in our kitchen occasionally. The mouse came through a space slightly less than an inch wide at the base in the corner where the kitchen cabinets came together. I learned how to set and bait the trap with a small piece of cheese. It was a relief catching the mice, but I always felt sorry for them when I dumped them in the trash. Once we caught a mouse, another showed up months later. You would think someone would have the common sense to jam a piece of wood in the hole to plug it up, but we never thought of it. I wound up having more empathy for animals than people. Animals seemed more helpless and defenseless – probably the reason why I expected so much more from people as an adult.

Off to the side of the hallway from the kitchen were the living room and our one small bathroom. The living room furniture was set around the RCA Victor console radio where we spent each night listening to the news and our favorite weekly programs like *Duffy's Tavern*, *Edgar Bergen and Charlie McCarthy*, *Fibber McGee and Molly*, *Green Hornet*, *Lone Ranger*, *The Shadow*, *Gangbusters*, and *The Whistler*. When the radio stopped working, I had to take the tube with the burn mark on it to the radio shop and get a replacement, which I used to fix the radio.

At the end of the hallway was the landing at the top of the front stairs that was used as our dining room. We had a heavy, highly carved dark brown mahogany table that could extend to accommodate up to 12 people. The upholstered high back chairs were also highly carved. On the wall was a chalk landscape sketch done by an old friend of Mom's. It was not until years later when I learned it was not a painting. Had I known it was chalk, I probably would have smudged it accidentally as kids always like touching things with no glass covering. Also in the dining room was the telephone, which meant whenever we heard the phone ring from the living room or kitchen in the back of the house, we had to run from there and down a long hallway to get to the phone on the far side of the dining room. All those years, I guess no one ever thought of having the phone moved to the center of the house in the living room, but everyone else must have thought private conversations were more important.

The two bedrooms in the front of the house and accessible from the dining room were divided by a floor to ceiling pair of sliding doors. They were pretty common as I saw them in a number of the flats my friends lived in. Mom, Dad and I slept in one room and Kathy and Joe in the other. I slept in a crib and was thinking that I was too old to still be sleeping in a crib because my feet touched the foot of the crib, not allowing me to stretch out completely. I also thought I was getting too old to be sleeping in the same room as Mom and Dad, since I was a "big boy" now at age four. I had suggested moving my crib to a different room, but I suppose Mom wanted to be sure she was there if I had trouble sleeping. One night I woke up. It was very dark, and I could not see anything as there was no streetlight outside that could be a source of light. I lay there and heard what sounded like squeaking metal box springs. There was a little bit of mumbling, but I could not make out what was being said by anyone.

Eventually I recognized the voices being Mom and Dad's. The next morning I told Mom and Dad that I heard various noises that night. Mom asked, "What noises?" They were very interested in knowing what I heard and I told them. After they asked me a couple of times what I specifically heard and getting no response, they finally accepted the fact that I did not hear anything specific. A couple of days later Mom said the landlord was going to seal up the two sliding doors between the bedrooms and create a solid wall. Once it was done, I was to move into the second bedroom with Joe, and Kathy was to move into the storage room on the other side of the dining room that was being converted into a bedroom by the landlord. Kathy had been trying to convince Mom that she should have her own bedroom and was too old at age 11 to be sharing a room with her brother. She finally got her wish. Even if there was barely room for a bed and dresser in the room, at least it was her own room.

Mom in turn told me I was too old to be sleeping in a crib and should have a regular size bed, while letting on it had nothing to do with giving Mom and Dad privacy. Having my own adult size bed made me feel so grown up. But as the ancient proverb warned, "Be careful what you wish for, lest it come true!" For the next few years, I found that I disliked the darkness, and I often pulled the covers over my head until I went to sleep, but before going to sleep, I said a prayer that was actually a ritual that mentioned everyone important to me.

Mom's shopping exploits were legendary in our household. She was a very opinionated and determined person. Nothing was too good for her kids no matter how long it took her to shop. Once she had her mind set on finding something, she continued shopping until she found it. "Second best" was not an option, no matter how many stores, days or weeks it took to find the object of her search. Whether it was food, clothing, house supplies or Christmas presents, she continued until she found that specific item, color, material or style in mind, and many times it required looking in a lot of stores. She came home and told us how tired she was from all the shopping and what she was looking for. I suppose that was another reflection of her compulsive tendencies. I eventually inherited the same shopping tendency. I also shopped forever until I found what I wanted.

First she shopped locally. The center of shopping in the neighborhood was the stretch of Mission Street between 16th Street and Army Street called the "Mission Miracle Mile" or "The Miracle Mile." It was second only to downtown and Union Square as a shopping destination. Mom shopped a lot at the large New Mission Market, two doors beyond the New Mission Theater on Mission Street between 21st and 22nd Streets for the meat, fish and other items not carried at Jack's. Mom was only 5'0" tall but had to be strong. We had no automobile so she would cart two full paper shopping bags of groceries home from the Market and had to use a small handkerchief in each hand to prevent the paper cord handles from cutting her hands over the five block walk. If she had to shop downtown, she would lug shopping bags of groceries from the Crystal Palace Market [6] on Market Street between 7th and 8th Streets. She would walk down to Mission Street, catch the bus, and walk four more blocks from the bus stop to the house, sometimes in the rain.

To replace any of the secondhand furniture in our house, Mom always shopped at the large Redlick Newman furniture store at Mission & 17th Streets, which had a huge "17 Reasons Why!" sign on the roof that could be seen day and night from afar. What were the "17 reasons" to shop at the store? There were none. The sign was merely used to attract customers to the store. [7]

Age 5: Life Began – Last Year of Being a "Little Kid"

My life really began by age five. I had accumulated enough toys to amuse myself at home; I started to experience more of life outside of the kid's section at Folsom Park; and kindergarten would prepare me for no longer being a "little kid" to eventually join the "big kids" in first grade.

In our living room I had a large drawer at the bottom of built-in drawers that was used to store all my toys. Most of the toys were things that I could use to play by myself, as opposed to games that required playing with others. My favorite toys were plastic soldiers, cowboys and Indians to create and carry out battles. I loved creating forts and buildings with various types and sizes of building blocks and log cabin sets with their dark brown logs and corner pegs and green wood roof strips that had grooved edges for joining the roofing pieces together. I played on the floor for hours and was never bored. My other toys consisted of marbles, comic books, a kaleidoscope, toy cars and trucks, Indian feather head dress with bow and arrows with suction cups on the end, and a cowboy holster with a silver chrome six-shooter that had white ivory plastic handles that had a raised long horn cattle head on both sides of the handle. On my View Master, I could look at reels of 3-D pictures that took me to exotic places around the U.S. and in foreign countries. I think so much playing by myself helped to create my independence in life, knowing that I could cope on my own. I had no games until I got older. My brother and sister were not interested in playing games with me as they had no interest in doing things with a kid so much younger than themselves – especially out in public. Mom and Dad loved to play whist at the church Whist Night. I never learned whist, but I learned Solitaire and played card games like Fish, Hearts, and Old Maid with Mom and Kathy. By age seven I was playing board games like checkers, Chinese checkers and chess with kids in the Park. I was pretty good and could beat some older kids who stopped playing games with me.

Benefits of Hiding Places

Another place at home I spent a lot of time was under the large dining room table, which was in the heart of foot traffic in the house. I could

27

see everyone going in and out of the bedrooms and coming and going from the house. It was the beginning of my constant search throughout my childhood for new hiding places, whether they were under the table, in a tree, in a bush or a cardboard fort. They gave me a sense of independence, privacy and quiet surroundings in my own dwelling to watch the world go by and to be alone with my own thoughts. Later in life, I found I did my best thinking in similar environments.

On rainy days, and there were a lot of them in San Francisco, one of my favorite playthings to do was to sit inside a large cardboard box and slide down the flight of carpeted 20-odd steps that led to the front door. It was like riding the Shoot the Chutes at Playland at the Beach, except there was no splashing in the water at the bottom. I had to center my weight toward the back of the box, otherwise the box and I would tumble down the steps head over heels, but that only happened a few times. Fortunately, I was able to kick the box off of me on the first tumble and my body just lay on the steps while the box made its way down to the front door – lesson learned.

One of my favorite forms of entertainment at home was when Mom showed me the family picture album. Throughout the early years, I asked her to take me through the album. Later I went through on my own. Our family was not big on taking pictures because we did so little traveling and seldom did things together other than attend special holiday meals with our relatives. We had a box camera that required a roll of film to be loaded, unloaded and developed. Joe, Kathy and I always made a fuss about having our pictures taken, so maybe Mom and Dad just gave up finally and left the camera at home. That would explain why we had less than five pictures from our annual vacations at "Seiglers" – Seigler Hot Springs in Lake County just south of Clear Lake. In the album, there were mostly pictures of friends of Mom and Dad that they knew here and in Ireland. There were some pictures that Mom had no idea who they were. She just said, "They must be friends of Dad." Dad could only identify about 85 percent of them, but I always wondered why those other pictures were even kept in the album. Years later I regretted not having a lot more pictures of the family. It was a natural curiosity to remember how we all looked over the years, and future generations of our family would be curious about what their family, ancestors and relatives looked like. Audio recordings would have been great to hand down through the generations too. You can tell a lot about someone from their recorded voice as to whether they were articulate, educated, confident, outgoing, cheerful…or none of the above.

Mom started to take me places besides Folsom Park. One of the most unique features of the Mission District, compared to any other residential area of the City, was that there were five movie theaters on Mission Street between 19th and 23rd Streets, which included the El Capitan (19th-20th), Tower (20th-21st), New Mission (21st-22nd), Crown (21st-22nd), and Grand (22nd-23rd). It was a movie fan's paradise. These five movie theaters formed "one of the greatest cinema rows in all of San Francisco." They showed a double bill with a cartoon, previews and newsreel.

To promote the premiere of extra special new movies, large spotlights scanned the sky out in front of theaters mostly downtown and on rare occasion out in the Mission. It did give a Hollywood feel and a sense that something special was going on, however Mom and I never chose to attend a premier because of the hoopla. Like reading a book, we made the choice based on content. It was a movie era of extravagant musicals with singers like Frank Sinatra and dancers like Fred Astaire and Gene Kelly, chorus lines, epic war movies, westerns, slap stick comedy, and especially extravaganzas with "casts of thousands" – long gone movie experiences.

Mom took me to the movies once a week – usually the El Capitan (second largest theater to the Fox Theater) or the New Mission. She always picked out the movie and that was fine with me. Going to any movie was a special treat. She got all dressed up in a nice dress and a hat. I had to wear something other than my play clothes. The Tower Theater gave away dishes on Wednesdays. Each week it was a different type and size of chinaware with the object of attracting customers interested in collecting a complete set of dishes. Mom had collected quite a few of the pieces over time. These were the days when candy bars were five cents and there was a large assortment of penny candy. My favorite five-cent candy bars were the U-No bar (a smooth candy bar with a rich, milk chocolate, truffle-like center, covered with milk chocolate before they added ground almonds) and 3 Musketeers (another melt-in-your-mouth candy, chocolate-covered fluffy whipped nougat made of egg whites). Not having sweets at home, it was special when she bought a small five-cent

29

box of candy at the concession stand, and we shared our one vice during the movie unbeknownst to the rest of our family.

Occasionally we dropped into the local Bank of America at the corner of 21st and Mission Streets. It was my favorite shopping stop. Inside the front door was a uniformed security guard. He always offered little kids like me a piece of candy – often licorice. He was plump, had gray hair and would have made a wonderful Santa Claus. I also did my banking there. The Bank had given me a metal piggy bank that was in the shape of a small book about 3/4 inch wide with a thick green paper stock cover. There was a slit for inserting coins and two springs inside along the slit to prevent me from shaking out the coins like typical piggy banks. There was a lock that could only be opened at the Bank whenever I wanted to deposit the contents into my personal bank account. Maybe it was just a coincidence I worked eventually for Bank of America for 20 years, but I like to think there was a link to my fond childhood memories at the Bank when it was the first and only company I applied for a job after college.

I got used to wearing floppy clothes because Mom always bought clothes and shoes a size larger than I needed so I could grow into them. Shopping for shoes was sort of fun. Mom always took me to Thom McAn's on Market Street. She felt it was the best shoe store in the City and nothing was too good for her kids. The store had a machine with a step I stood on, put both feet inside two holes, looked through a viewer on the top of the machine, and I could see all the bones in my feet. These shoe-fitting fluoroscope machines used x-rays to show how well my feet fit in the new shoes, whether they were too tight, too large or just the right fit. [8] The x-rays also made it evident that I had flat feet, so Mom took me to a foot doctor and he fitted me for chrome metal arch supports. Each six months he tightened them so they pinched more into the sides of my feet. Each time, I eventually got used to the supports squeezing into my feet. By the time I was 10, I no longer needed the supports. Whether they helped me run faster, I am not sure, but I like to think they helped.

Like all kids, I used to go through shoes more often than my parents wanted. So Dad, Joe and I put cardboard in our shoes when holes wore through the soles. When a hole also wore through the cardboard, we just replaced the cardboard. Eventually, when the heels wore down or the soles started to come apart, Mom got them replaced at Zinke's, the shoe repair shop on Mission Street around 23rd Street. I was also rough on the toes of the shoes, so Mom had metal toe plates and taps nailed to the toes and heels of the shoes. Later she had taps nailed on each side of the soles for added protection. Eventually, she had horseshoe taps put on the heels, which covered three sides of the heel. If I ran down the sidewalk and lifted my toes slightly off the ground, I could skid along the sidewalk several feet at a time.

The Cruelest Thing Done in My Lifetime

Mom started taking me on visits to friends' homes when I was five years old and able to sit still for an hour at a time. The most memorable visit was one that I regretted for a lifetime. Mom wanted to visit a friend up the street and insisted I come along, as she could not leave me all alone. I certainly did not want to sit around while two women sat talking about things I had no interest in, but I had no choice. They lived on Folsom Street, a few door down from 22nd Street. When we got there, I met the woman's daughter Marilyn for the first time. She was cute and about my age. I had no female friends up to that time. She was the first person I ever met with chrome metal braces on both legs. I had no idea why she was wearing braces, until I learned years later about cerebral palsy. No one had explained it to me or warned me before we arrived. She could walk around stiff legged but a little slower than most kids. We all sat around for a while, then Mom said, "Why don't the two of you go out and play."

I never played with a girl one-on-one before. I had no idea what we would do, especially on the sidewalk out front. I could think of nothing that did not involve running or jumping when it came to play. I repeatedly said I wanted to stay with them, rather than go outside. Mom kept after me to change my mind. Finally out of frustration I blurted out, "She cannot run around and play," and I pointed at the braces. Marilyn quickly responded, "I can so," which was probably true. She was a gutsy girl, but I was too stupid to realize how much I should have admired her. We never did go out and play. That outburst by me has haunted me throughout my life for being so insensitive and cruel. So often in my life I thought back to that experience, always regretting that I was not nicer, more considerate, and how it could have been handled better. If Mom had told me about the girl having braces, we could have decided what we could do to play together. Or if the girl's mother had games in the house that we could play with and had offered them as suggestions, but it just seemed like an effort to get rid of the kids so that the mothers could be alone. It was handled badly all around. That was the last time I ever saw Marilyn and her mom. I do not know if it ended her friendship with my mom, but it probably did. It was the cruelest thing I ever did in my entire life – something I could never erase from my memory nor be forgiven for doing. I immediately knew that I was wrong and if any good came of it, the sick feeling in my stomach made me decide not to be cruel to others in the future. People either learned from mistakes or kept repeating them. I definitely learned to be more compassionate and understanding for things beyond one's control.

Mom loved going to the Beach. Her love for the ocean went back to her youth in Ireland when she and her friends took the train to the sea for a holiday (weekend). She loved the smell of the salt air and a chance to breath in the fresh ocean air. Mom often took me to Ocean Beach for the day. We took a bus downtown and transferred to the B-Geary-Ocean streetcar that took us to the middle of Playland at the Beach. We got off, walked across the Great Highway and a block to the Beach at the end of Balboa Street. She always picked the same spot and laid out a blanket at the base of the 12-foot curved cement wall to get the most protection from the winds whipping from all directions. The view seemed like we could almost reach out and touch the Cliff House and Seal Rocks [I always mispronounced it "Seals Rock"], although they were about three blocks away. I watched Seal Rocks for a while, but I lost interest quickly. The sea lions spent nearly all their time just lying still. It was like watching the sun rise. The rare "excitement" came when one waddled into the water.

Mom was not the only one who recognized that area of the Beach as being so desirable because there were always a lot of others sunbathing and playing in the water there. If the weather got overcast, chilly, or the fog came in, Mom endured the cold by bundling herself up and relying on her broad brim hat to keep her head warm to give me as much playtime as possible at the Beach. The 12-foot-high curved cement wall was too steep for me to run up, but it was fun trying.

Mom insisted I could not wander along the shoreline out of her sight, and I had to stay out of the water, unless she was with me, and just play at the water's edge. There was reason to be concerned. Every so often the newspaper told of someone who was rescued from drowning or actually drowned. A less frequent occurrence was a sighting of sharks off shore, but the most rare was a shark attack. When my brother Joe was less than five years old, he went out too far in the water and got taken out by the undertow. Fortunately, a man swam out and saved Joe from drowning. All of the locals knew about the treacherous undertow at the Beach. What we did not know was that the San Francisco Ocean Beach was called "the most hazardous piece of urban shoreline in the entire U.S." due to its treacherous riptides. [9]

I entertained myself for hours playing at the water's edge. As the waves pushed the water toward the shore, I ran at the same speed to stay one or two feet ahead of the ebb and flow of the water. As the tide went out, I ran out with the water, always not allowing the water to get my feet wet. It was like playing tag with the water, which was always trying to "tag" my feet, and I was always trying to avoid the tag. When I got tired of running, I dug holes in the sand, but far enough from the current so the water did not fill the holes. I was searching for anything that moved, which was nearly always sand crabs that were about an inch in size. I just set them aside as the challenge was merely to find them. I kept the sand dollars if they were near perfect without any chips. I also made little houses and forts with the wet sand, but I had to keep my distance from the waves to protect the structures. Digging a moat was a second precaution to safeguard my creations from the water. Eventually the water came in and filled the moat, making the fort more realistic.

There were always one or two fishermen along the Beach with a rod and reel surf fishing. They tended to stay away from the area where kids and swimmers hung out, probably for fear of hooking a person. I never did see any of them pull in a single fish. With their rod stuck in the sand and the heavily clothed fishermen standing on the side with their hands in their pockets to stay warm, it just looked boring to me and like a lot of wasted time. As I got older, I realized that we all needed some "alone time" with our thoughts, dreams and away from our everyday problems, job and family life.

On very rare occasions, we took Muni to the San Francisco Zoo. The closest I got to feeling like a cowboy was riding a Shetland pony at the donkey ride. It was fun riding along and holding on to the knob of the saddle even if I was strapped on like a little kid. There was no need to steer the pony because it was tied to a giant wheel that went around in a circle. I thought how sad that the ponies had to walk around in circles all day, day after day, unlike the frisky ponies at the Golden Gate Park ride.

What was much better than the Zoo was a circus. Although smaller circuses came to town, we only went to the Ringling Bros. and Barnum & Bailey Circus, billed as the "Greatest Show On Earth." They were held at the Cow Palace and the San Francisco Civic Auditorium. They not only had animals like at the Zoo, they had trained animals, clowns, trapeze artists, tightrope walkers, musicians, and jugglers in their three-ring circus. My favorite was seeing 10-15 clowns piling out of the small clown car. My second favorite was the high-wire trapeze artists, especially when they worked without a net underneath their performance.

Besides the circus, one of the few other outings I attended with Dad was to see an Irish football match. Dad enjoyed watching Gaelic (Irish) football at the far western end of Golden Gate Park between Playland and the Dutch Windmill. We called it the "Soccer Field" or the "Irish Football Field," (later called Beach Chalet Soccer Fields). The field was only large enough to play one match at a time.

Dad and Jimmy Reidy, a friend of the family, went to a lot of Irish football matches together. Jimmy was a well-built, high energy and probably a pretty good athlete in his day. They took me to my first Irish soccer game. Jimmy parked his car on the Great Highway and we walked about 200 feet through the trees and bushes to get to the field. The teams were part of a local league in the Bay Area. Dad took me to a couple more matches, but I just found it boring and never got interested. I am sure that was a disappointment to Dad. As I got older, I regretted not making an effort to learn more about the game and to develop an interest in it. Kids always expect their parents to be interested in their activities, but seldom consider developing an interest in those of their parents. At the time, I did not realize that a mutual interest in each other's lives would have created a stronger and longer lasting relationship between Dad and me – how sad. It was Jimmy Reidy who gave me a used Irish soccer ball (football), probably left over from a match played at the Soccer Field where he occasionally served as a referee. It was made of soft brown leather and not as firmly inflated as an American football, but it had a similar hole for pumping air to inflate the ball. I used it to play kickball as the kids did not play soccer in the neighborhood or the schoolyard.

Dad's other sports related interests were watching Friday night boxing matches held at the National Hall at 16th and Mission Streets and going to the horse races at either Tanforan Racetrack in San Bruno or Golden Gate Fields in Berkeley. The National Hall was known as the "Bucket of Blood" arena because spectators allegedly did not expect to see a clean fight at the Friday night fights. Dad took my brother Joe, who was a teenager, to the boxing matches regularly and to the horse races occasionally. Mom was adamant that I was too young to go to either, and by the time I was old enough to go, Dad's health discouraged such activities.

Another outing with Dad was when he and Jimmy Reidy took me to the top of Twin Peaks a couple of years later and Jimmy taught me how to shoot a .22 rifle. At the time, there were no houses built on Twin Peaks. It was just fields of grass and weeds in 1946. Jimmy taught me how to aim and slowly pull the trigger without jerking the gun. It was fun to do once, just like the shooting gallery at Playland, but shooting guns was not something I wanted to do a lot. It was 12 years later before I picked up another rifle and that was to be at the U.S. Marine Corps boot camp where I was an adequate shot but not outstanding – should have practiced more.

The only trips our family took together were the one-week vacations we took every summer during the 1940s to Seiglers. We stayed at a hotel where Mom loved being waited on by others. She did not have to do any housework, chores or cooking except to dress the kids for every meal. There was a pool and entertainment at night. When I was four or five, my sister coaxed me into the swimming pool. I could not swim. I insisted on staying in the shallow end, but she kept insisting I go with her into the deeper end. The first time I did, I got panicky when my feet lifted off the floor of the pool and only she and the water were holding me up. I had a flashback of her dropping me down the stairs when I was an infant. That day she got me over my fear and taught me to dog paddle on my own in the deep water – the first step to learning to swim. Dad also helped me become an adequate swimmer, but I never really enjoyed swimming – never understood what was fun with gasping for air to breath, swallowing water on occasion and never being able to swim fast.

Wisdom of Early School Admission

The Catholic grammar schools required a child to be five years old to enter kindergarten, so Mom enrolled me in a nursery school on Potrero Avenue when I was 4 1/2 years old. She thought it would help prepare me for kindergarten. On my first day I began to pout and clung to her side, knowing I was going to be left with a bunch of strangers, even if they were my age. I eventually, but never completely, accepted it. I was not enjoying myself and Mom saw that I was not happy, so Mom was in a hurry to get me enrolled in grammar school. The school year started in September 1945, but I would not be five until mid-November. Yet a few months later, she got me enrolled in kindergarten at St. Charles Grammar School at age 4 years and 10 months even though the other kids would be five. Mom pulled the "you-owe-me" card by telling the school principal, "My other two children are enrolled here and both my husband and I have been active in school and church affairs for a number of years." It worked, so I no longer had to go to nursery school.

Art Curtis, whom I met later in high school, enrolled in kindergarten at age four and by age five was too young for 1st grade, so he had to repeat kindergarten for a second year. Later, he jokingly boasted he was the only kid who flunked kindergarten and had to take it over.

Years later I debated whether it was best for me to start school a year sooner than most kids or not. I realized that my life would have been so different. It was one of life's forks in the road that would have drastically changed my interests, experiences, values and friendships. I concluded Mom made the right decision and that it was best the way it turned out. There are so many friends, opportunities and achievements that I would have never experienced. As they say, "Be thankful for what you got. The alternative could be a lot worse." I also learned years later that some of the best decisions for us were made by others so do not be disappointed if you do not get your own way.

Those were the days the first name of the saint was often used when churches and schools were named after them. For example, our grammar school and church were referred to as "St. Charles." I never did know his actual name was Charles Borromeo. The two-story school building **[10]** on the corner of 18th and Shotwell Streets was built in 1888 and eventually declared a San Francisco landmark. For the six years I was there, I loved the Italianate architecture of the wood frame building. I think attending a school in such a historical place gave me an appreciation for exceptional and unique architecture. To some it must have appeared as just an old building, while I thought of it as classical as I got older. Kathy and Joe were already attending St. Charles, so each day Kathy walked with me to and from school which was a short four-block walk from home.

A block away from the school, St. Charles Church was on the corner of 18th Street and South Van Ness Avenue. A few doors up from the church on South Van Ness, St. Charles held all of their social activities at St. Charles Hall. Most of the activities were for adults like the card game whist, Father's and Mother's Club meetings, Bingo games and festivals to raise money. It also served as an auditorium for gatherings that required all of the students at St. Charles to meet in one place. A block away on South Van Ness off 19th Street, the nuns lived at the St. Charles Convent, which was a gorgeous Victorian building.

The school uniform for boys was a white shirt with black and white speckled wool or flannel pants, and a dark blue pullover sweater. Girls dressed in white blouses, dark blue skirts and dark blue cardigan sweaters. I liked the idea of uniforms, as I had a very limited wardrobe as a kid – something that carried through my entire adult life. I just kept wearing my favorite things, so washing clothes was a frequent thing for me. When classes started at 8:00 a.m., a nun stood on the front steps and rang her large bronze hand bell to signal that school was starting. They also rang the bell at the end of recess and lunch to get us back to class.

My favorite and most memorable things in kindergarten were the snacks and naptime. Each day we got a free half-pint carton of white milk and a cookie during snack time followed by a 15-30 minute nap. We sat at long tables arranged in a U-shape, as we were too young to be assigned individual desks. We had to rest our head on our folded arms that served as a pillow on the tabletop to go to sleep. If the nun saw anyone lift their head peaking or fidgeting, she called them out by name to quit it and get to sleep. With all of the name-calling, it was surprising how we ever got off to sleep. Since the breaks were so short, there was not much sleeping going on, but it gave us kids time to calm down and enjoy peace and quiet.

Kindergarten was fun. There was picture coloring, learning the letters of the alphabet and having stories read to us. Our kindergarten teacher was a civilian or layperson, someone who was not a member of a religious order. So it was a significant change when our teachers for the 1st to 8th grades were nuns in their black headdress (veil), white collar and floor-length black robe with large rosary beads hanging from their waist. I think their dress helped quiet the kids down due to the new respect we had for the nuns. They appeared to be more sacred. Being closer to God carried some weight too. Their clothes made them untouchable, so it was quite unnerving if I accidentally ran into one of them during recess. It was as if I dropped the host (wafer) from my lips while receiving Holy Communion.

We learned to fold paper to make simple origami figures like cootie-catchers. It was never the intent of the teacher for the boys to use them for chasing the girls around the schoolyard attempting to catch imaginary cootie bugs in their hair. The girls would scream and the boys just laughed.

The school provided small cartons of white and chocolate milk for lunch. My favorite was chocolate milk as it served as my dessert for lunch. The school had no cafeteria so everyone brought bag lunches. My bag lunch for school was always a sandwich cut in half and wrapped in wax paper and a piece of fruit but no sweets or desserts. The sandwich usually contained bologna lunchmeat, which was the cheapest, but often I asked for peanut butter and jam because the jam partly satisfied my craving for sweets. By the 2nd grade, I took my lunch to school in a metal Lone Ranger lunch pail that had a small thermos bottle to bring my own milk when the school stopped providing milk. Any time I dropped the thermos by accident, the glass liner shattered and the shards of glass made my milk undrinkable. I went through several thermoses during grammar school.

During lunch, the kids sat almost shoulder to shoulder on the benches that surrounded the schoolyard. Sometimes I ate my lunch under the short flight of backstairs leading from the school building to the schoolyard that I thought of as my secret hideaway. It was somewhat darker and definitely private from the others. Eventually, some of the kids came over and asked what I was doing under there. My secret spot was no longer secret so its appeal to me disappeared, and I never returned to eat lunch alone, which was probably a good thing.

Noel Murray, whom I met later in high school, said his mother made him a celery and mayo sandwich one Friday while in the 1st grade because his father did not get paid until Friday and there was not much in the house to eat. When Noel returned to school after eating lunch at home, the nun asked him what he had for lunch. Being a bit embarrassed to have eaten such a paltry meal, he said, "A hamburger." She replied in disbelief, "On a Friday?" At the time, it was a mortal sin to eat meat on Friday.

Age 6: Life Began as a Student of Learning

The 1st grade was a big transition from being a "little kid" attending the play world of kindergarten to being a "big kid" and attending a scholastic classroom as a student of learning. We began to carry around our blank sheets of paper and notes in golden yellow Pee-Chee folders that had sketches of competing athletes on the covers. Each student now had their own desk instead of sharing tables with others. The desk had a groove across the top for placing my pencil, which was the writing tool of choice until we could be trusted with fountain pens that sucked up ink into a rubber tubing. (This was before ballpoint pens.) There was a hole in the upper right corner of the desk where a glass inkwell with a hard cork stopper was provided when we got older. I would not trust first graders with ink either. Under the desktop was a shelf for storing books, making us very self-sufficient to get through our classes as we stayed in the same classroom all day. The sides of the shelf were fancy grills made of black wrought iron. When ink was provided to us a year later, it was one of those things that was destined for comedy and catastrophe. Every year at least one or two students bumped the inkwell hard enough for the bottle to pop out of its hole in the desktop and spill all over the desk on to the floor and sometimes on the kid's clothes. It was often followed by laughter from the class. It was more of a nervous laughter of relief while thinking, *I'm glad it did not happen to me*. I always felt sorry for the student who never meant to do it, and I was just thankful it was never me. The class came to a halt while the nun got paper towels to clean it up. The ink on the hands was the student's "red badge of courage" for a day or two.

In the 1st grade, coloring was still part of the curriculum and possibly my best subject. I meticulously stayed within the lines when I colored with the crayons. It was probably my compulsive trait to be neat and orderly. And as part of our spelling lessons, we were told constantly that Christmas was all about honoring Jesus Christ and we must always spell out "Christmas." It was sacrilegious to use "Xmas" because "it left Christ out of Christmas." For the rest of my life, I felt guilty if I even considered writing "Xmas."

When we were learning the letters of the alphabet and how to write, the nun tried to get all of us left-handers (10 percent of the class) to print and write with our right hand. She said it would improve our penmanship. Some of the students may have made the change, but she gave up on me eventually and said I could go back to doing things with my left hand. Some other Catholic grammar schools were stricter. If the student tried writing with their left hand, the nun just tapped their knuckles with a ruler. I suspect my teacher was looking for left-handers who showed promise and some improvement trying it right-handed, but I was not one of them. The nun was right about her assertion that left-handers had poor penmanship, which I can attest to over the years. The other thing she said was that I should relax my hand when I wrote – so relaxed that she could come along and remove the pencil from my hand with ease, which I could never do. I always bent my wrist and gripped the pencil so tightly as if someone was going to steal it from me. I just felt that I could control the motion of the pencil better. Years later I finally got rid of the tight, awkward looking writing grip.

The most memorable classmate I had at St. Charles Grammar School was a little person by the name of "Dolly." I always assumed that was her real first name. In hindsight, it was probably a nickname, which may or may not have been a disparaging name given to her by someone. But it was a time when kids just accepted others for whom they were – we did not think in terms of age, race, color, or economic status. Dolly was three to four feet tall and had a very large head, tiny hands and tiny feet. She had poor balance and seemed to trip and fall a lot, bruising her knee, elbow or forehead. She was always cheerful on the outside but must have lived with the pain inside of not being able to participate in the schoolyard games like the rest of the kids. I ran into her 20 years later. She looked much older with some wrinkles but her body had not changed much, if at all. I regretted not taking more time to find out what she had been doing for the past 20 years. I still had not developed good social skills and the ability to carry on meaningful chitchat.

Other memorable classmates of mine at St. Charles were two Latino brothers. They kiddingly were called "Herman the German" and "Tony Baloney." Herman was the quiet one and Tony was the explosive one. The nicknames had no racial overtones. No one believed Herman was a German or Tony looked like a role of baloney. Well after leaving high school, I realized that many, if not most, nicknames used during the school years left life-long scars with those called those names. We meant no harm. We did it for fun, but we were too stupid to know the harm they did to kids and how long lasting those memories were ingrained in them.

But for the most part throughout grammar school, students were well behaved while the nun was in the classroom, whether it was before, during or after class. I respected the nuns and thought of them as being holy – someone who deserved my respect. If any student acted up in class, the nun threatened, "If you do not behave, you will be sent down to the principal's office." It was never explained what that meant in terms of punishment, but there was no need for an explanation because it seemed to work. If a kid did not behave in class or in the schoolyard, their parents were called in to talk to the principal and were told in so many words their child needed to change their ways. That seemed to straighten out the kid because the parents were either disciplinarians or they did not like the embarrassment and inconvenience of being called to the principal's office. Hard-nosed parents who took the advice badly were also told the school had a waiting list of parents who wanted to enroll a child in the school, implying that their child could readily be replaced. It was true. Catholic grammar schools could never accommodate the number of applications each year for kids who were Catholics much less the non-Catholics. That got the message across to belligerent parents.

Throughout grammar school, we were always moving back and forth as a class in single file or a column of twos directly behind the person in front of us, whether we were going from the classroom to the schoolyard, the church or running fire drills. We were not allowed to talk in line so we traveled in a quiet and orderly manner. It also focused our attention on going up and down stairs and across intersections safely. It reminded me of soldiers marching in drills, except we were not marching in unison.

Schoolyard games consisted of hopscotch, dodge ball, basketball, and kickball. The three Catholic grammar schools I attended eventually did not have gym lockers, much less their own gym, so we played at recess and during gym class in our school clothes in the schoolyard. There was no changing into shorts like at the public schools that often had gym lockers. We could care less. We could not feel deprived if we did not know any difference.

Throughout grammar school, collections were taken up to assist and feed poor children around the world. They were called "pagan babies." Although the term referred to un-baptized children, the emphasis was on those living in poverty. These were mainly African, Asian and Latino non-baptized children taken in by Catholic missionaries around the world. The nuns showed us pictures of these kids living in rags and squalor. The pictures were heartbreaking, especially for six-year-olds in the 1st grade. They instilled in us a sense that we were very fortunate to be living in America with plenty of food and water while many children were starving and dying. It was a good way to instill charity and caring for others in kids through something practical like fund-raising at an early age. The teacher provided an envelope in which we could donate any amount of money. After donations from the entire class reached five dollars, we officially had adopted a pagan baby. We could also adopt our own personal pagan baby with a five-dollar donation. The teacher suggested various names and the students voted for one of them. A certificate with the child's name on it was posted on the class bulletin board. Bragging rights went to the class with the most pagan baby certificates. I, and probable most kids, put the bite on our parents for some change. It would be one more year before I could donate from my own money earned from turning in empty soda bottles. Some kids went door to door in the neighborhood for donations to adopt as many babies as possible. At this early age, I felt uncomfortable asking people for money, regardless of the cause. I felt that way all my adolescent and adult life. I think that attitude contributed to my being independent and self-sufficient, doing everything possible myself, and not looking for handouts and help as I grew up.

At Christmas time, we were asked by the nuns to sell Christmas seals. Although the school suggested everyone sell them door-to-door, some just went to their parents for a donation. There were prizes for the biggest sellers – mostly religious items like rosaries, statues and pictures. I again avoided asking for donations. Mom usually bought some to help me out. The donation drives only contributed to my desire to get a job as early in life as possible so I could make the donation out of my own money.

The 40-day period (excluding Sundays) before Easter Sunday was called "Lent" in the Catholic religion. It was a period for fasting and making sacrifices to strengthen us spiritually. Kids usually gave up things like candy or movies. Most parents preferred that we gave up being a pest around the house. Some nuns suggested the money we would have spent on candy be donated to the pagan babies. I am sure there was a significant spike in donations worldwide during Lent. The money certainly went to an excellent cause.

When I graduated from the 1st grade in 1946, my brother graduated from the 8th grade. Twelve out of 33, a little over one-third, in his class were Latinos, which was one measure of the neighborhood's ethnicity.

Our family was pretty involved with St. Charles. My brother, sister and I were all students there. Mom was active in and eventually president of the Women's Guild (Mother's Club) for two terms. They raised money for the church through various parish activities. Mom had an Irish brogue (accent) that she never lost her entire life. She knew she had to give a thank you speech when she left office as president of the Women's Guild, so she went to a woman who taught public speaking. Mom asked the woman to get rid of her brogue. The woman convinced her otherwise, that "You're an individual; you're someone different. You do not want to talk like the rest of the Americans." The woman also told her, "Start off with a joke and by the time you are done, you will be relaxed." As a departing gift from office, Mom asked for a rosary made of amethysts, which was her birthstone. When she got up to speak at the farewell luncheon, she said, "Thank you for the lovely rosary made of amethysts, my birthstone. Be thankful that my birthstone was not diamonds." She got a big laugh and applause, which did relax her.

Dad helped take up the collections at Mass every Sunday and was eventually president of the Father's Club – the male counterpart of the Women's Guild. Years later, my brother told me how he sat by Dad at Father's Club functions and how very proud and impressed he was by the way Dad could make speeches in front of crowds. I suspect that period was the zenith of my dad's life. This was a far cry from the first time Dad had to make a speech when they were honoring him for his service as president of the Hibernians. He got up to speak and froze. Mom was pulling on his coat and said, "For God's sake, sit down." Finally he got his bearings and got through the speech. The honors and speeches were a side of Dad that I never saw because I was too young at the time. Although there were the good times, so much of my memory of him was from the downside of his

44

life involving heavy drinking, alcoholism treatments, and a life of silence and staring into space. It gave me a distorted image and memories of Dad. He deserved better for being such a gentle and affable man who had the respect of his many friends, relatives and strangers.

Emancipation and Independence

By the time I reached age six, Mom felt comfortable enough letting me go across the street to the Park alone because my older brother and sister always hung out there. Mom made them promise to keep an eye on me, which they most assuredly said they would. In reality, they had no intention of babysitting me as they had their own circle of friends to hang out with. That was fine with me. It was a critical moment in time that gave me a kid's emancipation from my parents to come and go on my own and to choose buddies who would have the greatest impact on making me a good kid and keeping me out of serious trouble for the next six years. Not being under the close scrutiny by others made me more independent, self-sufficient and able to make decisions at a young age. It gave me the opportunity to make my own friends that led to a circle of buddies to play with, memorable childhood experiences, and the chance to develop social skills in getting along with others. For better or for worse, the person I became was influenced by those closest to me. As I grew older, I found lots of kids had pretty sad childhoods because a number of them had no close friends in their neighborhood to pal around with.

Since I was now walking the streets more by myself, I habitually walked along the curb looking in the gutter for loose change that fell out of the pockets of people getting out on the passenger side of automobiles. Occasionally I found a penny, nickel or dime along the way. On rare occasions I found a quarter or a crumbled up dollar bill. I checked under benches where people may have lost change when they sat down. There were pay phones everywhere in those days. Seldom did I pass a pay phone without checking the change slot for returned coins. That was where I had the best luck finding a coin or two. It was like looking for buried treasure. I never expected to hit it rich, but I had to keep trying. As I learned later in life, the most successful people experienced a lot of failures along the way, only to reach success eventually. Even as an adult, I was never too proud to bend down and pick up a coin, even a penny. Wasting the chance to pick up loose change was like wasting food left after a meal. We were always told we could never leave food on our plate by the end of a meal at home. Being Catholic, we constantly were reminded of "…all the starving children in China" to give us a reason to eat all our food. It did work and was a lifelong lesson I followed.

As I was always looking for a way to make money, one Saturday when no one was going to be home, I had a garage sale of toys – the only things I owned. Everything was small like trading cards, comic books, soldiers, cars and marbles, so they did not take up much room outside where I sat on our front doorstep. A man stopped and asked the price of a toy car, and I had no idea. I never gave any thought to how much I would ask. I finally said, "A penny." He immediately said, "It is worth more than that" and gave me a nickel. I was so excited. It was my only sale that day. I never had another garage sale.

I grew up in a different world from most kids. Folsom Park was a kid's world within an adult's world. Kids lived within a block of the Park and we could walk there in two or three minutes. It was a place to form close friendships with six to eight other kids, something I found was not typical of kids I met from other neighborhoods. The Park had every form of game and recreation for kids to play on sunny and rainy days. Our "playground" extended beyond the fences of the Park into the sidewalks in front of our houses where we played more personal games away from the kids in the Park. Having friends close to home allowed us to get out of the house and away from our parents to become more independent and adventurous than typical kids.

Home was where I had breakfast, lunch, dinner and spent the evening listening to the radio with the family. Folsom Park was my second home where I spent my time during the day when not at school. It was at the Park where I started to make friends. There was Kenny Atkins, who lived across the street from me, and a few doors down from the Park. Bobby Gray lived in a flat a few doors down from Atkins, and Robbie Hall lived in a flat behind Gray. Tommy Lynch lived in the middle of my block on my side of the street, and Joey Sandoval lived a few doors down from Lynch. Bobby Ellington lived around the corner from me on 21st Street off

Treat Avenue. They all lived on my block or just around the corner. On my block and surrounding blocks, there were some Victorian, Queen Anne, Italianate, Edwardian and Mission Revival buildings – probably where I got my interest in homes with character later in life. Nearly every building on our block on both sides of the street was a two or three unit flat with just two exceptions, one was Sandoval's Victorian house. **[11]**

I never knew the ages of my buddies because the topic never came up. We never talked about school, so we never knew each of our grades in school. Kids cared nothing about what we were – only about who we were.

My St. Charles classmates were not the kids that I went around with because they did not live within a block or two of my house and Folsom Park. Tommy Lynch was the only exception, and he was more of a family acquaintance. All of my other friends went to public school. I asked Mom if I could transfer to Hawthorne Grammar School (now Cesar Chavez School) where my friends attended. She said public schools were not as good as Catholic schools. Whether or not it was true, I would have rather gone to Hawthorne, but I had little say in the matter. It turned out that it probably would have been a bad idea because then everyone's age would be obvious. Some of the guys may have been at least a year older than me and they might have thought I was too young to be around. We never knew or asked how old each other were. I always passed by Hawthorne on the Folsom Street side of the school building where the schoolyard and fancier side of the building was, so I always thought it was the main entrance. I never realized the entrance was on Shotwell Street off 22nd Street nor did I ever wander through the school's hallways. As a matter of fact, I was never curious enough to wander through any school I was not attending, whether it was a private or public school. They just did not seem like interesting places.

Like any collection of young friends, my buddies made up quite a variety of characters, each unique in their own way. Bobby Ellington reminded me of the All-American boy – blue eyes, blond hair, solidly built as if molded to play football for Notre Dame. He went on to play center at Mission High School and made All-City on all three *Chronicle, Examiner and News-Call Bulletin* 1958 All-AAA football teams. Bobby Gray reminded me of Gary Cooper – slender, quiet, confident and good-looking. He had a real cowboy hat I always envied. Robbie Hall had a man's body, a child's emotions and a peanut brain. Atkins was the kid none of the parents wanted their boys to play with. He supposedly was in and out of trouble, which was not true as long as I knew him. Kenny had a glass eye that was a different color than his real eye. I never did ask him how that happened. Kids just did not care. Joey Sandoval was a Latino kid who eventually gave me the idea of how to get easy money. Richie Lucas was a quiet mild mannered kid, who later had a mental breakdown before he was 10. Tommy Lynch did not go around with us, but I knew him because his mom was friends with my mom. He was the typical rough neck, molded by hard times, lean from nervous energy, hard headed (literally) and often chewing through string or rope with his teeth. Bobbie Breckle lived on my block in a flat on Folsom Street off 20th Street, and we saw him at the Park occasionally, but he just did not fit in with our group. His nose was always running and he wiped it with the sleeve of his shirt or sweater – not something we wanted to see day in and day out. It was sad that his parents did not change his habit. He may have fit in quite well otherwise. Only goes to show that parents can affect their kid's social life by how they raise them.

I look back on my childhood and am so thankful my parents allowed me the independence to wander around our neighborhood on my own by age six, although they never knew exactly how far I wandered. I know it had a big influence in making me a self-sufficient, independent person and developed my confidence in so many ways. Up until then, Mom pretty much confined my activities to the kid's section of the Park, but now that I was going to the Park on my own, a whole new world opened up to me. The clubhouse had a separate room for the Park director's office. That was where I had to go to check out equipment like basketballs, ping pong paddles, bats, softballs, and all board games like chess and checkers. I had to leave a piece of clothing as a deposit to make sure I returned the item. Just outside the director's office door was a big wood box where the sports equipment was stored and I helped myself to whatever I checked out with the exception of ping pong balls that were kept in the director's office. The director hung a blackboard outside of the clubhouse where notices to the public were written, e.g., sign-ups for activities, Park areas restricted due to scheduled games and competition, temporary changes in hours, and maintenance being performed.

Hardball was not allowed on the baseball diamond at the Park due to the small confines of the Park and for fear that someone walking around in the outfield or around the clubhouse would be hit, so softball was the game of choice. I always envied the older kids who got to play baseball at the Park due to the challenges it presented. The "wow" excitement was if someone hit the ball over the first 15-foot fence in left field about 130 feet from home plate. It was the height of the fence that created the challenge. On rare occasion someone hit a ball 250 feet that cleared the second fence that was 20 feet high at the far end of the Park. That was a jaw dropping shot that brought real cheers. Only one or two kids were known to have done it with any regularity. The other challenge was to hit a home run 110 feet over the 13-foot-tall Park clubhouse roof out in right field, which was done mostly by left-handed batters. That was one of the reasons for the metal wire screens over the clubhouse windows – to avoid long line drives from breaking the windows every few weeks. If I was walking through the Park or by the clubhouse while kids were playing softball, I always had to keep an eye out for a ball coming my way. The players were pretty good about yelling to get our attention if they saw a ball coming close to others in the Park.

If the baseball diamond was not occupied, kids my age used it to play kickball. The rules were the same as baseball. The pitcher rolled the ball to home plate, and the kicker tried to kick the ball through the infield or into the outfield. If the batter missed the ball, it was a strike – three strikes and you were out, which never happened unless it was fast pitch. In that case, the pitcher rolled the ball as hard as possible to strike out the kicker, or at least have them kick foul balls. The object was to run the bases and come home to score a run eventually. Those in the field caught the ball and threw the ball at the runner before they reached the base. If you hit the runner, he was out.

Since the high school kids pretty much "owned" the baseball half of the Park, it left the other side of the left field fence where there were two basketball courts and a tennis court for kids my age to play. About the only thing we used to do on the tennis court was to bounce up and down on the tennis net until the Park director blew his whistle for us to get off. As for basketball, on occasion we played a normal basketball game with each other where we were trying to block shots and make baskets.

There was room on the north side of the courts to play dodge ball when no one else was around. One kid stood in front of a wall and tried to avoid being hit by the basketball being thrown by another kid who was about 15 feet away. On the basketball court, we played a variety of games like H-O-R-S-E, Twenty-one and Around the World.

Most, if not all, of the ground in the area of the baseball diamond was dirt. So a favorite pastime was to dig 1-inch-deep holes to play marbles in the foul ball area of the diamond in right field. We dug three holes in a straight line about 3 feet apart. Then a fourth hole called "purgatory" was dug off to the right about 4 feet from the furthest hole. The object was to shoot our marble from hole to hole and the first one to sink their marble in all four holes in one direction and the three holes back to the first hole was the winner. If we missed the hole, then the next player shot his marble. Occasionally we intentionally aimed our marble at the other guy's marble and tried to hit it as hard as possible to knock it far away from the nearest hole so he did not have an easy shot. If we missed his marble, we could wind up out in the "boonies," but it was a risk we took. We played with marbles of different sizes and materials. The large marbles were called "boulders." Steel ball bearings were used as metal marbles and called "steelies." Boulders were harder to shoot with the flick of a thumb, but we could knock the other guy's marble further into the boonies.

The Park was where I learned to play ping pong, checkers, chess and even Jacks. Although Jacks was considered a girl's game, I enjoyed the challenge. I learned ping pong from my sister, who was very good. At first, I could not find anyone to teach me the rules and to play the board games with me because I was younger than most of the kids, so I learned to play from the Park directors. He or she sat on the wood bench outside the clubhouse and played games with me. On rainy days, we played inside. Playing those older than me made me a good player. By the time I played with kids my own age, I usually won. Confidence was built on success. Every kid should find things they excel at or are good at doing, whether it be in games, sports, scholastics or other activities. The more wins in life, the greater the confidence.

Mom was a creature of habit and strict schedules – probably where my obsession with order, efficiency and planning came from. Dinner was served religiously at 5:00 p.m. every day. If Joe, Kathy or I were across the street in the Park, Mom leaned out the bedroom window that looked out on to the Park and called us each from across the street by name – Terrrrrence, Kathleeeeen, Joooooe. She repeated the same calling at least three times. If there were any stragglers, she went to the window and called some more for them. Some of the kids in the Park mocked us. "Terrrrrence, your Ma (or Mommy) is calling you." After a while, the other kids in the Park got tired of the mocking and just accepted it as the way things were going to be, so they just came inside the clubhouse to tell us our mom was calling us. By then, the repeat calling to dinner made the Quinlan kids known to everyone in the playground as they could place our first names with faces. Initially it was embarrassing for us, but soon we just realized this was just her way to get us to come home on time. It was the most effective and efficient way of getting us to dinner.

At age six, my main form of transportation was by foot. I also rode my homemade scooter on occasion. It had a wood crate body, a 2" x 4" deck, wood handles nailed to the top of the crate, not for steering but to hold on to, and wheels from a disassembled roller skate. Santa must have felt sorry for me, because I got a real scooter for Christmas. It had rubber balloon tires that had to be inflated with an air pump at the gas station. There was a seat that folded down flat on the floorboard when not in use, and I rode the scooter on flat ground by repeatedly pushing off with my right foot. The most fun was riding it down the steep driveway next to Atkins' house. I could pull up the seat and ride it full speed down the incline but careful not to drive out into traffic.

Roller skates were my preferred way to get around. My roller skates had leather straps to hold them on my feet and a pair of clamps by the front of the foot to attach the skates to my shoes. A skate key was used to adjust the clamps to tighten and loosen the skates from the shoes. Often the skates came off because the sidewalk cracks and rough street surfaces worked the skates loose from the shoe. More times than not, I could stay on my feet, but at times I fell to the ground skinning my knees. A little iodine and a bandage took care of the knee, but the hole in my pants meant Mom had to patch the hole for me.

Good, Bad and Ugly of Ancestry

There were a lot of Irish get-togethers. I was dragged along to attend Irish parties and celebrations throughout my childhood. They were events mostly for the enjoyment of the adults with little for kids to do. There was always lots of laughing, music and drinking. The parties were usually very crowded, as too many people were invited to share a space too small for them in a basement or living room. These were not rich people. Their flats and homes were small and simple, so kids had no room to run around. Everyone towered over us small kids, making us feel unimportant and in the way of the adults.

But one of the fun gatherings for our entire family was the Hibernian Irish Picnic held each year in Marin or Sonoma County, usually in the summer when the weather was nice. Kids and adults competed in different events like 3-legged races, racing with a raw egg in a spoon, and wheel-barrow races with one person holding the legs off the ground of the other person who moved as fast as possible with one hand in front of the other. There were tenor singers, men in kilts, Irish jig dancers with tap shoes, and lots of chatter, food and drinking – mostly alcohol for men and sodas for women and kids. It was a chance for adults to see friends they knew back in Ireland as well as those they met here. The music was the unique Irish tunes from Ireland played on accordions, fiddles and bagpipes with their high-pitched sounds. The Irish jigs, usually danced by young girls in Irish dresses or men in their kilts, were fun to watch. The drinking was mostly hard liquor like whiskey. I was surprised that my dad being a bartender all his life said his favorite drink was Early Times whiskey and a little water. I thought he would prefer a more special brand but he was simple in taste in everything about life – food, drink, habits, and lifestyle. But he did pride himself on his appearance in a suit, tie and hat.

Mom always reminded us of our Irish heritage: "Our blood is 100 percent Irish" because Mom, Dad and their parents were from Ireland. Being pure Irish was something she was very proud of, and she wanted her children and their children to experience the same pride, so it was natural later in life that Mom tried selling me on dating Irish girls. When none of her children married someone who was Irish, I think she realized it was more important that we married someone she respected regardless of their heritage. I was always proud to be Irish, but Mom occasionally complained Joe, Kathy and I never showed any interest in Irish activities and history, especially since we were "100 percent Irish." And she was right, but she did not tell us stories about life in Ireland unless we asked questions about it. She admitted she did not like talking about her days in Ireland because of all the bad memories she had about their house burning and the deaths of family members. Mom and Dad took us to Irish picnics, parties and family gatherings, but we seldom heard much about the Old Country and what the relatives and friends did in Ireland. Conversation was mostly about current events. We never got to know kids our ages at these events to carry on the Irish culture. It was all "old people" who had little interest in kids, our thoughts or opinions. When we did ask questions and got information about Ireland, it was learned in short intervals spread over years. There was no continuous flow of information about the Irish culture, stories, heroes and life experiences that might lead to a strong interest in the culture. I wish I had asked more about life in Ireland and knew more about what Mom and Dad did all their lives before coming to America. Years later Mom explained, "The interest in Irish culture was dying out because the Irish were no longer meeting frequently like when the Hibernians were a more popular organization. And the younger generations were not joining the Hibernians."

As proud as I was of being Irish, there was a challenge to growing up with parents who emigrated from another country whether it was from Ireland or any other country. For immigrants like Mom and Dad, it was natural for them to bring with them their preferences for Irish music, dances, sports, drinking-with-the-boys, and socializing with others from the same country. However, many did not realize that by not adopting the interests of Americans, they could hurt their children's ability to grow up in America. Their children were growing up with American kids, taking on their values, interests and customs. Immigrant parents would be of greater help if they also learned to accept the American ways. Mom and Dad clung a little too much to the Irish ways. This partly explained why Dad never took me to baseball or football games and why my parents never attended my baseball and football games and track meets in high school with the exception of two football games. These were things that were important to me when I was growing up, but I never got much encouragement or support from Mom and Dad. Without support from parents, kids relied on self-motivation for our accomplishments. Kids still wanted their parents to be proud of them. That was why we tried so hard to impress them. If they were not present, it denied kids a chance to show them how good we could be at what we worked so hard to do.

I always thought Dad just never knew how to be a father and never took Fatherhood 101, so he did not know how to spend time with his kids. At least Mom took me to the movies, but Dad never took me to places like ballgames, Playland or the Zoo. I suspect he felt that was for Mom to do. To be fair to both of them, Mom was in her late 40s and 50s, eventually working at a job where she was on her feet all day. Her shopping was done all on foot. Since Dad never helped with the housework, she used the weekends to do all the household tasks and to rest up a bit to return to work on Monday. Dad had a job where he often worked the night shift and slept in late. By the time he woke up in the morning, a good part of the day was over. Under the circumstances, Mom and Dad did their best to put food on the table and to raise us kids the best they could. It was a tough physical life for them, so I accepted that they did not have a lot of time for me. Besides, I had my buddies who were in a similar boat and we did just fine.

On the other hand, there were many values my parents brought from Ireland that I was so thankful to experience as I grew up. There was Irish pride – it was easy to be proud to be Irish in a city with a large Irish population. I loved the Irish songs, bagpipe music, jigs and wearing of the green. Parents worked hard, coming from nothing, to feed their children well, provide them a good education, and raise them to be a good person. My favorite meals were an Irish breakfast and a corned beef and cabbage dinner. There was the custom of the family and relatives living nearby so we got to know each other over the years. Kids were encouraged to be self-reliant and independent – to work hard to be all that we could be. There was the importance of a Catholic education with discipline in the classroom and surrounding us with "good" kids. St. Patrick's Day was an expected celebration each year. The local church was excellent for soul searching and thinking about life. Confession beat visiting an expensive "shrink." There would be no sex until your wedding night. Kids were expected to care for their aging parents.

The Mission District was known to have the best year-round weather in the City. When it was overcast in other parts of the City, it was likely sunny in the Mission. A big cause of the nice weather was that Twin Peaks to the west often kept out the fog that caused the overcast and dampness, leaving the sky a clear blue. It was actually quite pretty with the billowing white clouds sitting along the entire rim of Twin Peaks. It looked like someone dropped a huge pile of cotton all along the hilltops. Mom often referred to the fog that crept over Twin Peaks at the end of a warm day as "mother nature's air conditioner for the Mission." Since our neighborhood was the warm-belt of the City, Mom thought it appropriate to dress me in shorts and sandals whenever we went out, especially on nice days. And that was fine until age six when I was going to the Park trying to make my own friends. As the Mission was a somewhat rough neighborhood, I got lots of ribbing from other kids about not wearing "big boy" pants and shoes. I pleaded with Mom to buy me some long pants for play. Although she could not see why, she finally let me wear long pants to the Park and to shed the sandals.

Now that I was going out on my own into the real world, I started to get more self-conscious about my physical appearance. When I looked in the mirror, I just saw a kid with big ears and a face covered with freckles. That included one big freckle just above the tip of my nose and out front where everyone could see it. What was bothering about freckles was that other kids did not seem to have them, and kids wanted to be like all the other kids. My sister had lots of freckles but they seemed to have skipped my brother. After a few years I asked Mom if the freckles would ever disappear, and she assured me they would, which was a small consolation when most other kids, with the exception of a few other Irish kids, did not have freckles. So I could accept the freckles because I was not alone and some of them were my good friends. It helped bond those of us who looked different. I did not know if the freckles would grow together to give me a nice tan look or just fade away, but I believed Mom. Eventually most of them did fade away during my high school years.

Another flaw in my appearance was that I started to lose my baby teeth by age six, but it was worth it. Mom told me if I put my tooth under my pillow, the good fairy would replace it with money. Sure enough, when I woke in the morning, my tooth was gone and there was a quarter in its place. It really did take some of the pain away, which I suppose was what the fairy had in mind. Lucky for me, I was nowhere near being interested in girls at that early age, so it did not matter how silly I looked with missing teeth in the front of my mouth.

I never was interested in chewing gum, probably because I kept envisioning the gum pulling out the few fillings in my teeth, but I loved bubble gum. For those of us who could walk and chew gum at the same time, it kept me amused trying to blow a bubble bigger than the last one. In the confines of my home where there was no wind to blow the bubble onto my face, I tried to blow a bubble that exceeded my personal best – another case of trying to excel, even if the competition was only myself. One evening, Dad brought home two pockets full of bubble gum from work – probably a customer paid for a drink or two with them. It was the first time Dad ever brought home a gift for me for no reason. I was so excited, but Mom said not to expect it as a regular thing. Although I heard her, I did not believe it. I at least had hope for future treats. She turned out to be right. There were never any more treats from work again.

Going to the horse races was Dad's one escape from work and family life. It was his only form of amusement outside of attending an occasional Irish football game or boxing match. Dad may not have stayed within the limits with his drinking when he was behind the bar at work, but he did stay within his limits with his gambling. He told me he never bet more than two dollars on a horse. Whether that was true or not, no one ever knew how much he bet or whether he won or lost for the day. Mom never cared as long he turned his $100 weekly paycheck over to her for the food, rent and family living expenses, with the exception of the $20 he was allowed to keep. No one including Mom knew how much he made from tips at McCarthy's, but she did not care as long as we ate well and could afford the necessities. Dad was always frugal. He never made decisions about buying things for the house or family because he hated spending money. Mom made nearly every financial decision. I suspect that frugality contributed to Dad being one of the most prepared gamblers when it came to horse racing. He took it very seriously. He never went to movies with Mom and me, but handicapping the horses was his passion. It was his only form of relaxation and entertainment.

Every Saturday that horses were racing in the Bay Area, Dad spent hours Friday night studying the race forms, handicapping the horses and making his picks for the next day. I suspect I got my math aptitude from Dad's analytical skills and his father, who was a teacher of all subjects including math. There were many nights that Dad was at the kitchen table doing his homework for the races and enjoying a cigarette well after everyone else went to bed. The next day he went out to Tanforan Field in San Bruno or across the Bay to Golden Gate Fields in Berkeley to make his bets and watch the races. He never talked about how he did at the track or if he had a big winner. It was not something he wanted Mom to know about. At most he said, "I broke even." As much as I would liked to have known how he picked his horses, I doubt that he would tell me because Mom was against her children having anything to do with horse racing and would not want him to encourage me. She did not even allow Dad to take Joe or me to the races until we were over 18. Joe and Dad eventually went to the races, but by the time I was old enough to go, Dad's health was suffering and he was no longer enjoying his favorite leisurely pastime. I always regretted not showing more interest in his "hobby" and passion. It could have given us a topic that we could talk about and bring us closer together. But all kids probably had regrets of some sort that they wished they did things differently regarding their parents – too many missed opportunities, unspoken conversations, and experiences not shared.

Dad and I got our haircuts at the barbershop on 21st Street just off Mission Street where a friend of the family, Ed Daubeneck was a barber. He and his family lived two blocks from the shop on South Van Ness Avenue just off 21st Street. Up until age six, I had to sit on the little kid's seat when I got a haircut. It was a board laid across the arms of the barber chair with two handles to grab to keep me still. By age five I was getting embarrassed by all the older kids and adults in the shop thinking of me as a kid, so each time I asked Mr. Daubeneck if I could sit in the chair without the board, he kept telling me I was not old enough. But by age six, I must have been wearing him down because he finally let me sit in the barber chair like the big kids. I felt so grown up. I never realized it was only because he was doing a favor for my dad. If the barber was anyone other than a close friend to my folks, I would have been confined to the board much longer.

Age 7: Financial Independence

I had never ventured outside of the Mission District on my own. The Mission District was my entire world, but I was about to embark on the greatest adventure of my life at age seven. One Sunday I set out to walk as far as possible toward the ocean, which I knew was somewhere over the "mountain" (Twin Peaks) but not sure where. I started up 21st Street going west and just stumbled across Clipper Street, located between 25th and 26th Streets, which happened to be one of the few streets over Twin Peaks. I wandered through the West Portal District as if traveling along the Yellow Brick Road and entering the Land of Oz. I had emerged from a neighborhood of houses showing a lot of wear and tear to a world of well-kept and expensive houses. I was so surprised by the new Parkmerced apartments across from where San Francisco State (College) University was built a few years later. They were so modern with clean streets and no one around, so unlike where I lived. I continued west taking jigs and jags and finally reached the ocean. It was a fun adventure, but now I had to return, which was a very long walk. Ugh! I doubled back the way I came except I walked the full length of Sloat Boulevard. I was so impressed by how wide Sloat Boulevard was compared to the streets I ever saw. I later learned that it was the widest street in the City. I got home while it was still light out, and never told Mom and Dad where I was that day. I knew they would not have approved. But for me, there was such a feeling of independence and accomplishment – the feeling that I could do anything if I wanted it badly enough. It just involved taking one step at a time, keeping focused on my goal, and enjoying the trip along the way.

By 2nd grade, boys had developed the nerve to add spitballs to their repertoire of weapons for harassing the girls and playing war with the boys. A small piece of paper was chewed up into a ball and spit through a paper straw for distance. Girls got so upset with the whole idea and thought it was disgusting, which it probably was. Half of the time, the girls never knew the spitballs were in their hair until a friend pointed it out to them. It was tougher hitting a kid who was jumping around to avoid being hit, but the fun was just in trying.

The nuns posted a board in the classroom with each of our names on it. Across from our name, the nun placed gold, blue and red stars to reflect good things we did in our classwork and conduct (how we behaved). It was her way of motivating us to do well in our studies and behavior in the classroom and schoolyard. Gold stood for Excellent, blue was Good and red was Satisfactory. The object was to get the most stars – the most gold and the least red. At the end of the school year, there were no prizes given. It was just the self-satisfaction of achievement and that we did better than most. None of the kids did poorly for very long because the nuns would "straighten them out" long before the school year was well along.

My sister was taking piano lessons at St. Charles and was pretty good. Mom decided that I should take up the piano too. I fought the idea for as long as I could until she insisted finally. The piano lessons were given at the St. Charles Convent where the nun's lived. It was a beautiful three-story Victorian building but very foreboding to a 4-foot-tall second grader having to ascend 23 steep steps from the sidewalk to the imposing front door. Talk about creating a sense of power and intimidation on the part of the nuns – not their fault. The wood paneled interior was something seen only in the movies. I found playing the piano laborious to learn, and I was never good at it. I finally convinced Mom after six months that it was a waste of the money she had to pay for those private lessons. She agreed.

I started doodling in class about now and it extended throughout grammar school and into high school. I frequently doodled during class on a pad of paper used for taking notes. I hid the pad behind an open book for fear the teacher would see what I was doing. With so many war movies being made during and after WWII, it was no wonder I drew war scenes while the teacher was talking. Many of my doodles through 5th grade were air battles where the American fighter planes were shooting down the German planes. I drew stars and swastikas on the wings to distinguish the good guys from the bad guys. Of course the Americans were always winning. The reason that German rather than Japanese planes were used was because swastikas were easier to draw than the Japanese Rising Sun emblem on the wings and sides of planes, while the U.S. planes simply had five-pointed stars on their planes. I always thought the swastika was an interesting design – not for what it stood for but for the design features, and it was easy to draw. I did not know it was used earlier as a symbol of good luck and prosperity by various religions, major U.S. companies, the Boy

Scouts and Girls' Club of America, and the American military in WWI. **[12]**

Not everything was about goofing off. The nuns taught us that "All animals and insects are creatures of God." For the rest of my life, I always had second thoughts and a reluctance to kill any creatures even as small and insignificant as ants. If I could release an insect to the outdoors, I did it throughout childhood and adulthood.

Another of my doodles was a sketch of a baldheaded face with huge eyes peering over a wall with his huge nose hanging over the fence, his fingers clutching the wall, and the caption underneath "Kilroy was here." Sometimes I drew a single curled hair on his head. This popular cartoon was used by servicemen as graffiti wherever they went including on the beachheads. I also played countless games of tic-tac-toe by myself during class. I could pay attention to the teacher and doodle at the same time, so it was a win-win for both of us. At the Park, we played tic-tac-toe in the dirt as none of us carried paper and pencils around. Over time, I learned patterns to where and when to place my Xs and Os on the grid to win on a regular basis.

Cowboys and Indians was another popular subject of movies, so at home where I had more time for drawing, I sketched battles between the cowboys shooting guns and the Indians shooting arrows – often flaming arrows. The figures were always stick characters with a round head and straight lines for the body, arms, legs and a feather on the back of the head of the Indians. They would be riding horses or hiding behind rocks. No one was winning. They were just battle scenes, sometimes with burning covered wagons and buildings.

Combat Bullies With Laughter

One night we were at the Park and this Latino kid, Danny Machado, told us to come with him. He had something to show us. He was two or three years older than the rest of us. We had seen him around the Park trying to look tough but never seemed to talk to anyone or to have any friends. We thought it was strange, but we had nothing to do, so we went with him, since there was just one of him and a bunch of us. We walked out through the back gate of the Park, across the street to his house on

Shotwell Street. We walked up some steps to his large front yard, which was all dirt, weeds and no plants. There was a 3' x 4' pit about a foot deep. There was a black dog lying by the side of the pit. He put his dog "Blackie" in the pit. The dog was a black cocker spaniel and did not look menacing, much less vicious – just looked like a house pet. Danny tried to make Blackie vicious by poking a stick at him and getting him to snarl and bite the stick. It was a pathetic attempt to make a friendly dog appear vicious. In the middle of this, Danny warned us, "If any of you cross me, you'll be put in the pit with Blackie." The idea was that Blackie would tear us to shreds. It was almost comical. The pit was only 12 inches deep and hardly big enough for a dog and a "victim," as if we could not jump out and run away. We kind of laughed, turned around and walked back to the Park. It was a strange way for a stranger to try to make friends or create a new gang, if that was his intent. Anyway, we never saw Danny, Blackie or any of his theatrics again, even though they lived so close to the Park. He just disappeared. I suppose the lesson learned was that laughing in the face of a bully was the best solution when in a crowd.

Folsom Park offered a summer day camp for kids, which I attended that year. They took us on a bus ride, and I was thinking how far it was and it must be somewhere out in the country. It turned out we were still in San Francisco, just on the other side of Bernal Heights, a 400-plus-foot-high string of hills to the south. On the other side of these hills, the landscape was as if we were in the country where the grass and weeds were two to three feet tall. The "camp" consisted of a competition to see who could collect the most bugs and the winner got a prize. All day we scoured the hillsides looking for anything that was small and moved. There were points assigned to each type of creature, for example, five points for a grasshopper on up to 100 points for a garter (garden) snake. The values were probably a reflection of scarcity because grasshoppers were all over the place and I never saw a single snake all day. Everywhere I stepped, several grasshoppers jumped on my pant legs, so no one had trouble earning points – boys and girls alike. I turned in my catches in their provided containers, and they supposedly recorded my points. I was too naïve to realize there were too many insects to count for everyone, so I assumed they released all the critters at the end of the day, if not sooner. They never did announce the winner, but it was a fun day. If I was at all squeamish about bugs, I overcame that feeling by the time I returned to the Park.

Now that I was doing a lot more running around and playing away from the sandbox, slide and swings, I was going through the knees of my pants and soles of my shoes a lot faster. Although other kids had holes in the knees of their pants, Mom was a very proud person, so I was never allowed to go outside if there were holes in my pants. Mom cut off one of the back pockets on my pants and sewed it on the inside of my pants to fill the hole "as good as new." When the heels wore down beyond the heel and into the sole of the shoe, it was time for me to walk up to Zinke's on Mission Street where I could get my shoes repaired while I waited. One of the Latino shoemakers sewed on a new sole and nailed on a new heel. They had a lot of guys working on shoes, so I could take a seat, after picking up one of their small blankets to put over my feet to keep them warm, and waited for the shoes to get done – it usually took less than an hour. One of the gossip rumors among Mom and the neighbors was that the sister of one of my buddies was sleeping with the fellas at Zinke's. That was hard to believe because she was a really heavy unattractive girl and I figured those guys could do a lot better.

Start of a Six-Year Business Career

In our family, we did not get allowances. We were expected to do tasks around the house without getting paid to do them. I had to ask Mom for money, just like Kathy and Joe did when they were younger, but Kathy now had a job after school at the Public Library. Joe could not work much during the week as he was commuting about 30 miles to and from Serra High School in San Mateo. Joe made his money from summer jobs. When I asked Mom for money, she either said, "No" or "We cannot afford it" or she sent me to Dad, who always repeated whatever Mom said. Mom was financially practical. Dad was just cheap. If I wanted something that was not too expensive, Santa might bring one or two of them to me at Christmas time. I always hated the need to depend on others for money or the things I wanted. My resentment to depend on others for anything was something that stayed with me my entire life. This feeling drove my determination to be as financially independent as possible as a youth and completely independent later in life. So starting at age six and for the next couple of years, I went around the neighborhood looking for empty soda bottles to turn in at Jack's across the street for the two-cent deposit on each bottle. I looked in the Park, outside grocery stores, in doorways, along the sidewalks, and down alleyways. Selling recycled bottles for two cents each was fine, but they were not easy to find. It was far from a steady income.

I could now afford to buy my own candy. A novelty candy for me was chocolate cigarettes consisting of a 3-inch role of chocolate wrapped in white paper like real cigarettes. Walking around with one hanging out of my mouth made me feel like a grown up as I pretended to be smoking. Mom told me to take it out of my mouth and constantly reminded me that smoking was a disgusting habit. This was not surprising as Dad was a chain smoker who eventually died of cancer over 60 years later at age 69. Growing up around Dad's habitual smoking eventually was enough to turn me off of cigarettes. There was nothing attractive about watching someone who was addicted to constantly sticking something in his mouth. It was the same as someone with an eating disorder who was constantly eating except smoking also provided the repulsive smell of smoke in the air, on the furniture, in the clothing and on the breath of the smoker. Yet, with all of that, my sister also had a smoking habit that contributed to her death at age 73. I think what saved me in my teens was the adage at the time that smoking was bad for athletes, and it was more important to me to be a good athlete. Maybe that was the secret to avoiding or breaking bad habits – to find an alternative that was more important.

I was now seven years old and had seen kids selling newspapers on the corners along Mission Street, so I asked Mom if I could do it too. She was against it and said, "You are too young." I said it was a way to earn money so I would not have to pester her and Dad for money. I pleaded my case and she finally gave in on the condition that it did not interfere with my schoolwork. I said it would not. Of course I would have said anything, which is what kids did to get their way.

At the time, San Francisco had four daily newspapers. They were the *San Francisco News*, *Call-Bulletin*, *Chronicle* and *Examiner*. The *News* was the only option for me to sell after school because the other papers were either morning editions or sold by men who were in the newspaper union. So I hung around a corner where a kid was selling papers on Mission Street and waited for the paper distributor, Al Levine, to drop off the newspapers. I asked him for a job. He took my name and called me a few days later and said I could sell papers on the corner of 20th and Mission Streets in front of the Granat Brothers – the same corner Leo McCarthy sold papers. Papers sold for seven cents and I kept two cents and gave Al the rest when he drove by to pick up my leftover newspapers at the end of the day. If papers were ever stolen, I still had to pay him. The kids took the loss for thefts, which seldom happened and only when we left our stands. I started at 3:30 p.m. after school and ended at 6:00 p.m. after people got home from work. On Saturdays I worked all day. At least the *News* did not put out a Sunday paper, so I had that day to myself. Besides, only men in the union could sell the Sunday *Examiner* paper as they received a lot more than the two cents I got for each daily paper sold.

Granat Brothers was an interesting location for me to work. It was a combination retail jewelry store and manufacturing workshop. It was fascinating to look in their side windows along 20th Street and watch them repairing watches and creating new pieces of jewelry. There were four or five men with their magnifying glasses perched on their foreheads while working at small tables up against the windows so I could see up close how they used their tweezers to work with such small watch parts.

Selling papers probably was the most important thing I did in my youth by starting me to be on my own and independent of others at such an early age. From that point forward, I never had to ask Mom or Dad for any spending money. If I spent money, it was my money, which meant more than if my parents just gave me money to spend. Their money did not have the same value as my hard earned money. I could now afford to do my own shopping, even if the price range of many purchases was more appropriate for the F. W. Woolworth's store on Mission off 22nd Street. Having a five and dime store was great for finding cheap toys and comic books but not candy – a luxury still beyond my means, plus, candy and desserts were never around the house, so I had no craving for sweets.

Obviously my folks continued to provide the big stuff for me like food, lodging, clothing, and school tuition. For those things I remained eternally grateful even if I took them for granted at the time. That was why later in life I felt that I owed it to them to take care of them in their old age if it was necessary, and it turned out that it was for my Mom (Dad died before he needed home care). It was sad to see, as I got older, that less than 10 percent of children took care of their parents in their old age. I always believed that *I should take care of my parents in their old age to pay them back for what they did for me while growing up, and that did not mean putting them in a nursing home.* Looking back at my youth, I regret not offering to help pay for some of the household expenses or my tuition, but I suspect most kids were pretty self-centered like me. It never even crossed my mind at the time because those expenses were transparent to us kids. They were not expenses I personally incurred as a kid. Mom and Dad never discussed money in front of us kids and never threw in our face "all they were doing for us." They worked hard, lived frugally and did the best that they could for their kids without complaining. I respected both of them for that.

Power of Constant Suggestions

Besides getting my first job selling newspapers, another thing that influenced my life a lot was that Mom kept reminding me and telling all her friends and our relatives that I was going to be an engineer. By the time I did go to college, it was what I set out to be. Even though I changed my major from mathematics to finance, Mom's constant reinforcement that she expected me to go to college throughout my 10 most formative years kept that idea focused in my mind and resulted in me taking college preparatory classes throughout high school. This was pretty extraordinary for Mom and other mothers to be pushing their kids toward college at the time. Although the average San Francisco adult completed nearly 12 years of schooling, only 19% of those in San Francisco went on to college. [13]

So my new job got me used to making change and dealing with adults, both of which benefited me later in school and the business world. I made about 60 cents a day for three hours of my time, which came to $15 a month – this beat hours of searching for bottles for a lot less. On rare occasions a customer gave me a dime and told me to keep the change. That was a big deal to me, sort of money I did not have to work for. I saw more of that at Christmas time, especially from my regular customers.

There was some on-the-job training. Al Levine kept reminding me to hold the newspaper across my chest with one hand at the bottom so everyone could read the headlines and to yell out "Hail late *News*, get your late paperrrrr" or "Hail late *News*, get your 4-star edition." The early (1:00 p.m.) edition had 3-stars in the masthead on the cover while the later 4-star (4:00 p.m.) edition had the latest news. Most people coming home from work wanted the 4-star edition. Sometimes I lost a sale when 4-star editions were dropped off late due to printing delays. If there was a major headline that day, Al gave me the line to yell out, like "Hail late *News*, new mayor elected." On rare occasions, he told me someone from the *News* was driving around, and if he heard me yelling out the headlines, he would give me a dollar. I was always good about yelling to draw attention to my presence, but I only received the one-dollar bonus once. All that early yelling for a good cause may have been why later I turned out to the holler guy in baseball constantly cheering on our pitchers.

One of the paperboys told me how other newsboys made fun of Al with a Jewish slur. I never heard the slur from anyone, except that one time. I cannot believe it was frequently, if ever, said among newsboys, or that there was prejudice or hatred of Jews behind it. I had no idea there was such a thing as hatred and prejudice against those who were Jewish. Years later I learned nearly all prejudice came from adults and parents. Sad. Kids our age just said and did stupid things, often parroting what they heard at home. I never knew the Greenbergs, friends of the family, were Jewish because it was never mentioned nor relevant to anything. If there was any prejudice, it was against some of the Latinos in the Mission District. They were the gang members, but I never saw their presence or violence around Folsom Park. They hung out around 24th Street – one gang was even called the 24th Street Gang.

Key to Becoming a Millionaire

While still seven years old, I set a lifetime goal for myself to be a millionaire by age 40. I chose 40 because it was about the age my parents had me. I knew I did not want to be poor and I did not want to struggle for money. It was not that I wanted a lot of expensive things or to do a lot of traveling. I just wanted independence and not rely on others for money or have money be an issue when I did need something. I set the figure at one million dollars because anyone rich in those days was called a millionaire. I never lost sight of that goal as I grew up. It was not that I thought about it every day, but I did remind myself every few months. I never thought about how I would become a millionaire, but the key for me was the constant reminder of my goal and believing I would figure out the "how" along the way. It turned out that I did reach my first one million dollars in my 30s – the equivalent to about $4 million today. My continued pursuit to being a multi-millionaire would have amassed more, but I was too stubborn to adopt one of the keys to making a lot of money and that was to use human leverage – employing lots of people to create and grow a business. For various reasons, I preferred to be a one-man operation with complete control of the decision-making and avoiding employee issues. It was all about quality of life for me as a business owner. Besides, it was easier to make money through investments rather than run a business.

Over the years I learned that if I wanted something bad enough, I had to keep reminding myself of the goal. Too many people got busy with their everyday lives and lost sight of what they really wanted out of life and set out to do, but what I found most common with people was that they never set long-term goals in the first place. They grew up without any specific expectations, ambitions or concept of success, which simply is the achievement of a goal. Since everyone has different lifetime goals, "success" is something different for each of us. Goals may be experiential, educational, financial, physical/health or may deal with personal development, career or a relationship. The sooner one identifies their lifetime goal in specific terms, the sooner they can get on the road to success to face the numerous forks in the road along the way. By waiting too long, they will miss some of the early key forks that may have taken them to their intended destination.

I always liked Horatio Alger type stories. Kids who went from rags to riches were my role models as I grew up. I always pictured myself in their likeness. As a kid, I kept a sketch of a boy in knickers selling newspapers on the inside cover of my scrapbook. I never envisioned the exact road to my lifetime financial goal, but I never forgot my roots and where I came from – that was enough of a motivating factor.

The Neighborhood Sandbox

Growing up in the Mission was a world of adventures for me. There was a playground across the street. Movie theaters were within walking distance only five to seven short blocks away. There were rooftops on my block that I could jump across from building to building. A Boys Club was just several blocks away. There were industrial lots and a railroad yard to explore. It was a world of fun, legal ventures and curiosity from illegal trespassing, although I never knew what trespassing meant – all were just more places to play.

If I got to the Park early and none of my buddies were around, I could check out a basketball at the clubhouse and practice playing H-O-R-S-E, Around the World and Twenty-one. To add a little thrill to playing ball by myself, I counted down the clock for the game winning shot from the top of the key or practice taking the "winning jump shot" before I finished counting down the clock 5-4-3-2-1. Swish!

"H-O-R-S-E" was a game that required us to make the same shot from the same distance from the basket as the other shooter. Shooter 1 called his shot, e.g., 30 footer from the top of the key, left-handed hook, over the head with his back to the basket, or a between his legs shot. If he made it, shooter 2 had to duplicate the shot. If he made it, then shooter 3 must make it. This continued until a shooter missed the shot, and that shooter got an H against him. If shooter 1 misses his original shot, shooter 2 called his own shot. The next time the shooter with an H missed, he got an O, then an R, then an S, and finally an E. Once a player had five letters against him, he was out. The last player still in the game won.

"Around the World" involved shooting the basketball from seven different positions moving in a counterclockwise direction around the key from under the basket, to where the 6-foot-wide free throw lane met the circle, to the perimeter of the circle at the free throw line, to the top of the circle 20 feet from the basket, and on around the key. The first shot of Shooter 1 was from under the basket. If he made it, he took a shot from the second position and kept moving around the key until he missed his shot at which point he had two options. He could stay at that spot and wait for his next turn while Shooter 2 took his first shot from under the basket, or Shooter 1 could chance it and take a second shot from his spot. If he made it, he moved onto the next spot; if he missed it, he went all the way back to the starting spot. Chancing it on a second shot got a lot riskier the further we moved away from the basket. The first player who got all around the key (world) and back again in reverse order to the original starting spot won the game. This could be the end of the game unless Shooter 1 was the first to reach the end. In that case, the other players got a chance to make all their shots to reach the end so that all had an equal number of turns.

In "Twenty-one," players took their turns shooting from the top of the key (or the free throw line for smaller kids). If we made the first shot, we got a point. If we missed, we ran to retrieve the rebound. If we made our second shot from where we caught the ball, we got a point. We continued until we missed a shot. Each player in turn did the same thing. The first player who got 21 points won the game.

To give everyone an extra incentive to win whatever game we played, we added the rule to the game that the loser(s) had to get down on his hands and knees and bend over as far as possible against the wall with his hands behind his head with his butt serving as a target. Everyone else had one shot at throwing the ball as hard as they could from 20 feet away and hit the loser in the butt.

Dad was a chain smoker and my brother was a smoker, so I thought smoking was such a grown up and cool thing to do. Joe, who was 15, taught me to blow donuts with cigarette smoke, which I thought was so cool too. So at age seven, I used to steal Chesterfield cigarettes from Dad when he was asleep. As I rummaged through his pants and jacket pockets, I could feel specks of tobacco on the bottom of the pockets. He must have kept cigarette butts there until he had a chance to smoke them at work or before going to bed because I never ran across any butts in his pockets; or, he may have just thrown them out at night to have empty pockets to start the storing-of-butts cycle the next day.

One day I invited my buddies to have a smoke in my new hiding place I had found recently. We climbed up one of the 15-foot-tall trees on the 21st Street side of the Park in the middle of the block. The tree had sturdy branches we could sit on in the open space in the center of the tree. It was like a hideout for us. We lit up and started smoking the cigarette that was passed around, never realizing that the smoke started streaming out of the tree. Eventually, the Park director came over to investigate and made us put out the cigarette and get down from the tree. He also told us how dangerous smoking in a tree can be due to the possibility of a fire, and that we were too young to be smoking. He said he would tell our parents if he ever saw us smoking again, and we were never to climb the trees again; also, we had to promise not to do it again, which we did, but I did find other places to smoke. Looking back, it must have been a pretty comical scene for the director seeing all this smoke pouring out of a tree as if it was on fire, only to find these three mischievous kids smoking a cigarette. I never climbed the tree again, probably because my hiding place was no longer a secret. Later that year, I stopped smoking forever – another novelty that wore off fast, especially around Dad's chain smoking.

Free Transportation Around the City

The 36-Folsom streetcars with cattle prods on the front and back ran on Folsom Street from 1945 to 1948 when the line was discontinued due to low ridership. That was too bad since they provided free transportation for kids like me who were willing to jump on the rear cattle prod until the conductor kicked us off, which usually was a block or two later. I just waited for the next streetcar to ride it as far as I could. Streetcars ran on electricity. They had a pole with a roller on the end that ran along an overhead wire of electricity. There was a rope that ran from the trolley to the pole on the back of the streetcar. Another way to get a free ride was to pull on the rope in the back to disconnect the roller from the wire, causing the streetcar to come to a stop, which required the conductor to get off and make the reconnection, while we crouched down to sneak on the back. It was more effective if we did this as the streetcar slowed down to make a turn at a corner where it would appear that the trolley disconnected on its own, so the conductor was less apt to be looking for kids jumping on.

From 1941 to 1950, every one of the Mission District's streetcar lines was removed and replaced by bus routes, which was no deterrent to our lack of character for wanting to get free rides around the City. A matter of fact, buses made it easier for us as there were no conductors on the back serving as watchdogs. We just waited for people to get off the bus through the back door, and before the door closed, we jumped inside and stayed

70

low so the driver did not see us, while we scooted to the closest open seats. Surprisingly, no passenger ever complained to the driver or told us to get off – probably felt empathy for us. There was the chance that the driver saw us in his rearview mirror, but he generally was busy with riders getting on through the front door. That was why I only got caught once and was told to get off, so it was not a big deal getting caught. It worked best with just two or three of us at a time as there was less time to be spotted. I suspect some drivers did see us sneaking on but just said to themselves *what the heck* and just ignored us – like those conductors who were not sticklers for punching a kid's Muni card and enforcing the time limit on transfers.

Streetcars had dark redwood seats for two with brass handles and were hinged so the conductor could flip them to reverse the seats at the end of the line so all of the seats faced forward. If there were no other riders just before kids were getting off, occasionally they would flip a couple of the seats just to be annoying, something that did not appeal to me – strange where I drew the line as to what was and was not acceptable behavior for my mischief.

Mecca of Entertainment

Being just four short blocks from Mission Street that had five movie theaters was a kid's paradise for a cheap entertainment afternoon. Kids were not concerned about movie schedules. We just showed up whenever we got there, often in the middle of a movie, which did not bother us; or we could check the schedule hanging inside the ticket booth, and if the movie was half over, we had the option of checking out another theater; if almost over, it was worth waiting 5-15 minutes. Tickets for kids usually were 20 cents at most theaters but only nine cents on Saturdays at the Crown Theater. For the admission I saw a double feature (two movies), a cartoon, a newsreel, and previews of coming attractions that actually gave me an idea of what the movie was going to be about. Some theaters also showed a 15-minute short comedy and a chapter from a weekly serial that lasted for 12 or 15 episodes. Some of the cartoons were a sing-along involving a bouncing ball jumping from word to word in the lyrics shown on the screen. Nearly everyone sang along. It was one of those feel-good moments that added to the ability for adults to escape their problems and humdrum lives at home and work. A few doors down from the Crown was a small store that sold caramel apples and popcorn drenched in butter. It was as if the popcorn was dropped in a bath of hot butter. The smell of the caramel and buttered popcorn acted like a magnet to pull me inside. It took a stronger willpower than mine not to take treats into the theater. For the teenagers, the balconies in the theaters were the places to go to make out. Being a kid, I found it gross watching everyone making out, so I tried to stay out of the balconies – especially after theaters restricted smoking strictly to the balconies. The stench was just too much.

The San Francisco Boy's Club, at the corner of 21st and Alabama Streets, was just four blocks from my house, so it was an easy walk for me. Club membership was free, so even kids like me could enjoy all of the activities they offered. Activities like basketball, gymnastics, and the trampoline were dominated by the older kids, especially during certain times of the day and evening, so kids my age participated when there was room for us to play. I tried bouncing on the trampoline a few times, but could not get the hang of doing flips, even though there was an assistant who used pulleys to pull ropes attached to a harness that fit around my waist so I did not bounce or fall off the trampoline. Doing a somersault in the air was just beyond me. After failing to complete a somersault, I had to get off and let others have their turn. In hindsight, I wish I had the gumption to ask if I could have more time to get good on the trampoline when others were not around. I wish I was less shy and more aggressive to ask more questions and make requests of older people. Worst case was that they just would say "No."

The Boys Club each year provided free bus transportation and access to a "Playland Day at the Beach." They gave us a tag that we tied to a shirt button that allowed us on all rides and access to all concessions at Playland. Kids ran all over the place with the paper tags flapping in the breeze as we tried to beat the crowd to the next ride. There also was free food and beverages. It was the best day of the year for my buddies and me.

The Boys Club showed chapters from movie serials. There were 12 to 15 episodes, each 15 minutes long, just like at the theaters on Mission Street. There was always a thrilling ending to each episode to get me to return next time. The ending might be the hero driving off a cliff or a buzz saw about to cut the heroine in half. But my favorite activity at the Boys Club was the craft classes they held. Most of the classes involved working with wood like making and painting kachina dolls [14] and making Moorish scimitar swords from a single piece of plywood. The most memorable event was their Halloween Night. We lined up outside and had to be admitted one at a time. I never knew what to expect, but I knew it would be scary and fun. Although I knew the layout of the Club, where the doors and staircases were, and the location of the rooms, it was easy for me to lose track when there were no lights and was pitch black. Each door I went through closed behind me and I was always in the dark. Although I did not see them, there were people inside to guide me by hand if necessary so I did not bump into things or hurt myself. In the dark, I sat on the floor and slid down two flights of stairs on slick tumbling mats. By pushing myself along, the slide descended a U-shaped staircase. At the bottom, someone helped me up and told me to walk forward in the dark. I felt my way along the walls and scary monsters appeared with flashlights to their faces. There were lots of scary noises, yelling, groaning, rattling chains and cobwebs in my face. There were a number of other scary encounters until I finally reached the end of the chamber of horrors. It was fun doing once, otherwise I would know what to expect if I went back through and things would not be as scary and full of surprises.

It was always fun looking forward to Halloween night. My buddies and I could never afford costumes, and it seemed such a waste of money for something we outgrew in a year or two. So we went around in our street cloths trick or treating our first few years. Eventually, I created my own costumes and my favorite was when I put on one of Dad's old wide brim Fedora hats and wore over my clothes a pair of Dad's long john underwear that had a seat flap on the back that could be unbuttoned. Mom thought the idea was outrageous and would be too embarrassing for her and Dad because neighbors would know it was me. So I disguised myself by drawing eyeglasses and a full beard on my face using charcoal from burned wood. I suspect the neighbors still knew I was the Quinlan kid.

One year I trick or treated the Greenbergs. She must have recognized me because she gave me a quarter, which was a lot of money for me and no one had given me money before, so that was special. I brought my buddies by the Greenbergs on Halloween the next year. They only gave us candy, which was a huge disappointment to my buddies after telling them we might get money. Mrs. Greenberg showed no sign that she recognized me this time, as I probably just blended in with the other kids. I never went back to their house again on Halloween.

If people did not answer the door on Halloween, we were big on playing tricks on them by marking the windows with soap – something that was easy to clean off. We never used wax because it was harder to clean off. Even soaping windows was a rarity because most windows were on the second story in our neighborhood. Something we never did, but heard of others doing, was to put dog poop in a paper bag, ring the bell, set the bag on fire and run away, so the person coming to the door would put out the fire by stomping on the fire with their foot. My most memorable experience was going to the door with four buddies and ringing the bell. A man in his twenties came rushing to the door yelling and screaming at us and we all ran off in different directions so he could not catch all of us. I crawled under a car and stayed there for four to five minutes to be sure the guy was nowhere around. Only thing I could figure was some kids came by his place earlier and did something that really irritated him like ringing the doorbell and just running away. Most likely, he was just a jerk scaring kids away so he did not have to hand out candy.

A big treat was buying a five-cent ice cream cone at Jack's. It always seemed like a lot of trouble for Jack or his wife to come from around the counter to go over and make a single scoop cone for me, but they always did it with a smile as if I was one of their big spender customers. I could not eat a cone like others who simply chewed and ate the cone from top to bottom. After I licked the ice cream down to the rim of the cone, I bit off the bottom and sucked the ice cream through the cone. It was a way of making the special treat last longer.

Mom sent me to Jack's to get her shopping list filled and to bring home the shopping. It was a period when collecting trading cards, marbles and bottle tops was popular with kids. While waiting for Jack or his wife to gather my items off the shelves, I rummaged through the bottle top container at the bottom of the Coca-Cola soda box in search of certain bottle tops. The underside of these soda bottle caps had a piece of cork, and when pried off, there was a picture. It made the caps a collectable, so I tried to save up a complete set of all the possible pictures. I sat on the floor until I went through all the caps in the container, and Jack never complained or shooed me away, even if customers had to walk around me to pull sodas out of the soda box.

There was another grocery store on the corner of 20th and Folsom Streets. It was run by Latinos and seemed to get mostly Latino customers. Although only a block apart, Jack's never got robbed as far as I know, but the Latino store seemed to get robbed regularly.

There was a cigar store at the corner of 21st and Mission Streets that had one of the few pinball machines around and was rumored to be a bookie joint where bets could be placed on the horse races. It was across the street from Bank of America – sort of a one-stop shopping corner where you could withdraw cash at one and place your bets at the other.

Homemade Toys

Now that I was working, I could shop at stores that sold things I could never afford to buy in the past. There was a hobby shop on 24th Street where I bought 3-inch cylinders of compressed air used for operating a variety of tools. I tied them to toy cars and airplanes, punctured a hole at one end of the cylinder with a tool for such purposes, and the car or airplane shot across the field at the Park. As exciting as it was to create and launch my own jet vehicles and have a homemade toy that none of the other kids had, I soon lost interest because they were one-time toys. The cylinders could only be used once and it was too expensive for me to continue buying them for three to five seconds of excitement.

The hobby shop also had model airplanes hanging from the ceiling that I could build from kits. I built a number of them over the next two to three years. All of the parts were balsa wood. Most of the body and wings were made from thin balsa strips. I covered them with tissue paper that shrank and tightened smooth when I sprinkled water on the paper. A coat of clear dope and paint created the hard surface. A thick, long rubber band was strung from the tail to the propeller. I kept turning the propeller until it was tight, and when I released my hold on the propeller and threw the plane in the air, the plane flew for 50-60 feet. I either tried to catch it or have it land on grass to prevent the plane from crashing and breaking off parts. Eventually, I had to do maintenance work to piece the plane back together. After getting tired of repairing the models and patching the torn wings and broken wheels, I just set them around my room so I could appreciate the work I did.

I then moved on to making kites, which were sturdier and lasted longer. They were simpler to build and took way less time to assemble, so if they ever got broken, I did not have the regret of spending so much time on construction for nothing. To assemble a kite, I just had to connect the two thin pieces of balsa wood to the four corners of the tissue paper kite, tie the wood strips together where they crossed for sturdiness, and attach a 4 to 6-foot-tail made out of a strip torn from an old bed sheet on to the bottom corner of the kite. Folsom Park did not have a lot of room for flying kites and there usually were too many kids around to have space to run around to lift off the kite into the air. So when I eventually got a bike, I held the kite, tail and ball of string in one hand and steered my bike with the other hand and pedaled my way to Mission Dolores Park about nine blocks away. There I had all the room I needed to launch the kite and there was no chance of crashing the kite into a fence or telephone line. Also, the ground was grass, so if the kite dove into the ground, it would be a softer impact and less likely to cause any damage.

The simplest and most fun flying toys were airplanes about 12 inches long that were almost feather-light in weight and made entirely of balsa wood, except for a small metal cylinder imbedded in the front for balance. They consisted of four pieces of 1/8-inch-thick wood: a body, wings, tail and rudder. The wings and the tail slid through a slit in the body and the rudder slid into a slit in the top of the tail. Setting the wings perpendicular to the body, the plane would fly straight ahead when I threw it. If I set the wings forward, the plane flew in a loop-the-loop pattern. If I set the wings back in a more balanced position, the plane flew in a level pattern and for distance. If I angled the wings to the left, the plane flew in a loop to the left; if angled to the right, the plane flew in a loop to the right. Because they glided in the air and made soft landings, there was no crashing to the ground, so they lasted forever, unlike model airplanes and kites.

Then there were paper airplanes. By the end of the 2nd grade, we had a couple of years of schooling behind us, and that gave us the confidence to push the envelope a little. So before the class started, one of the boys sailed a paper airplane across the classroom. Then a couple of more boys jumped on the bandwagon by quickly creating planes and throwing them into the air. One paper plane design was to fold up one end of the paper three or four times, not more than 1/4-inch wide, to give weight to the front of the plane. Each side was folded once to create wings, and two small tears depressed at the rear of the body created a cockpit. But my favorite plane design had a dart shape to it with a long pointed nose and sleek wings that I could quickly make with five folds in the paper before the teacher arrived. Students were pretty good about picking up planes that landed by them, but if a nun saw any on the floor, she demanded to know who threw them and sent him to the principal's office. One visit to the principal's office was usually enough fear of God for the kid to stop. Over time, plane making and flying was usually limited to the schoolyard. The school still frowned on throwing paper planes for fear of a pointed plane nose hitting a kid in the eye.

I only knew our landlords by their last name – Sacco. They lived in the other upper flat in our building. I never met the people living in the other unit under the Sacco's flat. I assumed no one lived there, as there was never any comings or goings. On occasion, I had to drop off the rent cash payment with the Saccos. One evening I dropped in while they were having dinner. Being Italians, they offered me a small portion of wine in a wine glass. It was the first time I ever had liquor of any sort, even if it was only two or three swallows. Eventually, I must have innocently mentioned it to Mom, God knows why, which was a dumb thing to have done in hindsight. The next time I stopped by the Saccos during dinner, and they said Mom had told them to not serve me wine again. The entire family seemed as disappointed as I was in hearing the bad news. I then realized that the Italians and the Irish had a different attitude about liquor and kids, at least where wine was concerned.

The Sacco's son Steve had an orchestra that practiced in the basement. The musicians all had day jobs, so they practiced and performed in the evenings. The room was made soundproof so we never heard them in our flat, but when I went down the backstairs past the door to the basement is when I could hear them practicing. Occasionally I went in and just sat on the steps to watch and listen to them. Sometimes they had a good-looking female singer with them. Much of their music was dance and swing music. I stayed longer when I was lucky enough to hear them playing swing music. Steve never kicked me out all those years. I never knew at the time that he and his Steve Sacco Big Band Dance Orchestra played at such places as the Fairmont Hotel in the City and featured guys like Paul Desmond on alto saxophone and Joe Dodge on drums who went on to fame with popular groups like Dave Brubeck. I always thought they were some struggling band that just practiced all the time and never got a gig.

About this time, I started to dream in my sleep that I could fly. It was an exciting experience but also scary as there was always the fear of this being the dream in which I would not be able to land. Over time I could control the flying in my dreams, whether it was taking off, maneuvering in the sky or landing. In some dreams I was aware that I was dreaming and wishing I would wake up to escape some scary situation. Surprisingly, I woke up almost as quickly as I had wished it.

One night I was having a bad dream and woke up really scared. Mom and Dad asked what was the matter and I told them I had a nightmare after watching a horror movie. Dad told me, "It is just a movie. They are just actors in the movie and none of it is real." Whenever I watched a scary movie that was starting to get to me, I just remembered Dad's advice and said to myself "They are only actors. It is not real." That made it easy for me to watch the rest of the movie and it stopped the nightmares.

One day Dad asked me if I wanted to visit the local police station. Many times I had walked by it at 17th and Treat Streets but was always afraid to go inside. I felt safe with Dad, so we went. It was a big room with a few policemen hanging around. Dad took me up to the officer at the duty desk and introduced me to him. He seemed sincerely interested in meeting me. I suspect he was one of Dad's customers at McCarthy's. Seeing wanted posters were probably the most fun, but I did not recognize anyone. I felt a little relieved when we left. The visit was intimidating, a little scary but thrilling. It gave me a respect and admiration for police officers that I held dear to me all my life.

Age 8: Age of Exploration and Adventure

Although our flat was on the corner, I never crossed Folsom Street at the intersection just 20 feet from our front door. Instead I always took a shortcut by running out the front door and straight to the Park entrance. Although I made that crossing hundreds of times on my own, on this particular morning I ran out between two parked cars and heard a loud screeching that turned out to be a panel truck driver who slammed on his breaks to avoid hitting me. His front right fender just glanced off my left leg. I stood there confused as to what had happened and wondering where the truck had come from. The driver was by my side almost immediately asking me in a panicked voice if I was OK. I said I was and proceeded across the street as if nothing happened. I assume Mom heard the brakes screeching outside and came down and talked to the truck driver because a day or two later, Mom had taped a sign to the wall at the top of the stairs leading from the dining room down to the front door. The sign was from the San Francisco Police Department and it was a list of eight or nine things I needed to do before crossing the street in the future, such as I will not cross the street between parked cars; I will cross the street at the nearest intersection; I will look both ways before crossing the street; I will yield the right of way to any traffic before crossing, and so forth. I never did ask where the sign came from, whether Mom went to the nearest police station, which was seven or eight blocks away, or if a police car arrived at the scene and had copies in their patrol car. Mom insisted I had to read the entire page of warnings every time I was leaving the house, and I did do it religiously. After a week, I had memorized the entire page and recited it word for word as fast as I could as I ran down the front steps. I was done before getting to the bottom step of the staircase. At some point, the sign was taken down after Mom felt that I learned my lesson and had changed my ways of crossing the street. Initially, I did walk the 20 feet from our front door to the intersection at the corner, looked both ways as it said on the sign and crossed when it was safe. That lasted a month or so. After that I just jaywalked in front of our house, but I was careful to be sure there was no traffic coming. I did learn that lesson.

The Mysterious Room

Although the Park directors came and went every few years, there was one constant that gave the Park its own personality. It was "Jim," the gardener and maintenance guy at Folsom Park. No one ever knew his last name, but kids could care less about things like last names. Jim had white hair and a white beard and always looked old my entire childhood. He was always nice to everyone – a non-authoritarian type, unlike the Park directors. Jim had a gardening shed on the side of the clubhouse next to the children's play area. It was always a mysterious room as no one was ever allowed inside, and Jim never turned a light on, so it was always dark except for the sunlight from outside. It was the only place at the Park that we had to keep out. I guess it was a kid's thing, but any place that was taboo created the enticing challenge to get inside. We were no different.

The Park was locked up at 5:00 p.m. when the Park director went home. Although there was a 20-foot galvanized steel chain link fence on all sides of the Park to keep kids out after closing, it was easy to climb over and access the Park by the time I was eight years old. Kids my age had narrow feet so our shoe fronts easily fit the holes in the fence. One night, a bunch of us climbed the fence with the intent to finally see what was inside Jim's maintenance shed. We had a screwdriver that was used to unscrew the metal screen protecting the shed window on the back of the building where no one could see us from the street. The window was left ajar, probably to let air into the musty shed. We climbed in and could not find a light switch – probably why it was always dark inside during the day. There was enough sunlight outside that we could look around inside. It was filled with tools, brooms, hoses, and other unexciting things. It was quite a let down, but it was still an exciting experience – going where no other kid had been. It was a secret place we shared with our buddies, and that made it all worthwhile – even if we got caught, it would have been worth it. We screwed the screen back in place and no one was the wiser. After climbing over the fence at night a couple of more times, there was no need to do it again since there was nothing to do at the Park at night. Besides, we proved to ourselves that we could do it, and there was no challenge too tall for us.

There were some games that we played with the girls on our block, but never at the Park. Hopscotch was one of the games. The girls never seemed to hang around the Park and the guys preferred doing things with other guys at the Park. "Heats" was another game we played with the girls. It was a two-team tag game that involved capture, jail, jail breaking and lots of running. The two sides took turns being the jailers and the convicts. When the jailers tagged a convict, they had to go to the area designated as the jail. If a convict could avoid the jailer by running around them and touched an imprisoned convict, the convict could run and escape from jail. The object was to get all of the convicts in jail.

A more adventurous thing the guys did was to play on the rooftops on our block. We got on the roofs by going up the back stairs of my buddy's flat, climbing the access ladder and pushing open the trapdoor to the roof. All of the flats were two-stories high and the roofs were three feet apart above the adjacent bay windows. We got a running start and jumped from rooftop to rooftop. There really was nothing to see up there. It was just an exciting "death-defying" thing to do. No one ever missed or got hurt, but it definitely provided a great thrill. Initially, we had estimated the distance, marked the distance with chalk on the sidewalk and had done some trial jumps to be sure our short legs could make it before trying it two-stories up. We were foolish risk-takers but not stupid.

I loved going over to Sandoval's house. It was only one of two houses on the block that had not been turned into flats. It was a large Victorian house with fancy dark wood paneling on the walls and a wonderful staircase leading to the second floor. In their backyard, they had a huge bush in the far corner that was covered with blackberries. I had to be careful not to get pricked by the thorns, but the berries were free, plenty of them, and ripe for the pickin'. There were lots of bees around, so I needed to avoid them, but the effort was worth it – free snacks.

We all had comic books. They eventually piled up so I took a stack over to a buddy's house and traded with him. We were not collectors as no one ever told us that they were a collectable item. We just wanted to read comics we had not seen before. On the back and inside covers of comic books were ads for sending away for stuff like decoder rings, Charles Atlas exercise programs for "97-pound weaklings," magic tricks, and toys of all sorts. Ads in comic books were used to get kids to spend their allowance money. Those were the days when I could send cash through the mail since kids did not have checking accounts, so I did buy things from the comic books, but these purchases were often expensive for me because there was postage to pay, so I relied more on prizes out of the cereal boxes for a lot of my small toys.

My staple of literature was comic books, but I eventually matured from looking at pictures to reading stories from my collection of Big Little Books that were 3 5/8" x 4 1/2" x 1 1/2" in size with bright colored covers. The subject matter came from radio characters, movies and comic strips like *Dick Tracy, Flash Gordon, Lone Ranger, Popeye, Red Ryder, Tarzan*, and my namesake *Terry and the Pirates* was my favorite. The books sold for a dime (later 15 cents). My buddies were happy to trade for comic books but not for such literary works as my Big Little Books.

A carry over from comic books was my limited interest in reading the newspaper. When Dad was not working late, he sat in his cushy, padded cloth upholstered easy chair after dinner and read the newspaper. We were never allowed to read any section of the paper until Dad was done with it. I mainly wanted to look at the comics, so I had to wait the longest for my section of the paper. The comics were about all I ever looked at in the newspaper during grammar school. In high school I got interested in the sports page and local news but never had any interest in the international news, which was so foreign to me in many ways. I had little knowledge where most foreign countries were and had no idea what went on in their cities. Since I seldom left the City and had never traveled outside of California, I never had any interest in what went on in the rest of the U.S. and no interest in anything outside of the U.S.

My most memorable book at the time was *The Little Engine That Could* with its vivid turquoise blue steam engine pulling a string of much larger cars up and over a mountain – a seemingly impossible task. The little engine's repeating comment "I think I can, I think I can" and its never give up attitude until it succeeded crossing over the top of the hill were ingrained in my head throughout my childhood. It was the earliest book I read that helped develop my senses of self-motivation, focus, never-give-up attitude, risk-taking, self-confidence, and positive thinking for the remainder of my life.

My brother and his friends at age 16 were not very sensitive when they gave nicknames to their buddies. Once my brother and his buddies told me to go over to one of their friends and call him "Homo." It made no sense to me and I wondered what was the big deal, so I did after some prodding. Joe and the others just laughed when I did. I always thought it was his real name until I realized in high school it stood for homosexual. In all likelihood, he really was not gay. Kids my age knew nothing about the gay and lesbian scene in the City or familiar with the derogatory names they were called – an example of the innocence of childhood. Sad that some had to grow up and develop prejudices against them. Another friend of Joe's was "Dumbo." I was invited over his house years later on a business matter, and I addressed him as "Dumbo." He smiled and said, "Now that's a name I haven't heard for years." Until then, I had assumed his real name was Dumbo, but it was a nickname Joe and the others called him because of his size and took the name from the cartoon *Dumbo* the elephant. In those days kids called their buddies names for the fun of it, and it did not affect their friendships. I am sure kids preferred not to be labeled with derogatory nicknames, but being one of the guys was more important.

I was eight years old when my brother was hanging around out front of the Park's clubhouse. Somehow the subject of Santa Claus came up, and that was when my brother said there was no Santa Claus. I could not believe it. Even his buddies got on him for saying such a thing. The only reason I thought there might be some truth to it was that he was 16 years old and he should know and he had never lied to me before. But his buddies were not denying Santa's existence. I went home and told Mom what Joe said. She denied it was true and told me to forget about it. I was not around when Mom confronted Joe when he got home, but I was there when my 14-year-old sister got in Joe's face and told him it was a terrible thing to say. My belief in Santa was back intact because I knew it had to be true and his existence was definitely confirmed by Mom and my sister.

Biggest Contributor to City-wide Exploits

Up until age eight, I mainly hung around the Park and roamed around one or two blocks from the house. But the biggest thing that led me to develop the courage to try new things and a sense of independence to not relying on others was having parents that were not around much to micro-parent me because Dad worked days or slept late after working the swing shift, and Mom was caring for the house. So I could expand my "sandbox" to include the entire Mission District and much of San Francisco.

These adventures would not have been possible until I acquired a bicycle, which allowed me the vehicle to travel afar and into the nooks and crannies of the City. I bought my first and only bike from a kid in the neighborhood for four dollars. It was as stripped down as it could get – basically a frame, two wheels, handlebars and needing a paint job. It had no front or back fenders or chain guard. The first thing I did was paint it black, the coolest color I could think of. The bike gave me the mobility to ride anywhere I wanted in the neighborhood and much of the City. Most bicycles in the neighborhood had no chain guard, and without one, I often got my pant leg jammed between the chain and the chain wheel, causing me to get off the bike and walk the bike while I dislodged my pant leg from the chain wheel teeth as the chain advanced along the chain wheel. The worst part was that it left grease on my pants and the teeth punctured two or three holes in the pant leg. I would not roll up my pant leg or use a pants clip because I would look like a sissy, so I wore pants with thicker material like Levi's® and made cuffs too thick to get caught in the chain.

Not having fenders on my bike, I often got a streak of water spattered up the full length of my back when riding around during and after a rain, which often happened in San Francisco. To get people's attention so they had time to get out of my way and also to be a nuisance, I fastened a playing card to the rear bike frame with a clothespin so the card flipped against the spokes of the wheel to create a constant rat-a-tat-tat. The faster I peddled, the louder the rat-a-tat-tat. If there were bicycle helmets in our day, only wimps and sissies would have worn them.

I made all of the tire leak repairs myself. The first thing was to locate the leak by filling the tire with air from my pump and rotating the tire in a pan of water until I saw bubbles rise to the surface, which identified the location of the leak. Next was to patch the hole. Tire patching kits came in small cardboard containers with a metal top that had a grater for rubbing, cleaning and roughing up the area where the puncture was located. Pieces of rubber were included for cutting a rubber patch about 1" x 1". The glue that was provided was rubbed around the leak and the patch was held over the hole until the glue dried. When I got rid of the bike five years later, there were over 20-plus patched holes in the tires – talk about taking my life in my hands, but what did kids know?

My initial expanded sandbox covered the area bound by Twin Peaks on the west of my house, the San Francisco Bay to the north, Potrero Hill to the east, and Bernal Heights to the south. In other words, as far as the eye could see, since the Mission District was in its own valley surrounded by hills on three sides. The most adventurous neighborhood for me was the industrial area to the east. Some of the area had no interest to me. There were lots of very large buildings, many made of brick with no particular style or character. There was US Steel Supply (16th and Folsom), Cement Factory (17th and Harrison), Bethlehem Steel Company (20th and Illinois), and Ford Model T Factory (21st and Harrison). There were tracks left over from the San Jose-San Francisco Railroad that ran the length of Harrison Street. Many of the buildings were dilapidated with broken windows and must have been unoccupied because I never saw people coming and going. Little did I realize a lot of them were very productive businesses during the war. But amongst this wasteland of a bygone era, there was plenty to explore in these backstreets. An exception was the Levi Strauss factory on Valencia Street off 14th Street where they still made Levi's®, but I never saw anyone coming or going the various times I went by. I wore Levi's® most of my youth. I was told I could get a free pair if I cut off and turned in so many of the red tags attached to the back pants pocket that showed "LEVI'S®." For a few years I did collect the tags until I realized I had no idea how many I needed or whether I should turn them in at the factory or a retail store.

Exploring Long-Gone Places in the City

On Harrison Street between 20th and 21st Streets, there was a property locked up with a chain and 15-foot wood fence across the front. From the street, I could see the top layer of stacked large bundles wrapped in burlap. Always wondering what was in the bundles, I set out one Sunday to find out. The fence at the front was not climbable, so I found an entrance to the backyard of flats on 21st Street that took me to the rear of the property of interest. I climbed over the fence in the back, which was shorter than the one out front. I suppose they never figured someone would trespass from the rear. I crawled around on top of the 5' x 5' x 5' bundles. They were stacked three and four high. The burlap wrappings only covered the sides of the bundles, so I could see the content from their tops. It was all clothing. This must have been a rag storage lot. Most of the bundles had military uniforms. WWII had been over a few years, but there was no telling how long these bundles were stored here. I dug into a bunch of the bundles and pulled out military shirts, jackets, overcoats, hats and pants. Many still had arm patches, ribbons, emblems, buttons, and buckles on them. I had stumbled across a gold mine of military memorabilia. I went home, got a pair of scissors and a razor blade, and came back the same day. I removed and cut off those that were the most interesting. I took all of the medals, a variety of arm patches and anything that reflected exotic or foreign camps and cities that I could find. A week later, I brought back some of my buddies, but they showed no interest as they never bothered to look for any souvenirs. I guess I owned so few things, finding so many free neat things was a big deal, or some people were just born collectors.

Three blocks away at the corner of 18th and Folsom Streets, there was a company that made wood products like nutcracker bowls and hammers. They left their discards with minor and major defects out on the sidewalk. I went by occasionally, rummaged through the pile, and pulled out the good stuff. Lots of times I could not tell what was wrong with some of the pieces, so I wound up with some pretty good nutcracker bowls that had a nutcracker platform in the center as well as wood hammers for cracking the nuts. That venture ended when supply exceeded demand, as I ran out of friends and relatives to pass on these treasures.

A triangular shaped railroad yard was between 17th and 18th Streets between Harrison and Treat Streets. It was a playground unlike any other. I went there frequently to climb on the trains and walk through the cars containing sand, gravel, stones, rocks – anything small that could be poured into the open top cars. I climbed up on the first open top car and worked my way through the rest of the train, jumping from car to car, just to see what was in them and to find some new exciting stuff I had not seen before. The boxcars were often locked, so I was not able to see inside a lot of them. I suppose they were trying to discourage the hobos from sleeping in them. I ran across a hobo or two, either sleeping in one of the cars or walking along the tracks to leave before the train guard found him. The guard was generally trying to keep them out of the yard so they did not get hurt or run over, since they sometimes slept under the cars and between the tracks. The hobos probably knew that trains usually moved during the day and not late at night. Other than an occasional hobo or train guard, no one was ever around. Sometimes, the guard stopped and warned me about the dangers of playing around the trains. One time he said the bottom of a car could open up and I would be sucked down with sand choking me to death. I thought, *fat chance that would ever happen.* The warnings were my cue to walk off in one direction while the guard walked in the other direction. After he was out of sight, I would go back to finish my climbing and searching.

Half a block away from the train yard was the Mission Police Station on 17th Street between Harrison and Treat Streets. Funny that it never crossed my mind that if someone called the cops because I was playing on the trains, the police would be there instantly and there would be no chance of getting away. It was not that I was causing damage to property, but the guard was just concerned about my safety. More importantly, I am sure Southern Pacific Railway did not want a lawsuit if I got injured, since they never put fences up to keep kids out.

Although the term "hobos" referred to those who traveled around by stowing away on trains, we called anyone who was down and out a hobo, whether they were those in the doorways along 3rd Street or those sitting on the sidewalks in front of and on the side of the Greyhound Station on 7th Street between Mission and Market Streets. I always found a few who were sound asleep on the benches inside the Station. I assumed they were told to leave when customers waiting for a bus could not find a place to sit down, but I could never tell whenever I was there.

My parents always told me to stay away from 3rd Street because it was considered the City's Skid Row, even though one of the McCarthy's bars was also located on 4th Street off Market Street where Dad occasionally worked. Between Market and Harrison Streets on 3rd Street was where the winos and bums hung around outside the flophouses. The reputation was that guys could get mugged and women could get attacked. Of course anything my parents told me not to do was an invitation to go find out what it was all about. So on occasion, I found myself wandering along 3rd Street just for the heck of it. I always found it safe during the day but had no idea what it was like at night when I was not allowed out at night.

The SPCA (Society for the Prevention of Cruelty to Animals) animal shelter was located on 16th Street between Alabama and Florida Street. It was called "the pound." (This was before the term "animal shelter" was popular.) I loved going through the pound. Although there was a stench in the air where the dogs and cats were caged, I ignored it for the bigger picture – seeing all the cute animals lounging, playing and sleeping. The kittens and puppies were my favorites. The hard part was to see those with their paws up on the wire screen desperately begging for me to take them home. Initially, I went home and asked Mom if I could have a pet, but she was adamant about no pets in the house, at least large pets like a dog or cat. Dad went along with her as usual. They were convinced that I would lose interest in caring for it, and Mom would have to do all the work of taking care of it. So after a while, I gave up asking and just sucked it up when I made my visits to the pound. Dad did bring home a baby chick once – not sure where he got it or why he brought it home, but he must have convinced Mom to let me keep it. A couple of weeks later the chick and its box were gone. I never quite believed Mom that it died and they had to get rid of it, but she had never lied to me in the past. That was the only pet we ever had in the house except for a goldfish I won at a carnival a short time later.

The only thing my brother ever brought home was something that looked like a long colorless balloon. He said he found it on the front step of our house. He and my sister chuckled. I asked what was it. Mom said, "It's nothing," and told Joe to throw it away. A few years later I realized it was a condom. It was my first introduction to sex education – something never discussed in our household.

A block from the SPCA was the AAA minor league San Francisco Seals Stadium [15] at 16th and Bryant Streets. Only 10 blocks from home, it was an easy walk. Admission tickets were 50 cents but the cheap seats for kids in the right field bleachers were only nine cents. There were no seats in left and center fields, so right field was it for cheap kid seats. The view was not great from that distance, but there was always the eternal hope of catching a fly ball, which I never did – never had a chance. The stadium held less than 20,000 but it sure looked plenty big to a little kid. It was not a period of great players who made it big in the majors, but it was exciting for a kid to enjoy baseball at such a high level, since we had never had a major league team before. At a game in 1950, I did get to see the real seal (sea lion) used as the ball club's mascot. The keeper threw tidbits to the seal from a metal bucket to entertain the fans. [16] Nothing like an animal act compared to a guy parading around in a seal costume making a fool of himself.

My brother had a summer job during high school at Seals Stadium selling snacks in the stands. One day he got caught sitting down watching the game instead of walking the aisles. He got fired from a job that any kid would have given anything to have – working in the sunshine, making money, and attending the games. What a waste. The Seals era ended when the National League approved the move of the New York Giants to San Francisco in 1957. It was the end of affordable prices for us kids to see professional baseball up close at home and the end of an era of many cheap or free kid attractions disappearing from the City.

Almost next door to the Stadium and towering over the area was the Rainier Brewery on Bryant Street off 15th Street, home of Rainier Ale. Four years later, Rainier was bought by Hamm's Brewery with its 39-foot rooftop neon display of an ever filling and emptying beer glass. As far away as my house at 21st Street, with a northerly wind, I could smell the beer in the air. One of the most vivid memories of attending a Seal's game was the yeasty smell from the brewery and the fresh roasted coffee beans from the nearby Folgers and Hills Brother Coffee Companies. Funny that we remembered the smells from the area more than any one notable game. Perhaps it was because the Seals did not have memorable players [17], with the exception of Frank Malzone, or championship teams when we attended games post 1946. More than likely, it was because my buddies and I spent too many days trying to sneak in for free and not making it inside to see the games.

Seals Stadium was a block from Potrero Avenue, and up five blocks between 21st and 23rd Streets on Potrero Avenue was the Zuckerberg S. F. General Hospital or San Francisco General Hospital, but usually called "S.F. General." It was a large brick imposing building. It had a reputation of being a place where the poor and those who had no medical coverage went to be helped, and it was the last place I wanted to be a patient. I went through it just a few times out of curiosity. It was dimly lit and everything looked old and outdated. It looked like it had not been updated since it was built in 1915. Sick old people were sitting in wheelchairs in the halls. It was a scary place. It made me think of an insane asylum from the movies. I was so thankful for our family using St. Mary's Hospital for all of our medical needs. I never went inside any more, but I did play in their empty lot on the north side of the hospital that was a haven for garter snakes and grasshoppers – a naturalist's playground for little kids like me. I romped through the high grass and looked for lizards to play with – not the kind of pet Mom wanted around the house.

A couple of blocks from home, there was an empty lot on the corner of 19th and Folsom Streets (later the site of Firehouse Station no. 7). In the middle of the lot, there was a 6-inch-deep hole about 4' x 4'. There were some large empty cardboard boxes sitting around, so I built a cardboard house. For the first few days after building it, I went back to be sure it was still there and sat inside by myself. It was neat having my own house, but it was not much fun sitting there alone by myself. So I went and got Sandoval, Gray, Atkins and Ellington – all of my best buddies. I told them I had something for them to look at. When we got to the cardboard house, everyone squeezed through the cutout doorway, and there was just enough room for all of us to sit around the "room." They thought it was pretty neat too, but there was not much to say as we just looked at each other for a while. So I said, "Let's form a gang and this can be our clubhouse." The neighborhood and surrounding districts were known for gangs, so it was a natural, as I knew of no other gangs in the Folsom Park area, at least not our age. I said, "We should think of a password to screen who can come in." It never struck me that it would be obvious if a stranger poked his head in the doorway of our clubhouse that we would not let him in, and if gang members showed up, we would let them in, whether they had a password or not. Ellington finally asked, "Yeah, but what does our gang do?" I had not thought that far ahead. We sat there in silence until I said, "Well, we would hang out together" and Ellington said, "We do that now." I responded, "Well, let's think about it," and we all single filed out on our hands and knees. Even at that age, I was trying to organize a group. When

I went back a week later, the clubhouse was gone. Only a few pieces of the cardboard were sitting around. That was the end of the gang idea.

I learned my lesson about the temporary nature of clubhouses sitting out in the open, so I moved on to a less obvious hiding place. It consisted of a hollow space in a clump of bushes in the front yard of the house two or three doors from the rear entrance of Folsom Park and just across the street from the "dog Blackie in the pit" incident the previous year. One day I noticed that on the backside of the bush there was a crawl space to the center of the bush that was hollowed out. It turned out to be my new private hiding place. I never told any of my buddies about it. I just liked the solitude of lying inside with my thoughts, the idea that I discovered this neat hideout no one knew about, I would not be disturbed by outsiders, and it was "all mine" – my own home away from home. It was another case of wanting something unique that only I had.

Kilpatrick's Bakery was on Folsom Street off 16th Street, but on the South Van Ness backside of the building, I could look through big picture windows and watch fresh bread being cut into slices and going through the wrapping process on conveyor belts. I could smell the aroma and feel the warm heat from the freshly baked bread through the vents that ran the full length of the windowsill. On days when there was a slight breeze in the right direction, I could smell the bread a block or two away.

Around 23rd and Folsom Streets was a large hall that was used as an indoor archery range. I stumbled across it one day, went in, and saw five or six people shooting arrows into targets attached to a wall of bales of hay. The bales were about three feet long and 18 inches deep. I noticed none of the arrows were going all the way through the double layers of bales. There was enough room behind the bales to walk the length of the target range where there were arrowheads on the ground that had broken off when the arrows were pulled out of the hay. So arrows must have penetrated the bales on occasion. I went in back of the bales and picked up the arrowheads and feathers as souvenirs. On my second visit, a guy saw me back there and got very upset. He told me that I could get killed, but I thought he was overreacting, especially when he told me not to come back. Since I had plenty of arrowheads by then, I never returned.

Valencia Street from 17th to 25th Streets was lined with "junk shops" where used furniture was sold. On rare occasions I wandered through the stores, not that I was in the market for furniture, but there were interesting things like old books, pictures, knickknacks, memorabilia and neat stuff that appealed to kids. Some shop owners got annoyed with a kid looking around and probably thought I would steal something. Anything I liked cost too much for me – not that prices were high, but I was just too frugal with my hard-earned money. I never did buy anything, but it was more interesting than wandering through the aisles of department stores. I saw things that all the other stores did not carry, and it may have been the breeding ground where I developed my life-long appreciation of the style, design and quality of old things over new modern things.

Although I never knew the ages of the guys I went around with, some of them had to be a year or two older than me, which was a good thing. They were more adventurous than most kids my age, which led us to go places on our own early in life. For example, the City's Mission Pool at Mission Playground on 19th Street between Linda and Valencia Streets was called "Nickel's Pool" or "Nickels." I paid a nickel to enter and they in turn provided a pair of grey trunks and a towel to use. There was a large dressing room for males and another one for females. I hung my clothes on a hook and never thought about people stealing my clothes or property. One of my all-time favorite things to look forward to at the time was to stop at the small corner Mexican store on the corner of 21st and Shotwell Streets on the way to the pool for a snack and buy a slice of baloney in a warm tortilla for five cents. There were no condiments, but who cared?

Each year a carnival came to town and was set up at Bernal Park (now Precita Park). I just walked around and looked at the rides, concessions, and "carny" (carnival) games, which was no comparison to Playland, but it was only a 6-block walk from home. Maybe I saw too many movies or heard too many stories, but I suspected the carny games of being crooked, so I never played any of them. Among the rumors was that the Ring Toss supposedly had rings that were just a smidge wider than the block of wood that needed to be cleared to win the prize, or the ring was made of plastic to give it more bounce. The game operator showed how it was done, by using a larger ring than customers used. Or he dropped it from directly overhead, a move that also was necessary in the Basketball Shoot, which was difficult to make from the shooter's angle. In Coin Throw games, there was barely enough room for the coin to land in a square without touching a line, which was required to win a prize. I did break down and threw ping pong balls into small round fish bowls to win a goldfish, which I brought home to Mom's regret and previous warning that pets were not allowed in the house. Even though I put the goldfish in a larger container and fed it well, it did not live more than a month or two. I never realized that goldfish could be mistreated and handled harshly by carnival organizers, resulting in early deaths. On the other hand, it could have been my lack of knowledge of how to care for fish, having no prior experience or help with caring for animals.

Downtown on Market Street between 5th and 10th Streets, there were at least 12 movie theaters, such as the Centre, Crest, Embassy, Esquire, Golden Gate, Orpheum, Paramount, St. Francis, the State, United Artists, Warfield, and the opulent Fox Theater, "one of the grandest theaters ever built" with plush furniture, art, and ornate staircases, walls and ceilings. Those theaters were fine if we just wanted to watch the movies, but we preferred the Fox Theater at 8th and Market Streets where we could play hide-and-seek. It was the biggest theater in the City with two stories, long wide staircases, huge lobbies on both floors, a large main balcony, side balconies, and endless rows of nearly 4,700 seats to hide in. It was a huge theater, especially in the eyes of kids. We were too young to appreciate the gold-leaf ceilings, rich tapestries and antiques in the lobby. Seldom did we ever find each other. After getting tired of literally running around and not finding my buddies, I just took a seat and watched the movie. We eventually met each other in the lobby when we left the theater at the end of the movie.

Three Hours of Cartoons, Shorts and Serials

Many Sundays I took the Mission Street bus from home, jumped off at 7th Street and walked up to Market Street where Centre Theatre showed 20 cartoons, 15-minute comedy shorts and serials for three hours. I really looked forward to those afternoons and went on a regular basis by myself. Our generation was raised on the violence in cartoons, slapstick comedy, wars, gangsters, cowboy movies and characters like Bugs Bunny, Daffy Duck, Tom and Jerry, Laurel and Hardy, and the Three Stooges, yet we were never more violent than later generations shielded from violence by their parents.

If I was ever in a hurry to go downtown or there was a Muni problem, I caught a jitney. Jitneys were privately owned cars, mostly limousines that covered a fixed route, picking up and dropping off passengers. They ran up and down Mission Street more frequently than the buses, which beat waiting for a bus and stopping at every intersection. The jitney fare was 10 or 15 cents for a ride compared to the 14-Mission 10 cents bus fare at the time. They were great for getting downtown to go to movies or coming home during rush hour in a small jammed car compared to a large jammed bus.

The downside of being downtown for any reason during rush hour on rainy days was that on Market Street I had to stand on the island in the rain while the conductor slowly collected a fare from each person one by one, gave change and handed out transfers when necessary. Every island at every intersection from the Ferry Building up to Van Ness Avenue, the equivalent of 1st Street to 11th Street, was filled with people waiting for a streetcar to get home from work. As many people as possible crammed on to the 6' x 6' space in the back of the streetcar to get out of the rain, which slowed down the fare taking and boarding process, but no one cared as long as they were dry inside and everyone still outside was getting drenched. Waiting for a bus or jitney on Mission Street was no better. There were few, if any, doorways to seek shelter, so I just hugged the wall until my ride came along.

Golden Gate Park World of Adventure and Exploration

Golden Gate Park was about four miles from home. Although I could ride my bike from home to the park, it would have been a grind and time consuming for an eight or nine-year-old to go back and forth in the same day. When I learned that I could rent a bike near the park, a whole world of adventure and exploration opened up for me. On Sundays when I did not have to sell newspapers, I could catch the 33-Ashbury bus at 18th and Folsom Streets to Haight and Stanyan Streets, a couple of blocks from bike rental shops. There were a couple of them in the middle of Stanyan Street between Oak and Page Streets, across from the park entrance.

Always going by myself, I went and rode around the park for five to seven hours. The bikes were special in that they were new, 3-speeds with no scratches on them and tires without punctures – so different from my four dollar bike. I felt so proud riding around on their bikes. I visited some combination of the various park attractions, which were all free except for the Playground and Playland concessions. I had the luxury to see all or as many as I liked amongst Children's Playground, Japanese Tea Garden, de Young Museum, California Academy of Science, Music Concourse, Conservatory of Flowers, Botanical Gardens' Strybing Arboretum, Steinhart Aquarium, Strawberry Hill in the middle of Stow Lake, Spreckels Lake, Polo Field, Bison Paddock, Fly Casting Pools, Dutch and Murphy Windmills, Soccer Field, Ocean Beach, Playland, Cliff House, Seal Rocks, and Sutro Baths. Since I paid 35 cents per hour to rent the bike, I watched the time so I always returned the bike before the final hour was up so I did not pay 35 cents for a fraction of an hour.

The Children's Playground entrance was on Stanyan Street at Haight Street, and the playground was behind Kezar Stadium. There were swings, rings, double-dip slides and a carousel. The slides were fun going down headfirst. Only girls and sissies went down feet first. The carousel had an organ, decorative benches and 62 animal figures such as a camel, dragon, giraffe, tiger and lots of horses. This was not a place where I spent much time because I had most of those things at Folsom Park except for the merry-go-round that I did not like as much as the one at Playland where the atmosphere was more festive. Playland was a place to spend the day. The Children's Playground was a place for me to visit only a half an hour.

Just beyond the Children's Playground carousel were the tennis courts, which never interested me since we had our own at Folsom Park. Next to the courts were the lawn bowling greens and the 1915-built clubhouse for the San Francisco Lawn Bowling Club. [18] Only club members and their guests could use the bowling lawns. At times I watched the lawn bowling matches for five minutes, but the game was too slow to hold my attention as the bowlers were a bunch of "old guys" in their 40s or older. Kids preferred being around those of a similar age and interests.

The Conservatory of Flowers (1st Avenue) and Botanical Garden's Strybing Arboretum (12th Avenue) were places I went to once. I just was not into flowers, which explained why I never enjoyed doing garden work.

I spent the greatest amount of time on each trip to the park at the Music Concourse area around 9th Avenue, which was a sunken open-air plaza. If the Spreckels Temple of Music, also called the "Bandshell," had a performance, I listened for five minutes, or ten minutes if I really liked the music. Since time was money (35 cents an hour bike rental), I had to move on to what I really came to see. On the west side of the Concourse was the de Young Museum and on the east side were the Academy of Sciences (a natural history museum), the Steinhart Aquarium, and the Simson African Hall. Later additions to the complex were the Morrison Planetarium (1951) and the Science Hall (1952). I could spend all day in any one of them, and they were free like so many other things in the City. My least favorite was the Planetarium. I only needed to be taken to outer space to see the stars once, but as I got older, I always thought it would be a great place to take a date for necking under the stars and way too dark for anyone to see you – something I never got around to doing.

My favorite was the African Hall that contained dioramas with life-size stuffed animals from Africa displayed with their own floor to ceiling painted landscape mural backdrops reflecting the animal's original habitat. Among the animals were antelopes, elephants, giraffes, hippopotamuses, hyenas, leopards, lions, monkeys, rhinoceroses, water buffaloes, zebras, and my favorite giant gorilla. The animals were grouped in scenes such as lions hunting an antelope, deer in the snow, and birds being stalked by prey. It was like visiting these exotic foreign locations and seeing the animals up close. They were actual life-size stuffed animals and I was just on the other side of the glass from them as opposed to seeing them at the Zoo as far away as 100-150 feet.

The 16th century Spanish Renaissance designed de Young Museum contained four wings: Central Wing (American and European art), West Wing (artistic history of San Francisco), North Wing (Asian collections), and East Wing (paintings, sculptures, photographs). I was lucky to live in a city that had the de Young, considered to be the most visited museum west of the Mississippi. Kids got bored quickly, so seeing the same type of art, like at a modern art museum, got repetitious. The de Young not only had some of the best art in the world but it had such a variety to view among the paintings, sculpture, pottery, furnishings, textiles and costumes. My favorites were the African, Oceanic and Native American collections where I took more time looking at things more carefully. I found those to be the most different in the museum, and the rest of my life was impacted for wanting to see things, have things, and do things that were different.

In the Steinhart Aquarium's hall of gems, I was fascinated with how the color of stones changed as they passed under purple and other colored lights. But the real attractions were the live fish, reptiles, amphibians, and marine mammals. My favorite stop was inside the front door and peering over the 3-foot-high iron railing into the Swamp Room, a large pit filled with live alligators. Their habitat was a flat rock surface with some large stones scattered around and a few inches of water to keep the alligator's underside wet but shallow enough for the spectators to see their entire body. There were lots of coins thrown in by the visitors, many resting on the backs of the alligators. Against the walls that surrounded the pit were built-in glass cabinets filled with snakes, reptiles and amphibians, adding more danger and adventure to the visit for me.

The snakes had their own appeal. The movies gave them a bum rap in that they were always trying to bite and kill you with their poisonous venom. So seeing them up close was exciting yet consoling that there was a sheet of glass between them and me. It was very anticlimactic in that the bigger, scarier snakes were always asleep. I often wondered if they were alive or just stuffed specimens for display. I stared at the fish and watched them swim in circles from one end to the other end of the tank and often wondered what they thought about their entire life of getting nowhere, doing the same thing day after day, just eating and swimming. It made me think a little about life – wanting to do something worthwhile, not boring, and not following the crowd like a school of fish. I wanted to be unique and somehow better than the rest, otherwise, what was the purpose?

On the western edge of the Music Concourse was the Japanese Tea Garden. It was also free, but a pot of tea with cookies cost 25 cents. Being Irish, I never wanted any as I got plenty of tea at home. I had never been outside of California much less the country, so the Japanese Tea Garden made me feel like I was in a different country. Being a kid, I never fully appreciated the plants, flowers, bonsai trees and landscaping, but I loved the oriental style gates, benches, arched drum bridges, stone pathways and unique architecture of the structures like the tea house and pagodas. There were ponds with koi and other fish. The use of so many stones and rocks gave the landscape a different and more decorative feel. The peace and quite was the best part as compared to the noise and crowds of Chinatown.

Stow Lake extended from 13th to 18th Avenues in the park where rowboats and pedal boats could be rented. This was where I learned to row a boat, which was not a very easy task for an eight-year-old kid and why I preferred the pedal boats. They were easier to steer, maneuver and power with my legs. They also moved faster on the water, however, they were too much like riding a bike and moved much slower. Since I was paying to rent the boat, I was always in a hurry to pedal under the Stone Bridge, which gave me the feeling of entering a land of castles in the days of King Arthur, and finish pedaling around Strawberry Hill out in the middle of the lake in order to get back before the next rental hour kicked in. The good thing about learning to doing things like rowing a boat when I was young was that no one laughed at me if I looked foolish since I was only a kid. It saved the embarrassment of trying these things for the first time as a teenager or adult as your friends would be a lot more critical.

The Polo Field in the park was between 30th and 35th Avenues just off Lincoln Way. As a kid, I could never figure out why it was called Polo Field, because I never saw any polo horses, players or matches there. It turned out that there were none because the sport was losing popularity and moved to other cities. I never saw the Polo Field being used for anything other than for an occasional jogger.

On the other side of the Polo Field was the S.F. Police Department Stables where the police housed their horses. In the morning I could see all these well-groomed horses that filled most of the 52 stables before they were taken out to patrol the streets of San Francisco. I never worried about getting kicked out. The police never minded me watching or petting the horses as long as I stayed out of the stables. I think the police officers got a kick out of a young kid showing an interest in their horses. I grew up in a period of being able to pet the horses of the mounted police whether we saw them patrolling Golden Gate Park or Market Street parades, or directing traffic at a downtown intersection. The mounted police always looked down at us and smiled. There was a rapport. The police were our friends who everyone respected, and we were kids who admired them and their equestrian "partner" with a smile. I doubt the police could ever get enough well deserved smiles during the day.

Across the road from the Police Horse Stables was Spreckels Lake that extended from 33rd to 36th Avenues in the park. I enjoyed stopping at Spreckels Lake to watch the model boats being cast adrift. I seldom saw young kids there unless they were with an adult. It was usually grown men sailing their model boats and yachts. I always thought of them as guys who never grew up, but maybe they did not want to grow up. It gave them a break in their day to get away from the family and job and do something they probably could not afford to do as a kid. Nearly all of the models were sailboats, which I enjoyed the best because they were so graceful on the surface of the lake. The model motorboats generally went in straight lines and moved faster as if they were in a hurry. I felt the Lake was a place where you should relax, slow down and take in the peace and quiet of the park, like cruising on a sailboat.

Bison Paddock was between 36th and 40th Avenues in the park. It gave me a feeling of being in the old west. Being raised on cowboy and Indian movies, I could see buffaloes up close to appreciate how large they were and imagine what it was like to be riding alongside a stampeding herd. But it was sad to think of them being killed for their meat and fur. It was comforting to see these buffaloes grazing peacefully and protected from such harm, but the shedding of their winter coat each spring was gross.

Across the Main Drive from Bison Paddock were three Fly Casting Pools and the wood-and-stone Angler's Lodge, home to the Golden Gate Angling and Casting Club, an offshoot of the San Francisco Fly Casting Club, which dated back to 1894. [19] There were concrete steps at each end of the pools leading into the pool for those with waders to practice casting in waist-high water. If you forgot your waders, there were steps leading into an empty pit that allowed casting at the same water height. Although it was not the place to look for excitement, I always enjoyed dropping by. It was such an elegant sport with the pole being flicked back and forth through the air in a smooth, rhythmic motion. In the casting pools were accuracy targets or floating rings about 8 inches wide. They were 10 to 40 feet from shore. The object was to cast a line so it landed inside the circle. The novices used them to learn how to cast, while the experienced men and women worked on honing their skills and improving the accuracy of their cast. It looked like quite a challenge but was amazing to see the frequency the veterans were able to hit their mark. I very much appreciated watching things that I could not do.

The Dutch and Murphy Windmills by the Ocean Beach were a couple of eyesores for years. They were boarded up and many wooden parts had rotted or disappeared. There was nothing appealing about them to tempt my buddies and me to pry off the boards to peek inside. If it looked so bad on the outside, the inside could not have been any better not to mention just seeing darkness inside.

Playland for Confidence, Risk-Taking, Aggressiveness and Winning

Playland at the Beach was 10 acres that extended from Cabrillo to Balboa Streets along the Great Highway. It was the most fun place a kid could have in the City – the local Disneyland of the day. I caught a bus on Mission Street to downtown and transferred to the B-Geary streetcar that went directly to Playland. There was no entrance fee, so I could easily spend the day just walking around and watching others playing the games, riding the rides and trying to win prizes, but the real fun was doing the things that charged an admission. I paid individually for each ride and game. For example, the Fun House cost 25 cents, but I could stay there all day, which I never did. On the Roller Coaster, I could pay the operator for another ride without getting off to avoid standing in line again. The same was true of the Merry-Go-Round, but I had to get off and back in line for most, if not all, of the other rides.

The most memorable feature of Playland was Laffing Sal standing in a bay window at the corner of the Fun House on the second story next to life-size revolving human characters. The papier-mâché character swayed forward, backwards, and sideways while cackling. Although she was 6'10" tall, she looked a lot taller looking down at me from the second floor. Her laugh brought a smile to my face every time and her rocking fat body was comical, however I found her sort of creepy and her face sort of scary with her curly red hair, huge freckles, and gap-toothed smile. It was the combination of the laughing, comical and scary features that imbedded this animated figure in my mind forever.

The thing I enjoyed doing the most was playing in the Fun House. There was so much to do. As I entered, there were holes in the floor that blew air up women's skirts to their embarrassment – pretty risqué stuff for an eight-year-old kid. I went through a maze of full-length mirrors that made me look tall, short and fat, and squiggly. I had to feel my way with my hands so I did not bump into the glass, which was usually unavoidable. After exiting the maze, I squeezed through rows of spin-dryers. These were revolving cloth rollers that extended from the knees to the chest if you were an adult, but for an eight-year-old, they were at my face-level. Fortunately, the rollers were soft in the center, so no harm was done.

My favorite plaything was the three-story-high wooden Giant Slide that was 138 steps up and 200 feet down with two big bumps along the way. [20] It was said to be the longest indoor slide in the world. I had to sit on a sheet of burlap on the ride down and not allowed to go headfirst, which I did when I saw no one was looking.

The Barrel of Laughs and the Joy Wheel in the Fun House were made for guys like me who wanted to compete and be the best. The 8-foot-tall Barrel of Laughs looked like a huge stone polishing machine. The object was to walk through without falling down. The secret of getting through the Barrel that was rotating counter clockwise was to zigzag through by walking up the left side, then walking with the rotation to the right side, then back up the left side, and back across to the right side, repeating this until I got all the way through. There usually was some jerk insisting on staying in the middle of the Barrel holding everyone up and preventing us from entering the Barrel. When my buddies and I got a couple of years older, we just barreled our way through, and if we bumped such jerks and knocked them down, so be it. If they were obnoxious jerks, we threw an elbow into them to intentionally knock him down and just say "Sorry" while they tried getting back on their feet. This may have been when and where I developed the belief that jerks should be punished or called out.

The Joy Wheel was a wooden spinning turntable approximately 15' in diameter that people crowded onto in hopes of staying on as long as possible. The secret of staying on the spinning wheel was to be the first one on so I could sit in the very center. The further I sat from the center, the easier it was for the centrifugal force to spin me off. Everyone rushed to be in the center of the wheel where there was only room for one person and if that was not me, my only hope was to use my hands and rubber sole shoes like suction cups to stay on. Most of the time I spun off, slid across a slick floor and wound up against the cushioned wall. When there was only one person left on the wheel, the operator brought it to a stop. There were times I was the sole survivor, which made me feel great, since most times the others were older than me. The feeling of accomplishment was like running through the finish line first in a foot race. I proved to myself that I was the best. In the rush for the center spot, there was the occasional jerk who rudely pushed his way to the center. I always took a special delight grabbing their leg as I was spun off the wheel, dragging the jerk with me, as if it was an accident. I could always run around, get in line and ride the wheel as often as I wanted.

My second favorite place at Playland was the penny arcade. I could spend the day playing games that only cost a penny or a nickel, which fit the pocketbook of even a kid my age. Again, winning at these games were more types of competition to prove to myself that I was good at things.

The Merry-Go-Round had music from a Wurlitzer band organ and 68 animals to ride. The stationery animals and chariots for sitting were for wimps, sissies and "old people" over 30. I always picked out the best looking horse that went up and down and was on the outside row to try to grab the ring to earn a free ride. Even leaning as much as I could to my far right without falling off the horse, I was too short to reach the ring. I knew it was futile, but my never give up attitude made me keep trying. One year I grew enough and I was successful. After that, the challenge disappeared and I lost interest. The fun came from the challenge. When the challenge became easy, the fun was gone. [21]

It took me a couple of years before I had the nerve to go on the Big Dipper. It was the most rickety, scary looking and sounding ride anywhere. I had heard that the wood was rotting from the ocean air and looked real old (actually less than 30 years old). Hearing the creaking chain pulling the train of cars up the incline, I always envisioned the cars coming loose and rolling backwards to everyone's death, which never happened. When I eventually did go on the ride, the thrilling part was descending the steep 80-foot drop with the girls and women screaming to let out their emotions. Guys were too busy wondering if this was a mistake and why we had not reached the bottom yet.

One day my brother came home from Playland and said some guy got decapitated when he stood up while riding the Big Dipper. He hit his head on a sign overhead, and his head fell in some other guy's lap. I could not tell if it really happened that day, or if he heard a story and let on that it happened that day. On the one hand I doubted it happened, since I did not remember any overhead signs on the ride other than one at the top of the incline before it started a steep descent, but I was not sure. On the other hand, why would Joe make up such a story? He never told wild stories in the past. Then again, he was a teenager going around with a bunch of other teenagers, and it turned out that he was a pretty gullible guy. Actually, there had been a couple of reported deaths on the ride, including one similar to Joe's story that happened three years earlier. [22]

When I rode the Dodger bumper cars with sparks flying from the car's pole scraping across the electrified ceiling, I tried to avoid ramming kids smaller than me or girls whom I felt sorry for. I tried to focus on adults, especially men. The satisfaction of broadsiding an older guy made me say to myself "Gotcha!" as if I was shooting down airplanes in a penny arcade game, and I was beating fella who should have an age advantage over me.

Shoot the Chutes was a boat ride that took me through a tunnel of love that was obviously popular with couples. The boat was pulled up a steep grade while I listened to the constant clanking of the pulley mechanism. After the U-turn at the top, there was a moment to enjoy the panoramic view of the ocean, and then a sudden breathtaking plunge down a steep drop into the water that always caused a big splash, and it was nearly impossible to avoid getting wet. I hated getting wet because the water did not dry off quickly when the temperature was usually in the 50s and 60s out by the Beach. The thrilling part of going down the ramp was over in a few seconds, which left me thinking "Is that all there is?"

Although the Ferris wheel was a pretty tame ride and offered a great ocean view, I never liked the idea that I could rock the compartment back and forth if I was not careful. I always envisioned it doing a 360-degree rotation or coming loose and falling to the ground. That was why I never got on with any of my buddies who I thought might be rockers.

The Diving Bell was probably the eeriest ride. I got in this round metal chamber that was about eight feet wide, had about 10 portholes and looked like a prison gas chamber from the movies. They jammed more than 10 people on at a time, so I had to get on ahead of others if I wanted a clear view out of my own porthole; otherwise, I wound up trying to look over people's shoulders, which was tough for an eight-year-old to see out the portholes 5-foot above the ground. It was hard enough to see things in the murky water, even if my nose was pressed against the glass. As we descended, an alarm sounded like a submarine dive alarm. I would have preferred a recording of "Dive! Dive! Dive!" like in the submarine movies. The challenge was to get a glimpse of the shark in the tank. There was never the fear of not returning to the surface safely, but it made me realize that I never wanted to join the Navy and be assigned to a submarine. I was not claustrophobic, but having so many people on board made it more confining and difficult to move around. After sitting on the bottom of the tank with everyone's attention elsewhere, the chamber shot to the surface without warning, causing a big splash before bobbing on the surface like a cork. The screams from those inside were heard over loud speakers on the surface for the amusement and entertainment of those standing in line to get on board.

Among other favorite rides of mine was the Octopus with long metal arms constantly revolving and the attached cars at the ends swinging freely while the cars moved up and down at the same time as stomachs turned and people screamed for fun or fear. Tilt-a-Whirl had cars that revolved in alternating opposite directions while riding over an up-and-down surface and moving in a circle at the same time.

There were a lot of sailors taking their dates, who were often picked up at Playland that day, on various dark rides that had two-passenger cars like the African-theme Dark Mystery Ride and the Laff in the Dark Ghost Ride that had interior views of luminous painted wall murals in pitch-black tunnels. The rides were jerky, the cars spun around without warning, things from nowhere were popping out at me, and I never tired of seeing the same murals or felt the ride was too short.

Besides the rides, there were midway games that gave me a chance to win prizes like stuffed animals and chalk dolls and statues. I never played most of these games because the prizes were not things I needed. I had plenty of toys that were more fun, and the games reminded me of those at the carnivals that had the reputation of rigged games. [23] I had no reason to believe any rigging was done at Playland, but I was not going to take the chance, especially when I saw how seldom people won.

Games I did enjoy playing were Horse Racing and Skee Ball. Horse Racing had a winner every time, but I had to wait until enough people showed up to make it financially worth their while to run a race. I rolled my ball into one of the nine holes, which moved my horse one or two spaces toward the finish line. I had to wait for the ball to return before my next roll. The loud ringing and flashing lights that went off whenever my horse crossed the finish line first made winning even more exciting.

Skee Ball was a game where I won points that were turned in for prizes – the more points, the more expensive the prize. I rolled a ball up an inclined lane and over a hump that jumped the ball into concentric rings – the smaller the ring, the more points earned. The key was to get as many balls as possible in the smaller, higher value rings. This required banking the ball off the side rail at the right spot so the ball went the right distance and had a spin that stuck the landing.

Our family did not go out to restaurants to eat, so I grew up feeling that I could not afford to buy food at Playland with one exception. I often bought an It's-It Bar, which was the only place I found them. It remained one of my two favorite desserts all my life.

Sutro Baths: Solution to the City's Cold, Rainy Weather

Sutro Baths was built in 1896 and located at the north end of the Great Highway just beyond the Cliff House in the Lands End area. It was the largest indoor swimming pool house in the world with a glass roof, seven pools, and a museum. Since the weather in the City was below 70 degrees 75 percent of the time [24], the baths were the place to go on cold or rainy days. For my dime admission, I rented a locker, a small white towel and an old fashion black woolen two-piece tank top-style swimsuit. Everyone complained about how much these suits itched. The wool also held a lot of water that added more weight to lug around. The stairway at the front entrance led down to the museum that contained things Adolph Sutro picked up on his travels or elsewhere, such as Egyptian mummies, lots of stuffed animals from Africa, a grizzly bear standing on its hind legs, horse drawn carriages, statue of a Chinese man who plucked each hair from his body and inserted it into his likeness, clothing from Tom Thumb, the midget from the P.T. Barnum Circus, penny arcade machines, buggies, rickshaws, mechanical sports games, a miniature motorized amusement park made out of toothpicks by a San Quentin Prison inmate.

On the lower levels were the pools and an ice skating rink in the south end of the building. I placed my valuables in an envelope provided by a clerk. I sealed it, put my name on it and left it with the clerk. I stored my clothing in my own dressing room that was numbered and matched the number on the corresponding tag I had to show the attendant to access my room again. I started in the really cold-water pool then jumped into the 80-degree warm pool. Going from one extreme temperature to another made the water feel even hotter in the warm water. The water in six of the seven pools came from the ocean, so I always disliked the salt water in those pools. It had no redeeming qualities other than it helped me float, which was good if I was just learning to swim. The salt water burned my eyes and tasted terrible. The best part was going down the two-story slide. To an eight-year-old kid, the ride down the slide seemed to me to be longer and steeper than it actually was. But I always had an eerie feeling every time I went down. There was a story that a kid drowned while he swam under the slide. His trunks got caught on a nail in one of the support beams and he could not get loose. I did not know if it was a true story, but I believed it, so I always felt a little uneasy whenever I went near the slide.

Zoo: Bar-less Exhibits for Up-Close Animals

The 100-acre San Francisco Zoo was located at the west end of Sloat Boulevard at the Great Highway. There was Monkey Island, Lion House, Elephant House, a sea lion pool, an aviary, bear grottos, a petting zoo and so many animals on display. When it was built in the 1930s, the moated enclosures were the first bar-less exhibits in the country. Admission was free until the mid-1950s. In April 1960, five girls from a City College of San Francisco sorority were caught wandering around on Monkey Island as part of a scavenger hunt gone wrong. The newspapers called them the "monkey girls." They climbed over the 3-foot fence, waded across the moat and walked around on Spider Monkey Island. Some girls received monkey bites. Some guys admired them for pulling off such a caper and showing chutzpah for girls, but as cool as capers are, things can go wrong. In this case, a dead female spider monkey was found floating in a duffle bag. [25] One of the participants, who might still have been in high school, eventually married a guy I played with on our high school football team.

Fleishhacker Pool for Chionophiles and Eskimos

Next to the Zoo was Fleishhacker Pool. The Pool was the largest salt-water pool in the world and one of the largest heated outdoor pools in the world, so large that lifeguards paddled around in rowboats in case anyone needed rescuing. It was 1000 feet long and 150 feet wide, which allowed people to spread out so it felt like there was hardly anyone else there, as if I had the pool to myself in spite of its capacity to hold 10,000. [26] Like Sutro Baths, the water was pumped from the ocean on the other side of the Great Highway and it tasted as bad and burned my eyes as much as at Sutros. The pool temperature was supposed to be 65-75 degrees, which everyone doubted as we were just a block from the ocean, and the temperature was in the 50s and 60s or colder from the fog and constant overcast. It was when I got out of the pool and walked around in the cold air that made me dry off as quickly as possible with a towel or jump back in the pool right away to warm up. The diving pool had a high diving board and a tower with two diving platforms – high and very high (about 18 and 30 feet). I only had nerve to jump feet first from the lower of the two platforms as a teenager.

Now that I was working and able to buy my own clothes without Mom having to shop for me, I moved on to wearing Pendleton shirts and argyle (diamond pattern) socks with Levi's® – cool guys wore Levi's®. My brother told me when you wore Levi's®, the folded up cuffs had to be as tight and small as possible. If your cuff was more than 1/2 to 3/4 inches high, you were considered a "nerd," "geek" or "square." It was alright if girls had 2 to 3-inch cuffs because they were…well, girls who had their own fashions. No one wore jeans. I loved Pendleton shirts with Levi's®, giving sort of a rugged look but Pendletons were so expensive I could only afford a couple of them. When my elbows wore through, I cut the sleeves above the elbow and made a short sleeve shirt out of it. I still have one of them nearly 70 years later.

When the discussion of gangs in the Mission came up, the push button knife was all the talk as the weapon of choice. Whether it was true or not,

I had no idea, but I was fascinated by how they worked, so I bought one. Even an eight-year-old kid like me could buy them at the store. The knife had a 4-inch blade and a metal tab I slid to lock and unlock the blade so it did not pop open in my pocket. It was sort of empowering when I flipped the blade open instantaneously. I never carried it around because the last thing in the world I wanted to do was to use it for anything, so I just kept it in my toy box with the other toys.

I also mailed away for a Daisy Red Rider BB gun through an ad in a comic book. It had a lever cocking action and leather thong hanging from a saddle ring on the side by the trigger. I would stick my hand through the thong and twist my wrist to help steady my aim. Unlike in the movies where the cowboy could cock the rifle repeatedly after every shot, I had to hold the barrel in my left hand with the stock of the rifle braced between my legs and pull the cocking lever toward me with my right hand – not cool, but the rifle was not designed for a 55-pound weakling. The only place I felt it was safe to shoot BBs was out the 12" x 12" window with its sliding wood panel in the coal shed on our back porch. I fired the gun from the second story window at the neighbor's plants and marks on their wooden fences for target practice.

Math Can Be Fun

Jimmy Reidy, who took me to my first Irish soccer game and taught me to shoot a rifle, was a custodian with the San Francisco School District most of his life. He was very pro-education, probably from being around school kids all the time. I learned a lot of good values from him early on. He emphasized the importance of education, physical fitness, and posed mental math challenges for me. I always looked forward to seeing him when he came to visit, as he always challenged me to add up columns of numbers in my head as he rattled off eight or 10 single-digit numbers. When I gave the answer, Mom would ask Jimmy if I was correct, and he always said, "Yes." I liked to think that I was always correct, but years later I wondered if he even knew the right answers or whether he was just creating my interest in math with this game and building my confidence in handling math. In any case, it worked.

It was the first time I had a feeling that math could be fun, and he made me at least think I was smart and good at math and had an aptitude for it. Jimmy instilled a positive attitude in me about math, unlike the negative attitude lots of my friends had toward math over the next eight years. All kids should be led to believe they are good at things. That is what gives them ideas of what to pursue. I found when the guidance and advice came from someone other than my parents, I was more likely to believe that they were telling me the truth rather than parents who were willing to fib to make me feel better about myself.

On the other hand, at age eight, I realized that I needed help along the way. If I faced something that I thought was beyond my control, I added to my prayers at night a promise to God that I would do something good or stop doing something bad if God did as I requested. Seldom, if ever, did I get my wish. By my senior year in high school, I just accepted the fact that I should not be looking to others to solve my problems and I had to depend on myself. As long as I would be on earth, I needed to solve my own problems and work harder to avoid problems. It helped me become the independent adult I finally became. Being self-reliant allowed me to make my own decisions without other's permission to act or chance of others to slow me down to act to achieve my goals, which in turn led to self-confidence.

I accepted the fact that bad things happened and had nothing to do with fairness. There was no reason for unpleasant things happening. They just happened. It was just part of life, as unfair as it may seem. Life was never intended to be fair – it all started with birth and knowing life was not forever. The lesson I learned was to do all I could to limit the number of unfair things that happened to me and do all I could to make things have fair results. That was one reason I studied law later in life so I knew my rights to stand up to others for fair outcomes.

At St. Charles the nuns formed choirs made up of the students. Most of the time we practiced in the choir balcony in the rear of the church. It gave us a break and a chance to get out of class and do something that was "important." We were preparing to give praise to God and to entertain the parishioners at Sunday Mass. In all the years of singing in the choirs, none of us were ever singled out for singing poorly or for having a terrible voice, even though there must have been some besides me. Occasionally, the nun asked someone to sing softer, which was their way of eliminating the off-key singers.

Joe was 16 and had bought a 1940 black 2-door Ford coupe from money he made working weekends at the butcher shop at the Stonestown Market at the Stonestown Shopping Center, out by San Francisco State. The car had an ooga horn that Joe used to blare out "Ooga! Ooga!" to get the attention of girls and pedestrians. He had a pair of large felt dice hanging from his rearview mirror. Although it was illegal at the time for anything to dangle from rearview mirrors for fear of distracting the driver and blocking their view of other cars, kids ignored the law. It was way more important to be cool. If they got stopped, the police made them take the dice down. I was never allowed to ride in his car because it was only for his big kid friends. Joe and his best buddy drove around wearing flat sports caps that were popular in the 1940s especially with golfers. They did look cool.

Riding on a Bumper at 65 mph

A year later, one of Joe's buddies drove him and some others to Santa Cruz, which was popular with kids due to its amusement park and beach. Joe got separated from the others who had the car. It was over 70 miles back to San Francisco. In those days some car models had a spare tire metal container that sat on the rear bumper. Not having any money to get home, Joe snuck on the back of a car driven by a woman who must not have looked out her rearview mirror much. He wrapped his arms around the tire container and put his feet up on the rear bumper where he stayed for almost the entire way home. He hitchhiked the rest of the way. It must have been some sight – this kid hanging on the back of a car, speeding down the highway and the driver completely unawares. That had to have been one funny scene – dangerous, but funny.

The coal shed on our inside porch had a 4-foot platform about eight feet off the ground. Kathy invited a bunch of her friends to the house from Folsom Park. The boys and girls climbed up onto the coal-shed platform to tell each other ghost and horror stories. I asked my sister if I could join them and she emphatically shouted, "No." I continued to pester her and finally some of the guys talked her into letting me stay if I kept quiet the whole time and I agreed. Some of the stories were really gory with lots of blood and decapitations. After a few stories, they said that was the end of the stories, so I could leave, which I did, but they stayed. I suppose they spent the rest of the evening smooching, which probably was the main reason for getting together.

When the storage room was converted into a bedroom for Kathy three years earlier, she demanded a lock be placed on her door and absolutely no one could enter. I thought it was a strange request since everyone could enter any rooms in the rest of the house including the other bedrooms. A door lock was installed and no one ever entered her private space. Three years later, my curiosity got the better of me, always wondering what was so special, private and secret about Kathy's bedroom, so I decided to take a peek inside. There was no one around, so I turned the doorknob, the door was not locked, and I slowly opened it. There was Kathy in her bra and underpants getting dressed. Boy, was I dumbfounded. I had never seen any girl or woman that naked and in underwear. Kathy turned around, screamed and tried to cover herself up. I slammed the door shut and ran to Mom for protection. As soon as she got dressed, Kathy stormed out of her room and really read me the riot act. I knew I deserved it. I did something I was not supposed to do, but I was thinking through the whole outburst, what was the big deal? She looked the same as she did in her two-piece swimsuit, and there was nothing special about the few things I saw on her walls, but I promised never to go into her bedroom again. I always felt if she just let Mom and me in once to appease our curiosity, there would never have been a problem like this. Years later, Mom told us that Dad never saw her naked their entire lives, implying that was the way things were in Ireland, but I suspected that was her personal sense of morality. Hopefully, Kathy was not of the same ilk when she got married.

Mom was very critical all her life about people and things. Small things bothered her – things that most people ignored or overlooked. I just thought she was very opinionated, but I think it was her compulsive nature. She loved to play whist. It was her one form of recreation. Once there was a man she did not know playing at her table and his mustache came below his lip. That bothered her so much, she told him, "You should cut that mustache even with your lip." He said he would.

Not Following in Dad's Footsteps

Dad was old school when it came to husband and wife responsibilities. He was to work to bring home the money, and Mom was expected to do everything else. I never saw Dad wash or dry the dishes, wash the clothes, vacuum or dust the house, do the shopping, mow the lawn, or cook a meal for the family. He did make the drinks when we had guests. Why not, he was a bartender. It was something he could handle and it was a guy thing. Even after Mom went to work full time when I was 10 years old, nothing much changed, except on nights that Mom worked late, he cooked a chop and baked a potato in the oven for each of us. I was surprised he knew how to do that until I realized all he had to do was turn on the gas by setting the oven to 350 degrees. He still never helped with the household chores. I always thought that was so selfish of Dad not helping out Mom more when she was out working from age 48 to 65. That probably was why I turned out to be so much different. Years later, I spent all of my married life doing most of the chores around the house as my wife worked all of her adult life. I learned many things from my parents – many things I should emulate and things I should do differently. Parents could be the best teachers without knowing it. I sat on the sidelines and observed while picking and choosing the attributes I wanted to adopt myself. My brother developed the habits of Dad – not to help around the house as a child or in marriage. My sister took after Mom – doing the housework and working full time. The difference was that two out of three of us kids were hard workers by nature. We worked hard at whatever we did – sort of a drive for excellence.

One night the doorbell rang after 3:00 a.m. It rang a few times. I got out of bed and met Mom at the top of the stairs. I guess Joe and Kathy slept through it or just ignored it. Instead of opening the door with the handle at the top of the stairs, Mom and I went down the stairs to see what was going on. The chain was on the door, which meant Mom put on the chain after Dad had not gotten home at his regular time so he could not sneak in the house. Mom pulled back the curtain to see who was there, unlatched the chain, opened the door, and there stood Dad. I had never seen Dad drunk before. He had lipstick covering his face. Mom would not let him in the house. He pleaded and said, "I have nowhere to go," and she said,

"You are not coming into this house tonight," and she closed the door and put the chain on the door. I was stunned to hear Mom say that to Dad, but I agreed with her. I thought how proud I was of her for standing up to him and punishing him. He deserved it. Later I wondered how often this must have happened over the years with Dad working in a bar, often the night shift with constant drinking going on and lots of lonely women. Dad never came home in that condition again. But the sight of Dad with lipstick kisses all over his mouth and cheeks left that image indelibly ingrained in my brain for a lifetime. I am sure that experience helped form my attitude about relations and wanting to date only wholesome girls.

In celebration of Christmas at home, the Christmas tree had to be as perfect as possible. It started with shopping for a tree that was as near perfect as possible. We did not have a car, so Jimmy Reidy or one of my parent's friends took us to a tree lot to pick out a tree. Mom insisted we have a real tree – not an artificial tree. She wanted the smell of real pine, which added to the Christmas atmosphere. Mom was so particular that the branches had to be balanced from all angles. It had to be symmetrical from the wide base of branches to the pointed top. There could be no bare spots as if a branch was missing.

There was always a particular order for decorating the tree – first the lights, so all the cords got hidden by the branches, then the silver tinsel, and finally the ornaments. Mom and Kathy strung the cords of multi-color lights and hung nearly all of the ornaments. The lights had to be strung on every branch so they each cast enough light to show off the ornaments that had to be evenly distributed on all sides of the tree. My sister was the ideal decorator, because she wanted the tree to be perfect too. I helped Mom and Kathy hang the tinsel on the branches – only one or two strands of tinsel at a time so they hung straight down and did not cluster together. No kinks were allowed. The tinsel was placed on every single branch, regardless of how small they were. Finally, the ornaments were evenly spaced along each branch with the smallest ornaments at the top of the tree and the largest at the bottom. By all standards, the ornaments were plain, but no one cared. There were enough sets of 6-12 ornaments to create a nice variety in color, size and style to make the tree perfect. Joe inherited from Dad the tradition of doing nothing other than sitting off to the side and occasionally making suggestions.

I was allowed to hang my favorite ornaments first, wherever I wanted. The nativity scene was centered under the tree and placed on sheets of white cotton to replicate snow. There was a Holy Family, the Wise Men, a few shepherds, a cow, a donkey, some sheep and lambs. I got a train set at age seven that became an addition under the tree each year. We started decorating right after dinner at 6:00 p.m. and ended around 11:00 p.m. or later if necessary, but Mom always said, "It was worth it." By Christmas morning, there would be lots of presents under the tree, since there were five of us, but no one got more than two or three presents. Kathy, Joe and I were never expected to give presents, so they always came from Santa Claus or my folks. Mom admired the tree the most of all of us throughout the Christmas season. It was her annual opportunity to decorate something. If she could have any job in the world, she once told me it would be as an interior decorator. She had an eye for colors, detail and perfection. She was an example of someone not getting a job early on in a field that she would excel. So many people took whatever job was available instead of deciding early on what they would enjoy or be good at.

Santa Dropped by for a Highball

This Christmas Eve, the doorbell rang. Dad went to the door to see who it was, especially since we never had anyone come unannounced after dinner. A couple of minutes later he said, "Look who's here." It was Santa Claus who had come to visit us personally. I was so excited, seeing him up close and in our own house. He never personally brought us kids anything, but who cared. This was better than any presents. Eventually, Dad took Santa into the kitchen and closed the door behind them. They were in there for a while, so I got curious what they could be doing and taking them so long. I went over and peeked in the kitchen and saw Santa had lifted up his beard and was drinking a highball (Dad's favorite drink to serve guests – whiskey with water or 7Up). I went over to Mom and told her what I saw and said, "That is not Santa." She assured me he really was Santa and I was mistaken. I really wanted to believe her, but I was not completely convinced. After Santa left they admitted it was Jack, from the grocery store across the street, who dressed up as Santa. I was all right with that, since it did not mean there was no Santa Claus. As everyone said, "Santa had a lot of helpers."

At Christmas time, the store windows downtown were a must-see as they went to extravagant lengths to outdo each other every year. Macy's, the Emporium, the City of Paris, Gump's and Podesta Baldocchi were in the top tier for exterior or interior decorations. Macy's windows were each decorated with moving animals and figures in elaborate Christmas settings. Window watching was great for adults who could look over the heads of people standing four to six deep, but it was the pits for me being four feet tall. At least I could appreciate the huge trees in the Emporium and City of Paris rotundas and in the center of Union Square that were ablaze with lights, decorations and the smell of real fir and pine in the air.

The City of Paris department store at Geary and Stockton Street, a couple of blocks up from Market Street, had the largest indoor Christmas tree. The 60-foot-tall tree reached the fourth floor of the 6-story building and was decorated from head to foot with beautiful ornaments, bright lights, garlands and festive decorations. The tree stood under the 2,600-piece stained-glass dome ceiling depicting the *Ville de Paris* ship in full sail that dated back to 1918 (later moved to Neiman Marcus at Geary and Stockton). But my favorite store over the holidays was crowding into the jammed Podesta Baldocchi florist shop on lower Grant Avenue. It was a magical place with floor to ceiling wreathes and decorated trees with handmade and custom made ornaments and wreaths for sale from all over the world that you did not find anywhere else. We could never afford them, even if we went there the day after Christmas when they were half off, but it was a dreamland for kids at that time of year. It was nostalgic to see this familiar shop appear in Alfred Hitchcock's 1958 film *Vertigo* later.

Part of the fun of being downtown was to see the police officers in the center of busy intersections directing traffic, waving their arms behind their head to keep the cars moving and blowing their whistles with the other hand to warn pedestrians and drivers that traffic flow was changing. There were also foot patrolmen standing on the corners, spending most of their time giving tourists directions to find the street or store they were looking for. There was a constant sense of feeling safe when there was a policeman in sight wherever I was downtown.

Besides receiving presents each year, the other thing I looked forward to at Christmas time was the family jumping into Jimmy Reidy's car and driving along Sloat Boulevard, the Marina and 17th -18th Avenues between Vicente and Wawona Streets, seeing block after block of houses covered with bright lights and decorations. It took two to three hours to get around the City to see everything but well worth it. Nearly every house on the blocks we visited had lights all over the house fronts but the special ones also had their front lawns decorated with scenes. There were some blocks that had lines of 30-50 cars long inching along so they had the time to see everything. It was great for the passengers but not so enjoyable for the drivers. We never bothered to get out to look closer because there was no parking available. In Lindley Meadow at Golden Gate Park, there was an illuminated night display of a life size crèche scene with real sheep and actors playing the Holy Family, the three wise men, and shepherds. Like so many things that got too popular, the traffic over time got unbearable and visiting these areas at Christmas lost its charm, but it was memorable as long as it lasted.

The firehouses also elaborately decorated the front of their buildings. "1948 was the San Francisco Fire Department's first Christmas decoration contest, a tradition that was to last only three years. Each firehouse was limited to a total expenditure of $50 and the grand prize winner received $1,000 and a gold loving cup...Many of the decorations were animated and often reflected the architectural pattern of the firehouse's particular neighborhood." [27] We never toured the firehouses at night because we did not want to sit in traffic at each stop while cars inched along to view their decorations. Passing by a few of the firehouses in the surrounding neighborhoods during the day was good enough for me.

Ruination From Alcohol

If there was one word for describing Dad, it was that he was a nice guy – maybe too nice. He was always a soft-spoken man and only showed his anger once, and that was when I upset Mom by not letting her know that I would be home late. He was nice to his kids and especially to Mom all their lives, letting her make most of the decisions and not questioning them. He was nice to his boss by always working wherever and whenever he was needed. Dad moved around among the three McCarthy bars but worked mostly at the 8th and Market Streets bar across the street from the Fox Theater. Whether it was Dan or Dad's idea, Dad often worked the night shifts until 2:00 a.m., which left him no time to have a family life with his wife and kids. I am sure the more generous tips at night when customers were drinking more influenced his willingness to work nights, especially since Mom let him keep everything over the $100 he brought home each week. He was too nice to leave his boss and take a different job than one in a drinking environment that lead to his alcoholism. He was too nice to his kids to discipline them for pushing the limits or ignoring the advice of their mother. On the other hand, I was so thankful that he let me do my own thing and did not worry about me, which let me grow up to be independent and able to make decisions on my own. It was years later, that I realized I preferred to be completely in charge to make all the decisions rather than being on committees seeking a consensus of opinion.

I could appreciate the social life Dad must have had at work, seeing customers on a regular basis, some talking about common Irish memories, and those just out from Ireland updating him about the Old Country, hearing a lot of jokes, and seeing people feeling good after a few drinks. In his eyes, he must have preferred it much more than selling clothes at a men's department store, and it was some relief from being homesick for Ireland. But Mom never had an alcoholic drink in her life. She once said it was because she saw so much drinking and drunkenness in Ireland that she wanted none of it. It must have been doubly hard for her to be married to a man who loved to drink, spent eight hours a day in a bar environment, and frequently coming home a bit tipsy with the smell of whiskey on his breath. On top of this, she saw her two sons later in life drinking so much. I drank too much as a teenager. How sad it was that I did not recognize the grief I caused Mom all those times that she saw me following in Dad's footsteps and wondering if I would eventually wind up in a sanitarium for alcoholism too.

By the time I was eight years old, Dad had the first of three breakdowns due to alcoholism at the age of 48. Mom must have noticed Dad coming home after 2:00 p.m. tipsy or drunk more and more often and decided Dad needed help. I was asleep whenever he came home, so I had no idea of his drinking problem. Somehow Mom convinced Dad to let her commit him to Agnews Insane Asylum (Agnews State Hospital for the mentally insane), since we could not afford a private sanitarium. Dad was an alcoholic, not mentally insane, but the hospital was one of the least expensive administers of electroshock treatments, a common method for treating those with addictions and the insane at the time. I looked back over the years and felt sorry for Mom. She often had to make the Sunday bus trip to visit Dad in Santa Clara by herself. I knew that I did not want to make the trip. The thought of visiting an insane asylum and seeing depressing sights of patients in wheel chairs, on benches and sitting up in their rooms was so sad and kind of scary for a kid. Mom never pushed me to make the trip, but did try to make me feel guilty, as well as I should be, with statements like "He is your father." I wound up visiting Dad more often than Joe and Kathy, probably because I was the youngest and Mom only needed one of her children to keep her company on the trip.

I always regretted that Dad's best years were behind him when I was a kid. The shock treatments took a lot out of him physically and mentally. Over a 10-year period, Dad checked into Agnews three times for a "cure." After he was released each time, he seemed less and less himself – less outgoing, more withdrawn, with less energy, and less communicative, which were things needed for doing father-son things together, whether it was going out together or just having conversations at home. I was always envious of Joe and Kathy to have grown up with the man whom Mom originally married. My brother later followed the same path of being an alcoholic like Dad, but he got help through Alcoholics Anonymous (AA). One day Joe quit drinking cold turkey, which lasted a lifetime. For my buddies and me, we just needed to get married to change our ways.

No Excuse for Being Sick

With Dad in the hospital and out of work for months, Mom had to go to work to support us. She looked everywhere with no luck. She was 48 years old with no experience, as she had not worked since she got married. She went into Livingston Bros. department store for women's clothing at Grant Avenue and Geary Boulevard, and told them how desperate she was as she looked everywhere possible. They were just opening a Stonestown store and they offered her a temporary job for six months. It led to her working for them at their downtown store until retirement. Going to work for the first time in her married life was not what she expected at her age. She was raised with the belief that a mother's job was to be home in order to care for and raise her children.

For the 17 years Mom worked at Livingston's, she never took off a day for sick leave. The only exception was when she fell and broke her wrist. Her nearly perfect attendance record was a combination of things – her gratitude for being given a job at her age, her admiration for the owner Carl Livingston, and the fear of being replaced by someone who was younger than her. So we were raised with the attitude that it was almost against our religion to be sick and miss a day of school.

Most Selfish Thing Ever Heard

When Mom eventually retired, she was to receive a $17 per month retirement check, but they only wanted to give her $16 a month to dock her for the year when she missed six weeks when she was out with a broken wrist. I thought that was the most selfish thing I ever heard. Not only was the retirement program pitiful only paying one dollar a month for each year Mom worked for them, the thought of cheating her out of one dollar per month for something beyond her control was so ungrateful. They eventually agreed to the $17 per month figure.

When I saw how unfairly the store was treating Mom, I knew then that I did not want to depend on an employer to determine my financial future. I was determined to be self-sufficient, independently wealthy, and to march to my own drummer some day. I eventually achieved those goals later by buying and remodeling income property on the side early on and also investing in the stock market later on. I found success in real estate was the least challenging and the stock market a little more challenging. The secret to real estate investments was not so much *what* I bought but *where* I bought property. With the stock market investments, it was less about *what* I bought but *when* I bought stocks. My success rate in real estate was 100 percent and after age 40, I only lost money on one stock, and that was just a fluke.

Age 9: The Young Entrepreneur

Standing Up to Adult Bullies

After a couple of years selling papers at 20th and Mission, I got the much busier corner of 24th and Mission. It was on the eastside of Mission Street, while an older man was selling on the west side. All of the best corners were given to men who were supporting themselves and often a member of a union. Kids like me were given the corners with the least business. On my first day, the man selling across the street came over and told me to go away and stop selling there because it took business away from him. In the past he had both corners. On my corner, people used to drop the seven cents in the newsstand slotted coin tube and helped themselves to the paper. At the end of the day, the newsman unlocked the tube and removed the money. Al Levine must have figured that having a kid at my corner would sell more papers than a self-service stand and I could sell to those waiting for a green light to cross the street, which was probably true. Although I was only nine years old, I told the threatening newsman I was not leaving. He grumbled but never bothered me again. I felt pretty good standing up to someone, especially an adult, when I knew I was right. Whenever I left my corner to try selling papers in the nearby bars and restaurants, people could still drop coins in the slot and take a paper. Occasionally, I found people short-changed me by dropping in a penny or two for appearances. Very seldom did I find that people just stole the paper – probably because people were always walking by. Rainy days were the worst. There was no shelter on my corner and the edges of the papers got wet in spite of the sheet of clear plastic that was provided by Levine to cover the papers. So I had to decide which customers to slip a partially wet paper. If I did not, I had to turn down sales later when I ran out of the dry papers. I usually slipped them to those with kinder faces, hoping they would not complain if they noticed. By now I was making 75 or 80 cents a day with the heavier foot traffic.

Doing Business With the Dead

Later that year, I got the corner of 22nd Street and South Van Ness Avenue in front of Driscoll's Mortuary. This time I had an awning and large entryway to stay dry on rainy days. It also had more business. There was way less foot traffic than on Mission Street that had a lot of shoppers, but South Van Ness had lots of car traffic with people leaving downtown to get home. So customers pulled over to the curb with the window rolled down, as I dropped the paper inside and they paid me. I had more regular customers than at the other corners because they drove this same route every day and got in the habit of stopping at my corner for the stoplight to change. It really helped that the mortuary had a white zone in front so cars could not park there, leaving plenty of space for customers to pull over. Tips were better, especially at Christmas. Also, some people were in a hurry to get home and did not want to wait for three pennies change for a dime. I was averaging $1.00 to $1.25 a day, so I was moving up in the world. I had a few customers that I dropped off the paper at their front door each day and they paid me at the end of the month – wonderful to have a hardcore customer base.

One day I was out yelling "Hail late news…" and the mortician came out and asked if I would stop my yelling until the service inside was over. I felt so badly. I never thought about what went on inside. Later I asked if they would let me know ahead of time so I never did it again, but they never did. For whatever reason, they never came out to tell me to be quiet.

Like most funeral parlors, there was a bar across the street from this one. I went in there every day to sell papers. I walked the length of the bar and back, not so much hoping to sell papers but to have just one customer who had a couple of drinks and feeling good to give me a generous tip. It occurred only once in a while, but not as often as I expected. I was always amazed that the bartender did not run me out. If someone bought a paper, they probably stayed there longer drinking. If I had been smarter, I would have tried convincing the bartender to buy one or two papers to hand them to customers for that purpose. All the years I sold newspapers, I was never smart enough to try selling papers to those working in the bars, restaurants and other small retail outlets. The sales clerks were probably bored to tears when there were no customers and likely would have been happy to spent seven cents for a newspaper. I probably could have created a bunch of regular customers like on a newspaper route. It was not until college that I learned about identifying and creating new markets and product differentiation like newspapers were the best rag for wiping dry their store front windows because they did not leave streaks (a lesson learned from a passerby while washing my car later in high school).

Operating My First Casino

Always thinking of ways to make money, I created games of chance that were difficult to beat, so I tried different games that looked easy but hard to do. I made a board game out of empty egg cartons connected together. I colored certain dimples (individual egg holders) and the object was to throw a coin into a colored dimple. I colored enough dimples to make it look easy to win but had to repeatedly test the game until I was convinced that it took a lot more than five tries to win. That was my gauge for setting the odds of the game. I went over to the Park and brought back several of my buddies by telling them that I created a game for them to win money. I explained how it worked, that the game paid 5:1 if their coin landed in a colored dimple, and they could throw any coin – penny, nickel, dime, quarter – from one foot away. They were all hesitant until one of them threw a penny. He lost so he gave up. A second guy threw a penny and lost. I had to egg him on to throw another penny that he lost. That was it for him. No one else wanted to try. I was disappointed the game was not a moneymaker and they all expected to try once and win a 5:1 payoff – a case of a market that had little disposable income.

Trading card collecting was big at the time. We normally collected just baseball cards, but over time I ran across other types of cards that were free, so I held on to them. Those of us with baseball cards tried winning them from each other with a couple of games. One game required throwing the card closest to the wall in front of our houses or in the tennis court at the Park. We stood about 10 feet from the wall, and the closest card to the wall won the other guy's card. If I got a leaner where the card wound up leaning against the wall at an angle, that was a sure winner, unless the other guy knocked it down and his card wound up closest to the wall. With

122

time, I got very good at throwing cards so they generally slid and touched the wall, which was impossible to beat unless the other guy got a leaner.

Another game was to flip cards to the ground so the card fell to the ground as it continually rotated head over heels. The picture side was heads and the text side was tails. We declared who was to match whom. If I matched the other guy, I won his card; if they were not matched, I lost my card. We usually played with common cards that had no value. If we had duplicates of rare or more popular cards, each player had to use cards of similar value or demand. It provided a way of increasing the value of my collection, assuming I was lucky enough to win. With a lot of practice I found that if I flipped the card as hard as possible and with the same force and from the same height, I could control whether I flipped a head or tail based on which side of the card was face up when I started the flip. That increased the frequency I won by a lot.

Street Corner Hustler

An offshoot of throwing cards was to throw coins against the wall in the schoolyard, but we had to watch out for the nuns. It was hard finding kids to play at school or at the Park, especially those in our neighborhood, since they had no money or were not willing to gamble with loose change. So most of my competition was on the corner I sold newspapers. I played against kids who sold papers and had money in their pockets. We just played for pennies, but the closest penny to the wall won. After playing this game for a few months, I could throw a penny up against the wall or within a quarter of an inch from the wall with some regularity. In the long run, I wound up an overall winner in this money making venture.

Handicapping Horses on the Side

I had been selling newspapers well over a couple of years and started to look at the horse race section of the newspaper each day when sales were slow. I just looked at the names of the horses that placed in the top three positions, and I began to recognize the names of the horses that normally were in the money and whether they came in at win, place or show. After this period of learning the regular moneymakers, I made my own mental picks on the races. Most times my picks did win or at least finished in the top three spots. One day at Jack's grocery store, I happened to mention my handicapping successes, so he offered to place a two-dollar bet for me (never did learn if he was a bookie or if he just knew a bookie). In any case, I gave him two dollars and sort of forgot about the bet, and days later when I was in the store Jack said my horse won. I had asked him to make a two-dollar show bet (horse to come in third). I knew the winnings would be less but this was my first gambling bet and I wanted to play it safe. Instead, he said he placed the two dollars on the horse to win, and it did win. He paid me the $10.70 of winnings (versus less than four dollars for show-place money). He never told me why he chose the horse to win. He claimed that he misunderstood my request. For all I know, he may have placed a show bet but paid me the difference out of his own pocket. I thought that was the case. Jack made the mistake later when he mentioned my good fortune to Mom, who got upset with Jack for placing the bet and told him never to do it again. I was crushed when Jack told me. My new path to wealth had ended after only one "investment." If nothing else, it would have given Dad and me something in common to share. That was too bad.

After Dad was released from Agnews Hospital and had returned to work, Mom was regularly working late Monday nights at Livingston's and Kathy worked late at the Public Library, so I had to depend on Dad for dinner on Mondays. So, I took a bus downtown and met Dad for dinner. He usually worked at McCarthy's at 8th and Market Streets, three blocks down from Zim's Restaurant. We always ate there, as I loved their thick hamburger with everything on it and a thick chocolate milkshake. While I waited for Dad to get off work, he made me a fancy nonalcoholic drink like a Shirley Temple or a plain Coke. McCarthy's had a pinball machine, but the law required that you be 18 years or older to play. At first Dad was strict about not letting me play, but with the egging of some of his regular customers, Dad eventually let me play a game or two on occasion. I imagine that Dad knew every policeman that walked the beat in the area, so I doubt the bar would get into any trouble over me. Enjoying myself at the bar and eating out with Dad was the only thing we ever did together on a regular basis. That was why I so looked forward to that time with Dad each week.

Radio Quiz Show Victory

One day Mom told me she was going to a live radio show being held at one of the local radio stations and I had to go with her, as she could not leave me alone. She wanted to see and hear the guest speaker who was appearing on the show. During the show, they asked if any children in the audience wanted to participate in a quiz competition to win a prize. Mom nudged me, so I stuck up my hand. A girl about my age and I were both selected. As we stood on stage, I kept wondering what kind of question they would ask. It never entered my mind that it could be on a weak subject of mine, but I did like the idea of competing. The moderator was to ask the question and the first one who blurted out the correct answer won. When the moderator asked the question, I seemed to freeze for ages thinking how simple the question was – that this could not be that easy. There must be some mistake or trick to the question. Meanwhile, I was wondering why it was taking the girl so long to give an answer. This was all going on in my mind in a matter of nanoseconds. The question was "What fraction of a dollar is a dime?" The one subject that I was good at was math. The answer came to mind immediately, but I stood there silently for what seemed like a long time before I gathered my thoughts and said to myself, "I better answer before she does." I responded, "Ten percent." "That is correct," said the moderator. I was elated at winning but stood confused as to whether the young girl did not know the answer or just froze worst than I for a longer period of time. Whatever my prize was, it certainly was not memorable, as it did not leave a lasting impression with me. Besides, victory and applause from the audience was enough.

With the exception of basketball, my buddies were not into other sports. We never played football or baseball. So I had to play a lot of games by myself. I did not own a football, but on our back porch, I took grounders by throwing a tennis ball against the side of the flat in back of our flat. Our porch had five clotheslines for hanging the wash. Washday annoyed me with the wet clothes hanging on the lines as they prevented me from taking infield practice. The floor of the porch consisted of wood planks 1/4 to 3/8 inches apart over a tar and gravel flooring. Occasionally, I found a penny, nickel or dime between the cracks that had fallen out of the pocket of clothing hung on the line to dry. There was just enough space for me to pry up the coin using two kitchen knife blades.

Over time I was throwing the ball harder and harder to create hard groundballs and forcing me to move far to my left and right to improve my reaction time. One day the neighbor came to our front door and asked Mom if I would quit because someone was sick. She was very polite and almost seemed apologetic for asking. I never knew the neighbor or even seen her before, which was why I continued throwing the ball against the wall until Mom came out almost immediately and told me to stop. Later in life I often thought back to how inconsiderate and selfish I was that day. But it would not be the last thing I regretted about my childhood and wished I had done things differently.

Solution to Handling Kid Bullies

I was shooting baskets with a few kids at the Park when a Latino kid wanted me to throw him the ball. I had never seen him before so I ignored him because we were in the middle of a game and we never invited him on to the court. This kid was much shorter than me and looked a little younger than me, but he started a fight with me, probably to impress the others. Maybe he felt he might be accepted quicker in hopes of making new friends. It was the first time I ever encountered any threat of violence, as I had never been in a fight before. I tried ignoring him but he kept pushing me. Not wanting to hurt him or look like a bully because I was bigger, I wrestled him to the ground and we rolled around on the side of the basketball court. He finally got me on my back only because I was not putting up any kind of struggle and just wanted this to end. That was a mistake. It resulted in him pinning me to the ground. He asked if I gave up and I said, "Sure," meanwhile a crowd had gathered to watch and I was so embarrassed for letting a much smaller kid get the upper hand of me.

Over the next few months at the Park, he called me aside to separate me from my friends. I suppose it was his way of going on a power trip. He was always alone, so I never got the feeling he ever made any friends at the Park. I never understood why he thought I would do what he wanted each time. He never had anything to say to me or seemed to want anything, just the satisfaction of interrupting my life and having someone do his bidding.

I did start to wonder if I could beat him up, and I certainly did not want to be embarrassed again on my home turf. After a couple of months of this harassment, I just got tired of him bullying me and finally told him, "No, I am not coming over." He came over to me, looked up at me, and said, "I respect you for that" and he walked away. I never saw him again. Over my lifetime, I have relived that entire experience in my mind and it has served as a reminder never to underestimate a bully nor be intimidated by one. As a matter a fact, it caused me to stand up to others to protect my rights and those of others. There were many times I got after people trying to cut into line or picking on kids smaller than them. I think every kid should get beaten up once. There are many things you learn and take away from the experience that makes you a smarter person, a better person, unless you are stupid enough to fight someone much bigger than you. Winning or losing a fight reveals a lot about yourself and how you will react to future challenges in life – whether you are a shrinking violet or a fighter.

This was such the opposite experience I had with Latinos at school. Race was transparent to us kids. The only distinction we saw were boys and girls – not Italians, Irish, and Latinos. In fact, my first crush was with a Latino girl named Rosario. I thought she was the prettiest girl in our 4th grade class – possibly the prettiest girl I had ever seen. I probably spoke to Rosario a handful of times and only briefly, which was why I was surprised when she asked if I wanted to go over to her house after school. I was so flattered that she chose me over all the other boys in class. Her house was across the street from the school. Her mother was there and Rosario introduced me to her. Her mother was not expecting this and appeared displeased by the look on her face. At the time I did not realize it, but it may have been their custom to check out any new friends. I never was invited to her house again and we never did create a close friendship that year or any other year. I never knew whether it was because they did not approve of boys as friends at her age or that I was not Latino. In any case, it never bothered me as I only thought of her as a classmate and nothing more afterwards. There were plenty of other kids at school and in my neighborhood for making friends.

No Fear of Gangs and Derelicts

The Mexican gang members in the Mission were called "pachucos." In some circles, it referred to young Mexican-Americans who had a taste for flashy clothing, such as zoot suits. But that was not the image kids who used the term in our neighborhood had in mind. It referred to guys who wore black pants and black leather motorcycle jackets like the motorcycle gangs and got into fights, carried switchblades and other weapons. Mom told all her kids a few years earlier to stay away from the 24th and Mission Streets area. Even when I was selling newspapers at that corner, I never felt threatened. On the other hand, I never walked around that area at night. At the age of nine, it meant nothing to me if I saw guys wearing head bandanas, club shirts, gang jackets or visible distinguishing marks. They certainly did not hang around the Park, probably because it was mostly a white playground. Latinos only made up 10 percent of the Mission population at the time. I doubt the pachucos ever wanted to stray from their familiar surroundings, just as I felt more comfortable staying around the Folsom Park area. My friends and I never worried about going anywhere in the Mission – probably because we were just too small and not a threat for anyone to bother with.

The really scary parts of the City were outside the Mission. I stayed out of the predominantly Black Fillmore District until my adult life. The rumor was that there was an average of at least one murder every night, but we never knew how many assaults, muggings, and robberies went on. Hunters Point was another rough area that I never even drove through as a teenager. Daytime may have been fine, but definitely not at nighttime.

The Tenderloin District that was bound by Geary, Van Ness, Mason and Market, was a creepy area to walk through with run down buildings and the tacky frontage of the burlesque bars. I tried to avoid that area by walking around it where there were more entertaining storefronts and picture windows. Although it had a lot of bars and strip joints, it was also home to the Black Hawk Jazz Club at Hyde and Turk Streets where a lot of the jazz greats like Dave Brubeck, Miles Davis, Gerry Mulligan and Thelonious Monk performed.

"Skid Row" referred to the area of bums and winos, which we called "3rd and Howard Street," although it was most of lower Howard Street and several blocks east of Market Street (eventually along 3rd, 4th, 5th, 6th and 7th Streets). What I did not realize was that the area was the home for a lot of retirees and out of work guys just trying to get by on disability or meager pensions. I also never saw the violence, robberies and prostitution that existed in that area. All I ever saw were guys hanging around and sitting on the sidewalks and in doorways, often with a bottle in their hand. However, I was never bothered by any of them. Occasionally, they asked for change, which I never gave them because it seemed like a problem that I was not going to solve with what I could afford.

Sad Loss of a Buddy

Richard Lucas, one of my buddies, lived on 21st Street across from Folsom Park. We saw each other at the Park nearly daily. My buddies and I had not seen Rich for quite a while. We thought he may have moved away, but we were sure he would at least say goodbye to us. Nearly a year passed and one day his mom came by the Park and told me to tell the other guys that we should drop by their house to say "Hi" to Rich. She gave no explanation where he had been. In retrospect, I always wondered why we did not drop by a long time ago to see if he was still at home or had moved. Atkins, Gray, Sandoval, Ellington and I went over to see Rich. He was sitting in a large cushion chair sort of staring at us. His eyes looked different – sort of lifeless. Rich's mom said he had been in the hospital – that he had a breakdown. I did not know what that meant or involved, but I did know there were insane people where Dad went for his shock treatments. Rich had that same dazed, non-communicative look Dad had after his treatments, but we never received any details of Rich's problem. We kids were too young to even know what to say or what we could talk about. There was very little talking, which was why our visit was so short. We told Rich that we would see him at the Park. His mom assured us that he would. We never saw or heard from Rich again. My guess was that his mom saw from our reactions that things would not be the same and somehow did not encourage Rich to get back to his old stomping grounds. Maybe Rich could not function normally or maybe he was readmitted to the hospital. We never found out. Once again, we never made any effort to visit him, and maybe his mom interpreted that to mean that we did not want to play with him again, which definitely was not our intent. We kids were just not socially adept to do the right thing. That was too bad. Rich deserved better.

Learning From Our Own Mistakes

One day Atkins had some matches and suggested to me we set a small fire just for the heck of it. I had never gone camping, so making a fire was new to me. The only place we could think of that was out of the way and might have some twigs to burn was the fenced in area behind home plate at the Park. Atkins and I climbed over the 6-foot chain link fence at the corner of 21st and Folsom Streets behind the wood baseball backstop, and he built a small fire with twigs and dry leaves. As he added more leaves, the fire started to grow and got out of hand. The fire started to scorch the wood backstop. We panicked. Neither wanted to try stomping it out for fear of our pant leg catching fire, so we scurried over the fence yelling at each other to put out the fire, but no one stayed. Instead, we ran in different directions. When I got home later, Mom said the Park director came to the house to report he saw what we did and wanted to talk to each of us. A fire truck had been called, the baseball wood backstop got singed, but the bushes surrounding the Park were hardly damaged. We would never do anything intentional to bring fire trucks out, unlike some kids who pulled the lever in the red fire alarm boxes at the corner intersections throughout the City. There were just some things we did not do to cross the line being mischievous. I went over to the Park to see the director and felt really bad about what happened and I liked him a lot. He was a nice guy. I told him what happened and that we never meant to cause any damage. He was very understanding and said there was no serious damage, but I needed to stay away from making fires, especially near the hedges that surrounded the Park. I agreed and never played with matches again. Kids will be kids and we will do things that we should not do, which was fine as long as there were no serious consequences. As long as we learned from our mistakes, we became better for it – best to screw up on a minor incident to learn a lifetime lesson.

Weirdest Thing That Ever Happened

One day we were standing around in front of the Park clubhouse. Some kid came over with a few others, and told us we needed to go with them because they wanted to show us something. We said we were not interested, especially not knowing these guys and unwilling to tell us what we were going to see. After a little more pestering, we went with them. They led us from the Park, across Folsom Street, down 21st Street to a set of flats between Folsom and Treat Streets near Ellington's place. We went in a dark alley passage that led from the street to the backyard. Then the kid who dragged us there turned to one of his Latino buddies and kept saying, "Show 'em, Benny! Show 'em!" Finally, Benny slowly lowered his pants and shorts and showed off the largest penis I ever knew existed. We just stared for a few seconds in weird amazement. None of us said anything. We just left and went back to the Park. It was the strangest thing that ever happened to me up until then – complete strangers displaying a penis to a bunch of other strangers. I never understood what they expected us to all do. Applaud? Take pictures? Make a big fuss? It was just a very weird experience.

Birth of the Fart Flamethrower

On another occasion, a couple of my buddies said they wanted to show me and another buddy something. They took us into the men's bathroom at the Park. They made sure no one else was in there. One guy bent over, spread his cheeks and farted while the other guy held a lit match by his butt, creating a flamethrower affect for a second or two. We all got a good laugh out of it except for the farter who could not see anything, but it was his idea in the first place. I never thought to ask, but it was always amazing how and what ideas kids came up with to amuse themselves and others. How would you ever think of doing such a thing?

Although I had roller skates and a balloon tire scooter, I just wanted something that more resembled a car, so I built a coaster – a lot cheaper than having to buy a manufactured version. It consisted of a 5-foot board to sit on, a 2" x 4" rear axel nailed to the board, and a similar front axel that swiveled on a screw and bolt attached to the front of the board. A wood orange crate was not used as the front of my coaster like other kids' coasters because it required a longer coaster than I wanted and it might interfere with the rope nailed to each end of the front axel for steering. The wheels were ball bearings I got from the PG&E (Pacific Gas & Electric Co.) shop a couple of blocks away. The wheels slid over carved out axel ends. I nailed on a couple of pieces of wood where my feet rested with a strip of thick rubber attached to each to serve as breaks so I did not wear out my shoes from stopping and slowing down the coaster. A couple of pieces of plywood in a wedge shape and nailed to the 5-foot board served as the driver's backrest. The coaster was fun but noisy with the metal wheels rolling on the concrete sidewalks and driveways.

PG&E had a building on 20th Street between Folsom and Shotwell Streets. Their vehicle maintenance garage was on the Shotwell side of the building. That was where I got the wheels for the coaster. They gave me choices of 1/2 to 2-inch-wide ball bearings. I picked up four of both 1/2" and 3/4" thick wheels and said the other set was for my buddy, which was not true. That gave me a choice and replacements if needed. Across the street from PG&E on the northwest corner of Shotwell and 20th Streets was a long metal half-dome building. I just assumed it was a homemade commercial building. I learned later that it was a Quonset hut, the last WWII era structure in the Mission District – not a landmark, but it was nice to know we lived so close to such a historic structure.

Once I got my coaster built, we took turns pushing each other along the street. That got old quickly until we began using a steep 55-foot-long driveway between Atkins' house and the neighbor's house that ran the length of the houses. One day I was riding down the driveway on the coaster, as we frequently did, and the neighbor came out and asked if we would please stop because someone was sick inside. We were not going to stop, but Atkins asked us if we would stop as a favor. We did stop and actually felt good about it afterwards.

Not Settling on Being Second Best

I had played with yo-yos since I was six or seven years old. As they grew in popularity, the San Francisco Park & Recreation Department eventually started to offer yo-yo competitions at the parks around the City.

I was able to do all of the basic tricks by age nine like the Sleeper, Rock the Cradle, Spank the Baby, Walk the Dog, Around the Corner, Shoot the Moon, Around the World, but there were lots of difficult tricks that I only saw in pictures being done by older kids and adults – a more professional group. My fear was always that they would require some of those difficult tricks in the competition. I entered the competition that was held initially at Folsom Park. It was the beginning of a long history of serious competetion during my youth, possibly to compensate for my sense of inferiority in other matters in order to prove I was better than others including my older brother and sister. Not many competed, but I was the final winner. That qualified me to compete across the Bay in Oakland, where Mom drove me. I did better than a number of other kids, but I did not win. They required some tricks I only saw in pictures. Too bad I did not know that ahead of time so I could practice them. I was discouraged by why I lost the event and the unfairness of the City in not preparing contestants better, so I never competed in the Park & Recreation yo-yo competition again. Strange that I gave up at such an early age, but even in later years, I only focused on sports that I could be first string.

Setback to Acting Career

There was a San Francisco Community Chest Center on Capp Street off 19th Street. The building had the most attractive architecture on the block – something that should be in the country instead of in a major city. It had a weathered dark brown shake shingle cedar wood exterior. When walking by the Center one day and being curious what was inside, I went inside and got information about their programs. They asked if I wanted to be in a play. They needed kids to be extras for a *Wizard of Oz* one-night performance. They said it was an easy part, so why not, I agreed. I was assigned to a five-kid dance chorus line. We practiced a few times and learned a simple dance step. On the night of the performance, I was a little nervous, even though I knew our routine. But less than 10 minutes before the curtain was to go up, we were told that we were being replaced by a second number by the tap dancer, who was the only talented guy in the performance. They must have decided he was more professional and entertaining than us, which was true, but I thought it was unfair to those of us who had shown up for practices and to those who had parents in the audience. It was a good thing Mom and Dad were not there. I left a little disappointed but somewhat relieved. It was a new experience and nothing happened to deter me from trying other new ventures in the future.

End of a Stinkin' Business

Once in a while I went with one of my buddies to Fisherman's Wharf to go fishing, but most times I went by myself. I never had a fishing rod, but I did not need one. I had a drop line consisting of a nylon line wrapped around a wooden spool. I used bread as my bait because it did not cost me anything – I got it from home. I rolled a small ball of bread, put it on the hook, and dropped it off the edge of the pier that was in back of Alioto's Restaurant. It never took long to get nibbles, but the fish were either way too small to keep or the larger fish were catfish, which were so ugly. Older guys walking by told me catfish were not edible and Mom said the same thing, so I always threw them back. The crabbers in the same fishing spot always pulled up one to several crabs in their crab pots.

One time I caught enough regular fish that appeared to be enough to cook, so I took them home for Mom in a bag I found on the wharf. For the entire trip home, I really stunk up the bus and streetcar. Mom was not impressed by my catch, but she said she would cook them. When I came home for dinner, she said, "After cleaning them, there was not enough meat to cook." She was particular about what she fed us, so she probably figured anything caught off a pier could not be good for us.

Most Memorable Trip Not Ending Well

The most memorable trip of my young life to date was visiting Atkins' mother. His parents were separated. His mom lived in Pacifica. Atkins invited us to take a bike ride from the Mission District to Pacifica to see her. She was no one we had ever met, but this was something buddies did for each other. I knew Pacifica was near San Francisco but had no idea how far it was and how to get there. It was a 20-mile bike ride, each way. We set out about mid-morning. The trip took us over Twin Peaks, out Sloat Boulevard, along Skyline Boulevard, and out Highway 1 along the coast.

It took us a few hours to get to the border of Pacifica where we started our steep decent into Pacifica as we hugged the edge of the busy six-lane freeway. It was a pretty scary ride with cars whipping by us at over 65 miles per hour with our backs to the traffic. It took another hour to find our way through Pacifica to our destination. The trip was further than peddling back and forth across San Francisco – certainly the longest bike ride I ever took. We went inside and met Kenny's mom. She must have been an artist because she had a large mural of a South Seas beach and ocean covering her entire living room wall. I had never seen a wall mural in someone's house. We were there for a while and it was now late afternoon. I kept thinking there was a long ride to get home, up a very steep highway, and I was going to get home late. I had always been home when it was still light and never been late for dinner. Then Kenny's mom offered us milk and cake, which was the last thing I wanted. No one complained. I had the feeling that Kenny did not get to see her that often. Finally, we got on the road and it was a really tough ride up the hill. None of us had lightweight multi-gear three-speed bikes. For much of the hill, we had to walk our bikes up the steep grade. I got home well after 7:00 p.m., probably closer to 8:00 p.m. I had never seen Mom so upset and emotional. I was thinking, *what is the big deal if I got home late for dinner?* I figured it was not my fault, and it certainly was not my intent to be so late, so I explained what happened. She asked why I did not phone her. The idea of phoning never crossed my mind since I never faced a situation when I needed to phone her. At that point, my brother, who was 17 at the time, came to my defense, probably because he had done things just as dumb and saw there was no harm. It was the first time I ever saw Dad show his anger, as he had always been an extremely quiet and mild mannered guy. Dad yelled at me that Mom was almost out of her mind with worry that something bad had happened to me. Then Dad turned and started beating Joe for sticking up for me. I had never seen Dad punish any of his kids, much less strike one of us. I never forgot those three huge events in my life – the first time Dad ever emotionally supported Mom, the first time he ever struck any of us, and the first time my brother stood up for me. Never was I ever prouder of Joe for being the kind of big brother that any kid could hope for.

Age 10: The Birth of Competition

Dad's Only Advice Over 17 Years

Dad did little fathering with me including giving advice, and maybe that was good in that it left me to make my own decisions – right or wrong, at least they were my decisions, and I did not wind up blaming others all my life for mistakes I made along the way. Dad gave me advice only two times in my life and once was when I went in the bathroom one morning to see what Dad was doing as he was getting ready to shave and go to work. I knew in a few years I would start shaving, so I was curious what it was all about. I watched him with the greatest of interest, as I had never seen someone shave up close. He poured a little hot water in his shaving mug that had a small bar of soap on the bottom. He applied a hot washcloth to his face to soften his whiskers. He swirled his shaving brush inside the mug and covered his day-old whiskers with the warm shaving lather. He took a few swipes of whiskers off with his double-edged razor and then stopped in the middle of shaving. He looked down at me and said, "Do not start to shave. Put it off as long as you can because once you start, there is no ending to shaving every day." I did not follow his advice. I just wanted to grow up faster like all kids. I started shaving in my sophomore year of high school as soon as I saw some peach fuzz appear on my face. As I learned later, growing up was not all it was cracked up to be in some ways. Dad's shaving mug was one of only two keepsakes of his that I kept after his death years later. (The other was an 1877 silver trade dollar later stolen in a burglary.) I suppose it reminded me of a time when Dad gave me some advice, something I think all kids should cherish. It was strange how we cherished advice over tangible things – wisdom over property. The only other advice he ever gave me was the following year when we were walking together to get a haircut, and he told me to always walk erect. "Hold your head high and keep a straight back when you walk." He took pride in his appearance. That was why he always dressed well and walked so proudly for years.

Up until now, I went to Sunday Mass with Mom and Dad. By the time I was 10 years old, Mom and Dad preferred attending 7:00 a.m. Sunday Mass and I preferred attending a later Mass, so I began to attend Mass by myself. Going to Sunday Mass at St. Charles Church offered two options. I either sat in the pews with everyone else, which was not my preference because I did not like the idea of being wedged in by others and confined until the end of Mass. The other option was to stand in the back of the church, which was the only option to those arriving late when all the pews were taken. I preferred that option regardless of when I arrived, which generally was when Mass was just starting or a few minutes late. By then the pews on the ground level and in the rear choir balcony were pretty well filled. There was a chapel to the side in the back where I always headed because it was always less crowded. That got to be my regular hangout during Mass even though I could not see the altar or what the priest was doing, but I could still hear him reciting the Latin and giving his sermon. The nuns had told me I still met the obligation of attending Mass on Sunday if I was anywhere in the church, including the chapel, even though I could not see everything. I thought that was strange, but with the church always so crowded, they had no choice but to allow it to be acceptable. To a kid like me, the chapel was a more interesting place to hang out with all of the statues, lit candles and pictures. Often adults had to tell a classmate and me to keep quiet, as there was a lot of chitchat and moving around by us during the services. My attention span at Mass was on the short side – always looking for things to amuse myself. Being in the back, I could also leave a little early. I knew that I met my obligation to attend Sunday Mass if I arrived before the priest read the Gospel and stayed at least until people received holy communion. To miss Sunday Mass was considered a mortal sin, which was serious enough to condemn me to eternal hell. Something I did enjoy about attending Mass was taking in the Church's Spanish architecture, beautiful stained glass windows and the feeling of familiarity. It was the feeling I got years later when I went on vacation for two or three weeks – that I was glad to get home to my familiar surroundings.

Always the Loser on Sadie Hawkins Day

Besides the guys I palled around with, there were three girls about our age on our block that we knew. One was a really pretty blond, one was plain and the other was really unattractive. The girls suggested we all play

Sadie Hawkins Day, just like in the popular comic strip *Li'l (Little) Abner*. At age 10, I was looking at girls differently and not as silly annoyances. The girls hid somewhere on Folsom Street between 20th and 21st Streets but always in the middle of the block on the east side of the street. There were doorways, sunken driveways, side passages under the flats leading to backyards, and behind cars to hide. Gray, who was the best looking of all the guys, always found the pretty blond. I suspect she picked the same hiding place each time and he knew exactly where to find her. If I found a girl, it was always one of the less attractive girls. As much as I squirmed about kissing an unattractive girl, at least I got away with a quick peck on the cheek by the plain girl. But the really unattractive girl usually grabbed both sides of my face and planted a big kiss on my lips. Ugh! Looking back, I often thought that was for sure an all right thing to do in that I was contributing to the girl's self-confidence.

Stage Competition for the Illusive Bike

I went to the Crown Theater on Mission Street one Saturday when admission was only nine cents for kids. Before the movie started, they had a yo-yo contest on stage and the winner received a new bicycle. I was pretty good with the yo-yo having won a bunch of badges and saw the tricks the winner had to do. I thought, *I could do those*, and I had as good a chance as anyone to win. The next Saturday, I went back and entered the competition on stage. There was no age limit, so I figured the older kids probably were a lot more experienced than me. Again the required tricks were pretty simple, like the Sleeper, Walk the Dog and Rock the Cradle. To my surprise, I wound up being the winner. As I waited on stage with great anticipation for them to wheel out my new bike, a man walked out carrying a small box that contained a black plastic model airplane that you swung around on a long set of cords. I was so, so disappointed, which showed on my face to the moderator and the audience. I went back stage and told the moderator I thought the prize was a bicycle like the previous week, he said they gave away a bike every other week and I should try again the following week. I was so miffed. I never did go back to compete. In hindsight I do not know why. My anger and pride outweighed common sense. I probably was passing up a sure chance of winning a brand new bike for a nine cents movie ticket. Years later I always regretted not returning as I had a very good chance of winning, especially since I was still riding my stripped down hand-painted black bike with a bunch of patches in the tires. My pride was more important than material things. It was one of several bad decisions I would make in my childhood.

In Search of a Pot of Gold

I always wondered what was at the end of the rainbows, and we saw lots of them in rainy San Francisco. One day I decided to find out, not with the intent of finding a pot of gold as the stories mentioned, but just to see it up close and at ground level. There was a rainbow and it looked like the rainbow's end was about a mile away. So I set out on my bike going east along 21st Street toward Potrero Hill. Just beyond the S.F. General Hospital, the rainbow petered out. It disappeared – that I did not expect. It was such a disappointment, but I learned something – not everything in life was achievable, so if you do not get what you want, suck it up!

Absence of Prejudicial Name-Calling

Growing up in the Mission, I heard references to all of the derogatory slang names for every nationality under the sun: Chink (Chinese), Dago (Italian), Honky (Whites), Jap (Japanese), Kike (Jews), Kraut (Germans), Mick (Irish), Spade (African-American), Spick (Spanish), but it was always spoken in the third-person. I never heard anyone call people these names face to face, especially inside the fences of Folsom Park or the schoolyard. Some of these races were not around, but the Park was a place where color was transparent. Kids may have given others nicknames that were not very pleasant, but they were not intentionally racial references. My friends and I looked at kids in the playground and at school as just kids and never thought about racial differences. Everyone was an equal. No one was better or worse than another. The common denominator was that we were all on the poor side and about the same age. I guess that was the glue that bound us together. As I grew up, I heard the racial slurs being cast by the adults. I could see the prejudices in them and wondered why. Since I did not respect those making the comments, I never paid any attention to them – just let it go over my head. If I heard them from someone I had respected, I certainly lost that respect for them.

Dropping Like Flies at the Playground

Several of us kids were hanging around in front of the clubhouse at the Park and an older kid showed us younger kids how to hyperventilate to knock ourselves out. It was something we had not seen before and sounded like fun. My buddies tried it and they were dropping like flies. So I tried it a few times, and each time I would ask "How long was I out?" as if I was trying to break a record for being out the longest. Usually, I was out several seconds. It was another one of those comical moments of kids standing around in front of the clubhouse and all of a sudden, they were falling to the ground and lying there as if they were dead for a while. And that was exactly why we stopped doing it. The Park director came out and saw what was going on. He said, "Do you realize that one of these times you kids might not come out of it?" The thought never crossed our minds, but he was right. Whatever snapped us out of the deep sleep may not work every time, so my buddies and I never did that again – definitely for the best. Years later I learned that it could have caused brain damage and brain death.

Another thing we did at the Park and in school was to look cross-eyed at kids to taunt them or just to be funny. One day I did it at home. Mom told me never to do that again. "If someone hits you on the side of the head, your eye's could stay that way forever." I did not know if it was true, but I was not going to take a chance, so I stopped it forever. As I got older, I realized that Mom told little lies to correct my bad behavior. In spite of being Catholic and lying was a sin, I am glad she did – the end did justify the means.

While the baseball diamond at the Park was a teenager hangout, so was the Park clubhouse. The clubhouse at the Park was just big enough to hold a ping pong table with some seats on the sides for chit chatting. Because the clubhouse was mainly used by teens to socialize, most of them did not play ping pong. So kids of all ages had a chance to play, but kids my age pretty much stayed out with all the older kids inside. I had a brother and sister who were in the clubhouse a lot, so I felt comfortable going in and playing ping pong. The older kids knew me as Joe and Kathy's younger brother, so they left me alone. I never saw Joe play ping pong, but Kathy was very good among the older kids and had a reputation of being very difficult to beat. Boys did not like losing to her.

Benefits from Winning, Success and Positive People

I was very good at ping pong for my age too and even gave my sister a run for her money. One of the reasons I got good was because it was mostly older kids who played ping pong. So I had to play with a lot of kids who were better than me, only because they were older. It was a classic example of the principle "If you want to improve faster to become a winner in the long term, play against competition that is better than you." If you only want to win in the short term, play against those worse than you for a false sense of confidence.

The San Francisco Park & Recreation Department had a competitive ping pong tournament throughout the City park system. Kathy had in the past won their All-City Ping Pong Tournament. I entered when I was 10 and won the championship for my age group at Folsom Park. The next level of competition was held at James Rolph Jr. Playground at Army Street and Potrero Avenue. It was a long 12-block bike ride on my way to do battle for a 10-year-old kid to make by myself. I knew that no one would be there rooting for me. I never spent any time at that park and had no friends there. None of my family or friends would be there. So by the time I got there, I was mentally at a bit of a disadvantage. Although the Chinese kid I played against was good and could serve the ball hard and put a spin on the ball, these were all things I could do too, so there were no surprises in how he played. In the final two-out-of-three games, I lost 21-19. While those in the clubhouse were congratulating the winner, I left as fast as I could. I was not used to losing and I took defeat badly. That was how I was all my life. I always thought the sportswriter Grantland Rice's cliché "It's not whether you win or lose, it's how you play the game" was for losers but had good intent – to help losers accept the defeat to move on. The problem I had with the quote was that kind of thinking led kids to continue playing a sport or participate in an activity that they just were not good at. If one was not very good at something, they should try something that they can be better at or experience more successes – the more successes, the more self-confidence. If possible, quitting a bad team and playing for a better team was another option. Also, I learned later in life, one should surround themselves with as many successful and positive thinking people as possible, rather than hanging around with a bunch of losers or negative thinking people.

Self-Worth Not Based on a Single Attribute

It was the first and last time that I participated in the citywide ping pong competition. I never saw a need to try to get better just like with the yo-yo. I was content proving I was the best at least once at an activity that was not popular with my friends or apt to be a useful skill in the future. There would be other challenges ahead for me. I did learn a lesson that competition gets tougher when I step up from one level of competition to another, so I should not pin my self-worth on that form of competition or activity. Rather, I should enjoy my past successes as there will be other opportunities in life that offer different and greater possible successes inside and outside of sports.

I never appreciated Mission Dolores Basilica Church between 16th and 17th Streets on Dolores Street, which was the oldest building in the City and oldest original intact Mission in California. Like so many local landmarks, kids just took them for granted. I peeked in once and strolled through its historic graveyard and garden, but never knew its historical significance even though I was Catholic. However, I did get a lot of use out of Mission Dolores Park or "Dolores Park" two blocks away that covered the two square block area of 18th to 20th Streets and Dolores to Church Streets, across from Mission High School. The park had 16-acres of rolling grass hills. I would walk there with some of my buddies and spend a half-hour rolling down the hills. We lay on our side and just rolled. After descending one hill, we rolled along the flat ground to the edge of the next hill, and rolled down that one too. Whoever got to the bottom first was the winner. Sure it made us dizzy, but that was part of the fun, wobbling around afterwards like a drunk. Once an old woman told us that was not good for us. I thought *what does she know?* Kids got dizzy regularly on the spinning Joy Wheel at Playland.

On the edge of Mission Dolores Park at the corner of 19th and Church Streets was the entrance to a tunnel for the streetcars to pass on the west side of the Park. We stood above the top of the tunnel entrance and as a streetcar entered the tunnel, a couple of us dropped a handful of rocks on its roof making the passengers wonder if it was a hail storm outside. The conductor could see what we were doing, so he was never surprised – probably expected it. We then ran away to escape being caught. We did not try this with streetcars exiting the tunnel for fear that the conductor would stop, get out and chase us, even though there was no chance that anyone was going to do it. But we were not too bright in such matters. If someone did chase us, that would have been scary but exciting.

My favorite panoramic view of the City of San Francisco was from the top of Twin Peaks, but my favorite up-close view of the San Francisco skyline was from the corner of Mission Dolores Park at 20th and Church Streets where I could see all the office buildings in the downtown area. Also at this corner was the most famous fireplug in the City. **[28]**

Once I went to Dolores Park with two of the girls who played Sadie Hawkins Day with us. One was the really attractive girl that I could never find in the Sadie Hawkins Day search and the other was the unattractive girl. We were sitting around on the grass and eventually I pretended I was asleep. They whispered a couple of time "Are you asleep?" I said nothing and kept still. Then one of the girls kissed me on the cheek. I so hoped it was the attractive one, but I just knew it was probably the unattractive one. After a short while, I let on that I was waking up. Still hoping it was the attractive girl, I waited until we were alone and I asked her to go to the movies on a date. She smiled and said as nicely and considerately as she could that I will find someone my age down the road that I will make very happy. Up until that point, I had never realized that she was older than me, possibly by two to three years. I was so disappointed, but I understood – first because she was older and secondly, I never expected anyone so good looking wanting to go out with me. The latter I could live with, but the age thing really threw me.

Duped to Shill for My Sister

San Francisco was a great port of call for the U.S. Navy to drop off sailors on furlough. When the fleet was in, there were sailors everywhere. Where they were noticeable to me was at Skateland at the Beach on the corner of Balboa and Great Highway, across the street from Playland at the Beach. It opened in 1947 and the sailors must have thought it was a great place to pick up girls, because there were always a lot of girls there when the fleet was in. Music was played during freestyle roller-skating, when I ventured out on the rink. Mom dragged me there because my sister and her friend went there a lot when she was in the last year or two of high school. Kathy and Joe were the good looking kids in the family, and she did have a pretty good figure, but I think she and most girls there liked showing off their legs in their skimpy 12-inch skirts. Kathy owned her own skates, but I rented mine since I did not go as often as her. I never enjoyed roller-skating because the skates were so heavy on my skinny legs. As much as I hated it, Kathy made me skate with her during pair skating. I suspect it was to use me for bait to attract the older guys to skate with her. Skating with me showed them that she wanted to skate with someone and to be rescued from skating with her kid brother. It must have worked because she always found skating partners all evening. Skateland was a place she could meet older guys. She always seemed boy crazy to me, which was too bad, because when she graduated from high school, she passed up a full scholarship to Lone Mountain University. She told me later that she was tired of school. I think she just wanted to leave home, get married and have kids, which she did shortly after graduation.

The Korean War (1950-1953) was going on and the military draft was in effect. My brother decided to enlist in the U.S. Air Force. I was in the 5th grade at the time and he would not be returning until I was in high school. I never thought anything about it, since he never had much time for me when he was around. I never thought much, if anything, about the war that was going on, including that Joe may be in harm's way at some point and never return.

Picking Pockets for Spending Money

Until now, Joe and I shared the same bedroom, but with him gone, Mom decided that Dad should move in with me. She was tired of living with Dad's snoring and wanted to get good nights of sleep so she was not so tired at work. That meant I had to listen to Dad's snoring, which was not a problem as his bed was on the other side of the room and most nights he did not get home from work until 3:00a.m.

One Sunday Joey Sandoval offered to treat me to a day at Playland, but I asked him where he got the money. He said from his mother's purse. It was the first time I ever heard of someone stealing something, but who was I to turn down a free day at Playland. Days later, I felt that I was obligated to treat him to Playland in return for his paying my way, but where to get the money? I never thought of stealing from Mom's purse because I knew everything she had was spent on the family. But I always suspected that Dad was getting more than $20 a week for spending money. So a few weeks later, while Dad was asleep, I snuck over to the chair where Dad hung his pants and long johns and took $20 from his wallet. There was about $85 in the wallet, so I figured he would not miss it. I did know it was wrong but I told myself Mom and Dad owed it to me because I was not getting any spending money from them, and I was out working at a much younger age than all the kids I knew. After treating Joey to Playland, I told him I did not think it was right for either of us to be taking money from purses and wallets, so we both agreed that was the end of our free trips to Playland. I learned something else from that experience. Mom once said Dad turned over his entire paycheck to her with the exception of $20 for spending money. I always suspected Dad might have been holding out on Mom, which was evident from the $85 I saw in his wallet. I never told Mom – never even thought of telling her. I could not fault him for needing more than $20 spending money since he worked for it and our family never was deprived of the necessities in life.

Age 11: New School, New Experiences

Freedom From Sibling Chaperoning

Kathy had been attending St. Paul's High School for girls for the past three years. Mom must have gotten nervous about me going to St. Charles by myself, so she decided to transfer me to start 6th grade at St. Paul's Grammar School at Church and 29th Streets, just across the street from Kathy's high school. This was at the same time when some of my buddies were transferring from Hawthorne Grammar School to Horace Mann Junior High on 23rd Street off Valencia Street for kids in the 6th to 9th grades. They had to move to a new school but stayed in the same neighborhood and attended school with most of their friends they knew at Hawthorne. But Mom was telling me to attend school in a different neighborhood with all new kids. I made a fuss because I did not want to leave my school friends, and my sister made a fuss because Mom was requiring her to take me to and from school each day on the bus – the last thing a junior in high school wanted was dragging along her 6th grade baby brother. What would the other girls think? But that worked out fine since we parted ways at the bus stop at 29th and Church Streets. School was half a block away for her and I just had to cross the street to school, so I was out of sight quickly. Both of us got out of school at 3:00 p.m. when we caught the bus home together. On days she was going to be late, I got a soda at the creamery catty corner to the bus stop and waited for her. This lasted about a month or so until Kathy insisted I go to school on my own because taking me home was making her late for her afternoon job at the Bernal Heights Public Library at the corner of Cortland Avenue and Andover Street. We assured Mom it would be fine because it was only two short blocks to and from the house to the bus stop at 21st Street and South Van Ness Avenue, and I had gotten to know the same bus drivers each day. Mom agreed to let me go by myself on the 41-Van Ness trolley bus that connected to the 29-Noe bus on the condition that I always took the seat behind the driver. I felt so grown up having that independence. On the ride home, I got to know the bus driver really well and I really liked him. He always greeted me like we were old friends. We talked a lot, so I took the seat across from him so it was easier to speak to each other. If I was late and missed his bus, I was so disappointed. I never knew why Mom thought it was alright for me to go by myself to St. Paul's, which was a lot further away, than going to St. Charles by myself. I suspect Mom thought it was a better school in some way and had my best interest in mind regarding my education.

If I left the house on time, I always arrived at school about 30 minutes early, so with nothing to do and nowhere to go, I frequently dropped into the corner creamery at 29th and Church Streets for a Green River drink. The syrup used in the drink was made by the maker of Green River soda, which must have been more popular on the East Coast as I had never heard of it. It made me feel so grown up placing an order, being waited on, and paying with my own money since our family never ate out. A Green River soda was neither the Breakfast of Champions nor did I need it every morning, but it made me feel special.

St. Paul's Grammar School was different than St. Charles – not better, just different. Each had their redeeming qualities. St. Charles Grammar School was a historic Italianate architecture wood frame building built in 1888. St. Paul's was a more imposing building made of concrete blocks, which made it look more institutional, but that was offset by standing next door to the beautiful St. Paul's Church on Church Street between 29th and Valley Streets. It was a Gothic Revival style church built in 1911 of gray Romanesque stone with two slate-clad steeples. I loved attending Mass at St. Charles Church with its Spanish architecture and beautiful stained glass windows, but St. Paul's Church gave me a special feeling. It was much larger than St. Charles Church with an impressive towering exterior, and the inside had more stained glass windows, artwork and a very high ceiling compared to St. Charles. [29]

Boys wore to school a white shirt, blue tie, "salt and pepper" corduroy pants, and brown or black oxford shoes. It was a period of experimenting with tying different knots in my tie. My favorite was a double Windsor knot that I wrapped around twice as many times as normal to make a knot twice as large, leaving the remainder of the tie hanging way above my belly button. Only Dennis Leahy had a shorter tie appearing even smaller on his bulky body. Girls wore navy blue pleated skirts with a white middy top that had a large button-on blue collar that had three thin white stripes

147

along the edges that gave a Navy-look to them, along with a loose blue tie that slipped through a white cloth tie holder.

From Twenty to Zero Cavities

Mom always took me to our family dentist near the New Mission Theater. He was a prematurely white haired, professional-looking guy – always happy, smiled a lot, gentle, and patient with my clinging to the padded arms of the chair. I hated both the drilling noise and the smell of my burning teeth. But he drilled in very short bursts, so he made it more bearable. I used to go annually but stopped going for two or three years. Getting a toothache finally made me return. He said I had 20 cavities and needed three teeth pulled. I had the teeth pulled first and the remaining cavities filled over several visits. When I was having my teeth pulled, they placed a mask over my nose and mouth to feed laughing gas to me. I will never forget the smell of rubber. It was so pungent and unpleasant. For the rest of my life, whenever I smelt raw or burning rubber, I remembered the gas used to remove my teeth. The surprising number of cavities and lost teeth taught me a lifetime lesson. I brush my teeth whenever I wake up, go to bed and any other time when I eat something during the day. It must have helped because at the age of 50, I went to a dentist after not seeing one for nearly 30 years and he found no cavities. He asked if I brushed my gums in addition to the teeth. I said, "Yes, because I use a toothbrush forever," and the bristles got very soft, so it made for a gentle massaging of the gums. The implication of the dentist was that brushing the gums was a good thing, which I did ever since. By age 80, I did not have a single cavity over a 60 years period.

Flirting With a Nun

One of my favorite nuns was my 6th grade teacher. She was pretty, young and known as a "boy's nun" – one who appeared to enjoy working with boys more than with girls. One day after school, we were alone, and during our conversation, I thought I saw her blink several times in a row at me. I innocently did the same thing in return, when she said, "Why Terence,

I am so surprised!" I did not mean to flirt, but I realized that was how it must have appeared. I turned beet red in the face – something I did when embarrassed until I was 14 or 15. She smiled at me and I felt better that she thought nothing of it – made me comfortable in an uncomfortable situation.

TV Stardom Lost Opportunity

My favorite subject in school was math – probably because I always enjoyed it and got good grades in grammar school. Plus, I was good at it. It was not until I was a freshman at City College of San Francisco that an administrator told me the results of my entrance exam or IQ exam in order to motivate me to participate in a Saturday local television program about students who were exceptional at mathematics and to discuss a new math program. He said I was in the 98-99 percentile in math. I always regretted I had promised him I would show up for the show, but I never did. I told Mom I was not going to participate and she said I should go or at least phone the counselor to cancel, which I never did. It would have been a memorable and very worthwhile experience, but I was too immature to appreciate it at the time.

Secret to Winning Math Competition

Our 6th grade class held a competition each month to determine who accurately add up a column of numbers the fastest. The teacher wrote two identical columns of 10-15 double-digit numbers on the board. The two finalists were always the same girl and me, and I won every time. What allowed me to add numbers so quickly was that I added in groups of numbers instead of individual numbers. For example, if I saw 2, 3 and 5 appearing together in a column, I read them as 10, which was added once to my running total, rather than changing my running total three times had I added the three figures separately. So in a column of 10 double-digit numbers, I could be adding a total of eight or nine combined-numbers, while my competition was adding 20 individual numbers – the approach taught by teachers at the time.

Let Kids Follow Their Interests

The girl in the math competition finals loved drawing wonderful horses and was constantly being asked by the teacher to try drawing other things, but the girl never drew anything other than horses in class. Years later, I often thought how the teacher was right academically but wrong motivationally. Allowing her to draw her horses motivated her to continue doing something she loved, enjoyed and was passionate about. Had she been required to draw other things, she may have not been as interested and dedicated. She was still very young and had plenty of time to develop her art. Kids may not know the right thing to do, but long-term harm can be done if they are not allowed to develop their own self-motivation. In college I wrote Alfred Hitchcock type stories for my freshman English class. They had clever twists at the end like Hitchcock movies, but my teacher eventually told me to develop my own style and gave me C+ grades to force me to change, which I did eventually. My grades improved but my heart was not in the papers, so I spent a lot less time thinking about the story line, using my imagination, and writing the papers.

I was always concerned about how I thought my appearance made me stick out at school with my freckles and big ears, but they were nothing compared to a couple of my classmates. I never gave it any thought at the time, but at St. Paul's there was only one African-American [30] boy and girl in our class – Ralph Versey and Julie Newman. They were the first African-American kids I ever had as classmates, and there were none who hung out at Folsom Park. It must have been tough for Ralph and Judy. We were all friendly to each other, but I never felt either of them had really good friends at school. They seemed to be each other's closest friend and hung out together at school, which was why I was so surprised that one day the two of them got into a shouting match. I never knew why they were arguing, but I felt sorry for them being upset with each other in a world where they were in many ways by themselves.

Years later I asked my sister about her friends in high school, and she said that she only had a couple of good friends. I suspect it was because she had to rush off to her job after school each day and did not have time to participate in extracurricular activities to socialize enough to create good friends. That would have been too bad if that was the case because maybe if she had more friends who were going to college, she may have been more motivated to go to college too.

Giving up Is Not an Option

It was the same way with my brother. His friends in grammar and high school were mostly from his Folsom Park connections. He never mentioned more than two or three guys he was close to at school. It may have been different if he had made the frosh-soph basketball team in his freshman year at St. Ignatius (SI) High School. Mom told me years later that when he got cut during tryouts, he seemed to lose his interest in school, sports and ambition. He never went out for sports again. She said he was too short to play for them. If anything, he was just up against a lot of excellent athletes. In those days, SI had one of the better, if not best, basketball programs under coach Phil Woolpert and players like George Moscone '47 and Albert "Cap" Lavin '48 [remember that name]. I learned while going from grammar school to high school to college, the level of competition in sports and academics increased considerably at each level. He may have been king of the basketball court at Folsom Park in grammar school, but he would have encountered some of the best from other playgrounds at S.I. The test for every kid going from level to level was how well he faced challenges, difficulties, defeats and disappointments along the way.

Joe, like me, made mistakes and faced defeats during our school years school. The important thing was not the mistakes and defeats that we experienced, but how we recovered and started over again. Joe seemed to let defeat affect his outlook on life and his image of himself. I chose to admit my mistakes, accept my defeats, made sure I did not repeat them or be discouraged, and moved on to be good at something else. In the business world, it was well known that nearly every really successful person experienced failures multiple times. They learned from those failures, made sure they did not make the same mistakes, and tried a new venture until they got it right.

In hindsight, I suspect Joe's life would have turned out a whole lot better had he attended St. James High School, the major Catholic high school in the Mission, not far from our house, instead of SI. Going where his buddies went did not work out for him. If basketball was so important to him, going to a school that may have had less competition would have been wiser. Eventually, Joe transferred from SI to Serra High School in San Mateo because two of his buddies who were good football players were transferring to Serra. Every day he drove the 30-45 minute commute each way. Some buddies made big sacrifices to keep their friendships.

On St. Valentine's Day, we celebrated at school by exchanging our Valentine cards. We could address a card to anyone we wished, whether it was to one girl or all the girls. It was optional whether we signed our name to the cards. Everyone in the class received at least one or more cards. I suspect the teacher must have addressed one or more cards to each student so that no one was left out. The more exciting cards were the unsigned ones. Those cards left it to my imagination as to who may have sent them. I always hoped the card was from the girl I admired from afar and was too shy to speak to, especially if she sent hugs and kisses by signing it "XOXOXO."

Most Sickening Thing Ever Seen

Since I was born, our family wore green on every St. Patrick's Day as if it was our family colors, but I was surprised to find that St. Paul's really pushed St. Patrick's Day. The Irish made up a significant percent of the San Francisco population, and that was especially true among the kids attending the schools for the Catholics, the religion of the Irish. So on the week of St. Patrick's Day, our class had footraces between the Irish vs. the World (all other nationalities). The races were held in the schoolyard. For the two years I was at St. Paul's in the 6th and 7th grades, the Irish won both years. I never had an opportunity to participate in sports up until then because Folsom Park and St. Charles never offered sports due to lack of funds and I was selling newspapers after school, so I had no time to participate in organized sports in the school system. This was the first time I learned that I was a fast runner. The major events in the class competition were relay races between Irish vs. World teams and a race between the fastest boy and girl in our class. Once our teacher learned who were the fastest runners in the class, she placed them as the relay anchors and pit each against the other in the race between the fastest boy and girl. I always ran in the anchor position in the relays and ran against the fastest girl, who was the one who drew the horses in class. Thinking back, it seems she and I could have been a twosome, but she was too pretty and I was too shy. I never lost a race. I always beat the fastest girl and boy in the class. Ralph Versey was my closest male competition. The most unforgettable race was when Ralph was running in a relay. We had to run around the outside of the four metal basketball poles at each corner of the schoolyard. He was running around one of the poles, leaned in too much to cut the corner and his head hit the pole at full speed. There was a loud clang and a huge welt on his forehead for a long time. It was the most sickening thing I had seen in my short life to that point.

One of the kids in class was in the Boy Scouts of America. He told me about what they did and got me so excited about camping, learning about survival and making crafts – things I had not done before such as pitching a tent, building a fire, archery, diving, and tying knots. I went to the Boy Scouts office and acceptance was much easier than I thought, since I assumed there was some screening process and I would not qualify. Then they talked about uniforms, supplies and other required purchases. The total cost came to a huge amount of money in my eyes that I could not afford, and I knew my parents could not either. So that was that.

Something I could not do because I was selling papers after school was to be a traffic boy. Only boys were allowed to act as traffic monitors at the nearby intersections. As a result, all the girls and I missed out marching in the City's annual Traffic Boys Review and Parade at Kezar.

Acting Career Comes to an End

I did get to be in the 6th grade Christmas pageant because it was held at night. I was one of many angels that stood around in the background chorus. It was a no pressure experience as I just blended in with the group of angels and sang familiar Christmas hymns. Since I had an insignificant role, Mom and Dad probably came to the stage performance only because they did not want me out by myself at night, but I was too young to realize it. I was just happy they came – made me think someone cared.

Getting ready for 4th of July was an adventure. I would take a streetcar down to Chinatown by myself to buy firecrackers. There were a number of stores that sold them to anyone at any age. Once I knew which store to go to, the rest was easy. I just asked for whatever I wanted. They normally carried an assortment of fireworks. If I walked the back alleys in late June and early July, the storeowners knew kids walking through Chinatown without their parents were shopping for fireworks. They stood in their doorway and asked passing kids, "Buy firecrackers?" Some pronounced it "firecrackee." Generally, they asked for their money upfront and then disappeared. That was unnerving, but what choice did I have in a business that had common sales practices among the stores. I never got stiffed. They always came back with the goods. I liked the ladyfingers because they were small but I got a lot of them on one string. Our most popular game was to light them individually and throw them at each other. The ladyfingers were so small and not that explosive, so no one ever got hurt because we threw them away from the face. Ladyfingers lost their appeal as I got older, so I bought the regular size firecrackers and cherry bombs, which we put in the dirt, inside cardboard boxes, tin cans, or any kind of container to blow them up or to see dirt fly in the air like mortar fire. The effect was to see things flying in the air as opposed to just a loud bang.

Charlie Montague was a buddy of mine at St. Paul's. I went over to his house to play occasionally. He lived a few blocks from school and nearby was a toy store on 30th Street beyond Sanchez Street that sold magic tricks. The store was modified from a garage that was part of a house. I did a lot more looking than buying, but I did buy a few items like a wood disappearing coin box. I dropped a coin into a tray, slid the tray into a box, pulled the tray out, and the coin disappeared. There was the sleight of hand vanishing coin trick and vanishing items behind a small curtain. Once I did the tricks a few times, the magical novelty disappeared. Although it was not magic, I learned that using a pen and lemon juice worked as invisible ink. I could not see what was written on the paper until I held the paper over a flame, which caused the writing to turn brown so I could read secret messages. I just had no one to send me messages.

An Untapped New Tourist Attraction

In the 7th grade, Charlie Montague set out on his bicycle and visited all of the Catholic Churches in the City over several weekends. I thought that it was a great adventure and something all kids should do, but I never got around to it. I thought the trip would also make a wonderful tourist attraction, since I doubted there were any bus tours to view so many wonderful church interiors with their unique architecture, stained glass windows and artwork. Charlie was the nicest, most gentle kid I ever knew, but he had some medical problem when he was young. His skin had wrinkles and looked dried out. He later went to Riordan High School like me. He passed away right after after our sophomore year. I suspect he was fighting some medical condition most of his short life.

Different Sibling Reactions to Same Role Model

Mom and Dad had no more than the equivalent of a high school education. The difference was that Dad had no desire for more education, while Mom was always trying to improve herself, whether it was from radio programs or adult education classes. As a result, she was the one who constantly pushed her kids to go to college. I suspect my brother and sister were turned off by her efforts because she eventually gave up trying. While I just accepted it as good advice and the best way I knew how to some day be rich. It turned out that I was the only one to graduate from college along with a Master's Degree, a law degree and 6-units short of earning a second Master's Degree.

Most Influential Book in My Life

Mom listened to a lot of radio programs dealing on self-improvement. Unlike Dad, she was determined to improve herself and the life of her family. On one of those programs she heard Dr. Norman Vincent Peale talk about his new book *The Power of Positive Thinking*, and she followed up the following Saturday to visit a local radio station where Dr. Peale was lecturing about his book. He later became known as "the father of positive thinking." Mom was not a big reader as she was busy raising her family, keeping the house spotless, and eventually working full time to make ends meet. However, she knew what Dr. Peale was preaching was something special. Maybe she saw a lack of positive thinking in Dad and wanted better for me. So Mom asked me what I wanted the most in return for reading the entire book by Dr. Peale, as long as it was not outrageous. I was 11 years old and had not read an entire book before – just comic books and Big Little Books. So to read a 240-page book from cover to cover was not really appealing to me. I went away and gave it a lot of thought, since I had to receive something really special in return. I thought about it for a couple of days and told her, "I would like a Lone Ranger jacket." I had seen it at a department store on Mission Street. It was a dark brown leather jacket with a patch sewn over the left breast showing the Lone Ranger on his horse Silver that was rearing up on his hind legs. She agreed without hesitation. It took me some time, but I eventually got through the book, which turned out to be the most influential book of my life. I enjoyed the various true stories of people and the recurring message that I could overcome difficulties and do just about anything that I set my mind to do. It was the right message at the right time. It implanted a positive mindset in me at an early enough age for me to accept and practice what I read during my formative years to develop into a "glass half-full" guy, rather than a "glass half-empty" person. It influenced my outlook all my life. When I got my jacket, I wore it proudly on special occasions. Eventually, the jacket hung in the closet after a couple of years, but the content of the book lasted me a lifetime. I learned that attitude was not something taught in the regular course of studies in grammar school, high school or college, so I believe every kid should read a similar book – the earlier in life, the better, before they got polluted by insecure parents, teachers and friends.

Dad made two trips back to Ireland during my youth. Mom thought they would cure him of his homesickness, but the more he went, the more he wanted to go back again. He especially liked the fact that those in the Old Country waited on him hand and foot while he was there – not much different from life at home, as Mom did all the work around the house except for Dad putting out the garbage. I suspected the yearning to stay in Ireland was to escape the responsibilities supporting a family and raising kids. It may not have been that he thought Tralee was better than San Francisco, but he may have preferred being single again. Dad's distaste for responsibility was probably the reason he once told me, "Enjoy your youth with all the free time you have now to play and have fun because it will be a lot different when you get older. When you grow up, you will have responsibilities and a job that will take up most of your time." It was

156

good advice but went completely over my head because I only knew about playing, having fun and going to school "all my life." I could not imagine a different lifestyle.

I went to a few funeral services at funeral homes with Mom and Dad to pay our respects for their Irish friends but only attended a service a couple of times at Holy Cross Cemetery in Colma (South San Francisco) where the Catholics were traditionally buried at a burial site with their spouse. A person's life was normally "celebrated" after the funeral at a wake held at the home of the deceased with food, booze and shared stories about the deceased. On the way to the wake after the funeral service, many stopped at the nearby historic Molloy's Tavern. The tavern interior had dark wood paneling, walls were covered with historical pictures and articles about sports (especially boxing) and politics. There was even banners of each of the San Francisco all-boy's high schools – Sacred Heart, St. Ignatius and eventually Riordan.

Dad stayed for a couple of quick ones only because Mom never liked the bar scene. I wanted to get out as quickly too when I heard someone joking, "Only 700 of Colma's half million residents are upright", which was true – creepy!

One late afternoon Jimmy Reidy showed up at the house at dinnertime. He insisted we go with him. He would not tell us why or where we were going, but we had to leave right away. We finished eating in a matter of minutes, and piled into his car. He sped away and was taking us across town. We wound up on the Great Highway and parked facing the ocean. The surprise was a beautiful sunset. Jimmy lived about 15 blocks from the ocean, so he could tell whether there were clear skies and the likelihood of an exceptional sunset. Sure enough, he was right. Mom and Dad probably enjoyed it more than us kids, but it was just a special experience of a nice guy thinking of others to brighten their lives.

1953 was an eventful year for Kathy. Shortly after graduating from high school, she got engaged to a sailor whom she either met at Skateland at the Beach or the USO (United Service Organizations) Club where they held dances for servicemen. Mom never felt any of her children should get married at such an early age of 18. Something did not seem right to Mom, so she tracked down the phone number of the guy's parents and learned that he was already married. Kathy was devastated and it was the first time I ever saw Kathy cry.

Harm From School Being Too Easy

Kathy had given up a full scholarship to Lone Mountain College to get out of the house and on her own, and she finally made it a year later when she married a different sailor she met at the USO Club, He had been in the U.S. Navy (1953-1954) when they got married. I thought giving up a scholarship to college was the dumbest thing she could do. I would have given anything for the opportunity. If Mom was right that Joe and Kathy did not have to study much to do well at school, it may have been a sign of not appreciating something that was too easy for them to do. Those like me, who had to work harder for success, appreciated education more. The other part of the equation (achievement = goal + effort) was the difference in goals. Neither of them set college education as a major goal, while I did.

Just before her wedding day, Kathy was going through her scrapbook that had pages and pages of photographs of guys she had known or dated. Most were military servicemen, usually in the Navy. When I saw it, the first thing I thought was, *this must be her trophy case*. I found it hard to believe that she could have known so many guys, so maybe a lot of them were pen pals. I got the feeling that her main interest in high school was to meet and date as many guys as possible, because she spent her time either working at the library after school or studying, and she had no time after school for high school activities. It probably was a good indication that she probably would choose to get married after high school, since there was nothing more to prove in being able to attract boys. Now it was time to move on to having children. She said to me, "I guess I should get rid of all these pictures," while she thumbed through them. I never responded as I did not know how important they were to her. When she was done, she removed the pictures of all past boyfriends one by one. She had closed a chapter of her life – tough to turn the page on so many memories. Years later when she got divorced, I wondered if she regretted throwing away all of the pictures. I kept pictures of my old girlfriends, as few as they were, with no effect on my happy life-long marriage, because they served as confirmations that I made the right choice.

Dealing With a Child Molester

Just before moving out of the Mission in the summer of 1953, Robbie Hall had me over his house. He was much taller and bigger than me. For all I know he was a couple of years older than me. He dropped his pants and wanted me to perform a sex act. I was so naive, he had to explain what I was supposed to do, which made me livid and disgusted. I said, "No". Then he wanted me to fondle him, and I said, "No" again. I had no idea what this was all about. I was too young to know about how guys satisfied their sexual desires, but I just had a feeling that this was all wrong and not all right. I told him I was going home and he said with a stern grimace on his face, "If you tell anyone about this, I'll beat you up. You'll be sorry." And he could do it, as he was big enough, and I had never gotten a real beating in the past, so I had no idea how much I could defend myself. I went home with no intention of telling anyone at home, as they showed no history of ever taking action when we should stand up for ourselves. So I decided to tell Bobbie Gray. I knew he could take care of himself, and I believed he would have a solution. Bobbie lived across the courtyard from Hall's flat and had gotten in Hall's face numerous times in the past. When I told him what happened, he looked at me for several seconds and calmly said, "I will take care of it." The way he said it, I knew exactly what he was going to do. This was why it was so important that all kids be raised to develop the courage to tell someone about abuses and be tough enough to stand up to bullies, even if it means getting into a fight. We moved from the neighborhood shortly afterwards, before I saw Bobbie or the old gang again. I just wished I could have been there when Hall got what was coming to him. Kids should be taught to say "No" and mean it when someone crosses physical boundaries. I would have forever regretted not saying "No" more than being assaulted. A classmate of mine later in high school succumbed to molestation for what he thought was an acceptable reason but regretted the loss of his self-esteem his entire life – never worth it.

In Search for a Better Life

After WWII a lot of Irish and Italian families moved from the Mission to the Sunset District and more Latinos were arriving in the Mission. The Mission District was a lower-income neighborhood and Mom, with so many others, wanted a roomier and nicer home in a newer and safer area of the City. Although we never knew anyone who encountered any violence in the Mission, Mom wanted better for us. She was a very proud person and occasionally liked putting on airs. She was always concerned about what others thought and how they perceived our family, so she wanted to improve our stature among her friends and our relatives. She would give anything to have a nicer house in a better neighborhood than her friends. She also was a practical woman and saw monthly rental payments as money down the drain when those payments were better served if they went toward building equity in a house. If she had her way, we would have moved a long time ago, but we never had the down payment to buy a house when the median value of a house was $11,930 in the City. [31]

How to Determine a True Friend

So Mom and Kathy went out house hunting and found a place in the Sunset that they liked very much, but it required a down payment that they could not afford, but Mom and Dad were sure that Dan McCarthy would help; otherwise, Mom would not be out shopping for a house. So Dad approached Dan for the down payment, and Dan said, "Are you crazy?" He was referring to Dad taking on the burden of debt payments and buying such an expensive house for someone from the Mission. Dan turned him down. I can understand his position because if he did it for Dad, other employees may have expected it too. But Mom never forgave him for not helping them out. She felt it was the least he could do for them since Dad knew him in Ireland as a youth, worked for him nearly 15 years (eventually 25 years until age 65), never missed a day of work unless hospitalized, worked terrible night shifts that gave him no time for the family, served as manager on many occasions, was honest as the day was long, and worked in an environment of drinking that already sent Dad to a mental institution for shock treatments. Dan never dreamed of lending the money to Dad and that taught me a life-long understanding of what "friendship" really meant. It was not what people said when you did not need them; it was what people did when you did need them.

Good Deed Leads to Lifetime of Helping Others

The San Francisco Police Department had a lot of Irish policemen at the time, and a number of them dropped into McCarthy's when they were off duty. One of them was an ex-policeman and a regular customer where Dad worked. Dad mentioned to him how Mom had found a house she loved, but he did not have the down payment and was turned down for a loan by Dan. It must have emotionally moved him, because he offered to lend Dad the down payment without hesitation. Here was a guy who was just an acquaintance and did not know our family and wound up lending the money at a very low interest rate. It was unbelievable. This was the first time I learned that there are people who are generous beyond all reason. It was something that motivated me to work hard toward complete independence of others for money or any other purpose. I suspected less than five percent of those I knew would help me if I needed significant financial help. When I got older, I found that to be true of people in general. I was eternally grateful for the generosity of that ex-policeman and it caused me to adopt the practice of helping friends and relatives all my life if they needed money for a good reason. Each time I did, I said to myself, "This is in memory of that ex-policeman." They say you never know the extent of a good deed. This was a case when a good deed by a stranger resulted in a lifetime of generosity by another stranger.

When Dad came home and told us about getting the loan, I was so happy for Mom who deserved her own nice home after sacrificing and putting up with all of Dad's drinking, his mental breakdowns, and paying rent for over 25 years to have nothing to show for it. They financed the house with a 30-year mortgage with Bank of America – something else that influenced me years later to work for them after college.

Valuable Lesson From Stupidity

Over the years of selling newspapers on corners, I handled a lot of coins on my job, and I occasionally found a coin that looked different. It was a penny or nickel made before WWII, so I started to collect old coins. By the time we were moving to the Sunset District, I had a stack of old coins about 8 inches tall and stored in a round toothbrush travel container. I kept it on a pantry shelf in a corner with all of the drinking glasses. Mom had a moving company pack nearly all of our things. When everything was delivered to our new home, we unpacked the boxes, but I could not find my coin collection amongst the glassware. I asked everyone if they saw a toothbrush container that had my coins. No one said they saw it, which got me so upset. I collected those coins for years. The age of the coins were pre-1900 and into the 1930s. I was sure the movers found them and kept them. It was my own fault. I was naïve and forgetful, but it made me more careful with my valuables in the future.

When I moved from the Mission to the Sunset, I assumed the entire City was warm and in sunshine most of the time. The Mission District was shielded by Bernal Heights Hills on the south and Twin Peaks on the west. Both hills were undeveloped and covered with green vegetation with little housing at the time. That was when I learned that Twin Peaks that stood between the Sunset and Mission acted as a barrier that shielded the Mission from the cold sea air and fog that covered the Sunset. The irony was the Mission, the older part of the City with the lower cost housing and less maintained condition, had the best weather compared to the more affluent neighborhoods in the City. I wondered how long it would take people to understand that and start moving into the Mission to demolish, rebuild and renovate the area to bring up property values. (It took over 50 years.) But I could not complain about the Sunset weather. When I was living in the Mission, the sun was out most of the summer and when it got warm, my skin broke out in a heat rash on my arms and body. Small red bumps appeared and they itched. Fortunately, they disappeared when it got cooler by the end of the summer. When I moved to the Sunset, the rash never came back, thank goodness.

Age 12: A New Sandbox for a Better Life

Life Changing Sandbox – Sunset District

The Sunset District had been built mostly on sand dunes, which made it one big new "sandbox" for a better life for me to play and grow up. But the sand dunes were disappearing about this time with the exception of isolated plots of land like the site where St. Ignatius High School was later built after its purchase for $2 million in 1964. [32] Henry Doelger had built about 3,000 homes in the Sunset and Richmond Districts. My first impression of my new digs was seeing rows and rows of stucco houses set shoulder to shoulder with no space between them to breath. Our fear was that we would hear our neighbors 24/7 but that was not the case. On one side was a quiet, older couple, and on the other side an empty lot. Nearly every house in the Sunset had a lawn in front of it, compared to concrete sidewalks that ran in front of most houses in the Mission. Not only were there all these green lawns, half a block from our house was the four-lane Sunset Boulevard called "the Boulevard." It ran 20 blocks from Golden Gate Park on Lincoln Way out to "the Circle" at Lake Merced Boulevard. Along the Boulevard were rows of large trees, mostly cedar, cypress and pine, and solid walls of bushes on both sides of the street. There were dirt-walking paths the length of the Boulevard too. It was like walking in a park with all of the greenery. How much more country could a kid want living in the middle of a major city.

Good and Bad of New Digs

One of the scary parts of moving to a new neighborhood on the other side of the City was that I knew nothing about the Sunset District, which was the largest neighborhood in the City. I was concerned about finding my way around and having to learn new street names. Fortunately, there was nothing to worry about. The City was so logically laid out in 1909, making it easy to find your way around the City and to remember the location of places. In the Mission 1st through 31st Streets ran numerically north to south from downtown through the Mission District, while the Richmond and Sunset Districts had 1st through 49th Avenues (1st, 13th and

49th were changed eventually to Arguello, Funston and La Playa Streets respectively) going numerically east to west and the streets going north to south were pretty much in alphabetical order. Beyond 48th Avenue was the Lower Great Highway and beyond that was the elevated four-lane Upper Great Highway built on sand dunes that served as a wind blocker for the nearby residences. We just called the latter the "Great Highway," which was the only one we ever used to get anywhere. Why would the City want two streets running parallel to each other called Great Highway?

I did not realize how much I would miss the Mission District until there was something to compare to it. It had the playground across the street, all my buddies lived just a block or so away, the fun of exploring the train yard and manufacturing sites, space between buildings, access to people's backyards, a grocery store across the street, Nickel's swimming pool, loads of movie theaters just blocks away, Mission Dolores Park, the Boys Club down the street, the interesting Victorian style of houses, and the weather was sunny and warm. The Sunset District was completely the opposite. In the Sunset, there were plain looking houses shoulder to shoulder – all looking the same and no space between them. Everything was spread out – friends, parks, movie theaters, stores, and the weather was overcast and chilly. But I learned to bundle up to keep warm and these differences were things that only kids missed. What the Sunset District offered were things that were more important to meet the needs of high schoolers for a better future. It had comparable schools but less crime, kids and families that valued education and a college degree, a middle class environment that promoted culture and the better things in life. It was my salvation and a huge opportunity to be a better person in the long run. I always missed the guys I grew up with in the Mission. It was a fun time in my life, but the Sunset was going to be a whole new experience – hopefully for the better.

Although everything was spread out in the Sunset, I could use the City's Muni system, which had the reputation for having one of the best public transportation systems at the time for getting around the City. There were buses and streetcars that went everywhere. They came in a timely fashion as they stuck to their schedules. Most importantly, they came frequently, so there was little wait time – especially important when it was raining. The fares were always reasonable. Muni fares for adults were seven cents (1940-45), 10 cents (1946-52), and 15 cents (1952-58). Starting in the 1930, kids could buy Muni student car tickets with 20 rides for 50 cents. In the 1950s, the car tickets offered 10 rides for 50 cents. The 72-Sunset bus ran along Sunset Boulevard and was a half a block from our house, which got Mom to Stonestown for shopping. The N-Judah streetcar was one block away and went to the Ocean Beach, Playland, and got Mom and Dad downtown to work.

Dad went to work during off-peak hours, but Mom commuted during rush hours to and from work, which she found challenging. San Francisco had many rainy days, and Mom bundled up each morning, walking the block and a half to the streetcar stop at 35th and Judah, and huddled inside the only open doorway at the corner of 35th Avenue and Judah Street that offered 4' x 5' of shelter, assuming three or four others did not get their first. There often were more people waiting there than there was room to stay dry. Mom usually could get a seat going to work, but coming home, she had to stand on the island in the middle of Market Street to wait for her streetcar. At rush hour when she and the tens of thousands of workers were leaving for home, the islands were always overflowing with people standing shoulder to shoulder and belly button to belly button, so some people had to stand off the island on the street with cars and buses driving by. The islands provided no shelter on rainy days, patience got shorter, so people crammed onto the streetcars, even when there was no room for them, just to get out of the traffic, off the island, and out of the rain. Mom nearly never got a seat and had to stand almost the entire way home on the 40 minute ride after being on her feet all day – no way for someone in their 50s and 60s to have to commute. Mom worked at Livingston's for a long 17 years. I know I never fully appreciated the sacrifices she made for all of us – especially for me. I was too young, selfish and stupid, but I did get a chance to give her a comfortable life in one of the best sections of the City while living with us for the later years of her life.

Benefits of Cutting Ties to Past

When I told my friends we were moving to the Sunset District, they all said they would never see me again. I assured them I would come back regularly, but they said I would not. They were right. I always regretted it. I felt I should have kept in touch, but looking back, it probably was for the best. I may have gone to a different high school and not gone on to college due to their influence. Years later I ran into Joey Sandoval and asked about everyone. He was working for the telephone company and the last he heard, Bobbie Gray was selling flowers at one of the stands around Union Square – possibly the one on Powell Street by Union Square. He suspected Robbie Hall went on to become a fisherman like his father. In the five years I knew Bobby Ellington, he never talked about his dad, who was killed in WWII, nor did I ask about it. I just took it for granted. I felt it was none of my business. I knew he was too young to remember his dad, but I thought there might have been stories passed on by his mom.

We moved to the Sunset in the summer of 1953. Our new house was on Kirkham Street between 35th and 36th Avenues. Mom loved the house being on a side street where there was little traffic. It was 1,400 square feet with 2 bedrooms and 1 1/2 bathrooms. The diminutive backyard was about 16 feet deep, 34 feet wide and constantly in the shade of our two-story house. On the west side was a fire access strip of land 16 feet wide that was owned by the City of San Francisco. It ran the length of the block between the backyards of houses aligned from Kirkham to Judah Streets. It was there to provide the S.F. Fire Department access to the rear of the houses on 35th and 36th Avenues in case of fires, which never happened in the nearly 40 years my folks lived there, but this empty lot did allow plenty of sunshine into our kitchen and breakfast nook to keep it warm when the sun was out. I could look down this strip and see sand left over from the undeveloped sand dunes. Eventually, our neighbors and my parents split the cost to put up a fence at the rear of their houses to cut off this ugly view. That left the area between our house and the neighbor's house with a 60-foot strip of empty land that was covered with weeds. The neighbors had no interest in taking care of it, so Mom had a lawn installed and a sprinkler system we controlled from inside our garage. There was also a small strip of lawn in front of our house including one palm tree. As the tree grew, it got to be a pain in the butt to drag out a ladder and pull off the dead spiky leaves, often with Mom teetering on the ladder to remove the hard to reach dead leaves. Good thing I took over the job. I could not see poor Mom continuing to do it on her own. Since my sister and brother no longer lived with us, and Dad had no interest in doing anything around the house other than sleep, eat and watch TV, poor Mom initially had to mow the front and side lawns too. Shortly afterwards, I took over the mowing. The previous owner of our house had intended to finish off the basement by building another room, but it never happened. But he did build in about 45 feet of beautiful knotty pine closets along the entire wall of the garage.

It turned out that our house in the Sunset was on the very edge of "Doelger City," the concentrated area of houses built in the Sunset by Henry Doelger between 27th and 39th Avenues between Kirkham and Ortega Streets, where most houses had two bedrooms and one bathroom with living quarters upstairs from a street-level garage. Our house was a mile from the Pacific Ocean, and when the wind was right, I could smell the salt air. I loved that smell from the first time I got a whiff of it. It was one of the redeeming qualities of the Sunset District, since we seldom saw the sunshine. Some nights before drifting off to sleep, I could hear the foghorns in the distance. At first they were annoying, but I eventually got used to them and thought of them as part of the charm and appeal of San Francisco that helped make it so unique.

Our house had a fireplace, unlike our flat in the Mission District, so Mom could show off how many friends the family had by displaying Christmas cards across the fireplace mantel and hearth just like most others did in the neighborhood. I know the cards added to the festive look at Christmas, but I always thought it was a little pretentious of people who followed the custom as if to say "Look at how many friends we have." Mom never used the fireplace so it was always clean. It was part of her obsession with a clean, tidy, smoke-free house.

Where Those With No Dreams and Interests Wind Up

Dad was a chain smoker and Mom was a nonsmoker all her life. He died of lung cancer at age 69 and she lived to age 89. It was Kathy who pointed out to her there was a smell of cigarette smoke in the house, which Mom got used to all those years in the Mission. So Mom made Dad go down to the Boulevard to smoke because she did not want her home reeking with the disgusting smell. I often saw Dad sitting by himself on the 8-foot-long wood park bench at the bus stop on the northwest corner of Kirkham Street and Sunset Boulevard smoking a cigarette and left with his deepest thoughts about God knows what. Since he was gone for at least an hour, I suspect he was having more than one cigarette. A few times I asked him what he was thinking about when he sat in silence at home or smoking a cigarette on the Boulevard, and each time he replied "Nothing." At first I though he just did not want to talk about it, but with time I began to believe him, especially as he got older. With all the time he spent alone during his treatments for alcoholism, I suspect he got used to just staring into space and at best observing life as it went by. He had no plans in life, no dreams ahead of him, and no outside interests to look forward to. I only hoped that he was at least mentally returning to his earlier life in Ireland, where he was the happiest and could relive the good times and his friends back there.

There was only room in our basement for a washing machine but no dryer, so Mom hung small washes on a line outside the bathroom window that stretched diagonally across the yard to the top of a two-story wood pole. The wind helped dry the wash in spite of the frequent fog, overcast and cold air, but the thicker items had to be hung again in the garage overnight where we had two lines stretched the length of the garage. On those rare warm days, most things got dry outdoors.

Moving meant changes for Mom too. We now lived further from our relatives to visit on the holidays; the best shopping for food and clothing was at Stonestown; and we had a garage to park a car off the street. Mom decided it was time to buy a car. In the Mission, there was no place to keep a car except on the street, and I do not think Mom thought that was safe. Mom went to driving school to learn how to drive at the age of 51. Dad never did learn to drive. More power to Mom for tackling such a daunting challenge at her age and being only 5'0" tall, she had to sit on a 2-inch cushion to see over the dashboard. On top of all that, she got sold a bill of goods buying a 1941 Chevrolet 4-door sedan with a vacuum stick shift, supposedly the latest in automotive technology. The concept was that the vacuum supposed to pull the shift into the desired gear without having to shift all the way into that gear. I never noticed that ever happening when I was old enough to drive. What actually happened was that I had to shift from third gear to first gear before stopping for a red light or at the top of a hill, and San Francisco had lots of steep hills, otherwise I was stuck in third gear on the steep incline, and third gear had very little power to get me over the hill. Also, if I parked perpendicular to a curb and did not get shifted out of third gear into reverse gear, a buddy or I had to get out of the car and manually try to push the car away from the curb so I could get a rolling start to shift into reverse gear before hitting the curb. As a result, Mom never parked perpendicular if she was alone, and she went far out of her way to drive around the hills rather than drive over them. It was hard to believe that vacuum shifts were used for ten years in Chevrolets.

Now that Mom had a car, we could go watch the fireworks on 4th of July at the Marina Greens. We had to leave early to get a parking place that faced the Bay over which the fireworks appeared. If it was really cold out, which was the norm, we stayed in the car and everyone peered out the front window the best we could, especially difficult from the back seat. Weather permitting, Mom stayed in the warmth of the car and the rest of us stood outside leaning against the car. Fog was the norm, rather than the exception, so lots of the fireworks appeared as if looking through frosted glass. Patches of fog took on the color of the bursting rockets. The crowd oohs and aahs came out for the largest and loudest of the explosions. It all lasted about 45 minutes and ended with a thankful applause from the crowd. That was the good part. The bad part was getting home. There were only two routes to take and both were bad. Either go left and work our way along Nan Ness Avenue and over Twin Peaks or turn right and get on the Golden Gate Bridge approach to go out 19th Avenue. Either way, we just inched along most of the way because everyone was leaving at the same time. It was a little better when they moved the fireworks to Candlestick Park, which was not built until right after I graduated from high school. By then the novelty of watching fireworks lost its appeal due to the hassle of getting home afterwards.

In our new house I was still sharing my room with Dad. He still snored and Mom still had to get a good night sleep in order to go to work each morning. As a result, I never felt it was my room and I certainly did not want to deface the freshly painted walls with scotch tape or nails for hanging things on the wall. I was at that age of being attracted to pinups and movie stars. The attraction was seeing pretty girls I would never meet.

So I gathered a bunch of pictures of my favorite movie stars and taped them onto the closet doors that ran the length of our garage downstairs. When Mom saw them, she was not happy. Even my sister said I should take them down. Mom was afraid her friends might see them. I argued that I did not have my own room for hanging things on the wall. Besides, her friends never came down to the garage when they visited. Mom let me keep them up. Eventually, I hardly noticed that they were there any more.

Obsessive Compulsive Behavior: Lemons into Lemonade

In less than a year, I took the pictures down. The novelty of looking at the pictures wore off. Mom and Kathy knew I would eventually outgrow them, but I was glad Mom let me make the decision. Right or wrong, it was my decision and I learned from the wrong ones. I found that seeing the bare pine closet doors was more attractive to look at day after day. It was neater. Later in life I realized that I had a compulsive nature like Mom. It was nothing extreme or interfered with my life, but I needed things to be neat, straight, lined up with each other, or symmetrical. Specks of lint were annoying. I assumed it had something to do with my high math aptitude or enjoyment of learning Geometry or there was something different in my brain or genes. The good news was that it made me a neat person and I was thankful for that as it helped make me a very organized person, which in turn led me to be very productive and efficient in life. Mom was also a neat freak by always keeping the house immaculate with nothing out of place, beds always made, leaves removed from the front lawn, house always vacuumed, and dishes put away. There could be no clutter like newspapers, magazines, clothes, or dirty dishes. It was a house of minimization – only the bare necessities of furniture, almost like no one lived there. My sister once said she always felt embarrassed after getting married to come and visit. It made her feel guilty for the untidiness of her own house.

One rainy day I went down to the garage and saw wet cat prints all over the floor. We did not own a cat, so one must have gotten in when Mom brought in the car. I looked all over, but no cat. I put out some food and milk and saw some was gone the next morning. I hoped it would feel safer and come out of hiding, but no luck. That night I poured flour in different areas of the garage in the hope the cat left a trail. The next morning, there were lots of white cat prints all over but one trail led under the front staircase where there was wood flooring for storage that sat four inches off the ground. That must be the cat's hideout. It had stopped raining the day before, I opened the garage door, got a broom, stuck the handle under the raised floor and with a sweeping motion the cat flew out and shot outside to search for a new adventure and shelter.

Avoiding Boy-Crazy Girls

The Cronins, whom Mom lived with when she first came from Ireland, brought their eight-year-old daughter when they visited one day. Gail was five years younger than me, and was being a pest that day. I went all around the house to get rid of her, but she kept following me. I finally left the group in the living room one last time, ran down the steps to our garage and hid in one of the closets. I waited and could hear Gail coming down the stairs. She must have looked around, but could not find me. Then she started opening each of the closet doors one by one. There were about 12 doors. When she got to mine, she opened the door, looked inside and saw me standing there. She let out a blood-curdling scream and ran up the stairs to her parents. I had slipped on a Halloween horror monster mask and scared the crap out of her. Actually, I felt badly. She was only a kid. When I went upstairs, Gail was softly crying, which made me feel even worse. I told them what happened and why I did it. I doubt it made anyone feel better. Gail never followed me around again. It was too bad because she turned out to be an attractive young girl when she got older.

A new family moved in next door and had a daughter who was probably a couple of years younger than me. She was old enough to have an interest in boys and I was still at an age that I felt uncomfortable around girls. One day she convinced me to sit in the front seat of her father's pickup truck parked in front of their house "to just talk" as she said. We got in the truck and I really got uncomfortable when she said she liked me. I sensed this was leading up to kissing. I thought, *this does not feel right* with her much younger than me, so I made up an excuse that I needed to get home for some reason. As soon as I got in the front door, Mom asked what I was doing in the truck with her. I knew Mom looked out the front living room windows through the curtain and venetian blinds a lot but never dreamed that she was watching where I went and what I did outside. I told her we were just talking. She told me to stay out of their truck and away from the girl. Her instincts were right as usual, and I did avoid the girl, as I had no desire to make friends with a 10-year-old when there were 12-year-olds at school. Knowing Mom, I would not be surprised if she went over to the neighbor's house and had a few words with the girl's parents on the matter. I never did see their daughter again except coming and going with her parents.

Strong Legs to Look Young

There were a number of things I was doing by myself now. In the Mission, I could just walk across the street to the grocery store or the Park, and the movies were just a few blocks away. But in the Sunset, everything was further away. It was then that I started jogging everywhere. I was just too impatient to walk. If I did walk, I always took long strides and walked briskly. It was a good habit because I did that the rest of my life. I learned early on that strong legs made me feel and look strong. When I saw people who looked old regardless of their age, it was because they walked so slowly. Walking briskly made me feel young, healthy and confident.

First New Friends – Future All-Stars and Hall of Famers

Since we moved to the Sunset during the summer it was too early for me to meet new friend from my new school, but a week after moving in, someone rang our doorbell. There was a kid standing there. He was taller and more solid than me, but looked about my age. His name was Dan Fitzgerald. Wouldn't you know it – he was Irish. He said he lived a couple of doors away at the corner of 35th Avenue and Kirkham Street and saw us moving in and wanted to know if I wanted to come out and play some catch. I said, "Sure, but I don't have a glove." He took me to his house and gave me a crappy flat beaten up trappers (first baseman) mitt from his garage, which was plenty good for me. Dan was my first new friend in the neighborhood and the first person I ever played catch with, since my buddies in the Mission had no interest in baseball. Dan was a year younger than me, but seemed much older. He reminded me of Tommy Lynch from the Mission District – a tough, down in the dirt type of guy, and hard as steel. We played catch in front of his house regularly. Dan was a catcher and pitcher who always threw very hard without any effort or even trying. It just came naturally to him. My hand stung from his throwing but I never let on that it hurt.

Dan lived next door to Bob Farber on 35th Avenue. Bob was another catcher whose father was really into baseball. He joined us whenever he saw us outside. Bob was another guy who threw hard without trying – so hard that I had to catch the ball in the web of my glove. I cringed a little whenever he wanted to join us. Little did I know at the time that Dan and Bob would be exceptional ballplayers later in high school, but I could tell right away that they were both special athletes. Dan eventually was a San Francisco AAA (Academic Athletic Association) All-Star pitcher at St. Ignatius High School, who later turned down a professional baseball contract and went on to be a very successful head basketball coach at Gonzaga University with a record of 252-171, and he won the West Coast Conference title in 1994. Bob was my age and was an exceptional baseball catcher and was a San Francisco AAA All-Star outfielder at Washington High School the same year that Dan made the All Stars in 1958. Bob went on to be elected to the San Francisco Prep Hall of Fame.

Free Golf for Early Risers

Golf was another sport I had never played. It was Dan who introduced me to the game. He often played at the Golden Gate Park Golf Course on 47th Avenue off Fulton Street, about a block from the Ocean Beach. He asked me if I wanted to join him. I told him I had never held a club, much less swung one, and had no clubs. He gave me an all-wood driver that he had no use for, and we set off for the nine-hole golf course on the western edge of Golden Gate Park the next morning at 5:30 a.m. before the sun rose so we could play a few free holes. Although the entrance to the Golden Gate Golf Course was at 47th Avenue, we just cut through Golden Gate Park and started to play on the closest hole we came across around 43rd Avenue. We had to finish as soon as possible before the golf course employees showed up, so we could not be choosy which holes we played.

The price was right. The course had just opened the year before and was shaped by the sand dunes on which it was developed. Using the same club for driving and putting was a challenge for me, but it made no difference to me. I never expected to play well. It was just a chance to try something new, have some fun with Dan, and the chance to beat the system by not having to pay for our fun. I only played one or two more times in my youth – seemed like a waste of time to do something that I was not good at. It was a trait I followed the rest of my life. For whatever reason, I was never good at golf or basketball. I kept the all-wood driver for 20 years because it was a classic from the 1930s or 1940s, but sold it in a garage sale eventually.

Mom had transferred me from St. Paul's to Holy Name of Jesus Grammar School at 40th Avenue and Lawton Street to attend the 8th grade. The school principal was Sister Mary Claude and Father Richard Ryan was the first and only pastor of Holy Name since the first Mass was held in 1925 in a rented community hall on Kirkham Street at 45th Avenue. Father Ryan was originally from Bartlemy, about 20 miles from Cork in Ireland. Having someone in charge with an Irish brogue made my folks and me a little more comfortable in our new surroundings as we listened to his sermons each Sunday. I was told years later Irish Monsignor Harold Collins at nearby St. Cecilia's parish had the best line for bringing in the largest collections each Sunday. From the pulpit, he routinely reminded the parishioners he wanted "a silent collection – God did not want to hear the jingling of coins in the collection basket!" Monsignor Collins was also outstanding in uniting the parish by drumming into the parishioners from the pulpit that St. Cecilia Parish was, and will always be, "The Finest, The Greatest, The Best." And he meant it. This was something every grammar school and high school should have done to establish morale and pride among the students.

Attending Mass at Holy Name was different than at St. Charles. There was no chapel in the rear to hangout. I often went with Mom and Dad while I was still in grammar school. They liked sitting up front, and I was more of a sitting in the rear type guy. I paid more attention to the sermon and services at Holy Name, but at St. Charles, I enjoyed watching who was coming and going and if I recognized anyone. Standing in the back of the church allowed me to see who was staying seated in their pew and

Sunset District standards. Uniforms also allowed kids to be judged on their inner personal qualities and not based on external superficial appearances.

Changing Appearance to Be Accepted

Before moving to the Sunset, I was at an age that I turned the collar of my shirt and jacket up because I saw older kids at the Park doing it. The nuns did not allow it at school, as everyone was supposed to look the same, but I did it after school and on weekends. For a while I wore a key chain that hung from my pants belt loop with the other end in my pocket like in the pictures of zoot suit characters from the 1940s. I also spent a lot of time combing my hair in the morning. I had long hair so I could create a big wave in the front. For a period of time I replaced my pompadour hairstyle with a curl so it slightly hung down my forehead. I combed the hair on both sides straight back until each side met in the center of the back of my head, then ran the comb down the back of my head toward my neck to create a D.A. – short for "duck's ass" (also called "ducktail"). None of my friends had a D.A., but maybe that was what made it special and unique to me. All of this clothing and hairstyle were so cool to me, until I moved to the Sunset District where kids did not dress or look that way. I realized I just looked like a punk or hood. My opinions about what was cool quickly changed. What was now cool was to look like normal kids. It certainly made a positive difference in the new company I kept.

Take Charge by Doing Things Myself

The Mission was a neighborhood that did not care much about how kids looked, so I normally wore pretty ratty old clothes unless the family visited relatives or friends. But when I started school in the Sunset, I was more concerned about how I looked. Kids dressed better and I so wanted to fit in. Mom worked during the day, cooked our meals and did the wash, so if I wanted something ironed out of the wash I learned it got done quicker if I did it myself. So Mom gave me some pointers about setting the iron temperature for different materials and how to maneuver the piece of clothing around the ironing board for the best angle to iron different sections of my shirts and pants. Mom also showed me how to operate the washing machine in the garage so I did not have to wait for the weekly clothes washing.

School was just a short five-block walk from home. On rainy days, it was a quick jog whether I had a raincoat or not. There was always a line of cars dropping off and picking up kids on rainy days. I always thought, *what a bunch of wimps*. I always walked to school down Kirkham Street and left on 39th Avenue, instead of along the Boulevard, and right on Lawton because I did not want to get attacked by the birds. Along Sunset Boulevard, black birds dove at me and pecked at my head. I was told they were just trying to protect their chicks in a nest. Ten years later, I saw the Alfred Hitchcock movie *The Birds*, and it brought back those dreaded memories of the Boulevard birds.

First Business Kid at Haight-Ashbury

Before the move, I asked Al Levine if I could get a corner to sell newspapers closer to my new home as I could never commute back and forth to the Mission every day – could never get there in time after school. He gave me the corner of Haight and Ashbury Streets. This was before Haight-Ashbury became so renowned. Haight-Ashbury was a nothing, unremarkable corner with plain architectural buildings. It was a new site for selling papers, and I was to be the first to try making a go of it. I often wondered why they chose this corner since I always felt the newsstand was out in the sticks – too little foot traffic and no place for cars to stop. It turned out not to be a good spot, but it was fun years later looking back at what turned out to be a landmark corner in a legendary neighborhood during the Hippie days. I was glad to get there before that movement started, as I doubt there would have been much demand for newspapers in that market.

A few months later I was moved to the corner of Masonic and Anza Streets which was catty-corner to a large red brick building, the location of St. Elizabeth's Infant Hospital, a home for unwed mothers (now called Mount St. Joseph - St. Elizabeth's Home). I always watched to see what these girls looked like and somehow expecting them to have a certain common look I guess. Were they generally attractive, unattractive, sweet

178

looking, hard looking, young, old? During the few months I worked there, I never saw any young girls ever go in or out of the front door, so I just assumed there was a back door or the comings and goings occurred at night. In any case, I always felt sympathy for them, even though I never saw any of them.

After a few more months, a better corner opened up at Haight Street and Masonic Avenue. There was decent foot traffic, lots of car traffic along Masonic, and a bus stop for cars to get out of the traffic. It was the best of both worlds and I was making $1.50-$1.75 each day. Compared to the Mission, it took longer to and from work as I had to catch a bus both ways, but the money was 40-50 percent better, and the tips were better in the more affluent neighborhood.

There was a war surplus store across the street from my newsstand and a few doors down Haight Street. I was looking for some new cool clothes. I wound up buying a black shirt. I matched it up with a yellow gold silk tie. I also picked up a cowboy shirt that had ivory buttons down the front and two buttons to fasten each sleeve cuff closed. For a 12-year-old, I felt so cool. I think it was a carryover from the gangster and cowboy movies I used to watch. In retrospect, I must have looked like a dope to the middle class kids in the Sunset – at least like a wannabe who was too short and young. There was little call for wearing those clothes in public – bad investments.

Age 13: I Am Those Around Me

Our 8th grade class did not have any famous parents that I was aware of, but there were some local celebrities. Wendy Nelder was the daughter of Alfred Nelder who was a colorful homicide detective and became chief of police and on the police commission of San Francisco. Richard Carberry was the son of Matt Carberry who was a San Francisco supervisor and later became the sheriff of San Francisco. Bonnie Pischoff's father, Darrell, owned Pischoff Sign Company, the largest commercial sign company west of Chicago and was best known for their gigantic and opulent lobby displays of featured movies in theaters around the country.

Lifetime of Humility From a Quotation

Don Sherwood was probably the most popular radio disc jockey in San Francisco during the 1950s and 1960s. He got hired by radio station KSFO in 1953 and later was billed as "The World's Greatest Disc Jockey" during his 6:00-9:00 a.m. weekday program. Don Sherwood signed off his radio programs with "Out of the mud grows the lotus." That quote stuck with me my entire life. I repeated it frequently to remind myself of the humble lifestyle roots I came from and what I wanted to become. It was a reminder in my case that the mud was needed in order to create the lotus. It also was a perfect symbolism for a kid who grew up in the Mission in the dirt and in the Sunset built on sand. I would be perfectly happy to have the quote engraved on my headstone when I go – as fitting a tribute to me as I can think of.

Path to Most New Friendships – Sports

Moving from the Mission to the Sunset was a major social change for me. Coming from a poor section of the City to a more affluent middle class neighborhood, I felt inferior to everyone. I became even shyer and humbler than before the move. I knew no one; kids dressed better, and their parents had better jobs than my parents. Houses were nicer, streets were cleaner, and cars were newer. I had this image of moving in with a bunch of spoiled rich kids, but it did not take long to find out that the kids were just normal guys. They were richer than us, but not excessively so. More importantly, they were just regular guys who accepted me as an equal. How I lucked out to make friends with a lot of the popular guys was that they were involved with athletics at Holy Name and tended to hang out in the schoolyard on weekends, when I was free to hang out too. Fortunately, I also went out for sports, even though I had never played organized sports in the past. I found this also was the path to meeting most of my new friends in high school. Sports were the only activities that allowed kids to spend time together after school to create friendships, unlike high school that offered loads of other activities. Although I made a lot of friends in my 8th grade class, eventually, a handful of us became friends for life when we went to the same high school and stayed involved in the same extracurricular activity – sports.

There was Tim Applebee who lived on 35th Avenue off Noriega Street. His Dad was really active at Holy Name and one of the two coaches of our 8th grade baseball team. Dennis Beyma, who moved to San Diego in the 8th grade due to his father's government job, came back into our lives when he enrolled at Riordan High School in his freshman year. He lived a block from the Beach on Judah Street. Rich Canas lived on 39th Avenue off Lincoln Way. Barry Sullivan lived on 38th Avenue off Noriega Street. Gerry Hipps lived on 34th Avenue off Moraga Street and Terry Carmody lived in a flat on 32nd Avenue off Judah Street. Little did I know at the time that I would be a reflection of the "Holy Name gang," my closest and lifelong friends for which I was eternally grateful – I am those around me.

The kids I grew up with in the Mission referred to each other by first names, whether talking to them or about them. But in grammar school and especially high school, we used the kid's first name when talking to them and their last name when talking about them, because we knew more kids with the same first names like Terry Carmody and Terry Quinlan.

Lesson Learned From Bully Put to Practice

The weirdest encounter I had in making friends was when I met Canas for the first time. It was shortly after the school year started. I was shooting hoops in the schoolyard. Some Latino kid was standing under the basket at the opposite end of the court and told me to throw him the basketball in a threatening manner. I may have seen him around school, but I did not know his name. He was just trying to bully me to give him the ball and possibly trying to start a fight, which never happened. This was a flashback of the encounter I had at Folsom Park when the much shorter, younger kid picked a fight with me. I thought to myself, *what was it about basketball courts and bullies…and why did I bring out the worst in them?* He looked a little shorter than me and not particularly tough. Little did I know at the time that he would one day carry a gun for a living as head of a variety of law enforcement and intelligence operations at all levels of the government. All I knew was that I learned my lesson from three years earlier, when I got suckered by a bully shorter than me. At first I just ignored him, thinking he would go away. When he continued to stand there, I threw him the ball. He bounced it a couple of times and threw it back to me. I invited him to shoot baskets with me, which he did. He turned out to be Richard Canas, a kid who had a similar background as myself. He came from the Mission District, was trying to make friends at a new school, and shy and insecure like me.

Age 13: My New Found "Twin Brother" (continued)

Canas turned out to be one of my two closet friends the rest of my life, partly due to our similar backgrounds. He also wound up overcoming a lot of challenges in order to achieve a lot of successes in his lifetime – none greater than coming from El Salvador and speaking no English. This was his adventurous and difficult life before we ever met as told by Canas himself.

My father, Ricardo Cañas Carranza, was born in March 1913 in San Salvador, the capital of El Salvador. His father, León Cañas Orante was a businessman and his mother, María Luisa Carranza, managed their home. Ricardo, the youngest of three brothers, was three years old when both parents died from unrelated illnesses less than a year apart. Urban aunts, Concepcíon and Catalina Cañas, adopted their three orphaned nephews in 1917. The sisters were spinsters and lived comfortably while managing their substantial inheritance. They were strict, conservative, and pragmatic. They also paid close attention to current events, especially politics, which included maintaining close ties with influential people.

It was in this environment that my father developed his values and direction. His early years shaped his temperament and personality. One joyous adventure often followed another in school. His innovative school pranks and other nonsense soon became a school legend and challenged the patience of the religious brothers all through secondary school.

Other friends and relatives commented that my father had a romantic and soft side that reminded them of his mother who died shortly after her husband of a broken heart, they speculated. Early on, the aunts decided on the professional education and directions their three nephew-wards would take. Rafaél, the meticulous one, to become a teacher; León, the analytical one, an engineer; and my father, the free-spirited adventurer, a dentist.

My father received his doctorate in surgical dentistry in 1936 at the age of 23. He was an imposing figure physically and intellectually as he was over six feet tall, strong, big-boned, and with the bearing of an athlete. (The average height of a Salvadoran male was 5'4".) He was the type of man other men wanted to look and be like. He loved fast cars and horses and was expert in both. He was an avid reader, especially swashbuckling classics of Alexandre Dumas and Rafael Sabatini, and the news of world affairs. While he was confident discussing most subjects, he was neither arrogant nor hurried with his opinions. Even his gait reflected this trait – slow and deliberate.

But it was his inner size that set him apart. His greetings were festive and his smiles and laughs contagious. You were cheered by his presence and drawn into it – you missed him when he left the room. Some said his handsome looks resembled the popular Mexican *charro* (cowboy) singing actor, Jorge Negrete. He was unsure of the comparison, but admitted he did love to sing, especially with friends. He enjoyed being around people and they enjoyed him. It was said the party did not start until he arrived.

At the university, he excelled in long-distance swimming, basketball and marksmanship. He eventually represented El Salvador in these sports at the 1930-31 Pan American Olympics, medaling in both swimming and marksmanship. His swimming style was similar to that of the American Olympic swimmer and actor, Johnny "Tarzan" Weissmuller. He held and expressed strong opinions on various subjects including the often-shunned topic of politics. Being well read, he confidently defended his arguments. His presence and self-confidence alone compelled others to listen and take heart. These traits resulted in him having an abundance of coveted friends.

My mother María Teresa Olivares Contreras was born in September 1915 in San Vicente, El Salvador, a small-town east of San Salvador. She was the youngest of seven children. The family lived in a modest home outside San Vicente where her father, Manuel Olivares, managed the crops for a landowner and her mother saw to the children and tended the home. When Teresa was just six months old, her father tragically drowned, swept away by a flash flood while trying to cross a stream. Her mother Anita Contreras Olivares carried on with the help of the older children. The youngest daughter, Sara, died at the age of 12, and the oldest sibling, Manuel, was born a quadriplegic. In 1927, when Teresa was 12 years old, her mother unexpectedly died of pneumonia.

Because of her youth, Teresa was sent to live with spinster aunts, Juana and Gertrudis Olivares, in the "distant" town of Santa Ana 57 miles away. There, sponsored by a family relation and parish priest, Father Jose Vides, Teresa attended primary and secondary schools at the Colegio María Auxiladora (Mary Help of Christians College) run by the strict Salesian nuns and priests.

Teresa was not rebellious by nature, however, she developed an independent adventurous spirit. Occasionally, she snuck out of school, and in the evenings, climbed out her bedroom window to seek out the rebellious youngsters of the *barrio* (neighborhood). In that setting she learned to smoke, speak in the vernacular, and embrace the same social directness, instincts, and contests of the less privileged. She was a devout Catholic, mainly because of the love and guidance shown her by Father Vides. But by the time she completed secondary school, the contradictory lessons of street-life and church teachings made her devoutly religious but socially independent.

When she turned 18, Teresa had blossomed into a stunning young woman. She was just over five feet tall and exhibited a slim curvaceous figure. Her wards realized that she now needed a different type of tutelage and supervision. They quickly arranged for Teresa to live with an older sister, Juana Olivares de Imeri in San Salvador, who was married to a very successful photographer. With time friends and acquaintances began to compare Teresa's features and looks to the new American movie star, Ava Gardner. An everyday topic of discussion was who would eventually land this prize catch. It was the combination of her boldness and beauty that attracted a young dentist friend. When my mother and father first met, it was preordained that the most eligible bachelor and the most desirable debutant would marry, have beautiful children, and live idyllic lives.

Escape From Death Squads

It was June 1945, and all the wars of the world were ending. Germany and the other European axis powers had surrendered. Japanese aggression in the Pacific was being defeated; their surrender was imminent. But in many Latin America countries, internal struggles against tyrannies, which had raged for decades, continued despite regime changes. In one such country, El Salvador, the oppressive practices of ousted President General Maximiliano Hernandez Martinez, a "closet" admirer of the European fascists, endured – the policies aimed at exterminating every political dissident. My father. Dr. Ricardo Cañas Carranza, one of the main leaders of a group of young professionals opposing Martinez and his brutal regime and a target of death squads, was forced to flee to neighboring Guatemala

185

without his family as extremists extended the violence against key rebel exiles into bordering regions. My father petitioned asylum in the U.S., and his projected destination for his family was San Francisco, CA.

My mother did not discuss politics; in fact, she abhorred the subject. She was also a teetotaler. The year that my father was forced to flee the country, her resilience was tested to its limits. She was terrorized weekly at her home by soldiers searching for Ricardo, the image of which was burned into his mind forever. The soldiers even shot their pet dog while she was holding it and verbally threatened her and the children. As she lost sleep caring for their sickly daughter, as well as losing weight and physical strength, she continued to focus.

Any news from home was the high or low-point of my father's day. For a year he had waited for word that it was safe for his family to join him. Finally, the news arrived from the travel agent, and it was positive. So when the opportunity came for my mother to escape the country to the U.S. with the children, she did not hesitate despite doctor warnings that my frail sister, Ana María, might not survive the journey. Hidden in a vegetable truck with her sedated children, she crossed the border into Guatemala and joined my father. Meanwhile, rumors, the frustration of the desperate, continued to circulate about increased round-ups. The Cañas's flurry of activity was accompanied by the anxiety of last-minute surprises. The unknown was usually confusing and terrifying. Throughout the 30-minute ride to La Aurora International Airport, my father's eyes scanned parked cars and other vehicles along the road. He knew from experience that Martinez' spies were everywhere, but they were also lazy about reconnaissance and surveillance work.

My father calculated that it would take them and my mother's older brother Tomas Olivares approximately two days to reach Nuevo Laredo, Mexico, across the river from Laredo, TX. Despite his planning for the Mexico journey, he was unsure of what to expect at the northern border, and beyond that, more unknowns. None of us spoke English and the Americans had a reputation of arrogance when it came to dealing with Latinos. Our Spanish/English dictionary had to do.

A few miles north of Mexico City, the bus made an unscheduled stop. The emotion of the passengers ran from anger to apprehension. Two uniformed police officers boarded the bus and announced they would be inspecting papers. Mumbles by the passengers signaled that the police were probably looking to elicit bribes for any anomalies they discovered. As the officers approached us, my father gathered our passports and my mother unexpectedly jumped up. *"Ah, gracias a Díos, oficiales"* (Oh, thank God, officers), she exclaimed loudly, catching both of the officer's attention. "The baby is sick and has soiled herself. I need to change her. May I go outside to find some water? My husband has our papers." It was a diversion to prevent the officers from finding the gun my father hid in their handbag, which she took with her when the officers said, *"Esta bien, señora, pase usted* (Very well, Misses, you may pass). There is water just outside the guardhouse. Ask the officer there."

Immigrants Viewed as Second-Class Citizens

In a day and half, after making dozens of stops in each state, we finally reached San Diego, CA. That same day, we transferred to a new Silverside Greyhound bus that serviced the route from Southern California to San Francisco. We had finally arrived but remembered the advice of my father's good friend Dr. Jose "Chepe" Molina who often warned those who sought refuge in another country, "An immigrant always travels with guilt as a back-seat passenger. Also, immigrants will always be viewed as second-class citizens away from their native home, so they must focus on their children and live vicariously through them." *And Chepe being a psychiatrist knew about those things*, my father thought. And his words proved true over the next 15 years and that made the City and its island-like setting easier to accept.

As soon as we arrived, we immediately took a taxi from the bus terminal at 1st and Mission Streets to Missouri Street off 23rd Street in the Potrero Hill District. It was the home of my mother's sister Concha and her husband, Silverer Von Kroll, a journeyman plumber. The Von Kroll home was sandwiched between rows of other similarly constructed residences in the hilly neighborhood. Although fatigued, Ricardo ventured a look up and down the rows of old wooden framed and simply trimmed two-story homes. *It is an old architecture; not very impressive*, he thought, but as glanced down the steep Missouri Street, he was struck by the view of San

Francisco Bay and an island in the middle of it with a dominating large concrete building with tiny windows at its center.

After a few days, my father and Tomas found employment, painting warships at the Hunters Point Shipyard. But with WWII winding down, they were laid off a few months later. Tomas then found work washing dishes at a nearby restaurant while my father toiled on an assembly line at the American Can Company facility, which had opened on 22nd and 3rd Streets near Potrero Point. With the help of a saintly doctor, Andrew Ryan, who made house calls and charged little for his services, my sister regained her strength.

During these months, Concha introduced my mother to other Latino wives and mothers who lived in the neighborhood, and through word of mouth, my mother heard of an apartment for rent on Bryant and 26th Streets at $45 a month. Having lived four months with the Von Krolls, my parents jumped at the move, although the rent and utilities strained their budget. The Von Krolls, also anxious to have us move on, lent them the money to cover the rent for a few months and to buy some used furniture.

I was born Ricardo León Cañas Olivares in San Salvador, El Salvador, on January 24, 1941. I was four years old and my sister was one when we arrived in the City. The only references I had of our life in El Salvador were my parent's stories and the hundreds of black and white family photographs pasted into two tattered photo albums that they prized and safeguarded over the years.

My first recollection of a home environment, circa 1946, was a one-bedroom apartment on Bryant Street between Army and 26th Streets. The three-story building had a two-car (end-to-end) garage on the first floor and four apartments on the two floors above. Two apartments faced the street and the other two faced an enclosed concrete open area that was shared with three adjacent apartment buildings. Our apartment was on the second floor facing the rear yard.

My sister and I shared sleeping space on a couch that made into two beds in the living room, which was connected to the bedroom by French doors. Together, the rooms served as living space, where in the evenings the family and visitors listened to Latin music on 78 rpm records or played their favorite card games, Casino, Poker, or Canasta. My mother was an enthusiastic card-game participant. The kitchen area could hold only small appliances and a chrome legged redtop Formica table with four chrome-framed chairs with matching red vinyl seats – very 50s.

Neither of my parents were avid cooks, but we did not miss any meals. Beans were a daily staple and meats were the cheapest my mother could buy at the meat market two blocks away. My mother hand-washed our clothes and hung them on lines strung from the bedroom window to a pole on the other end of the yard. Clothespins were one of my first toys.

Living Among Other Salvadoran Immigrants

The Mission District became our world. My parents quickly identified, mainly through word-of-mouth, other Salvadoran immigrants who lived in the Mission and they became life-long friends. They also kept in touch with Salvadoran distant relatives who had migrated to the City years before. Weekly parties at alternating homes became a tradition within their inner circle. We also now had a telephone that required an operator to make the call and included a shared party line with another subscriber. The latter created a constant battle, since my mother talked with friends for hours and occasionally had to be called off with a barrage of name-calling by the angry co-subscriber. There were also angry skirmishes with the neighbors upstairs, the Hayes, who banged on their floors during our more raucous parties. The entire ceiling of our kitchen was dotted with retaliatory indentations from the end of my mother's broom handle.

But any clashes with neighbors and on telephone party lines were laughable compared to the relatively comfortable and safe existence these gatherings generated. They became my parent's lifeline to a world that held their contented memories and blocked the suffering of the last few years. They joyously celebrated with the toast of every expatriate: "Next year in [wherever they were from]."

A few of the younger Salvadoran relatives and friends were married to North Americans and these spouses, mainly men, viewed the social interactions as Latino affairs. The husbands of my mother's sisters, for example, were not part of my parent's inner circle, partly because one spouse was a haughty medical doctor and the other a busy tradesman, both with their own subdued circle of friends. Also the age difference between my mother and her older sisters was more than 10 years. The Americans who partook were readily accepted and the love was mutual.

Key to Drinking – Knowing When to Stop

During these times, my father was at his best. He thoroughly enjoyed himself talking, singing, dancing, and all the time with a drink in his hand; his favorite was scotch but he did not discriminate. He did not drink to excess and often chided others who did so. He was not a prude, but "Knowing when to stop," he said, "was the key to knowing how to drink." My mother, on the other hand, privately abhorred drinking, as did most of the other wives. Long ago they were privy to the nonsense and sometime abusive behavior of drunken men. Still, they celebrated the gatherings with equal vigor, singing, dancing, and conversing. They accepted a highball here and there but the ice melted long before they accepted another. Discussing politics was discouraged. If an occasional alcohol-induced debate developed, it was not to any major disagreement.

But when politics did surface, my father went on the alert. So far, he had not heard of any strong opinions that might signal a possible political danger to him or his family. *Anyone who claimed to have any inside information was either exaggerating or misinformed,* he thought, *much like Salvadoran cab drivers.* Occasionally, an unknown person attended their parties having heard about them through a Latin grapevine. My father always did his due diligence with visitors by engaging them (he only worried about males) in a conversation over drinks. But these casual exchanges never produced any troublesome information, only indirect references to possible activists and where they might congregate.

One place he heard about was a Latin dance hall downtown called the El Patio Ballroom above the Les Vogel Chevrolet dealership at Van Ness Avenue and Market Street. As much as he liked music, dancing, and the camaraderie of Latin get-togethers, he avoided ever taking my mother to the El Patio and encouraged his friends to do the same. The place had a bad reputation for hosting Mexican pachucos and young dissidents from other Latin countries. In such an environment, the odds were against him that he could avoid calling attention to himself. Years of avoiding danger had made him circumspect.

One evening Tomas, who more than enjoyed his bouts with liquor, came to our apartment drunk and bloodied about the face and hands. He explained that he was living with a Colombian woman he had met at the El Patio and they had gone there that night. Some innocuous comment about his national origin and someone else's girlfriend had turned into a fistfight. During the telling of the tale, my sister and I were wide-eyed and worried; it was our first introduction to real-life violence. My mother calmed us with stories of how brave Tomas was defending some girl and how everyone was happy now. We needed happy closure or our questions were never-ending.

Holidays and special occasions were especially celebratory and the festivities were not complete without a distinct Salvadoran nourishment. While the women cooked, the men's chore was to keep the children away from the kitchen. If the number of invited guests was large, tamales were the favorite choice. But preparing tamales demanded organization. First, the number of tamales to produce had to be determined – usually 75-100 salt and 50-75 sugar tamales were the targets. Then, the fixings, *masa* (cornmeal dough), paper wraps, lard, chicken, and other condiments, had to be purchased by a team, and each were dispatched to carry out their specific purchase. Then, the two-day assembly was scheduled.

On the appointed day, the *masa* mixed with tons of lard was cooked in huge vats. Once cooked, the assembly line formed around a table. One-by-one a measured quantity of the cooked cornmeal dough was passed from one worker to the other for stuffing with different ingredients, and finally handed to the wrapping and binding crew for placement into more vats for the final steamed cooking. The daylong process was a festive occasion with raucous songs, jokes, and gossip.

To keep the children occupied, the men usually took them on short excursions around the City. A favorite car trip was visiting the warships that were anchored along the Embarcadero piers near Fisherman's Wharf. The battleships were the most dramatic and always a favorite. On special days, a limited number of the public was allowed onboard. At other times, the men took the children to the Zoo or the Aquarium in Golden Gate Park. Late afternoon, they took their children on the streetcar to Market Street to see the bright lights adorning department stores and the large movie theaters. By the day's end, all the children were soundly sleeping in their father's arms on the ride back.

The end game, of course, was the party that was usually scheduled for the following evening. The hand prepared food and drinks were always the centerpiece and would be the envy of any chef at a gourmet restaurant. Food, dancing, liquor, and chatter dominated the fiesta. The children were in a room nearby and, as evening came, were put to sleep together. During the following week, left over tamales, hangovers, and related gossip about who flirted or danced too long and too close with whom, were discussed with great pleasure.

Pawn Shop Visits During the Hungry Years

For the first few years, other than the occasional get-togethers, life for the Cañases was a relatively quiet affair while my father worked and my mother took care of the children. They did not have a car so they relied on public transportation. Fortunately, the Bryant streetcars [33] ran directly in front of our apartment. They were convenient for work commutes, and occasionally, even served as a cheap attraction for my sister and me. The Bryant Street line ran the length of Bryant from Army Street, where the cars reversed directions, all the way to the Embarcadero past the City's downtown area. The line provided direct transportation from the Mission to shopping on Market Street. But there were other times when my mother took my sister and me on that streetcar to 5th and Bryant Streets and then walked the 10 mostly short blocks to 5th and Mission Streets during the "hungry years." There, she occasionally needed to hock her wedding rings at a loan/pawn shop across from the *San Francisco Chronicle* newspaper building to pay for monthly outlays.

A couple of years later, the Muni began removing the streetcars made in 1917 and replacing them with electric buses on some lines and newer electric streetcars on others. Bryant Street was to receive electric buses so the rails were being removed from the street and the overhead wires were reconfigured. The job caused a muddle for months along the street, which in turn and to the delight of the neighborhood kids, turned the area into a humongous play area for rock fights and mudslinging after the workers left for the day.

My mother's daily activity included taking my sister and me for walks during the day. Both sides of 24th Street, between Potrero and Mission Streets, were full of shops and restaurants, and some, but not many, of them were Hispanic stores. The best place to buy handmade tortillas and other Latin American staples and delicacies was on 24th Street. Since it was two blocks away from the apartment, my mother almost daily walked us there for exercise and some relief from her need to speak English.

Accepting Unjust Social Inferiority Without Protest

My mother was self-conscious about being seen as a poor Latino immigrant. She fought the feeling by stubbornly criticizing the Americans for their informal and often abrasive manners. She rationalized that our family's plight was temporary. After all, her husband was a prominent dental surgeon, educated and respected, and it was just a question of time before they returned to El Salvador to a life that was familiar and where she could contribute more, perhaps even take a respectable job or study at the university. More than anything she loathed not being able to fight back these feelings of social inferiority, which was her nature. So, she decided to rebel in the only way she could, like her compatriots had done to force Martinez from power: *con los brazos caidos* (accept without protest). She did nothing. She did not try to learn English or have American friends, and she did not learn to drive or even write a bank check. She would wait. She knew that it was going to be an imposition, especially since I was about to start grammar school and her involvement with my education was necessary. It was a daily pretend game using smiles and gestures to communicate and hide her true feelings. But she knew that she was a survivor and she would persevere.

Pride in Being Different

Meanwhile, my father was oblivious to any change in my mother because there was none. Her attitude of resignation was not obvious; she merely chose to not be proactive; her duties and demeanor remained unaffected. He knew that she was not intellectual when he married her. He, in turn, was studious by nature; things interested him. Language, customs, new friends, trends were all on his radar. He knew Americans saw him as being different, but then, that was not a negative – he was different. He was also confident in himself and had the ability to assimilate and not repeat mistakes. He took to reading newspapers and books in English. He also felt that it was only a matter of time before they could eventually return to El Salvador and he kept reassuring my mother of this fact. His optimistic nature did not allow him to waste an opportunity to learn from this extraordinary experience. His intelligence and ability to charm served him well in advancing in his job at American Can Company; he was already teaching the assembly line to other laborers. He volunteered for overtime to help repay his brother-in-law Tomas. Other than food and rent, we did not have any other expenses. His assuredness allowed him to enjoy his family and show them all the love he could render.

At the age of five, I was very attached to my parents but still confused about their reaction to going from one "world" to another. A five-year-old child could sense through moods, words, or just osmosis when a loving parent was unhappy. Clearly, we were not on a fun vacation.

Learning English From Scratch

I was just getting settled into the newfangled routine of playing, eating, and sleeping at our apartment, when I learned that I had to start school right away and learn English. I asked my parents, "What is school?" "Fun with children your own age," they answered. But I had to learn to speak their language – more confusion and apprehension.

Because I was five and born in the month of January, I was too young to qualify for the 1st grade at St. Anthony Elementary School at Army and Folsom Streets, and too old for kindergarten at Le Conte, the public elementary school at Army and Harrison Streets. Since St. Anthony did not have kindergarten, and Le Conte considered me too old for their kindergarten, the latter accepted me into their 1st grade. A year later, when I transferred to St. Anthony, the nuns did not find it necessary for me to repeat the 1st grade and placed me in the 2nd grade. Thus, I was destined to be the youngest of my classmates, which went a long way to explain my immaturity to this day.

My first day at Le Conte was predictably traumatic even though my father accompanied me and spent hours consoling and assuring me he would be there to pick me up in the afternoon. I spoke only Spanish and felt self-conscious among the mostly Irish and Italian students. Until that time, my frame of reference for practically everything was Hispanic; the rest of the world was, well, foreign. In the 1940s, the Mission was not yet the Latino experience it is today.

I do not recall being laughed at or called names; not that I was able to understand what the other students were saying anyway. Although finger-pointing and dirty looks were a universal language, they were not directed at me. Those first school days involved playing games during recess like red rover and tag. When I learned a little English, I appreciated one of my schoolmates David Kurtz, a chubby funny kid who told me jokes while walking in formation in silence up stairways to our classroom. One of his jokes was a witticism that mimicked an ominous voice behind me saying he was my conscience warning me about my bad behavior.

Play Had No Language Barriers

My pretend play also began to get more complex at that age. Specific fantasies about heroes started when I was more comfortable with English, and they were in full bloom by the time I was six years old. They involved characters and scenarios on the radio and in comic books. They also manifested themselves in the games I played in the backyard with my neighbor friend, Pat O'Brien, whose family lived in an upscale apartment building next door. Pat and I met almost daily after school either in the backyard or at Castelli's grocery store, which was on the corner of 26th and Bryant Streets. Pat's uncle, Tony Castelli, who ran the store was a friendly young man, gave our family credit for groceries and even turned a blind eye when they sent me to pick up cigarettes for them. After school Pat and I spent hours immersed in whims, assuming the various roles of spaceship commanders, cowboys, or soldiers. My fledgling English was no impediment; kids had their own language when playing.

Choosing White Over Latino Heroes

In those days, heroes displayed their bravery and superhuman powers not only on the radio and in comic books but also in Saturday matinee serials, which I occasionally attended at the Roosevelt Theater at 24th and York Streets. My favorite serials with real actors, not cartoons, were the *Adventures of Red Ryder and Little Beaver*, *Batman*, and *Superman*. As hard as I tried to enthusiastically recount these episodes to my attentive parents, I am sure they just patronized me because they did not go with me to the theater or even understand the premise. But one Christmas, Santa Claus brought me the best gift ever, a Daisy Red Ryder BB gun. No question now who was the best cowboy in our backyard "ranch." My mother was not thrilled, but it had my father's full endorsement.

Christmas was a big deal every year, not only because of the great toys Santa brought but because the nuns and my parents emphasized the spiritual significance: "Baby Jesus was really responsible for gift giving." The irony that most of what "the prince of peace" brought us were cap guns to shoot the Indians and military toy rifles, pistols, and grenades to kill "Japs" and "Krauts" was lost on most parents, let alone me.

Back then heroes shared the same characteristics. They were male, strong, fast, independent, tall, grounded, admired, righteous, and, more poignant to a Latino immigrant boy, all white. At the Hispanic movie theaters, there were serials with Latino superheroes donning capes and masks, but my parents did not relate to those serials and neither did I. Young boys imitated their real-life hero who was usually his father, and the tastes of his peers, and I was no different.

Impact of Radio Hidden Persuaders

During the pre-television years, when I was seven and eight years old, most evenings I was pinned to the radio listening to half-hour programs such as *Lone Ranger*, *The Cisco Kid*, *The Green Hornet*, *The Fat Man*, *The Shadow*, *Inner Sanctum Mystery*, and *Space Patrol*. Each passing day I understood more and more of the plots and the English. Unbeknownst to me, these radio fantasies were designed for kids where the practice of aiming the "hidden persuaders" of advertising towards kids had its origin.

I begged my parents to buy (the more expensive) Kilpatrick's bread, Ovaltine, Kellogg's Rice Krispies, and Colgate toothpaste just because they were the advertisers of my favorite shows.

At the time, nothing dominated and promoted my fantasies more than those radio programs. Music, clothes, politics, current events, and trends did not resonate with me consciously. But, like the hidden persuaders, nothing was lost in the subconscious of a child. Any thoughts I had about mature topics mimicked my parent's sentiments, tastes, and prejudices, all in Spanish no less, and with Latino prominence. The songs they sang and the music they played at parties and at home were Latin ballads and refrains. If they were going to dance, it was to Latin beats. My sister and I even learned a tango dance complete with dips and turns; like trained monkeys, we frequently performed on request at get-togethers. For years the embarrassment it caused followed us around like an unnoticed piece of toilet paper stuck to our shoes. The hey-days of Sinatra, Dorsey, Miller, Goodman, and other popular American music-makers blew right by us like a subtle breeze. Regarding politics, I recall my parents claiming to be Democrats, although what that meant or how it affected us directly or indirectly was unclear to me, and probably unclear to them. My parents often said a Mexican taxi driver knew more about U.S. politics than they did. I did not know how they knew that.

We were part of a small and growing Latino minority in the City, but I was not aware of its significance at the time. Expressions of cultural insensitivity were not common around us. My parents did not utter derogatory remarks about other minorities directly in my presence. But there were Spanish words I overheard that stood for gays of both genders and other minority groups. I also heard pseudonyms to use when in public. For example, the Spanish word *negro*, denoted the color black and not a race of people, but because the word was similar in English, I was warned to not use it when referring to African-Americans, and instead use the word *conejo* (rabbit). On this subject, my parents were more discreet about political correctness, certainly more than what I overheard from the mouth of white adults and students. I knew the insulting significance of the English words "micks," "spics," "niggers," "kikes," "wops," "chinks," "dikes," and "fags" even at a young age. At the same time, I did not learn any slang or comparable words in Spanish. Even the word *conejo* was not used disparagingly but rather as a disguise. It was much later I realized that it was a distinction without a difference.

While on the subject of lexicons, it bears noting that my mother was very fond of using the vernacular and telling bathroom jokes – not to my sister and me, but to close friends in our presence. "Part of her charm," friends commented. It was said Salvadorans in general were renowned for their use of gutter-speak, and that was true in the case of our mother. While we were not allowed to use that type of language ourselves, we hardly celebrated her jokes and uncouth references along with my father and their inner circle of friends. At the same time, and more poignant to our schizophrenic rearing was her frequent invectives that were directed at the American life-style and North Americans in general. During those times, my bicultural sister and I were put in awkward situations, but we were wise enough not to challenge her during one of her outbursts. We did not understand her biases. It was much later that we traced her motive to having been forced away from her cultural comfort zone. As ungrateful as it sounded, given our refugee status, her biased expressions were more venting than expressions of her true feelings, and were directed mainly at those she felt were prejudiced against Latinos. In most cases she was expelling anger, and as I later learned only begets more anger. Regrettably, this disorder followed her for the rest of her life.

Bilingual But Unable to Share My Americanization

After a year in school, I was functionally bilingual; I could now speak, read, and write Spanish and English, and that meant I understood English and American practices better than my parents. [Vocabulary growth was proven to be rampant at this age according to pediatricians.] But this skill was double-edged. While I gleaned an appreciation for both cultures, clearly a plus in the well-rounded person, I could only share the Latino end of that fortune with my heroic parents; likewise, I could only share my Americanization with schoolmates and a few American friends. My parents, especially my mother, had no interest in American life-styles, so they could not share or give advice on *my* American interests, such as tastes, fantasies and heroes. Without this counsel, a bicultural child could

198

grow up confused and feel he or she was without a country, or perhaps worse, chose one side exclusively.

Better Living Conditions Traded for Freedom

During the first years of their marriage in El Salvador, my parents had been respected and popular members of the Salvadoran community and economically stable. Their future was nothing if not bright. And while my boyhood ruminations did not question why they left Salvador in the first place, the subject was often alluded to during their adult conversations, and overheard, if not understood, by me. I do not recall hearing details or discussions about my father being engaged in such things as seditious idealistic pursuits, being a fugitive, or anything related. The reason(s) for our immigration in the first place merely hung over our daily lives like a murky cloud.

It also seemed to me at the time that their Latin friends and family members living in the City had individual "clouds" about their reasons for being in the U.S. Comparing life in the two countries was a frequent topic of discussion, much like the weather, and how in their "beloved" native country, the food, ambience, and living conditions were so much better than their current living conditions in the U.S. It was only much later that I learned that many of these immigrants had fled those "better living conditions" because of political reasons or unemployment. Any banter about likening was disingenuous. During the late 1940s and early 1950s in the City, we may not have been at a poverty level but we were certainly in a lower socioeconomic stratum, which was also true for the friends and families we knew.

Overcoming Unjust Denial of Prosperity

One impediment to improving our financial and social situation was that my father could not practice his profession because the American Dental Association (ADA) did not provide for non-U.S. college-educated applicants a path to licensure. [This was an unjustified rule that was found prejudicial and unconstitutional in the late 1960s as no such obstruction hindered medical doctors.] In the 1940s and 1950s, this bias relegated my

199

father to seek work as a common laborer for the first three years of our time in the City. As a result, we ate sparingly, cooked the cheaper meats, such as tripe, brain, tongue, rabbit (all considered delicacies today), and shared Salvadoran native meals with other Latin friends. To their credit, one by one, these immigrant families began to pull themselves out of their dire circumstances, all the time vowing their offspring would never know such hunger. My father's breakthrough finally came in 1947 through pure serendipity. Providence's name was Edgar R. R. Parker.

Edgar R. R. Parker, an American dentist, was famously known by his *nom de guerre* (false name), "Painless Parker." [34] By the 1940s, Parker, in his late 60s, established more than 70 dental offices nationwide, most of them on the West Coast, and his wealth was in the millions. While he was remembered for his showmanship style, his endurance was attributed more to his innovativeness. In 1947, while searching for qualified dentists to service his increasing number of offices, he heard about the plight of immigrant dentists prejudiced by the ADA. Ever the opportunist, he devised a plan that benefited the immigrant dentists while denigrating the ADA's bias – he employed as dental technicians experienced immigrant dentists, which did not require ADA licensure. Parker paid the technicians a higher wage and assigned them to back up his increased dental workload. Parker knew that without meticulous oversight, the ADA could not police technicians performing minor dental work. He knew that the immigrant dentists would jump at the opportunity to practice their profession. My father heard of this opportunity and wrote Parker a letter with the help of a family friend. He heard back almost immediately. Parker agreed to meet with him in the City. Parker decided to interview my father while sailing on his yacht in the Bay, and he invited our entire family to accompany them. Parker immediately appreciated my father's background, especially his odyssey so far and the lengths he had gone to protect his family. He offered him a job at his Seattle, WA office that same day.

My ecstatic father leaped at the opportunity. So for the next year, he commuted monthly to Seattle where he learned the dental-chain business and polished up his English. He laughingly told the story that for months he survived on cheese sandwiches and coffee, which were all his limited English let him order off a menu. After his year of internship, Parker offered my father the job of managing the Stockton, CA office, which he immediately accepted.

I was 10 years old at the time, and my family was poised to move to Stockton. My father worked at Parker's office there and came home on weekends. We made a house-hunting trip in our 4-door dark grey 1937 Chevrolet, which my father had bought with his new salary. In those days, the trip was not pleasant; it took hours to drive through the hot San Joaquin Valley to Stockton on a two-lane road. The heat, the road, and unrefrigerated bean sandwiches had Ana and me carsick most of the time.

For a time, my parents seriously considered a permanent move there, but in the end decided to stay in the City. I never learned why. I surmised that it was at the insistence of my mother, who relied heavily on friends and relatives in the City who helped her cope during my father's absences. We knew no one in Stockton.

We continued living at the Bryant Street apartment and in time my father transferred to Parker's Market Street office, now with an above average salary. This enabled my parents to add new amenities to improve our lifestyle. One was trading in their pre-war 4-door Chevrolet for a 1948 Chrysler Windsor sedan with its distinctive harmonica grille, automatic transmission, and comfortable seating and ride. There was new furniture for the apartment and fixing up a storage room as a bedroom for me. But biggest of all was no longer needing my mother to make further gloomy trips to the 5th and Mission Streets pawn shop.

My sister and I were caught up in the high-spirited mood of our parents, but best of all, my father was emboldened by practicing his profession and not having to travel. He bought me a new bike and my sister comparable gifts. Outings with friends and families were now more elaborate – Pine Crest in the winter, Clear Lake in the summer, and trips around the City every weekend. My father recounted over the dinner table fascinating stories from the life of Parker, who he would affectionately called "*el viejito*" (the old man). Even the actor Bob Hope was filming a 1948 comedy called *The Paleface* based on Painless Parker's life. The number one hit song was "Mañana (Is Soon Enough for Me)" by Peggy Lee that served as a poignant reminder of this latest twist in our journey.

Meanwhile, I was interacting more confidently with students and teachers. I joined the Cub Scouts (Pack 132) and received the Blue and

Gold, a monthly award for student achievement. At home, relations with my parents were loving. They took us everywhere with them – to evening parties, picnics, and late-night Spanish or English movies. We were never left with babysitters, probably because they could not understand or afford the concept. Plus, they were still in protectionist mode from El Salvador days. I suspect the latter was more likely because when I was an adult, my father gifted me a Super .38 Colt automatic that he said he had kept from the old days and asked me to not mention it to my mother. He never explained why he kept it all those years and why it was meticulously maintained with two full clips of ammunition. Any discussions about the times before moving to the City were still avoided topics of conversation.

Personal Outlook Influenced by Action, Romance and Humor

When my father was working in Seattle and Stockton for Painless Parker, my mother, no doubt bored with the care of two active school children and looking for distractions, took us to see American films at the Roosevelt Theater, especially historic action films that she could follow despite not speaking English. Thursday nights were special because the "Roosie" handed out dinner plates and other incentives to patrons; my mother was collecting a set. My parents favored certain American actors and they were permanently embossed in my memory and sentimentality. Most prominent were John Wayne, Jimmy Stewart, Humphrey Bogart, Errol Flynn, Ingrid Bergman, and Gene Kelly. There could be no greater tribute to some of these stars with kids everywhere mimicking John Wayne's "Pilgrim" salutation, Jimmy Stewart's stutter and displaying your upper teeth when imitating Humphrey Bogart. We must have seen the movies *Sands of Iwo Jima*, *The Three Musketeers*, *Captain Blood*, and *Casablanca* dozens of times at the Roosie. Likewise, memorable Latino actors like Pedro Infante, Jorge Negrete, Libertad Lamarque, Arturo de Cordova, Pedro Armendariz, Maria Felix, and my mother's favorite, Mario "Cantinflas" Moreno also stemmed from that era, which today is referred to as the "Golden Age of Mexican Films." We saw these edgy movies, all in Spanish, at the Sutter Theater on Sutter Street in the Laguna Heights District, and at the historic Victoria Theatre on 16th Street. Those movies and many others in both English and Spanish greatly influenced my

202

personal outlook of that period. Even today, I do not pass up any chance I get to nostalgically see them. The standard we used to classify a movie as "good" was that it had to have action, romance, and humor.

Having a foot in each of these two separate, distinctive international movie genres no doubt cemented my bicultural and bilingual values and appreciation, which I took into the next phase of my life, preadolescence. They were testament that parental tastes and discriminations can have lasting effects on developing minds.

When my father was not traveling, life at home was exciting. Having a new car gave our family added choices of trips. We were able to travel to beaches up and down the coast and to a place we regularly visited for the next 15 years, the Russian River area or, as City-folk referred to it, "The River." The picnic and swimming area of choice at the River was Raines Resort on the west side of Guerneville. So, the "bestest" day ever for my sister and me consisted of picnicking/swimming at the beach along the River, eating at a restaurant on the way home, then taking in a double feature with a Tom and Jerry cartoon at the Geneva Drive-In adjacent to the Cow Palace on Alemany Boulevard in Daly City or the El Rancho Drive-In on Hickey Boulevard off El Camino Real in Colma – all shouts of joy.

This family lifestyle during the post-war period became routine for the next five years. As children we were oblivious to the limitations imposed by the war. We collected bits of aluminum foil from discarded packaging, even gum wrappers, to bring to school as a contribution to the post-war effort, but that was about the extent of our contribution and understanding of the program. My parents still visited distribution sites to get gasoline rationing stickers and rationing books of stamps for food and other consumables. The practice continued through my grammar school years until the early 1950s.

Evil of Pigeonholing at an Early Age

In the meantime, I was comfortably adapting to grammar school at St. Anthony. I enjoyed the teachers, who were all Dominican nuns, especially Sister Mary Peter who I had for my 5th and 6th grades. One day, she said, "Ricardo, you are an above average student; a solid B student. Continue to work hard." I stayed in contact with her for the next 10 years, and even though I knew she meant well, in retrospect, her limiting words were a self-fulfilling prophesy, *Ricardo, the solid B student.*

Athletics were not stressed at St. Anthony or perhaps my lack of sports prowess gave them little importance. I was an enthusiastic member of the Altar Boys Society and the Traffic Boys, both of which were managed by the Franciscan brothers. Annual picnics exclusively for both activities were particularly enjoyable. The annual Traffic Boys Review and Parade at Kezar and sponsored by the S.F. Police Department was a highlight and a moment of pride when our squad, marching in formation, entered the stadium and took its place among seemingly hundreds of other squads. My proud parents (and my father's camera) were annual attendees.

Socializing with other students at St. Anthony was egalitarian. There was no obvious social discord among students or their families because of race or nationality, at least from my vantage point. Perhaps it was because there were so few of us minorities. No one felt threatened enough to single us out. Non-Catholics, however, were another story. In fact, I do not recall ever meeting a non-Catholic until I was a young adult. The good brothers and sisters made a point of scaring the crap out of us if we even befriended a non-Catholic or even thought about attending a non-Catholic service (a venial sin if I attended, a mortal sin if I participated). Ouch!

Discipline Using "Sin" Label and 12-Inch Ruler

St. Anthony students came from the immediate neighborhood, which consisted of blue-collar working families; most were of Irish and Italian descents. I do not recall any bullying or name-calling, but then, such behavior was a sin and the good sisters efficiently controlled our behavior with platitudes, early warnings, or the sharp snap of a ruler to the knuckles. The fact that unkind conduct was un-Jesus-like carried little weight compared to the description of hell, eternity, and stinging knuckles.

Bragging that my father was a dentist was a haughty "badge" I could display if needed. I do not recall using the conceit but I definitely felt it; it did wonders for my self-confidence (which means that I probably did use it). My father was a hero in my eyes and I was proud to be seen with him. My mother was beautiful and I was delighted when they both attended school functions. They were always formally dressed for formal affairs, my father in a dark double-breasted suit and my mother in a light perfectly fitted dress or suit that accented her slim waist. Naturally, her outfit was always accompanied with a matching hat and high-heel shoes, which she wore all her life, even at home. I was proud of their appearance and demeanor. *If they had both only spoken English.*

I was socially comfortable at St. Anthony for the five years I attended school. I recall no anxiety or major preoccupations during that period. The setting allowed me to walk safely on Army Street the five blocks to and from school to our apartment, occasionally catching grasshoppers that fed on the minty weeds that populated the vacant lots en route. Girl ogling started during the 6th and 7th grades although it was not infectious or memorable. Darleen Burch and Sandy Shombert were on my short list of favorites. They were popular girls, personable and easy on the eyes. Sex, like our heroes, was limited to characters and events in the movies, not part of our reality. Hormones were still on hold, but that dynamic soon changed. While that time period and school days remained uncomplicated, it was no doubt influenced by the contrast of what awaited me. In 1952, my world was again turned upside down, only this time the anxiety was more acute and personal.

By the end of 1951, my mother's daily routine was caring for my sister and me, keeping house, and cooking – the latter she did not enjoy or do well. Prompted by another of her sisters, who lived in the Richmond District, my mother took a couple of part-time jobs as a seamstress at Lily Ann's and Ransohoff's, women clothing stores downtown, while we were in school. Those employed as seamstresses were mainly Latinos and the experience did not enhance her ability or desire to speak English. It did break the monotony of her duties at home where she had a propensity to change the furniture in different configurations at least once a month during her adult life.

Never-Ending Yearning to Return Home

My father had his own idiosyncrasies to ward off anxieties about feeling like a second-class immigrant from a foreign country. He stayed busy in his quasi-profession, but still found time to reflect on returning to El Salvador. He knew my mother wanted this as much, perhaps even more, and for different reasons. The prospect of moving back sang to him like Homer's Sirens of Greek mythology. He knew that it was dangerous, but he needed to atone for getting my mother involved with his political causes and leaving her alone while he fled from the tyrants in power and their death squads. She had to survive alone while the police broke into homes, killed pets, made illegal arrests and performed the worst atrocities. On top of that, my father eventually uprooted my mother from all her friends and relatives to move to the U.S. He felt guilty for all of that for the rest of his life.

Failure Viewed as Success in Progress

My father also knew my sister and I were reaching an age when serious thoughts and impulses would begin to fill our imaginations. He could see that I was trying to meld his Latino background with American values and customs, the latter a subject that he did not feel comfortable advising me on one way or the other. A major decision had to be made, and soon. The clock was ticking. Then, the sudden death of one of the aunts who raised him provided an unintended opportunity to explore the prospect of returning for good. Dr. Parker agreed to lend him the money for the trip to El Salvador, and he could repay it from a small inheritance coming from his aunt. He did attend the funeral and did come back safely. He brought back photos and stories and gifts – a marimba for me and native costumes for my sister. He also brought back the news that my mother had silently feared. They were both disappointed, but pessimism was not his master. He often quoted Winston Churchill, who said, "As for me, I am an optimist. It does not seem too much use being anything else." My father was also an accomplished scientist and agreed with Einstein who said, "Failure is success in progress."

My sister and I did not know what he had learned, namely, that it was still an unsafe environment for their permanent return. He had checked the information from various sources and tested their reliability. Others had been betrayed recently. Martinez' former henchmen were lurking in the background and clinging to their fascist philosophy. Returning was not to be, not now, perhaps never. My mother took the news hard, but she had anticipated it. She had to be strong and make personal adjustments if they were to move forward. *The children*, she thought, *think of the children.*

Resigned, they began to make plans for the future. First, my father applied for U.S. citizenship. My mother acquiesced to remain the loyal wife and mother and accept living in the U.S., but she would not consider citizenship; her reasons remained private. They also decided that the time was right to buy a permanent home in the City. They did not feel that the change of schools and its effect on Ana and me was a major consideration as long as it was another Catholic school. Regarding this decision, they did not see past the life-style benefits. Neither did they anticipate the unforeseen "train wreck" around the corner that almost derailed their socioeconomic standing.

After my father returned from my great-aunt's funeral, the search for the right house to buy was on and in earnest. After months of searching and much negotiation, in late 1952, my parents settled on a two-bedroom home on 39th Avenue in the Sunset District. The house was four houses from Lincoln Way, which bordered the south side of Golden Gate Park, and it was a mere 10 blocks away from the Pacific Ocean. My parents made an offer of $12,500 for the house and it was accepted. So, almost every morning for the next seven years I heard the moan of the foghorns that were mounted on the Golden Gate Bridge and elsewhere to aid in the safe passage of ships and fishing boats traveling in a low fog under the bridge and around the Bay.

The monthly house payments required that my mother seek a full-time job but they determined it was worth it. My sister and I were old enough to come home to an empty house after school, but everyone was going to do their part, and the revelry was contagious. Already many of their friends had moved from the Mission to the Sunset District and considered the decision a step-up socioeconomically.

Parental Love Was Not Enough for Americanization

But as we toured the unfamiliar neighborhood, the stark reality of the change set in. For me, the dreaded unknown was four blocks away at 40th Avenue and Lawton Street, and it had a holy name. I was entering the awkward age of adolescence and my parents did not recognize that the

Americanization experience was already traumatic enough. America was a refuge, not a home to them, especially my mother. To be fair, they were experimental parents, that was, both were orphaned very young and had not inherited child-rearing models. Both believed that parental love was the only necessary ingredient in raising children. As a result, they reacted to my social interactions at school and educational development in general terms and based mainly on what I described to them, not from an innate understanding of the dominant system and culture. If a school activity made us happy, it must be good, let's do more of it, and conversely, if a subject was distasteful, then it must be bad, unimportant. The language barrier was also a crucial impediment in this regard. My father spoke some English but did not recognize colloquial expressions or slang that he often tried to imitate much to my chagrin. Ana and I only spoke Spanish to them and English to each other and with our friends. All during this time, I had no Latino friends my age.

Although I loved and respected my parents, I kept any description of interactions with *my* friends superficial because any profound discussions would have been fruitless. The divide between us was growing. I began to have inexplicable urges to rebel against their overtures of affection. They kept treating me as a child; kept me "dancing the tango with my younger sister," so to speak.

Significant Difference in Pre vs. Post-Adolescence Migration

It was years later that I realized the significance of this rift and its implication on generations of any youth migrating to the U.S. or to any country from their birthplace for that matter. I came to believe that the age of the child migrating was paramount in influencing the quality of the relationship with the parents because pre-adolescence or post-adolescence migration determined the nationality that the youth identified as his/her own. Pre-adolescent children favored the trends and values of the new country, and likewise, post-adolescent immigrant youth, essentially young adults, retained the values and guidance of their immigrant parents and native country. My parents were oblivious to this significance, and so were ineffective in explaining changes in my behavior and physiology. As conversant as I was in Spanish, I did not know the clinical names for genital parts or the stages of puberty until I was in college. There was no effort on my parent's part to have this discussion, nor would I allow it if they had tried.

At the time, however, I did not analyze these incongruities, but the cumulative effect of *not* openly discussing such personal matters tended to alienate me further from my parents. These inconsistencies applied to all immigrant adolescents, especially pre-adolescent immigrant youth where the parents were unable or unwilling to understand their divergence in values. If there are lessons to be learned, they are well documented by social scientists as the causes of, among other things, youth gang activities, alienation, and other anti-social behavior. Although the effects are known, parental education of this phenomenon has not significantly evolved despite the escalation of immigrants today.

To add to my confusion, my generation was in the midst of the 1950s counterculture movement (rejection of conventional social norms) at the time. Parents, let alone immigrant parents, of that period never understood the intricacies of the social injustices that had caused that revolution. In their eyes, America had won a world war against world despotism; my parents also had survived tyranny; and none were in the mood to sanction a "civil war" by ungrateful youth. It was easier just to dismiss any discord to the idealism of the young, which they knew was nothing new and this cavalier dismissal only widened the gap between us.

Family-Suffered Train Wreck

The aforementioned "train wreck" my family suffered was reported in the May 1952 edition of Life magazine: "Famed Vaudevillian-Dentist Painless Parker Dead in San Francisco at the Age of 80." The brief obituary read: "If Parker was not the best dentist in the world, he was certainly the most famous. He lived a life of contrasts: he was famous and infamous, a shameless self-promoter and patient advocate, a celebrity and a scoundrel, a quack and an innovator, and a provocateur and a victim; he was admired, respected, and hated for what and how he did it." [35]

My parents were stressed over what would happen to the Parker dental chain. They had just bought a house and a new car. My mother's salary at an insurance company was a pittance. A month later they learned the

Parker business was being liquidated and my father had a few months to finish any pending business at the S.F. office. He received a two week's salary severance package. Meanwhile, prospects for a similar job were nil; no other dental office would risk a similar arrangement to what Parker had made with the immigrant dentists. The ADA's strangle hold on licensure remained solid.

My father began applying to every dental office in the Bay Area and statewide for a job as a dental technician; it was the only card he had to play. Meanwhile, the financial burden on them was severe, to the point of asking for loans from friends. After four months at working at odd jobs, my father received an offer from the U.S. Army Depot at the Alameda Naval Air Station, across the Bay Bridge. They were recruiting dental technicians for an expansion of their services. My father could start within two months, pending a security background check.

With an income again, albeit a reduced one, my parents began to dig themselves out of their economic hole. My sister and I never knew about these economic burdens, only about the new job and different routine for our father. *Another challenge*, thought my father; *another cross to bear*, thought my mother.

Compared to the cramped apartment in a cramped building in the cramped Mission District, the home on 39th Avenue was a dramatic and exciting change. It was a spacious two-story, two-bedroom, single family home with a two-car garage and an unfinished basement on the first floor, and located in the middle-class residential Sunset District. The formal entryway, the large picture window in the large living room, the separate dining room, the large kitchen and a backyard was now *all theirs*. The Sunset did not promote outdoor living and gardening like in the Mission because the backyards for such purposes were much smaller. The fact that all the homes were of the same general size and appearance (two-story, box-shaped stucco facing), and were built with no measurable space between each other did not detract from the tranquil setting. If someone criticized the almost daily fog and overcast days, the counter praises were the proximity of the ocean, the N-Judah streetcar two blocks away on Judah Street, and the amenities of Golden Gate Park right across the street.

Although my parents spent considerable time touting to Ana and me the advantages of attending the larger Holy Name Grammar School in an affluent area, there was the concern with both parents working, that we would have to walk the four blocks to school by ourselves and care for ourselves until our mother arrived in the afternoon. By now, my parents knew that in the City, neighbors were not inclined to be friendly. However, they had close friends and relatives living in our neighborhood, and at least one of them was available for any emergencies.

Loss of My Latino Identity

Despite assurances by my parents that we were transferring to a similar Catholic school, albeit mid-year, and that we would make new friends and continue similar interests and activities, I was dubious. No one accompanied my sister and me on our first day at the new school, and although we were older, both of us were nervous. These nuns seemed officious and regimented. Other rude awakenings were evident as soon as I was introduced to one of the two 7th grade classes. Each grade at Holy Name had approximately 100 students and was divided into two classes, A and B. In contrast, St. Anthony had about 25 students in each grade. Most shockingly, I was presented to the class as "Richard Canas," not Ricardo León Cañas, as I was known at St. Anthony. (Ethnicity and the "ñ" had not made it past Twin Peaks to the Sunset District.) Entering this new world meant that I would no longer be known as Ricardo. I would be called the Anglicized name of "Richard," whether I liked it or not. There were almost no Latino students in my grade or in all of Holy Name, as far as I could tell; in fact, it seemed like most of the students in my class turned out to have Irish surnames. I had never seen so much red hair and freckles. The teachers were from the Order of the Sisters of Mercy and quite modern and brash compared to the modest, servile manners of the Dominican nuns. The parish priests were secular (no specific religious order) and wore black suits and drove parish cars, totally dissimilar to the dark brown monk robes and sandals worn by the Franciscan fathers and brothers at St. Anthony who used public transportation. Sunday sermons were more concerned with stimulating donations in the collection basket than religious direction. Oozing humility and poverty, it seemed, were not prominent in a secular priest's vows.

Popularity Based on Sports and Cliques

During my first recess, "Rich" (not Ricardo) was handed a basketball by another student, presumably to test my athletic competence. After determining that I could neither pass, dribble, or shoot, I was left alone. It was obvious to me that the popular boys favored sports and exuded confidence. And the popular girls, it seemed, were constantly flirting with the popular boys. I was making mental notes about all of these traits and habits. Back in the Mission, Darlene and Sandy might as well have been in another city with the number of steep hills that divided us.

The popular girls formed cliques, informal and select groupings that the nuns disapproved, while the girls denied and ignored the claim. Girls' parents allowed them to wear makeup on weekends and some were even dating older boys. At school, the girls wore uniforms like at St. Anthony. Boys wore brown instead of blue corduroy pants worn at St. Anthony.

The Sunset was populated by middle and upper-middle-class, white, predominantly Irish families. Being a Latino was neither a novelty nor a hindrance unless I chose to make it so, which I did not. I also realized that having a dentist father was not a bragging point; many of the students' parents were professionals and well to do. I was taking more mental notes.

My parents had miscalculated or exaggerated our acclimation period. With no frame of reference, they could not support my concerns about fitting in that no doubt seemed trivial to them but humongous to me; *Americanization* for me remained an autonomous process. In retrospect, adjusting to Holy Name had more to do with timing in that I entered Holy Name at what was known in public schools as Junior High School, rather than the stark differences between the traits of St. Anthony and Holy Name students. Entering this adolescent age group greatly added to the many challenges of the physical move. Holy Name students had been interacting for years. For them and their parents, puberty was just part of the circumstances one faced growing up. Meanwhile, these social and biological changes peppered me at a fast and furious pace, and I could not separate them from the physical move; adjusting was like trying to change the oil in a running engine. I had not been shy until this period in my life.

Imitation Key to Fitting In

As part of my social survival "tool box," I found imitation was often helpful and, as the saying goes, was also a form of flattery. If not overdone, a certain amount of insincerity was tolerated, and any slight adverse reactions were balanced out by shared experiences. So by the end of the 7th grade, I had finally adapted to the Holy Name experience. I was not invited to any of my classmates' homes, but I did not think it unusual, since I was not inviting anyone to my home either. My socialization with classmates would have progressed further had I more time to interact with them after school or weekends, but as it turned out, I accepted a job after school to make a humble contribution to the family income. The job involved delivering the *San Francisco News*, one of the two afternoon daily newspapers, to people's homes.

Running My Own Business

I picked up my bundle of newspapers (marked route G-52) at Judah Street and Sunset Boulevard along with six other boys with different routes. At this location, we individually folded our papers in "tomahawk" triangular shapes for throwing them to front doors and stuffed them into poncho-type canvas double bags that we either put over our head to walk our route or draped over the handlebars of a bicycle. If the edition was not too thick with pages, it usually took me only one trip around the route to complete the deliveries. Maneuvering the bag on the bike was a bit tricky, but with some practice, I could ride along and throw the papers with accuracy to front doors without stopping. On rainy days, the process was slower and more complicated because the paper could not be delivered wet because I was evaluated by the number of complaints I received. I had 32 serves (customers) on my route that ran along both sides of the seven 1300 blocks between Irving and Judah Streets, from Sunset Boulevard to 43rd Avenue. It was a lot of ground to cover for so few customers but a job was a job. I collected the subscription money from customers and paid for the papers on a monthly basis. I also received bonuses for every new subscription I acquired. The company bragged that this system allowed us in effect to "run our own business." Of course, deadbeat customers were *our* problem. On a good month, I netted $25, which I dutifully turned over to my parents. I did not get a regular allowance, just on an as-needed basis.

At my age, job options were scarce. Some classmates delivered the weekly *Progress Shopping News*, a free neighborhood advertisement newspaper, which was delivered to every home on a route. The pay was about the same, but the number of deliveries was much greater. Once in a while, I substituted for a classmate, Peter Brucato, on his *Shopping News* route and he returned the favor when needed.

Solutions to Whining Irritating Kids

While waiting for our newspapers to arrive in the afternoon, which were often late, our idle minds proved dangerous. On one occasion, we tied and gagged the whining and all-around irritating Keefer boy to a tree after the papers were delivered. Not cool, as his mother later threatened the newspaper distributor with charges against all of us, but nothing ever happened. Another time some of the other boys got the bright idea of putting the contents of small sample boxes of soap detergent, which they confiscated from the front doors of neighborhood homes, on the tracks of the N-Judah streetcar. Judah Street had a significant grade between 33rd and 36th Avenues and when the streetcar tried to stop, the crystallized soap sent it skidding, forcing the streetcar driver and other motorists to panic. The police were called, but before they arrived, the other scared boys and I scattered to deliver our papers. No one identified who was responsible, but our delivery site was moved away from streetcar tracks to Irving and Sunset Boulevard where we were checked-on frequently by our distributor. Of course, Keefer was part of that stupid prank but the little weasel vehemently denied it, drawing more of our irritation. Insincerity was considered serious buddy abuse.

An advantage of the *S.F. News* having a stable of cheap child labor was they could hire paperboys to distribute free sun visors with political election propaganda at Kezar before football games. Kezar was located at the east end of Golden Gate Park and home to the San Francisco 49ers pro football team and the annual Shriner's East-West All-Star college football game. After half-time at the 49er games, those of us distributing sun visors with "Vote for Murphy," or whomever, were allowed to stand in the stadium aisles on the visitor's north side to watch the game. Most fans had thrown the visors away but after halftime the seats on the north side were usually engulfed in sunlight, and fans gladly paid us a dime for one of the discarded visors, which we had cleverly stockpiled. We spent little time watching the games, since earning pocket change not turned over to my parents was more satisfying.

Eventually, Kezar became part of my beat in the Sunset. While I was not yet a pro football enthusiast, I did follow boxing because of my father's interest in it. One of my heroes was the "Rock," Rocky Marciano, who had beaten Jersey Joe Walcott for the heavyweight boxing title on September 23, 1952, just when I started to attend Holy Name. The bout was considered the 16th Greatest Title Fight of All Times by *The Ring* magazine. The Rock was knocked down for the first time in his 49-0-0 career in the first round. A couple of years later at the Kezar Pavilion in May 1955, my father and his best friend bought seats for my friend Ed Finn and me to accompany them and witness firsthand Marciano destroy the European champ, Don Cockrell, in nine rounds, although during the last three rounds Cockrell was unconsciously walking through the motions while Marciano whaled away.

By now, I had taken "ownership" of Kezar and Golden Gate Park. Living just a few houses away from the park, I went there daily to walk my dog, Sandy, and on weekends with friends to explore the plethora of activities in the park. I recall playing with a classmate, Vince Davis, and being literally thrown out of the park's Bamboo Island, as we called it, by a bunch of older kids who had taken ownership of the hidden island as their fort. We vowed to come back with our gang of ruffians to reclaim it. We never did.

Occasionally, some of my friends and I rode our bikes through the park to the west end and the foot of the Richmond District. That was the site of Playland at the Beach that was packed with as many as 50,000 visitors on weekends. My parents loved the red-sauced Mexican tacos that they sold to go at The Hot House. As kids, we rarely had money to spend at Playland but it was a place to go and hang out with friends. It was one of many things available in San Francisco, an enchanted place for kids to explore, play, develop and forget our place of origin – El Salvador.

Age 13: The Brother I Never Had – the "Wild Child" (cont.)

In addition to my "twin brother" Richard Canas, there was another kid in my 8th grade class, Barry Sullivan. I guess I took a shining to him because his name was Sullivan and looked as Irish as can be with his red hair and freckled face. He also had an electric personality with high energy in how he talked and acted – sort of a "wild child." He immediately became my lifelong "brother" I never had – someone my age that I could pal around with while sharing his parents and their home. This was his wild and turbulent youth before we became brothers as told by Barry himself.

Lessons From the Great Depression

Barry James Sullivan was born January 13, 1941 at Saint Francis Hospital on the corner of Hyde between Bush and Pine Streets in San Francisco. I was the first child of Doris and Jim. My mom was a native San Franciscan born in 1918, and my father was born in Paris, KY in 1916. He was a product of the Great Depression and never graduated from grammar school. He worked for 10 cents an hour to help his poor family, which was why he later insisted I develop a good work ethic at a young age. He often said, "I don't care if you're cleaning toilets or mopping a floor, I always want you to do your best." Of course, he never let me forget that no one had ever worked as hard, or gone through as much as he had during the Great Depression, which was truly one of the worst periods in American history. It may have been why it was so hard to satisfy him in whatever I did – the bar was just set too high.

Dad left grammar school and took any job that was available to help the family. He eventually left home when he was around 15 and joined the U.S. Merchant Marine when the jobs dried up. But when WWII was declared on that Day of Infamy, Dad would never see service. He was exempt because of a severe handicap. As a boy, a cart ran over his right foot shattering all of his bones, so he had only one big bent front toe. Medicine in the 1920s in Kentucky was rural to say the least. Speaking of medicine, one of Dad's childhood friends was an African-American kid who ended up becoming a doctor and the first African-American San Francisco police commissioner. His name was Washington Garner and he was a guest at our home on many occasions. My parents called him "Wash" but the two men sometimes called each other different "endearing" names, which were never taken personally or seriously.

Yearning to Return to the Womb

When my father first saw me through the glass at the hospital, he thought I would become a drummer since my hands were pumping furiously – the first signs of my high-energy personality. In reality I was probably yearning to get back inside the womb as soon as possible since my infant psychic powers already deduced that it was going to be a rocky ride with Doris and Jim. It also may be why one of my regrets by the time I graduated from high school was that I never learned to play the drums.

At that time, we lived on the corner of Arguello and Frederick Streets where Lincoln Way began, but we always called it 1st and Arguello, which were their original names. We lived on the top floor of an old Victorian across the street from Kezar Stadium and Polytechnic High School. Poly was a frequent participant in the annual Turkey Bowl on Thanksgiving at Kezar for the San Francisco AAA high school football championship, which it seemed they won nearly every year in the 1940s and 1950s. High school football was a big deal those days, and the games attracted tens of thousands of fans. Poly was also considered a tough school in terms of the attending students and their football teams.

Every year the Shriners conducted their massive and colorful parade. We sat in the living room and looked out the front window, as a stream of Shriners wearing their tall red fez hats with the black tassels marched down Frederick Street past Poly and around the perimeter of Kezar into the stadium. The parades were colorful and dramatic, with bands, clowns, costumes, cars, motorcycles, and even Shriners riding tiny bikes. Some were dressed in full Arabian garb, since the Shriners were members of the Ancient Arabic Order of the Nobles of the Mystic Shrine. If the letters A.A.O.N.M.S. were rearranged, the anagram spelled out "a Mason." The Shriners were a noble organization helping thousands of crippled children. Their hospital was built in 1924 on 19th Avenue at Moraga Street in the Sunset District. It was one of the few remaining hospitals in the City erected before World War II. The brick building had a beautiful Italian

Renaissance and Baroque style. I had a friend who had seven operations at a Shriners hospital at no cost to her parents. They were truly a fraternity of good souls.

My earliest memory was when I was two years old. Mom had given birth to my sister Nancy at the UC Hospital (University of California, San Francisco Medical Center) that was only a couple of blocks up from our home. Mom slowly climbed our stairs as Dad followed carrying Nancy. Mom opened the sliding front room door and closed it behind Dad. She pulled me aside and said in a hushed tone, "Here's a Hershey candy bar. Don't let your sister see it. She might get jealous." Mom was 25 and already a master of psychological manipulation.

The war years for our family were filled with saving stuff and never throwing anything useful away. We were the original recyclers. We balled up all rubber bands and tin foil, and saved all our bacon and food grease in a coffee can, which we took to the butcher shop on 3rd Avenue and Hugo Street. It was our patriotic duty for the war effort. The bacon grease was used to make glycerin, which was used to make bombs. The tin foil was used to make aluminum parts for airplanes and rubber to make tires.

Effect of the Green Glove Rapist

There was a lot of tension in our house, not only due to the war, but because there was a "bad man" in the neighborhood. The newspapers referred to him as the "Green Glove Rapist," and this fear must have permeated my childhood imagination, since I had a recurring nightmare that haunted me for years. In my dreams I would be asleep when suddenly I would hear a loud thumping noise coming closer and closer to my room, the sound of heavy menacing footsteps. Thump, thump, thump. My heart began racing to the pounding of the noise. I then jumped out of bed and raced down the hall. Bursting into the kitchen, I dove under a red and white oil tablecloth hoping to avoid the threat. The noise became louder and louder until the thing was inside the kitchen, and slowly, very slowly, a hand reached under the table to lift the tablecloth, then suddenly I would wake up, my heart pounding but thankful I was still alive. In February 1944 the Green Glove Rapist who raped five women was arrested. Joseph Finkel, a 29-year-old married shipyard worker, was sentenced to 21 years to life in San Quentin Prison. I slept better after his capture, but that nightmare continued occasionally into my teens.

Collection Box Money Spent on Candy

Every neighborhood in San Francisco was unique. At the time, I did not realize we were living at the beginning of the Inner Sunset District, an area populated mainly by Catholic and Protestant white families. Dad had been a Catholic and Mom a Protestant, but my earliest memory of religion was going to Sunday school at the Seventh Avenue Presbyterian Church a few blocks up from Golden Gate Park. Mom would give me a nickel and a dime for the collection. But I was a bad little boy as a kid, so I spent it on candy, which I figured was no big loss for the church. I cannot even remember one Sunday school lesson. Religion did not become a part of my life until we moved later to the Outer Sunset in 1948.

As a kid, I had a rambunctious mischievous look and to capture a picture of me with my curly red hair, freckled face, and my large gapped two front teeth smile, Mom took me to a photographer to have pictures taken. One was a picture of me drinking a glass of milk and another of me eating an apple. He said he was going to have them used in a calendar, but we never heard if the pictures were ever published.

Origin of Interest in Writing

Dad was a great writer and storyteller and every Saturday or Sunday morning while we were still very young, Nancy and I would run into their bedroom and jump up and down on the bed, begging for a story. Dad then told us stories about Backy-Whacky Barry, and Ansy-Nancy in the Land of the Wog-Wogs. He had traveled the South Seas as a Merchant Marine, so we loved listening to his South Sea tales filled with danger and drama in the style of Jack London. He told thrilling tales of life among the natives on Bora Bora. In one story he told us, "When I was at the back of the ship, I looked over to my left and saw one giant eye looking up at me. I did not know what it was, but it fascinated me. I then looked to my right and saw another eye. It was a giant hammerhead shark following the ship for food being tossed off the back." Of course he was exaggerating, but we did not know the difference. This may have been the origin of my later interest in radio, television, movies and eventual pursuit of writing movie scripts after college.

Our family indoor activities consisted of playing card games like canasta, board games like Monopoly, and listening to all the wonderful radio shows – the imaginative theatre of the mind: "Faster than a speeding bullet! More powerful than a locomotive! Able to leap tall buildings with a single bound! Look, up in the sky! It's a bird! It's a plane! It's Superman!" Everybody loved Superman who was an American icon, along with the Lone Ranger and his Indian sidekick Tonto.

But they were not the only popular radio shows. There were so many good detective shows, action thrillers, variety shows, and comedy shows like the *George Burns and Gracie Allen Show*. Gracie was a native San Franciscan who attended Star of the Sea, a Catholic girls grammar school, so she was one of us. I loved radio. Although I was told to turn off my lights by ten and not listen to any programs, I was habitually disobedient. I put the radio under my covers, turned the volume down low, and listened to shows like *The Whistler*, which started with footsteps and someone whistling a very haunting tune. *The Whistler* was a commentator who usually followed a crime and talked about where the people were going wrong or right. Then there was *Inner Sanctum*, a spooky show that opened and closed with a creaking door. The show sometimes entered the realm of horror, other times the supernatural. And, of course, one of my favorite shows was *The Shadow*. The crime show always began with "Who knows what evil lurks in the hearts of men? The Shadow knows." Then the creepy laugh. At the end, the Shadow signed off, "The weed of crime bears bitter fruit! Crime does not pay...The Shadow knows!"

Some of the comedy shows I enjoyed were *The Great Gildersleeve* about a pompous know-it-all water commissioner, his family and friends. *Fibber McGee and Molly* was also very popular. There was a standing joke that every time the absent minded and messy Fibber opened a closet door, a ton of clothes and boxes fell out. It truly was the Golden Age of Radio. More of my favorites were *Amos 'n' Andy*, a comedy about two African-American men living in Harlem, but played by two white guys. There was *Dragnet*, *Duffy's Tavern*, *Edgar Bergen and Charlie McCarthy*, *Bing Crosby Show*, *Green Hornet*, *Suspense*, *Adventures of Sam Spade*,

Lights Out, Sergeant Preston of the Yukon, Johnny Dollar, Bob Hope Show with his traditional "Thanks for the Memory" closing, and the *Jack Benny Show* with his sidekicks Rochester, Dennis Day, and Don Wilson, who had to endure Jack's dreadful violin playing. Jack always complained about money. He was radio's ultimate cheapskate.

But for kids, the real entertainment and adventure was out on the streets. There was a small shop next door to Poly High School that I loved because it was stocked with every kind of candy imaginable – licorice pipes with white and pink sprinkles on the bowl's top, black licorice strips with beads of colored sugar, licorice wheels, bubble gum cigars, Bazooka Bubble Gum, Bit-O-Honey, Mallo Cups, Necco Wafers, and an endless supply of goodies. My favorite sweet, however, was the round Cho-Cho chocolate malted ice cream on a stick.

Living across the street from Kezar was always an adventure. The San Francisco 49ers won their very first game 34-14 against the Chicago Rockets at Kezar before 45,000 fans in 1946. Crowds were always big. The parking was hideous around the stadium so families that had homes with a garage rented the front space out for the day. We had a garage, but I was disappointed that Dad never rented it out for the games. It would have been a great job for a five-year-old to do.

Good Shaking for the Little Bastard

One day I was playing on the sidewalk when a kid across the street fired a rock from a slingshot. It hit me in the face. Mom streaked across the street to nab the little bastard. She caught him and gave him a good shaking. Today someone who doing that in public would probably be arrested for child abuse, but he deserved it and more.

Protesting Injustice Developed From Dad

Our landlady, Mrs. Brown, lived below us. One day she came up the backstairs to show us her new kitten. When I reached out to pet it, it scratched my arm, but that did not stop me from becoming a big-time cat lover. I had several cats in my lifetime, and they always broke my heart when they died. I cried more when my cats died than when people close to me died. I always felt I had to stand up for the weak and defenseless – probably why I complained about the government all my life and wrote so many "Letters to the Editor" complaining about injustices.

San Francisco in the 1940s was a magical city. We were schooled never to call it "Frisco" – only low-class people and sailors used that nickname. There were so many exciting adventures when I was little, especially after getting a bicycle. Owning a good bike was a source of pride, and Dad bought me a brand-new red Schwinn bike with all the bells, whistles, and white wall tires. The first thing I did was to strip down the bike. I removed everything except the pedals, the frame, the wheels, and the handlebars. I then attached a playing card with a clothespin to the frame so the card created a loud sound like a rapidly shuffled deck of cards. It was a bare bones bike that I raced around on all day. Dad did not appreciate me removing the parts, but he never reprimanded me. I think he actually enjoyed watching me whip around out front.

Being the Best We Could and Winners

We rode bikes without wearing helmets. The thought of wearing any protective gear was not what kids did. If we fell, cut ourselves, or injured ourselves, we just got up, wiped ourselves off, and went on with playing. We played games without being overly supervised by parents or teachers. We could make our own rules, fall down, get up and punch the classroom bully. We were free to develop life skills. We strived to be the best we could be and to be winners. Our certificates and trophies were earned by winning and excelling in competition, and not just for participating.

Just inside Golden Gate Park at 5th Avenue across Lincoln Way was "Whiskey Hill." We appropriately called it Whiskey Hill because of all the booze bottles tossed about by the bums. San Francisco had always been a haven for the down-and-outers, drunks and deadbeats. They have always been a part of the San Francisco landscape, and I always felt very sorry for them. One day a fire broke out on the Hill and a bunch of us kids scampered up to help the firemen. It was not a big fire so the firemen did not mind if we picked up their large white hoses, as long as we stayed away from the fire. While I was helping with the fire hose, a bumblebee stung me inside my nose. One of the firemen came over and told me to put some wet mud on the sting. God Bless all firemen!

Rebellious Nature Came From Mom

When I was five years old, I got into the family car, sat in the driver's seat, released the brake and the car rolled out of the garage and on to the street. Mom was hysterical, but she did not spank me. I believe she saw in me the rebellious nature that she herself possessed. She was a redhead too.

The first school I attended in 1946 was Laguna Honda Elementary on 7th Avenue between Irving and Judah Streets. I was five years old and, unbeknownst to me at that early age, I was already following in Mom's footsteps. When she was 10 years old, the teacher, who was a pompous bore, was out of the room. She jumped up on his desk waving her arms dramatically in the air and loudly mimicked the teacher as she proclaimed, "Four score and seven years ago our fathers brought forth on the continent a new nation..." Suddenly, the teacher appeared and tried to grab her, but little Doris jumped off the desk and ran around the classroom much to the delight of her classmates. The teacher chased her around the room, down the hallway, and out into the schoolyard. But she escaped and ran home.

I also was a scamp. One morning the class got into a crayon fight and I broke the glass on the bookcase at the back of the room. But that was not enough. We had to create more hysteria before our teacher Miss Claire returned, so we turned our attention to tossing crayons out the window at the cars speeding up the street. The class was in an uproar. Thirty years later my wife said, "I've never known anyone who could incite people to riot faster than you." I never told her that story so I am clueless why she thought that. Years later Terry Quinlan said it was because I was a high-energy guy all my life – just channeling it in different directions.

Discipline From Coat Hangers and Smacks

Mom's brother Ed Nicol and his family lived two blocks away from us on 2nd Avenue between Lincoln Way and Hugo Street. Ed and Mary had three children: Brad, Gayle, and Ronnie. Uncle Ed, like many parents of that generation, literally believed in the adage "Spare the rod, spoil the child." So, hanging on the kitchen wall next to the door was a long wide black razor strap. I do not think the kids were whipped excessively, but my parents also never shirked from using corporal punishment on my sister and me. Mom preferred coat hangers, and Dad just smacked me. However, I never was punished for breaking the bookcase glass or starting the riot at school. My punishment usually came from talking back to my parents or disobeying them. I never held it against them because they both disciplined us. If only one parent did it, I may have resented it. I guess the lesson was that both parents should discipline the children.

Once when my grammar school friend Frank Glynn was visiting me, my father and I got into a violent fight because I talked back to him. We smacked each other but it was over in seconds. We did not hurt each other, but it was traumatic and it left a lasting memory – probably because my friend was watching. I always felt nervous around Dad. Even in my adult life, whenever I visited my parents, my heart began to pound as I drove closer to their home. I did not like to think about the non-physical violent arguments my parents had, but they both did their best to raise us in their own way.

In 1948 the green and cream white N-Judah streetcars ran from King and 4th Streets to Judah Street and 48th Avenue, which was the last avenue before the Great Highway along Ocean Beach. When the N-Judah was introduced to the City on its initial voyage, my cousins, Brad and Ronnie, and I caught the streetcar as it made its turn around the bend at Frederick and Arguello Streets, just below the UC Hospital. I could smell the tan leather seats of the new car and the shiny painted interior. If we were old enough to drink, we probably would have broken a bottle of champagne across the car. It was a very special occasion for us kids.

Impact of Seeing Extreme Gore

The most traumatic event happened a block away at the corner of Arguello and Irving Streets. An armored truck hit a little boy, around my age. He was lying on the N-Judah tracks screaming with pain, and the bone from his left leg was sticking out of his bloody pants. I watched the medics attending to the poor kid until the ambulance took him away and thought a lot about his extreme pain. It influenced my behavior regarding safety much more than witnessing the normal bruises and scratches from growing up.

Throughout the early years on Arguello Street, we took many trips on the N-Judah down to Ocean Beach and walked over to Playland at the Beach. We were fortunate to experience it at its best. There was so much to do there, but first we had to say hello to Laffing Sal at the Fun House. She was as iconic to us kids as the Statue of Liberty was to New Yorkers.

Upon entering the Fun House, we got lost in the Hall of Mirrors where it was difficult to find the way out to the rides inside. As I made my way through the mirrors, I always thought of the 1947 film noir classic *The Lady from Shanghai* with Orson Welles and Rita Hayworth and the climactic scene inside the Hall of Mirrors. The final gunfight involving Welles, Hayworth and Everett Sloane (the later two got killed) was a masterpiece with each shooting at the other but hitting mostly mirrored images of each other and shattering glass.

In the Fun House we played endlessly on the slide. We were required to sit on a gunnysack, as it propelled us quickly down the long slide. When we reached the bottom a rush of air blew up through the holes in the floor. It was a special challenge for the girls sliding in their dresses. An exciting ride was jumping on the Joy Wheel. We tried to stay on while it spun around and around in order to be the last person on the wheel when it finally came to a stop.

Self-Confidence From Taking Risks

If we felt brave and wanted a real thrill, we rode "The Dipper." The Big Dipper, by today's standards, would have been considered a safety hazard because it was built of wood and looked like it could collapse at any moment with all the clickety-clack and squeaks. Even though we thought it was probably unsafe at the time, the "danger" was part of the excitement of the ride. Sometimes we clung to the handle across our laps as the car was slowly pulled up the steep slope with the creaking and clanking on the metal tracks only casting more doubt on the safety of the contraption. As we reached the top, the cars paused for a moment, and we got a magnificent view of the Pacific Ocean, but then, the rapid plunge down and around, up and down until we finally reached the bottom. The thrill ride was worth the risk, and we were proud we had the guts to ride it.

After a ride on the Dipper, if we wanted to do something a little more physical, we drove the Dodger bumper cars and tried desperately to smash into each other while avoiding getting smashed. It was great fun whizzing around, avoiding my pals while trying to outmaneuver them. Sparks flew above the car and there was always an electrical smell in the air from the car's electrical pole contact at the ceiling.

There was so much more to do at Playland, but when we got hungry there were the best tamales in San Francisco at The Hot House. We then finished the day off by eating an It's-It Bar, a delicious dessert of two oatmeal cookies filled with vanilla ice cream and dipped in chocolate. This ice cream sandwich was invented by George Whitney who was one of the owners of Playland.

Many people who moved to San Francisco arrived with the idea that the City had great beaches and warm sunny weather. Unfortunately, they were sorely disappointed. Ocean Beach rarely had hot weather and was not conducive to sun bathing or swimming. The neighborhoods near the Beach were usually shrouded in fog. The Pacific Ocean, was usually very cold (53-60 degrees). If the weather permitted, we played on the Beach and even swam. But we could not swim very far since the rip tide could pull us out to sea in no time. If we really wanted an exciting swimming venue, we went to Sutro Baths. The swimsuit was uncomfortable, but it did not stop me from loving the pool. I preferred the warm saltwater pool, and I loved swinging on the ropes and sliding down the slide. I still remember the strong saltwater smell.

In the 1940s and 1950s it was a tradition for many San Francisco families to spend their summer vacations at the Russian River that was about 80 miles north of San Francisco. The Russian River was in Sonoma County among the majestic redwoods and was dotted with many small towns and enclaves from Rio Nido to Guerneville, from Camp Meeker to Occidental. Every summer when I was in grammar school, we spent part of our summers at Camp Meeker, which was located between Monte Rio and Occidental. We rented a cabin for about two months, and Dad came up on the weekends. It was great for the mothers who could get away from their husbands. They had all that time to visit their summer friends and raise their children in a wonderful rustic environment. We had the best of both worlds – summertime in the country, and school days in the most beautiful city in the USA.

Although Camp Meeker was not on the Russian River, it had a great swimming hole about 10 feet deep. We spent our time sun bathing and swimming. This was where Mom taught me to swim. Mom was a great swimmer, but she once dove off a board and hit her head on a rock, so she never dove again. It really freaked her out, but she still managed to teach me how to swim eventually.

Our family became friends with the Prossers. They owned their own cabin, but we always rented the same cabin every summer to be near them. Mr. Prosser was an Oakland police officer, and his son Ron and I became good summertime friends. We explored the countryside, picked wild blackberries, and played with our BB guns. Dad bought me a Daisy Red Ryder BB gun, which was the cream of the crop. It was the ultimate for boys who liked to play cowboys and Indians. One summer, several of my buddies and I decided to have a BB gun fight. As I was running down a hill, a BB caught me in the middle of my back. Just like in the movies, my arms flew up, the gun went flying and I fell to the ground, but I was not injured. No one was ever injured because we never tried to hurt each other with the exception of my friend Gerry Hipps who was shot and almost lost an eye from a BB – an example of a "toy" that was not at fault as it was the misuse by another kid.

Sometimes we cut a branch, stripped it, attached a fork to the end to make a spear, then hunted for frogs and fish. We were young adventurers let loose to explore everywhere. At night we slept outside in our sleeping bags, sometimes in the forest on our porch. The smell of the redwoods and chimney fire, the chirping of birds, forest sounds, and the sky studded with a million stars, made our summer nights unforgettable.

Dad Saved My Life

On Saturday night the summer residents could attend a show at the Armand Girard Grove. The Grove was like a miniature Hollywood Bowl. The Camp Meeker Players sang, danced, and performed skits, providing the entertainment. Sometimes residents got up on stage and performed their own material. It was innocent entertainment in a simpler time. One of the treats of spending summer time at Camp Meeker was its proximity to the town of Occidental. Occidental was only a mile away and had some of the best restaurants on the Russian River. Our favorites were Negri's Original Italian Restaurant and the Union Hotel Restaurant, but we all especially loved the Union. It specialized in a family style Italian menu. The tables were traditional red and white oil table covers. We usually ordered meat or chicken, but the meal consisted of a non-stop course of fresh bread, minestrone soup, salads, raviolis, plates of salami, cheese, and then the entrees. They also had a wide variety of desserts, but my favorite was their custard. Once I thought I was going to die. I took a big bite of a chicken leg and got some meat lodged in my throat. I jumped out of my chair, choking, turning blue, and became the center of attention for the whole restaurant. Dad quickly got up, wrapped both arms around my stomach, and kept squeezing until the piece popped out. The audience clapped, as I sheepishly sat back down. I was beyond embarrassed, and to this day I sometimes still have problems swallowing.

Athletes Did Not Smoke

The family went to Camp Meeker for the last time in the summer just before I entered high school. That was where I smoked my first cigarette. I pilfered a Camel from Mom's pack in her purse and had my one and only cigarette because I did not enjoy it. My friends and I never did smoke because most of us were into sports, and athletes did not think smoking was smart or cool.

I also had attended Captain Ed's Boyland, a summer camp for boys at Felton Grove in the Santa Cruz Mountains. The only major highlights of that experience was two wild boars running through camp and me falling out of a tree and hurting my back that bothered me for years – no wonder I only went for one summer.

In 1948 we moved to the Outer Sunset. Dad paid around $13,000 for our house on 38th Avenue between Noriega and Ortega Streets. Our new two-story house had three bedrooms, two bathrooms – one with a shower the other with a bathtub – a living room, connecting dining room, and the windows were covered with venetian blinds. The kitchen had a built-in booth, gas stove, and our first refrigerator, which was a boon for Mom, since our previous home only had an icebox in the back-porch closet. Our phone number was Lombard 66442. Mom loved that number because it was easy to remember.

Never Died From Drinking From Milk Bottles

The first room I visited when coming home was the kitchen. I opened the fridge and took a long drink from the milk bottle. All boys did it and were reprimanded for doing it, but many continued that habit in adulthood. Kids were just in too much of a hurry to get a glass. I suppose our views as to what was right and wrong did not all change over time. We never saw anyone in the family get sick or die from it, so what the heck.

Mothers Served as Neighborhood Sentries

It was unusual for the mothers in our neighborhood to have an outside job. Most stayed home and took care of their children's needs and kept their homes a sanctuary for the family. Mom was a stay-at-home mom who cleaned, cooked, and tended the garden. Sometimes she helped us with our homework. She also spent hours on the sofa reading, sewing, listening to the radio, and occasionally looking out the window at any sound that piqued her interest – keeping an eye out for unusual strangers. She was a first-class sentry, always on the alert. Perhaps that came from her days when the Green Glove Rapist was on the prowl. Those were the days when mothers kept their eyes on their kids playing in the street. So, there was always someone like Mom watching out for us but without interfering in our games.

Mom was a social butterfly. She was very fashionable and always wanted to dress to impress. She was very active in supporting Holy Name Church and in raising money for the new Saint Mary's Church. She held fashion shows at the school, and she was a den mother for the Brownies and my Cub Scout pack. She was a very creative lady and became an excellent ceramist. She had my sister and me take old coffee cans, wrap colorful yarn around them, fill the planter with dirt, and make a wooden top on two sticks to shelter the plant.

The ground level of our house had a one-car garage with an electric garage door. Carpentry and garden tools were stored on the walls and shelves. Dad had a large closet built in the back where he stored a myriad of canned foods and other household essentials. A year later, the garage housed the new 1949 Hudson Hornet that Dad had flown back to Detroit to buy and drove back to the City. The car was dark green and was the sharpest car on the block.

Beyond the garage we had a rumpus room for recreation. There were two knotty pine cabinets built into the wall. One contained a .22 rifle (an eventual gift to Terry Quinlan decades later), and a .38 Smith & Wesson revolver given to Dad by an FBI friend. There were boxes of ammunition, a swastika flag, and a German officer's black helmet with a silver eagle insignia on the front and a spike on the top. Dad's brother brought them back from World War II, but the helmet looked like it came from the First World War. Years later when my parents moved to San Rafael, the helmet and flag disappeared in transit. The back door of the rumpus room led to our backyard where the ground was covered with cement, and the sides were rows of flowerbeds.

The rumpus room had a green tile floor, rattan chairs, and a rattan table with a glass top. The walls were knotty pine and the room was decorated in a Hawaiian motif. Mom surprised Dad by having a small bar built-in with two rattan stools for visitors. Behind the sink there were four shelves of every kind of liquor imaginable, and above the bottles was a large mirror with a greenish light that accentuated its Polynesian scene. As I grew into my teens, that bar became a source of trouble. I sometimes pilfered a bottle of booze for my friends and me.

Music at home was a very important part of my childhood. We loved to listen to our collection of vinyl records, especially the haunting songs of the 1940s Swing Era: "Green Eyes," "Perfidia," "Begin the Beguine," "Sing, Sing, Sing," "My Blue Heaven," and so many more. Dad loved Artie Shaw and thought Shaw was the best, even better than Glenn Miller. We also had an old five-cent slot machine, since both of my parents were avid gamblers. Mom loved the slot machines, and Dad poker. When they entertained the neighbors, everyone drank, listened to music, danced, and played cards.

Next door to our house was a sandlot preparing for the construction of an apartment building, which created a very deep hole. I was always a good big brother, and Nancy looked up to me for protection. So, it was my responsibility to keep her from ever falling in that hole. As she got older, she became her own person as we each had our own friends and social activities.

Teasing Like Father, Like Son

There was one thing that I regret doing with my sister. I was a terrible tease like Dad. I would hide in her bedroom closet and when she opened the door, I scared the hell out of her. Also, at the dinner table I sometimes hid a rubber spider or a snake on her plate. I know some people, particularly children, get a big kick out of teasing others, but I think one should think twice. I never appreciated the teasing Mom received from Dad. What one person finds funny just might make the other person feel really lousy. Once I slipped on the proverbial banana peel and my friend laughed his ass off while I was in agony. I was in pain, and he thought it was hilarious. My attitude changed toward him and remained less than friendly. Teasing was a playful thing to do between friends, but when the person on the receiving end did not find it funny, it became bullying.

The Howard Hughes' movie *The Outlaw* starring Jane Russell first came out in 1943. The Hays Code was responsible for banning any film that they deemed immoral and for a woman exposing large sexy breasts, well that just was not proper. So the censors banned the movie, but it was re-released in San Francisco in 1946 and set records almost everywhere it was shown. A billboard across the street from our house on the southwest corner of 38th Avenue and Noriega Street promoted *The Outlaw* with Jane Russell in all her glory to the delight of the neighborhood kids and me.

When I was eight years old, Dad took me on my first plane trip to Reno. It was a twin-engine prop plane. We hit a snowstorm and it was an extremely bumpy flight. As I got off the plane, I threw up on the tarmac. Welcome to Reno! We stayed at the Mapes Hotel, one of Reno's finest, but I just could not stay out of trouble. When Dad left me alone, I printed on the hotel's stationary "Zorro was here" or "Zorro is watching you" and signed it with a big slashing Z. I went through the hallways on our floor from room to room and slipped the notes under the doors. No one ever caught me but later, Dad hired someone to watch after me, so I suspected someone squealed. I never got punished for it, so I figured Dad thought it was funny too.

Dad had many jobs during my childhood. He was a Yellow Cab driver, a bartender, and finally a salesman for Tiedemann & McMorran, a wholesale grocery business. Their main product was Sunset Foods, known as "The Brand of the West." Every visitor to our house left with a large bag of groceries. Our garage storeroom was well stocked with a variety of canned goods: peas, spinach, creamed corn, peaches and other grocery items. I suspect Dad did not have to pay for the cases of food he brought home because he was so generous with giving away so much. We were certainly well stocked for any emergency. He had his own company car so the food was perhaps just another perk. He believed canned foods were literally far superior to frozen food, and he loved to talk about food. Whenever we went to a restaurant, Dad inevitably regaled the waiter or waitress with a dissertation on the type of olives being served or some other fact about the food on our table. Mom, Nancy and I would squirm with embarrassment and thought *Oh God, please Dad, don't talk about the beets.*

Dad not only stocked grocery stores with their goods, but he supplied many Chinese restaurants and the restaurants on Fisherman's Wharf, so he became friends with their owners. He was particularly close to the Fisherman's Grotto #9 owners and a Chinese lady who owned a restaurant in Daly City. Every time he visited her, she gave him cartons of the most delicious food: jumbo shrimp, noodles with chop suey on top, and other delicious containers of food. When he came home from his visits to Fisherman's Wharf, we inevitably had a superior lobster thermidor with a creamy white crust with mushrooms. We never wanted for good food, but some meals were nothing special with a few exceptions. Mom's specialty was creamed tuna with peas on toast and salmon croquets. My favorites were the cream tuna and her meat loaf. She really did not like to cook, but when she put her mind to it, she was a great cook.

The first time we ate at a drive-in restaurant was when Dad drove us out to Ocean Avenue to order hamburgers and milk shakes at Tick Tock. My sister and I were sitting in the back seat, and a girl on roller skates took our order. The hamburger and milk shake tasted like nothing I had ever tasted before. The food back then tasted fresher because it contained fewer additives. I never ate processed food. The cakes were made with fresh ingredients and butter, not margarine.

Discipline Cured the Wild Child

After moving to the Sunset District, my parents enrolled me in Holy Name Grammar School even though I was not a Catholic. I could walk to school each day as we lived only four blocks away. My parents thought that I would get a better education, and perhaps some needed discipline by the Sisters of Mercy, since I was a wild child in public school. It must have worked because I eventually received a certificate of merit that read, "This certifies that Barry Sullivan by reason of Regular and Punctual Attendance, Well Prepared Lessons and Good Behavior, is ranked among the Honor Pupils of the Month," which may have been the only certificate I received, as I was not especially good academically at Holy Name.

Red-Face Period From Embarrassment

Shortly after enrolling at Holy Name, our class was attending Mass in the church, and when all my classmates got up to take Holy Communion, I also got up and started up the aisle. One of the nuns quickly stopped me and told me I could not receive communion as I was not a Catholic. I felt so humiliated and embarrassed. I wished they had informed me earlier of the rules, since I had yet to be baptized. That was to be the beginning of my red-face period.

Neatness Used as Security

Holy Name had a dress code to give us a common look. I was happy to wear a uniform because it made it much easier to dress for school, and it stopped any cruel comparison between those kids who could dress well, and the others who were not as cool. My sister was the messiest in our family. She would come home and toss her uniform all over her bed, while I, "Master Neat," emptied my pockets and placed everything in a precise order on my dresser. First, my wallet was placed on the top left side of the dresser and my neatly folded handkerchief placed next to the wallet, followed by my change and keys. I then hung up my pants and shirt, and changed into my play clothes. I could always tell if someone had been inside my room and messed with my stuff, because everything was in a specific place in a particular order. One day I discovered Mom had opened a box and found some risqué French postcards I thought I had hidden – so much for my privacy.

The Catholic nuns in San Francisco were always revered for their historic service during the April 1906 Earthquake. Anytime a nun dressed in her habit boarded a bus or streetcar, they got on for free. However, my earliest Holy Name classroom memory involved Sister Mary Veronica, my fifth-grade teacher. She, like most of the Sisters of Mercy, was a good teacher and a stern disciplinarian. We had to behave or else we felt the wrath of her "magic wand." Sister used a round wooden pointer, one like the classroom American flagstick, to crack our knuckles or palms when we were disobedient. Like most of the nuns and priests, she was old-school Irish. Father Ryan was the pastor and rather stern, but Father Patrick Keane and Father William "Bill" McGuire were just good guys. Father McGuire was the most interesting of all the priests, and a good friend to my parents. He came from a wealthy family and was quite handsome. He arrived at our home driving his new red Ford Thunderbird (T-Bird) sports car with porthole windows. We often wondered why he was a priest since he could have been a movie star. He was in his 40s, tall, ruggedly handsome with premature whitish hair. He once dated actress Lana Turner when she lived in San Francisco, and according to my sister, he had a screen test with Judy Garland.

Priests Can Be Human and Superhuman

I was shocked one evening while eating dinner in the dining room when Father McGuire used a swear word. He said, "Damn!" I had never heard a priest use that word. Those were the days when certain words were considered naughty. We just did not say them. Several years later Dad and Father McGuire went on a gambling trip to Reno. It was snowing heavily, and on their return they encountered a bus that had driven over a cliff. It was icy, cold, and windy, but they got out of their car, stopped the cars behind them, and formed a human chain to assist those trapped over the side. It was no big deal to them. That was the honorable thing to do, and I really respected both of them for their heroic act.

Perfect Time to Die

When I was 10 and my sister was eight years old, my parents finally agreed to have Nancy and me baptized. We could not stop giggling when the priest spoke Latin, but we made it through the ritual and were now certified Roman Catholics. Mom was baptized soon after us. I quickly learned to love the Latin Mass. I loved the ritual, the Gregorian chants, Holy Communion, and the confessional. After confessing my sins like swearing and having impure thoughts, the priest usually required me to say 10 Our Fathers (Lord's Prayer) and 10 Hail Marys for my penance. Sometimes leaving the church I could not help but wonder if it was a good time to get hit by a car, since I would instantly go to heaven having just been absolved of all my sins.

Sneaking Sips of the Sacramental Wine

I took my religion seriously and became an altar boy. I learned how to assist the priest before Mass and recite all the necessary Latin during Mass. As altar boys, we arrived at the sanctuary wearing proper pants and shoes. We changed into our black cassocks and white surplices, and then lit the altar candles, and occasionally even helped the priest on with his vestments. We made sure the sweet sacramental wine was ready for the chalice, and if the priest was pre-occupied, we sometimes snuck a sip of the generally sweet and sticky wine.

As the priest performed the service, we answered his prayers in Latin. We assisted him when he gave Holy Communion by holding the gold paten under the chin of the communicants to catch the host (thin, round, unleavened bread wafer) if it should fall. Before the Church changed some of the customs of the Latin Mass, the host was considered so sacred only the priest was allowed to handle it, and it should never fall on the floor because it was the body of Jesus Christ and the blessed wine was his blood.

When the Mass was over, the priest said, *"Dominus vobiscum"* (The Lord be with you) and we answered, *"Et cum spiritu tuo"* (And with your spirit).

No Place for Bosoms at Church

The one ceremony that frustrated me the most and caused me some embarrassment was when I carried the cross during the Friday service of The Stations of the Cross. The Stations depicted the path Christ took on his way to his crucifixion. I carried a metal cross and walked by the priest, going from station to station that hung on the church walls depicting Christ's journey. We stopped, said some prayers, and continued on. My heart began to race as we approached the picture of Christ being taken down from the cross. When the priest said, "And they took Jesus down from the cross and placed him on Mary's *bosom,*" I instantly turned 50 shades of red. "Bosom" for some reason terribly embarrassed me.

Appearance Does Not Win Awards

Besides being an altar boy at Holy Name, my friend Frank Glynn and I decided to become traffic boys. We had the responsibility at an early age of standing at the school intersections to stop traffic and watch out for the kids as they crossed the street. We wore our traffic boy "uniform," a "Sam Browne" style white web traffic belt across our waist and secured with a belt over our shoulder and across our chest. We also wore General Eisenhower "Ike" garrison style military caps. It was fun stopping the occasional car and waving the girls across the street. And if we were good at our job, we were rewarded with a trip to the yearly Traffic Boy Review and Parade at either Kezar or the Polo Field in Golden Gate Park. All the grammar schools in San Francisco assembled on the field and marched around like professional soldiers on parade. Bands played, banners waved, and sometimes City Hall dignitaries attended, along with all the families. We may not have won any awards, but the Catholic school kids seemed to look sharper than the public school kids, which only went to show that appearance is not the most important thing in life.

Speaking English Important to Immigrant Assimilation

In 1950 when I was nine years old, a new boy entered Holy Name. He was a German, and he wore lederhosen. We had never seen anyone before dressed in short pants, stockings, and a white shirt with suspenders, and he did not speak one word of English. Some kids teased him because of his accent and others because he came from a country we had just defeated in the war. The nuns were kind to him, but they did not baby him. They made him sit in every class, and he learned English simply by listening, studying, and talking to his classmates. When he graduated from Holy Name, he spoke good English but with an accent. It was a time when people who came to America were expected to learn and speak English. That may be why they had an easier time assimilating into our culture.

Good Manners and No Pampering

Kids were not pampered at home or at school. Parents taught their children good manners and teachers could administer corporal punishment. We were taught to say "please," "thank you," and "you're welcome." We were taught to open doors to let the person behind us go in first, especially women, and Mom was a stickler especially for good table manners. She made sure we used the proper utensils and did not slurp our soup or talk with our mouth full. Once, while eating dinner, I reached across the table to pick up the butter tray. Mom quickly cracked my knuckles with the back of her table knife. "Don't ever do that again. Next time ask please pass the butter." She had a way of pursing her lips tightly and casting a stare that went right through me. But I appreciated her for raising me with good manners and for not cutting my knuckles.

Part of the Sunset in the 1950s was still undeveloped. Our house was only a block away from the sand dunes, which later housed A.P. Giannini Middle School on Ortega Street off 39th Avenue and Saint Ignatius High School on 37th Avenue off Quintara Street, which were both just a block away from us. The former was named after the Bank of America founder and the later after Saint Ignatius of Loyola, a 16th century Spanish Basque priest who founded the Society of Jesus – the Jesuits. A few years late, my first visit to A.P. Giannini was to get a polio vaccination. Doctor Jonas Salk created the vaccine in 1953, which was a major discovery since parents dreaded the idea of having a child end up in an iron lung. I hated going to the doctor or the dentist because the needles always seemed so big and long, but the visit to the dentist was always the most traumatic.

Stoned on Laughing Gas

During my years at Holy Name, I had two dentists – one was in the neighborhood and one was downtown. My neighborhood dentist ran his business out of his garage around 42nd Avenue and Kirkham Street. He did not use novocaine; he used laughing gas. He placed the mask over my nose and mouth, and I was lulled into happy land. Little did I know that when I walked back to school I was one stoned 7th grader. My dentist downtown was at the landmark Phelan Building on Market Street off Grant Avenue. After one visit Mom took me across the street to the Pig & Whistle Restaurant. It was a great experience for children because the walls were covered with murals of the Three Little Pigs prancing about, playing their flutes and whistles. Unfortunately, during our meal, I took a bite of spinach (Popeye's favorite vegetable) and crunched a large piece of my new silver filling. Mom was pissed, and to this day, I still have a hard time eating spinach without an image of crunching pieces of filling.

Dad believed in putting me to work at an early age. During my years in grammar school, I was a paperboy for all three of the San Francisco newspapers. I delivered the *S.F. Chronicle* while it was still dark in the morning. The papers were delivered to a corner where I began my route. There were two ways to fold the papers. One was the tomahawk method and the other was the easier fold over method. I then packed the papers into the front and back of my canvas delivery bag, which hung over my shoulders. I liked the tomahawk method the best because it made the paper easier to toss to the front doors. I prided myself on making my toss as close to the door as possible. It was also my responsibility to collect the monthly subscriptions. I never had any problems collecting.

Whenever I had a *"Chron"* left over, I always checked out Herb Caen's column "It's News to Me." He was the ultimate San Francisco insider, knowing every politician, bar owner, sports figure, and character in the City. He championed the multiculturalism of the City and never wanted for a free drink. If your name, bar or restaurant appeared in his column, you got some great free publicity. He not only wrote about the latest gossip but occasionally he said something pragmatic like "A good column is one that sells papers. It doesn't matter how beautifully it is written and how much you admire the author…if it doesn't sell any papers, it's not a good column." The implication was that you should be a person based on substance over appearance, real over phony, and action over talk.

Working for a Celebrity

I later got an afternoon paper route in the early 1950s, which turned out to be quite memorable. I would go to the paper shack around 42nd Avenue and Judah Street to pick up my papers from the paper master, who was a U.S. Marine Corps veteran. He had served in the South Pacific and saw action on Guadalcanal and Tarawa. His name was Leon Uris and he was writing a book entitled *Battle Cry*. There was a rumor that he was using some of our names as his characters, but I did not end up in his novel. The book became a sensation because of its realistic portrayal of the Marines. When the movie came out, it was the first time anyone had given the middle finger salute on film. Of course, after the publication of *Battle Cry* he was no longer our paper master. He became one of the most popular and prolific writers of his generation, from *Exodus* to *The Haj* to *Topaz* and his books became successful movies. He was a no-nonsense guy, but I never had any problems with him nor he with me.

Most Fun Job for Kids

My most fun job was working at Kezar. Sometimes after the games my friends and I collected cushions and returned them for 50 cents each. We could make up to $30 if we really worked fast. There was one game where I was too excited to pick up many cushions. There was a brutal fight that broke out between the Philadelphia Eagles and the Forty Niners at the 1953 season opener. There was bad blood between these teams in the past, and during the game, Niners linebacker Hardy "The Hatchet" Brown, known as one of the 10 meanest defensive players in league history, flattened an Eagles running back in the game with one of his infamous shoulder tackles, causing him to leave the game with a broken cheekbone. In the third quarter, an Eagles receiver picked a fight with Niners defensive end Charlie Powell. During the ensuing melee, the Niners 1952 Rookie of the Year Hugh McElhenny was attacked by a couple of helmet-swinging Eagles. The benches cleared and notoriously rowdy Niner fans stormed the field to defend their team. After 15 minutes, order was restored when the Niner band played the National Anthem. [36]

During the 7th grade, I had a loving crush on my classmate Wendy Nelder, who was as cute as a button. She was socially active, an excellent swimmer, and one of the most popular girls at Holy Name. She lived two blocks away from me on 39th Avenue. Wendy eventually followed in her father's political footsteps, became an attorney, and later a member of the San Francisco Board of Supervisors. Among her other accomplishments, she introduced legislation that protected the environment for non-smokers.

In the 1940s and 1950s nearly everybody was smoking. Mom smoked Camels and Dad smoked Lucky Strikes. My sister and I hated to use the bathroom after Dad had spent some time on the throne, because the room smelled of smoke and poop. Complaining was useless. We had a neighbor who lived across the street. She smelled so bad of smoke that when she opened her front door, no amount of mints, gum, or mouthwash could stem the stench of her breath. It was overwhelming and disgusting.

When Harry S. Truman ran for the U.S. presidency in the 1940s, his opponents chanted "L.S.M.F.T" that meant "Lord Save Me From Truman." This chant was a take off on the Lucky Strike commercial slogan: "Lucky Strike Means Fine Tobacco." Mom was a big supporter of Truman, and when he was elected, he sent her a "personal" letter thanking her for actively supporting him. Dad was not a Truman supporter so he got a kick out of using the Truman version of "L.S.M.F.T." He enjoyed teasing Mom, which sometimes did not end well.

As for Wendy Nelder, I do not believe she ever knew I had a crush on her. I was too shy to approach her even at Holy Name dance classes. One day after class I was walking up the stairs to our house, Mom opened the front door and asked me, "What's wrong?" I was blushing and blathering how difficult it was for me to dance with girls, and all she could say was "You're too sensitive!" Truer words were never spoken, but Mom was not

240

very helpful. With time I became a very good dancer, but I still had the problem of blushing.

Elmer Fudd Speech Impediment

I also had a speech impediment. I sometimes sounded like the cartoon character Elmer Fudd. "Kill the wabbit, kill the wabbit." Actually, my impediment was not that bad, but I had a hard time saying words like "wolf," because I dropped the "l" and it came out "woof." So Mom took me to a convent in a Victorian mansion in the upscale neighborhood of Pacific Heights where some nuns worked on my speech. Strangers still asked me if I came from Boston or New York, so I never lost the San Francisco accent that sounded like I came from the East Coast.

Escaping Unpleasant Dinner Experiences

Two subjects were never discussed at the dinner table: religion and politics. It was considered bad taste to ever bring up either of the subjects, particularly with guests at the table. Most conversations centered on school and friends. Mom knew I had a crush on Wendy Nelder but she did not push talking about her. Dad, however, always had a way of making dinner uncomfortable. He liked to needle Mom, and they had too many unnecessary arguments that made dinner an unpleasant experience. Nancy and I learned to eat fast and excuse ourselves. We rarely played together, but we were both on the same page when it came to our parents.

Getting to a Mother's Heart

San Francisco in the 1950s was still a magical city. Whenever Nancy and I went downtown with our parents we had to dress-up. Dad wore a suit and tie, and sometimes a fedora hat. He had a beautiful head of black wavy hair, a handsome face, the body of a tough fighter, and a nose that had been broken several times. He was 5'10" and 230 pounds – the reason we called him "Big Jim." Mom was a good-looking redheaded lady with green eyes, 90 pounds and 5'2" – the reason we affectionately called her "Lil Midge." She was a spunky, feisty, fun-loving, warm-hearted woman who loved her children deeply and always supported us. I know I got my "wild kid" high-energy from her. She always dressed like a fashion model, and she would light up when I told her how great she looked.

Market Street and Union Square provided a multitude of stores for the upscale shoppers and the middle class alike. The very popular Emporium was right across the street from the Powell Street cable car turnaround. It was a massive department store with a high glass ceiling, 110 feet above street level. The locals referred to the Emporium as "The Big E." And every Christmas the roof top was turned into a small carnival with various rides, a Ferris wheel, a little train, and a jovial Santa Claus for the children.

During the Christmas season the City was ablaze with lights. Colorful lights were strung across Market Street along the two-mile stretch from Van Ness Avenue to the Ferry Building. People went downtown just to enter the stores and view their massive decorated trees. The store exteriors were decorated with lights, and in the window was a tree with presents underneath and sometimes a nativity scene. Union Square, the center of many of the upscale stores, had a 40-foot-tall Christmas tree and a large nativity scene. There was never any pressure in the stores to buy anything. In those days the Christmas spirit thrived in San Francisco.

Closet Hunting for Christmas Gifts

Christmas at our home was always special. A few weeks before Christmas we spent hours decorating the tree with ornaments, lights, tinsel, and an angel on top. I loved the smell of our tree. Underneath the tree we had a nativity scene and piles of presents. Mom really loved Christmas and she loved buying us lots of presents. I was sometimes an impatient and sneaky child. I hunted for presents in closets, in drawers, under beds, and anywhere I thought I might find one. Once I even took a knife and slit open the wrapping paper to see the contents. I suspect they knew because I did not do a very good job of re-taping it.

We opened our presents on Christmas Eve and then went to midnight Mass at Holy Name. In the morning we unpacked our big red stockings with our names sewn on their side. The stockings hung on the mantle and were filled with small gifts, candy canes, and fruit. After breakfast we prepared for our annual trip to Grandma's across the Bay in Alameda. Dad often complained Mom was always in a hurry because she wanted to be the first one to arrive. I suspect she did not want to miss any gossip, or if anyone said something about her. Being such a fashionable lady, Mom wanted to be the best dressed, and she always was. I believe she was my grandfather's favorite, but I do not think Grandma liked her as much as her other children. It might have been a simple case of jealousy.

The trip across the Bay Bridge at Christmas was the only time we visited the East Bay. In those days native San Franciscans considered the East Bay to be, as Gertrude Stein said about her hometown of Oakland, "There is no there there." And we made no distinction between Oakland and Alameda because they were only two miles apart. The East Bay was the East Bay and not our beautiful San Francisco. Besides, the Bay Bridge could never compare to "our" Golden Gate Bridge.

Grandma originally came from Nova Scotia in 1909 to Arizona, then settled in San Francisco. When she, Hazel Fraser, met and married Edwin Nicol, they bought a cozy two-bedroom house in Alameda on Santa Clara Avenue. Grandma was a no-nonsense-woman who regaled us with tales of Clan Fraser and our notorious Scottish ancestor Simon Fraser, known as Lord Lovat, nicknamed "The Fox." Simon Fraser was a Jacobite who supported Bonnie Prince Charlie and the Stuart claim to the throne. Simon, unfortunately, became the last of the British Peerage to be executed for high treason and was beheaded in 1747 at age 80.

My grandfather, Edwin Nicol worked the graveyard shift as a security guard for International Harvester. Every morning when he returned from work, he hung up his holster in a closet off the kitchen. All the grand kids were sternly forbidden to play with the gun, and nobody ever did. I think Grandpa was born and raised in San Francisco, but we knew very little about his life because Grandma dominated everything. I loved Grandpa. He was a kind man. Grandma, however, was as tough as nails, and her six children, particularly Mom, always wanted to please her.

Living Under an Alias All My Life

I never knew my grandparents on my father's side, and we were never quite certain of our heritage. In the late 1950s, my parents received a strange visitor. He was a colonel in the French Army, perhaps the Foreign

Legion, who claimed my father had property in Lebanon. Nothing ever came from it, but we did learn that our real name was not Sullivan but was a derivative of Suleiman. When immigrants from other countries entered Ellis Island, the Irish agents changed the immigrants' ethnic names to a more English/Irish name. All my life I never identified with the Irish, but with the Scots, since we knew so very little about Dad's side of the family. I definitely took after my mother's Scottish side of the family. I later thought that families should research their family tree to find the heroes and colorful characters in their family line like Simon Fraser "The Fox" so kids could take pride in their family name and history.

My grandparents on Mom's side had six children – five girls and one boy. One daughter, Phyllis, married Jack Gerkensmeyer, the lead artist and famous cartoonist for the *San Francisco Examiner* and illustrator for the book *San Francisco Say It Isn't So*. Years later we learned Uncle Jack had been an orphan and was raised at St. Vincent's School for Boys in San Rafael. He was a great family man and beloved by everyone. Another daughter, Virginia, married Ken Robertson, a senior executive with the Standard Oil Company. Their only son Doug, even as a child, was a born entrepreneur. He was the kind of kid who set up a lemonade stand and had a great sales pitch. Often his customers bought an extra glass because he was so persuasive. After he graduated from the University of Southern California and worked in radio, he ran his own advertising agency that did the advertising for Tower Records, founded by his friend Russ Solomon. Doug also owned five percent of five of their retail stores.

Just Ask – Works 50% of the Time

Doug lived in Sacramento and became a promoter of many rock concerts. In the early 1960s when the Rolling Stones were on their first American tour, Doug booked them as the second act to The Turtles. He picked them up at the airport, and as they drove to the motel, he said two of the Stones were kissing and acting up in the back seat as if trying to shock him. When their gig was over, and he picked them up at their motel, he said their room was a mess. It looked as if they had a Chinese food fight since the walls were covered with noodles. I loved my cousin Doug. His motto was "It's an asking world." So, with that in mind, he was never afraid to ask for an upgrade at a hotel or first class on an airplane. "All they can say is yes or no." For him, the odds were 50/50, and he usually got what he wanted – the better room, the better seat on the airplane.

So, with 14 adults and 15 cousins, Christmas at Grandma's was a very active event. The boys were expected to play, and the girls were expected to help in the kitchen with serving food and cleaning the dishes. The ladies chatted and helped, and the men told jokes and played poker for nickels and dimes. When my sister was about 13 she decided she had enough of working in the kitchen, so she pulled up a chair and decided to play poker with the men, and they loved it.

The dining room table at Christmas was filled with goodies: cinnamon walnuts, creamy fudge, Toll House cookies, pickles, olives, and celery sticks stuffed with cheddar cheese. The parents sometimes had a hard time calming down the kids as we placed 10 big seedless black olives on our fingertips and ran around acting like monsters. After the turkey dinner, Grandma brought out a big grab bag and we all picked a present and opened it. The gifts were usually small and simple things like shampoo, notebooks, cards, pens, puzzle books, and cosmetics. Then the trading began. If we did not like our gift, we traded with someone else.

Learn From Parent's Traits and Habits

Just as Mom wanted to be the first to arrive at Grandma's, she also wanted to be the last to leave, which always frustrated Dad. Inevitably, he ended up complaining all the way home. Dad always complained about almost everything, which led to numerous arguments between my parents. Sometimes their arguments even got physical. Once my parents were screaming and pushing each other as Dad was attempting to leave home. Nancy and I were still in grammar school and we were shocked. We were crying and pulling Dad's legs to keep him from leaving, but he stormed out anyway. Unfortunately, I have just as many painful memories of my childhood, as I do fond memories. Perhaps that was one reason I left home at age 17 and joined the U.S. Air Force, but I still have lots of very fond memories. I inherited some of Dad's complaining nature starting with my stories in the university school paper, articles to the editor and verbal comments about the government. Dad became an enthusiastic contributor to Letters to the Editor, and I later followed in his footsteps. As the adage goes "The apple never falls far from the tree." As kids, maybe we needed to look in the mirror frequently and ask ourselves what we liked most and least about each parent. Then make up our mind which traits and habits we wanted to develop and emulate and which to avoid, remembering that it takes practice, practice, practice.

Dad was always great with kids, and the neighborhood children loved him. Unfortunately, I believe he got along better with other children than his own. He was wonderful when Nancy and I were small, but as we grew up, he changed. I believed he resented the attention Mom paid to us and we became the wedge in their relationship. I really thought he was jealous of us. Mom, unfortunately, was a master of manipulation.

Generosity Stemmed From Hard Times

Dad did his best to be a good father and person. One day while we were playing a round of golf at the nine-hole course in Golden Gate Park, a down-and-out man approached us with some golf balls to sell. The man showed us the balls and Dad took one, examined it carefully, and gave the guy some money. He did not shun him; he treated him with respect. It was obvious the guy had been roaming the course and picking up lost balls, and if spotted, he would have been chased away. I was moved by Dad's compassion, and I cannot help but wonder how he must have suffered through his childhood during the Great Depression in Kentucky. Those experiences made him such a generous person as an adult. I think that was true with kids I knew who were raised in families that were just getting by. Kids learned to appreciate what little they had and were motivated to make a better life for themself, their spouses and children.

Good Business to Be Generous

Another time Dad gave me some good advice when we visited a local ice cream shop that had a big owl sign and was called Hoo's on Judah Street at 28th Avenue. They usually gave us a huge scoop for 25 cents and then dipped it in chocolate. But this time the boy gave me a very small scoop. Outside my dad said, "Never do that. If you ever work in a job where you're serving customers, do not skimp. You'll lose a customer by being cheap. Be generous and they'll come back."

One of my favorite stores was F. W. Woolworth, the famous five and dime on the corner of Powell and Market Streets. The store opened in 1906 so it had the feel of old San Francisco with its wooden floors and long rows of glass cases. The candy case contained every kind of sweet imaginable, but my favorite was the large blocks of milk chocolate. The clerk took an ice pick and chipped off a hunk or two, weighed it, and put it in a paper bag. There was a soda fountain where I could order lunch or pizza, but my favorite food was the Woolworth Hoagie. It was a sandwich on a long soft roll filled with turkey, ham, salami, cheese, and some kind of dressing. It had a taste all its own, and I never tasted any sandwich that came close to that delicious Hoagie.

Independence Led to Best of Times

Although I had some painful childhood family memories growing up in San Francisco during the 1940s and 1950s, I was blessed to have experienced the best of the City. It was a time when kids could go out on their own and roam around to explore and play in the neighborhood and farther if they had bikes. We played touch football, tossed baseballs, and built underground forts in the sand dunes. And during the housing boom that was going on in the neighborhood, we explored the partly finished buildings with the smell of new wood and sometimes jumped out of the second story windows into the sand. I once landed on a broken Coke bottle and ripped open my right knee. I still have the scar to show for it. In those days we did not wear helmets or kneepads, and when we hurt ourselves we just got up and carried on. Nobody ever thought of treating an accident as a means to a lawsuit. We took blame for our mistakes and did not look for others to blame. That's just the way it was.

I loved watching the 1958 movie *Vertigo* with James Stewart and Kim Novak over the years because it brought back so many fond childhood memories as Stewart followed Novak all over the City including Ernie's Restaurant, Mission Dolores, the Palace of the Legion of Honor and Fort Point. Kids growing up in San Francisco, where so many movies were made, uniquely experienced the blessing of reliving our childhood and experiences whenever we watched those movies over our lifetime.

Some of my friends really loved *The Three Stooges*, but I was not a fan. I found Larry, Moe, and Curly and their overly aggressive slapstick antics to be just a tad too hostile, but to each his own. I did, however, love some of the Abbott and Costello movies. I saw the 1948 movie *Abbott and Costello Meet Frankenstein* at the age of seven. When Frankenstein first appeared on the screen, a friend and I both jumped out of our seats and ran screaming hysterically up the aisle and into the lobby. We were laughing our asses off, so we were not that scared. In the lobby we could buy popcorn, candy, and the usual treats. Some theaters poured Coke or orange soda into a paper cup with a wooden stick and then froze them. They were delicious.

The only movie I saw with Dad was the 1951 film *The African Queen* with Humphrey Bogart and Katharine Hepburn. I was only 10 when we saw this movie and there was one scene that really disturbed me. After Bogart got out of the stinking water while trying to push his boat through the muck, most of his body was covered with black slimy leeches. As Hepburn helped him remove the filthy creatures, I squirmed, and Dad made a point to remind me "Son, I always want you to remember that when you watch a movie it is not real. Remember, there are always people with cameras standing in front of the actors filming them. It's make-believe." As an eventual movie aficionado, I often forgot his sound advice.

I found the museums educational and thrilling as well, but nothing could compare to the thrills we received when visiting Chinatown. San Francisco's Chinatown was the largest American congregation of the Chinese outside of China, It was a mysterious and exciting area for kids to visit. From the Chinatown entrance (now Dragon Gate) on Grant Avenue to Broadway and Columbus Avenue, both sides of the street were filled with every kind of Chinese store: butcher shops with ducks and chickens hanging from hooks, fish tanks with carps and sea anemones, stores with trinkets, jade jewelry, statues, incense, red lanterns, exotic gowns, tea shops, and restaurants. But my favorite shop was Wing Ducks situated on the east side of the street a couple of blocks from the China Gate.

Safari Into an Illegal World

As grammar school and high school kids, Wing Ducks was our safari into the illegal world of fireworks. The shop fronted as a small grocery store, but beneath the facade was a cellar filled with every kind of illegal celebratory explosive. One-time my friends Terry Quinlan, Gerry Hipps and I were escorted down the stairs to a secret room in the cellar by a clerk who could hardly speak English. The room was covered from wall to wall with the most beautiful display of fireworks. The Red Devil firecrackers and cherry bombs came in pastel packages of pink, lime, red, yellow, and green with exotic labels. The labels were works of art – beautiful Chinese women dressed in long gowns, tigers, lions, birds of prey, and fiery dragons, all surrounded by Chinese symbols. The labels were exquisite. The clerk put our contraband in large brown paper bags, and when we left the store, we looked around to make sure the cops or FBI were not following us. We really did feel like we were criminals and we hugged our bags until we hopped on the streetcar to take us home.

Age 13: I Am Those Around Me (continued)

Life With My "Second Parents"

Barry was more than just a "brother" to pal around with, but to live with, as I spent so much time at his house throughout 8th grade and high school. He once said, "For teenagers growing up in the 1950s, San Francisco was beyond exciting." There was no one I would rather have "lived with" and experienced the excitement during those years than Barry. His parents became my "second parents." Initially, I had been going over Barry's house on occasion to watch television, so I got to know his parents Doris and Jim a little.

Key to Successful Speaking: Know Nothing About the Subject

The Holy Name Women's Group asked our teacher to pick three kids to give a short presentation at their next meeting – one on the married life, one on the religious life, and one on the professional life. I was picked to speak on the married life – stuff like why people got married, where babies came from, and what married life was like. What did I know about such things? My experiences revolved around a mother who was gone during the day and a father who was gone at night with their jobs. I should have interviewed Mom and Dad, but I did not. I just made things up in my head. Doris, who heard my talk at the meeting, must have told Jim about it and he called my mom to see if it was alright for me to make the speech for the school's Men's Group. Jim must have said how much the women laughed and enjoyed it, but Mom must have felt that they were laughing at me because she was really against me doing it for the men. Jim must have worked on her and finally she left it up to me. I agreed to do it in spite of my fear of speaking in front of people, but there was nothing to prepare and I wanted to do it for Jim and Doris. I gave the speech again and remember the men laughing a lot. Afterwards, Jim asked if I had written down the speech, and I told him I had not, so the speech was probably different in some ways. In the speech I gave a distorted image of parental responsibilities at home, a very naive version of how couples had babies and where they came from ("stork" may have been mentioned). Years later

I realized that no one was laughing at me but just enjoying the innocence of a very young, naïve kid talking about something he knew nothing about. I was glad I did the speeches as they gave people a memorable experience. My teacher also announced in class that the Men's Group had requested me to do my speech again, which made me proud to be singled out.

Barry came to our house occasionally, but not nearly as often as I was at his house. As he recollected, "Sometimes I went to breakfast at Terry's house and his mom cooked the traditional Irish breakfast of eggs, bacon, blood sausage, fried chopped onions, tomatoes and toast. It smelled great and tasted even better. I never got close to Terry's dad because he was so quiet and seldom spoke around me."

I spent a lot of time over Barry's house, often watching television programs in the afternoon that became a ritual through high school. The Sullivan's had recently bought their first television set, which was a brown RCA with a greenish screen. At the time, important things were being broadcast on radio and television like the House Un-American Activities Committee hearings being held by Senator Joseph McCarthy in Washington, D.C., but current news often went over the heads of us kids or we had no interest as we did not understood the magnitude and danger of what was going on. Instead, Barry and I watched the *Mickey Mouse Club* with emcee Jimmie Dodd in our freshman year and the *American Bandstand* with host Dick Clark in our sophomore year. Another program we occasionally watched was the body builder *Jack LaLanne* fitness program televised from San Francisco on KGO TV. In our freshman year, Jack LaLanne was handcuffed and with a 1,000-pound boat tied to his waist, swam from the south side of Alcatraz to Fisherman's Wharf in only 56 minutes, where he knocked off a dozen one-handed pushups. [37] It seemed like every year he was doing some unusual feat of strength to prove that he was the best body builder around and why we should watch his program. I enjoyed watching him on television with his high energy and enthusiasm for promoting exercise and healthy diets – my kind of guy.

Barry fondly remembered our early television years together. "In the afternoon after school, Terry and I often watched the popular *Howdy Doody Show* starring Buffalo Bob Smith and his puppet, the freckled-faced Howdy Doody. They sang songs and performed skits with Clarabell the Clown acting crazy and honking his horn. Walt Disney's *The Mickey Mouse Club* was another one of our popular afternoon programs. We were 14 when the show first appeared in 1955. I enjoyed watching the kids dance and sing while wearing their Mickey Mouse ears. Annette Funicello was my favorite Mouseketeer, who was about our age and cute as a bug. And it was fun to sing along with their closing number. 'Who's the leader of the club that's made for you and me? M-I-C-K-E-Y--M-O-U-S-E! Hey there, Hi there, Ho there. You're as welcome as can be…'"

"The innocence of *The Mickey Mouse Club* soon passed, and Terry and I wound up watching *The Dick Clark Show*. It was the first television program to showcase the most popular musical groups of the 1950s. Clark had every top performer from Johnny Cash to Sam Cooke, from the Big Bopper to Chuck Berry, from Buddy Holly to Fats Domino. The show did not discriminate. Black artists and white artists, it did not matter. There were so many memorable songs – swinging rock songs to slow dance-up-close songs. It was a most chivalrous era when boys and girls could slow dance to very romantic songs."

Strong Willpower From Saying "No Thank You"

Occasionally, Doris asked me to stay for dinner. At first I always turned down the invitation and said, "No thank you" and gave some lame excuse about my mom expecting me home. I always thought it was like a handout or receiving some form of charity. I came from the Mission, which I always considered a poor part of the City, to the Sunset where people had more and lived better than me. Turning down something offered to me made me feel pride in myself for being able to show people that I did not need it – I could afford my own. How stupid. I was an insecure kid, but I think the ability to turn down things, even desserts, at such an early age led to a strong willpower later in life to control my eating habits to stay thin, to stay focused on projects, and to remain focused on my ambitions.

With time I started staying for dinner at the Sullivan's and watching television with the family until 10:00 p.m. On weekends I often stayed until the *Steve Allen Tonight Show* was over after midnight to keep Doris company, as she always stayed up to watch the late shows after the others went to bed.

By my sophomore year in high school, I was having dinner at the Sullivan's most nights. It was so great sitting down with a family of four others and carrying on conversations. It was a much more sociable family life. At home, Dad never spoke and Mom was so tired after working and standing on her feet all day, then coming home to cook dinner, while Joe and Kathy had married and were long gone. Best of all, the Sullivan's always had a dessert, something that was nonexistent in our house.

Critical to Have Second Parents

The Sullivan's had taken to me as a second son. They even referred to me as their "second son" and to themselves as my "second parents." This was one of the things that influenced my future and me the most while growing up. Barry's mom was 5'2" tall, about the same height as my mom by coincidence. Whether it was true or not, I felt that she loved me as much as her own children. His dad was a big guy. I always thought he looked like, but was better looking than, actor and boxer Max Baer, who was the World Heavyweight Champion during 1934-35. I was always amazed by Jim's uncanny palate at meals to be able to taste a dish, dissect it, and tell us the various ingredients used to make the dish. He filled a huge hole for me as a father while my dad was going through his years of mental and physical problems.

As much as I loved my parents and as hard as they worked at being good caring parents, I was fortunate to have a second pair of parents while growing up. I often wondered how much easier it would have been for kids from other countries like Canas if they had exposure to second parents who understood American values, beliefs, customs and life-style. Life with the Sullivans was huge in molding me into a much better person. They were positive adult role models for me to advance in life socially, career wise and financially. Most importantly, they provided a home where we were constantly communicating. They helped instill confidence in myself by teaching me table manners, social skills, different viewpoints and new ways to think about things. It was a chance for me to talk to adults about adult things, learn from their experiences, and share good times with a family. They taught me things like keeping my elbows off the table when I ate. They gave me advice that I could accept or reject without hurting their feelings, unlike advice from my actual parents who were hurt if I did not accept their ideas and opinions. I am sure this helped me to not depend on others, as I got older, by making more objective decision on my own. Jim occasionally sent me home with a bag full of canned food from work. Barry and Nancy were the brother and sister that I never had at home during my teens. They were both closer to my age and had more things in common with me. More importantly, they were more willing to share their thoughts and ideas with me. That was the major downside of being born six to eight years after Joe and Kathy.

Mom once asked why I spent so much time at the Sullivan's, but I did not have the heart to say it was a stimulating atmosphere compared to her coming home tired from work, having to cook our dinner and wash the dishes, and Dad sitting mute in front of the television with nothing to say. I never begrudged them for their lifestyles. I loved them dearly, but they were living a tougher life under more difficult physical and financial conditions than the Sullivans. The Sullivans were about 20 years younger than my parents – at an age that I never experienced with my own parents because I was born so late in their lives. It was a chance to live with parents when they were younger and living an active life and had the energy to do things with their children. For me, it was like traveling back in time and experiencing an active family life. Not long after that, at a time when I was not showing appreciation for what Mom had done for me, she told me, "When I am gone, you will miss me." I learned later in life that there were never truer words spoken about her and Dad.

Secret to Parenting – Earn Respect of Children

Having a second family was like what happened often in the business world. It took a certain type of person to start up a company and make it successful in the short term over the early years. But it took a different type of person with different skills and experiences to continue the growth of the company over the long term. That was why so many founders of companies were moved aside, if not fired, to make room for the new breed of executives and managers – always a sad situation. At least I had the good fortune to have both sets of parents – one to bring me into the world and nurture me, and the other to develop me. I never felt I was a good son to my actual parents – certainly worse than they deserved. I was a much better "son" to the Sullivans – probably due to what they brought to the table in "raising me." I suppose the basic difference was that I had a different respect for the Sullivans. I respected Mom for taking charge at home and her hard work. I respected Dad for his fight against alcoholism and his homesickness for Ireland. These were respects for survival, but with the Sullivans, it was a respect for them being role models for my self-improvement. Doris provided me with social skills and Jim provided career and financial skills to succeed in spite of our humble beginnings.

I got to know Barry's relatives at family get-togethers including Doris's mother. I never knew any of my grandparents, but I got to call her "Grandma" like everyone else. That was special because she was such a sweet old lady who took a shine to me too. This expanded my family circle by another 15 or so relatives – sort of like marrying into a large family. One of the bigger than life visitors to the Sullivan's house was the assistant pastor at Holy Name, Father Bill McGuire, who occasionally dropped over to chitchat and have a drink. He had the good looks of a movie star. I always wondered if Doris had a crush on him, as she tended to act like a little girl around him. Of course, that also was probably true of hundreds of other women in the parish. My friend Terry Carmody's dad was a liquor distributor. Father McGuire and the other young priest Father Keane at Holy Name occasionally dropped by Carmody's home to pick up liquor on Sundays when the neighborhood stores were closed. Carmody's mom had several jobs but Terry's favorite, for obvious reasons, was her job at the donut shop around the corner on Judah Street.

Barry Sullivan had become the brother I never had. I grew up with him through high school, while my real brother missed much of my youth while he was in the U.S. Air Force and married shortly afterwards. Barry always reminded me of the movie actor Mickey Rooney as a kid in his hyper personality, energy and appearance. Barry was not as short as Rooney but he was a redhead, showed a lot of teeth, had freckles and a mischievous look on his face.

Barry and I used to sing an excerpt from the song "Harrigan." It all started on St. Patrick's Day in 1954 and we did it regularly when I came over to watch television. Then it became a frequent routine when we were having a few beers. We never did learn more than the first four lines of the lyrics, but that was enough for us. Each time, it was a binding moment that we shared for being Irish. As we grew older as adults, we just sang the first line: "H - A - double R - I - G - A - N spells Harrigan." It was our form of greeting each other just as others used a handshake. It was a reminder of our youth and a friendship that has lasted over seven decades.

No Need to Lie to Real Friends

I was too young to own a car, but I always wanted to own a Vespa motor scooter. They were sleek in style and pea green in color. I think they cost $395. I told Mom and Kathy I wanted to buy one when I saved enough money, but they said I should save that money to buy a car, which I would want in three years when I was old enough to get a driver's license. Three years seemed like an eternity at the time, and I wanted something to impress my new classmates now, none of whom owned anything other than a bicycle. I realized they were right, so I dropped the idea. But I still had to try to impress my new friends so I appeared as good, if not better, than them. I had been going to Holy Name for about a month and during recess one day I told the guys I owned a Vespa motor scooter, but no one believed me. They told me to bring it to school so I could show them. I told them I would bring it by Saturday. I went home and wondered now what am I going to do? I showed up Saturday where five or six of the guys were hanging around and playing basketball. I told them I flipped the scooter Friday and it was not drivable. No one believed me, but I stuck to my story. I learned the lesson never to lie to my buddies. They would like me regardless of my possessions. Material things were not important to them. Friendships were built on who and what you were all about.

Money Less Important Than Friendships

About that same time, Holy Name was having a paper drive to raise money for the school. They were recording the number of pounds of paper contributed by classroom in order to create competition among each class in the school. Stored under the stairs in our garage at home were over 20 years of back issues of National Geographic magazines dating back to the 1920s and 1930s that were left there by the previous owners. No one in the family wanted them, and I so wanted to make some type of impression with my classmates so I was accepted as an outsider from a poorer section of the City. So on Saturday we loaded the Chevy up with the magazines and Mom drove me to the schoolyard. We had to make two trips. When the men who were unloading the cars saw what we brought, they asked if we really wanted to give them away. They said some of them might be worth some money. In hindsight, it would have been smart of me to do some research about them to pull out those that were most collectable, but no one in our family were into collecting things or knew old magazines might be worth something. I said, "Yes, we want to donate them." Even if I knew the potential worth of the collectables, I still would have given them away. It was more important to me to impress my classmates than receive money. Besides, I had a job selling newspapers, which provided spending money for me, but it was my first experience realizing that doing good and showing character were easier to do having money – a reason to make a lot of it in my lifetime.

When School Allowed Copying

One day in class, we were asked to draw anything that we liked. I was a doodler but by no means an artist. If it was going to be anything special, it had to be a mechanical drawing type picture that I could do with a ruler and pencil. I thumbed through our English textbook and found a picture that was almost entirely straight lines. It was a window over a window bench that looked out at a boat on the water. I must admit when it was done, it looked pretty good. The next day, the nun returned our drawings to us with a letter grade, but she held on to mine until the end. She showed the class my drawing as an example of something she thought was special. I sat there so proud that she had praised me but felt so guilty because it was not something from my own imagination. I kept debating whether or not to say something. I finally raised my hand and the nun acknowledged me. I stood up and confessed I copied the picture out of a book. The class laughed and the nun smiled and said it was all right to use pictures in books for ideas. I was so relieved and felt good that I was honest about it.

Money Was More Important Than Embarrassment

Each week, one student in our class was asked to bring a small wreath to crown the Virgin Mary statue that rested on a shelf in the front of the classroom. About two to three months into the school year, it was my turn. All of the previous wreaths appeared to have been created by professional florist. They were made of small flowers, greens and held together by a wire frame. I went to a florist on Irving Street to get a price quote and they wanted five dollars. I was selling newspapers on a corner in the Haight-Ashbury District and made about $1.50 a day. Paying three or four days of my earnings was way too much. Instead, I built my own wreath from wire around the house and some small flowers I picked from the yard. Inserting some greens was beyond my feeble skills. It wound up to be nearly round and looked pretty good, but when I picked it up, the whole thing went limp. I figured if I handed it to the teacher on a stiff surface, maybe she could slide it on the statue's head and it would be all right. As I handed it to the nun, she picked it up, the fragile wreath went limp, and the entire class laughed. It was obvious that it was homemade and not done well. I was so embarrassed, but the nun said, "The Virgin Mary appreciates all wreathes equally well." I felt better and comforted myself by thinking *I got through this and saved myself five dollars.*

Each month students who made the Honor Roll received a small certificate for "regular and punctual attendance, well prepared lessons and good behavior." I made it six out of the nine months. Not sure why I got it six times nor why I did not get it the other three times, but it made me feel special being honored.

For several months Holy Name bused our 8th grade class across town where we took dance lessons at Lakeside Dance Academy on Alemany Boulevard on Fridays for weeks. I had never danced before much less held a girl close to me. The girls enjoyed the classes, but the boys were like fish out of water. The boys stood around on the opposite side of the room from the girls, pretty much the same as school dances later in high school. When I learned from some of the girls at school that Barbara O'Reilly liked me, I would pick her as my partner in dance class. She was one of the prettiest girls in my class – certainly in the top three in my eyes. I could not believe one of the best looking and popular girls would go for me. I was excessively shy and insecure when I was around girls. I never approached good-looking girls to dance even in high school. In addition to our dancing together in class, I did take Barbara to a couple of Holy Name functions. For the first one, I had to call for her at her home on 37th Avenue where I met her parents. They were an attractive couple, but I had no feel whether they liked me or not. I never asked Barbara out on a date until the end of the school year knowing we had to take a bus wherever we went, and my Mom worked during the day, so she could not drive us anywhere. When I finally did ask her out, she said she wanted to go out with older guys now that she would be going to high school. I felt badly. My first really good-looking girlfriend, but I certainly understood. Guys knew girls in high school always tried dating older fellas. The memory of our brief friendship was extended through high school because I had carved our initials in the wood bench at the corner of Kirkham Street and Sunset Boulevard across from her house. As for the dance lessons, the only thing that stuck with me was doing the box step and slowly moving clockwise. It got me through all slow dances for the rest of my life.

Secrets to Getting the Girls

Decades later at a Holy Name 8th grade class reunion, some of the women said some girls in our class had a crush on me. I was stunned because I had such a poor image of myself at that age. I asked why and they said, "Because you were different from the boys they grew up with in their classes. You were unlike so many of the boys with their bravado and cockiness." I guess I was just much more unassuming, shy, unaggressive, quiet and humble – virtues I probably inherited from my dad. I was different and something of a novelty. I hoped that I was cute in some way, but I did not think so. If I only knew then that physical looks, especially with my big ears, mattered so little and that demeanor was so much more important, my confidence in myself may have developed faster. It was certainly not my personality. There was a lesson to be learned here for shy kids of every generation. As for dancing and dating, if in doubt, just go ahead and ask the girl to dance or to go out on a date. If she turns you down, she really was not for you. You only want girls who are attracted to a person with your unique qualities.

Pride is Less Important Than Safety

Some of the girls in class suggested we go horseback riding one weekend. There was a horse stable out by the Zoo where people could rent a horse and go riding along the Beach, down the sides of the Great Highway and throughout Golden Gate Park. There were 10-12 boys and girls who agreed to go, and I said I would go only because some of my buddies were going. When we got to the stables, each kid was asked whether they had been horseback riding before and how experienced we were. I originally assumed all the horses were the same – gentle and slow walkers – but realized I was wrong when we were getting asked all these questions. I did not want to appear weak in front of the girls and wanted to look as good as the other boys, so I told the guy, "Sure, I've ridden horses before." He asked, "How much?" I said, "Quite a bit." After lying, I could not ask about how do I start up, stop or turn the horse, so I tried to hear what the novices were being told. I was so relieved when they brought my horse after all the novice riders got their horses. My horse was good looking, mild mannered and remained perfectly still as I mounted with some help. So far, so good, but I suspected this was going to be different than riding ponies in a circle at the Zoo, which was my only previous experience. It turned out, the horse pretty much just moved with the string of horses across the Great Highway and on to the Beach. The guide from the stables was up front and set the pace, which was just walking along slowly. A few times my horse started to act up as if he wanted to gallop, but he quieted down thank goodness. We went about a mile down the Beach, staying on the soft sand as opposed to out by the ocean where the ground was wet, compact and harder. We turned around and about two-thirds of the way back, I could see a sewer pipe 3 to 4 feet off the ground that extended the full width of the Beach into the ocean. God knows why, my horse broke out into a gallop. I said to myself, "Oh shit!" I was never so scared in my life. All the other horses stayed back and we kept getting closer and closer to the pipe. I had no idea how to ride around the pipe, and I knew I could never get the horse to jump over it, nor would I ever try, even if I knew how. When we were about 40 feet from the pipe, the horse slammed on the brakes and I went flying over his head. Even he had better sense than me. I got up on my feet feeling so foolish. I embarrassed myself in front of everyone, but I suspect they were just relieved I was all right and it did not happen to them. Hopefully, they were blaming the horse and not my incompetence. The rest of the way back to the stable, the guide rode along side holding on to my horse's bridle bit to prevent the horse from acting up. It was the only time I ever went horseback riding for the rest of my life, but I learned a couple of lessons – always tell the truth and pride has consequences.

The 1954 Golden Gate Park Road Race was being held, so I walked over since it was just a few blocks from home. They asked for a one-dollar a head donation for the Guardsmen to send underprivileged kids to camp. About 60 sports cars raced at speeds well over 100 mph along the straightaways. Bales of hay were stacked on the curves to "protect" the tens of thousands of spectators and me. We literally stood on the edge of the roads and inches from the cars speeding by with nothing between them and us. This was the last of the three years this race was held due to complaints from the neighbors and the Society for the Preservation of Golden Gate Park. Like most things, it was fun seeing once, but this sport was way too noisy for me.

I saw my one and only Soap Box Derby Race, which happened to be held in the Sunset. I would never have known about it except Mike Chapman in my class was participating. Mike started participating in the 6th grade. His dad sold Chevrolets, the company sponsoring the Derby, and he was appointed the Derby coordinator that year, so it would not do if his son did not participate. So with help from his dad, Mike built his first coaster that had to meet rigorous specifications especially regarding physical dimensions, weight, steering and braking. Chevrolet provided all of the wheels and steel axles for all of the coasters. On race day, the coasters all parked on Sunset Boulevard between Taraval and Ulloa Streets. Hundreds of spectators came and checked out the cars before the races began. The race was held on Sunset Boulevard between Ulloa and Vicente Streets, which was the steepest block to go down to pick up speed. At the end of the block, the coasters went up another steep hill from Vicente to Wawona Streets to slow them down to a stop. At the top of the hill, a starting launching ramp was temporarily put in place. The ramp added a few degrees of slope to the hill and three coasters at a time were pushed up onto it and gently rolled against a drop gate that held them until drivers were loaded. When the drivers were set, a trip lever was pulled and the coasters began their roll down the hill. Winners of heats were trucked back up the hill and got to run in second heats. Mike placed third in his heat that year. The same happened in his second year when he learned adding more weight to the coaster was not the solution. In his third year, the race I saw, he finished second in a sleeker style coaster that looked great, but in three years, he only beat one car. He never raced again, but he did come across a kid working on his coaster who had won multiple heats. He told Mike the secret was to break in the wheels to get them to roll faster. He showed Mike the electric motor that had been spinning his four derby wheels for the past three months. These coasters were a far cry from the coaster we made in the Mission out of a wood crate, a board, a couple of 2x4s and four ball bearing wheels. I envied the kids competing in these races – lots of proud kids and parents regardless of their standings in the races. It brought a lot of kids and fathers together.

Many of the trees along Sunset Boulevard had large sturdy branches. There was a huge cedar tree at the northeast corner of Lawton Street and Sunset Boulevard that looked climbable with wide spacing between its branches, so I decided to climb it to see what the view looked like. Reaching the top about 60 feet above the ground, there was a clearing where three or four kids could sit and look over the roof tops at the view of the ocean a mile away – a new hideout like the ones I had back in the Mission, except this had a terrific panoramic view. I was moving up in the world. I told a few of my buddies of my new discovery and we made a few visits up and down the tree until one day a gardener saw us. He told us to come down and not to do it again because it was harmful to the tree. That was something I never thought of – another neat hideout hit the dust.

Each year, Holy Name held a picnic for the altar boys. Just so I could get a day off class and attend the picnic, I asked to be an altar boy about a month before the picnic. In order to qualify, I had to serve as an altar boy for at least one Mass, so I learned some Latin and the moves to prepare. On the day of the Mass, I was paired up with Barry as the other altar boy. I was a fish out of water. Things just seemed different than the practice sessions. Barry had to mouth some directions to me and the priest used hand jesters to position me around. I got through it, attended the picnic, and was never asked to serve at another Mass, which was just fine with me. It just was not my thing. However during Holy Week, I did serve as cross bearer at the Holy Thursday and Good Friday evening services, which was no big deal. I just led a parade of participants up to the altar and stood on the sidelines during the services.

It was during the 8th grade that the nuns tried to recruit the boys and girls to be priests and nuns because the religious orders had seminaries and convents starting at the freshman high school level. Even I got called into the hallway during class when there was no one else in the halls and asked by the nun if I ever considered being a priest, because she said, "You would be a good priest." I felt special and thought maybe there was something to her belief about me if it was worth her while to take me away from class time to discuss it with me. I told her I had not thought about it and that was it. There was no pressure; she did not show any disappointment; it was more about planting the idea in my mind to think about it. A number of the popular girls did go to the convent the next school year and some of the popular boys went to the seminary. Most of the guys left before they finished high school, but at least they tried it and could look back without any doubts or regrets.

Stealing Not Worth the Risk

One of the guys in class told me he had built up his mostly jazz record collection by stealing them at a local record store. He offered to show me how easy it was, so we went down and he gathered a bunch of 45 rpm records because they were small and the easiest to hide under his clothing. We took them in a booth where we could play and listen to them. He waited a while, as if he was playing some records, then stuck several in his pants under his belt, shirt and jacket. He convinced me to do the same. I took three 45 rpm records. We walked out, he put the other records back and we left the store, giving the illusion that we played some records, did not like any of them and left. It was certainly easy – too easy. There was no one watching out for shoplifters, but it was not for me. When I got home, I felt so guilty. It was that Catholic education. Even when I was older, my friends kidded "It's your Catholic background" whenever I felt guilty about some minor thing. A couple of days later, I went back to the record store and left the three records for someone to find. It was the last time I shoplifted anything. As easy as it turned out to be, I only needed to get caught once to get in real trouble – the risk was just not worth it.

Sex in the Eighth Grade

This was the same guy in our 8th grade class that supposedly was having sex with a seventh grader. I had never heard of kids having sex. He said they went down to the Beach to some secluded spot. He was boasting she probably would have sex with any of us, but no one took him up on the offer. Besides, we were not sure if he was telling the truth or just bragging, since he knew it was something none of us had ever done.

The San Francisco 49ers played their first NFL season in the City three years earlier. I never thought about the 49ers until I moved to the Sunset. The kids I knew in the Mission could never afford to go to a game nor collect 49er memorabilia. But the kids in the Sunset not only went to games with their dads, but collected football programs for the professional teams and especially college teams. They told me how to write away to the universities and ask for free copies of their football programs mostly from past years. In no time I had quite a collection of my own. If I was lucky, I received copies that included players who made All American teams or went on to play pro ball.

In the Mission, we never played at each other's house. Parents did not want kids underfoot, so they sent us out to the Park. But things were different in the Sunset. The parks and schoolyard were a good walk from where we all lived, so we often played games or watched TV at each other's house. Carmody often watched *Victory at Sea* episodes in the afternoons after school. The only time I ever watched the program was when I dropped by his place. There always seemed to be a sea or land battle going on. His dad was a war veteran and Terry's interest in guns stemmed from a friend of the family who had a house full of guns – the kind of thing that probably fascinated any young kid. Carmody also enjoyed hunting because it allowed him to handle and fire weapons. The combination of these interests had to have contributed to him joining the U.S. Marine Corps after high school, and I joined with him – an example of how early interests of a friend can influence future lives of others.

I played an electric football game for endless hours at Carmody's place and especially at classmates Bill and Phil Diehl's house on the corner of Lawton Street and 37th Avenue. We each owned our own game, but we mostly played with Bill and Phil's set. Each side had 11 metal players on a metal field. Turning on the electricity caused the board to vibrate, which caused the players to move forward. The quarterback had a spring lever that held the football (a small ball of wool). Squeezing the lever projected the miniature football toward the player I was trying to hit for a completion. On running plays, I had to designate who was carrying the ball. A receiver or runner was tackled when a defensive player touched the offensive player.

Carmody and I used to play catch in front of his house with a baseball or football. Sometimes we played two-man (him and me) touch football in the street and were only occasionally interrupted by car traffic. The offensive player with the ball had to toss the football in the air before the other person touched him and was considered tackled as soon as the offensive player caught his own toss and was touched by the defender. The object was to work my way down the street to the designated end zone for a touchdown before four incomplete passes to myself or the ball got intercepted. Although the street was flat in front of Carmody's place, most of the block was a steep slope leading down to Irving Street. Occasionally, the ball got dropped or overthrown and rolled down the hill. The person responsible had to trudge down the hill to recover the ball. If it was no one's fault, we took turns retrieving the ball. We usually stopped playing catch or football immediately after the ball had to be recovered a couple of times.

One of the kids in our class was Jerry Hipps. Barry recalled the day he made a lifetime change in his identity. "One day he got up in front of the class and told us he was changing the spelling of his name Jerry with a 'J' to Gerry with a 'G'. He so admired Jerry Coleman who graduated from Lowell High School and played second base for the New York Yankees – the same position Hipps played on our school team. There always was some confusion if Coleman really did spell his name with a 'G'. His first name was Gerald and his name often appeared as both Gerry and Jerry in baseball articles and on memorabilia. But Hipps did not care. Gerry was his name ever after, so why bother to argue the point."

Barry also remembered "Gerry's dad installed a basketball hoop on the pavement in front of their home. We played many one-on-one games, but unfortunately Gerry had a series of accidents. One day he tripped on the curb and broke his ankle, and he managed to break his ankle three more times before graduating from high school. But breaking ankles was not enough. He got shot with a B.B. in one eye and the doctors thought he might lose his sight. Fortunately, the medical staff at Stanford Hospital used a new laser technique to extract the B.B. and he did not lose the eye."

Celebrities in the Neighborhood

There were a couple of famous athletes living in the Sunset District at the time – Jim Gentile (pronounced Jen-TEEL) played for the Dodgers and Orioles. Carl "Bobo" Olson was the World Middleweight Champion. Barry thought Gentile lived on 33rd Avenue between Moraga and Noriega and Bobo Olson at 34th Avenue and Judah in a flat. Hipps was friends with both Gentile and Olson according to Barry. "Hipps was befriended by Bobo and they ran on the Beach together. He also was close to Gentile and they played pick-up basketball games. Unfortunately for me, I was always doing something else."

Hipps told us Bobo Olson was fighting one night and said we should go over to his family's house that night, which was in Holy Name parish. Bobo Olson, a transplant from Hawaii, was a top contender middleweight boxer in those days. By 1952 his record was 55 wins and six loses. His parents lived a few blocks from us and they always invited all of the neighbors over after any of Bobo's fights. He had just won the World Middleweight Championship. I went with some of the guys and wandered through crowds of people, mostly adults, who seemed to know each other and everyone was having a good time. I picked up a 5" x 7" photo labeled "World's Middleweight Champion" with Bobo in his trunks and boxing stance with his "Mother" tattoo prominently displayed on his left arm, but I did not eat or drink anything. Bobo Olson went on to defend his title October 1953 to December 1955, the longest reign of any champion in that division during the 1950s. It felt special having someone famous living in the neighborhood.

Failure Was the Road to Opportunity

Holy Name was the first school I had attended with organized sports that competed against other schools. Competing against kids who had played on teams all during grammar school was intimidating. Some of my new friends said I should try out for basketball, so I did. The team had lots of good shooters and guys who played organized basketball since the 1ˢᵗ grade. The starters were Hipps and Jim Smith at guard, Bill Nocetti and Chuck Chudzinski at center/forwards, and Brian Cahill and Vince Davis at forward. To say the least, they were very good and went on to win the Catholic League championship that year. Although I was only briefly on the team because I had to work, I never did get to play much, if any, in the games. I was actually sort of glad. I knew I was no good and the last thing I wanted to do was embarrass myself in front of my friends, or worse than that, do something to lose the game. I felt badly about not being good at basketball like my brother. But instead of quitting sports all together like he did in high school, I realized the folly of his decision and turned out to be the opposite. Failure was just an opportunity for me to try again at the same or different activity. The lesson I learned was that if I was not very good at a sport or activity, I probably should not be on the team. If I was not confident in getting the job done, it put too much pressure on me with all my doubts in myself when I was called into the game. I thought of all the parents who pushed their kids into sports that were not on the first or second string. So many of them probably had their stomachs turning the entire time they were sitting on the bench, hoping that they were not put in the game. No kid wanted to do badly or fail in front of their friends, family and a grandstand of spectators. Hopefully with perseverance, they would overcome their fear from doubts about their capabilities to perform.

Carmody, and nearly everyone else, was better than me in basketball thank goodness. There was a Holy Name game that could go either way at the end. We were down by one point. I sat there thinking *please don't send me in.* Instead, Carmody was sent in and immediately got fouled. The opposing coach probably thought *foul a benchwarmer as he will most likely miss the shot, but certainly will not hit both shots, which would at least let us go into overtime.* Carmody stood on the foul line, bounced the ball a few time and shot an underhand free throw like I used. You rarely saw players use underhand free throws. It was considered sort of "nerdy." His first shot went in. I was really impressed. To make a shot under that pressure was somewhat amazing, especially for a second string player. The score was tied. Carmody looked straight ahead, ignoring the mixture of cheering and booing from the stands, stared at the backboard, bounced the ball a few times and took another underhand free throw. Swoosh! He made the second and winning shot. I felt so proud to be his buddy.

Every February over the previous five years, the boy's basketball teams from Holy Name played St. Cecilia's for the annual Pastor's Trophy. There were six weight classes represented: 70s, 80s, 90s, 100s, 110s and 120s. The teams were made up of 7th and 8th graders. Barry was on the 90s, Hipps, Carmody and I were on the 100s, and Applebee was on the 110s. Our coach was 20 years old Jim Gentile who had signed with the Brooklyn Dodgers and was playing professional baseball in their minor league system. The basketball tournament was played at City College of San Francisco gym, which was a big deal. We were used to playing in gyms at grammar schools and city playgrounds. I was praying again in this game that I did not have to go in, especially for such an important game and with the largest crowd ever to attend our games that season. My wish came true. I never got in the game. However, our team did lose and St. Cecelia won the tournament trophy.

Try New Things to Find Your Niche

When baseball season rolled around, my buddies suggested I tryout for the 8th grade baseball team. It was not a real tryout because everyone made the team, just like the basketball team. We just might not play much. I had never played organized baseball, but since I found out that I was not very good at basketball, I thought, *what the heck. At least I would be around my buddies.* I did not even own a glove, other than the crappy glove I got from Dan Fitzgerald, because we never played baseball at Folsom Park other than softball, and that did not require a baseball mitt. So I went to Free-Minetti Sporting Goods Store on Haight Street by Masonic Avenue, a few doors down from where I had been selling papers on the corner. It was the first time I was ever in a sporting goods store, as I never had a reason to shop in one. I did not know what I was looking for, but I found a nice glove that had a bigger pocket than the others – a glove that would make it easier to catch the ball. Another sports store that became a favorite was Hirsch & Price on Sutter Street off Market Street where Joe DiMaggio was known to shop. [38]

We used Big Rec (Big Recreation Ball Fields) for our tryouts and practices. Big Rec was located just inside Golden Gate Park off Lincoln Way between 7th and 9th Avenues. Big Rec was the premiere ballpark for high school, sandlot and semi-pro baseball, so for grammar school kids to play there was something special. That probably was why the coaches chose it rather than use a field at one of the playgrounds that was closer to school. It worked out because the coaches drove us from school to practice and back. There were two diamonds. On the left (west end) there was Big Rec Graham and on the right (east end) was Big Rec Nelson. We never knew their real names. We just called them the "big diamond" and the "small diamond," respectively. Our 8th grade baseball team practiced at the small diamond. The small diamond had spectator stands, just like the big diamond, but the field was not as well maintained – more apt to get funny bounces on the infield. It was the big diamond that was the ultimate field for kids. The stands had five sections with nine rows of seats that wrapped around the infield from first to third bases. When the diamond was not reserved for a game, a sign on the pitchers mound said to stay off the field. The infield was immaculate and maintained by a corps of Golden Gate Park gardeners. The outfield went on forever as there were no fences, and the stands always had a good turnout of fans – some were parents of players but most were just older guys from the area that liked baseball and could see a good game for free, whether they were sandlot, high school or semi-pro teams. We could see it all.

At our first baseball practice, we were told by the coach to go out in the field to the position we wanted to play. Never having played hardball before, I had absolutely no idea if I would be good at any of the positions. I waited on the sideline to see where there was the least competition. First base looked the easiest to me and there was only one player there, but it was Applebee who was a really good athlete, plus his dad was one of the coaches, so I knew I had no chance at first base. There were two or three kids at every other position except centerfield, so I went out there. I did a lot of running around chasing fly balls hit to center. Not having the hang of getting a jump on balls, I made easy plays look hard by diving for balls and catching balls over my shoulder because I misjudged them. It must have worked in my favor because I won the starting centerfield job.

Humility From Not Knowing Better

It turned out that the centerfielder had to cover the most ground, which I did not know at the time. Although I was never beaten in races in grammar school, it never sank in that I was especially fast in running. If someone asked me if I was fast, I would have said, "I don't know." I think most kids, who were special at anything, did not realize it. It was not something they worked at to get that way. It was just the way they were. It was why kids at that age were so humble about themselves. They were just one of the guys – nothing more, nothing less. It was only later in high school and college when the exceptional kids realized they were special in sports, academics, skills and talent as they faced stiffer competition. Anyway, my speed was enough for me to get the job done. If I could get to the ball, I could catch it. No one hit a ball over my head and I never committed a fielding error.

When I came in from the outfield after our first practice, a couple of the guys said I was using a first baseman's glove. When I bought the glove, I just thought it was a neat looking glove, was different than all the other gloves in the store, and might be easier to catch balls with its large pocket. This was one time trying to be different may have been a mistake. I asked the two coaches about it, and they had no problem with me using the glove as long as I could play my position without any problems. I still felt stupid for not knowing better, and I did not want to take the chance of the other guys kidding me about it, so I went back to Free-Minetti and bought another glove and baseball shoes with spikes. I had been running around on damp grass in tennis shoes, slipping and sliding. The two salesmen were really nice guys. They asked what kind of glove I needed and I said, "Anything besides a catcher's mitt and first baseman's glove." I loved the smell of the leather in the glove section. They had all sizes of fielder's gloves and autographed by a star player. I finally picked one that was the smallest glove (7" x 8") with a perfectly formed pocket. It seemed just right for a small kid with small hands. It was made by Rawlings and had a Mike Schmidt signature printed in the pocket. I never heard of Mike Schmidt, but it was the glove itself that was most important to me – not who endorsed it. It turned out that Mike Schmidt was a third baseman who played for the Philadelphia Phillies for 17 years and eventually was inducted into the Baseball Hall of Fame in 1995.

Work to Your Strengths

At batting practice, I saw most kids holding the bat at the bottom against the nub of the bat. I suppose everyone was hoping to hit a home run, but I found it hard to control the swing because so many bats were top heavy. If my wrists were stronger, maybe that would not have been a problem for me. So I choked up with my hands about an inch or two from the nub, depending on the balance of the bat, so I could make a consistent level swing each time. I was just trying to get the ball over the heads of the infielders to get on base. In my first year of playing baseball on the Holy Name 8th grade team, I batted .286 for the season – not outstanding but it was a start.

The assistant coach was Ralph Applebee, Tim's dad, but the head coach was Joe "Mule" Sprinz who was a former catcher for the Cleveland Indians (1930-31) and St. Louis Cardinals (1933). Thirteen years earlier when Joe Sprinz was 37 and a catcher for the San Francisco Seals, he attempted to beat the world's record for catching a baseball dropped from a great height that was set by a member of the 1938 Cleveland Indians. Joe attempted to catch a baseball at 154 miles per hour that was dropped from a blimp 800 feet in the air. It was a stunt performed at the 1939 World Expo on Treasure Island. On the fifth attempt to catch the ball, there were two stories as to what happened – either the ball broke through his mitt and into his face or the ball slammed his glove hand into his face. In either case, he broke his nose and upper jaw in twelve places, fractured five of his teeth, and was rendered unconscious. Although there are mixed views as to whether he caught the ball, the Guinness Book of World Records thought so, since they acknowledge his record for the "World's Highest Catch."

Most Memorable Person Ever Met

Joe Sprinz' son, Leroy, was three years older than us, and he worked out in the outfield shagging flies during some of our practices. "Leroy had polio as a youngster and was left without the use of one of his arms, and though the doctors wanted to amputate the arm, the boy fought to keep it, saying he would figure out a way to live with it." **[39]** He went on to be a teacher and coach at Newark Memorial High School in Newark, CA. Leroy had one arm tied to his side and shagged fly balls by catching the ball with the other hand. He slid the glove and ball under his stump, grabbed the ball from the glove, and fired the ball back to the infield, all in one continuous motion. He was a real inspiration to me, and the most memorable person I ever met. His presence was a "hidden persuader" for me to improvise, adapt and overcome like a good Marine.

That season I learned how to take care of my baseball glove. It was my neighbor Dan Fitzgerald who told me about rubbing down the leather of the entire glove with linseed oil to keep it soft and flexible. He showed me how to create a tighter pocket by pulling and re-knotting the rawhide lacing around the edges of the glove. This pulled all the fingertips of the glove as close together as possible at the top to curl the fingertips inward to complete the pocket. He was the one who got me to keep a baseball in the pocket of the glove and tightly wrap several large rubber bands around the glove, when I was not using the glove, in order to create and maintain a curved pocket the size of the baseball. The glove turned out to be the one I used throughout high school, and by my senior year, I was using the smallest glove on our team that made it to the league championship game. By then everyone else went with larger and longer mitts to make it easier to catch grounders and fly balls. I took pride in playing with my small glove. I liked to think of myself as a throwback to the early 1900s when professionals played with gloves not much bigger than their bare hands.

Our Holy Name baseball team did not have a great record, but I sure developed a passion for the sport. I should have known I would from two of the earliest pictures of me – one of me at age 3 holding a ball while having my picture taken in a professional photographer's studio and one at age 4 when I was photographed holding a bat on vacation at Seiglers.

Surprise Visit With Ty Cobb – Who's He?

The highlight of the season was a trip we took with Applebee's dad, Ralph. He scheduled the Saturday trip for the team, but he would not tell us where we were going, just that it was to be a surprise. So the coach and 14 players took off down the peninsula 30 miles to Menlo Park. There was Tim, Barry, Hipps, Ed Finn, Gene Cooney, me and other Holy Name team members. We stopped in front of a small, unassuming house in a nice neighborhood. We went inside and Ralph said, "I would like you all to meet Ty Cobb." I stood there waiting for more of an introduction and thinking, *who is this old, pudgy, kind looking guy?* I had never heard of him. Ralph asked him a few baseball related questions, so I assumed that he had something to do with baseball. Then Ralph mentioned he was in the Baseball Hall of Fame and held so many records in baseball. When Ralph asked us if anyone had questions for Mr. Cobb, not a single person spoke up. It was understandable that I had no questions, but I was really surprised the others had none – most of them knew who he was and the outstanding career that he had. Barry knew all about him. "He was the legendary Detroit Tiger's Baseball Hall of Famer known as the 'Georgia Peach.' He was born in 1886, so he was 67 when we met him. [40] He was considered the 'bad boy' of baseball. Some said he sharpened his spikes to scare players when he slid in stealing bases. It was an uneventful day. He did not even play catch with us, and he sure did not run imaginary bases for us, but it was memorable."

I would have loved to get tips on Cobb's hitting and base stealing exploits, but I would have been too shy to speak up even if I knew his history. Ralph asked him a question to confirm one of his statistical records, probably to impress us that he knew something about Cobb, but that was it. Then Ralph took out some paper and a baseball for him to autograph and told the rest of us we could get an autograph. I knew he wanted this trip to be a surprise, but it resulted in none of us having pen and paper to get an autograph. I felt uncomfortable the whole visit – being in a stranger's house, people not having anything to say, and leaving in such a short period of time after traveling all that distance. It would have been really special to get a ball autographed but at least Ralph brought a camera for a team photo with Ty Cobb outside a rather ordinary house with a simple interior and furnishings – a far cry from the later references of him living in an Atherton mansion. We each got a copy of the 5" x 7" photo, which we all treasured over the years. The lesson learned was that surprises can be fun, but keeping things from kids fails to prepare them to get the most out of trips and events. I never forgave Ralph for not advising us to bring a ball and pen.

Pride of Underdog Ragamuffins

When I was not playing for a school team and in between seasons for organized school competition, I could play sandlot ball to stay in shape. We found out about baseball teams by word of mouth. They were self-organized teams that scheduled games amongst each other. A lot of the better teams had sponsors, like real estate companies and restaurants who paid for the uniforms and equipment for the kids to have their company name plastered across the back of all of the players' uniforms like walking billboards. None of the sandlot teams I played on from age 12-17 had uniforms. We just showed up in our Levi's® and baseball jerseys, some with blue 3/4-sleeves, others with red 3/4-sleeves and others in sweatshirts – a bunch of ragamuffins, but we always had good teams. We had one outstanding pitcher, but that was all we needed since we often played just one game each week. When we played against teams that wore uniforms, which was more often than not, we felt like the underdog in our street clothes versus the impressive sponsored uniformed players. That was a good thing because we felt no pressure to win. We were there playing for the fun of it with every intention of winning. There was a little something extra in beating a team that wore uniforms – the idea that money could not buy success and clothes did not make the man. It was the man inside. It took working harder to be better than others to be a winner.

Throughout the year, we could watch a lot of excellent games at Big Rec that included high schools in the San Francisco AAA League, sandlot teams and semipro teams. I got to see a lot of players who got signed by major league teams. That included Jim Gentile who was a star at Sacred Heart Cathedral Preparatory High School in 1951-1952. Gentile was our Holy Name 8th grade basketball coach in 1954. There may not have been any better than him from those Big Rec days. He signed as a pitcher and first baseman with the Brooklyn Dodgers right after high school in 1952. Jim had a cannon for an arm and relied heavily on his fastball. He was 6'4", weighed 215 pounds, and had a ferocious swing. He uncorked monster home runs, some of the longest home runs hit at Big Rec. I heard that he was the only player to ever hit the steps out in right field on a single bounce at Big Rec's big diamond. The steps were about 600 feet from home plate. [41]

More Character Rooting for Underdogs

After the baseball season was over at Holy Name, Carmody, Barry and I started playing sandlot ball. The guys at Holy Name were all into baseball long before I got interested in 1953. Carmody was a huge New York Yankee fan, and why not. The Yankees were the powerhouse of major league baseball having won the World Series 12 out of 19 times since 1936 including 1953 and the previous four years under manager Casey Stengel. That was the one thing I held against Carmody – being an avid Yankee fan. It was easy to jump on the bandwagon and be a fan of a constant winner so he could rub it in the face of his buddies, so I was always pulling for whomever played against the Yankees, which meant rooting for the Brooklyn Dodgers most of the time. It was like playing for ragamuffin teams against teams that had "pretty" uniforms. I preferred "taking the road least traveled" and being the underdog – the challenge was greater and it showed more character.

We went to Sunset Playground at 29th Avenue and Lawton Street to play basketball and West Sunset Playground at 41st Avenue and Quintara Street to take batting practice. We only needed a pitcher, hitter and outfielder. Actual sandlot games were played at city playgrounds that had baseball diamonds with grass outfields and dirt infields. If we were lucky, we could play at the small diamond at Big Rec and hardly ever at the big diamond, usually reserved for the more organized, established leagues.

Quit Before Failure Becomes a Habit

We took a lot of batting practice at West Sunset Playground and got to know the park director Ed Kelly pretty well. He was a really nice guy, sort of a Santa Claus build and an easygoing personality. West Sunset was a brand new playground had opened that year (1954) and Ed had not yet organized any teams. Since my buddies and I worked out there regularly, he asked us if we wanted to make up a basketball team. None of us were very good at basketball, so we had nothing to lose. No matter how bad we played, no one on the team could do much better. We practiced a little, and Ed gave us some fundamentals and plays. Our first game was against the Sunset Recreation Center on Lawton Street at 29th Avenue. We just called it "Sunset" or "Sunset Park." They had a history of fielding the best team in the league. We had to play there, as it was one of the only indoor basketball courts around. The gym had a half dome Quonset hut shape with a seating capacity for 600 spectators. It was tall and big – pretty intimidating for the visiting team. We never had predetermined positions on the team, so Ed said I would be one of the guards and always the one to take the ball down the court. I had never played the guard position, much less been coached at the position, but I figured how hard can it be? All I had to do was dribble the ball and move down the court. From the outset, the home team quickly got down the court to set up their defense and never applied any pressure as we brought the ball down. They never needed to. Every time, the referee blew his whistle and called me for "traveling" (carrying the ball), causing us to turn the ball over to the defense. I kept doing the same thing each time. I concentrated on my right hand to be sure I pushed the ball from the top toward the floor rather than placing my hand on the bottom or side of the ball in a lifting motion before the dribble, but nothing worked. I kept looking to the sideline at the coach for help, put he ignored my pathetic look of desperation and just kept encouraging me to stay at it, hoping I would eventually figure it out. I suppose this was his approach to players learning on the job. The ref probably got tired of calling me for the foul, especially after the other team had a large lead, because I got through the game. I knew Ed meant well, but I never did like doing anything I was not good at, and this was the first time I encountered failure. I told the other guys I was not going to play any more and that led to the others dropping off the team that no longer would have five players. It was not a matter of not "getting back on the horse," but we just were a really bad team. And it was not worth my time to continue when we had baseball that we were much better at. This was the first of several periods during my youth that I followed my belief that it was better to move on to something I was good at, rather than waste time on something I was bad at. It was better to quit being a failure before failure became a habit. It was one of the attributes that led to building my confidence, positive thinking, and drive to be a winner and successful.

Self-Confidence and the Will to Work

I started a scrapbook now that my name was appearing in baseball box scores in the local newspaper. In those days, the major San Francisco newspapers published box scores of sandlot baseball teams. On the inside cover of my scrapbook, I taped a large picture of a boy selling newspapers with one hand holding papers under his arm and holding a paper up with the other hand. On the cover of the newspaper I printed "Self-confidence and the will to work" – the two things that were most important to me at that age. I wound up being a big collector of motivational quotes all my life. The first one I put in my scrapbook was:

> *I was early taught to work as well as play,*
> *My life has been one long, happy holiday;*
> *Full of work, full of play –*
> *I dropped the worry on the way –*
> *And God was good to me every day.*
> *– Rockefeller the elder*

Never Too Proud to Accept Criticism

One day Bob Farber's father was giving Bob, Dan Fitzgerald and me a ride home from playing a game at Big Rec. It was the only time his dad ever saw me play. He said I had quick wrists, which allowed me to wait until the last moment to swing, giving me a longer look at the pitch. I felt good hearing that from him, as he knew a lot about the game. Then he asked if I had a sore arm. I had been playing centerfield and it was the first time anyone commented about my arm, implying that I did not have a strong arm and it was too weak for the outfield. I sheepishly said, "Yeah, sort of" to cover up my weakness and to not let on that I was not as good as the other players. He just let it go. But he was right. I could not throw the ball from deep centerfield to home plate with much on the throw. At that point, I knew I was not an outfielder. I had the foot speed and agility but not the arm. That was when I decided to consider a position that required a shorter throw. I was not a power hitter, which ruled out first base. Second base required the shortest throw to first, but it was not an exciting position. Third base required a very strong arm, which was not me. So at the next sandlot game, I asked if I could try playing shortstop, which worked out fine. Shortstop got lots of action and in hindsight I had been preparing for the position back in the Mission when I took all those ground balls off the neighbors house on our back porch. So began a career of playing shortstop throughout high school.

Besides reading the book *Power of Positive Thinking* by Dr. Norman Vincent Peale two years earlier, the other most influential event in my young life that gave me the incentive, motivation and confidence to be successful was just before graduation from the 8th grade. The previous year we moved from the Mission to the Sunset, from a lower-income neighborhood to a middle-income neighborhood. So it was my belief that kids at my new school were much better than me. I was shy to begin with and was even shyer now. I assumed their parents were better than mine in terms of education, job position and finances, which was true. At the end of the school year, our class was asked to vote for the recipient of the 1954 American Legion Awards. There was one girl and one boy chosen from each of the two 8th grade classes of nearly 50 students. (There were 97 students in our class but we were divided into grades 8A and 8B). The awards were for the students we felt had the most promise and admired the most. Although the words "most likely to succeed" were never used on the Award, it was the gist of the Award according to my teacher. As with every class, there were those who were most popular, most attractive, most athletic and most studious, so there was a lot of competition. A week later, our teacher announced the winners in our class. Norma Haller was one of two winners among the girls. She beat out Judy Carle, who became a nun, by one vote. Norma went on to be the owner and operator of the Granlibakken Resort and Conference Center in Squaw Valley. Wendy Nelder was the other girl who got the Award. She went on to be an attorney and on the San Francisco Board of Supervisors for a number of years and serving as the Board President following the likes of John Molinari, Diane Feinstein, and Quentin Kopp. I certainly understood why Norma and Wendy got the Awards, but when I heard that I had received the Award as the male recipient of the Award in my class, I could not understand how and why that could have happened. I could not believe it. I was not good looking, extremely popular, or exceptional in academics or sports. In any case, I received a small medal, a paperweight trophy and a Certificate of Distinguished Achievement, although both my first and last names were misspelled. For years afterwards, I wondered if our teacher Sister Mary Carmela swung the decision in my favor because of my humbler background than most of the others. That Award turned out to have possibly the greatest impact on who I became and what I did with my life. It gave me the incentive and motivation to succeed by making something of myself – to be the best that I could be in everything I set out to do over the next 50 years. I believed that I could never do enough to have earned that recognition, and I frequently reminded myself during my entire life that I would be letting down my classmates if I did not achieve as much as I could. Every six to nine months, I relived the experience in my head and reminded myself "I owed it to my classmates to succeed and I cannot let them down." Some kids had that feeling of wanting to not let down their parents, especially if parents were constantly pushing them to succeed or overachieve. Although I wanted my parents to be proud of me, I especially felt I owed it to my 8th grade classmates to succeed. When things got tough or my life was not advancing very fast, I never forgot or lost sight of the need to succeed for my classmates.

Awards and Degrees Are Not the End – Just the Beginning

While I viewed the Award as something that I used to motivate me to be all that I could be in life, another Award recipient told me years later she viewed it simply as an honor. The moral was that the importance of an award, certificate or degree was not receiving it or the honor; it was what we did with it. Some hung it on the wall; others used it as an incentive. It was like making a lot of money. Accumulation of money should not be the purpose. It should be what you do with the money.

Encouragement Only Effective If From Those You Respect

I often thought that every kid by age 13 or 14 should get a vote of confidence from their peers, a favorite relative or respected teacher that they will be successful or something special when they are mature enough to grasp and appreciate the compliment. Although parents tried to instill that in their kids, kids did not pay too much attention to the desires of their parents. But kids listened to those whom they respected, knowing that they really believed what they said as opposed to being told what parents are suppose to say. What kids did with the compliment was up to them. Like so many options we faced in life, we may choose correctly or incorrectly, but we all deserved a chance to face that fork in the road.

Upon graduating from the 8th grade, my sister surprised me with a gift, a 17-jewel watch from Granat Brothers as a graduation present. She had an accounting job at the jewelry store on the corner where I first sold newspapers five years earlier. She was working there since she graduated from high school two years earlier. When I thanked her, she said, "I get a discount at Granat Brothers" rather than "You deserve it." For being a sister who did not have much time for me, I was really surprised when she gave me such a nice graduation present. I did not know kids got presents for such things. It changed my whole attitude about her and being my sister. She turned out to be a very caring and generous person all her life. She was my last resort and lent me the money for the down payment on my first house 20 years later – interest free. It was my start in real estate investments – in St. Francis Woods no less.

Now that I would be starting high school, I had to give up my job of selling newspapers on the corners because I would always be late for work. Applebee and I were sitting at his kitchen table wondering how we could make money during high school. He came up with the idea of a morning *San Francisco Chronicle* paper route (the *S.F. Examiner* put out the news section and Sunday magazine of the Sunday issue). It could be done before school and would not interfere with our classes. I thought the hours were ideal. I would finish work before going to school, leaving the afternoons free to do stuff, especially for playing sports. The idea that the free afternoons would be ideal for studying never even crossed my mind. Tim went ahead, looked into it, and got himself a route near his house. He told me how to apply for my own route, and shortly afterwards a route became available close to where I lived.

Historic Houses in My Own Backyard

My paper route covered the blocks from 35th to 40th Avenues between Judah and Lawton Streets. I did not know, but my paper route included one of the historical blocks in San Francisco on 39th Avenue between Judah and Kirkham Streets. "In 1927, Henry Doelger built his first house in the Sunset District, a barrel front, single-family house on 39th Avenue between Judah and Kirkham Streets. Later that year, on that same block, he began construction of the first tract of Doelger-built homes." [42]

Across the street from my house was the square block of 35th and 36th Avenues between Kirkham and Lawton Streets, which was on my paper route. It contained 47 of the homes built by the Rousseau Brothers. Another 50 of their constructed homes were in the adjoining square block of 34th and 35th Avenues between Kirkham and Lawton Streets. These homes were excellent examples of Oliver and Arthur Rousseau designed houses that got away from the building of identical-looking Doelger tract homes by using a range of architectural styles such as Spanish Colonial Revival, Tudor Revival, French Provincial, Mediterranean Revival, and Storybook styles. These two square blocks comprised the 97 houses that were the Rousseau Brothers' most ambitious and final development in the Sunset District and contained the largest and most expensive of the firm's houses. Their especially large and expensive houses were located on the street corners at 35th and Kirkham Street, 36th and Kirkham Street, 35th and Lawton Street, and 36th and Lawton Street. Even some of the interior of smaller houses on 35th and 36th Avenues between Kirkham and Lawton Streets had special architectural touches.

Coincidentally, my paper route also included two other noteworthy houses. Oliver and Arthur Rousseau settled with their families in this development immediately after its completion. "Oliver Rousseau resided in the large Spanish Colonial Revival corner building at 36th Avenue and Lawton Street from 1933 to 1937. At the other end of the block, Arthur Rousseau resided at 36th Avenue at Kirkham Street, in a Storybook style, Tudor Revival corner building, from 1933 to 1937." [43]

Character Building Four-Year Boot Camp

Never did I realize that the paper route would be an early version of a boot camp for me – I rose early in the morning, worked seven days a week rain or shine, followed the same daily routine, did lots of physically strenuous work, perfection was expected, learned self-reliance, dedication, responsibility, dependability, endurance, and how to deal with people, all to prepare me to be a better person. It was a character builder for sure.

Every morning that I attended high school, I got up before 5:00 a.m., seven days a week, and jogged five blocks to the corner of 39th Avenue and Judah Street where the newspapers were dropped off. Thank goodness there was just enough shelter from the rain in the 30-square-foot triangular doorway of the storefront. During the week, I just had to stuff the papers into my canvas bag, but on Sundays I had to insert the news section into the rest of the paper before starting out. This allowed the newspaper to print the bulk of the paper earlier and wait until the last minute to print the news section so they could report the latest news. The paper route had over 125 customers. There was no way to carry all the papers at the same time (50-200 pounds of newspapers), so I made two trips on weekdays and three or four trips on Sundays with the thicker and heavier issues. On rainy days, I draped a rain poncho over me and the bag of papers hung down my front and back in order to keep the papers dry. By the end of the route, my pant legs, shoes and socks were soaked. I had to wring the water out of my socks. These were fond memories when doing the same after high school in the U.S. Marine Corps. On any heavy raining Sunday mornings, Mom drove around with me to keep the papers dry. If it was just a light rain, I let Mom sleep in. I always felt badly when she got up at 4:30 a.m. for me. I was done delivering around 7:00 a.m.

As I walked along my route, I folded the papers in between houses using a double roll fold, rather than the tucked sandwich or tomahawk fold, because it was faster to fold and would get me done in the least amount of time. Customers expected their newspapers to be convenient to retrieve and dry on rainy days. Many of the Sunset houses had straight staircases to the front door on the second floor, so it meant I had to throw the papers onto the top step. Unfortunately, a lot of the houses had tunnel entrances with security gates, so on rainy days, it was a hassle having to walk up to each security gate along the way to throw the newspaper in the tunnel to keep the paper dry. If a paper got wet or a person had to walk "too far" to get their paper and they called in to complain, I got a notice to that affect. I tried my best to keep everyone happy. Since subscriptions were not prepaid, I had to collect payments at the end of the month. More importantly, I did not want to lose a customer because I would make less money in the future.

Another thing that caused extra time to delivering the newspapers was that I was not supposed to walk across the strips and plots of lawns extending from the houses to the sidewalk, so I had to walk around the lawns, otherwise the "pain-in-the-butt" customers phoned in a complaint that was passed on to me and my supervisor. On rainy days, there was no visible evidence of me walking across the lawns, but on cold days when frost covered the grass, customers could see a visible trail of footprints.

Many of the houses that had tunnel entrances had security gates that caused me to walk an extra 15 feet to drop the newspaper inside the gate on rainy days. A few years later I found out the flaw in the security gates, at least the one on the front of a buddy's house. It was after attending a party and having a few beers, I was successful in bypassing the gate on the front of his house. The next morning I told his dad how I did it. Not only was he surprised, he was also grateful.

As I walked my route thinking about money and how hard I was working, I often thought about someday working on Montgomery Street, which was the financial center of the City. I always imagined it as the Wall Street of the West Coast and thought of working there because that was where the money was and I wanted to be rich someday. For my first job after college, I was among the first inhabitants of the newly built Bank of America 52-story world headquarters building located at the corner of Montgomery and California Streets in the Controller's Department on the 5th floor, so I achieved my daydream – just in a different occupation.

Ambition From Seeing How the Other Half Lived

At the end of the month, I had to go around in the evenings to all 125 houses when people were home from work to collect my money. I always went after dinner when they were well fed and more relaxed in hopes of getting more tips. Most people were home, but I had to go back once or twice to catch some people at home, and three or four times for the deadbeats who repeatedly asked me to return when their husband came home or wait until payday. I was sometimes asked to step inside to get out of the rain and cold while the person went to get the money or a check. Many Rousseau-built houses had some combination of Mediterranean architecture, arched doorways, very large sunken living rooms with extra high and decorative stencil-painted wood beam ceilings, ornate hardware, stained wood wall paneling, wall murals, polished hardwood floors, and arched picture windows. The inhabitants of these homes were ordinary people like everyone else on my paper route, but their house and car in the driveway were more expensive than their neighbors. That made me think when I got older, I wanted a house like their houses that were special. Twenty years later, the first house I bought was in St. Francis Woods, an exclusive area in San Francisco. At the time, my wife and I were just a middle class couple, but I kept that dream in mind, and after looking at over 300 houses, we found one that met my expectations and we could afford with the help of Bank of America. Throughout my life, whenever it came to investing and buying property, if I looked at enough options (at least 300 properties), I would find the right one. It only took one out of 300 to find the best house or income property at the best price.

Once I went to collect at one of the corner houses on my route. I had to ring the bell a couple of times and a tall guy came to the door with a scowl on his face, which was pretty common with men answering the door. I probably interrupted them while watching television. I looked at this guy for what seemed like ages and said, "Paper bill." He went back into the house, and I thought he looked like Randolph Scott, the movie star who made so many western films. To this day I relived that incident and kept kicking myself for not asking him if he was Randolph Scott – one of the many times I regretted being so shy as a kid. He was one of my favorite movie stars – one of my few chances in life to meet greatness.

Collect Money Fast to Avoid Deadbeats

I made $125 a month – far better than $35 a month selling papers on the corner. If I added all the hours I spent delivering the papers and collecting my money, I may have been making less per hour, but I was too young to think in those terms. Besides, gross revenue was all that mattered, especially since kids never paid income taxes. Tips were better from my paper route because I had more regular customers. I was lucky to have a route in a middle class neighborhood. There was never anyone who did not pay me, in which case, I would be out the money and have to pay for my papers out of my own pocket. If someone cancelled because they were moving, I collected from them on their delivery cutoff date rather than waiting until month end and have deadbeats move early or skip town.

Always Greet Ingrates With a Smile

At Christmas time, a couple of my customers gave me a paper plate of cookies as a gift, but what I really wanted was cash. Although a few gave me a two or three-dollar Christmas tip in an envelope, no one during the four years of delivering newspapers ever gave me a large enough tip for me to say "Wow, that is really generous of you!" Being a middle class neighborhood and some customers owned expensive homes or cars, I was always disappointed how few people tipped me each month and how small the Christmas tips were and from so few customers. When I sold newspapers on the corner, I had customers who gave me a dime for a seven cents paper and told me to keep the change – a 150 percent tip because I only made two cents from each paper. I just expected a little more appreciation on my paper route after getting up before 5:00 a.m. every morning, seven days a week with the weather always cold and generally damp at that time of morning because we were so close to the ocean and having to carry 125 newspapers on my shoulders (two loads of over 60 newspapers) 32 blocks every morning and in the rain 75 days out of the year with the customers' expectation that not a single one of the 46,000 newspapers I hand-delivered during the year ever got wet, went undelivered, or was thrown anywhere except on the top doorstep under the eaves out of the damp and wet weather, especially challenging on Sundays when the papers weighed three to four pounds. Although I was not perfect in my job for four years, I was pretty damn close to perfect, even with a hangover after drinking too much the night before. Yet, whether the customer paid me with no tip or a pittance of a tip, I always said "Thank you" with a smile. I learned from their stinginess to be a generous person myself later in life.

Business Principles Learned From Paper Route

The paper route taught me to be independent by making my own money, and I learned a lot of basic business principles that I did not learn grammar or high school classes. I was a "self-employed" entrepreneur and operating as such – report to work on time, provide good service, be courteous and smile when I asked to be paid. It turned out I was involved in production (preparing the papers), service (paper delivery), customer relations (excellent service), accounts receivables (collecting payments), and accounts payable (paying the distributor their share). I may not have known those terms, but I understood the concepts.

High School – The Most Important Sandbox (1954-1958)

Age 14: Freshman Year – Time to Adapt and Improvise

Months prior to graduation, kids had to decide where they would go to high school for so many most important experiences. Boys had choices of three all-boys schools (co-educational currently): Sacred Heart, Saint Ignatius (S.I.) and a school I never heard of called Archbishop Riordan High School. Actually, the first Riordan class in 1949 transferred from St. James Boys High School. [44] Even though St. James was just 10 blocks from Folsom Park, I had never heard of it either – probably because it was on a narrow street that was just five blocks long on Fair Oaks Street at 23rd Street, between Guerrero and Dolores Streets. Riordan and Sacred Heart were the blue-collar schools and S.I. was for the upper crust non-blue collars. Sacred Heart was established in 1852 and St. Ignatius in 1855, so they had lots of history, city wide alumnus, excellent athletic teams, and famous alumnus in sports and other field. Archbishop Riordan was a new upstart high school that had been open for only five years. Without the longevity of Sacred Heart and S.I., Riordan sports teams got little respect from the local newspapers and the other high schools.

Beliefs Are More Important Than What Others Say

During most of the 1950s, Riordan was considered a "second-class citizen" when it came to sports in the City because they were in the Catholic Athletic League (C.A.L.) and all of the other San Francisco schools, including the other two boys Catholic schools, were in the San Francisco AAA League. Although the C.A.L. was tougher because it had more strong teams, the local newspapers gave the AAA teams all of the publicity. The local papers never even allowed the San Francisco Riordan athletes to qualify for their high school All-Star teams until 1957, my junior year. Nine schools made up the competitive league: Riordan (San Francisco), Bellarmine (San Jose), Bishop O'Dowd (Oakland), Junipero Serra (San Mateo), Marin Catholic (Kentfield), St.. Elizabeth (Oakland), St. Francis (Mountain View), St. Joseph (Alameda), and St. Mary's (Berkeley). Each school was a powerhouse in basketball, baseball and/or track. The competition was from the entire Bay Area, not almost entirely from the City like the AAA League, so it had a larger base of outstanding athletes. Athletes in the C.A.L. knew they were generally as good as, if not better than, the AAA teams in spite of how they were treated by the local press. Their beliefs were more important than what others did or did not say about them. Disrespect only fueled motivation to win.

Happenstance of the Origin of Best Buddies

If my parents had not moved to the Sunset and we still lived in the Mission, I probably would have gone to Sacred Heart. I always wanted to go there. It was my kind of school – kids-from-the-Mission and blue collar. And how could any Irishman turn down a school with a "Fightin' Irish" mascot versus St. Ignatius "Wildcats" and Riordan "Crusaders?" My brother went to St. Ignatius for two years, probably because it had the best reputation for scholastics and one of the best schools for athletics. But for me it all came down to where my best buddies were going – Applebee, Beyma, Canas, and Carmody – except Barry and Hipps chose to go to the seminary but not for long. The Holy Name gang all chose Riordan, and it stemmed by happenstance from the fact that Applebee's older brother was attending Riordan and his dad was involved with the school. So if Tim was going, so would Carmody, and so would the rest of us follow along. Barry joined us in our freshman year and Hipps in our sophomore year. We were told Riordan had a reputation for scholastics at least as good as Sacred Heart and no one wanted to be an "S.I. Cherry", which was what we called those who attended St. Ignatius. It was our endearing name for "wimps." So it was clear that I would go to Riordan along with 20 others from Holy Name – all of us living and raised in the same "sandbox" in the Sunset District.

Unsuspecting Ripple Effect's Unpredictable Outcomes

A few months before we all decided to attend Riordan, Applebee's dad installed the new inner auditorium doors at Riordan for $1,800. It was one of a series of his winning bids to do carpentry work at our new school. That working tie to Riordan along with Tim's brother attending Riordan resulted in the rest of us going to Riordan. It was an example of Michele Bardsley's "ripple effect." The pebble you throw into the water is your action – the only thing you can control. The ripples you cause cannot be controlled. It was the perfect word of advice for us as we set out on the four most formative years of our lives. We would never know whether our actions would positively or negatively impact others – so choose wisely.

Adjusting Was Difficult When Alone or Different

I was lucky to be going to a new school where I knew others from Holy Name, St. Paul's and St. Charles. I never thought of the loneliness and insecurity of those who knew no one because their grammar school friends went to other high schools. Guido Mori-Prange and Noel Murray came from public schools, and most of their friends went on to public high schools. Guido experienced discrimination in his neighborhood for being partly Japanese – the lingering prejudices from WWII, so he did not know if he would encounter the same at Riordan, which he did not as he found out later. Noel was small and shy, so he felt too small to go out for sports, which he loved, and too shy to make a lot of friends. It was a lot more difficult to adapt to a new surrounding with all strangers when one was shy and alone versus being shy among friends. I learned years later that both of them "felt lost and isolated." Along the way they had made a few friends, but they really felt part of the school and made a lot of friends when they both went out for sports – Guido in track and cheerleading and Noel in football.

Canas wrestled with a different problem. He came to Riordan from Holy Name with the rest of us, so he had friends when he arrived. But he felt uncomfortable bringing girls home to meet his Latin parents for fear that the girl would hold that against him. So he took his girlfriends over to meet a couple that was friends of his parent's whom Rich really respected and were like second parents to him. They were Americans. Rich never took the girlfriends to meet those who were Latinos in order to give the appearance that his family and friends were Americans.

I started at Riordan in September 1954. **[45]** It meant traveling across town instead of walking five blocks to school, but that would have been true for attending any of the three Catholic boy's high schools. Not being old enough to drive made public transportation the only way for me to get around. I caught the N-Judah streetcar at 35th and Judah and transferred to the 10-Monterey bus at 9th and Judah. Kids under 18 could use Muni student car tickets that cost five cents per ride. I could use the car ticket from 6:30 a.m. to 6:00 p.m. Monday to Saturday and for fewer hours on Sunday. Most conductors did not enforce the time restrictions, and they sometimes punched over a punch or missed the car ticket so I got a free ride. I could use a transfer three times within a limited two to three hour time frame, so I could get anywhere in the City for a nickel. Some kids were driven to school by their parents. But some guys were embarrassed to have their parents drive them where they would be seen being dropped off by their classmates, so they were let off a block or so from school. They did not want to be viewed as a "mama's boy."

Other kids commuted on the 36-Teresita bus that dropped them off at the front door of Riordan. Noel Murray said, "The bus driver often was a parent of one of the Riordan guys, so he pretended to punch our Muni card and gave us a free ride." Other kids caught streetcars that took them to the Phelan Loop on Ocean Avenue. As Art Curtis described it, "In 1954, the 15 'temporary' buildings of the World War II U.S. Navy WAVES (Women Appointed Voluntary Emergency Service) facility that had been constructed in 1945 on the 30 acres next door to Riordan were still on that site, and we went through them on the two-block walk to school."

The 260 incoming freshmen were divided among six freshman classes (9A-F). The faculty was mostly Marianist Brothers with 19 brothers and only 9 lay teachers. Of the Holy Name gang, only Sullivan was eventually in my 9A class.

The Riordan school mascot was the Crusader and their logo was a courageous crusader mounted on a horse and proudly holding his lance upright. It was an appropriate mascot for our school as most of us came from families that started out with so little, but adapted and overcame like many Crusaders during medieval times who were the least affluent and considered underdogs as a result in their day.

A common form of poking fun at our classmates was fashioned after *Crusader Rabbit*, a popular cartoon show on television during our high school years and about a toothy rabbit dressed in a crusader outfit. Since Riordan's mascot was a Crusader, students formed rabbit ears with their forefinger and middle finger in a V-shape to resemble rabbit ears and stuck them behind the head of the guy next to them for group photos.

Our freshman year was all about entering a new environment that presented new social and academic challenges not faced in the past. Like being in the U.S. Marine Corps, it was a period to "improvise and adapt" to a larger school with larger classes, making new friends, challenged by new school subject matter and activities, being treated differently by teachers and students, and greater competition in academics, sports and the other activities. The freshman year was our high school scholastic boot camp. Some washed out, everyone else survived, but we all adapted differently. By the end of our senior year, there was a range of feelings from "high school was the best years of my life" to "I do not want to talk about those years." The latter group made up a small percent of our class. As in life, not everyone was willing or able to adapt successfully. For the rest of us, it was onward and upward.

In Search of My Impossible Dream

The first month of school was as if an epidemic of shyness overcame the new freshman class. I felt nothing like Richard the Lion Hearted and more like Don Quixote in search of my impossible dream to find my place in this new, overwhelming environment. We were the "low men on the totem pole," the smallest people walking the hallways, and thrown in with a bunch of strangers. It was a time of searching for the handful of guys we knew from grammar school, whether it was in class, in the hallways or at lunch. Fortunately, I knew about 20 from Holy Name, 15 from St. Paul's and one from St. Charles – an unforeseen benefit from having transferred so frequently. It was even more unsettling if you were the only one from your grammar school class and knew no one. Even though I knew some guys from grammar school in my freshman year, I should have joined some extracurricular activities but none of the guys I knew from Holy Name did. At best they played sports. Applebee played frosh football and baseball and Beyma played JV basketball as the tallest kid on the team. Some of the friends we made that year ran track (120s) like Mike Duffy, Al Latour and Maurice Lafayette whose first choice was football, but being only 90 lbs. and his mom refusing to let him play, he went out for track because he could run fast. He ran the 75-yard dash, 220 and 440. He also did the low hurdles, broad jump, and pole vault – a pretty versatile guy and he was good at them. I never considered running track that year because I was playing sandlot baseball and never considered football because I felt I was too much of a lightweight at 110 pounds soaking wet. Besides, I might have gotten discouraged if I was not a starter in football and got turned off from trying out the next three years. Sometimes the best decisions are the ones we do not make.

Sincerity: Main Characteristic of Being "Cool"

Canas had a unique challenge attending Riordan. He was one of only a few Latinos in the freshman class. As he recollected, "Those of us who were devoid of wit, humor, originality, or any God-given talent in the arts, sports or hobbies (*my name is Ricardo and I am a solid B student*) had to work a tad harder despite adopting most of the props to appear cool. So, when the occasion required a 'splash' of coolness, I pretended to have it and my friends were generous enough to let me get away with it. Trying so hard to be cool blinded one from seeing reality and wholesome values like sincerity. I was not being the person I really was by pretending to be cool. It was not until after high school during a physical for the Marine Corps, I learned I was not 5'10" tall and had no resemblance to the actor Troy Donahue. I recall my uncle Bob advising me about pretense: 'Face it, you're Latin, so you have to try harder.' In retrospect, I could have saved myself a lot of anxiety had someone convinced me that being a *real* Ricardo and a *solid B person* was head and shoulders above mediocrity, and thus cool. And although that elusive key to self-worth was within arm's reach at the time, it might as well have been on the moon. I was just another adolescent who did not accept who he really was. *Not* seeing one's identity was part of the camouflage that my friends and I wore to church when we needed to confess our sins."

In retrospect Canas said, "No description of coolness during the 1950s would be complete without referencing interpersonal relationships. True, the dance varied according to the music. Just as some of us were more car and girl crazy than others, the jocks remained aloof about both. To them women, and later cars, were of secondary interest. I was a hybrid. I did not conform to any particular group but rather embraced them all like the Stephen Stills song goes, 'If you can't be with the one you love, love the one you're with.' Perhaps the reason for adapting to the situation was that I was a Mission transplant and bi-cultural. I loved sports and women. I did not know that I was *not* fast, tall, or strong, but hung around people who were. I was drawn to and was mediocre in every cool sport. And although when sides were being picked, I was usually chosen last, but at least I was chosen and that allowed me to maintain the illusion. I was not as tall or strong as Beyma, as fast as Applebee, as smart as Carmody, as motivated as Quinlan, as enthusiastic as Sullivan, or as white-assed as any of them. Yet, I pretended my best to be cool despite occasionally venturing outside the truth. Over time, the Holy Name gang recognized that sincerity was the main characteristic of coolness, and that superficiality was the mark of mediocrity, lameness, and the uncool."

Applebee wound up being our freshman (and later sophomore) class representative on the Student Council. This was the student governing body that worked with the faculty to get things done. Tim got elected to the position for being a class officer, active in sports and other activities, and being such a likable guy with a mild demeanor.

I was not big on wearing hats, probably because Dad and so many other men at the time wore hats. It was an old guy's thing. On normal days, I wore a beige cloth McGregor Drizzler jacket that zipped up the front, buttoned the collar around the neck and did a good job protecting me from the cold and rain drizzle all four years of high school. On rainy days, I wore a gray plastic raincoat that was easily folded up and stored in my school locker. My head always got soaked, but that was fine – a "guy thing" to do. Rainy days caused the crowded streetcar to smell of wet clothes. I transferred to a bus that left me off five blocks from school, which left a short walk or jog depending on the weather.

Secret to a Good Education at Affordable Prices

Riordan had about 900 students. Since the school roots stemmed from St. James High School in the Mission, it was not surprising that the make up of the students reflected much of the general population of that neighborhood. We were primarily of Irish, Italian, and German descent but only a few Latinos. There were almost no African-Americans and Asian students. For Catholic white kids from the Sunset, the first contact many of us had with African-Americans and Asians was at Fleishhacker Pool in a city of 90% whites and 5.7% blacks. [46] The school was named after Archbishop Patrick William Riordan, born to Irish immigrants, who devoted his life to education, the growth of the Catholic Church and a huge impact on San Francisco and the Bay Area. A good education at an affordable tuition was dependent on the large contribution of services by those in the religious order. Teachers were 65 percent from the Brothers of the Marianist (Society of Mary) order and 35 percent lay teachers (two-thirds were also coaches). This was in stark contrast to grammar school where all the teachers were nuns. I liked the idea of having some lay teachers, otherwise school would feel like a seminary. The positive of having brothers from a religious order was that it was the school's way of providing a good education at affordable tuitions since the brothers received a much lower salary than laymen.

Teacher salaries must have been in the ballpark of those paid to city schoolteachers, which was a $3,000 annual minimum. [47] The monthly tuition was $10 in our freshman year, $17.50 in our sophomore and junior years, and $20 in our senior year. To put this in perspective, the annual median income in San Francisco was $3,000, and monthly rent was $40. There were not many in our freshman class from public schools. Since there were so many parents wanting to get their kids into the Catholic high schools where there was more discipline, no violence, good teachers and emphasis on college preparation, there just was not room for everyone. Being Catholic and coming from a Catholic grammar school were two things in our favor for admission.

A tuition of $20 a month or $180 for the school year would be the equivalent of $1,600 for the year today – a bargain by any standard and certainly worth every penny of it for the education, values, discipline and friendships we received all thanks to the nuns and brothers willing to work for so little for the benefit of the kids and their parents. [48]

Unprepared for First Career Fork in the Road

During the school enrollment process, we were given the choice of a four-year college preparation curriculum or not, so we were assigned to the appropriate classes where college-prep subjects would be taught. It was the first fork in the road we faced regarding the direction and choice of a career. Some families pushed the idea of their kids eventually going to college more consistently than other families, so by the time we got to high school we had a general idea of whether we or our parents wanted us to go to college. The decision was based on what our parents wanted and our buddies wanted, but the decision was not based on facts about why we should go and what options were available. Most importantly, students generally waited until their senior year to think seriously about college – if they were going and which college to attend. It would have helped in our freshman year to invite some guest speakers to talk about the pros and cons of junior vs. four-year college, local vs. out of town schools, in-state vs. out of state issues, prestigious vs. non-prestigious schools, financial aspects, and obtaining grants. We may have been too immature to grasp everything, but it would have set benchmarks for those who might aspire to attend the better schools. Probably the most important lecture would be on the importance of good grades for getting into various schools and their impact on doing well in college. Parents and teachers just assumed that kids wanted to put in the time to get good grades. It just was not so. We needed reasons. We needed specifics. It was not enough to just tell kids "You need to get good grades to get into good colleges." What about the impact extracurricular activity participation had on the entrance application evaluation? Which activities had the greatest impact? How does attending a school with a national academic reputation or influential alumni impact getting a good job and moving up the ladder? The same sessions would be good also as a reminder in our junior year.

Most kids were probably asked in grammar school "What are you going to be when you grow up?" Most of the time their parents answered the question for them, since kids did not think much about those things since adulthood was so far away. But by high school, that question got a lot of thought. I was always being asked that question, and like most kids, I just did not know other than what Mom told everyone, which was "an engineer." At least I did not have a dad pushing me to take over the family business. It was sad that a family worked all of their lives to create a successful business with the expectation that their kids would take it over. I suspect most kids who took over a family business did it out of respect for their parents and it was expected of them all those years they were growing up. Sad how many of them may have had their own dreams but not given a chance to make such an important decision until they were older and wiser. To give kids some ideas and information to make such career decisions, it would have been helpful if practitioners were invited to school early in our freshman year to talk about their career or job, both the good and bad, what was involved to qualify to be a doctor, engineer, teacher, accountant, mechanic, real estate agent, self-employed, whatever. It was decades later that I realized being an entrepreneur or self-employed was an option. I just assumed I had to work for some company all my life.

Need for More Speaking Opportunities

School started at 8:00 a.m. and ended at 2:30 p.m. The day opened with 30-minute homeroom to study, followed by six 43-minute classes, and ended with a 30-minute study or activity period. The curriculum consisted of four years of religion and English, three years of history and science, and two years of mathematics (optional advanced math offered in 11th and 12th grades). Business courses also were offered in the 11th and 12th grades. Physical education was held one day a week. We had the option of taking a language from among French, German, Latin and Spanish. I chose Spanish because it was considered the easiest of the four to learn. I envied Canas who spoke fluent Spanish. I always thought he had an unfair advantage over the rest of us and should have been required to take one of the other three languages. All freshmen took a year in speech and typing. Looking back, I always wished that we were required to take four years of speech. I found that in the business world, writing and verbal skills were the two most important attributes for doing a good job. We received four years of English and only one year of speech, but that was common in high schools at the time. Schools could have required students to speak in front of the class or illustrate at the blackboard more often in the other classes –

anything to get us to get comfortable speaking before groups.

The school provided lockers to each student to store our textbooks because we moved from room to room for the different classes. I took out only the books needed for my next class or two. At day's end, I took home only the books needed to do the next day's assignments. In San Francisco it rained 25-30 percent of the time during the school year, so keeping the books dry was a challenge. I usually stuck them under my raincoat, but on days when the rain was a surprise, I just ran fast between school and the bus stop. I was self-motivated to do as much homework as possible during the study period to eliminate at least one book I would not have to carry home, especially on rainy days. If I had to take a lot of books home, I used a duffle bag that I used to bring my lunch and sports gear from home.

On our first day of school, we only knew those who came from the same grammar school. I was lucky. I knew nearly 15% of the freshman students from my three previously attended grammar schools, so I usually saw familiar faces during the day even though there were six freshman classes, 9A through 9F with about 45 students in each class for a total of 264 students. By the end of the school year, there were 234 after students left for various reason.

Students were moved around among the five or six classes from year to year, so this helped us meet classmates we did not know in the previous years. By my senior year there were still a lot of kids in our senior class of 177 students that I never got to know. There also were about five percent of our senior class pictures in the yearbook that I did not even recognize as attending Riordan. The one thing those classmates had in common was their lack of participation in extracurricular activities – a sure way to remain anonymous throughout high school.

Necessity of Extracurricular Activities

Riordan was about studies, sports and activities. Riordan had no gangs. We just hung out together, not looking for any trouble. Throughout high school, I focused on sports and studies in that order, and little interest in extracurricular activities. I learned to regret that decision later in life.

My circle of friends during and after high school was completely limited to those who played sports. If I joined different activities, I would have made closer friendships with a wider group of kids including the smart kids, which may have led to me doing better scholastically. Besides, they were all great guys whom I never got to know well. Sad!

The most important challenges in grammar and high school were those mostly faced outside of the classroom. They were the activities that resulted in successes, failures, wins, losses, triumphs, disappointments and especially fun experienced from extracurricular activities after school, at work and at home. These were the things that molded character, attitude, perseverance, and the other qualities that result in being successful in our family life, work environment and social environment. The more times we faced challenges in and out of school, the more we learned and benefited from the experiences to deal with life successfully. Those who were sheltered during those years often would be ill prepared to do well in life unless they found people to take care of them as adults like a strong and protective wife, boss, secretary or assistant.

It would have been helpful if on the first day or two of the new school year each student had to stand up in class and introduce himself, tell which school or neighborhood he was from, describe his interests/hobbies, how he spent his leisure time, and any interesting things he had done. These introduction sessions would be especially useful in the freshman and sophomore years when we knew so few kids. It would have been nice to have the religious and lay faculty members do the same. It would help break down the barriers between teachers and students. The students would have had greater respect for the teachers. I knew nothing about our teachers other than what was heard through gossip and rumors. Faculty and student competition would have been fun and made the teachers more human. It could be board games, spelling bees, quiz shows or athletics – everything in a competitive spirit but just for fun.

What was beneficial for new students each year in December was an assembly to acquaint and remind freshmen and sophomores of the various organizations and activities offered by the school such as art club, band, drama club, library staff, photography club, school newspaper, science club, service club, sodality (religious club), speech club, and sport teams. Fifteen percent of my classmates participated in less than two activities

298

during their high school years – all nice guys but seldom, if ever, seen again at our class reunions. Maybe they had after school jobs or family obligations, but I found it was the after school activities that facilitated making friends as there just was not enough time during classes and lunch hours for such purposes. Maybe schools should offer social activities during class hours to develop friendships and a lasting connection with their school. Maybe exposing kids to volunteer services and apprentice programs would give them real world experiences and possibly stimulate an interest in a future career. In any case, the key to making friends was doing things together. What was beneficial each year in December was an assembly for freshmen and sophomores for new students to be acquainted with and reminded of the various organizations and activities offered by the school.

Misguided Detour to Leave Home

Barry took a different road than the rest of us. As he told it, "Most of my friends from Holy Name went to Riordan High School. I, however, having the naive desire to be a priest entered St. Joseph Seminary in Mountain View, CA. It also was a chance to move away from home. There was a priest named Father Joseph Riddlemoser who taught Latin and had a very distinct and loud voice. When he spoke quietly he was upset, if not downright angry. He was portly, smoked a pipe, and became my spiritual advisor. I loved his room that was filled with beautiful oak furniture and a nice thick rug. The room always smelled of sweet pipe smoke. Father Riddlemoser instilled in me a love for reading, especially the classics. I loved visiting the library with all the old books covering the walls. I was particularly fond of the older books with pictures of knights and classical Greeks and Romans. Some books were so old the pictures were covered with thin rice paper to protect them."

"There was not much that was memorable about my short residency at St Joseph's. I had a room on the fourth floor, and we all ate our meals in a large dining room. We sat at long tables while an older student read a Biblical passage from a podium, and then we said grace. Once someone decided to put milk of magnesia in the big silver milk pitcher. I knew about the prank so I did not have to run to the toilet every 10 minutes. If we unfortunately ever ended up sitting at the end of the long table, we became the 'scraper.' As every plate was passed down to him, he scraped the left overs into a bin and then stacked the plates until another student took them to the kitchen. That was one chore most seminarians hated."

"Shortly after arriving at the seminary, I fainted in church during Mass. It was hot and stuffy and I suddenly blacked out. I felt myself falling in slow motion and crashing down loudly in the pew. I woke up outside on a bench with someone telling me to relax and breathe slowly. This happened several times during my time at the seminary. Perhaps that was the 'sign' that I was not meant to be a priest."

"So after my 10-week stay at the seminary, Dad picked me up and drove me home. I told him I was not cut out to be a priest and that I was going to say the rosary every night since I did not want to displease God. He wanted to know why I wasn't cut out to be a priest, but I had no rational reply. I simply did not want to stay at the seminary, and I wanted to go to Riordan to be close to my buddies. He accepted my rationale and that was that. Considering the combustible relationship between Mom and Dad, I believe they were both happy to see me return home for someone else to focus their attention on rather than each other. Nobody made a big deal out of it, and I was immediately enrolled in freshman class 9A. I was now a proud Riordan Crusader – so proud that I sang the Riordan alma mater all my life as a greeting to classmates I had not seen for years:

> Sing from the top of the mountain, of Riordan's hallowed name.
> Ring through the soft green valley, our alma mater's fame.
> Our purple is our loyalty, our gold is tried and true!
> All hail to Riordan High School
> Hail! Alma Mater. Hail! Alma Mater. Hail! All hail, to you!"

Discipline: The Mettle That Molded Uncool Kids

In the 1940s and 1950s the Catholic schools enforced discipline, which was why many parents desperately tried to get their kids into Catholic schools, but the schools gave preference to Catholics. Many of the public schools had an opposite reputation for lack of discipline and violence in some cases. The nuns and brothers conducted classes with a firm hand

and swatted a kid if they became raucous or were disturbing the class in any way. Some nuns used a ruler to swat our knuckles. A buddy of mine at Holy Name had his mouth taped shut for talking too much [my kind of nun]. Some teachers were stricter than others, but I always agreed with the swatting by nuns in grammar school since it was someone else being swatted – sort of like law and order, where the public wanted laws and punishment, the criminals did not.

Things got a little more physical in high school where we had all boys and no girls. We were older and many of us were playing contact sports. Boys were at an age when they were trying to be grownups so they should be able to take discipline like a man, but the form of discipline varied by teacher. Kids behaved pretty well in class by our junior year, but in our freshman and sophomore years, if a kid was talking in class enough to disturb the teacher, it was likely disturbing the others around the kid, so a teacher might have him stand in the corner for the rest of the class to make him feel like a little kid and experience some embarrassment. However, the most common form of discipline was being given an hour of detention, which meant staying after school an extra hour. I was never sent to detention, but the guys just used it to do homework or study. Some teachers preferred a more physical approach, which all of us agreed was the most effective means of getting our attention and changing our ways. For example, the nuns told the kid to put out both hands, palms up, and they gave each hand a couple of swats with a ruler – not too much to hurt anyone but just enough to quiet the kid for the rest of the class. Guys got a lot worse at home from some of their fathers, so this was no big deal. Not only was it effective in straightening out the kid who was disturbing the class or the teacher, it sent a message to the entire class, which kept them disciplined without experiencing the physical punishment. Some teachers came down the aisle, and in a couple of cases, storming down the aisle. That was when we knew there was going to be trouble. The teacher either got in the kid's face or let him know in so many words to keep quite. For regular troublemakers, he might be pulled out of his seat and given a little shove. Both worked well.

I never got to know much about the teachers during high school, which may have been a sign of the times. They were there to teach, keep discipline, but not to be our buddies. It was not like a small town school where we stayed in the same classroom with the same teacher all day. When our class was over, we moved to a different classroom to be taught by a different teacher. It was a transit system of education. There was nothing wrong with it because each teacher taught his subject of specialty. An aspect of a quality education, which Riordan was known for, was to have teachers who knew their subject matter well. Often it was their major or minor in college. Buddies of mine over the years looked back at their high school days and said, if nothing else "Riordan gave me a good education." Contributing to that quality education was that the teachers maintained discipline in the classrooms and school events. They did not tolerate disruptions from the students. We could focus on what the teacher was saying with very few disturbing conversations or antics to distract us.

The most effective teacher was Brother Carl Spooner. He must have weighed 300 pounds or more. Barry told me numerous times how he did poorly in algebra class because he feared Brother Spooner so much. As he said, "He scared the hell out of me. He sat behind his desk and glared at us with his beady eyes. I always felt nervous, hoping he would not call on me but of course he did. I flunked the class. It was the only time I ever got an 'F' and I ended up having to spend part of the summer being tutored by a neighborhood lady. I improved enough to get a passing grade eventually, and it was not until I was in my 20s when I became proficient at fractions, which was a reflection of poor math instructions long before entering Riordan. Ironically, I did very well in geometry."

Instilling Fear of God Always Worked

I never believed that fear was the real reason for Barry's "F" since lots of kids like him who did well in reading and literature but did poorly in math. Too bad Barry never told me, as I could have helped him, as algebra was my favorite subject. Too bad we did not have study groups to help each other. I actually thought Brother Spooner was among the most effective teachers as he instilled discipline and the fear of God in students, which goes a long way at an all-boys school. One day a kid in the back of the class went too far and really upset him. Brother Spooner just had enough of this kid's frequent class disruptions and stormed down the aisle pushing desks aside with kids in them. It was an image I will never forget. I wondered what kind of strength he must have had to push desks aside with kids weighing 120-180 pounds in them as if they were empty cardboard boxes. That was impressive, and that was something that got a guy's attention and convinced him not to misbehave in his class. Brother Spooner never needed to lay a hand on a kid – just the look on his face that was steaming when he told the kid to go to the principal's office. The kid did not think twice, scurried out of the room and probably stopped off at the bathroom to clean out his underpants. We nearly all came from Catholic grammar schools and were used to the fact that there would be consequences if we talked out loud or misbehaved in class like a whack on the hand. Regardless of the method used in grammar school or high school, it effectively sent a message to the rest of us to be quiet and behave. It was good that teachers did these things. I often thought that these methods were less about the kid being disciplined and more about teaching the rest of us to behave, which we did. School was for learning, not only what was in the books, on the blackboards and coming out of the mouths of teachers, but learning to be a better person – one who was considerate of others and that there was a time and place for different behaviors. The classroom was the place to learn. Recess, lunch and after school were the places for talking and horsing around.

At the time, we never knew that Brother Spooner was limited to a light teaching schedule for health reasons at the end of our freshman year. There was no telling how much of the stress caused by students may have contributed to his condition. Kids never thought how our conduct could affect the health and mental state of our teachers – something that deserved more consideration.

Respect for Teachers and Drill Instructors Required

There were a lot of teachers who had the respect of the students by their mere presence in class to keep kids quiet and attentive – much like U.S. Marine Corps drill instructors. Most of them looked like they played college football and could be tough if necessary, and there were teachers who had impressive backgrounds to earn that respect, such as baseball and football coach Visco Grgich, basketball and track coach Edward Fennelly, baseball and basketball coach Albert Lavin, and teacher Ross Giudice.

They each had two things in common – all nice guys and had a history of personal success in sports. Too bad we never knew about the academic background and personal achievements of the other teachers to show more respect on a different level.

Visco Grgich weighed 217 pounds when he played for the Santa Clara University football team and eventually guard as one of the first stars on the San Francisco 49ers from 1946-1952. "He was known as a tough and sometimes vicious two-way lineman who loved to intimidate…and also known for his rousing pep talks prior to games." [49] As head football coach at Riordan and with everyone knowing his professional football background, he did not have to intimidate or punish students to keep them in line. His mere presence was enough to maintain order and discipline. Barry said, "Grgich was a big man, and he loved to show us how strong he was. He taught U.S. History to our freshman class. One day he picked up a 16-pound sledgehammer at the end of the handle with one hand and held it straight out while he taught class. Then, unexpectedly, he raised the end of the sledgehammer and scratched his nose. When he left the room after class, we all tried to do what he had just done, but no way. The guy was a stud. We could believe that he could eat nails and spit them out."

Ed Fennelly was an outstanding athlete in basketball, baseball and track in high school. He attended the University of Santa Clara on an athletic scholarship and was a starter on the basketball team with a record of 21-4 in his senior year. It did not hurt knowing that he also served in the U.S. Marine Corps during WWII and was a 1st Lieutenant in the Marines during the Korean conflict. In addition to teaching, he was the basketball and track coach.

Albert "Cap" Lavin went by "Cappy". His son Steve Lavin became a successful basketball coach at UCLA and St. John's University. As a player at St. Ignatius High School in the 1940s, Cappy was named San Francisco's High School Player of the Decade. A guard who was noted for his ball handling, he played for the University of San Francisco (USF) during 1949-1953 and was inducted into the University's Hall of Fame. Cappy taught English and eventually wrote 19 books.

Most students' favorite teacher was Cappy Lavin. That included Barry who had these fond memories of him. "Cappy was a very dapper dresser. He wore beautiful tweed suits, stylish shirts and ties. He was, by far, the best-dressed person at Riordan. However, he had a crappy car – 'Cappy's crappy car.' He drove a 1941 Buick that often did not start in the morning. So my friend, Gerry Hipps, after leaving the seminary, was living near Cappy's home on 34th Avenue and sometimes had to assist Cappy by pushing his car to get it started in order to get to school. Cappy was the best teacher and my favorite because he had a great sense of humor and instilled in me and others a love for reading and writing. I read *Mad Magazines* hidden behind my textbook in some classes but never in Cappy's class. He had us recite passages from William Shakespeare to Samuel Taylor Coleridge, as he stood at the back of the room urging us on." "Barry," he asked, "What is your favorite passage from 'The Rime of the Ancient Mariner?' I replied, 'Water water everywhere, nor any drop to drink.' And thus began a class discussion on the meaning of that line. Cappy Lavin will always be remembered as a great teacher."

Ross Giudice was in the U.S. Navy and fought in WWII on the USS California. He later played for the USF Dons from 1945-1950 along side Cappy Lavin. Giudice was remembered for sinking an underhand free throw in the final minute to secure the 1949 NIT Championship against Loyola-Chicago. I wondered why Giudice did not coach basketball at Riordan. I heard he was a good player at USF earlier, but I did not know he was the lone assistant coach for USF's varsity basketball team at that time and the freshman team head coach since 1950 under legendary coach Phil Woolpert. During the 1950s, Guidice was the assistant coach of the powerhouse 1955-1956 teams. Basketball great Bill Russell credited him with the real refinement and development of his game. **[50]**

While coaching outstanding basketball teams at USF, Giudice brought K.C. Jones and Hal Perry to speak to us for one of the basketball rallies held in our gym in January 1955 – pretty special to see and hear local celebrity athletes up close. K.C. and Bill Russell eventually signed with the Boston Celtics. Perry signed with the Harlem Globetrotters but was told he was too short (5'10") to play in their barnstorming environment by the team's owner, Abe Saperstein. However, Abe paid Perry's way to law school, leading to Hal's own law practice. **[51]**

Had I known about Ross Giudice's playing and coaching background, I would not have thought of him as just my typing teacher. I learned years later that being an assistant coach at USF did not pay well, so he taught at Riordan High School and helped operate a furniture store at the same time.

The lesson learned from these examples as to what led to order and discipline in the classroom by the teacher's mere presence was that the background and accomplishments of all teachers should be revealed to the students before the school year begins, possibly in the form of a Teacher's Directory. I am sure many of the teachers and coaches had experiences that would have gained a special respect of their students if the students only had known their background.

Going through high school was like going through the U.S. Marine Corps boot camp with the exception of the "in your face" drill instructor type confrontations. They were both about improving our mind, body, character, discipline, teamwork and respect with the goal of producing a better person to face future challenges. That was why I never minded the teachers getting after students who were disruptive or trouble makers. Just as I learned in the U.S. Marine Corps, drill instructors can change the ways of decent kids with intimidation and a little verbal abuse without much or any force or violence. But there will always be one or two who will go over the hill – just not cut out for the challenge.

With the high demand of parents wanting to get their kids into a good academic school that enforced discipline, not everyone was able to qualify. Noel Murray was one of many whose scores on the entrance exam were rather low for acceptance. So his dad went over to Riordan and played the "his brother is in the seminary" card, which was true, and Noel was accepted provided he attend summer school at Sacred Heart High School, which he did. It was the first of many times that I heard about Riordan faculty showing compassion and understanding to the students and their parents.

Toughness and Courage from Tragedies

Noel Murray and I eventually and coincidentally played side-by-side, running back kickoffs and playing in the same offensive and defensive backfields, not knowing that we had a similar upbringing. We had similar economical backgrounds, family life, interests and experiences as kids, but we barely knew each other in school. It would be so useful in creating friendships in school if kids in various school activities and sports would have to break up into smaller groups like frosh-soph versus junior-senior, position on teams (backs, linemen, ends) and school activity groups, to introduce each other by talking about their backgrounds, interests, and so forth, just like the football coach did with the white and African-American players in the movie *We Are Marshall*. In our case, we went through school knowing so little about the personal life of our classmates. It would bring kids closer together and create friendships otherwise not made.

Noel came from the Outer Mission, a working class neighborhood a lot like so many kids in those days. The fathers worked as carpenters, teamsters, electricians and plumbers. Most mothers stayed home and took care of the kids, and there were lots and lots of kids playing outside on the sidewalks and in the parks. There was a little larceny in him, like the rest of us. His neighbor grew a vegetable garden in his yard, and one day, he good-naturedly accused Noel of stealing some of his strawberries. When Noel denied it, he gently lifted Noel up and planted him squarely in some footprints in the dirt next to the berries. Busted!

Like me, Noel also enjoyed museums, especially the Junior Museum (later the Randall Museum) in the summer. **[52]** His favorites were the Reptile Room with the snakes and turtles, the library and the woodshop. The fellow running the woodshop gave kids a part of a model airplane, usually the fuselage, which they sanded thoroughly; then they received another part to be sanded and eventually put them together. The airplanes were model B38s. On Wednesday afternoons, there was a reading hour – all reading, no talking.

At age five, Noel had just come home from school for lunch and saw an ambulance from Alemany Emergency, his father's truck and neighbors. Later, a black coroner's wagon arrived. His brother Jackie, who had been sick with a bad cold, had died in his sleep. It turned out that he had died from bronchial pneumonia. He was not quite three years old. Noel sat on the curb outside his house watching the coroner remove Jackie's body. He just said, "Bye, Jackie." Some kids had to face tragedy at too young of an age, but they were tougher and more understanding for it.

Each June during his grammar school days, Noel's mother began lay-away purchases of clothes at J.C. Penney's for the coming school year – a pair of tans, a pair of grays, usually a size larger, with deep hems so he could grow into them. At school as a traffic boy he was entitled to a traffic boy rate at the local theaters – just three cents at the Granada and Amazon Theaters instead of 20 cents. There also was a traffic boy discount at Seals Stadium baseball games.

At Balboa Park on San Jose Avenue, just north of Ocean Avenue, he enjoyed playing in the park's "Jungle" – a wooded area that was mostly eucalyptus trees next to a big field. The Jungle was taken out in the early 1950s and replaced with two baseball and two softball fields, as well as a new soccer field, and then a pool.

Noel never owned a bike, but he borrowed a neighbor's bike that was too big for him. He could not quite reach the pedals when they were at their lowest level. He got going fairly fast down Niagara Avenue and could not stop at the bottom of the hill. He broadsided a car going through the intersection, flipped over the car, got up and ran away before he could get in trouble. The poor woman driving the car was frantic, and the owner of the bike was not too pleased either.

Noel got his dog Laddie as a pup. He was part dachshund, part cocker spaniel. Dogs in those days – like the kids – ran free. Noel never walked him on a leash because Laddie followed him everywhere. He was also, unfortunately, a car chaser. One day Noel was on an errand to the butcher shop on Ocean Avenue. Laddie followed and was hit by a truck that he was chasing. The driver stopped and brought Laddie to a nearby vet but Laddie did not survive. Some kids had more than their fair share of heartbreaks, especially at such a young age. Sadly, Noel was one of them.

To Study or Not to Study, and How?

It was an interesting philosophical question whether I should devote my time to getting good grades, focus on extracurricular activities, or do both – one developed my academic knowledge and the other developed my social skills. But how should I split my time? 50-50? 75-25? Since extracurricular activities was an important aspect of being accepted by a college, which activities were the best choices? Speech Club and Drama developed public speaking skills, one of the most important skills in the job market. Working on the school newspaper developed writing skills, another important skill in the job market. [Today, technology skills would be a third important skill.] Being a class officer developed leadership skills and so would leadership on the sports field. Any activities involving a team or group developed social skills and the ability to work as a team, which was critical in the many jobs involved with working on group projects. Loners were less likely to succeed in those environments.

I never thought about how much time was the right amount of time to devote among work versus studies versus socializing versus sports. My emphasis unfortunately was on delivering newspapers, going out with my buddies, visiting the Sullivans and playing sports whenever I wanted and squeezing in studies with the remaining time, which resulted in always cramming for exams and writing papers at the last minute. In the back of my mind I kept thinking of the academic axiom, *give me the "A" students for my future teachers and the "C" students for my financial donors.* The implication was that the "A" students had the greater interest in the academic world and the best grasp of academic knowledge that could be passed on to students as teachers, while the "C" students spent their time developing their social, communication, teamwork and risk-taking skills that led to being financially successful and entrepreneurs. [53]

In grammar school, there always seemed to be enough time for my studies, probably because we were given less homework to take home. The Catholic school system knew it was important for kids at that age to be out playing and enjoying their young life. But high school was a lot different than grammar school. There were more classes, a greater variety of subject matter, harder subjects and more assignments. Although my brother and sister were excellent students, I never thought of asking them for tips on how I could be a better student. It would have been interesting to know what I was doing differently. That was why years later I thought of a couple of critical classes or sessions that should be offered for all freshmen. One would be on "How to Develop Habits to be a Better Student." What, where and how to study? Where do we find the time to study? How many hours per day and on weekends to study? Finding time for part-time jobs. How to study for different types of classes such as math/science versus literature/history? How to take notes and determine what was most important? How to prepare for exams? What software was useful for class assignments? Another class or sessions would be on "How to Read, Study and Research." How to read for comprehension and speed?

How and when to skim textbook chapters versus read in detail? How to research for and write good papers? How to do research on the Internet and other major sources and methods of doing research? These could be among the most important class sessions of our education.

It would be more effective if we got advice from high school seniors who were good students – advice from peers goes a lot further than from adults. It would be great to get advice from students who were good in all three: scholastics, athletics and extracurricular activities. How did they manage their time between studies, sports and other activities? What did they do that I did not do? A session by students for students would create a bond between them. Athletes would lay off teasing and stick up for the smart kids because they would know they were nice guys, and more importantly, owed them for the favor.

Taking notes of the lectures was always a mystery to me. Trying to determine what was important and likely to be on the exam was a constant guessing game. If I read the assigned chapter before class, I would have known better what material in the textbook was being covered in the lecture, which likely would be on the exam. No one ever said, "Focus on the lectures because the textbook gives a lot of unimportant background information." Some of the lecture was new material not in the textbook. Should new material be considered a candidate for appearing on the exam? I had no idea? Paul Scannell, one of the brightest kids in our class, told me years later that there just was not enough time to write down an entire 45-minute lecture, so he wrote in a shorthand, e.g., words, phrases, dates. He also assumed everything the teacher was lecturing in class was the most important material from the text and likely to be on the exams.

I also asked some of the really good students years later about their study habits. They generally could not remember anything special they did to get good grades other than review the material before the exams like the rest of us. They were not always fast readers, but they seemed to absorb a lot of what they read because they concentrated on what they read. I came to the conclusion that possibly their minds absorbed written material better than I did – possibly something unique to their brain and how it worked. Over the years I learned that there are a small number of those who are good at both mathematics and verbal (reading, writing and speaking), others not good at either one, and the rest of us good at math and poor at verbal or good at verbal and poor at math. I suspect those who absorbed written material well, were those who were good at verbal skills. Classes were mostly a one-way lecture from the teachers with occasional questions to the students. Teachers should break up the class into smaller discussion groups to generate an exchange of ideas, brainstorming and creating relations and friendships among kids with different interests, which would remove the divide between athletes and scholars. These social skills, which are so crucial to success in later life, are also developed through participation in school activities, whether we are working in a group or part of a team, and should be required of all students to qualify for graduation.

Not everyone can be an outstanding student, athlete or leader, but we can all be the best we can be in any of those traits. Just as average athletes can be super-achievers by practicing harder, becoming stronger and playing smarter, average students can out perform some of the smarter kids if they [54]:

• get organized	• take good notes and use them
• schedule their time	• speak up and ask questions
• set priorities	• study together
• learn to read fast	• test themselves
• study anywhere and everywhere	• do more than is asked for

Some criticized school systems for placing too much emphasis on grades at the sacrifice of other aspects of molding kids, and that focus was turning out employees like lawyers, doctors, corporate presidents and teachers but not entrepreneurs. Some kids fell into being an entrepreneur by taking over their family business, but kids were not instructed on being dreamers, creative, and risk-takers to become self-employed entrepreneurs who were good at identifying and solving problems and filling needs. High schools should try to develop those interests and abilities more. Years later I realized it required a certain type of person (entrepreneur) to start up a successful company, but it took a different type of person to manage and grow the company to the next level.

Mom bought a second hand 3-foot-wide desk for me to study at home. I varnished it to hide the years of wear and tear. At least it looked a lot better. It had a fold down desktop and various compartments for storing things at the back. There was a drawer for storing paper and supplies. The only place it fit was against the wall of my bedroom, since there were two beds and a chest of drawers and dresser taking up most of the space. I sat on a wood chair with a straight back and no padding. It was hard to sit there very long in an uncomfortable chair and staring at a wall two feet in front of me. It took a year or two to realize that I studied longer in a comfortable chair and environment that was not so claustrophobic. I also studied better where there was no clutter to distract me. My obsession with neatness and order led to my bedroom at home having no clutter around. Everything was neatly put away in drawers and in the closet.

Kids Needed Their Own Sanctuary

Most teenagers felt they were old enough to deserve privacy with their own bedroom, but that was not possible in our two-bedroom house. Dad and I were still sharing a bedroom. As a kid, I was always looking for new hiding places to get away from the adult world and the unpleasantries that went with it. Instead, my sanctuary turned out to be the Sullivan house. If I had my own room, I probably would have spent a little less time at the Sullivan's and more time in my own sanctuary like Canas described his experiences: "I was two years older than my sister. We were close as children but as I entered adolescence, our personal interaction lessened. She was still socially dependent on our parents and continued to enthusiastically participate in family gatherings, while I avoided them when possible. When my mother complained about my distant behavior, her friends assured her it was a passing phase and all male teenagers were *bayunco* (silly, stupid). Part of my distant behavior had to do with our new 'entertainment center' – a Motorola television with an attached radio and phonograph. I found myself spending more time in front of the screen watching TV programs, mainly versions of the old radio action programs, which were being phased out with the advent of television, as were the Saturday matinees at the movie theaters. Weekly productions of the *Cisco Kid* and *The Lone Ranger* were my favorites. On Saturday nights, I did join my family for the weekly variety shows, such as *Show of Shows* with Sid Caesar and Imogene Coca, the *Ed Sullivan Show*, and the *Hit Parade*, which announced the top 10 pop tunes of the week. When my parents hosted social gatherings, I retired to my bedroom in the basement and listened to my favorite rock 'n roll music on my 45 rpm record player. Listening to music in the confines of solitude at home and eventually in cars was typical of the times. I was left to develop my own customs, styles, and values independent of my parents. I took to mirroring those of my buddies, all of whom attended Riordan."

Unlike most public schools, Riordan had a *Creed for Riordan Men* that included "In our four years of high school we will endeavor to be a model student in studies, in sports, and in activities." As much as Barry and I may have wanted to live by that statement, it was easier said than done. We may have been model students in sports but not so much in studies. There were many distractions from our studies, some not all that important like this story by Barry: "One of my favorite comedy shows was *Laurel and Hardy*. Unfortunately, the show sometimes aired in the afternoon on a school day. I loved their movies so much that I did anything to stay home. The night before a movie I made it a point to tell Mom, 'I'm not feeling too good.' She touched my forehead and told me that I did not have a fever. The next morning, I went to the bathroom, locked the door, quietly turned on the hot water, and put the thermometer under the water. I made sure it was not 120 degrees, so I let it cool to about 100 degrees. I then put it in my mouth and while sitting on the toilet I opened the door and called Mom to show her my temperature. Of course, I got to stay home, and in the afternoon, I cuddled up on the sofa with a warm blanket and enjoyed the antics of my favorite comedy duo. To this day I still remember their secret greeting when they attended the Sons of the Desert Convention. Upon meeting a fellow conventioneer, both men placed their right hand on the right shoulder of the other man and their left hand on the left shoulder of the other man, so their arms were crossed, and then they both slapped their hands up and down on each other's shoulders. It was really funny, and for years I greeted some friends and family with the same secret greeting."

The Loneliness of Being Gay

I knew of Art Curtis but I never knew anything about him, since he was never in any of my classes. It was only years later that I got to know him and what a strong individual in principles and character he was –

not surprising, as he had to endure the solitude of being different from everyone or nearly everyone else at school.

His youth in the Richmond and Sunset Districts was much like every other kid's. He dreaded going to the dentist at a Painless Parker office, who was not painless according to Art. He did his fair share of pranks like pulling the lever on the fire alarm box, and he and his friends watched with excitement as the fire engines came screaming down California Street to the location of the alarm box, looking for a fire that never was. There was exhilaration and guilt – sort of the good and bad of the prank. It was a one-time thing for Art. As with most kid pranks, it was a learning process of experimenting and pushing the envelope – once tried, never done again because the virtue of guilt taught to us by the Catholic nuns won out.

Art built a battleship out of wood and painted it gray. His dad went to an Army-Navy surplus store and bought him a World War II gray Dixie Cup style sailor cap to wear while playing with it. Who knows if it was his early interest in playing with ships or attending Star of the Sea Grammar School that influenced him to join the U.S. Coast Guard after high school to serve his country.

He had his share of memorable nuns and priests but most memorable was St. Cecilia Church pastor Right Reverend Monsignor Harold Edward Collins, often referred to as "Happy Harold." He was almost larger than life to the youngsters, whom he called his "little pigeons." He turned out to be a very powerful influence in both the Archdiocese of San Francisco and the City & County of San Francisco. Art was told later that back in those days, it was the Catholics who had the most say in choosing the chief of police, while the Episcopalians had the influence in the selection of the fire chief. Harold also got a U.S. Post Office mailbox placed in the middle of the block in a residential neighborhood. It was unheard of in those days. To this day, that mailbox is still on 17th Avenue, in front of the St. Cecilia Rectory, midway between Ulloa and Vicente Streets.

Like all kids looking for the easy way out when going to confession, Art only went to Father Daniel Riordan, the "easiest" priest to confess to at church. He was the quintessential old Irish priest, harking from the "old sod," with a brogue to match. No matter what they told him were the most egregious sins just committed in their young life, the penance was always an easy five Our Fathers and five Hail Mary's. No rosaries from him.

Art's home on 15th Avenue off Ulloa Street was on the L-Taraval streetcar line, and every time the streetcar went by, the house shook because the neighborhood was built on sand. Whenever they had first-time company, they thought it was a small earthquake, but the family got used to it. Some of those living on Judah Street had the same experience.

From ages 10 to 13, he and his cousin had part-time jobs on Sundays at the Golden Gate Park Band Shell, also known as the Spreckels Temple of Music, where they set up and tore down the chairs and music stands for the Golden Gate Park Band concerts. Listening to the band play was a bonus. He also had part-time jobs at Flying A gasoline stations pumping gas, cleaning windows, and checking the engine oil and air in the tires.

Smoking cigarettes seemed to be the cool thing to do. Art tried one but did not know he was supposed to inhale. Less than impressed, he did not see what the big deal was. Then he was told he had to inhale the smoke into his lungs to get the great feeling they gave. So he did, only to cough and hack and said to himself, "What the hell is this all about – yuck!" It was another kid's experiment down the drain.

Between grade school and high school, Art shot up almost 6 inches in height. Within a year, he topped out at 6'4". Why were no coaches talking to him about playing a sport? I do not think any of the coaches were asking kids at school who had the physical appearance of being an athlete to try out for the teams. They relied solely or mainly on sport tryouts. Years later I learned that most people did not volunteer to participate in things, whether they thought they did not have the time or were not good at it. But if I asked people, many would volunteer. The biggest source of good athletes was often the students sitting in our classrooms and coaches did not take advantage of it.

Art developed a passion, and some said an obsession, for the Muni streetcars, cable cars, trolley buses and motor coaches. His classmates knew about it, thought it strange, but never bothered him about it. As in basketball, "no harm no foul." Much of his spare time was involved with riding the streetcars, in particular, and getting to know the motormen who let him operate the streetcars for a few blocks at the outer end of the lines, something incredibly exciting for a young railfan. Inspectors, especially at West Portal Tunnel, let him help them turn the streetcars around in the intersection by changing trolley poles, throwing track switches, or passing messages to motormen when the Inspector was real busy after significant service delays. Art got to know enough conductors so when he boarded with his student Muni car ticket, most punched at a hole that had already been punched. One time he had used a car ticket so many times that the entire number was literally punched away. If his classmates knew all of this was going on, they would have thought it was pretty cool. Only went to show that our stereotyping and prejudices usually stemmed from ignorance on our part.

All of his years at Riordan, Art kept a personal secret to himself. It was the realization that he was actually attracted to other guys. He kept this to himself because he feared being taunted or bullied because he was now "different" from his classmates. In retrospect years later, he said he probably could have taken some comfort from the fact that in a class of our size, he was most likely not the only one hiding the fact of being gay. It was a period of ignorance and intolerance at the time regarding this matter. It caused Art and any other gays at school a lot of unnecessary guilt and masquerading. Whatever the form of prejudice based on one being different, whether it was how we looked, dressed, spoke, or thought, we should never have condemned them for being different. As much as they may have wanted to be like the majority, they had no choice in most cases, but we had a choice of not expecting, much less requiring, them to be like the majority – we should have judged people based on those things under their control, not on the things beyond their control.

I learned years later that Art and at least one other of our classmates were gay all those years. The classmate who wrote, "The boy I adore. Love XX" in my junior yearbook was probably gay too. Being attracted to other guys was something they kept to themselves all through high school and for years afterwards. As Art put it, "It was for fear of being taunted or bullied because I was different from all my classmates." It would have been interesting how we would have reacted if we knew. Would it have been acceptable knowing that our brother, sister or friend was gay? Like everything else, I suppose some would and others would not accept a homosexual. Like name-calling and making fun of others in class, it was too bad that more kids did not think for themselves and stand up for those being picked on for any reason – sort of a Don Quixote Club who set out to right the wrongs of others or achieve impossible dreams. Whether in classrooms or on the field, one could learn from the song "The Impossible Dream" to "…fight the unbeatable foe…to right the unrightable wrong…"

Heroes in the Shadows

From the outset at Riordan, it was obvious that athletics was going to be the center of attention in high school. Athletes who made junior varsity and varsity sports wore navy blue block sweaters. The only difference was that the purple with gold trim block letter "R" (reflective of the school colors) was larger for making the varsity. On the arm of the sweater were gold bands representing each year we made the varsity. The athletes could wear their sweaters any time, but we did not see them that often. It would have been a lot different if girls attended Riordan. The times we saw them the most was when the athletes were asked to wear their sweaters to a sports rally, when serving as ushers at special events or attending a Mass for athletes. With all this fanfare for athletes, there was no special clothing for students excelling in academics or other extracurricular activities like C.S.F. (California Scholarship Federation), Band, Speech Club, *Crusader* school newspaper, or the Sodality religious group. There were no special badges, hats, vests, shirts or sweaters for them. I always thought they should have their own badge of courage for being proud of their excellence and to create a presence of each group on campus. There were school rallies in the auditorium and gymnasium to support the sports teams but no rallies to support the other groups. The Riordan Band, under the direction of Verne Sellins, had a reputation for being among the best high school bands around and got recognition when they performed at games and school functions. It was the same for those in Dramatics, under the direction of James Lindland, who had the reputation for creating the most professional stage productions of any high school in the area in a state-of-the-art school auditorium that held audiences of 1,240. But only athletics got additional recognition beyond their performance on the field.

The athletes were considered cool because they were assumed to be tough guys, but a special group of tough guys went unnoticed during our four years. I call them the "Heroes in the Shadows." Excellence in grades was not emphasized in terms of recognition paid to the smart kids. Only sports drew crowds to cheer us on and support our efforts. There were rallies for the student body to promote a big game. But there was none of that for the intellectually smart guys, the "eggheads," the "brains," the students who made the C.S.F. honor roll each year. The athletes never appreciated the accomplishments of the smart kids who devoted their effort excelling in academics. They were as competitive as the athletes if not more so.

Their toughness was displayed every day in class, not just Friday night on the football field. They put up with the pressure not to appear smarter than the rest of us and took the harassment that went along with it. Theirs was a toughness of character – not necessarily a physical toughness. While the athletes were developing their physical skills and attributes, the scholars were developing their own mental and communication skills that were far more important and longer lasting than the skills of athletes that quickly diminished after high school. We use our mind our entire life but most athletes are not good enough for college ball and usually stop exercising and playing sports after getting too busy with their job and family. The scholars often were among the members of the Speech Club, *Crusader* newspaper, *Lance* yearbook, and Sodality religious group where they developed the three most important skills for getting ahead later in life – speaking, writing and morality skills. I came to realize that achieving victory in individual competition like debating, spelling bees, test grades, and grade point averages should receive greater recognition and admiration than excelling in team sports. There was just you and you alone competing in individual competitions, while sports teams depended on other players to be successful. I always felt that any negative attitudes the other students had against the smart kids was jealousy. Whether the smart kids knew it or not, the rest of us did admire and respect them because so often we elected them as our class officers over the four years of high school.

I always assumed that the "A" students all had higher IQs, better comprehension, better at note taking and read faster, which gave them a competitive edge over the rest of us. That may have been true for some students, but the common denominator was that they had to work hard at it, just like athletes did, to excel. Some lived with handicaps that most of us did not have to face like unpleasant family situations, time consuming family responsibilities, and physical problems. A few of the kids in our class were dyslexics. In addition to having to deal with their stigma, there was the feeling of being different from other kids. It at least would have been some consolation knowing that Albert Einstein, Thomas Edison and Leonardo da Vinci were also dyslexics. Rich Kirby, one of the kids in our class with dyslexia, not only graduated with honors but was also awarded a four-year scholarship and eventually graduated from law school and became a judge. There was as much heroics going on in the classroom as there was on the playing field.

There was another student with a reading problem who never received appropriate encouragement by the teacher and had to repeat first grade. When he entered high school, he was told he would not be able to handle the Latin class based on his entrance exam. If a kid was told he can't, he probably won't. If he was told to at least try, there was a good chance he would succeed. If he was given a chance and failed, he could always drop out early. But if he was denied the opportunity to try, he was denied the chance to succeed. This kid said years later, "I was crushed. I felt real dumb and to this day these events had lasting negative memories for me." Who knows how much this influenced him not to be a better student. However, when it came to taking things apart to find out how things worked or were built and fixing things, he was in his element and always excelled at it.

Learning From Successes and Failures in the Classroom

A dumb thing a lot of us thought was that cool guys sat in the back of the classroom and the "brains" sat in the front. To some degree it was true. I suspect the serious students sat closer to the front so they could concentrate on what the teacher was saying and not get distracted by the antics of the class "cut ups." The cool guys, who were often not good academically, sat in the rear half of the classroom so they were not as visible to the teacher for fear of being called on and being embarrassed by not being able to answer questions or interpret the literature. I found that sitting in the back of the room, there was a lot of fidgeting, horseplay and fooling around, especially when the teacher had his back to the class.

As a result, I often lost track of what the teacher was saying and missed the entire statement. Although it would be unfair to the good students, teachers occasionally should have switched those in the back with those in the front. It certainly would help the concentration of us poorer students.

Teachers told us answering questions in class would help our final grade. They were good about not randomly calling on people to answer questions, probably so they did not embarrass students like me for not reading the homework assignment or coming unprepared for class. Instead, they asked us to raise our hand if we knew the answer or they frequently called on the smart students who they knew read the material. About the only time I raised my hand was in the math classes. I could see that the smart kids stopped raising their hands as frequently by the time we were juniors and seniors. Either they were getting tired of carrying the class by always providing the answers or they felt it was not popular or cool to be the smart kid in class. That was the perspective of a lot of the average students. We did not consider it cool to raise our hand to answer questions. That was only for the "teacher's pets," which we did not want to be labeled. It also was a matter of feeling that we were showing up our classmates as if to say, "See how smart I am." Maybe it would have been better if teachers called on all of us randomly in the freshman and sophomore years, so by our junior and senior years we would have gotten tired of appearing like dummies for not being able to answer the questions. It may have been the motivation we needed to study more and come better prepared to class, but I suspect not. Telling us that answering questions would help our final grade was not enough of an incentive to study more, overcome kid's shyness of speaking up, or the stereotype images we had of those who did speak up. However, if they got more of the cool kids to participate, it may have helped change the mental labeling of others based on class participation.

Some kids developed a bad attitude toward certain subjects in their freshman year and it stayed with them for all four years. Whether it resulted from using the reason as an excuse for doing poorly in a class or because teachers could not change their attitude, some of my classmates complained they did not like certain classes because they did not see how they could use the information later in life. Often it was the science, math, Latin and foreign language classes. Kids would learn better from seeing

320

demonstrations, the use of props and explanations of how a measurement, calculation, theory or principle applied to a real life example.

Although I was not good at book learning, I found, as I got older, that I did possess a lot of common sense. Many of my decisions in life did not involve things taught in school textbooks. I could not always depend on my education and often there was no one around to help me. I found using common sense led to so many right decisions in life. Whether the decision involved people, places or things, my litmus test for facing the situation was to ask myself "Does that make sense?" Maybe I had more common sense than many others because of my analytical mind and propensity for mathematical problem solving, but I did find that I tended to question things more than others rather than just accept what one said, read or wrote. At the other end of the common sense spectrum was Mom who once defended her argument with me by responding, "If it appears in the newspaper, it must be true." Some say that common sense cannot be learned, but it comes from having many experiences, which I had at an early age. I probably learned from my many mistakes and successes – another reason for kids to participate in a lot of extracurricular activities.

Ross Giudice was my typing teacher. He gave us the option to learn the right way to type or to type with just two index fingers. For students who were interested and willing to practice, he taught them how to type properly. Years later many of those students said, "Typing served me well in life." But those like me who did not have the patience and discipline to practice, he allowed us to develop the hunt and peck method (two-finger typing). A big regret of mine about high school was that I did not learn to type properly. It was my own fault because I had a choice, and even though I prided myself on making my own decisions, I understood that some would be bad decisions and I should suffer the consequences. At the time, I just viewed typing as a secretary's skill, but it would have been such a valuable skill later in life when I wound up doing so much typing to write articles and books, and who could have foreseen the advent of laptop computers? [55]

Legendary James Lindland, Chairman of our award-winning Drama Department, turned out years of the best theatrical performances of any high school in the country, winning many awards along the way. One of his students, Joe Spano, television and stage actor, went on to appear regularly on *Hill Street Blues* and *NCIS*. One of the most valuable classes was in my freshman year in Lindland's speech class to develop one of the critical skills in life. Although nearly all of us dreaded to stand up in front of the class, he was a fun guy as a teacher. If Lindland needed to correct us for doing something wrong, he affectionately called us "Booby" for messing up. "Let's try that again, Booby." For one of his assignments, we were asked to get up in front of the class and do anything we wanted, whether it was sing, dance, recite, give a speech, anything. We were all in the same boat. We were never asked to get up in front of a class before, so we all sweated out what we could do. All in all, I enjoyed what everyone wound up doing. We saw a personal side of these guys that we never saw before. I had no musical skills, had a terrible singing voice, but I loved music, so I chose to mime a record that I used to sing along with at home, so I at least knew the words pretty well, which was easier than learning something from scratch. The song's name was "Gilly Gilly Ossenfeffer Katzenellen Bogen by the Sea." Of all the other songs I could have chosen, I thought this one was a fun one and each verse ended with the title of the song, which was kind of cute. I was so focused on remembering the words, I never thought about the audience or being scared. Later in life, I learned the secret to making speeches in front of audiences was to know the content so well that I did not need to memorize the speech or could use minimal, if any, notes so I could just talk off the top of my head – just remembering a list of key words so I covered the material enough. If I left something out, no big deal – no one would know the difference, so no need to sweat it. Another trick was to look at the back wall of the room just above everyone's head to avoid eye contact and seeing their facial expressions. Scanning the back wall back and forth above head level made the audience think you were speaking to them individually.

The one thing that Barry hated most at school was when he was told to get up and speak in front of the class. As he said, "I always had a fear of public speaking, not only because of my speech impediment, but because I was constantly teased. When the teacher called my name to get up in front of the class my heart slowly began to pound, and I hated that feeling. When I began to speak the class erupted into a chant 'Tomato, Tomato, Tomato,' when I turned my usual 50 shades of red. I felt the heat rising and my face turning hot and hotter. The fact that I was a lifelong blusher haunted me for years. It was not until a psychiatrist told me blushing was good for my face because it brought more oxygen and enhanced my complexion, that I stopped blushing. He said it made people realize that I could be trusted because, after all, if I could so easily allow my feelings to rush into my face, they could trust me. The other positive for blushing was that most girls found it endearing and sensitive. I guess they could relate to it. His advice made me feel much better, but it still hampered me later in pursuing a career as an actor."

Like Barry discovered, I also found later in life when I was doing a lot of public speaking, that another thing that women found attractive, was when men showed their emotions. Frequently, when I was speaking about something that I felt very strongly about or stirred my emotions, I would get teary-eyed and have to stop to gather my composure. As soon as I was ready to continue, I would address the men in the audience and tell them, "All you guys in the audience, never be ashamed of getting teary-eyed or showing your emotions. Women LOVE it." Every time it got a big laugh, so I was never ashamed of getting teary-eyed or choked up in public.

The most indelible memory that Noel Murray had of our freshman year was also in speech class. Noel said, "I was called upon to come to the front of the class to read aloud. I stumbled and stammered, broke into tears and fled the room. After that, the teacher understood the degree of my shyness and did not call on me very often to answer questions. One day, Lindland was the substitute teacher in the speech class. He skimmed through the list of student names and randomly called on me to read aloud. I felt like all eyes were on me but I took a real deep breath and read the assignment. When I finished, all the kids in the room clapped. It was a moment of relief…and the feeling of acceptance by my classmates." This was an example of how the faculty recognized the unique challenges individuals faced in adjusting to our new surroundings, allowed us to face challenges at our own pace, and let us reach inside ourselves to overcome our greatest fears when the time was right.

A common English class assignment was to write a book report or summary to prove that we actually read the book. I was a terribly slow reader. It took me weeks to get through a 150 to 200-page book, so I had forgotten what I read when I was finished. The idea of sitting down and reading an entire book in the same day was just beyond my imagination, so I was always looking for shortcuts to studying. Most of us were raised on comic books and we knew *Classics Illustrated* comic books provided abbreviated versions of many classic books. Some were selected by the teacher as the book to be reviewed. I sometimes wondered if this was one reason that teachers chose specific books for us to read, but I doubted it. So reading the *Classics Illustrated* version of an assigned book when possible was my forte for my entire four years in high school. I "never had the time" to read a book for a class assignment, so I often found a *Classics Illustrated* version at the magazine stand at the drugstore at 34th Avenue and Judah Street. Comic books were ten cents and the *Classics Illustrated* were 15 cents – a small enough price to pay to get a "C" or "C-" grade to save all the time to read an entire book. In hindsight, it was like cheating on an exam. My lack of interest in reading only hurt me by not benefiting from the enjoyment that came from reading great literature. Years later, a University of California survey found that Americans spent more money on comic books than all the country's elementary schools and high schools spend on textbooks. **[56]** Makes me wonder how many were for *Classics Illustrated* being used for book reports. My poor study habits and not devoting the time necessary to do well explained why I was a "C" student throughout high school – something I have always been ashamed of and regretted. For a guy who worked so hard to excel at so many things, I failed at the most important. Fortunately I got a second chance and made up for it in college.

Organizing a Fart Orchestra

In the physical education classes, we had to be careful in the gym locker room. If we were bending over and drying off, we needed to be sure no one snuck up behind us to snap a towel to hit our bare butt. It especially stung if it was a damp towel – something we learned at an early age. There was also Fart-making 101 going on in the showers. By placing our hand in the opposite arm pit and creating an airtight pocket, then jerking our elevated arm to our side we could make the sound of a fart. Once one kid started it and others in the shower did the same, we had our own fart orchestra bringing laughter to everyone in earshot of the "music." It was not until I went out for football the next year that I ever heard of jock straps and cups. The coach told us to bring one or the other to the next practice, whichever we preferred. One of the fellas asked the guy next to him what a cup was and the guy told him it was something to put over your nose to protect it.

Personal Dress and Grooming Misadventures

During the school year, there were various dances held in the school gym, each one with a different sponsor like the Block Society and Senior Class. Now that I was in high school, my taste in clothing was changing and I wanted at least to look normal and presentable at the school dances. I gave up the idea that a black shirt and yellow silk tie were cool, and needed something different. I asked my brother when he returned from the service what kind of sport coat he liked. He said a one-button roll (only one button on the jacket so both lapels rolled naturally outward) was the style that was popular when he was my age. I knew that was four to eight years earlier, but I figured styles must be pretty much the same. I saw a picture of one and thought it was cool too. Of course that was coming from a kid who thought being dressed all in black was cool. I went to all of the major department and men's stores, and they all told me "They no longer carry that style. They went out of style 10-15 years ago." I even looked into having one custom made. Even though I liked the look, I was afraid I would look too weird to the other guys. So, I settled for a more "conventional" sport coat. I bought my first sport coat at a time when charcoal and pink were a popular combination. Looking back, it was popular mostly with girls. In any case, I bought a charcoal sport coat with checkered thin pink streaks. I was the only guy in school with one. The jacket mostly hung in my closet because we just wore shirts or sweaters to the dances. For high school proms, I rented plaid jackets or cummerbunds. Once I wore plaid pants. Everyone else wore white or black tuxedo jackets, which seemed too dressy to me. I never liked getting dressing up, which was a trait that stuck with me all of my life, even the 30 years I was wearing a suit and tie in the business world. Maybe it was my desire not to lose sight of my early roots and upbringing in the Mission when I wore tattered clothes and well-worn shoes.

Cure for Insecurity

Going to school dances, I took more notice of my big ears. I asked Mom if there was some way I could make them stick out less, and why she did not do anything about them, since she did so much to correct my flat feet. She just shrugged off the suggestion and said, "There is no need. There is nothing wrong with them. Your ears are fine." I wanted to believe her, although I never quite believed her, but maybe she was right. I had no reason not to believe her because she never lied to me before. In hindsight, the big ears may have contributed to my "cuteness" as some grammar school female classmates described me decades later. Eventually, I simply realized that the cure to a lot of insecurities was to see how many successful, good looking and famous people had the same "problem" that I had, and the problem should not be viewed as a handicap or impediment. I noticed famous and successful people had big ears like movie and sports stars Clark Gable, Gregory Peck, Bing Crosby, Douglas Fairbanks Jr. and Ty Cobb. I also learned from their pictures that if I turned my head at a slight angle to the camera, portrait shots of me did not show my ears sticking out. This was why all of my yearbook pictures show an angle shot of my head. As I accomplished things and achieved minor and major successes along the way, I just did not give a damn any more, I finally learned that self-worth, character and accomplishments were way more important than being different like physical defects, peculiarities, and race. These were beyond one's control; I just focused on things within my control.

One morning I was in the bathroom combing my hair to get ready to go to school, and Mom said I should only put water in my hair and stop using Wildroot hair oil like Dad used. She told me a friend of the family, Pat O'Brien (not the movie star), had a full head of beautiful long white wavy hair, and he was in his late 70s. It was true. It was an impressive head of hair. Mom said it was because he never put anything in his hair except water. For a while I switched over to just water but my short hair stuck out on the sides like a porcupine, so I went back to the hair oil. Years later as I was losing my hair, I thought back and wondered if Mom was right until I learned that the loss of hair was not caused by hair oil but was more of an inherited gene thing.

Lessons Learned From Dad Beaten to Hell

The biggest thing that happened on the home front in my freshman year was that Dad had the hell beaten out of him. Illegal "pay-to-play" tactics had been a common practice in the beer distribution business since Prohibition. This involved offering incentives (bribes) to bar owners and managers to stock or push their beer over the competitors' beers. They in return offered to provide a new draft beer system, lavish gifts, cold hard cash, and occasionally, they used muscle if necessary. Dad was always a meek person, on the weak side, and never bothered anyone. He was 5'8", slender build, about 150 lbs., but more like the "97-pound weakling." One day when Dad was working the bar by himself, a driver making a delivery of one of the local major brewery beers came in and said to him, "How is it you're not selling my draught (draft) beer?" Dad said, "There wasn't much demand for the draught beer – just the bottled beer." I do not know what incentives, if any, the driver offered Dad to sell his beer and stop stocking the other beers, but the driver realized his arguments were not going to change Dad's refusal to do so. At that point, the drive jumped over the bar counter and beat the crap out of Dad. His face was battered with red bruises and dark discoloring around the eyes and cheeks as he lay in the hospital bed. I was only 14 years old, but I told Mom we needed to get a lawyer and sue the hell out of the beer company, but Mom seemed reluctant, maybe for fear that someone would come back and beat him up again. They did get a lawyer recommended by an Irish acquaintance – one of the customers Dad knew from the bar. The lawyer said to them, "The legal fees will be very expensive to sue the beer company, so I can negotiate a settlement." They took his advice. The "settlement" resulted in the beer company only paying for Dad's medical expenses. There was no compensation for Dad's pain and suffering. The lawyer told them, "You were lucky to get that much." Mom was so grateful they got the medical expenses covered. Back then and to this day, I am convinced that the beer company bought off the lawyer to settle out of court, since that was how business was often done. I also thought if Dad's employer did not provide medical coverage for their employees, the least they could have done was to hire a lawyer to sue the beer company. After all, they were friends from childhood and Dad worked for McCarthy's for the past 15 years. I was just a kid but Joe and Kathy were older and they should have convinced my folks to push for more or to at least get a different lawyer, even though I doubt it would have made a difference. It was just how my folks were – don't rock the boat and avoid confrontation.

Years later, Mom looked back at the beating and said, "Dad was never the same after that beating." Whether it was the injuries from the beating or heavier drinking afterwards to forget the beating that caused Dad to be committed to Agnews State Hospital for a second time for more shock treatments was not clear. From this experience, I learned it was always best to stand up for my rights, fight for what was fair, and speak up for those who were being taken advantage of, like my folks. I swore never to let someone take advantage of me and get away with it. That was why years later I got a law degree to learn my rights so that such things could not happen to my family or me again.

A Day With the Ghosts

The most interesting trip I ever took with Mom was to visit the Winchester Mystery House in San Jose. Mom used it as an incentive for me to go with her to visit Dad at Agnews. It was a smart idea of hers to use some form of entertainment to incent a kid to do something. I learned that construction of the Winchester House started in 1884 by the widow of the Winchester rifle magnate and continued until her death in 1922, taking 38 years to build the mansion with 160 rooms and thousands of doors and windows. There were 40 stairways (most with 13 steps), blind stairways that went nowhere, hundreds of closets (some opened into blank walls), trap doors in the floor and secret passageways. It was not a place to be without a tour guide. The millions of dollars to build this 6-acre complex came from the Winchester rifle fortune. Supposedly, the mansion was haunted by the ghosts of those killed with the rifles, none of whom did we see on our visit.

Dad was released from Agnews in 1954. On nights that Mom worked late and Dad got off work after 6:00 p.m., I met Dad at McCarthy's and we went to our old favorite – Zim's on Market Street. If Dad got off earlier, he came home and cooked dinner for the two of us since my sister was married and no longer around to cook our meals. We each usually had a lamb chop

328

with a baked potato. Dad was not a cook, but it only involved setting the oven, putting two potatoes in the oven along with two chops in pie tins to catch the grease, and occasionally poking the potatoes to see if they were soft inside. It was my first "cooking lesson" and something even I could handle.

This was the second time Dad spent two to three months at Agnews. He was more withdrawn and just sat in front of the television hour after hour at home. Mom thought calling in a local priest from Holy Name might help him snap out of it. The young priest, Father Keane, came over and spoke with Dad for at least an hour and then told Mom there was nothing more he could do. Mom was livid and told him she expected more help from the Church after all they had done for the Catholic Church all those years she and Dad had attended Mass every Sunday and religious days, contributed to the weekly collections even when they could not afford it, participated in Church functions, and she and Dad served as the heads of the Women's Club and Father's Club at St. Charles Church in the past. The priest kept his cool but left a little upset too. Like him, I did not know what she expected, but I felt it was unfair to blame the priest and the Church. Mom stopped going to Church for a very long time after that, which meant Dad did not go either.

Regrettable Welcoming After Return From Korean War

My brother Joe had been an air traffic controller and sergeant in the U.S. Air Force for the past four years. He was there from the start to the end of the Korean War. He never came home on leave, so I never saw him from 1950-1954 when I was 10-14 years of age. The day Joe finally came home, I was playing with toys on the floor of our living room. When he appeared in the doorway, I just stared at him as if he had just returned from shopping for groceries. I showed no great emotion, did not know what to say to him, and did not jump up to hug him or shake his hand because I just saw a stranger. I am sure it was not the "welcome home" he was expecting. Years later I felt sorry for the nonchalant reception he got when he arrived home. But our family was never a bunch of huggers. Mom, Dad and the kids were not raised that way. I never had strong bonds with my brother or sister because they were so much older than me, so they understandably just treated me as a kid whom they did not want to be seen with when their friends were around. I was never bitter about it. We just had different interests. I just accepted the fact that big kids did not want to be around little kids.

Once Joe settled in, he did give me a carved pool stick from Japan. He had never given me anything in the past, so it was a big deal to me. I kept it for 40 years as one of the few keepsakes I had from him and passed it on to his son eventually. I also kept a "Korea" arm patch, an air controller pin and his "Miho" baseball cap from clothing he brought home as well as a newspaper picture of the USNS General Nelson M. Walker transport ship that brought Joe back home and docked at Treasure Island. Later he told me the highlight of his tour in the service was a flight on its way to Japan. The pilot asked him if he wanted to talk to the movie actress Marilyn Monroe who was on board. Before he could answer, Marilyn got on the radio and spoke to Joe and the others in the control tower. It was the only thing he ever told me about his four years in the service other than they spent a lot of time drinking because they were under so much pressure on the job. His reason was probably true, but he had been a drinker before and after the service.

Learning to Drive in the Garage

Every teenager was in a hurry to drive a car. I was no different. One day I got in Mom's car sitting in the garage. I did not know how to drive and I knew I could not go anywhere, but I sat in the driver's seat to just get a feel for holding the steering wheel and putting my feet on the peddles. I shifted the gear into neutral to feel what it was like steering while the car was moving, even if it was just a foot or so. The car started to role forward and I had to put on the brake sooner than I thought, but it was too late. The front fender ran into the large furnace pipe and put a large dent in it. I had to leave the car resting against the furnace pipe and hoped Mom did not notice when she started the car in the morning. Mom never said anything to me, so she either did not notice it or thought she did the damage. I never asked.

No one on Mom or Dad's side of the family ever came out from Ireland to visit us until Mom's sister Chris Collins visited us that year. We thought

Yosemite National Park would be a good place to take her and she could see some of California along the way. It was a three to four-hour ride or 170 miles, the same distance as the entire width of the island of Ireland. Not used to traveling anywhere the size of California, she asked us every 15-20 minutes, "Isn't it time for tea?" It got to be the joke of the trip – a good laugh for all of us. We did stop once for tea along the way, to her great joy.

Tough to Live With Excessively High Expectations

Mom had a history of high expectations. She sent out birthday and Christmas cards religiously, and she expected to receive cards in return. The Daubenecks were close friends with our family for years. We went on vacations with them. My sister palled around with their daughter Betty. Her father Ed was our barber. This year Mom did not receive a birthday card from Mrs. Dauberneck. Mom was beside herself and went ballistic. She said, "After all our years of being such close friends, how could she forget my birthday?" I tried reasoning with her. I told Mom to phone her, but there was no forgiveness in her heart. Mom never saw or spoke to Mrs. Daubeneck again. I thought how sad. The card may have just gotten lost in the mail.

Even I did not escape her excessive expectations. I gave Mom a Best Mother in the World Certificate on Mother's Day. Since I always called her "Mom" I wrote in "Mom" where the recipients name appeared. She really got upset and thought it was terrible that I did not use her actual full name. Another time, I made the mistake of misspelling her name. Mom's full name was Catherine Frances Quinlan. She went by Frances Quinlan, but I always wrote and called her "Mom." On this occasion, I misspelled her first name as "Francis." Never having a need to write her given name when I was young, I could never remember the correct spelling. The same was true as to whether it was Catherine or Katherine, which I misspelled once too. In both cases, Mom got really upset with me, and I had no defense. It was unforgivable that I did not know the correct spelling of my own mother's name, but the spelling of names was not high on my list of importance things at that age.

Following sports during our high school years was fun and exciting to say the least, but Kezar, home of the San Francisco 49ers, was not where to go to watch football games. Of the 59,000 seats, only 18,000 (30%) were between the goal lines. [57] Also, there was very limited parking. Lots of the neighbors in the area rented out their driveways for game day parking. Fortunately for me, I just walked a half a block, jumped on the 72-Sunset bus, and got dropped off at Kezar about three miles away. On the way home, I walked a few blocks up Haight Street to get a seat on the bus home to beat the crowd waiting at the stadium bus stop. But I mostly watched 49er games on television. I saw the game much better than from end zone seats and snacks were much cheaper at home. I also avoided sitting shoulder to shoulder in the stands, standing shoulder to shoulder at the men's latrine, enduring the hassle of crowds in and out of the stadium, and trying to catch a bus after the game.

The San Francisco 49ers had Y.A. Tittle (replaced by John Brodie in 1958) at quarterback and a backfield of Hugh "The King" McElhenny, Joe "The Jet" Perry and John Henry Johnson. Among the linemen were Bob St. Clair and Leo Nomellini. R.C. Owens came to the team in 1956 and was part of the "Alley Oop" pass developed in 1957. It basically was a jump ball pass where Tittle threw a high-arching pass and the 6'3" tall, long-armed Owens outjumped the defender for a reception. Although they had mediocre records during my high school years, except in 1957 when they lost to the Detroit Lions 27-31 in the Western Conference Playoffs, the 49ers were exciting to watch with their "Million Dollar Backfield." Compiling record offensive statistics, they were considered possibly the best backfields in NFL history, as it still is the only full house backfield to have each member enshrined in the Pro Hall of Fame.

Seats at Kezar were $1.00 to $3.75 for end zone "nose bleed" seats, but if kids cut out the coupon on the back of a carton of Christopher Milk, which was owned by local politician George Christopher, we could sit in the Christopher Milk section in the northeast side of the end zone for only 50 cents. Not only was it hard to see the action on the field from the end zone, the sun was in our eyes if the sun ever showed up without overcast skies. The stadium was unconventionally laid out east-to-west because that was the space available to build on the available site of an old Park nursery and stable yard. It meant the sun was in the eyes of the 70% of the

332

fans sitting in the end zones. Less than 30% of the fans had seats between the goalposts because a wide six-lane track circled the playing field and the stadium was built too close to Lincoln Way. [58]

If we did not have 50 cents, there were the free seats on the rooftops of the houses and Polytechnic High School just across the street from Kezar. They had better views than the Chicago Cub fans who watched baseball games from the rooftops across from Wrigley Field. If we were daring, we could climb the Kezar light towers, step on the ledge at the top, climb over, and look for an empty seat.

The Shriner's East-West game at Kezar in 1955 cost me five dollars for equally bad seats (program was 50 cents), but I got to see one of my collegiate heroes Howard "Hopalong" Cassady from Ohio State, and the East was coached by "Woody" Hayes. The nickname "Hopalong" came from the western movie character Hopalong Cassidy, the same source Bob "Hopalong" Hoppe got his nickname. He was the other halfback in the "pony backfield" I was part of on the Riordan varsity football team in my junior year.

But the best team to watch and cheer for was the University of San Francisco Dons basketball team playing under Hall of Fame coach Phil Woolpert and assistant coach Ross Giudice. The Dons played in the Sweet Sixteen NCAA finals all four of our high school years (1954-1958). [59] The primary home court for the Dons was Kezar Pavilion, located next door to Kezar Stadium. Although the Pavilion held 4,000 people, it was a "breadbox" for watching games. Whenever I attended games there, it felt like the rafters were rocking and the floor was bouncing when the USF fans shouted and screamed their cheers for the home team and jeers for the opponents. The noise level brought an electric atmosphere to the game. The USF 1955-1956 team was recognized as a racial pioneer for being the first of any four-year collegiate or professional team to win a national championship with a majority of African-American starters.

Unlike the Mission District where I had at least five movie theaters within walking distance from home, the Sunset District had the Surf, Irving and Parkside Theaters. These were much longer walks or Muni rides until one eventually got their own car, but that was all right. My buddies and I only went to local movie theaters together. We never went to movies downtown because the theater ticket prices were higher and we had to pay for parking once we could drive. We generally went to the Parkside Theater on Taraval Street off 19th Avenue because they had the best selection of movies.

Up the street from the Parkside Theater was my favorite hamburger place, Zim's Restaurant, at the corner of 19th Avenue and Taraval Street. On many a night when I was in the area, I went there for a hamburger made of whole choice chuck steak, french fries and a chocolate milkshake made with real ice cream if it was still early, but if it was late, I ordered coffee and a slice of their thick apple pie à la mode.

Scared Straight Cure-All for Wise-Asses

While four of us were walking along Sunset Boulevard between Lawton and Moraga Streets, I was throwing rocks at the bushes like target practice. One of us, probably me, got the bright idea of pretending to throw rocks at passing cars as a joke. So we stood with nothing in our hands in front of the bushes on the walking path so passing motorists could see us. As a car drove by, the four of us faked throwing something at the car to see the reaction on the driver's face. We did that to three or four cars and the motorists looked startled and a couple momentarily turned their heads away from us as if something was going to hit them. But we tried it once too often because the next car we did it to, a carload of older teenagers yelled out the window at us. We laughed as we watched the car drive to the end of the block until we saw them start to circle back to come after us. As we ran off, I was thinking how I never expected this to happen to us, but I was not surprised, as I would have reacted the same way. We should have scattered in different directions instead of the same direction, which made it too easy for them to round us up. They caught up with us and asked what we were doing. At least one of us was scared – me. We explained we were just pretending to throw something to get reactions from people and not really throwing anything. Fortunately, they were not violent guys out looking to pick a fight because they could have kicked the crap out of us. They let us go, probably because they knew nothing hit their car, but I was so surprised that they did not throw any punches to teach us a lesson. I think we just lucked out to pick on nonviolent guys, and if they were from a different neighborhood, it could have been a different story. We never did that again – lesson learned.

One day a buddy of mine and I took the Muni to the Marina District and walked to the south end of the Golden Gate Bridge. It was a good thing it was not a real windy day. As we walked across the bridge, the cold wind blew in our faces constantly. Somehow the air smelled and felt fresher than on the mainland. There was a slit between the walkway and the road that allowed me to watch the surging tides far below with the hope of seeing a ship passing under the bridge. The scarier view was over the railing. It was a long ways down (245 feet at the highest point). I kept thinking, *I hope the wind does not pick me up and blow me over the side.* As I stared at the water, there was a touch of acrophobia at the beginning, but it went away the longer I gazed at the swooshing waves. It was quite hypnotic but entertaining because I could also see the boats passing under the bridge "up close" and from a completely different, sky view angle. At times I could feel the bridge sway in the strong winds over the Bay and hear occasional creaking, making me wonder if the whole bridge was going to collapse. By the time we reached the other side, I felt it was a great adventure every kid should experience and it was free. It did not get any better than that.

This year was the first time I went to the Main Drive in Golden Gate Park to watch the San Francisco Bay to Breakers Race. It was a hoot. The race started in 1912, but this day there were thousands of participants, many in outlandish costumes, running or walking the 7.5-mile race from the Ferry Building on the Bay to Ocean Beach. The route went up Market Street to Golden Gate Avenue, turned on to Divisadero Street, along the Panhandle, then through Golden Gate Park to the Great Highway. In 1940, Bobbie Burke ran disguised as a man because women were not allowed to participate. Little did she know back then that it would be common in this race for men to appear as women and vise versa after the gay and lesbian movement took hold in the City.

When my high school buddies and I were not doing things together, we were off doing our own thing. Beyma enjoyed fishing since 6th grade at Holy Name. When he fished in Golden Gate Park where it was not legal, he hid in the bushes with just the fishing pool visible. Later in high school, he went a couple of times a month fishing on Muni Pier (also called Municipal Pier and Aquatic Park Pier) at the end of Van Ness Avenue. He once shared his lunch with an old (70-plus) African-American guy. The fishing was good and his friend shared his thoughts with Beyma, such as "The only things in life that count are big breasts and a tight ass."

Carmody and Ray Andreini would ride down the highway in the back of Applebee's truck shooting their .22 rifles at anything in remote areas that served as targets. I suppose it was inevitable that Carmody's interest in guns and fast cars would lead him to a career in law enforcement. No one would do the same if they were uncomfortable around either of them.

Barry developed a new interest in music. "In 1955 I purchase my first 45 rpm record, 'Rock Around the Clock' by Bill Haley and the Comets. My heart got broken when I hurried into my room to play it on my small player, tossed the record on my bed, and when I sat down to take off my shoes, I sat on the record and broke it. Man, I was angry! I loved that song and it was the beginning of my lifelong love affair with rock 'n roll."

Canas also listened to music on his 45 rpm record player a lot of the time in his room. Rock 'n roll was his favorite music of choice. As Canas described it, "It blended the beats of boogie-woogie, country, gospel, jump blues, and rhythm 'n blues, such as 'Smokey Joe's Café' by the Robins. Ed Finn, who had a keen interest in this new music, and I went to a Saturday matinee at the Paramount Theater on Market Street featuring the Robins and other rhythm 'n' blues singers and bands. The audience was predominantly African-American and the place was rocking. Finn introduced me to up-and-coming artists and sounds that later became rock 'n roll hits. Only a few at Riordan initially had heard of the rockabilly style of Sam Perkins and the rebellious country music artists such as Elvis Presley, Johnny Cash, and Jerry Lee Lewis. And insiders like Finn and me knew that the real King of Rock 'n Roll was not Elvis but Chuck Berry, unbeknownst to everyone else at school."

Babe Ruth Autographed Baseball Down the Drain

I began a stamp collection only because someone gave me a used stamp album that had a few stamps already pasted in it. There must have been 60 or 70 pages for domestic and international stamps. I collected

336

stamps throughout high school. I have no idea how many I wound up with, but there were a lot of stamps that either matched the pictured stamps in the catalogue or stamps that were interesting in that they appeared to have manufacturing flaws or unusual designs. Just a few years later, I gave the album to Barry's sister, Nancy Sullivan, whom I started to date and so wanted to impress her. She was collecting stamps at the time, so I thought it made a great gift. Much later, I realized that was a real stupid thing to do. Not that my collection would have been valuable, but it would have been a nice keepsake with a history years later. More importantly, she broke up with me five years later. A few decades later I asked her what she did with my stamp album and she never even remembered me giving it to her, much less what happened to it. A more depressing story was a couple of decades later, I gave Jim Sullivan a Babe Ruth signed baseball, as I had two of them and he had been so good to me over my life. He later gave the ball away – not to Barry. I never asked why but I suspect he either assumed it was a forgery or he wanted to make points with the young son of a friend. He was a generous guy all his life, so who knows?

Restitution for Prank 60 Years Later

I never went out for football in my freshman year since I never played football and had no idea if I was any good at it. However, I was an avid supporter of the Riordan football team that played their home games at Kezar Stadium. Although I enjoyed rooting for the team, there had to be more. Cheering from the stands with everyone else only went so far. I had to do more to show my buddies I was a bigger fan than everyone else. So during the Marin Catholic game that October, I thought it would be a hoot to steal the Marin Catholic banner that hung across the wall in back of their cheering section on the other side of the field. I told the other guys that I would be back but did not tell them where I was going. I made my way around the field to the Marin Catholic side, climbed up the stairs to the top and started to untie the cords holding up the banner. I kept waiting for someone to ask me what I was doing, but no one did. I got the banner off the wall and rolled it up into as small of a bundle as possible and returned to my seat on the Riordan side. I explained what I did, and they could not believe it. I kept the banner for years and finally returned it to the school with a generous donation check – not just for my guilt for stealing their property but for the 40-6 Riordan victory that evening.

Friendship Ended by Age Discrimination

When I lived in the Mission, I went around with five or six kids who lived within one block from me. Everyone looked the same age as me, so the subject of one's age never came up. We went to different schools, so we had no idea what grade everyone was in. I was the only one attending a Catholic school and all the others went to public schools. At the first Riordan football game in my freshman year, I saw in the program a picture and the name of a guy I spent a lot of time with in the Mission –Tom Lynch. For the first time I realized that we were not all the same age in the Mission or even close to it. In this case, he was a senior and I was a freshman, but I was delighted to know he was at my high school – the first of my Mission friends whom I knew at any school I ever attended. Monday at school, I was so excited trying to spot him in the hallways. That week I did see him coming down the hallway. As I approached him, I cheerfully said, "Hi Tom." He just grunted "Hi" in an unemotional, monotone voice and continued to walk by me. I knew it had been a year since we saw each other, but he had to have recognized me. Maybe he knew before, but it certainly sank in then, that I was a lowly freshman and he was a popular senior, a starter on the football team, and one of the best runners in the 880 and mile. I was crushed. I never tried to run into him again, which I sort of regretted later, because I would have loved to talk to him about running track and playing football at Riordan. It was another lesson as to what made a "friend" and I realized he was not one.

In some ways I was no different than Tom Lynch. I ran into fellas at Riordan whom I knew from St. Charles and St. Paul's grammar schools. We were always friendly with each other but did not have the same interests as in grammar school. Instead, what seemed to determine whom we went around with on weekends and evenings was who lived in our neighborhood and if we participated in the same activities in high school. It would have been great if there was something the school did to bring kids together from the same grammar schools to keep those contacts intact.

Fairness in Life Depends on What Line You Stand In

During football season, I was still playing sandlot baseball and getting lots of experience until basketball season rolled around. I went out for freshman basketball only because some of my friends tried out for the team. The coach was Cappy Lavin. I used a two-hand push shot and never had the "touch" that the better one-hand push shot shooters had developed. I knew I was no good and never expected to make the team, but I thought Cappy had a strange way of cutting down the size of tryouts. After a few days of practice, he had one line of players taking layups and another line of players going in for rebounds. At an arbitrary moment during practice, he said, "Everyone in this line of players is cut and the other line report for practice tomorrow." I was in the cut line. Maybe he figured any good players that got cut would approach him to make a case why they should not be cut. In any case, I was not good enough to make the team anyway. It turned out that basketball was the only sport I did not participate in for Riordan, but I wound up being a starter on the other three varsity teams.

Confidence Booster From Nicknames

Volney "Skeet" Quinlan was a halfback for the Los Angeles Rams from 1952-1956. I never heard of a "Quinlan" who was a celebrity before, so he was someone I could emulate. He was never a star but he played a lot for three years. His best year was 1953 with 705 yards rushing with an average 7.3 yards per carry. Barry started to call me "Skeets" when I told him about Volney and the nickname stuck with me. I liked it. It reflected a positive role model for me.

Barry, Carmody and I decided to join the San Francisco Boy's Club, located on Page Street off Stanyan Street, so we could sign up for their basketball team. We had to take out a Club membership, so I used the name "Skeet Quinlan" on the membership application. It was neat to see "Skeet Quinlan" on my membership card. The basketball coach told me there was a Los Angeles Rams player with the same name. I played dumb and said I did not know that. The coach asked me a couple of times if it was my real name and I said, "Yes, it is." I could have just said it was just a nickname, but I so wanted to have the name of a celebrity – especially in sports. From then on, the name stuck with me. A lot of it was because Barry called me "Skeets" throughout high school, and some of the guys at Riordan did too, especially in sports circles.

Success From Trying New Activities

Although WWII had been over for nine years, there were still some lingering prejudices in San Francisco. Although I never saw any of it at Riordan, Guido Mori-Prange told me years later he especially experienced it in his neighborhood. His family came to the U.S. in 1944. Guido was German and Japanese. It was being Japanese that some parents and kids could not handle and were hostile toward. A lot of prejudicial comments were thrown at him while growing up. He felt a lot of the kid's prejudices came from their parents. At least one parent told their kid he could not play with Guido. By the time he came to Riordan, he had reason to want to fit in with others, but he was coming from a public grammar school and saw that kids were in cliques with those who attended the same Catholic grammar schools. By his sophomore year, he had made a few friends but felt he needed to get involved with some school activity to get closer to other students, so he went out for track. Coach Fennelly asked him what he wanted to try out for and Guido said, "I don't know. I have never run track. What do you need?" The coach said, "We are light in pole-vaulters," so Guido tried out for it. The coach lent him a pole but told him not to tell anyone. Guido built a pole vault pit in his backyard to constantly practice with his own pole. He competed in the pole vault in his sophomore, junior and senior years. Along the way he tied the pole vault record at Riordan, and he also beat Rich Kennealy who was the star pole-vaulter for Riordan, which was a personal triumph. Guido had the opposite build of typical pole-vaulters who were tall and thin, but with the motivation and drive to be part of a team of new found friends, he went on to excel in the sport and personal life by owning a successful company in the optics industry.

Quitting is the First Step to New Opportunities

After basketball season, I went out for the freshman baseball team at Riordan. Cappy Lavin turned out to also be the freshman baseball coach.

He was an outstanding basketball player and coach, but Riordan assigned less familiar sports to coaches in order to earn a little extra money. As the basketball coach he was familiar with his players who also turned out for baseball. I quickly saw there was a clique of freshman basketball players that were assigned starting positions on the team. I went to a number of practices and realized that I was not going to get a chance to start over a kid who was worse than me at shortstop. So during English class one day, I went up to Cappy and told him I was dropping off the team. I am not sure that he even knew I was trying out for the team, as he offered no reason why I should stay on. In hindsight, it was the best thing I could have done. I went on to play sandlot ball as a shortstop with and against a lot of kids who were older than me. I faced a higher level of competition than if I played freshman ball. When I went out for the junior varsity baseball team the next year I beat out the previous year freshman team shortstop and was first-string all season. The lesson learned was I should not settle for second best but to take a chance and try again the next season or join other activities. I batted .300 for the season on the JVs.

Success From Being With the Best

By turning my back on playing freshman ball at Riordan, I had the good fortune to play baseball that year for a sandlot team organized by Jim Riley's dad, Matt Riley. He was a calm, soft-spoken guy, the type of coach we enjoyed playing for. I played baseball with his son Jim on later Riordan teams, but Jim's real forte was being the school statistician for the various sports teams throughout our four years of high school. Who would have thought there was such a thing, but Jim received a full four-year scholarship from the University of San Francisco to be their sports statistician. Jim was a chip off the old block. Like his Dad, he was a kind, gentle, jovial guy, but I would not want to try sliding into home plate with the brick wall Jim created. The team was built around Jimmy O'Connor, an outstanding pitcher. He pitched just about every game we played. Most of the players were from Riordan and guys Jim knew from St. Philip's. Jim's dad got the grammar school to sponsor us. I either batted leadoff or fifth in the order behind O'Connor, who was also our best hitter. We lost very, very few games. Another lesson learned was to try playing on the best team possible. Like I learned in business years later, if you surround yourself with the best people, you will succeed.

A lot of the baseball players had their own bat, which made sense. It was better to use a bat that worked for them rather than randomly picking a bat from those provided for the team to use. So I went back to Free-Minetti and searched through all the racks of bats until I found one that felt right for me. It was an Al Rosen model. Al Rosen played 10 years with the Cleveland Indians and was a four-time All-Star even though he had to retire at age 32 due to an injury after a career batting average of .285 and 192 home runs. It was not that he was my hero. I liked the bat because it did not have a large barrel that made bats top heavy. Instead, the handle was a bit thick, giving the entire bat a more balanced feel with a 32-inch length, a narrow barrel and the right weight for a level swing. With my thin wrists, it was easier to take a level and faster swing with more control. No one ever explained to me home run hitters used bats with large barrels that had a larger surface area or "sweet spot" and more weight to power the ball further and higher. The other feature of bats was their length. Kids used bats 30 to 35 inches long – the longer the bat, the heavier the weight but the greater chance to reach more outside pitches.

I should have tried to strengthen my wrists so I could use big barrel and longer bats when I needed to hit for power, but I never had a coach who gave suggestions how to hit for power. To them, it was all about just getting on base. If a hitter was repeatedly striking out, the coach told him to try a lighter bat or to choke up on the bat, but that was about it.

Our freshman year was coming to a close, but the memorable events were not ending yet. Being late for class was a no-no. In March 1955, one of the freshmen in our class accidently broke one of the two large entrance glass doors to the administration building. He was running to class and assumed the door swung the other way. Just a few months earlier, a sophomore broke the other door. Hopefully, they both showed more smarts in the classroom. In April, 390 eighth graders took the entrance exam for the 1955-56 school year. Hopefully, they were a smarter lot.

In May, we were treated to viewing our first CinemaScope wide-screen movie *The Long Gray Line* in the school auditorium. It starred one of my favorite actors Tyrone Power. The movie was a great choice to show young boys how a kid went from nothing to becoming a successful adult – exactly what I wanted to do. It was based on the life of Martin "Marty" Maher, an Irish immigrant, who started as a waiter to become a non-commissioned officer (Master Sergeant) and athletic instructor during his 50-year career at the U.S. Military Academy at West Point. The phrase "The Long Gray Line" referred to the continuum of all of the graduates and cadets who ever attended West Point. As I watched the movie, I kept thinking of Riordan, the students, activities, sports and values instilled in us, and the visual image of the long purple and gold line of students matriculating out of Riordan over the years. I envisioned a long conveyor belt of students with all our imperfections and shortcomings going in one end of the processor, unacceptable ones being rejected, and the smarter, wiser ones coming out the other end. In the movie, Marty learned that he and his wife could not have children and the cadets became the children they could never have. How prophetic this story was as I began my high school years, as I and a lot of other classmates were later in life not blessed with children, which may be one reason why so many of us made financial donations to the school over the years.

Price of a Catchers Mitt – Bottle of Whiskey

There was other stuff going on during that movie. Barry wanted to try out for catcher the following year because there was less competition at that position, although he had always played second base and the outfield in grammar school. But he did not have a catcher's mitt, and he did not want to buy and break in a new stiff mitt. A classmate, Paul Waterson, had a used mitt that was already broken in so Barry offered to trade with him. Paul was a noted drinker, so Barry offered to give him a fifth of whiskey for the mitt. Barry purloined the whiskey from his dad's home bar, which Barry doubted he would miss. The nefarious transaction took place in the darkened auditorium while the whole school was watching the movie. Paul was seated several seats to his right. Barry had the bottle in a brown paper bag inside his duffle bag, so he simply passed it down the row, and Paul passed the mitt along to Barry. It was a fair transaction and nobody ever ratted on them.

Major Source of Friendships – Extracurricular Activities

I learned by the end of the freshman year that friendships in high school were different than those made in grammar school. Friendships in grammar school were driven by what class we were in (8A or 8B), while friendships in high school were often driven by what activities we got involved with, such as band, drama, speech, school newspaper, sports. Also, in grammar school there were only one or two classes, but at Riordan we were broken into six separate classes (9A to 9F), each with 38-40 students by year-end, and our classmates were reshuffled from year to year, so we did not stay with the same group of classmates throughout the four years. This was especially true of kids I knew well in grammar school, but if they were not involved in my class or school activities, which seldom happened, I saw too little of them to stay close to them. Sad. So I made new friends from other grammar schools. Also, the A, B and C classes at Riordan were the college preparation classes that offered the science, math and language classes. I was given the option of preparing for college or not. Old friends may not make the same choice as I made. So new friendships were made among those in my class or on the same sports teams.

The school cafeteria was a novelty from grammar school. Instead of eating lunch on a schoolyard bench and confined to talking mostly to the kid to the left and right of me, at Riordan there were rows of tables in the cafeteria that I could choose which table of eight students to join. It was a good chance to meet guys I did not know. As I got older, I tended to seek out tables where I recognized the most familiar faces. It was too bad there was nothing done to require us to do less of that in order to develop a breadth of friendships as opposed to a depth of friendships.

In early June, Applebee's dad and a few of the students erected a Carrera marble statue of the Blessed Virgin that arrived from Italy in the school courtyard. The white marble with its dark veins cast a slight grey-bluish tint, giving an air of elegance the Blessed Virgin so richly deserved. The statue has greeted seven decades of students coming and going.

Age 15: Sophomore Year – Standards Set
for Schoolwork vs. Socializing

The freshman year was over and we finally got used to the new school, the student body of about 900 strangers, more difficult classes, and greater academic and athletic competition. We were no longer the low men on the totem pole at school. With an increase in confidence and knowing the interests of our best friends, we used the sophomore year to solidify our friendships and participate in the various activities offered at school. It was a critical period in that it set patterns of how time and effort would be split between schoolwork and socializing for the next three years.

Cool Kids: Clothes Made the Man

As freshmen, no one or anything we did could be considered cool. We were now sophomores, mature enough to be making more of our own decisions, as stupid as many of them were, but we now knew how to be cool about it. Being accepted or cool in high school was important to us, but especially for Canas. It was one way for kids to fit in, whether they were Latinos or not.

Canas described the times and our experiences in being cool. "The jargon and morals of the young in the 1930s and 1940s had been censored by parents, the religious, and anyone with authority over the behavior of young people. Any descriptive word or expression beyond the word 'swell' was frowned upon. In the 1950s, the voice of the counterculture movement began and included the vernacular of so-called irreverent groups. One word replaced 'swell' immediately. It was a hip word that had been used by minorities and musicians for some time but took on an esoteric meaning of its own among the youth of the 1950s. The term 'cool' was used to describe any person, thing, or behavior based on the counterculture's judgmental style. For me and many other kids, there was an obsession associated with coolness, and I am convinced it shaped some of our personas *for eternity*. The apprehension was not about whether we were actually witty, attractive, natural or rooted, but whether we were perceived to be. As they said, 'Better to *look* good than *feel* good.' It sent a shiver down my back just thinking about being tagged 'uncool,' especially for a Latino in a white school. Being considered as uncool was as traumatic as having gonorrhea. Merely trying to be cool or copying the traits of the cool guys was by definition, uncool. Plagiarism of any kind was uncool. Likewise, imitating the life style of a different sex, race, color or creed was a major breech and totally uncool."

"One group of cool kids at Riordan was referred to as 'Ivy Leaguers.' The Ivy League reference came from a dress style started in northeastern schools and popularized by college folk-singing groups like the Kingston Trio of 'Tom Dooley' fame. The clothing consisted of button-down plaid or striped shirts, tight pegged trousers with a buckle on the back or plaid Bermuda shorts (also with the buckle on the back), and suede desert boot shoes or white, brown or black saddle shoes, later copied in golf shoes. Rich kids wore Florsheim shoes; anything Florsheim or Brooks Brothers was Ivy League and thus cool."

"These dress styles were most dramatic among young males. It just seemed to me that girls made subtle adjustments to their dress such as the tightness of their skirt and peddle pusher pants, the knot on their bandanas above, on, or under the chin, or the brightness and amount of make-up. Coolness rules of style were specific and attention to one's appearance was not understated. We would not be caught dead out in public without our 'uniform.'"

"The cool Ivy Leaguers were prone to play sports, embrace academia, and hang out in cliques. They did not hangout or mosey around the minority-dominated districts, such as the Fillmore or the Mission, where African-Americans and Latinos respectively had their own variety of cool, or Japantown and Chinatown where immigrants from respective countries congregated, or the Sea Cliff area near the Presidio where many wealthy Jews lived noiselessly in mansions and sent their kids to the quasi-public Lowell High School with its high academic standards that resembled the private schools. Another group considered to be cool, at least within their circle of friends, were those in social car clubs like the *Frisco Coupes* and the *Renegades*, who wore 'colors' (club jackets) but did not go for the outlaw image or practices. There were just a few of us at Riordan."

"Then there were those who copied the dress of the 'Barts,' who were school dropouts that joined gangs and adopted the dress of motorcycle club members. They wore jeans, crew neck T-shirts with the short sleeves rolled up, 'ducktail' oily hair with a curl in the middle of the forehead, and yes, black jackets with grease-stained collars turned up. The movie *American Graffiti*, and later TV's comedy spoof of the same film, *Happy Days*, depicted a fairly accurate snapshot of the period. Fonzie, in *Days*, for example, was a cartoon of a Bart; Richie and his friends were typical Ivy Leaguers. What was glossed over in the series was the abhorrence Barts had for Ivy Leaguers, although the feeling was not mutual. We both patronized Mel's Drive-In, whether on Mission or Geary Streets. When intermingling with other groups or just walking into Mel's for a shake and hamburger, I always made an assessment of the surroundings and the perception of other's demeanor and dress."

"Our generation thought soldiers were cool; parents and teachers were not. Rebellion against officious authority was cool; being arrested or injuring someone was not. Drag racing, smoking, drinking, punch-outs, stealing spinner hubcaps, being independent, and taking chances were also cool; burning the flag was not. They were boys and girls looking for purpose and playing at being bad – *rebels without a cause* (in case you did not know what the movie title meant). Our mantra throughout high school was frequently repeated by the 1960s radio disc jockey Wolfman Jack in his gravelly voice 'Remember your ABCs—Always Be Cool!'"

Carmody got a job at the Big Dipper Ice Cream Shop on Judah Street off 32nd Avenue. The shop was owned by Bert Farber. Carmody was the first of our buddies to get a job on his own in a store. He worked there part-time all through high school. We thought there would be some side benefits to his friends, but he never gave away free ice cream cones to any of us. Although we had to pay full price for a cone, the novelty was that we could have the cone dipped in warm chocolate sauce that hardened in seconds so the ice cream was encrusted in a thin coating of chocolate candy. That was the idea behind the store name "Big Dipper." It did not hurt that the locals were already familiar with the same name used by one of the major attractions at nearby Playland.

Barry was lucky jobwise to have a father with connections as he described his work experiences. "During my days in grammar and high school, Dad always had me working. In my sophomore year, he got me a job in a grocery store close to Riordan where I stocked the shelves, cleaned the floors, took out the garbage, unloaded the deliveries, and performed just about every menial task available. The next year, he had me working at Tiedemann & McMorran's main warehouse on the docks where the San Francisco Giants currently play home games. Every year John Tiedemann, the founder, gave my sister and me a brand new silver dollar. I ended up working in a clerk's office sorting mail, filing papers, and doing bills of lading, which gave me a knowledge of all the shipping companies and trucking companies in America."

Willie Mays Was White?

Until we could drive a car to school, we had to take a streetcar and bus to get to school. That did have social benefits because several of us caught the same streetcars and buses at the same time, which gave us time to catch up and kid around, like this conversation about the New York Yankees between Canas and Carmody while they waited to transfer from the N-Judah streetcar to the 10-Monterey bus as told by Canas.

"Yeah, and hey, have you noticed that all the great ballplayers are white?" Carmody asked a matter-of-factly.

"You mean for the Yanks?" I asked.

"No, actually in all of baseball."

I could not tell from his tone if he was serious or needling me because he was speaking over the noise of our flapping baggy pants. That was one annoying thing. If it was not foggy in the Sunset, there was a stiff breeze funneling up from the ocean. And on that sunny morning, everything was fluttering except our greased down glossy crew cut on top and long hair on the sides.

"Name me one who isn't," Carmody continued.

I thought about that for a while, and then said, "What about that guy Willie Mays who plays for the Giants?"

He did not answer right away, which was not unusual for Carmody. He was a "muller." You know, the type you hate to play checkers with because they mull over every move to the point of despair. When the bus arrived and we were boarding, Carmody turned suddenly and said, "Well, he [Mays] isn't really a Negro, you know." And he bounced into the bus and went about looking for seats. He found two on the aisle and we sat across from each other.

"Yeah, right," I said. "Like last week you told me Chuck Berry was related to Bill Haley."

"Hey, Maybellene, Rock Around the Clock...just the same ole rock 'n roll to me. But you can trust me about Mays though," he said with that smirk again.

"Oh," I said over the roar of the bus's diesel motor accelerating. I was not sure about his familiarity with pop music, but I knew enough to believe anything he said about baseball. I mean, he was the starting third baseman on the JV team in our sophomore year.

I nodded pensively, "Huh, I didn't know that. Cool."

Carmody just smirked.

Carmody was smart and liked playing defense in conversations. Once he was bantering politics with the galling know-it-all Eugene Cooney who had gone to Riordan with us after Holy Name and idolized Franklin D. Roosevelt, the former president. Cooney challenged Carmody's view on a new book that was coming out, *Profiles in Courage* by an obscure John F. Kennedy, a Democrat from Massachusetts.

"Why would anyone care what a Kennedy thinks, Carmody?" Cooney chided.

Terry did not respond, just tilted his head back and smirked...for a long while. He was a good smirker. But by class break time, he was ready.

"Unlike Roosevelt," Carmody said when we caught up to Cooney in the hall, "who probably staged Pearl Harbor with the Japanese, Kennedy is a war hero, and besides Kennedy's younger brother, Robert, is a trusted aide of another American hero, Senator Joe McCarthy. You see, Cooney, the Kennedy's are really Republican plants."

The retort turned Cooney apoplectic. But that is what I mean in that Carmody was calculating. By comparison, my efforts at being deep was biting my fingernails down to the cuticles and worrying about substance abuse (liquor was a rampant problem among many of our parents). I mean, we can be brainy and cool if we are natural about it. And Carmody had this urbane air that was often mistaken for haughtiness. Oh hell, we were all haughty in one way or another; some just carried it better.

Remain Grounded When in the Ocean

For a long time, I ventured out into the ocean no further than waist deep. I always remembered the story about my brother almost drowning. But now I was a teenager and old enough to swim in the ocean. This one time I was out in the water about 100 feet from shore and just far enough that my feet did not touch the ground. As I tried to swim back to shore, the water on the surface was flowing against me, making it much harder to swim than being in a pool. I felt a little panicky but at least it was not the case of the water below the surface creating the resistance. That was what I always heard was the biggest threat. Fortunately, more waves came behind me and gave my body the momentum to slowly work toward the shore. When I finally reached shore, I made up my mind that was the last time I would ever go out where my feet could not touch the ground.

Bad Parental Advice Regarding a Child Molester

One morning I was almost at the end of my paper route, and a man wearing a suite and tie drove up in a nice car. He asked when I was done and if I wanted to go for a ride with him. I thought *why would I want to go for a ride with a complete stranger? There is no reason for it, and I did not have time for such nonsense.* I lied and said I was only half done and it would be another 45 minutes. He said he would be back. I memorized his license number and told Mom what happened when I got home. I said that I should report him to the police, but Mom said not to. This was neither the only nor last time Mom did not want to get involved. I never understood why she felt that way. She never wanted to rock the boat, get involved or stand up to others. I learned from her what I did not want to be like regarding these matters when I grew up. I wanted to be just the opposite – report crime, catch the bad guys, get in people's faces, and stand up for my rights and those of my family and others.

It was the beginning of the school year, which meant picking up books and supplies at the school bookstore. All supplies were three cents to $5.00. The school paid the 3 1/2 percent sales tax and all profits went back into the student body fund. A large pack of binder paper that held 20-30 percent more than the average pack sold for 25 cents instead of the 39 cents regular price. Three ballpoint pens sold for 29 cents. We could save $5 on a pair of track shoes or baseball shoes and $1-$2 on sweat shirts. The warm wool school jacket inscribed with "Riordan Crusaders" and our graduating year sold for $17.50.

There were a lot of things going on at school in my sophomore year. The most tragic was the death of Charlie Montague at the end of the school year (June 1956). It brought back happier memories when I used to play at his house in the 6th and 7th grades and his constant smile even though he always appeared fragile and somewhat sickly. One of the blessings of being a kid was that we accepted other kids as just a kid and playmate – no concerns over age, physical or mental differences, color of skin, home life, parents, abilities or inabilities. Those were only concerns of adults. Although his classmates were never notified of his funeral services, some of the brothers from Riordan attended the wake – one of many things teachers did behind the scene and never got credit for from the student body.

The second tragic thing that year involved Ed Finn who was in my class at Holy Name and Riordan. He came to school one Monday with his jaw all wired shut. He looked terrible. He was still black and blue around the eyes and nose. He could not eat any solid foods; he had to drink everything through a straw. He was a frightful site like something out of a *Frankenstein* movie. He had gone ice-skating at Sutro Baths Ice Skating Rink with Beyma and Canas the previous Friday night. Beyma and Canas passed through the entrance to the rink and started to take a practice lap around the rink. When they got back to the entrance, there was no sign of Ed, but there was a pool of blood by the entrance. Den and Rich never did find Ed. Somehow Ed skated into the clear plastic wall without sticking out his arms – probably did not see it – and someone got him off the ice and to the emergency hospital. We only found out about it when Ed showed up for class Monday. I never went ice-skating nor had the desire to go my entire life after seeing what happened to Finn.

Classmate Jim Sweeney was president of the Art Club at Riordan and drew doodles on the blackboard before the teachers arrived for our classes. Sometimes they were little characters like out of comic books but more often it was an image that started out as one thing and metamorphosed into something else, like an M.C. Escher drawing – just much simpler. After gaining a reputation for his art work, a couple of the teachers called him up in the middle of class to draw a couple of doodles, probably to give us a break from the class material. I gained a little more respect for those teachers who knew there was more to being a good teacher than lecturing and giving tests. They needed to be empathetic and liked by the students to be most effective as teachers.

Pornography Was in the Eye of the Beholder

The most memorable student paper I heard read in four years of high school was one written by Gary Preston in Cappy Lavin's English class. When the papers were returned to the students, Cappy asked Gary to get up and read his paper in the front of the class. He read the paper with all the inflections in the right places to make the entire story sound sexy. It was about a kid describing her as being so beautiful with a curvaceous body, and sleek lines that would turn any guy's head, while he walked up next to her, bent down, and slipped his hot sweaty hand under her skirt as his heart was racing. The story lasted about 20-30 seconds, and the punch line at the end was that it was a kid talking about shopping for a car and finding the car of his dreams. Some of the class snickered. The topic was appropriate because Gary was into cars and hot rods, and I thought it was a clever writing style – sort of the surprise ending we were used to from watching Alfred Hitchcock movies. But Cappy thought otherwise. He really came down on Gary for writing such a risqué paper. I felt sorry for Gary being set up by Cappy and embarrassing him in front of everyone. Cappy wanted to use Gary as an example to prevent him and everyone else in class from writing such unacceptable literature, but it could have been done in private after class or Cappy could have read the paper and kept the name of the student anonymous. The depressed look on Gary's face as he slowly walked back to his desk was heartbreaking. He never returned for his junior year. I hated to think that it had anything to do with this incident, but I would not blame him if it had been one of the reasons.

Power of a Couple of Words of Praise

It was in Lavin's English class that Canas convinced himself that he could be as cool as anyone. As Canas remembered it, "I had written the words 'time and space are relatives' for an English composition paper on some existential topic. And, as we took our seats for English that day, the graded papers were waiting for us. I remember the phrase because it had been boldly circled in thick red ink and a line had been drawn to the margin where Lavin had scribbled, 'Great phrase!' It took a moment for the rare praise to sink in, but when it did, a warm glow started building and something caught in my throat. I do not recall if I even knew what the words meant or the context of their use, but I remember the exhilarating feeling. It was more than cool. The paper was only graded 'B,' but just being recognized by Mr. Lavin for something creative, something he considered *great*, was invigorating. He was one of the few really cool teachers we had and he took English comp *very* seriously. Still brimming with pride, I looked back at Cooney, who sat in the desk behind me. His round face was staring dumbfoundedly at his paper, which had a large crimson 'C-' accompanied by a similarly large question mark on the cover. Since I knew that his tank ran a bit low in the grit department, I reached back and snatched the composition right out of Cooney's hands."

"Gimme that," he protested trying to grapple with me.

I turned my back shielding his lame onslaught and started leafing through his paper. "Just wanted to see where you went wrong," I said smugly over my shoulder.

"Yeah, like you'd know, Canas." (He pronounced my name, can-ass.)

"Hey, good one, Cooney," I said ignoring him as I scanned the bold red comments on his paper.

I knew, because Cooney had bragged so much about it, that he had written his essay on the concept of eternity. I flipped the top sheet and saw on the second page that some of the words had been hacked up by Lavin's much-celebrated red pen. Cooney had used a phrase that I had heard from Sister Mary Carmela in grammar school. It was pure Mercy propaganda, right out of their Scare-the-Shit-Out-of-the-Little-Heathens training manual. *If once every hundred years a bird drops a bead of water on the top of the tallest mountain, when that mountain has totally eroded, eternity has only just begun.* Jeez…What garbage. I could not believe Cooney had regurgitated that tripe. The symbolism must have made an impression on the *little heathen* and no chance now that he would ever forget it. I did not bother reading further because Lavin's written barrage said it all. *Infantile, illogical* and *plagiarism* were scrawled everywhere with large exclamation points behind them.

"Not cool, man," I said gloating as I held the paper over my shoulder.

"Jerk off," he snapped as he grabbed the paper back. I sat there fanning my paper with the graded cover facing up. Bragging when I can back it up was always cool, like soaking in a warm bath of confidence.

High school was a time when guys were picked on by "pantsing" or giving "wedgies" to them. Kids unbuckled the kid's belt and pulled down his pants so he stood there in his underpants. I never saw kids pantsed during grammar school and rarely in high school, but occasionally outside of school hours. It was usually done in a private area like the locker room or an area where no one else was around. When it happened, it was only his pants to be pulled down – never an attempt to drop his underpants. The attempt was to embarrass him and not to humiliate him. It was done in the privacy of his "buddies" and close classmates to be a private joke, initiation or harassment just amongst a small group of four or five. Even among kids, there were some standards among pranksters. Although no one liked to be pantsed, we did not think the degree of embarrassment was all that great, but it was a cruel thing to do to anyone especially a friend. It was that type of thing that scarred some kids for life. They remembered those things all of their life – one of the reasons some kids said later in life "I did not enjoy high school." Sad. Giving a wedgie to a kid was a lot less demeaning as it involved grabbing each side of his pants and pulling them up to squeeze the testicles to make his crotch uncomfortable for a few seconds. There was no exposing him in any way. This more modest form of harassment could be given in any public area. It was on a par with a "noogie" – rubbing our knuckles back and forth on a guy's head for a few seconds – another friendly form of ribbing a kid. In grammar school there was the "Indian burn" where we grabbed a kid's arm with both hands and twisted in opposite directions, just to cause a momentary discomfort.

Lifetime Damage From Nicknames and Name-Calling

By our sophomore year, we had been around our classmates for over a year and got to know them and their idiosyncrasies. So some kids were given nicknames in jest, but kids always went too far in that nicknames stayed with those picked on throughout their high school years. Dodd Zakasky was a real nice, quiet guy. He came from Holy Name with us. Who started it, I did not know, but he was labeled with "Doddy-o." They chanted "Doddy-o, Doddy-o." The nickname probably stemmed from the 1955 movie *Blackboard Jungle* in which Richard Dadier played by Glenn Ford was called "Mr. Daddy-O" by the students in his class. As Canas recalled "If we wanted to see, hear, and feel the coolness emulated by male teen-agers of the 1950s, we only had to see the last scene of this movie. A teen-aged Sidney Poitier nodded knowingly to high school English teacher Glenn Ford and said, 'See you around, Daddy-O,' and walked cockily down the street to the iconic rock 'n roll score 'Rock Around the Clock' by the Comets playing in the background." The nickname also could have been reinforced from the slang "Daddy-O" that was popular in the mid-1950s among the beatniks and hipsters. Wally Coughlin was nicknamed "Wally Ballou" after the character by the same name used by the radio comics Bob and Ray (Bob Elliott and Ray Goulding) in their comedy skit of an inept news reporter conducting man-on-the-street interviews. (Ironically, Wally worked later for a newspaper all his adult life.) It was Jim Peterson who coined Barry's nickname "Tomato." Whenever Barry got up in class, several students chanted "Tomato, Tomato." Not only did he have red hair, but he also turned red whenever he had to speak in front of the class. Actually, only his cheeks got a little red, but it probably felt more widespread to Barry. Whenever Art Curtis did something stupid or made a weird comment, his classmates called out his name repeatedly "Art-Art-Art!" whenever he was called to the front of the classroom. As Art recollected, "It did not really bothered me, and looking back, I thought it was kind of fun." So some kids accepted nickname chants as all in fun but most took them very personally. It was all good fun for everyone else, but not for the likes of Dodd, Wally, and Barry. These were terrible things to do to anyone. Any form of making fun of a kid in front of others, especially among his friends and classmates that he regularly saw every day, was completely unacceptable. They left scars with many kids for the rest of their lives. I found negative memories were more likely to stay etched in one's memory much longer than the positive memories. Barry said it took him years to overcome those name-calling memories and to speak in front of groups without being embarrassed when he became a teacher, but he never lost his dislike of Jim Peterson all those years. Too bad that Wally, Dodd, Barry and Art did not respond initially by creating a nickname for the one who came up with their nickname. Had they, it may have ended all the "Doddy-o," "Wally Ballou," "Tomato, Tomato" and "Art-Art-Art."

But it was not their responsibility to right the ship. The real culprits were the students who allowed the name-calling to continue. As much as we may have abhorred the chants and sympathized with the victims, we said nothing and did nothing. It was a clear case of following the herd mentality. Just as those at the time claimed they were not prejudiced against Jews and African-Americans, yet they did not get in the face of someone telling a racial joke or using terms like kike or nigger. That made them part of the cause of, rather than the solution to, prejudice. We all owed Dodd, Wally, Barry and Art an apology. It was our fault the name-calling took a foothold and continued.

Some Did Not Turn the Other Cheek

On the other hand, at least one of the victims fought back against the harassment and got into fights at school – seven times. If caught by the coaches, the fight was moved inside where it could continue by using boxing gloves. There may have been no one who had more fights than Barry. Years later he could not remember whom or why he was fighting, but at least one of them was with boxing gloves in the gym. That shows that fights got the problem out of his system and never led to holding grudges if Barry could not remember the kids or reasons he fought any of those seven times. Only reason he remembered anything about one fight was because the guy he beat was one of the better athletes at Riordan – sort of his championship fight. This was how Barry described his fighting experiences: "Although I do not remember any of the other guys in the fights, I did get in seven fistfights. We called them 'punch-outs.' We had

356

an ethical code, an unspoken understanding that we never used a weapon, never kicked anyone, particularly in the groin, and never bit anyone. However, I did bite another football player while on the ground because he was trying to hurt me. In any event, one fight was on the lawn of a house behind Riordan where students parked their cars. Canas told me it was not a very dramatic fight, just lots of shoving and wrestling. The guy was from another grade, bigger than me, and a braggart. Why I got into so many fights, I do remember, but I was always surrounded by classmates who loved to egg me on. I had a bad temper at the time so I probably was fighting over some slight such as a 'Tomato, Tomato' taunt. I never lost a fight, but I never seriously hurt anyone." Good for him. His dad would be proud if he only knew.

Teachers were not immune from nicknames either. Their nicknames started in our freshman year and lasted through our senior year. Brother Maurice Miller was our principal from 1955 (his first year there) through our graduation in 1958. Bill Jovick in our class claimed he gave him the nickname "The Shark." When I asked him why, he said, "He seemed to appear out of nowhere and caught you when you got out of line. He gave the impression that he was on the attack." That tied into my assumption that it reflected the image of his constantly patrolling the hallways looking for kids being disorderly or tardy for class. On the contrary, I never saw him wandering the halls. I am sure he had more pressing things to do with his time. Brother Richard Roesch, an English teacher and Librarian, was nicknamed the "Duck," probably because of his long neck, which he had in common with me. Others said, "It was because he walked with his feet pointed outward." If kids passed him in the hall or saw him on stage, one of the kids blurted out "Quack! Quack!" Brother Donald Bradley was called "Big Don" for his short stature and Brother Paul Wessling was "Twig" for his tall thin body. The most popular teachers and coaches never seemed to receive a comical nickname – must be a lesson there for all of us including future teachers.

It was too bad that most nicknames were so negative. It would take the same amount of time and energy for kids to come up with positive nicknames for teachers and other students with a name based on the single most positive feature or characteristic of the person. Rather than adopting a derogatory one started by some insecure jerk in class, it would show class and coolness to be positive in how we treat others and being a "glass half-full" type of kid. When I heard these nicknames shouted out, I felt badly as did most of the other kids because the chants only came from a few kids. How refreshing it would be for the silent majority to not follow the herd mentality and stand up, turn to the rear of the class and shout back, "Cut it out!" Now that would be cool.

Giving Back Same Medicine Stopped Bullying

Al Martin was one of our class leaders and on the basketball court throughout high school as well as a cut-up at times. He and I both had big ears. If Al was sitting in back of me in the auditorium or snuck up behind me in the hallway, he flicked my ear with his finger, giving a stinging sensation to my ear. He laughed and I smiled. After he did it a few times to me and I realized this was not going to stop, I did it to him when he was not looking. His ear flicking stopped. Just went to show that giving back the same medicine could stop bullying by others. It surprised me that someone would pick on one's own imperfections. I concluded in life that we should never judge others for physical features, deformities, skin color, nationality or anything else beyond their control. We should just judge others based on things within their control such as degree of education, professional and personal achievements, living a healthy life, and being a good spouse or parent.

Greatness Is Evident at an Early Age

One of the most infamous alumni during my four years at Riordan was Warren Hinckle III. He graduated from Riordan in 1956 when I was a sophomore. Barry remembered him as being "...an original, very bright and rebellious. He was the first kid to wear khaki pants with a buckle on the back, and blue and white saddle shoes. He was blind in his left eye and later wore a black patch that gave him a rather dangerous but distinctive look." He was editor-in-chief of the *Crusader*, which was hailed as the "most controversial and outstanding high school newspaper in the nation, had a circulation of 4,000, carried more advertising lines than competitors, and adopted an editorial policy of commenting on world and national affairs." He was editor of the Riordan *Criterion*, a semi-annual literary magazine. Professors and teachers at nearby universities and schools called it "the most outstanding high school literary magazine" they had seen. Warren went on to be a legendary magazine publisher and award-winning journalist, editor of anti-war magazine *Ramparts*, and writer for the *S.F. Chronicle* and *S.F. Examiner*. One tribute to him was "Herb Caen was the greatest San Francisco columnist over the past 50 years, and Warren Hinckle might well deserve to be viewed as the City's most influential reporter." [60] Even a literature illiterate underclassman like me knew Warren was special from his contribution in so many areas of school life and made me feel special to be at Riordan where there were so many winners walking the halls.

At one of the school assemblies, the brothers had prepared to entertain us. They sang the song "Cool Clear Water" made popular by the western group Sons of the Pioneers. I really enjoyed their singing but some of the students started mocking and making fun of their rendition. I felt sorry for the brothers. They worked hard to prepare and practice and tried to do something nice for us. Kids could be so cruel and it only took a few to set off the others. The brothers never tried to entertain us again, and I could not blame them.

Car-in-the-School-Hallway Prank

A teacher had a Crosley, the smallest car in the school parking lot. Crosleys were subcompact cars, bordering on microcars. They weighed 1,100 to 1,400 pounds. He parked close to the rear entrance to the school one morning. Guys from our class, including Humbert Realini, lifted up the car, brought it through the 70-inch-wide rear entrance, and placed it down in the hallway. Everyone stood around and had a good laugh. The juxtaposition of a vehicle that belonged on the freeway sitting in the scholastic halls of education was one funny scene. After we all went on to our next classes, the teacher eventually drove the car through the two rear doors back out to the parking lot.

Cool Teachers for Student Counselors

Although the school had a student counselor (dean of boys), seldom was the faculty in those positions student friendly. With the exception of Brother Edward Immethun, they were not the cool teachers or the type we chose to sit down with and shoot the breeze. Each year each student should be able to pick any faculty member as their confidant – someone you felt comfortable talking to about your personal and school lives and getting their advice. I did not think most kids went to their parents for advice, so they needed someone to keep them on the straight and narrow and to motivate them to do better in everything they tried. Weekend or after school field trips could create a rapport with teachers to see them as a person other than a lecturer/disciplinarian. Coach Fran Hare took some of the football players hunting, but weekend outings were almost unheard of in those days. Unfortunately, teachers were not that well paid back in the 1950s, so a number of them had second jobs to make ends meet.

Piano Thrown Off Rooftop Folklore

There was a rumor that one of the cool teachers and a bunch of his college buddies threw a piano off the roof of a major hotel at a school dance. I never really believed it because people would have read about it in the paper. Also, lifting a piano over any balcony or rooftop ledge would be difficult. But it made for an interesting folklore to his legacy and added to his image of being cool.

Cheating Never Turned Poor Grades to Good Grades

There never seemed to be any cheating going on in grammar school. It probably was because Catholic kids thought cheating was a mortal sin, as well as, there was no pressure to get good grades in order to go to college. Even in high school, there was little cheating going on during exams, and it was often the same "C" and "D" students. Occasionally, we saw someone looking across the aisle and turning his head as little as possible so the teacher did not catch him. One or two were more blatant. They waited for the teacher to be immersed in reading before tapping the fellow in front of him to raise his answer sheet to copy. Depending how good of friends the two were, the reaction was either to cooperate or to shake his head "No," realizing that if he was caught as a party to the cheating, he risked getting an "F" on his paper too. Occasionally, teachers blurted out "Keep your eyes on your own papers!" We never knew for sure whether the teacher was suspicious of someone cheating, or it was his way of warning us that someone was watching us, so do not take a chance of getting caught. I think it was more of the later as only a few times over the four years did a teacher have to come down the aisle and take the exam from a student. The teachers probably should have done it more often, because it did send a strong message to the rest of the class and served as the stiffest deterrent. It was like in law enforcement – knowing that people do get caught and there are penalties for breaking the rules motivated us to stay on the straight and narrow.

I heard a couple of kids went through a teacher's desk, found the answers to the exam and made copies for others. Another story was that a teacher who had been grading papers left the room during the exam, and a student went up and found the answer sheet in the drawer. He tried to memorize as many of the true and false or multiple choice answers as quickly as possible. He did not have time to remember that many answers, so I never felt that the risk of getting caught was worth the few answers gained by cheating, but there were those who were not the brightest bulbs in the class. I suspected who those cheaters might be and in the long run, it never impacted their overall grades because they still wound up being poor students with poor grades. There were no shortcuts to success in school as there were none in life. Success just took hard work.

Others cheated by writing things on the palm of their hand, on their arm, or on a "cheat sheet" or small piece of paper in the palm of their hands, but there just was not enough room on a piece of paper to be of much help. The probability of having the correct notes on a small piece of paper that addressed the specific questions in an exam was so remote that the notes would prove worthless. From a term I learned later in life, the "risk-reward factor" was too great to take the chance of getting caught. One may improve their exam grade by a couple of points, which probably was not enough to improve the grade from a "D" to a "C", and if he got caught, he definitely went from a "D" to an "F" plus the embarrassment of being labeled a "cheater" – an image no one wanted to carry throughout high school.

I saw a couple of kids get caught with cheat sheets, but the most frequent method of cheating was to write notes on the surface of the desktop, which got wiped clean with spit and their sleeve or handkerchief. By our junior year, some teachers checked the desktops before or while they passed out the exams individually to each student. That seemed to cure that form of cheating, at least in those classes. What the cheaters did not realize was that whatever form of cheating they did, it just was not going to help their grade. There were so many questions or breadth of knowledge required to do well on the exam, that the odds were so against having the right notes, much less enough of them, to help the grade. My attitude was to take a chance on getting a "C" on my own rather than risk an "F" if caught cheating. There was also the humiliation if my parents heard that I cheated.

By our sophomore year, all of my closest buddies and I were playing sports at Riordan. Barry and I were on the frosh-soph football team and the JV baseball team. I traded in my pompadour (big-wave-in-the-front) for a flattop haircut. It was literally cooler under a football helmet, but it felt like a big hairbrush. Canas played frosh-soph football while Carmody and Hipps played JV baseball with us. Applebee was a running back on the JV football team. Beyma made the varsity football team, as well as the next two years, being one of the biggest and strongest in the school. He was on the varsity track team as a discus and shot put thrower and played center on the JV basketball team. Riordan Hall of Fame basketball player John Galten said, "One reason Beyma was on the basketball team was to be a strong aggressive rebounder against me and to make me tougher on the boards." It must have worked because John went on to play for the University of San Francisco along with teammate Bob Joyce.

Secret to Fitting In Socially: Imitation

Canas said, "If Quinlan and Sullivan played on the frosh-soph football team, so did I." Canas really felt out of it because he was a Latino in a class of white students, but "these guys made me feel comfortable being part of 'the gang' and I copied everything these white dudes did, from their cars, girls, dress, and music. It was inexplicable to me at the time why I was not as fast, strong, or bigger in sports but I tried. On the other hand, I did not have trouble dating the good-looking white girls." The moral was that whether you were in the majority or minority, you needed to make an effort to be similar in interests, actions and appearance as your peers if you wanted to fit in and be accepted. Participation in the same activities as our friends helped all of us to adjust socially in school.

By our sophomore year, we could tell that we never had bullies who physically picked on kids. There were tough kids, and a couple were rumored to be members of the Ocean Avenue gang, but even they were nice guys at school, probably because they were not the type who went out looking for trouble on the weekends but would not back down from a fight if ever called out nor took crap from name-callers. Many of the tough guys played sports, and that was one of the huge benefits of the sports program. It gave guys an outlet to show how tough they were on the field or court rather than on the streets.

Videos of Success to Teach Success

I quickly realized that coaches, like teachers, were asked to coach sports and teach classes that were not their forte. It was a way to reduce the cost of running a school. I understood that and was so thankful for the resulting low tuition. But to make up for any shortcomings of coaches' knowledge and experiences, it would have been helpful if they had videos of how the best professionals played the various sports, whether it was dribbling, shooting, throwing, catching, running, kicking, blocking, hitting, fielding, sliding and all the fine points of each position or event. Many of the greatest athletes told stories of how they improved by watching videos of other greats from their sports. It would be the poor man's solution to "hiring" the best coaches in the country – call it "Athletics 101."

Applebee, Latour, Beyma, and Coughlin were on the track team when they made friends with Maurice Lafayette, who was on the junior varsity (JV) track team with most of them. It was through those connections I got to know him. Lafayette did well on the JVs, but he noticed that some of his classmates that he used to beat as a freshman were now beating him. It was a stark realization that kids progressed at different rates in sports from year to year. At least we did not experience hitting the wall like going from high school to college, when competition consisted of outstanding athletes from a variety of schools. If high school kids realized this would happen, more of them may have studied harder rather than later have their dreams of playing college ball dashed and lose interest in their education.

Devil-May-Care Kid

Maurice Lafayette's parents were children when they immigrated to the U.S. – his dad came from Martinique and his mom from Belgium. They lived in the Excelsior District. Lafayette developed his devil-may-care attitude early on. He gathered couch cushions and pillows at home, spread them out, stood on an end table or chair, jumped off, bounced on the cushions, and flipped over. He did this for hours – great fun. While playing hide-and-seek in the house with his sisters, there was not a lamp that did not get broken by him. "Mom and Dad were saints to let me get away with this behavior."

To have a place nearby to play with his friends, Lafayette and his dad built a tree house in the trumpet tree in their backyard. His dad also built a small fishpond where Lafayette loved to chase the goldfish and sail his toy boat. I suspect some toys we played with did influence our interests later in life. With Lafayette, it was sailing and racing boats later in life. On vacations at Clear Lake, he discovered that on the lake bottom there was a soft slimy black mud that led to diving down, grabbing a handful of mud and slinging it at kids in their mud fights.

Toys and Neighborhood Terrain Affect Interests and Moxie

His mom bought him a Horner Marine Band Harmonica when he was six years old. He quickly learned to play a few songs and this was the start of his musical interest. He eventually became quite the musician – another example of how parents impacted their child's interests in life without realizing it at the time. A few years later, his mom asked him if he would be interested in playing the saxophone and join the band at Corpus Christi Grammar School. He said, "Yes," so she rented an alto saxophone and signed him up for music lessons. He liked playing the saxophone but

364

music lessons were boring. He would rather be outside playing football with the other kids, but the lessons paid off as it gave him the training needed to play later in his high school band.

What kids did and how they played had to do with what was in their local sandbox or neighborhood. Some had a park, gymnasium, museum, hill, or even an ocean. Lafayette happened to live on a hill. Baden Street was a kid's delight because it was the fifth steepest street in San Francisco (34% grade). His house was located midway up the hill with Monterey Boulevard at the top and Hearst Street at the bottom of the hill. Lots of the kids in the neighborhood built skateboards and coasters and rode them down Baden Street. Long before skateboards were popular, Lafayette nailed roller skates to a 2" x 4" board and rode around on the jerry-rigged skateboard. He also had visions of building a coaster that he could sit inside and ride down the hill. This was not to be any ordinary coaster. It had four large 6-inch ball bearings for wheels, a steering wheel, brakes, a seat and top. It weighed about 60 pounds. Because it was so heavy, it took two of them to push it up the hill. His maiden run would start midway up Baden Street, ride down to Hearst Street and maneuver a sharp right turn. He had a friend check for cars at the bottom of the hill. When it was clear, down came his hand to signal the OK. Lafayette released the brakes and was off. Traveling down the hill was fast and exciting but the ball bearings soon lost their grip on the pavement and he lost control. He spun around, hit the curb and rolled over. He got scared and bruised but he survived. That was the first and last coaster ride down the hill. Kids pushed their limits and learned their lessons.

For the next Christmas, he got a flexy racer, a sled with wheels. He lay flat on it and steered it with front handlebars that also did the braking. It had four 8-inch hard rubber lined steel wheels. It went really fast, especially down the Baden Street hill. Lafayette always needed someone at the bottom of the hill to be sure there were no cars coming. Initially, he started the ride halfway up the hill, and after a while, started at the top of the hill. On one of those runs, he lost control at the bottom of the hill, slid off the front of the flexy on his belly, his head hitting the pavement, and his front tooth was knocked out. The pain of a broken tooth, skinned-up hands and face were nothing compared to his dad's anger at him and the loss of his front tooth. "It certainly was a hard way to learn the limits of my riding skills." Parents being upset with their kids getting hurt was to be expected, but buying such a toy for a kid living on a hill...?

If a hill or mountain was within eyeshot of home, kids naturally wanted to climb it. Mount Davidson was the highest natural point in the City with a forest of eucalyptus and Monterey cypress. When Lafayette was nine years old, he and two friends with a sense of excitement and suspense set out to see up close the 103-foot concrete cross that sat on the top. It was a long and steep hike from his home. Once he reached the cross, the hike seemed like he was miles away from home. He never got lost on the climb, but it was sure an adventure that he never forgot. For the rest of his life, he enjoyed hiking and backpacking with his buddies.

Some kids had unique experiences that led to their lifetime interests. Lafayette's parents bought him a small sailboat when he was 10 years old. It was an 8-foot long racing class El Toro sailboat. He immediately joined the Lake Merced Sailing Club, making him the youngest member of the club. He quickly learned how to sail the boat and had some success in racing. The races were held at Lake Merced, Lake Merritt (Oakland), Lafayette Reservoir (City of Lafayette), Clear Lake, Lake Tahoe and San Francisco Bay. He won a lot of the races, and when he was not the winner, he was always one of the race leaders. Racing that little sailboat was quite an adventure and racing a small 8-foot sailboat in the San Francisco Bay was a real challenge. The boat was not forgiving because he was out of the race for all practical purposes if it flipped over – no greater challenge as getting the boat upright and back racing. One may remain interested in an activity if they frequently lost, but winning led to passion. Lafayette had a passion for sailing as he aged.

When Lafayette was 11 years old, he spent a weekend up the Russian River with a friend who had his own boat, a small 10-foot-long wood boat that was docked on the River just across the street from their summer home. One day they set out to take his boat five miles down the River to Jenner – the mouth of the Russian River. They told their parents they were going to Jenner to fish like they had done before, so it was fine with the parents. The boat had a 3.5 horsepower Johnson outboard motor that pushed the boat along pretty well. It took about two hours to get to Jenner and along the way they pulled out a pack of Marlboro cigarettes that they had hidden away and smoked. It made them feel like big stuff. When they got to Jenner, it just happened to be high tide and the ocean water was flowing into the River. They drove the boat to the mouth of the River and pulled the boat up on the estuary sand to check out the surf. It was an exceptionally calm day, so they decided to take the boat out the mouth of the River and cruise around the ocean for a while! They were lucky that the surf waves were not big, so it turned out to be a successful adventure. To this day Lafayette's parents do not know he did this really dumb thing, but he was a devil-may-care, easygoing, reckless kid. He was the only kid I knew in high school who had the nerve to jump off the top high diving board at Fleishhacker Pool. Some kids took chances and others always played it safe. Many of those who took chances as a kid, grew up to be the risk-takers that wound up successful in business, while many of the better-safe-than-sorry kids wound up in the government. Not that one was better than the other. It merely showed how these early years molded who we became.

Lafayette played sports in grammar school, and it was not the games that were as memorable as were the related experiences. St. Finn Barr Church did not have a gymnasium, so basketball games were played at Glen Park Gym. The coach picked up the team at church and drove them in his 1940 Ford to the gym. The car was so underpowered that it died halfway up some of the steep hills, so the kids had to get out and walk up the hill while the car chugged along without passengers and the kids just laughed and thought it was great fun.

Adult Prejudices Overcome by Kid's Exposure

The word around the neighborhood was that there was a Filipino family living nearby in a house on Monterey Boulevard. The older kids called them "spinach kids" and heard from their parents that they were mean kids and would beat you up, so "watch out when you go past their house." Whenever Lafayette was sent to the store, he passed the house and felt fear for the first time and each time – the threat of being attacked by toughs. As years passed, he never actually saw them but that fear stayed with him. All his friends were white kids just like him, so older Filipino, Mexican and African-American kids were viewed as possible threats. Kids were not born with these images. These stereotypes and falsehoods always came

367

out of ignorance and stupidity. The best cure for prejudice has always been to be given the chance to know people, and sure enough, it was not until his dad hired workers who were Mexican and African-American at the shop where Maurice got a better understanding and appreciation of them. In the 8th grade and all during his high school years, Lafayette worked as a general helper to the six workers at the shop. He worked part time after school and full time during the summers sweeping the floors, driving the truck, taking deliveries to job sites, and taking loads to the dumps for $1.50 per hour.

The perennial football powerhouse in our league was Bellarmine. The 2,500 fans at the Riordan-Bellarmine football game at Kezar in October watched Riordan lose again 13-20 – close, but no cigar.

The Night Rally in November for the football homecoming game announced the queen for the opening ceremony where the queen was driven around the track at Kezar in the police-escorted motorcade at the game against Serra. I always assumed queen selection was based on a vote, but in our case, the queen was the girl who sold the most tickets to the football game and she seemed to be from Immaculate Conception Academy (ICA) nearly every year, if not every year, I attended Riordan.

That same month, our frosh-soph football team finished with a 2-4 record and Coach Jack Buckley was quoted in the *Crusader*: "The five outstanding players during the season included Barry Sullivan and Terry 'Skits' Quilan." My last name was constantly misspelled in the newspaper the entire time I was at Riordan. This time it was even my nickname. Sometimes Beyma was called "Don" instead of "Den" in the paper.

Respect From a Deviated Septum

Barry recalled his most memorable game in our frosh-soph football season: "I stood 5'7" and weighed 135 pounds, but I was a starter as an offensive guard and defensive linebacker in the game against California School for the Deaf. Some of us felt sorry for them because they could not shout out their plays, but that quickly changed when one of them managed to smash his elbow across my nose giving me a deviated septum. In those days facemasks were simply one bar across the face, so we were sitting ducks for injuries. The only serious injury I suffered in sports was shin splints from catching on the baseball team. We ended up beating the deaf players, but we gave them great credit. They were tough and courageous."

Winning Strategy – Play to Your Strong Suit

Football was Barry's favorite sport, probably because it was his best sport, which meant he experienced his greatest number of successes. That was why kids should think twice about participating in an activity that they are not very good as compared to one that they are good at and might even excel in. Kids often joined things to be with their friends, which was admirable, but they may develop to be a more rounded person if they played to their strong suit and took the lead from what they would be most qualified to do.

David Took on Goliath to Right a Wrong

In December, a *Crusader* sportswriter wrote an article that expressed what was on the mind of every student whoever attended Riordan. The article was about the unfair treatment of outstanding Riordan athletes by the local newspaper's selection and publication of their All-City teams. Only players from the San Francisco AAA high school league were ever selected, including the two Catholic high schools St. Ignatius and Sacred Heart. The local newspapers ignored Riordan standouts like High School Football All American center Dick Max (1954) and others who received scholarships from Stanford and a host of other outstanding schools. The gist of the article was to either start recognizing Riordan athletes in their selection process or change the name of their awards from All-City to All-AAA. How much such articles and letters to the newspaper affected their thinking, who knows, but things did change in our junior year.

Be All You Can Be – Not at the Pleasure of Others

I was the starting halfback on the frosh-soph football team. Teammate included Barry, Canas and Mike Duffy. If we had played football in our freshman year, we probably would have made the JV's in our sophomore year. The lesson learned was one should go out for all activities of interest as early as possible. Neither football nor baseball teams that I was on that year were very good – the reason why we hardly got mentioned in the school newspaper along with the fact that the newspaper mostly covered varsity sports, since most students only went to varsity games. On the other hand, getting our name in the paper was not what it was all about. Once we stepped on the field, it was all about being all that we could be and not about doing something to please others. I lived by that principle all my life.

I loved playing football but there were those days I came home from practice with aches and pains from sore muscles or slight injuries that made it harder to study. Even after getting in shape after the first month of conditioning, I came home a little tired from practice, especially after eating a meal. Eating always made me sleepy, which was why later in college, I did not eat breakfast or lunch because they made me too tired to study. It was a habit I maintained my entire adult life.

Only Run on Grass and Dirt – Legs Last Longer

Now that I was playing football at Riordan, I often jogged over to the four blocks over to the Polo Field on the weekends after delivering my newspapers at 7:00 a.m. The Polo Field had a 0.8-mile long, ground level dirt track and a 0.7-mile sunken hard surface track. I jogged around the 0.8-mile dirt track three to five times. I broke up the jogging with 60 and 100-yard dashes to work on my speed. Because the dirt track was chewed up, bumpy and uneven, I ran cautiously when I jogged and even more so when running sprints so I did not do something stupid like twist an ankle, which I never did over the next three years. I never ran on the inner, lower track because I grew up with the belief that the worst thing for my legs in the long run was to run on hard surfaces like cement sidewalks and paved streets, and I should always run on grass or dirt. Years later, friends of mine who ran on hard surfaces for years developed back and leg problems, which may or may not have been a coincidence. Even the great golfer Tiger Woods said, "Running over 30 miles a week for my first five or six years on tour pretty much destroyed my body and my knees." [61]

It was our sophomore and junior years when we started to date girls and go to the Riordan dances. Some were more obsessed with it like

Canas who admitted, "That illicit of all drugs, invented by Satan himself, testosterone, the 'Big T,' had narcotized all of my pious conscious and unconscious thoughts. If they pulled me apart on the rack, I would have denied with dying breaths that I had ever had the least notion of joining anything that practiced chastity, poverty and obedience. By that time, my father's wisdom had taken a victory lap about discouraging me from going to the seminary, which had faded in my eyes, no doubt clouded by the Big T."

The first dance of the school year had about 900 Riordan boys and girl from San Francisco Catholic high schools. They checked school ID cards so only boys from Riordan and girls from Catholic high schools attended. The dances were held at 8:30-11:30 p.m. in the school cafeteria. Admission was 75 cents stag (singles) and $1.25 drag (couples).

Dating One of Seven Sisters, Oh My!

The most infamous dating couple was Maurice Lafayette and Colleen O'Toole. Lafayette got an invitation to play poker with Dave Sereni, who was also in the school band, and Dave's buddies who lived in the Sunset District. At one of the games, Sereni mentioned he was dating one of the O'Toole girls and was wondering if Lafayette might be interested in going on a date with her sister Colleen. He thought it sounded like a good idea and they planned to meet after one of the Riordan football games and go to a party at one of Sereni's buddy's house. He felt way out of his comfort zone meeting a girl. He just was not really interested in girls. Cars and sports and music were his interests. The date turned out better than he expected. Eventually, he met the O'Toole's – the parents Tommy and Margaret O'Toole, and Colleen's six sisters Sheila, Mary, Peggy, Bonnie, Nancy, and Kathleen. "Oh my, what an experience meeting a family of nine and so different from mine." They lived out in the Sunset Avenues and so far from Baden Street and the Excelsior District. There were all those sisters and so many guys hanging around whenever he visited, but there was this spark and an attraction as he and Colleen hit it off. He played in the school dance band so they had no chance to dance together except at parties. They dated all through high school, got married two years after high school, and are still together 60 years later.

Avoid Having to Get Married – Abstinence

Lots of guys in high school were really obsessed with girls, dating, making out and trying to get laid. The latter was more talk than action, sort of like the characters in the 1955 movie *Marty*. There was talk of getting a "hickey" as if it was their badge of courage. I never saw anyone with one, but I always thought it was stupid that getting a bite or bruise mark on my neck was something to be proud of – why not simply have a girlfriend bite off my earlobe if I wanted to endure pain?

Going to an all-boys school, I never heard about guys impregnating girls. It would be more obvious at all-girls Catholic schools if it ever happened. But the thought of having a baby in high school was one huge reason I was extra reluctant to have a steady girlfriend in high school. At the time, the rhythm method of birth control and condoms were the main forms of birth control among the Catholics. I heard too many stories of both not working. Abstinence and staying out of harm's way was my attitude until I got married 12 years later. As Barry said, "The idea of having intercourse with a high school girl was unthinkable, particularly a Catholic high school girl, although there was the myth that Catholic girls were really loose. But I never found one wanting to 'go all the way.'"

Lower Expectations at School Dances

At the first few Riordan dances in my freshman year, I just circled the room "checking out the chicks," especially the good-looking girls, and looked for guys I knew. I never asked a single girl to dance, good looking or not, because I was so shy. More importantly, I was afraid of being turned down in front of other girls or guys I knew. It was like going out for a pass in a football game and dropping the ball in front of all the fans in the stands. Here I could just take myself out of the game.

When I eventually got the nerve up to ask girls to dance at school dances, I found if the girl was with one other girl, she often said, "No thanks." But if she was one of the few there by herself, she normally said yes nearly every time. I never asked really good-looking girls to dance, avoiding the high risk of being turned down. I never considered myself good-looking enough and I sure did not want to set myself up for rejection, especially from a group of three or four girls. It was a long walk back across the dance floor after being rejected. I thought everyone might look at me and laugh or make fun of me, which was silly since couples dancing were into themselves – not watching guys walking around. So I always asked average looking girls who served as my pool for dates during high school. And why not, from the girl's standpoint, as I was only an average looking guy, so we both felt comfortable with each other. Besides, I was a pretty shallow and boring guy on the dance floor and on dates. I did not have a lot to say, but neither did the girls. There was not much going on in our lives to talk about. Also, I found that dating average looking girls was less of a temptation to go to bed with them, which was important to me because I wanted to stay a virgin until I got married.

All guys enjoyed slow dances with a chance to hold a girl close to them, but I especially liked fast dancing. I was more of an athletic dancer holding both hands of the girl, waiving them in and out to the beat of the music, twirling her in a counter clockwise circle, then back in a clockwise circle. I often thought that I was being too energetic and probably wearing out the girl, but I did not much care. I sure was having a good time. Besides, we usually just danced once together and we moved on looking for new partners. To try entertaining a girl for the entire two or three hours of a dance was way beyond my skill level. Carry on conversations during and between dances for that length of time, I could never do. If there was a big dance, like a prom, I tried to find someone at the last minute, yet the dates all turned out to be wonderful girls.

Motivation From Mistakes of Siblings

Mom told me several times while I was growing up how smart Kathy and Joe were and "they never had to study." I knew they were smart, but Mom never praised me for anything – sports, grades or math. My overall grades were never great, but occasionally they were better than average, especially in math. I never understood whether she was trying to motivate me in my studies or just felt Kathy and Joe were better than me in school. In any case, it did serve to motivate me to get my college degrees. Every time Mom mentioned how good they were in school, I envisioned the image of the little engine pulling the much larger cars over the mountain in the book *The Little Engine That Could* as a reminder that I wanted to achieve more than Kathy and Joe. I was determined to wind up better than them, and in many ways that was how it turned out. I was the only one to graduate from college and accomplish a lot with my life. But there was sadness with those accomplishments. Kathy and Joe probably were a lot smarter than me, but they both wasted the opportunity to do something with those advantages. Kathy had a full scholarship to college and turned it down because she wanted to leave home. Shortly thereafter, she got married and raised a family. Joe went into the service for four years, probably for the same reason, and got married and had children shortly afterwards. Right or wrong, I viewed their decisions as mistakes and used them to motivate myself not to get married before I finished college, which was what happened – best decision I ever made.

Single Greatest Influence on Lifestyle – Access to a Car

The biggest thing that influenced my lifestyle and that of my friends in high school was getting a driver's license and our own car, allowing me to go wherever I wanted, whenever I wanted. I was able to get a driver's permit at age 15 1/2 that allowed me to drive until I could get my driver's license at age 16. Mom had her 1941 Chevy, but she was not willing to teach me to drive. My brother was never around, but my sister's husband offered to teach me. We went to Golden Gate Park, just a few blocks from our house, where there were few cars on the road early in the morning. It took just a few lessons to get the hang of driving. But a driver's permit only allowed kids to drive with an adult in the car – a rule that I broke frequently – so I had to wait until I was 16 before the car became my new hiding place, meeting place, and clubhouse, all rolled into one – a place to share with my friends to explore the largest "sandbox" that included all of San Francisco and surrounding areas.

To get a 10 or 15 percent discount on my car insurance, I attended a driver's education class at Galileo High School on Francisco Street. One of the exercises was to test our reflexes. On the wall was a large poster with 12 squares, each numbered, in a mixed order. The instructor timed us as to how fast we could touch the squares in numeric order. I was the fastest in the class each time we competed. That was more rewarding and important to me than passing the class for the discount.

Barry learned to drive at a much younger age. As he told it, "Dad was a great teacher when it came to driving a car. When I was five or six years old, he let me sit in his lap as he drove around the City. He even let me hold the wheel and steer. So, when it came time for him to teach me how to drive for my driver's test 10 years later, we had already established a great rapport. He taught me how to drive 'defensively' and to always keep my eyes out for children running into the street. So I developed the habit of always looking under the cars from a distance to make sure no kid was about to run out and get hit. He also said, 'Don't worry so much about yourself, but be very wary of the other drivers. Be a good safe driver and drive defensively.'"

"I enjoyed driving so much that I went into my parent's bedroom early on a Saturday or Sunday morning and took Dad's car keys off the dresser while they were sleeping soundly. We had two cars – the family car and his company car, a 1950s two-door grey Ford coup. His company car was always parked in front of the house so I did not have to wake them by raising the garage door. I loved to drive around the neighborhood, and I always ended up on the long-deserted block on 37th Avenue west of Sunset Boulevard. The sand dunes were on one side and the trees along Sunset Boulevard on the other. I shifted into gear and raced back and forth along the four blocks of sand dunes from Ortega to Santiago Streets. One day a man jumped out into the street. He waved his arms back and forth for me to slow down, but I just whizzed by him and returned home. Nothing ever happened to me, but my early morning trips were curtailed."

Mom's Only Rule: 11:00 p.m. Curfew

Once my buddies and I got driver licenses, we got our own cars or had access to parent's cars to go out at night and do things. We were turning 16 years of age in our sophomore and junior years and starting to feel our oats for independence and adventure. We had reached one of the pinnacles of adulthood – the ability to drive a car on our own. Mom gave me a curfew of 11:00 p.m. to be home at night. I complained and made a fuss, but she said, "As long as you are living under my roof, I expect you to follow the rules." She was absolutely right. It gave her peace of mind knowing that I would be home at a reasonable hour and not getting into trouble. It was probably the only rule she set down for me, so it was the least I owed her in return for food and shelter, since I did not turn over any of the money I earned from my paper route. Mom once mentioned Kathy contributed some of her pay from her job at the public library for room and board. She must have voluntarily done that since Mom never asked me to do the same. I think girls were better about those things than guys. I like to think Mom felt sorry for me as I was making my money by delivering newspapers in the cold and rain while Kathy worked in a warm library. Who knows?

San Francisco was only 47 square miles, roughly a seven-by-seven mile square. Since my schooling and social life covered much less ground since there were areas that were bad-news places to be, I pretty much lived in a world that was about a five-by-five mile area, so it did not take much time for me to get anywhere by car. Gasoline was 20 to 25 cents a gallon. I always filled up at the GETs (Government Employees Together) station at 34th Avenue and Sloat Boulevard on my way to or from school. It had the cheapest gas around. Having a car allowed us ready access to such kid's gourmet places like Jumbo's Drive-In at the foot of Sloat Boulevard (between 44th and 45th Avenues) and across the street from the Zoo. They had 19-cent hamburgers, 24-cent cheeseburgers, 11-cent fries, 23-cent malts and 10-cent sodas.

This was a period with the best music of the century when I had the best of two worlds. I could still hear lots of the Big Band music from the 1930s and 1940s and live with the current rock 'n roll of the 1950s on the car radio. Among my Big Band favorites were Tommy and Jimmy Dorsey, Glenn Miller, Benny Goodman, Lionel Hampton, Count Basie, Duke Ellington, Artie Shaw, and the battle of the drums with Gene Krupa and Buddy Rich. I could not ask for cooler music for a high schooler driving around with my window open sharing classics with the public, such as "Rock Around the Clock" by Bill Haley and the Comets in 1954 to "At the Hop" by Danny and the Juniors in 1958. In between we had so many great songs like "Great Balls of Fire" (Jerry Lee Lewis), "Tutti-Frutti" (Little Richard), "Jailhouse Rock" (Elvis Presley), "Whole Lot of Shakin' Going On" (Jerry Lee Lewis), "That'll Be the Day" (Buddy Holly and the Crickets), "Good Golly Miss Molly" (Chuck Berry), "Cry" (Johnnie Ray), "All the Way" (Frank Sinatra), and "Tom Dooley" (Kingston Trio). You could understand the words; they had a great rhythm; they made me keep a beat with my hand or foot and made me want to sing out loud, even a guy like me who had no singing voice. It did not matter because I was "performing" with the greats of the day. One of my all time favorite singers was Johnny Mathis, a 1954 graduate of the George Washington High School in the City, where he was an outstanding track star. During my high school years, he made such hits as "Wonderful! Wonderful!" "It's Not for Me to Say," "Chances Are," and "Twelfth of Never." I liked traditional jazz from the 1930s and 1940s as well as cool jazz by the likes of Dave Brubeck, George Shearing, Woody Herman, Stan Kenton, and Miles Davis. I could listen to them from my record collection or go see them at the nightclubs and jazz clubs in North Beach. They let minors in but we just could not get served liquor. I did not like modern jazz being performed at a lot of the nightclubs and jazz clubs. To me it sounded like the guys picked up instruments for the first time and played together off key. Obviously, I just didn't get it because lots of people liked it or at least pretended to like it so they did not appear uncool.

One day I happened to be driving along 15th Avenue between Ortega and Pacheco Streets, and each house on the west side of the block had a mailbox by the street curb that was a mini-replica of the house. These were large detached houses built in 1939 by Henry Doelger. "The houses were set on oversize lots and featured a rear alley, expansive front lawns, and matching white picket fences." [62] Henry Doelger had lived in the Monterey Revival house on 15th Avenue at the corner of Pacheco Street, where he could look out at the thousands of houses he built in the Sunset. One of the current residents on the block said Doelger's daughter lived next door to her father on 15th Avenue during the construction and his "lieutenants" lived in the other houses on the block. This was where I got the idea to build my own mailbox that was a replica of the house I had built for my wife and me later in my life.

Never Knowing How to Read or Study

All through high school, I would cram for the tests. I had trouble remembering what I read earlier, so I just fell into the habit of waiting until days before the test to read the material. My biggest handicap was that I was such a slow reader, so I never enjoyed reading. While some people read to pass the time, I was trying to do things. I never thought of books as a form of entertainment like radio or television. Being a very slow reader, I did not have the patience to get through the pages of the story to keep my interest. When I studied, I never understood what was and was not important. Were dates and places important or was it the story that was unfolding? I studied with the purpose of answering test questions and remembering specific facts, so I was constantly asking myself "Is this important? Is that important? Will this be on the test?" If we had to read chapters and write down everything we remembered in the exam, I could have read for overall comprehension. Instead I read for pockets of information with no connecting relationships to each other. An exam about all of the chapters' content would cause a lot more work for the teacher and take longer to grade the papers, but I think I would have learned more and retained it longer. It was years later after getting married that my wife, who was an avid reader and a scholar, said I should initially have read the first sentence or two of each paragraph because they often were packed with important information. She said I should have read in groups of words rather than reading individual words, which would have increased my reading speed – just like my adding up columns of numbers.

Regrets of One and Only Runner Without Paying

We heard of guys pulling a "runner" at restaurants and drive-ins like at Mel's Drive-In on Geary Boulevard. Guys drove in, parked, ordered their food, ate up, and drove off without paying. It was riskier doing it at a restaurant because someone might run after and catch them. Or someone might see what was going on and block them from leaving. I only saw it happen a couple of times. Once when everyone ran out at the same time and the other time everyone walked out slowly and left one person to pay the bill. That gave the others a head start to get to the car. Then the last guy, probably the fastest guy, ran out without paying.

We were lucky to have a couple of outstanding pizza places in the Sunset – Villa Romana on the south side of Irving Street between 8th and 9th Avenues and Pasquale's on the northwest corner of Irving Street and 8th Avenue. If one was crowded, we could always go to the other. My favorite pizza place was Villa Romana that opened in 1955. It served the best thin pizza with the works along with other Italian favorites. Sitting in the cushy upholstered booths made waiting for our order transparent. One time we were there, one of the guys suggested pulling a runner. I thought, *why? We can all afford to pay.* But it had nothing to do with money or a problem with paying, and there was no talk about ordering more than normal to take advantage of the situation. It was just something to try for the first time. When we were done eating and all the staff was in the back, we all got up and walked out slowly and ran like hell once we got outside. It was something we got out of our system and never did again. Sixty years later, I saw a picture of the owners of the Villa Romana when they retired and closed the restaurant. They were a sweet looking couple. It was sad to think that I participated in something that cheated them out of money. At the time, the victims were viewed as faceless – a crime against a business, not a person. There was some solace knowing that everyone involved remained steady customers and tipped generously for years to make up for the crime.

Failure of a Great Student Recruiting Idea

In the January edition of the *Crusader*, the Sports Editor suggested students, alumni and supporters seek out good athletes among grammar school kids who were big, strong, fast and exceptional and ask them to consider Riordan as their future high school. I thought it was a great idea, but it was not a successful campaign due to its lack of visibility and longevity. There should have been a committee to establish a game plan to identify how and what needed to be done. The Sports Summer Camp established years later was one giant step forward but not near enough to create dynasties in multiple sports.

At the March Talent Show, Tom Belluomini and Ken Toscanini from my sophomore class won first place and the $10 prize for playing an accordion duet with their rendition of "Tea for Two." The most unusual entertainers were the freshmen Dave and Dennis Powell twins, dressed in their Scottish outfits, who won third prize for their Irish bagpipe duet – a big hit with the large Irish contingent in the audience.

In April, 525 kids took the entrance exam for the 1955-56 school year and Bob O'Neill from our class was an integral part of an outstanding debate team as a sophomore along with a lot of seniors. Another student in our class, Dave Sereni received the highest rating of Superior for his trumpet solo at the Northern California Music Festival in May.

The *Crusader, a* frequent award winner in the high school newspaper statewide and national competition, was awarded an All-American honor rating by the Scholastic Press Association in April. The following month, the *Crusader* was awarded the trophy for the best Catholic boy's high school newspaper in the West at the annual Catholic High School Press Convention. This was not a football game, but it was comforting to know we could beat Bellarmine at something, as they were the trophy winner the previous two years.

It was the end of the baseball season, and the *Crusader* newspaper quoted coach Frank Clark as saying: "Skeets Quinlan has been a standout at shortstop all season with his fine hitting and fielding." It was one of the few times the newspaper spelt my nickname correctly. In our freshman year, Ed Coleman and I played sandlot ball and not for Riordan, but we played on the frosh-soph team this year. We moved on to play varsity ball together the following two seasons.

Break Rules During the School Year – Not at the End

The Senior Sneak Day, which was a picnic held for the graduating seniors, was held in locations like Marin Town & Country Club in Fairfax, across the San Francisco Bay. This year 10 seniors were caught drinking beer by the local sheriff and some faculty members. As punishment, they did not receive the printed version of their diploma at the graduation ceremony or awards some of them were to receive. The message was loud and clear to us underclassmen. I learned over the next couple of years, penalties seemed to be harsher if we broke the rules close to graduation as opposed to breaking the same rules during the school year. That was the part I found unfair, and it became crystal clear when it happened to one of my friends in our senior year two years later.

At the end of our sophomore year, a major change was happening on the 30 acres on the south side of Riordan. The City was tearing down the WWII buildings used by the WAVES to build two huge Phelan Avenue Water Reservoirs on the property, which eventually served as a huge parking lot for Riordan and City College of San Francisco students. [63] This worked out perfectly for those of us beginning to drive to school, because there were only 50 parking spaces in the school courtyard. Once the project was finished, we had access to 200 of the 1,000 spaces on the roof of the Balboa Reservoir. [64]

It had been a year since the school traded in their Studebaker and bought a used 1954 Plymouth Plaza for $1,325. This summer they traded in the Plymouth and bought a new 1956 Fordomatic sedan for $1,605.

During the summer, I wanted to put on more weight for football. All the juniors and seniors looked bigger than me as I was only 140 pounds. So I started eating more food and increasing my calorie intake as well as lifting weights. We worked out in the garage of a friend of Al Latour out by Lake Merced. Latour ran track at Riordan while Beyma and I were focused on football season. We each spotted one another by grabbing the barbells if anyone struggled with the amount of weight they were trying to lift. Beyma never needed help, but Al and I did on occasion. This was years before Riordan provided a weight room for their athletes. The high schools did not push weightlifting and maybe it was an insurance issue for them. By football season, my weight was at 170 pounds, which was where I stayed for the rest of high school.

Barry had a number of OK jobs so afar, but his most memorable and favorite summer job was when he got to work at the Northwood Lodge in Monte Rio. As he described it, "Since Dad had accounts all over the Bay Area, he had contacts in restaurants, grocery stores, and hotels, including those at the Russian River. So he decided that it would be good for me to spend a couple of summer months away from home working at the Lodge. Saturday morning we drove up to the Russian River and Dad introduced me to the staff. He told me to do the best I could do and to remember that I was also a reflection on him. We said our goodbyes, and for the first time, I was on my own at the age of 15. I was first led to my room by one of the Chinese staff. It was a small room in a cabin at the back of the kitchen. The room was very rustic with a single spring bed covered by a blanket. When I pulled the blanket off, there were three small white scorpions enjoying themselves on the sheet. It was a shock, but I managed to dispatch them without injuring them. A positive thing about my room's location was that I was close to the kitchen. It was the first time I was in an industrial-sized kitchen with a freezer loaded with huge containers of one of my favorite foods, ice cream. Some nights after the guests finished eating and the restaurant was closed, I went to the kitchen and treated myself to a large bowl of cobbler topped with a very large scoop of ice cream. The Chinese chef made the most delicious peach and cherry cobbler and he gave me free reign to eat as much ice cream as I wanted."

"Fortunately, I was always on the move driving a jeep around the golf course, changing the sprinklers, replacing water bottles, and working as a lifeguard, so I never gained weight. I was always a really good swimmer so spending days at the pool, watching the guests, was not a problem. But one day I did develop a big problem. It was my job to help clear the bushes and shrubs around the golf course. It was a hot day with the usual summer critters skirting about so I was not paying attention. I was just wearing a pair of shorts and no shirt. In the course of cutting and shearing the shrubs, I did not notice I was touching a ton of poison oak. I ended up with a bad case of it all over my arms, face, and legs and wound up visiting the hospital. It was a painful experience but made me a much wiser lad when dealing with the native foliage."

Age 16: Junior Year, A Whole New World –
Mobility in the Biggest Sandbox

It was the start of a new school year and total enrollment at Riordan was 900 – 65 higher than any previous year. Among the new freshman class was Bob Buffin, the second or third African American to attend Riordan and the first while I was there. He was an all-around guy participating in the band (trombone), library staff, stage crew, track and football (guard). He went on to be an attorney.

It was time for me to shop for new clothes so I would have more of an Ivy League look. My favorite store was Roos Brothers (Roos-Atkins in 1957) on Market Street at Stockton and Ellis Streets, where I always went first for clothing. The tables, cases, paneling and partitions were made of mahogany inlaid with satin wood and ebony. Whatever I needed, I usually found it there, so it saved me from running around to a lot of stores. The store's electric eyes automatically opened the front doors as I walked toward them. It made me feel special, like being welcomed by a doorman opening the doors for me at one of the fancy hotels. Their Varsity Shop for teenagers on the fourth floor was selling Ivy League clothes like chino (lightweight cotton) and khaki pants with a buckle on the back below the waistband and tapered pant legs with no pleats. Shirts had a buttonhole in the back of the collar and at both ends of the collar to give a buttoned-down look. Pants and shirts sold for four dollars and up while men's suits sold in the $40 range.

Secret to Good Teachers – Being Respected and Liked

This school year was the first time when faculty ate lunch in the school cafeteria with the students at faculty-designated tables. I suppose that was a big step to bring the faculty and students closer together, and that sort of thing had to be done in baby steps, but it would have been more effective if faculty sat at the same tables as the students – maybe one or two teachers joining the other six or seven students. Unfortunately, some of the teachers were not people-oriented, but the others who could talk about things kids were interested in would have made a hit with a lot of us. I found later in life as an educator that students listened to me more if they liked me and/

or respected me. They could not respect me unless they knew something about me, and we knew next to nothing about our teacher's background, interests or achievements.

Applebee's dad built the two trophy cases in the school's entrance foyer over a two-week period for $2,000. They were just inside the two entrance glass doors that two students had broken the previous year. The cases finally provided a prominent place to showcase the 25 trophies that accumulated from 1949-1956.

'54 Merc Taught Financial Responsibility

By the time I was nearly 16 I saved up enough money for a down payment for a car. Mom took me shopping for a car at Auto Row on Van Ness Avenue where there was block after block of new and used car lots. It was surprising that I only went to a couple of car lots, with Mom and me being such particular shoppers, but once I saw the car, I knew it was the one for me. After being around Mom's clunky 4-door sedan family car, I wanted something with style, so the 2-door 1954 Mercury Monterey that I bought was perfect. It was only three years old, so hopefully there would not be any major, expensive mechanical problems for a while. It had a red top, light grey body with red and cream rolled upholstery and large whitewall tires. There was plenty of chrome on the front and back fenders, hubcaps, and three chrome strips in front of the rear wheels that gave the illusion the car was going fast in the wind. I was not excited about the grey body, so I had the entire car painted red shortly afterwards. Mom insisted I had to make all the $52 monthly payments for the three-year life of the loan and pay for repairs and gasoline because she and Dad did not have the money. I agreed since I was making $125 a month from my paper route. Financing the purchase of a car was my first exposure to being in debt and having the financial responsibility to make monthly payments and to live within my means. I never missed a car payment even when I went into the U.S. Marine Corps after high school and making only $76 a month, but I did pick up a little extra money by playing pool and blackjack for money – only with guys I knew I could beat.

The car was a big hit with my friends. It was cool looking inside and out. I think they enjoyed riding in it as much as I did. With my obsession for cleanliness, I washed the car most weekends and made sure I cleaned everything under the hood and removed any evidence of oil, grease or grime from the engine block and parts. It was a guy thing when I was in the gas station with my hood up checking the water and oil, and other kids looked under the hood. I always felt proud showing off an engine that was at least clean, even if it did not have any chrome parts under the hood and was not souped-up in any way. It gave the appearance that the engine was probably special in some way. I never hung things from my rearview mirror but did install a suicide knob on the steering wheel. I got the idea from my brother who had one in his car. I thought it looked cool, even though they were against the law to use. After a few months, I took off the knob because it got in my way while driving and became a nuisance.

Some guys wanted to draw attention to their car, so they punctured a lot of holes in their car tailpipes to create a roar when they stepped on the accelerator. Some kids thought the sound was cool, but I never tried it because I found it an annoying sound. Besides, I liked to hear and enjoy the music on the car radio. It was an era of great music for kids.

We all finally had access to cars, which was the single most important thing to us that year. Cars gave us the mobility to explore the whole new world of the wonders of San Francisco, Santa Cruz, Russian River, Lake Tahoe and everywhere within hundreds of miles – the largest and most exciting "sandbox" of our young life. Five of us had our own cars by now with no need to drive our parent's cars. I had a 1954 Mercury red coupe, Carmody a 1950 Ford yellow coupe, Hipps a 1949 Mercury black coupe, Canas a 1951 Mercury red customized coupe, and Lafayette a 1950 Chevrolet red coupe. Three other buddies had access to their parent's cars or pickups. Applebee had a 1955 Chevrolet lime green pickup truck, Beyma a 1939 Plymouth black sedan, Sullivan a 1957 Ford light blue and white convertible, and Coughlin had no car access. Carmody eventually got rid of his Ford for a Plymouth Fury. That was a smokin' car. It was sleek and fast, and he often dragged it on the Great Highway. He did not fear speed – something useful eventually in law enforcement.

Canas, having a hidden agenda, talked his father into buying himself a car that was cool and had flair. Canas described the car as "a red 1951 Mercury convertible, molded (devoid of factory chrome trim), hidden electric solenoid switches instead of door handles, frenched (recessed) hood headlights, Lincoln taillights, dual glass-pack mufflers, stick shift, and, naturally hanging from the rear-view mirror was a pair of red and white fuzzy dice, which had obligatorily been crocheted by my girlfriend. And while this description sounded cool, maintaining functionality of a car was a pain in the ass. My father bought the car on the rationale that he occasionally would use it to carpool his cronies across the Bay Bridge to work. I eventually told him it was only a matter of time before those wheels attracted hot-rodders wanting to 'drag' him along Lincoln Way or on the Bridge – very uncool. By the end of football season, the car and its reputation was all mine. And, when I drove down 19th Avenue across the Golden Gate Bridge and over the Waldo Grade on my way to the River with the top down, my hair frozen in place by half a jar of Vaseline, wearing my 'Frisco Coupes' black car club jacket with the back collar up, I defied anyone to challenge my owning a good chunk of coolness. Some of us just needed the props."

The movie *Rebel Without a Cause* came out in 1955. James Dean played a troubled teenager and was idolized by our generation of teens. Gerry Hipps was no exception. About a year later, he got his first car – a black 1949 Mercury coupe, just like Dean drove in the movie. The next year the movie *Giant* hit the screen. There was a scene where Dean was driving his limousine in a parade and made an S-shape wave out the window to Rock Hudson – pretty cool. Gerry adopted the wave as his way of saying "Hi" or "See ya." Gerry was also a cool, calm guy and snappy dresser. He had an endless collection of pullover sweaters of every color. The demeanor, clothes, 1949 Merc' and S-wave made Gerry the coolest guy in school – a combination that would likely work in any generation.

The 1950 Chevrolet coupe bought and paid for by Lafayette was generally in pretty good shape for a used car except for the engine. He and his dad pulled the engine and rebuilt it. He spent lots of time on the car, as he loved that kind of work. Like Applebee, he loved working with his hands. The new paint job was candy apple red, and the engine had duel carburetors and headers with straight exhaust pipes. There were large fat tires on the rear. The car was fast and he loved to drag race on the Great Highway and Sunset Boulevard.

Most of us liked to speed on the open road and none more than Canas. Not surprisingly, one of Canas's heroes was his cousin Bob Machon, who at the age of 17 survived D-day after a parachute jump and being shot in the chest three times by a German's submachine gun. Once he came home, Machon celebrated by scaring the crap out of Canas and his sister by driving through Golden Gate Park as fast as he could in his Plymouth coupe while they "shrieked in joyous fright." We sometimes imitate our heroes for better or worse. For Canas, the thirst for speed cost him a lot of money in car repair bills during high school. The moral was to be careful whom we select as role models.

Barry summed up our social life pretty well once we had access to cars: "The movie *American Graffiti* by George Lucas was a very accurate depiction of teenage life in the 1950s. We drank beer, played sports, loved cars, and most of us really loved to chase the ladies. One of the best places to drink beer was on the Beach or in our cars. We were not particular about the brand of beer, which we called 'reebs' because it spelled beer backwards, but Country Club Malt Liquor and Rainier Ale were popular. Country Club came in a small can, half the size of a regular beer, but it could quickly get us mellow with its higher alcohol content of 12 percent or more. Beer usually contained less than five percent. Rainier Ale came in a green bottle with a green label and was nicknamed either the 'green death,' based on its green packaging and strong kick, or 'panther piss' because of the discomfort it caused if consumed to excess. In other words, we sometimes wound up puking our guts out. After a night of drinking and 'hell raising,' consisting of simply cruising the streets trying to pick up girls, we sobered up with a great breakfast and cups of coffee at The Flying Saucer Restaurant on Geary Boulevard or Zim's at 19th and Taraval."

Badness Was All Talk, No Action

Canas described our actions from a different perspective: "Our friends had their own, albeit warped, idea of what constituted cool youth behavior. Being tough, for example, was an overrated attitude but considered cool. So, some of us spent a lot of time talking about 'getting drunk,' 'picking up women,' and 'punching someone out.' But any *badness* was all talk no action. *Punch-out after school today... Ocean Beach... pass it on.* These so called 'rumbles' were pathetic affairs of false bravado. To display any semblance of coolness, an occasional show of fortitude was required. I did not understand it but the Irish did, and so I copied the attitude. From what I had seen on a two-week summer trip to El Salvador, Latino youth there were more emotional and causing bodily harm to someone else was more certainly a possibility when provoked. In our group, suggesting that we use knives, clubs, chains, or guns would have been an exaggeration and viewed as ridiculous because we would be 'losing our cool.' In fact, our generation may have coined that feeble term."

Before we learned to drive, we had to commute by bus or streetcar to meet our buddies at an event like a high school basketball or football game. Then we had to go home the same way we came, so the only time we were together was at the event. But now with a car, we could spend the entire evening together from start to finish. We usually cruised the streets of Geary, Taraval, Ocean, Sloat, Geneva, Sunset Boulevard, and Great Highway. Our main highway in and out of the City was U.S. 101, the road toward San Jose south and to Fairfax in Marin County or the Russian River north of the City near Guerneville in Sonoma County. One of us volunteered on a rotation basis to use our car. We set a time and the driver came by and picked up each of us. He in turn dropped us off at the end of the evening. Since our cars only fit five comfortably and six if necessary, it was never the same five or six guys each night. Fortunately, not all ten of us wanted to do the same things all the time. The regulars in the car were Barry, Carmody and me. Frequent riders with us were Beyma, Canas, and Coughlin. Applebee, Duffy, Hipps, and Lafayette were on board depending on the night's destination like a game, dance or cruising. Because Applebee had a pickup truck that only sat three people, he, Lafayette and Beyma used to go to a lot of places together, such as Big Sur, Death Valley, waterskiing with Lafayette's boat, shooting cans and bottles in the canyons off the Pacific Coast Highway between Daly City and Half-Moon Bay, along the coast, and in and out of the mountains.

"19 Cents of Gas, Please"

Duffy recollected when we were riding in Beyma's car late Saturday night on the way to drop us all off at home. We were running on fumes and stopped at the gas station at 19ᵗʰ Avenue and Taraval Street. We had

19 cents among the five of us and Beyma was not happy. It might not buy enough gas to get us all home and it was late. More importantly, it was customary for the riders to help with gas money. When Beyma asked the gas station attendant to put 19 cents of gas in, the attendant sarcastically said, "I'll wring the hose out for you."

Socialize First, Beers Second Priority

Getting together was the main objective of the evening, having a few beers was secondary, and everything else was an afterthought. Now that we had wheels, we could drive around to find someone to buy us beer and then drive somewhere to drink it. Initially, we parked outside a small local liquor store, figuring they may be more desperate to sell to minors. We had better luck if the owner was oriental. They seemed more willing to bend the rules. Beyma was 6'4" and looked old for his age compared to the rest of us. It was a hit and miss thing. Sometimes they did not ask for an ID and other times they did. We only needed one success each evening. If Plan A did not work, we resorted to Plan B. We waited until some young guy came to the store that looked like a nice guy. We asked him if he would buy us a six-pack. He normally was just buying a bottle or a six pack for himself, so more times than not, he said, "Sure." For all we knew, he was doing the same thing at our age.

Barry's dad had a great bar in their basement. Instead of watching television in the afternoon, Barry occasionally poured me different liquors and liqueurs to sample when his parents were not home. Being around the Irish all my life, I was exposed to whiskey at home and Irish parties but not other liquors and certainly never saw liqueurs before. It was a crash coarse on developing my likes and dislike for various alcoholic drinks. It was a cheap learning process, but it soon ended. Barry's folks came home unexpectedly. While Barry was frantically cleaning out the glasses, I ran out the front door while his parents drove into the garage. The next day, Barry said his dad was pretty upset and told him he had to stop raiding his bar when he was not around. Well, it was fun while it lasted but an end to one of those adult things we experienced for a while.

There were a lot of times we all got picked up by the driver and sat at the last pickup spot to discuss where we were going. It was like a scene from the movie *Marty* with Ernest Borgnine that just came out the year before (1955): "Well, what do you feel like doing tonight?" "I don't know. What do you feel like doing?" It continued around the car until someone said something like, "Let's check out the Great Highway." Sometimes guys were having drag races there. Other times, we went to a bar, often in the Sunset, where we could get served when it got busy with less chance to get asked for a driver's license for identification. In the North Beach area, the Monkey Inn served beer in mason jars and had a free bowl of peanuts on every table. The floor was a thick carpet of peanut shells that never seemed to get swept up. There was a small Dixieland band and they served great cheeseburgers. Another bar in the area served unlimited free crab legs. It was too much work for me to find the meat, so I just drank the beer. A few of the small local bars in the Sunset seldom checked for IDs, especially when the place was jammed. They were too busy mixing and serving drinks.

Slap Across the Face After a Night of Drinking

I drank beer during high school because it was what my buddies did at the time. I always thought it helped me overcome my shyness, but there was no need to overcome shyness because girls were very seldom, if ever, around. I often regretted drinking the entire evening, rather than quitting after two or three beers, but the beers were there for the taking and I could not pass up "free" beers or take leftovers home. It was always a relief to wake up in the morning without a hangover, which was the norm rather than the exception because I normally had two to four beers but could drink a six-pack without getting hung over. I more likely woke up the next morning feeling a little dopey, so it felt good getting up and out on the street on the way to doing my morning paper route. The slight breeze was usually chilly and often brought the smell of salt air. It was like getting slapped across the face a couple of times. The colder it was outside, the better for me. After a half a block, I was back to normal and ready to get to work.

Those nights when I got home after my 11:00 p.m. curfew, everyone was in bed asleep. It did not take long to learn how to open and shut the front door as quietly as possible. After quietly turning the key in the lock,

I leaned my right shoulder against the door to help cushion the sound of opening it. I did the same when I closed the door from the inside. Years later in a college English class, I wrote up that technique in one of my papers. The teacher selected my paper with a couple of others as examples of what he admired. He told the class it was a very descriptive, detailed explanation of something that I must have had a lot of experience with. He praised my writing style and then took a shot at my excessive drinking. He picked me up and slammed me down at the same time. I expected a much better grade than the C+ that I got just for the fact that it was good enough to read out loud to the class as an example of good writing.

There were some nights I drank too much, and when I got home my head was in the toilet bowl puking my guts out. First, any food in my stomach came up. I often thought why did I bother having that delicious hamburger and milk shake – why not just get coffee and pie? After the food, yellow bile came up, which had its own unique, disgusting taste. Finally, I went through dry heaves. Each time, I swore I would not drink too much again, but things never changed. I often thought that this could not be good for my body. Being so serious about athletics, I wish coaches or someone had told me it would affect my ability to play sports. Even if it was a lie, it may have been the only thing that would have sunk in and got me to cut back on drinking.

It was always exciting to look forward to a new football season with fresh hope and wishful thinking of beating our perennial league rivals like Bellarmine and watching the Riordan games on Friday nights at the home field of the 49ers while getting charged up by the music played by the award winning school marching band.

Learning to Play the Sax Using the Think System

I thought I would try something new this year and join the school marching band. Their music always moved me at the football games and some of the guys like Lafayette and Sereni were in the band as well as in a small jazz band called the Spotlighters – a nine member combo from our class made up of two sax players, two trumpet players, clarinet player, trombone player, standup base player, drummer and the band director, Howard "Howie" Segurson, who played the accordion and wrote all the music for the combo. Howie went on to be a composer, arranger and alto saxophone player in the movie and entertainment music world. They had so much fun together that Lafayette had visions of making it a career after high school. They played for the dances at Riordan, the Catholic all-girl high schools, and other local high schools in the City. They got to perform in front of crowds and it would give me something to do in between the seasons that I was playing sports. God forbid that I would want to devote that time to my studies.

So I went to the band director and asked if I could try out for the band. He gave me a strange look and seemed sort of stunned for someone in the middle of the school year making such a request. He asked if I had any experience playing an instrument and I said, "No." I just assumed that they gave me lessons and I eventually would be good enough for the band. Little did I suspect that all of the band members had been playing their instruments for years. He asked what instrument I had in mind. Never having thought about it, I simply replied, "I don't know." I liked drums and figured that they might be easier to learn to play, so I said, "Drums." He disappeared for a while, then came back with a tenor saxophone. He said it was all that he had available. He handed me a music book and asked if I could read music, and I said, "Not in a long time." I had played the piano years ago for a short time and looked at music when in various choruses, but that was all forgotten. Besides, I expected to be getting music lessons, but I guess not. He told me to go home and practice by getting used to the keys and doing the best that I could. The musical *Music Man* came out that year, so maybe the director wanted to test out the "Think System" on me. I did practice off and on in our garage for a month at most and saw I was getting nowhere. The biggest challenge was the convoluted arrangement of the keys on the sax. Unlike a trumpet where you pushed a key and that key was depressed in a hole directly beneath it, on a sax I pressed a key and two or three keys somewhere further down the sax were depressed into holes. I never even thought of asking Lafayette, who played the alto sax, for help. So I brought the sax back to the director and that was the end of my musical career.

In hindsight, I would have loved to be a dancer in the school plays, but no one from the Drama Department tried to recruit dancers. There were no dance or gymnastic classes offered as extracurricular activities. Like all school activities, kids were expected to take the first step and show up for tryouts. Coaches and teachers could have taken the initiative to seek out those with the potential, whether they were physical, mental or inherent qualities. Many athletes would make very good dancers. I could picture myself being another Gene Kelly, Donald O'Connor, Gene Nelson, Russ Tamblyn or his other brothers in the 1954 movie *Seven Brides for Seven Brothers*. Others may want to be a Fred Astaire. If kids started in a dance class as freshmen, they could be pretty good by their junior and senior years, just like in sports. Who knows? We could entertain at the school dances during breaks – not a bad way for girls to check out my moves and me.

At one of the early Riordan football games at Kezar, some rowdiness broke out and caused by non-Riordan students. For future night games, faculty members and fathers of students were assigned designated posts around the stadium to maintain order and to make sure it did not happen again – another contribution by Riordan Father's Club members, parents and faculty that saved the school money from not hiring security.

Deaths Bring on Urgency to Succeed

I grew up going to wakes for older friends of the family, and it was easier to accept because I never really knew any of them. But when it happened to someone my own age, kids whom I knew or played with in the same mud on the football field, it made me question my immortality along with the urgency and determination to make something of myself. In my first year at Riordan, senior Gilbert "Tito" Aldecoa was killed by a falling giant redwood. At the start of my sophomore year, a teammate of mine Dave Smith died from a heart condition right after a non-contact football practice. He walked off the field at 3:30 p.m. on September 13, 1956 and into the gym where he collapsed. He died shortly after vain attempts were made by the coaches to revive him. Three months earlier, we lost another classmate Charlie Montague who died in the hospital in June after complications set in after a cold, and three months later, senior and varsity football player Alex "The Chief" Nava tragically died in a terrible highway accident. As a tribute, Riordan established the Al Nava Memorial Trophy in his memory. How appropriate that Beyma should be the first recipient of the trophy as Nava was described as a "quiet dynamo," which Beyma also demonstrated on the football field. This was well after Beyma at a muddy football practice broke his wrist tackling 250-pound guard Rich Horan during tackling practice when he fell to the bottom of the pile with his wrist under him. He did not know it was broken until he tried to take off his jersey in the locker room. I thought if a big, strong guy like Beyma could break a bone, what are my chances of escaping injury, never realize how prophetic that would be for me in my senior year. In our senior yearbook, Beyma was also designated Best Athlete in our class.

On the subject of deaths, I thought it strange for a funeral service owned by a couple of St. James High School graduates, where Riordan had its roots, to be taking out ads in the *Crusader* newspaper during my four years at Riordan. There were ads by retailers that catered to teenagers like clothing stores and hamburger places, but a funeral service? I admired their support of the school, but it seemed weird, eerie and macabre.

Football season was starting and Hipps was trying out for the varsity. Barry remembers more frustration for Hipps at a practice session. "Gerry took the handoff and was hit by two tacklers. He was hit so hard he could hear his collarbone snap with a loud crack. Gerry was told afterwards that Coach Grgich told a couple of the defensive lineman to hit Gerry high and low. There was no intent to cause an injury, nor could they know the history of his previous bone injuries. It was really too bad because Gerry could have been their fullback and kicker having made over 50 yard field goals at practice. Gerry spent the next two weeks in traction at St. Mary's Hospital, and when he got out he had to wear a cast from his neck to his lower body with his one arm sticking straight out. He was in that hideous cast for several months and his football career was over for the season."

In our junior year, Beyma again made varsity football, varsity track along with Coughlin, and junior varsity (JV) basketball. Applebee ran varsity track. Duffy, Lafayette, and Latour were on the 130-pound track team. Barry and Canas played JV football and I was on the varsity and JV football teams. Most of the time I was the starting halfback on both offense and defense on the JV team. The offensive running backfield on the JV team consisted of me, Tim Moffett and Bob "Hopalong" Hoppe. Noel Murray finally grew up and out physically by our junior year. He made both the JV football and baseball teams, which is where I got to know my new friend Noel. This was the same year when he used to walk, catch the Muni or get a ride from someone to get to school. Once in a while his ex-math teacher and future track coach, Ed Fennelly, came up from the Peninsula and picked up Noel several blocks away and drove him to school.

It was great that kids like Noel persevered to pursue their passions. Some studied more, others got involved with extracurricular activities, making new friends along the way, and others found time to do both. It was sad that some kids had to spend their extra time working at their family business or choosing to just go home after classes every day. Years later Noel said, "Football remained my favorite memory of high school." Others said, "High school was not an enjoyable period in my life. I do not want to even talk about those years." I learned over my lifetime that so much of what goes on in life was not based on the 80/20 Principle but on the 90/10 Principle – sometimes the 95/5 Principle. That meant we could satisfy people 95 percent of the time but could not satisfy five percent of the people, and that probably was true in the case of our graduating class. Fortunately, the five percent received a second chance to turn their lives around after leaving high school.

The school paper drive in October collected over 450 tons of paper, a new record, compared to the previous year's 400 tons. Riordan had the reputation for putting on outstanding stage performances and attracting large audiences thanks to James Lindland. The November performance of *The Man Who Came to Dinner* drew the customary 2,000 attendees over the 3-day Thursday to Saturday performances.

Early in the school year, a consultation night was held for all parents of kids who got less than a "C" in a subject. I doubt it was mandatory, as my parents never told me they ever attended, and God knows I got a few D's along the way. My mom probably was too tired after being on her feet all day at work and cooking dinner when she got home, and knowing that I probably was not going to do anything differently at her suggestion. On the other hand, the threat of having to attend summer school may have made a difference, but knowing me, I would have assumed that I could turn my grades around on my own to avoid summer school, which did not always happen. I always thought the school had the consultation thing backwards. The school counselor should talk to kids in our freshman year, but no one ever confronted me about improving my grades except once when I was called into the principal's office for a disciplinary matter and once in my junior year when the Guidance Center Counselor just said that I should be doing better with no advise about how to do it.

In the second half of the football season, the varsity coach, Visco Grgich, called up the JV starting backfield of me, Moffett and Hoppe to the varsity team as backup running backs. It was not only an honor to play with the "big kids," but we would be playing for a celebrity like Coach Grgich, who the month before the season coached the West team in the East-West All-Star high school game at Kezar to a 19-0 victory. The coach called us his "pony backfield." When he wanted us in the game he just called out "Give me my pony backfield." We did not get called very often, but it was a thrill to be part of the varsity. We played our varsity home games at Kezar, and it was pretty exciting to run through the tunnel like the professionals. As I came out of the tunnel, there was the initial intimidation of the massive high-rise stadium The football field looked a lot bigger than the one at Riordan, but once the game started, all those images went away. It just became another game on a 100-yard field that could be anywhere in the City.

Riordan played St. Ignatius (S.I.) in football the first Saturday in November at Seals Stadium. It was the first time Riordan played a city league team in football. Riordan tried for years to get practice games scheduled with the city league teams with no luck. Even the two Catholic schools refused. We got the impression they thought playing against such a new school was beneath them. Our opinion was that they were afraid to play us for fear of getting beaten, since we played in the much tougher Catholic Athletic League. Although Riordan lost 0-13, it began the intense rivalry between Riordan and S.I. no matter the sport, event or activity. The gauntlet had been thrown down by the Riordan Crusaders, especially after hearing the following Monday morning that the brothers found three tombstones taken from the Chinese Cemetery in neighboring Daly City and set up in fresh cement by the school's kitchen entrance. Each stone had the name of one of the star players on the Riordan team freshly painted on them. The two biggest stars were quarterback Mike Carson and halfback Jerry White, two of the top players in Northern California. The culprits were never caught, but the memories were not forgotten for years.

Confessions in the Shower

The most unusual aspect to the S.I. game was that in preparation for the game and after our team meeting in the Riordan gym, Father Joseph Priestley heard individual confessions in the showers. It was a one-time thing, but certainly the most memorable confession we ever experienced. This was a time when kids were committing more sins than they did in grammar school and those sins could be embarrassing when they went to confession. By now we had figured out which priest gave the easiest penance when confessing our sins at church. For me it was Father Keane at Holy Name. The penance was always a few Our Fathers and a few Hail Marys as opposed to having to say an entire rosary of six Our Fathers and 53 Hail Marys.

As much as I loved playing football, the only negative was getting tackled with four or five players piled on top of me. It always seemed like forever for everyone to unpile. Meanwhile, 600-800 pounds of weight was crushing my body while I was gasping for air and yelling, "Hurry up! Get off me!" The yelling never sped up the process. They got off in their own sweet time.

One of the highlights of our junior varsity football season was against Lick-Wilmerding High School. Both Barry and I scored touchdowns in the same game – a first for us. Barry intercepted a pass and ran it back for a TD and I scooped up a punt and returned it 48 yards for a TD. We won 23-6, one of the few wins for the season.

Teaching Character With Movies

The day before Thanksgiving and a long weekend for us, the seniors played the underclassmen in the Senior-Junior football game that morning. It was followed by a judo exhibition by two U.S. Marine Corp officers. After lunch, another one of my favorite movies, *The Fastest Gun Alive*, was shown at school. It was a great example of character to serve as a role model for me and the other kids. Actor Glenn Ford was the best at what he did, but he was shy, unassuming and not a braggart – as was every student I knew in our class, whether they were outstanding in academics, sports, speech, drama, or any other activity.

Physical Beatings but Never Mental Beatings

Our JV football team had a record of 1-5 and fared no better in the Senior-Junior game at the end of the season. The seniors had a backfield of Mike Carson at quarterback and Jerry White at halfback, two of the best high school football players to ever come out of Northern California. The juniors had a backfield of me, Bill Baker, Bob Hoppe and Noel Murray. Although we lost 20-0 and there was not much we could do about the physical beating, we did not take a mental beating. We still believed in ourselves, our teammates, and had the satisfaction that we would be back the following season, while the football days for all of those on the other side of the ball would be over for them after graduation. They would be "retiring" while we would be center stage in our senior year.

Faculty Celebrities Not Given Their Due

After Visco Grgich's career with the 49ers ended with a knee injury, he turned to teaching at Riordan and was their head football coach. He had the reputation of creating teams that bulled their way straight ahead down the field. That was a simplification of his style as Riordan over the years had some outstanding end-around runners and quarterbacks who could really air it out. Since he was a major player for the 49ers, you would think I would get his autograph, but it never crossed my mind – even knowing this was to be his last year at Riordan. I also never got autographs of other faculty "celebrities" like Ed Fennelly, Ross Giudice, Al Lavin, and James Lindland. There were some like Vern Sellin who we did not know about their background and future fame. He was a conductor, a violinist with the San Francisco Symphony nearly 50 years, and played with the Spike Jones and Xavier Cugart orchestras. I guess it was a case of taking people for granted when we dealt with them on a daily basis. The only autograph I ever got was at a 49er game from Mel Triplett, a fullback for most of his 8-year career with the New York Giants and on their 1956 championship team.

At the end of football season, Canas had trouble convincing his father that he could afford the insurance and car maintenance support of his own car, but the realization was that it meant getting a job. An opportunity presented itself, and although it meant giving up extracurricular activities during his last year of high school, he accepted a job delivering groceries in the Sea Cliff District for Korss Market located at 33rd Avenue and Lake Street. As he tells it "The pay was $1.25 an hour and I needed to report right after school until the store delivery service closed in the early evening. Now with the assurance of the extra income, I could take over 'ownership' of my father's hot 1951 Mercury. This freedom afforded me the final step in adolescence – social interaction on a broader scale."

Pedigree Made a Difference in Some Circles

"The Korss Market in the affluent Sea Cliff District had me driving from Riordan five miles north to the other side of the Golden Gate Park and just shy of the Presidio every school day and from home on Saturdays. The owner, Bud Korss, was Jewish, as were 27% of homeowners in the Sea Cliff area. [65] It was my first exposure to Jews, especially Jewish millionaires and their children. Their customs were a revelation. I learned about their approach to child rearing, which was not like that of the permissive parents of my friends. I do not include my parents in this comparison because they were in a category all their own in that they were oblivious to American customs let alone American teenage customs."

"I made friends with Tommy Horwitz, whose father was a famous surgeon and whose mother Frankie oozed liveliness, and with Joe Smolen, whose father owned a chain of pharmacies and just bought Joe a brand new Corvette. While I interacted with Tom and Joe while delivering groceries to their homes, they avoided going out with me after work for a hamburger or a movie. That evasion continued until one day I happened to mention my father was a dentist. Then, it was a brand new ballgame. Frankie began making Tom and me *matzah brei* (matzah fried with eggs) Saturday mornings, and Joe agreed to a road trip to Tijuana for a weekend. Joe later explained their parents strictly regulated their children's friends, and one way of doing it was to check their pedigree. They had thought my father was a common laborer. Hmm...very pragmatic, but wholly elitist. Still, when in Rome...So, dating a local rabbi's daughter, whom I met on my deliveries, was a stretch. But I tried anyway. Her name was Sarah and she was beautiful and attracted to me, but she confided one day *it would never happen*. Tom and Joe both already warned me of that possibility. Pedigree has limits, it seems."

"I did learn some Yiddish. For example, a *schmuck* (actually meant penis) was someone who knows he deserved a raise in pay but was too shy to ask for it. He eventually paid me a slight raise with an agonizing expression on his face. I learned much about business and relationships outside the Catholic/Irish circle where I had grown up. But I was not intimidated by Jewish wealth and status. Joe might have a new Corvette while in high school, but he did not work for it. He would inherit his wealth; I probably would work the rest of my life to merely break even. But I was just as proud of my lineage. I did learn that a different and vast world was out there and befriending such people was not a sin, at least it did not warrant absolution."

During the last quarter of 1956, there was a lot of excitement in professional and local college sports. A historic World Series was played and the University of San Francisco Dons continued their winning ways. Barry was fortunate to experience both as he told it: "On October 8, 1956 I had the great fortune of watching game five of the World Series between the New York Yankees and the Brooklyn Dodgers on television. Dad and I played hooky that Monday to watch the 11:06 a.m. game. (Meanwhile, Jim Riley was secretly listening to the game on his transistor radio in the hallway at Riordan as he kept students abreast of the game.) The Yankees had players like Mickey Mantle, Yogi Berra, Billy Martin, Enos Slaughter, Gil McDougald, and Hank Bauer. The Dodgers had Jackie Robinson, Jim Gilliam, Pee Wee Reese, Gil Hodges, Duke Snyder, and Roy Campanella. The manager of the Yankees was Casey Stengel, and the manager of the Dodgers was Walter Alston. The pitchers for the game were Don Larsen for the Yankees and Sal Maglie for the Dodgers. The Yankee announcer was Mel Allen and the Dodger announcer was Vin Scully. We saw that day Don Larsen pitch the only perfect game in World Series history – no runs, no hits, no errors. The crowd went wild and as Yogi Berra rushed to the mound, jumped into Larsen's arms with his legs wrapped around Larsen's waist, Dad and I hooted and hollered around our living room. Larsen achieved baseball immortality, and I got to see it live."

"The other memorable game I saw was on December 8, 1956 with several of the best college basketball players in history at Kezar Pavilion.

The Dons were playing Seattle University, led by their superstar Elgin Baylor. The game was tight, back and forth while each team struggled for the lead, but in the end the Dons won their 59th game of the season. They beat Seattle and Elgin Baylor 57-52. Baylor was fantastic but he was outmanned by a team of future NBA stars." Their next win against Loyola (Chicago) was their 60th and set the longest college win streak at the time.

Tough Group Those Marianist Brothers

On January 28, 1957, snow covered the ground in the San Bruno hills that bordered the City. The principal Brother Miller drove the new 1956 Ford the school just bought six months earlier to St. Mary's College in Moraga, CA. On his way home just outside of Orinda, he was rear-ended and pushed into oncoming traffic to be hit head on by another car. His car was totaled but fortunately he received only superficial injuries. The student body was never told of the incident. Tough group those Marianists.

The February Annual Talent Show had several entries from our class. Bob O'Neill sang, Howie Segurson played the accordion and saxophone with his Spotlighters quartet, with Dave Sereni on trumpet, Paul Breslin on bass, and Ray Andreini on piano. Also this year, Bob O'Neill and Paul Scannell were two of the best on the Speech Club in winning competitions.

Junior Class Miracle of 1957

Nearly all of us in school grew up with earthquakes in the City. They were regular things so we took them as a matter of course – nothing to get excited about because they eventually stopped and generally there was little damage throughout the City. It was just the magnitude that varied. In our lifetime of 17 years, the worst effects of the quakes were concentrated in a few areas built on landfill or sand. The typical reaction to earthquakes was "Huh! Must be an earthquake." I preferred an earthquake anytime compared to the hurricanes, tornadoes and forest fires in other parts of the country that always caused major widespread disasters. The earthquakes we experienced typically caused cosmetic damage to fronts of houses and occasionally structural damage confined to a few blocks of houses in a few neighborhoods. A good example of kids' and teachers' casual attitude toward earthquakes occurred on Friday March 22, 1957 just before lunch at 11:44 a.m. when there was an earthquake with a moment magnitude of 5.7 and a maximum Mercalli Intensity of VII (Very strong). It was called the "Daly City Earthquake of 1957" named after the center of the quake. It was the strongest earthquake since 1906. While some people downtown were running in the streets crying, we were calmly sitting in class, the rooms started to shake, and an amazing thing happened. It may not have been a miracle (or was it?), but a strange coincidence occurred in at least four of our five junior classrooms.

In Brother Elmer Dunsky's 11A math class, the 24-inch statue of the Blessed Virgin Mary (BVM) fell off the small platform 8 feet above the ground, and Jim Veal who was standing at the blackboard caught the falling statue. Randy Mellinger caught the BVM statue in my 11B class. After catching it and laying it on the ground, he patted her head as if to say, "You're OK. I gotcha." Art Curtis described his experience that day in the 11C class. "I was in Ed Fennelly's class. As the quake progressed, he told us just to stay calm. I looked at the ceiling that appeared to be shifting on the walls. Then I heard a classmate yell out 'Mr. Fennelly – the statue!' Fennelly, who was standing at the middle of the blackboard, looked up, ran over, and caught the statue in his arms just as it fell off its perch." In a fourth junior classroom, Brother Edward Immethun caught the BVM statue that was falling in their room. Those of us who witnessed these catches thought it was one of the coolest things we had ever seen. The "miracle" was that the fallen statues in our junior classes were caught without damage, while eight of the statues in the other 17 classrooms tumbled down and broke on the floor, while only two light fixtures were dislodged and left hanging by their wires above the students' heads – no one was hurt.

Even the Best Choke – Consolation to Us Mere Mortals

That same month Coach Cappy Lavin entered the San Francisco Boy's Club free-throw tournament by hitting 28 of 30 free throws using his famous one-handed push shot. By beating out 58 other contestants, he won a trip to Honolulu for two. He said he missed the 27th and 30th shots because he choked as he heard the fans counting each basket after he hit the 20th shot. Even the best got distracted while trying to mentally shut out crowd noises. Also, you did not have to be perfect to be a winner.

The entrance exam for the next year's freshman class was held again on a Saturday in April from 9:00 a.m. to 12:45 p.m. There were over 640 eighth graders applying for the 260 seats in the next freshman class. That meant the school would have to turn away 60 percent of the applicants. Just in my four years at Riordan, the demand for a good private school Catholic education was way up.

Barry, Carmody and I played varsity baseball in our junior year. The only time I ever got hurt in baseball was this season when I was turning a double play and the runner came in high with his spikes and got me on the side of my right leg. There was blood around the tear in my pants. I told the coach to wrap it, as I did not want stitches. I dreaded the thought of a doctor sticking a needle in and out of my leg to sew the sides of the cut shut. Had I let them stitch it up, I may not have had a scar to this day.

Most Interesting Athlete in My Four Years

The most interesting guy I ever met in sports at Riordan was Doug Johnson, who was a senior, the third baseman and supposedly the fastest runner on the varsity baseball team that year, although we had never raced each other. He told me that during the summer, he worked as a mercenary south of the border. Whether that was true or not, he looked the part – ruggedly handsome, serious, a tough looking guy. Actually, he was a nice guy – kind of guy I wanted to have my back. Once I saw him put a metal soda bottle cap between his thumb and forefinger and bend it in half. That was so cool. If nothing else, it showed a sign of hand strength I had never seen before. Maybe it was one reason for his rifle arm to first base.

Research Gene Pool to Scout Athletes

Bob Joyce, a neighbor of Mike Duffy, was one of the sophomores on our baseball team. His father was Robert Joyce, a professional baseball pitcher (1934-1949), who was the Pacific Coast League's Most Valuable Player in 1945 with the San Francisco Seals and went on to play for the Philadelphia Athletics and New York Giants. Young Bob went on and played basketball and baseball at USF – an example that genes can make a difference and something coaches should consider in recruiting players.

At the end of our varsity baseball season, Sports Editor Lou Ligouri wrote in his Baseball Profile column in the *Crusader*:

"Terry Carmody, 2b/3b, his inexperience was his big drawback. He can be an important factor in the success of next year's varsity." Part of that was due to the coach not giving him a full time position.

"Barry Sullivan, catcher, started to come into his own at the end of the season. His inexperience is his only drawback, but he is a highly spirited contender." His fiery, team-spirited rah-rah personality was evident in all his sport activities throughout high school.

"Terry Quinlan, shortstop, was a very fine defensive player. His speed and natural ability will find him a spot on the first team next year. His attitude toward the game helps his performance." That meant my head was always in the game and like Sullivan, my rah-rah attitude helped make the team a contender. As much as we appreciated the kind words, it did not erase the embarrassment of winding up with a 3-7 record and in last place in C.A.L. competition. That made it even more amazing when the following season we made it to the league championship playoff game.

As a junior, Applebee took second at the C.A.L. track tournament finals. Dennis Leahy, whom I knew from St. Paul's Grammar School, broke the school's shot put record five times, but he never was inducted into the school's Hall of Fame. Sad!

Historic Athletic Achievement for School and Athletes

The 1956-57 school year was monumental for Riordan sports. At the time, each of the three local newspapers selected their All-City AAA teams for the various sports. Because Riordan was not in the City's AAA league, no players from Riordan were ever selected. That changed in 1957. Quarterback Mike Carson and halfback Jerry White were the first Riordan players to be selected for the *San Francisco Examiner* All-City Football Team. This same year, Mike Carson was the first from Riordan to make All-City in basketball and Ed Coleman, from our class, was the first from Riordan to make All-City AAA in baseball. Mike and Jerry were seniors and Ed was a junior, which made Ed the youngest from Riordan to make an *Examiner* All-City team from Riordan. These three ballplayers finally pierced the athletic veil of the press, no longer treating Riordan athletics as a second-class program and finally gave our outstanding athletes their due. It certainly helped our image in recruiting future athletes to Riordan.

More Challenges, More Successes, More Rewards

There have been many arguments for and against playing team sports. Some argued kids should concentrate their efforts on studies and others argued the merits of team sports. There was always the chance of getting a serious injury, which was true for driving a car or crossing the street when cars were on the road. I never believed in an argument based on the worst possible outcome, otherwise I would never leave the house. Odds were so small that really bad things would happen to me specifically, but life was just a daily trail of chances. Bad things did happen to people. About 10 years after I played football at Riordan, one of Riordan's players received an injury that left him a quadriplegic for life. That could have been any of us. We went into sports thinking only the best. It was not until after our playing days were over and we knew the outcome that we could honestly answer the question "Would you do it all over again?" On the other hand, there were plenty of non-contact sports and other activities that provided groups for kids to make friends who made them feel like part of the school and student body. Being on a team or in a group activity did not mean we had lunch regularly with all of these guys or got to know any of them very well. It was the facial recognition of a team or group member passing in the hallway as we went to the next class, where we could just nod, smile or say, "See ya." Otherwise, four years would have been spent walking past a bunch of strangers, not seeing anyone we felt comfortable sitting next to at lunch. Not everyone could make the sports teams, but they could join the extracurricular activities where they met others with a common interest. Some fathers of students were too focused on sports and pushed their kids to play sports whether the kid was good or not. Kids would more than likely be better off in the long run if they were allowed to participate in activities that they really liked or were good at rather than being below average or no good and sitting on the bench most of the time. On the other hand, whether we were first string or third string, there were a lot of qualities kids developed that may not be available elsewhere. [66] However, if you or your team frequently lost, your expectations could be to lose the next time out. If you lost the desire to do your best, you could wind up being a procrastinator or quitter in the future, leaving your tasks half-done or accomplishing nothing. Kids needed to experience as many successes and achievements in these early formative years as possible. Successes led to greater confidence in tackling challenges in the future – the more challenges, the more successes, the more rewards in life.

Team Concept Applicable to Marriage

The concept of "team" greatly influenced my attitude about marriage throughout my married life with the same woman. I thought of marriage as a two-player team fashioned after professional ballplayers during the 1940s and 1950s when they stayed with their team most or all of their career. I viewed my wife as a player who gave me the best years of her life when she was young, energetic, and beautiful with a gorgeous body. But as we aged, we both lost some of those qualities. But rather than me quitting our two-player team for a younger woman like ballplayers left teams for more money and better benefits, I always felt that I owed it to my wife to stay on our team for life, because she gave me the best years of her life, something she could not get back. That was a hell of a price she paid to join our team, and she deserved better than a separation later in life. I owed it to her to live out our "playing days" to the end, which we have done so far after 50-plus years of marriage. It made respect, love and commitment the binding forces between us.

Call Out the Cheaters – a Good Feeling

Every once in a while when I was waiting in line to get into a movie theater, there were one or two jerks trying to cut in line. They never knew anyone in line; they just muscled their way in line ahead of us. By my junior year I felt morally righteous and physically confident enough to get in their face and tell them to go back to the end of the line. I was now 16 years old, in pretty good shape, 170 pounds and no longer a 110-pound weakling, plus there were one or two buddies in line who had my back.

In addition, others in line would jump on the bandwagon and shouted out "Yeah! Get outta here." They always left without an incident – probably because I was not stupid enough to call out anyone a lot bigger than me.

Even at drive-in theaters there was line cutting. I seldom went to the El Rancho Drive-In in Colma because it was "too far out" from the City. It was the main reason the Geneva Drive-In by the Cow Palace in Daly City was the most popular drive-in for my buddies and me. It was not uncommon for a line of cars to be backed up waiting for drivers to pay their admission to enter the drive-in, but occasionally a car sped around the line and entered through the exit lane on the other side of the ticket booth. The person in the ticket booth could not stop them because he or she was busy taking money from those paying to enter. By the time they could get help, the crasher found one of the parking spots that was in complete darkness. There was no way to identify who was the crasher. We never did it because we could have a beer while we patiently waited – no need to hurry.

Lifetime of Reliving Our Youth at the Movies

One of the things that made San Francisco such an attraction for tourists was the interesting things they saw just driving around the City. Being locals, we enjoyed the "sightseeing" whenever we wanted among: Golden Gate Park, Fisherman's Wharf, Alcatraz Island, Mission Dolores, Chinatown, Haight-Ashbury, Castro District, Lombard Street, Coit Tower, Golden Gate Bridge, Seal Rocks, Lands End Lookout, Legion of Honor, de Young Museum, Palace of Fine Arts, California Academy of Science, Japanese Tea Garden, Twin Peaks' city view, S.F.-Oakland Bay Bridge, Cable Cars, Cliff House, North Beach, and Ocean Beach. There were so many movies made in San Francisco during the 1940s and 1950s and gave us kids a unique opportunity to relive our youth for the rest of our lives like in *I Remember Mama* with Irene Dunne, *Maltese Falcon* with Humphrey Bogart, *Pal Joey* with Frank Sinatra and Rita Hayworth, *Race Street* with George Raft, *The Caine Mutiny* with Humphrey Bogart and Van Johnson, and *Vertigo* with Jimmy Stewart and Kim Novak. It was fun to see up on the big screen places we saw on a regular basis and part of our hometown. It made me feel special and proud to be from the City. Occasionally, while

I was driving through the City, I saw houses in areas such as St. Francis Woods, Nob Hill, Fisherman's Wharf, and the Marina District where there were cameras, lights, and people just standing around for a film shoot. I never saw any action taking place or cameras rolling. That must have happened when they blocked off car traffic.

Alcatraz: Crime Does Not Pay Reminder

But we were smart enough to stay out of the high crime and violent areas after dark like the Bayview, Fillmore, Hunters Point, and Tenderloin. It did not hurt having Alcatraz and San Quentin nearby as a reminder that there were places where we could wind up if we were really bad and that crime did not pay. But Alcatraz presented no fascination to us kids, since we could never go visit and play out there. Occasionally, we heard on the radio or saw in the newspaper that there was another failed jailbreak – a total of seven while I was growing up. San Quentin was more obscure as it was "out of sight, out of mind" since I did not even know exactly where it was located. Fifteen years later, I went to San Quentin annually for their Saturday Art Show to purchase artwork created by the convicts. Those in for forgery were the best artists.

Live and Let Live Led to Open-Mindedness

Interesting parts of the City were the Castro, Haight-Ashbury, and North Beach Districts where unique atmospheres were created by the gay, hippie, and beatnik movements. On the whole, not much attention was paid to those neighborhoods by the locals who did not live in them; they were mostly attractions for tourists. Some of that was due to those who capitalized on catering to the neighborhoods. Those benefiting most off these movements were the tour businesses, neighborhood business groups, restaurants, bookstores and parade organizers. Locals viewed these upstart groups just as people with different life styles and looks. They were people we lived with and around – not people to be stared at. Outsiders labeled us locals for our tolerance of these groups. It was not a matter of tolerance but acceptance – live and let live. One reason the City was so accepting of these groups was that they stayed in their own neighborhood for the most part, like we all did, giving us the choice to mingle with them or to leave them alone. They were loving, peaceful groups that left those outside their circles alone too.

Growing up in a city known for being a tolerant, open-minded city that accepted the gays, hippies and beatniks gave me an attitude of live and let live, have an open mind, especially when I was in the majority. It made me more aware of critics expressing their narrow mindedness and ignorance. Mom's frequent statement "If it appears in the newspaper, it must be true" was the same narrow mindedness by Mom and Dad when it came to politics and elections. They were Democrats from the outset, and once I asked Mom why she did not vote for a Republican governor. Her response was "We always voted Democrat." So all the campaign speeches and election promotion had absolutely no effect on their decision-making. It never made sense to me that one party always had the best and most qualified candidates according to my parent's viewpoint. Being a numbers guy, I thought, *what are the odds?* They were the same way about religion. Whatever the Catholic Church said, must be true and the way things should be. It was a few years later when our generation started to attend Catholic universities that we had teachers encouraging kids to discuss the rationale of some of the teachings, not with the intent to change our minds but to allow open discussions for a more educated generation.

A drive down Lombard Street was something we did on occasion, just to remind us of the free neat things we could do in the City. I often drove down what was considered the crookedest street in the world with its eight sharp turns, but I decided to really experience the street up close. Usually I was too busy looking around for fear of running off the road, and I could only drive down the one-way street in one direction. So one day I parked my car at the top of Russian Hill and walked down and back up the street. I got to see what it was like walking in both directions and taking my time to look closely at the houses and landscaping. I walked down the hill on the sidewalk used by those living on the block. I reached the bottom and saw there was no traffic because it was early Sunday morning, so I walked up the hill on the narrow single-lane street. I only encountered a couple of cars coming down the hill at the same time. One honked to let me know that I should not be there, which was not news to me – just something a kid had to get out of his system. I wish I had known that the "crookedest street in the world" actually was in the Potrero Hill District on the other side of the Mission District where I grew up. It was the southern end of Vermont Street (12 blocks east of Folsom Street) between 20th and 22nd Streets. It only had seven turns instead of eight, but its hill was steeper and had tighter turns than Lombard Street. It was one of the best-kept secrets from the tourists.

A Hung Bun Was Not a Chinatown Delicacy

When driving around at night, occasionally one of the guys in the car would "hang bun" (also called "mooning") out one of the car windows. It was not something we did because we drank too much beer. We did it just as a joke – usually when passing a theater that was just letting out where there was a large crowd. With the cold weather in San Francisco, there had to be a crowd to make it worthwhile to drop his drawers and expose his butt to the cold evening air. Most of the time, people did not know what was sticking out the window. It was not until we were past the theater that it sank in and too late to get a good look. But looking back out of the car's rear window, we could see lots of the crowd pointing at our car, telling their friends what just happened, and everyone in the crowd laughing including the girls.

The Most Kid-Friendly Police in the City

I heard from a number of kids in the Sunset and other neighborhoods that if we got in trouble with the police. got stopped or picked up by them for any reason, just hope that they were from the Taraval Police Station on 24th Avenue off Taraval Street. They had a reputation among kids of being the "most kid-friendly." Not that they looked the other away if we did something wrong, but they treated us fairly because they understood that good kids can make stupid decisions. We were lucky that by chance we did our carousing in the Sunset and West Portal areas, which were the precincts patrolled by the police from the Taraval Station.

One evening a bunch of us were driving around in Hipps's Merc' looking for a place to park and have a few beers. We stopped by the Sunset Playground on the dimly lit Moraga Street behind the gym. Hipps decided to skip the beers and go inside to shoot some baskets, but the rest of us stayed in the car shooting the breeze. After a while we decided to move the car to play a joke on Hipps. He loved his car and if he found the car gone, he would have a conniption. It just seemed like a good prank to play on him at the time. Beyma knew how to hotwire cars, so he went under the dashboard and did his magic and drove the car around the block. We figured if Hipps found his car gone, he would just go back in the gym and wait for us to get him. We sat in the car for another hour and finally some of the guys wanted to go home, so one of the fellas went in to get Hipps to take us home. He came back and said he could not find him. Beyma offered to drive each of us home and then drop off the car in front of Hipps's house. The first stop was across town in the outer Mission District. On the way back to the Sunset District where the rest of us lived, we were going along Portola Drive and the brakes gave out. Beyma took a sharp right on Vicente Street, which was a pretty steep downhill block. The car started to pick up more speed and at the first intersection, he took a sharp left on to West Portal Avenue to get on a flat street in hopes of slowing down the speed of the car. I thought we might tip over in the turn because the car was moving at a pretty fast clip by then. Although the wheels screeched as we made the turn, the car did not role over. While driving the length of the block, the car slowed down a bit but was still going pretty fast, so at the first intersection, Beyma took a sharp left on to 14th Avenue, which he saw was a steep street that went uphill and might bring the car to a stop. Two-thirds of the way up the hill, the car did stop and Beyma turned the wheel so the front tire rested against the curb so the car did not roll back down the hill. The police showed up – not sure where they came from at that time of night. Fortunately, we had gotten rid of all the beer and empty cans back at the gym. The two policemen were really understanding when we told them our story – that we moved the car just as a joke, could not find Hipps, and were in the process of dropping off everyone before returning the car to Hipps. The police told us hotwiring the car probably led to the brakes giving out. They said there were two options. They would call Gerry's dad, Manny, and ask what they should do with us – let us go home or put us in Juvenile Hall overnight. When the officer told us Hipps's dad told them to take us to the Juvenile Hall Guidance Center or "Juvie" on Woodside Avenue, both officers looked sorry for us as if they would have chosen to send us home. The police were really nice guys. They were from the kid-friendly Taraval Police Station. When I heard the decision, I was really surprised since we never intended any harm, the brakes giving out was unforeseen, we did intend to return the car that evening, and we offered to pay for any damages. I just thought it was an extreme punishment for a bunch of kids that were never arrested before and went to school with Hipps in grammar school and high school. We knew it was not Gerry Hipps's fault. I felt badly for him when he found out what happened to us. We were never asked to pay for the damage to the car by Gerry's dad – good man.

Every Kid Should Spend a Night in Jail With a "Bubba"

After getting booked into Juvenile Hall, we were each put in separate cells. Each cell had a thick solid door with a very small window, which let in very little light. The facility was actually pretty nice, since it was built just six years earlier. When they opened the door to my cell, I saw this big husky white "kid" inside who had all this hair growing on his back and upper arms. I thought, *Great! I get to spend the night in the dark with 'Bubba.' What if he tries to molest me? He was much bigger and stronger than me, and I was in no mood to be wrestling this guy off me all night.* As I lay down on an empty thin mattress, I did not say a word, hoping Bubba would ignore me. I waited a while, heard nothing, and hoped he just rolled over and went back to sleep. When I woke up the next morning, I was rather surprised nothing happened during the night and all my fears were for nothing. I never saw any of the other guys that morning so we must have been released at different times.

To be released from Juvie, an adult was required to appear to sign us out. Beyma's dad was out of town and his mom did not drive, so Den had them call the chaplain at Riordan. Father Priestley came and signed for Den, who was so embarrassed when he arrived. Mom came by and drove me home, but before leaving, the officer said after age 17, my juvenile record would be expunged if I kept my nose clean. Although I was bitter and held a grudge against Hipps's dad for what he did to us, I was glad years later that it turned out the way it did. It was a good lesson for me and the other guys. I always felt that every kid should be thrown into Juvie

412

for a night. It probably would stop most good kids from making more mistakes. Sometimes we got caught, sometimes we did not, but we all needed to be punished by someone or something other than our parents, whom we did not always listen to. Yeah, it was a good experience and having a "Bubba" in my cell was a bonus for teaching me a lesson – every cell should have one.

Respect Learned From Gross Dipshit Experience

Little did I realize at the time that one of the wilder kids in our class who deserved to be in Juvie, but never was held there, spent his career later at Juvenile Hall. As Barry described him "He was a first class dipshit. I never liked him, but he was a close friend with one of my buddies. He was a 'gear head.' He loved to work on cars so his hands and fingernails were always dirty. He was also a prankster, which I found to be disgusting. He was not only tasked with cleaning one of the most popular donut shops in the City but making the relish as well. Once my buddy and I visited him at the shop and got a good look at how he made relish. He put the usual vegetables into the pot and then, unexpectedly, he spit into the pot and swept some of the dirt from the floor and tossed it into the pot as well. Needless to say, none of our friends who knew him ever used relish if they ate at the shop. In fact, I avoided eating anything where he worked."

I heard stories about workers at restaurants getting back at unpleasant customers, but they were just rumors until I heard what this classmate did at the donut shop. If there was a customer who was rude to a waitress or treated them badly, he would spit in the food he was preparing for them. Obviously, the customer never knew, but it gave the staff something to laugh about and some comfort to the waitress involved. Ever since, I have always treated waiters and waitresses with the same respect I expected them to show me. It might be a good lesson for every city to spread similar rumors. It might deter more people from talking down to or being rude to those in service industries like fast food restaurants. The irony was that this guy went on to work at the San Francisco Juvenile Hall as a probation officer giving advise to wayward kids. "Who'd a thunk it" to quote the Edgar Bergen dummy Mortimer Snerd on the radio program *Charlie McCarthy Show* in the 1930s and 1940s.

Make Your Point With One Punch

The Oceanview District on the south side of Riordan was known to be the home of some pretty tough kids. Ocean Avenue was where they hung out a lot. Occasionally on Monday mornings at school, kids from the area told us a gang fight occurred there over the weekend. I never saw one, but one night a few of us were standing outside the El Rey Theater on Ocean Avenue. One of the fellas with a reputation for being among the toughest in the neighborhood was leaning against the wall, talking to a buddy at the theater entrance. This kid was slender, average height, about 19 years old and ruggedly good-looking. A car stopped for a red light on the other side of the streetcar island. A wise guy in the passenger side of the car flipped him the bird through the open window and yelled out something. The kid walked in a very slow and deliberate manner about 40 feet from the theater entrance doors, across the sidewalk, across the traffic lane, up onto the island beside the car and said nothing. The placid look on his face never changed nor did his steady, slow gait ever change. He was in no hurry, but he was on a mission. The red light still had not changed yet. When he reached the car, he threw a brutal punch squarely in the face of the smart ass. Before speeding off, I could see blood coming from the guys nose. It was so cool. One punch from the strong silent type – statement made.

Letting the Air Out of a Blowhard

Many cars had tire caps called "tire tube valve stem tool caps" that screwed on to the tire tube valves to prevent air from leaking out of the tire tube. I put them on my car tires too. On the end of the cap was a two-prong fork used to unscrew and replace tire valves. They came in handy to pay back those occasional drivers who were blowhards or acted like jerks. One time I was waiting to back into a parking space that was just vacated. Before I could back into the space, this older wise guy drove into the space behind me. I got out of the car and told him I was about to back into the space. He kept his window up, completely ignored me and continued to straighten out his car in the space. Seeing this was going to be a no win situation for me, I drove around the block and found another parking space. I unscrewed the cap from one of my tires, went back to this guy's car, and looked around to be sure no one was looking at me. I kneeled down and used the cap to unscrew the valve in his tire and let all the air out of it – justice served.

Hard Way to Learn About Rolling Stops

The only time I ever got a raw deal from the police was when I was coming up to an intersection on California Street. It was pretty busy with traffic so I slowed down looking for cross traffic to the point that I almost came to a standstill. As I started to enter the intersection, I spotted a patrol car parked on the side street as if they were looking for speeders or traffic violators. I stared right at their car thinking this was a strange intersection for them to pick to patrol. I continued to coast through the intersection and proceeded along my way. I got no more than a block away when I saw a police car with its flashing red light behind me. I thought that was strange. I pulled over and the officer said I went through a stop sign. I told him that I did not see any sign and I even saw their car parked on the side street, so if there was a sign, I definitely would have stopped with them sitting there. I said I nearly stopped as it was. He said, "You did a rolling stop," meaning I almost stopped but kept rolling through the intersection. He gave me a ticket, which I thought was unfair because my explanation sounded believable and I felt a warning was sufficient. They obviously could not have been from the kid-friendly Taraval Police Station. Anyway, I immediately went back to the intersection to see why I did not see the stop sign. There was an arterial sign, but there was a large tree branch in the way, making it difficult to see the sign until you were almost in the intersection, and who would be looking for a stop sign at the last second when your attention was on traffic coming from the left and right. Adding to the oversight was that my car was descending a hill that put the car at an angle so the top of the windshield blocked the view of anything 8 feet off the ground like an arterial sign. It answered my question of why police picked that intersection to look for traffic infractions. They knew many drivers were doing rolling stops with the obstructed view of the sign. It was in the same category of patrol cars that staked out speed traps. I did learn a lifetime lesson. When I came across an arterial sign, I reminded myself to come to a complete stop, rather than nearly stopping, as so many drivers did regularly.

A popular weekend destination was Guerneville on the Russian River where we stayed at a cabin owned by the parents of one of the guys in the car. We spent Saturday on the beach along the Russian River swimming, watching girls, drinking beer and working on our tan. Getting a tan was important, even to fair skinned Irishmen. Coconut oil was popular for speeding up the tanning. Unfortunately, I suffered a lot of sunburns. At the time, we either had never heard of SPF (sun protection factor ratings) or we did not care because coconut oil provided very limited screening against sunburns with an SPF of only eight. After the occasional weekend sunburn, I spent the week pulling the peeling skin off to speed up the skin shedding process. The most painful part was getting burned behind the knees. It was painful to walk, sit and stand, always thinking that I learned my lesson, but I never did.

Learning From Mistakes of Others Cost Us Nothing

We seldom tried getting a tan at the Beach in San Francisco because it was too windy and cold or there was no sunshine. Instead, we went to the Beach House at China Beach, a small cove by the Bay in the Sea Cliff District. China Beach, previously called James Phelan Beach, which was at 25th and Sea Cliff Avenues. I always felt a little uncomfortable driving through the Sea Cliff neighborhood because the houses were so large and luxurious – a whole different world for a kid from the Mission. I always felt like I was trespassing. The Bath House had a lifeguard station and workout and shower facilities, but we only used the roof of the Bath House for sun bathing, drinking beer and hanging around guys in their late teens and early 20s. This "social group" used the 26' x 41' east side of the roof. There was a chest-high thin wall to cut off the wind from the Bay, which kept it warm at ground level for lying around. If the sun was out and the temperature was less than 70 degrees, we still got good rays with the roof being sheltered. The view was tough to beat with the Golden Gate Bridge to the right, the Marin headlands straight ahead, and the mouth of the Bay and the ocean to our left. We could also watch the ships coming and going along the Bay.

Most of the guys hanging out on the Bath House roof were out of high school for the past two to six years. They sat around and drank beer, worked on their tan and caught up with what was going on with their friends. Most of them were cutting college classes or on unemployment, joking and boasting about what a great racket getting unemployment checks for six months was and reapplying for payments. They simply told the Unemployment Office they had been searching for a job, went for job interviews but could not find anything. With little or no documentation needed to support their stories, they qualified for six more months, and that cycle seemed to continue for as long as they liked. One guy had a job as a City gardener in Golden Gate Park. He bragged it was the perfect gravy train job ever. Each morning he punched in, went into the bushes to disappear, then took off for China Beach to spend the day. He said there was no one checking up on where he was or what work was getting done. So many of these guys were out and out deadbeats. They had no ambition, looked for the easy life, and did not want to work to earn money. I was glad that I was exposed to them because they set an example of exactly what I did not want to do with my life. It was wonderful when we learned from our own mistakes, but more rewarding to learn from the mistakes of others – it cost us nothing.

Some Just Prefer to Believe Con Men

I was downtown one day at the corner of 5th and Market Streets when a sad faced plump Hawaiian asked me if I could help him out. I never stopped for panhandlers before, but this guy reminded me of the "Poor Soul" character on the television *Jackie Gleason Show*. He said that he needed money to get him and his family home to Los Angeles because they got stranded in San Francisco. He was not badly dressed, so I thought there might be some truth to his story, so I gave him a buck. A few weeks later, I was downtown and walking by the same corner on Market Street where I saw this same guy soliciting an older woman for money. I went over to her and told her he was a con man and I told her the story he previously pitched to me. She looked at me like I was crazy. I saw in her eyes that she did not believe such a nice man could do such a thing. I just shrugged and went on my way. The lesson was that trying to help people

417

often goes unrewarded, but I should still be proud that I at least tried.

Preference for Personal Rather Than Pathetic Crowd Celebrations

I decided to celebrate New Year's Eve downtown this year. I had seen pictures of the celebration in the newspaper, but I never experienced it firsthand. I could not get any of my buddies to go with me, so I went by myself. I would be crazy to take my car downtown with all of the lots full, so I caught the N-Judah down to Van Ness Avenue and began my walk down the length of Market Street. I was surprised to see so many kids and servicemen. Confetti was just 10 and 25 cents for small and large bags. There were no cars, buses or streetcars on lower Market Street – just shoulder-to-shoulder and almost bellybutton-to-bellybutton people milling around with big smiles, blowing horns, swirling noise makers, talking loud or shouting over the roar of the crowd, and looking lost like there was nowhere to go. I could hardly move through the crowd, but there was no need to hurry. I was not going anywhere. Confetti and calendar pages blanketed the sidewalks and streets. Streamers were hanging on a lot of reveler's shoulders, many wearing some type of silly New Years hat.

I just did not get it. Maybe if I enjoyed being a loud drunk I would get it. People were wandering aimlessly, not able to hear each other talk, but maybe got lucky and picked up someone. It just reminded me of a lot of people who were lonely inside but acting like fun-loving happy people on the outside. I kind of felt sorry for them. I started home before 11:00 p.m. I had seen enough. It was the last time I did Market Street on New Year's Eve. My attitude toward such celebrations remained with me for the rest of my life. I preferred spending that evening with someone I really cared about and make it a personal celebration for the two of us. When I grew up, that was exactly what my wife and I did on nearly every New Year's Eve. We stayed at home, had a special meal with all our favorite foods, drank mimosas or champagne, reviewed each of our lists of resolutions we made the previous New Year's Eve, went over our personal financial statement and balance sheet to analyze progress from the previous year.

Curiosity of Semi-naked Women Cure-All

For 16-year-olds, the North Beach District was a mixed bag. There was the Broadway strip and the International Settlement. The latter was a carryover from the turn of the century's famous Barbary Coast days and was only one block long on Pacific Street between Montgomery and Kearney Streets. It was an eye-popping experience. We wandered through the streets packed with bars, clubs, dives, restaurants, and strip joints with pictures of large breasted dancers displayed outside. The bars with the strippers had barkers out front loudly claiming, "We have the best-looking women in the world," and "You will see things you've never seen before," but there was never any mention of the inflated price of drinks, much less the cover charge just to watch the entertainment. Once they got you inside, customers seldom got up and walked out. I guessed they counted on guys not wanting to appear cheap. After two or three visits to Broadway, the appeal of pictures of semi-naked women wore off. What was amazing was the greater number of sailors around compared to members of the other armed forces. I assumed all that salt air and time on a ship with a bunch of guys did something to them. Being kids, my buddies and I were always turned away at the door so there was no sense in trying to go inside, but the barker would always say "Come back in a few years," trying to lay the ground work for future new customers. By then we would outgrow the curiosity. The local neighborhood bars were a lot easier for teenagers to get served. They had a lot less to lose if they got caught and closed down compared to what the big money strip joints in the busy tourist section of the City could lose.

There were burlesque clubs in other parts of the City. Those that had no cover charge were harder for high school kids to get in, but there was no trouble getting into those that had a cover charge – that was part of their bread and butter, especially if there was also a two-drink minimum. After I saw one or two shows, I got it out of my system as something kids did just out of curiosity. Tell a kid you cannot do something and they want to do it, just to be more like an adult. Also the women all started looking the same. It was like dads who intentionally have their kids smoke cigars or get stinking drunk at an early age in order to kill the kid's curiosity and hopefully curtail future interest in smoking and drinking.

A must-do-once thing was to see what Sally Stanford looked like. She ran one of the City's notorious brothels on Pine Street off Jones Street on Nob Hill from 1940-1949. I took a date to see her Valhalla Restaurant in Sausalito for dinner. We saw the Victorian furniture, Tiffany lamps and art nouveau pieces, but no one with a huge rolled bun hairdo and puffing on a long cigarette holder. The teenage venture was not worth trying again.

Appreciation for Beatnik Freedom Lifestyle

The North Beach area was a whole lot more than strip joints. The Beat Generation was evident from the beatniks [67], artists, writers and poets hanging around outside coffee houses, bookstores, shops, cafes, bars, and restaurants. It was an area of an expensive city where they could find cheap apartments. Barry recalled it this way: "The generation of beatniks were non-conformists, artists, poets, writers, and social revolutionaries. Once I met Eric 'Big Daddy' Nord at the Bagel Shop on the corner of Grant Avenue and Green Street. According to columnist Herb Caen 'Big Daddy' was the face of the Beat Generation. He stood well over 6 feet and had an impressive beard. Unlike its name, the Bagel Shop did not make bagels. It was a café for all the artists, hip comedians, poets, writers, and jazz aficionados. They read poetry, played chess, drank coffee and beer, and generally regaled against the 'squares' (those not cool). Jazz was the music of choice. Turtlenecks, berets, beards, and black stockings on the ladies were in vogue. I was only 16 but I found myself attracted to their freedom. As for the Beat writers, many of them could be found at the City Lights Bookstore owned by Lawrence Ferlinghetti. City Lights was the first all paperback bookstore in the USA, and a great store for writers, poets, and the socially active political progressives and non-conformists. The store had a feel unlike any other bookstore in the City. There were tons of books by writers mostly unfamiliar to the general public. Poet Allen Ginsberg's 57-page book *Howl and Other Poems* was a national sensation for its so-called obscenity, but I bought it anyway."

North Beach for the Locals, Fisherman's Wharf for the Tourists

The entertainment scene in the North Beach spread along Broadway where famous clubs like the Black Hawk, Hungry i, Basin Street West, El Matador and others offered major headliners and great jazz. It was a place where teenagers could take a special date, have a good time and not have to talk if you were shy like me – I only had to talk during the performance breaks. Many famous standup comics, singers and musicians got their start during that period, and we could hear them at prices that even a kid could afford. One place I never got around to was Finocchio's, a world-famous nightclub of female impersonators – both gay and straight. There was still a phobia among teenagers about homosexuals. That was too bad because they put on a great show as I learned later when I took visitors there over the years. Other places I intentionally stayed away from were the restaurants at Fisherman's Wharf. Even teenagers knew that the big name restaurants on the Wharf should be left for the tourists. If I wanted the best meals, I took dates to more out of the way restaurants especially if they served Italian food.

I seldom went to nightclubs. Tables and chairs were shoved too close together so they could cram in as many customers as possible. The rooms were filled with smoke. I could not hear the person talking at our table with the loud conversational noise level from the crowd, and the price of sodas was more than I wanted to pay. Often there was a cover charge to get a seat, which was never revealed until I got inside.

But when Barry and I did go clubbing, the Hungry i, owned and run by Enrico Banducci, was our favorite nightclub in North Beach. They had the best performers and we never knew on any given night if we would see some new budding star get their start there. Woody Allen, Bill Cosby, Mort Sahl and Barbra Streisand got their start there. Comics Lenny Bruce and Ronnie Schell appeared there a lot. I got to see the Kingston Trio at the Hungry i, Dave Brubeck at the Black Hawk jazz club, and Smothers Brothers and Jonathan Winters at the Purple Onion Comedy Club where Phyllis Diller, housewife turned comic, began her career.

Daly City and Pacifica were the only cities bordering San Francisco, since the other three sides of the City were surrounded by water. There was never any reason to go to either city with the exceptions of Daly City's

Geneva Drive-In for movies and the Cow Palace for sports events and the circus. Across the Bay was Oakland, and we kept away due to the City's reputation for crime and violence. So for day and weekend trips, we went north across the Golden Gate Bridge to Sausalito, Marin, Russian River/Guerneville, and Lake County. We could count on warm weather, swimming, sun bathing and drinking a couple of cool ones. Napa and the wine country were of no interest, since we were too young to be served in the winery tasting rooms. A few years later, I found Italian Swiss Colony in Sonoma County had the most generous tasting room – unlimited tasting for free from any or all of the available 32 wines posted on the wall.

Some Ruts in Life Just Insurmountable

A bunch of the guys were going up to Lake Tahoe to go skiing. I had never skied before, but I was a pretty athletic guy, so I thought I would give it a try, especially since I had never been to Tahoe, unlike most of my buddies. After bundling up inside the lodge we were staying at, I went outside with my rented skis. It was freezing cold outside, but at least it was not snowing. After a buddy helped me put on my skis, he suggested that I try out the bunny slope set up for beginners. That sounded pretty good to me. I gingerly took four or five steps out to the street and wound up in a shallow trough in the snow. I tried to walk out of it moving one foot forward after another, but I just kept sliding back and forth like I was on a treadmill going nowhere. I kept this up for a couple of minutes but realized this was useless. I sat down in the snow, removed my skis, went back inside and never left the warm lodge for two days. That was the last time I was ever on skis. Little did I know that I would return to nearby Reno, NV on a regular basis in a couple of years.

Book That Helped Pay for My College Education

The book *Beat the Dealer* by mathematics professor Edward O. Thorp was published in my senior year of high school. It was the first book that described how to count cards in blackjack. After reading the book and lots of hours of dealing cards to myself, I took the Greyhound bus up to my favorite hotel in Reno and played blackjack, even though it was illegal for those underage to gamble. I always came home a winner and it helped pay my way through college. Years later all of the casinos changed the rules of the game and how they ran their blackjack tables to make it a lot more difficult to count cards. I stopped playing blackjack when I got married, even though I had always walked away from the table a winner to that point, because I was no longer playing with "my" money; it would be with "our" money.

What was the secret to my success at blackjack? As I was growing up, I practiced a lot to be good at whatever I did. More importantly, I knew when to stop competing when the competition was much better than me and the odds were against me being a winner or star player. It was the same with blackjack. I learned how to play the hands dealt to me well. Initially, I sat at "third base" (last person dealt cards) so I could see if the other players were dealt high or low cards in order to decide if I should take another card or not. After seeing how poorly most played their hands, not hitting when they should and hitting when they shouldn't, I never played at a table with other players again because I knew they could lose a lot of my money for me. Most importantly, I left the table when I had won a reasonable amount relative to the amount I was willing to lose. If I was playing with $500, I would quit once I won at least $250-$300 – more than enough to cover the cheap $10 Reno bus fares. I did not want to take the chance that I could not consistently beat the house if I played for a long period of time. Plus, I did not want to go home a loser after the long trip. That meant I would make the trip to Reno only to play blackjack for 15 or 20 minutes. I always gave 10% of my winnings to the church on Sunday in hopes it gave me an edge at the blackjack table on my next trip.

With so little time spent gambling, I loved spending hours watching so many inconsistent and desperate blackjack players. So many could not afford to lose their money as evident by the slight tremor in their hands motioning for another card. I also bumped into some celebrities like the time I wandered into an exclusive casino on the top floor of another hotel. It was dark but just enough light to see Harry James, the trumpet-playing bandleader. He was a big guy. As he came toward me, he was looking everywhere except at me. That was when I learned that celebrities did not need to walk around or step aside for common folks or kids as he bumped me aside. Served me right – being a minor, I should never have been there.

Sports, Beer and Cars – Glue of Friendships

Friendships in my freshman and sophomore years were mostly limited to those who attended Riordan from Holy Name, because we saw very few, if any, of the other students after school or on weekends, unless we played sports together. That all changed when some of us got our own cars or had access to our parents' cars, which started in our sophomore year when we could pal around regularly on Friday and Saturday nights, but most of our carousing was in our junior and senior years. Applebee, Barry, Beyma, Canas, Carmody, Hipps and I were from Holy Name. Those from other grammar schools were Coughlin, Duffy, and Lafayette. The two things the ten of us had in common were that we all played sports and liked beer. Hipps was a one-can drinker, Carmody and I were often a three or four can drinker, and everyone else was somewhere in between, depending on the occasion.

Sports, beer and cars were big parts of the glue that bound us together and directed our social activities. I often thought about those kids I was good friends with in grammar school but did not pal around with in high school. I often wondered why. Initially, I thought it was because they did not participate in sports, and that was a common bond among most of us. But it was years later when I realized the main reason was that they did not have cars in high school and were not able to reciprocate with "I'll take my car next Friday." Having access to a car was a huge factor in creating our circle of friends.

The basis of the relationships among our group of 10 closest friends in high school were common interests, treatment as an equal, humble personality, respect, and dependability. As I got older and we went our separate ways, my view of a strong relationship or friendship was based entirely on dependability – did you come through when someone needed something from you? It was easy to be friends with others during their good times when they needed nothing from you, but when they needed something during their bad times, were you willing to help? Whether it was siblings, relatives or friends, the most frequent need was financial. Would you lend money for a crisis? But there were other types of needs – need for advice, need to attend a special event, need to provide lodging for a visit, need for a favor, or need for forgiveness for acting like a jerk. And for the ultimate friend, you would take a bullet for him.

Marijuana and Narcotics Not on Our Menu

The ability to drive around the neighborhood to find a store that sold beer to minors started our whole beer-drinking phase of high school as Canas recalled: "During our junior year, I and my friends were regular users of liquor (some started the previous year). Liquor was available through older friends, fake IDs at liberal stores, or just boosting their parents' liquor cabinets. We were never hard up enough, like some kids, to go to 3rd Street and pay a wino to buy one or two six-packs. Drugs and narcotics were not on our 'menu' for partying because we bought into the dangers of the 'killer weed' and heroin addiction propaganda promoted by the media and Hollywood censors. Most of our parents were frequent users of liquor, some to excess, and these parents found it hypocritical to police their sons' behavior vigorously in that regard. It was questionable that even a do-as-I-say-not-as-I-do admonition would have an effect. Since we had cars or access to parents' cars, it was a wonder that drunk driving and vehicle accidents were not more pervasive. Only one of our buddies eventually became a drunk for a short period of time. Most drank because it was considered 'being bad,' which was a form of cool, and gave them an excuse should they do something uncool. Our token drunk recovered and went on to a career that made us all proud. The girls I dated were not into ruckus drinking parties either, so I escaped most of the dramatic encounters with the law. But there were a few times when I had to be taken home and propped against my front door by my friends after a drunken stag night. My father was aware when that happened but only warned me the following day to be careful about excessive drinking. The conversation about the perils associated with excessive dating, however, was never had by us."

None of us held parties for our friends at our houses, but having access to cars, we could crash those parties that we heard about from others. We never seemed to stay long since we never knew anyone there. It was just a bunch of strangers sitting or standing around that did not care whether we were there or not – just sort of weird.

By our junior year of high school, we had pretty well decided if we were going on to college or not. But, just like the nuns recruited students in grammar school, the brothers at Riordan were recruiting students for the religious life to be teaching brothers or working brothers. Among them were Ray Malley, one of the smart kids, and John "Jack" O'Neill, one of the really nice guys and a friend of mine from St. Paul's. (Jack served as the chaplain at San Quentin Prison for 19 years.) Other students developed a strong interest in a certain line of work. Lafayette eventually took over his father's business when he retired. Art Curtis had a passion for Muni transportation throughout high school and later got hired by Muni where he worked his way up to his dream job of chief transit control inspector. The rest of us had to wait until after high school and college to see what fate had in store for us.

Need for Early Counseling and Student Tutoring

In my junior year, I was called into the dean of boy's office and asked why I was not getting better grades. I suppose he was basing this on the school entrance exam and early IQ tests. We were never told the results of our IQ exams, which I thought was a mistake. If I was told as a freshman that I was in the 98-99 percentile in math, as I learned later in college, it may have motivated me to meet that high standard, since I was always so competitive. Anyway, the dean of boys was right. I was a "C" student throughout high school and I could certainly have done better – especially if I was not taking college preparation classes. As to his question, I told him "I don't know. I spend a lot of time on sports." I also should have said I was spending too much time carousing on the weekends. I never really thought about reasons for my average grades and certainly never set any academic goals for myself. Life was just a matter of playing sports, going out with the guys and cramming for exams to just get by. The dean never offered me any explanations or suggestions about what I could do to improve my grades like different study habits, tutorial help, or reading improvement techniques. It was too bad there was no effort to have smart kids tutor guys like me. It would have helped the athlete's grades and created friendships among those from the two different worlds – athletics and scholastics. I would have enjoyed getting to know the smart guys better to find out their interests, way of life, and most importantly, how they got such good grades. As I was leaving the dean's office, I wondered why he was asking me this in my junior year. I was getting C's since my freshman year. That would have been the time to question my study habits.

Prom Night Misadventures

The Notre Dame Des Victoires High School nuns asked the Riordan High School principal to find dates for a couple of their new students. As Canas told it, "The announcement for two volunteers was made in one of my classes. After a few moment of silence I looked over at Dennis Beyma, he nodded after a shoulder shrug, and we both volunteered to escort the girls to their prom. They gave us $50 each for dinner and we took them to Lupo's Pizzeria in North Beach – not memorable or cool."

Barry and Dennis Creedon were asked by two girls from St. Paul's High School to take them to their prom. When they arrived at the home of Dennis's date, she gave him an envelope with the prom tickets. We first had dinner at the Beach Chalet on the Great Highway. When the waiter brought the bill, Dennis fumbled for money, while his date said: "Dad gave you money for dinner." "No, he didn't." "Yes, he did. It was in the envelope." Dennis never saw the money and threw away the envelope after removing the tickets. We all had to scrounge to pay the bill, but we left without incident. At the prom, Dennis caused quite a ruckus when he was asked to sit on the floor for a group prom photo and a half pint of whiskey fell out of his jacket pocket to everyone's laughter. No one got drunk and they all got home safely. When he got home a little after 2:00 a.m., he punched the button to lift the garage door. As Barry recalled, "Mom was standing in the center of the garage doorway. If looks could kill, I would be six feet under. Expecting me home much earlier, she chided me with her lips pursed tightly and her eyes ablaze, but no matter. I had a night to remember."

Chemistry class in my junior year was the only class I ever had to repeat in summer school. I got a "D" in chemistry, which did not qualify for college preparation. There were some students in the class who said they got a "D" but deserved an "F". For all I knew I may have been one of them. It showed that the teachers had a heart and took into consideration factors besides numeric grades. I think they understood grading of papers required some arbitrariness and judgment calls, especially on essay questions, and that some students did not have a math or verbal aptitude. Whether it was a matter of never having a science class in grammar school or just being lazy, I just did not do well in Latin and the sciences with the exception of math-related material. Unlike one student who said, "I never understood how you combined numbers and letters together and came up with an answer in algebra."

Summer School – Academic Wakeup Call

When my teacher said I had to go to summer school to make up the grade if I wanted to go to college, I pleaded with him for some other alternative, but he insisted. In hindsight, it was the right thing for him to say. It was a wakeup call academically. I took classwork afterwards more seriously. Besides, there needed to be consequences for not studying enough to achieve a satisfactory grade. Kids needed rules, standards and penalties in their early years to not make the same mistake twice. I learned later in life that making mistakes in life and business was one of the ways we learned – through our mistakes, whether they were by learning the limits of pushing the envelope or learning what did and did not work. Just like incurring defeats in sports or intellectual competition, a person's character was strengthened by learning to quickly get over defeats and failures and to be anxious to face the next challenges in life. Those who could not bounce back after failures and quit trying, generally turned out to be losers in life. That was a lesson I learned from playing sports – we had our fair share of loses.

I did not look forward to spending six weeks of summer in school, but I had no choice. Riordan mentioned Drew High School at California and Broderick Streets was offering summer school, so off I went. The school was historic – something out of the turn of the 19th century and reminded me of my grammar school St. Charles but not as nice. Fortunately for me, but not for them, Duffy and Marchel Nelson were also enrolled there for summer school. Our days at Drew brought us a lot closer together, sort of like the three of us being alone on an island. They wound up being two of my good friends in high school.

Entertainers, Practitioners and Successful People as Teachers

Chemistry was not the only science class that I found difficult. I did not see how biology and physics applied to everyday life or how they were useful to me in the future. That was true of math classes for some other students. So much of the material was about memorizing things, and I understood that aspect of it, but interesting material was a reflection of a good lecturer. An audience paid attention much more and absorbed what was being said much better when the speaker used demonstrations and interjected humor and jokes. The speaker needed to be liked, otherwise he came across as being boring. That was why years later when my company organized and conducted conferences for the business, government and university sectors, I told speakers my lecturing motto: "You need to be entertainers as well as educators." Also, the conference attendees always wanted to hear more from the practitioners rather than the consultants and vendors. The reason was that they wanted to learn how to do things so they could actually apply the information when they returned to work. Consultants and vendors generally lectured at a high level, giving an overview but not the details. They talked about theories, principles and techniques and why we should do things, which needed to be understood, but not how to do things. Most people knew why but not the how. If this was true of adults, it was true of kids. They wanted to hear how to apply the sciences and math, and most importantly, what was the end result or product. What did it look like? What practical problem was solved? If the high school teachers looked beyond what was between the covers of the textbooks and brought in real life examples of how their science and math classes were used in real life, I think I and the other students would have been more interested in the lectures. I really enjoyed calculus in college because I calculated optimum solutions to problems like the maximum and minimum revenue, cost, dimensions, volumes and speed – not just solutions, but the best possible solutions. If teachers never had personal hands-on experiences, call in alumni practitioners as guest speakers.

For the same reasons that one became a better ballplayer if we played on the best teams, one did better academically being around the best students. Likewise, companies were more profitable if they hired the best people, and individuals became more successful if they socialized with successful people. Since that was so unlikely for most kids, the next best things would be to bring successful people to the students, even if for only 45-60 minutes – successful people from business, government, education, investments, entrepreneurs, and professional leaders describing their road to success from start to finish including what they did in high school, roads taken, challenges met, decisions made, and key takeaways would have been so beneficial, but none of the schools were doing it. On the other hand, kids could always read biographies of how people became successful and emulate the paths taken.

Barry described his most memorable moments that summer. "My pal Terry Quinlan and I decided to spend a weekend at Rio Nido. He picked me up with some of our other friends in his red 1954 Merc'. Rio Nido was a lively enclave and not as sedate as Camp Meeker. It was close to the River and had an outdoor stage where noted entertainers performed. We were walking around waiting to see a show and I bumped into this guy who turned and gave me a real cool movement with his hand like, 'No problem. It's cool man.' It was actor and singer James "Jimmy" Darren, a teenage heartthrob in teen-themed movies of the 1950s."

Quitting Bad Habits Through Excess

"That weekend turned out to be a very painful experience. I, like an idiot, stole a fifth of Jim Beam whiskey from Dad's rumpus room bar. During those days, my buddies and I drank beer and cheap wine. However, I decided that we needed to drink something stronger than beer or wine, so I proceeded to drink over half the bottle of whiskey and chased it down with Royal Crown Cola. I do not think Terry or any of the other guys drank any whiskey, but I drank enough for everyone else. Needless to say, I got so sick I could not stop vomiting. I spent the next day in bed, puking over and over until my friends made it a source of entertainment. They came by and counted every time I heaved. They mockingly shouted '45…ahhhh… there he goes again…46…ahhhh…' and they continued to urge on my puking. I was sick as a dog, but it amused them. Fortunately, it did not result in my death from alcohol poisoning, but it did cure me from ever drinking whiskey again. To this day the smell turns me off."

Land of Escorts and Prostitutes

"I did not work at the Northwood Lodge this summer, but my days spent up the Russian River were always memorable. Besides the weekend at Rio Nido where I got so sick and lucky I did not die from alcohol poisoning, there was the Surrey Inn weekend in Guerneville. We always called it 'Gurney Ville,' but the correct pronunciation was 'Gurn-ville.' It was a weekend when the Bohemian Club members were attending their annual three-week visit to the Bohemian Grove. The Grove was a very secluded 2,700-acre compound in Monte Rio, where the very rich and famous came to party and relax. It was founded in 1872 for journalists and artists, but over the years the all-male club morphed into a club for the elites of society. The campground was very secure and protected since U.S. presidents, famous artists, journalists, politicians, businessmen, and actors came to commune with nature, put on costumes, get drunk, frolic in the forest, pee on trees, and perform skits and secret rituals. The main ritual was called 'The Cremation of Care,' where the members came together dressed in robes and burned the effigy of an owl. There were many interpretations of this ritual, but it probably simply meant leaving their cares of the outside world behind. The motto of the club was: 'Weaving Spiders Come Not Here,' which supported the fact that this was a time to relax, have fun, leave all business outside, and misbehave. So of course, with all these famous and rich men coming to town, who should arrive but the bevy of 'escorts.'"

"It was at the swimming pool of the Surrey Inn where I met my first prostitute. My buddy Jerry Lucey and I were lulling in the pool admiring a group of gorgeous women in their twenties, shapely and friendly. I started a conversation with a very sweet young lady probably 10 years older than me. We just talked about general stuff like the weather and how I liked going to Riordan. I developed a small crush on her, but of course I did not have a chance in hell of ever having a date with her. We were in the pool talking, and she sent shivers through me when she touched my arm and playfully tried to dunk me. We had a lot of fun, but then we said our goodbyes, and it was not until much later when some older guy told me she was a professional call girl and probably here to visit the Bohemian Grove. I wondered how I could become a member."

Age 17: Senior Year – When Everything Came Together

By our senior year, we still had about 900 (886) total students and there were about the same number of new freshman (260), but the number of eighth graders taking the entrance exam jumped from 390 to 640. With the growing demand to enroll in a good private school, it was surprising to see the administration bending backwards to put up with the shenanigans of so many students like me. They, like the kid-friendly officers from the Taraval Police Station, knew how much slack to give good kids and the right amount of discipline to get us to change our spirited ways. That did not mean that kids were coddled. There was no room for bad kids and constant repeat breakers of the school rules as evident by the number of students who left the school for various reasons as reflected in the trend of class sizes during our senior year: freshmen (260), sophomores (246), juniors (199) and seniors (179). The faculty met at the end of each school year to discuss which students, especially the underclassmen, did not deserve to return the following September.

Classes still started at 8:15 a.m., ended at 2:30 p.m., and 45-minutes each with four-minute breaks to get to our next class. The first class was homeroom, which gave us time to finish our homework or to prepare for that day of classes. Lunch was 50 minutes. There was no clock watching during the break, as there was just enough time to get to my locker, take out the book for my next class, or go to the bathroom. Besides, who could remember the start times of classes following homeroom being 8:34 a.m., 9:28 a.m., 10:22 a.m., 11:16 a.m., 12:06 p.m. (lunch), 12:44 p.m., and 1:38 p.m. Since 886 students could not fit in the cafeteria for lunch, the seniors went after third period, sophomores and juniors after fourth period, and freshmen after fifth period.

Bob Cutone from our class got elected student body president for our senior year in 1957-58. The position represented the entire school student body, not just the seniors, so all students got to vote for the candidates. Bob had two brothers who had been elected to the position previously – Anthony in 1953-54 and Michael in 1955-56. With that pedigree and reputation, it was questionable if anyone could have beaten Bob that year. More to the point, would Riordan have allowed anyone to beat him? The three Cutone brothers had a history of being very good in football, held numerous class offices and heavily involved in school activities. If the vote was close, would the faculty choose Bob over the opponent as recognition for all that the Cutone family did for Riordan, or would they allow an unknown to win? Unless the opponent was one of my close buddies, I would say give it to Bob – the family deserved it. But this was a moot point because Bob won by a landslide. I thought Applebee could have given him a run for his money, but Tim chose to be the campaign manager for fellow track record holder Bob Fennell who was running for Student Body Vice President. Tim may have realized that Cutone's family history would make him popular with the underclassmen. I liked to think Applebee stepped aside because he thought it was the right thing to do.

Leader Qualities: Nice Guy, Liked Socializing, Excelled at an Activity

The governing Student Council in our senior year consisted of Bob Cutone, student body president, Bob Fennell, student body vice president, Dave Serini, band representative, Al Martin, block society representative, Howie Segurson, rally/publicity representative, Roy Barrone, *Crusader* representative, and Tim Applebee, secretary. Senior class presidents were Tim Applebee, Bob Fennell, Dennis Leahy, Paul Scannell and Al Martin. These representatives and class presidents were some of the leaders in our class, each with their unique qualifications, qualities, and interests. But the common denominators of these and other class leaders was that they were self-motivated to succeed in activities they relished, they enjoyed being around their peers, and they were nice guys. They had to be to get the respect and support of their classmates. Interestingly, they all excelled in some activity, whether it was academics, sports, band, speech club or school publications. It was the image students looked for in their leaders, and that was why kids who wanted to be leaders needed to find what activity they were best in if they had the ambition to be a leader.

Paul Scannell was also editor of the yearbook. I wish I had known that in advance as he had final say about which pictures were published to document our senior year for posterity.

Good Things Came to Those Who Helped Others

Ralph Applebee, Tim's dad, was actively involved with the Riordan Father's Club throughout my four years at Riordan, and he was finally recognized for his service by being elected Riordan Club President. Ralph took over from the previous year president Matthew Riley, Jim's dad. Whether it was coincidental or fate that my grammar school baseball coach should replace my sandlot baseball coach for the same position at Riordan, I liked to think good things came to those who helped me along the way.

The previous year's paper drive record of 450 tons was shattered in September of our senior year with over one million pounds (560 tons) of paper, but the recycler's purchase price of eight dollars per ton never changed during our four years at Riordan.

Love for Privacy From Being an Introvert

My senior year was all about sports. It was my last year to play varsity ball and to compete in the sports I so loved. There would be plenty of time to study when I went on to college, and I had no idea if sports would be in the cards for me in college. With football season starting in September, I started running more during the summer at my old haunt, the Polo Field four blocks away, to strengthen my legs and work on speed. Throughout high school, there was seldom anyone around, so I had the place to myself and could do whatever I wanted. I liked the privacy – probably from being an introvert. It reminded me of the days as a kid with my hiding places and forts. The track seemed like it was all my own.

Our varsity head football coach was Frank "Fran" Hare, a graduate of Santa Clara University where he played three years varsity football as an offensive fullback and defensive halfback. He was sought after by at least a couple of pro teams, but he chose teaching and coaching to our benefit.

Albert "Al" Sanelli was the new football line coach at Riordan. He had played tackle at Arizona State (College) University and threw the shot put. At the start of our football season, he said, "When I first arrived and saw what kind of material I had to work with (just 10 of us were returning players from the 1957 varsity), I felt like going home. But now that the team has come a long way, they now have the potential of a winning ball club." When I read that in the school newspaper, I thought that was a hell of a thing to say about the kids who went out for the team – sort of a "glass half-empty" statement and a hell of a confidence builder! I knew he meant well by implying what "miracles" he and the other coaches did with us no-talents, but the statement gave all the credit to the coaches and none to the players. We ended the season tied for second place in the tough Catholic Athletic League.

At the start of the football practice season, I was nervous about who might be coming out for the running back positions. There were Applebee and Bob Fennell, two of the fastest guys from the 1957 track team. It was a big relief when I saw neither tried out because they wanted to focus on track that year. Another candidate was Hipps, but he got another season-ending injury early in the season. By the end of the practice season, I had won one of the slots at starting halfback on both offense and defense. Also, I also was one of the two deep men for running back kickoffs.

Beyma and Bill Baker were two other returning varsity players and selected as co-captains of the team by the coaches. Beyma was one of the quietest, meekest and mildest guys at school – never showing his temper and always under control. But he may have been the tallest, biggest and strongest guy at school. On the football field, he was a different person. Beyma gained the endearing nickname of "Animal" for his ferocious hits and tough attitude at his tackle position on the field. The *Crusader* editor Roy Borrone joked in his "Riordanland" article: "Beyma can't dance like everyone else, he has to do the Hawaiian War Chant."

Seniors Beware of Junior Prospects

Bill Baker wound up sharing time as starting quarterback with Bob Connelly, a southpaw passer and only a junior. We all entered our senior year anticipating our opportunity to play on the varsity and knowing it was our last time to prove ourselves. We competed to win the starting jobs, just what we had hoped. We never considered the competitive variable that we were the "old men," and a younger junior might replace us to give him more experience in preparation for his senior year – a tough decision for

435

all coaches and a heart breaking experience for a senior. I think that may have happened to Bill Baker. Both deserved to start – tough call.

Hipps got hurt again early in the football season, but he became an assistant coach to the frosh-soph football team. The *Crusader* predicted that he would be the coach at Riordan in 10 years, which was not to be. He chose a tougher and more challenging career – union representative standing up to a lot of really rough tough guys – some mobster types.

Never Hesitate to Ask a Favor

The week before our first game, we were given our football game jerseys. I asked for number 21, which was the number worn by the L.A. Rams Skeet Quinlan. They matter-of-factly said, "That number was taken" and gave me number 20. I assumed the starting players would be given first choice of the number they wanted, but that was not how things were done. I was so disappointed. I really wanted the number of my namesake. But it was my own fault. I should have asked Reno Taini [68] to swap my "20" jersey for his "21" jersey. I doubt he would have cared, but I just did not think of it. Dumb! Sure enough, over 60 years later, I asked Taini at a class reunion if he would have swapped jerseys with me and he said, "Sure, if you only asked." The irony was that his assigned football jersey in his senior year was number 20. The lesson here was that we should never be too shy or hesitant to ask. All they can say is "No." Odds are that at least 50 percent of the time we will get a "Yes" response.

Most Character Developed on the Sideline

There was another "Terry" on our football team and his first name "Terence" was spelt the same as mine, so his name automatically made him a kindred spirit of mine. He was sophomore Terry Fischer. At the beginning of this season, he got sharp pains in his chest. They found that he had an enlarged heart, which gets bigger with continued physical exercise, so he had to drop out of sports that year. He showed a lot of character and the positive side of a "large heart" by accepting the tough news and continuing to attend the practices and games on the sideline, encouraging individual team members on every good play and supporting

436

them when things did not go their way. The sideline is where those with the most character were found – not those out on the field. Those on the sidelines practiced all week as hard as those on the field, so it showed lots of character to stand on the sideline patiently waiting for their chance to play, which may not happen, yet they constantly cheered on their teammates, congratulated them after making a good play, and supported the team in every way possible. Terry Fischer did return to play halfback on the football team the following year and made the All C.A.L. team. He went on to marry Marlo Gotti, daughter of the co-owner of the famous San Francisco Ernie's Restaurant where he learned the restaurant business and eventually his own restaurant. There were many leaders like Fischer who emerged from Riordan, and they showed their leadership in their own style – some at an earlier or later age than others.

Underrated but Always Admired

Many of the kids at Riordan came from middle income families that had small businesses and relied on their children to work at the shop, store or business after school and on Saturdays, so they had no chance to take part in a lot of the school extracurricular activities like sports. Ramon Calderaro was one of those kids. He enjoyed kicking the football and practiced at Cayuga Park in the Outer Mission, less than two miles from Riordan, even though he literally lived next door to Riordan. He had to work at his father's butcher shop on Monterey Boulevard after school until 6:30 p.m. every school day and all day Saturday, so there was no time for him to play football in his first three years at Riordan. But his brother was going to work at the shop in Ray's senior year, so his father let Ray try out for football. Ray turned out to be our regular kicker for field goals and point after touchdowns. What was unique was that he was probably the only kicker at any level who used a ski boot. The toe of the boot was relatively flat and an inch high. It was a good surface for kicking. He used his father's old ski boot originally, but the constant kicking caused the sole of the boot to separate and ruined the boot. So his dad bought him another used boot. The toe area had to be ground flat for kicking. This boot was heavier, but did a good job. When referees saw the boot, they took a long look but could not find a rule against the boot. His punts went about 40 yards, his kickoffs were within the 10 yard line and some in the end zone for automatic touch backs – such a valuable weapon to deny the opposition from running back kickoffs. In our first game of the season against Franklin High School, they scored first, but the extra point was missed. The teams battled back and forth until the fourth quarter when Riordan scored. Ray was excited to finally put his skills to use. The ball was snapped, it was placed down perfectly and the ball went straight between the uprights and just over the bar. Success!!! But wait – there was a penalty – 12 men on the field. On the retry, Ray lifted his head too soon and his toe made contact at the middle of the ball instead of below the middle and the ball went under the goalpost. The coach pointed out the head lift flaw – lesson learned! Ray went on to be as dependable and consistent a kicker as there was in the league, if not better. If Ray had the opportunity of three to four years of coaching and playing, he could have been kicking longer punts and kickoffs into the end zone every time, which would have been all-league stuff. I always felt it was an oversight that he was not featured in our senior yearbook pictures as he was truly an underrated player for us.

The most exciting thing second to playing our home games at Kezar was to watch 49er games there. Barry attended his most memorable game just about the time Riordan's football season started. As Barry described it, "It occurred in the Niners' second league game against the Los Angeles Rams. Dad and I were seated high in the west end zone. The Niners were driving toward the east end zone. End R.C. Owens stood 6'3" and was much taller than most defensive backs. Suddenly, he ran all the way to the southeast side of the end zone while Y.A. Tittle tossed the ball high in the air. Owens out jumped the defender, scored a touchdown, the crowd went wild, and the play became famous. The pass was nicknamed the 'Alley-Oop' after a cartoon character in the funny pages and just like the cry of circus acrobats about to leap in the air."

The opening game of the season was against Franklin High from Stockton. At the start of the second half, I was back with Tim Moffett, the other running back, waiting for the kickoff and to execute our kickoff return play. Prior to the kickoff, one of our linemen turned his back to the opposition and pointed which side of the field our linemen would peal off single file to create a wall of blockers along a predetermined left or right sideline, leaving a lane between them and the sideline for us to run up the field. Once one of us caught the kickoff, we turned and ran past each other to either handoff the ball to the other player or to keep it. It was to help confuse or at least slow down the charging opposing players. It turned out that I received the kickoff at the 32-yard line, "made a beautiful fake handoff" to Moffett according to the *Crusader* newspaper, "and ran all the way along the sidelines behind the wall of blockers for a touchdown." Due to a clipping penalty, the play was called back. Making a big play like that on the same field used by the 49ers was special, even if it was called back. The game ended in a 6-6 tie.

The Haunting Failure on the Field – I Choked!

The second most memorable football game for me was in the second game of the season against Albany High School on the Riordan School football field. The game had to be rescheduled the day earlier due to the rains on Friday that would have caused us to tear up the Kezar field for the 49ers. It was the only game of the season played on Riordan's own field, which did not have good drainage like Kezar. It was still raining at game time, the ground was soaked, and our uniforms were soaked. Early in the game, we were on our 40-yard line and Bob Connelly called a pass play. I ran through the line and Bob was looking for receivers. I suspect he had in mind a short completed pass to one of his ends or a flaring halfback. I found myself through the secondary, I looked back and Bob was scrambling. By now I was way beyond any defenders, and I was standing on the goal line waiving my arms frantically. He probably did not see me because he never expected anyone to be downfield, much less wide open. It seemed forever that I continued waiving my arms. Finally, he saw me and threw a beautiful pass, which I tried catching with my bare hands. I dropped the ball. I felt so badly for losing a touchdown for Bob and letting my team down. I lost count of how many times over my lifetime that I replayed that pass in my head and second guessing myself. "Were my hands wet? Why didn't I try to make a basket catch by cradling the ball between my arms and chest?" I do not know how much the rain was a factor, but there was no excuse since I never dropped a ball in all of the punts and kickoffs I received in the past or that season. I had too much time to think about getting Bob's attention and how I would catch the ball. I choked! I went back into the huddle, said I was sorry, but the blank look on Bob's face said it all. He never threw me another pass that game – could not blame him, but would have liked a second chance. We lost 32-0.

My Cherished Personal Record

What I liked most about football was standing back by myself in the cavernous Kezar Stadium to receive a punt or kickoff with everyone watchinga, hoping I would run it back all the way. It seemed like I was returning most kickoff in the games I played – probably 90 percent of the time. I never dropped the football on kickoffs once, which was a personal record I cherished. By our third game of the season, an away game against Santa Cruz High School, one of the top-ranked teams in Northern California, we had been using a slightly different kickoff return pattern with a lot of success. We eliminated the fake handoff to speed up the return process. After catching the ball on the five or 10-yard line, I ran straight up the field and at the last minute before the defenders reached me, I made a sharp turn toward the sideline and ran behind the wall of blockers like in the past. I always made it to our 35-45 yard line. We played better but still lost to Santa Cruz 33-45, which made it an even longer ride home after the night game. It was only a 75-mile drive, but we stopped off for dinner, probably paid for by the Riordan Father's Club, and got home way after midnight.

Field of Dreams – Disappearance of Racial Differences

Our first victory finally was in our fourth game of the season against McClymonds High School. This was a predominantly African-American school and had a reputation of students coming from a rough part of Oakland and playing tough football. Up until the McClymonds game, my only personal exposure to African-Americans consisted of knowing Ralph Versey and Julie Newman at St. Paul's Grammar School for two years. There were none at Folsom Park or in my Riordan classes. I suspect there were not a lot of African-Americans in other City Catholic grammar and high schools in the 1940s and 1950s. During our four high school years,

Sacred Heart High School probably had a few African-American students, and octoroon Fred LaCour, a great basketball player, was at St. Ignatius High School. Riordan had one or two in the early 1950s. All I heard about African-Americans was the violence in the Fillmore District. I was a little stressed, not knowing what to expect, and so were some of my teammates. My image of African-Americans changed in the McClymond game. Once the game started, they were just another team. It helped when we could move the ball and able to keep them from scoring a lot. I caught a 14 yard touchdown for the final tally and happy to contribute to the 21-7 victory. But the greatest take-away from the game was I left the game respecting them. They were just a bunch of ballplayers like us, trying their hardest to win. When the game was over, the McClymond players were smiling when they congratulated us and said, "Good game!" after their defeat. It was the night we played on a field of enlightenment and understanding.

Our senior year was when Barry had his best season in football. Still 5'7" and only 165 pounds, he did not make first-string offensive guard as those guys were well over 200 pounds, but he was first-string defensive guard and linebacker – something of a mighty mite. Being a wild child in his youth finally paid off – just needed the appropriate application for it. Kids never knew when their negatives could be channeled into positives.

Bigger the Challenge, Greater the Confidence

Barry also remembered the McClymonds game for a very good reason. As he recalled: "In those days we had very little contact with African-Americans. We initially were somewhat intimidated and afraid because our coach told us some of their players were very big. That immediately was confirmed as they came through the dark tunnel at Kezar dressed all in white and orange, which accented their bulk and height against the dark background in the tunnel. I played opposite a guy who weighed 260 pounds, a massive high school player in those days, but he was slow of foot. I was small and quick and could avoid his charging mass. I was no longer intimidated. Football taught me many lessons for being a better person and on that night, it was self-confidence."

Throughout high school I felt the single biggest reason why we did not have better teams in all sports was the lack of African-American enrollments. I believed it was the missing ingredient to create more dynasties. Riordan was heralded only for track, drama and the school newspaper at the time. It was just a short time after our senior year when African-Americans started to make their mark at Riordan in scholastics and athletics, making it is a completely different and better environment over the years, along with the eventual enrollment of girls at all three of the local all-boys Catholic high schools in the City.

Thursday following the McClymonds game was the Homecoming Queen Night Rally. A girl from Immaculate Conception Academy was homecoming queen again for the umpteenth time and third consecutive year. Al Corona, the very popular *San Francisco News* sportswriter who covered high school sports, boxing and 49ers, was the principal speaker.

Aspect of the Game I Never Understood

The next night we played our fifth game of the season against Serra High School in the homecoming game at Kezar with our flu-riddled team. There were 150 students out with the Asian Flu. 5,000 watched us beat Serra – the first time Riordan won a homecoming game. Barry got us off to the right start by blocking a punt in the end zone for a safety. He went on to play outstanding defense at linebacker and was selected the game's MVP. Beyma and Bill Baker were our regular team co-captains, but the coaches decided on different co-captains for the homecoming game. The coaches named Bill Baker, Rich Horan, and me. As co-captain, I was one of the players the referees went to for making the call as to whether or not to accept a penalty. I never received any instructions from the coaches how to do that. Do I accept the penalty or replay the down? I had no clue. I never really thought about those things when I was watching games on television or played the game for Riordan. Someone else always had to worry about those things. The few times in the game we were asked for a decision, I was trying to process the options in my head and never came to any conclusion. I panicked a little when the ref looked directly at me. Fortunately, one of the other co-captains spoke up and made the call, thank goodness. If it was left up to me, we would have been called for delay of game every time.

Level Playing Fields Allow Victories Against the Best

Serra High School was a perennial powerhouse in sports, producing professional athletes like Barry Bonds, Tom Brady and Lynn Swan. This year they had an all-purpose athlete in Jim Fregosi. On that October night, Barry had the game of his life, but one play really stood out. Barry said, "It was in the first quarter and the score was 0-0. We had stopped the Padres near the end zone and Fregosi, who played several positions, dropped back to punt. I rushed past their right tackle, my arms extended, and timed my dive perfectly. I blocked the punt and Fregosi fell on the ball for a safety. The crowd roared loudly and we went on to beat Serra 16-12 thanks to Bill Baker who took over from our starting quarterback Bob Connelly who was out with the flu." Competitive activities, whether they were sports, academics, debate, chess, or band competition, offered a level playing field where on a given day or night, a personal victory could be had by anyone against the best.

Seeking Personal Victories in Losing Battles

The following week we played our perennial rival Bellarmine in our sixth game of the season. They were a football powerhouse every year, one the best teams in the state, if not the nation. The coach assigned Barry to follow California Player of the Year and All-American fullback Jim Josephson wherever he was, whether he had the ball or not. Barry recalled "Before the game, Coach Hare told me to follow Josephson everywhere, to make him my primary target, but laughingly he was bigger, stronger and faster than me, so he simply ran right over me. Looking at the film of the game, well, it was almost comical." Josephson ran back the opening kickoff and a later kickoff for a 94-yard touchdown both times and ran through the line with ease. It just went to show that, no matter how hard one played, if the opponent was physically superior and played with the same intensity, he would most likely beat me, especially an All-American. They beat us 52-21 and Josephson went on to play for Oregon State. Two weeks later, we played Bellarmine again. We lost but the score was 25-7.

The cliché "Winning is not everything" was true in sports as well as life. Winning requires experience and improvement. Our defense that game improved 50% by limiting the opponent scoring by that amount, which was the macro view of what took place. On the micro view of the game, there were a lot of defensive players having many personal one-on-one victories against individual Bellarmine players. The team was only as good as the parts, but individual players were as good as they could be, and that was what team sports was about – we tried out for the team, did our best, learned from our mistakes, did better the next time, achieved personal victories, and hopefully, team victories followed. Every successful person has experienced failure, often numerous failures, but they kept trying. Those successful in life never gave up.

Decision Regretted for a Lifetime

Not only did Barry have a nightmare game but my football career ended that evening in the same game. It was to be the most memorable game of the season for me just for that reason. I was running a play along the left sidelines. I saw a defender coming on to tackle me. I had the option of running out of bounds just to my left or lowering my head and running into him or cutting inside and try running around him. I took the worst of the three options after not even considering the other two options. Even professional players would run out of bounds to avoid contact and injury. We never practiced changing directions quickly to avoid tacklers. Practice was more about lowering your shoulder to run over tacklers. So my first instinct was to lower my shoulder and run straight into the tackler. He hit me low, I flew over him and tried to cushion my fall with my right hand, and I wound up with a broken wrist. I relived that moment endlessly over my lifetime, because it ended my varsity football career as a senior. If I could have done it over again, I would have stopped on a dime just before the tackle, made a quick turn to the right and tried to run around him. I felt running out of bounds was the cowards way out – definitely a smart decision, but still cowardly. We lost the game, so even if I was not injured, we still would have lost. I loved football and I missed the final three games of the season. Bob Hourigan moved from his end position to halfback as my replacement and went on to make *S.F. Examiner* All-City Honorable

Mention.

Seeing Stars While Playing Against One

The next game was against Jefferson High School in Daly City. How much improvement Riordan gained from the second Bellarmine game was anyone's guess, but Riordan shut down Jefferson's quarterback, Paul Tapia, who was the leading passer in Northern California that year and a future Jefferson Hall of Famer. Riordan won 33-7 and intercepted seven of Tapia's passes. Noel Murray, our best pass defender, went on to be the team leader in interceptions, two of them from this game alone. Barry blocked two punts to set up touchdowns for us. Barry's recollection of the game was "At one point, I was sitting on the bench between plays looking around and wondering what happened to me. I did not know that I had a concussion. The only memory I had of that game was sitting on the bench wondering where am I and what am I doing here."

What It Took for Studies to Take Precedence Over Sports

I was only 16 when I played varsity football in my senior year. When my football days came to an early end due to the injury, it was the only time I half-heartedly wished I started school a year later so that I could play football the next year at age 17 like most kids. I continued to attend football practices after my injury, hoping to contribute from the sidelines, but I just was not a sideline type of guy, especially when I saw there was really nothing for me to do that helped anyone. Standing around, just doing nothing, just made me bitter about being injured and feeling sorry for myself. The coaches never gave me anything to do or recognized my presence. I figured the best thing for me was to get out of the situation, move on, and do something more constructive and positive like studying for a change.

Get a Job: Girls, Cars and Fun Not Cheap

While the rest of us were playing sports in our senior year, Canas was working to pay for car-related expenses and dating girls. According to

Canas "My senior year was pivotal in my young life. Up until then, I had played organized sports, tried out as a singer in the annual Talent Show (with no luck), was part of the rabble in the renowned *Riordan Passion Play*, was a member of the Alter Boy's Sodality Club, and participated in other intramural events. But following the summer of 1957, it was clear that I had to choose between extracurricular activities and supporting my demanding custom car and girlfriends."

"I was going steady with one girl or another most of the time in high school. My mother referred to my girlfriends by the disparaging slang *gringa* (American female) to her friends and often expressed a preference for me to date a nice Latino girl. The dates consisted mostly of rides in my car, drive-in movies, or just parking to make out. The police always drove through the 'parking' locations with their spotlights on to make sure that heads were seen above the seats. I am not sure how I would have handled dating without a car. Those dates and my inability to stop getting speeding tickets and beating up my Merc' were also stressing my pocketbook. And I was not alone with this dilemma. Most high school boys of similar age who wanted to enjoy having their own car had to work to support them, but none of us complained. The independence was well worth the effort."

"In my case, the heavy Merc' was not designed for racing. I ignored reality because I thought it was cool to drag race at the organized strips in Vacaville and San Jose, and at informal (and illegal) drag races on the Great Highway and other city streets. I suppose I inherited my interest in fast cars from my father's youth. The result was constant trips to the mechanic to have the transmission repaired and paying speeding tickets. Already, my father had informed me their insurance policy had been amended; I had to enroll in a mandatory 'assigned risk' insurance policy."

Stiff Price to Pay Having Two Jobs

"These expenses and a full-time girlfriend, a junior at Mercy High School, forced me to take on a second job, this one as an attendant at the Flying A service station at 33rd Avenue and Geary Street for 75 cents an hour. I went to work after my grocery delivery job at Korss Market. Working the evening shift, I pumped gas, took inventory of products, read gas meters, counted the money in the cashbox, secured the ledgers and the

446

money in the safe, and closed the station at 10 p.m. With the salary of my two jobs, I was able to maintain the 'red sled' and pay for dates. However, as a result, my grades dropped and I switched from college preparatory classes to the less demanding general education courses. Meanwhile, my parents did not fully comprehend the significance of these decisions that were made for the most part unilaterally. But my mother continued to tell her friends I was studying to be a lawyer."

Loved Getting in Love, but Not Being in Love

"I never took any of my girlfriends to my home or the summer cabin; the truth was that I was embarrassed about the perception of Latinos and the intensity my parents placed on our Latino roots. Some Latino cousins older than me were more representative of the bicultural status. They spoke English in their homes and were conversant on the latest styles and American trends. Two families that I often visited were the Linkas and the Johnsons. The Linkas lived down the Peninsula in San Carlos and the Johnsons lived in San Anselmo across the Golden Gate Bridge in Marin County. My cousins, Adelia Linka and Marina Johnson, had married North Americans and were raising three young school-aged children each. Although my cousins were 10 years older than me, I felt comfortable with them because they had been Americanized as I was and I considered their husbands to be cool. Both families took a liking to me and were flattered when I brought the latest girlfriend around. Since most of my dates involved taking the girls for rides in my car, I alternated between the Peninsula and Marin County. But the relationships with these girls were getting more and more tiring. The breakups and new romances were a roller coaster. I loved *getting* in love but not *being* in love. This regimen lasted my entire senior year."

In December 1957 the school put on the *Song of Bernadette* drama production under the direction of James Lindland. The play drew nearly 3,500 people, which included 125 priests, nuns and other clergy. Lindland directed 12 plays and wrote a handful of others during his eight-year tenure at Riordan.

On New Years Day of 1958, a prowler attempted to break into the Riordan faculty residence building through the kitchen entrance but they were unsuccessful. The poor religious faculty had their own problems to contend with besides putting up with us kids during the school year.

Riordan hosted the fourth Annual Marian Society Speech Festival with 15 Catholic High Schools participating. The Riordan team lost out on first place by only one point. The next month they took first place and won the sweepstake trophy at the tournament held at Serra High School – only goes to show the caliber of our classmates on the team like Paul Scannell, Sean McKenna and Bob O'Neill. They deserved more than the few lines of coverage they received in the school newspaper, which was typical for non-sports activities.

On Friday and Saturday nights we usually were just driving around town or going to Riordan varsity basketball games later that school year. On occasion we went to Riordan dances or the movies. Whenever or wherever it was, we picked up one, two or three 6-packs depending on the number in the car and whether we were going to an event or just parking and driving around. We figured two or three beers each was about right. If we were going to an event, we drove there first, parked, and had a beer or two before going inside. That way the driver was sober on the way. On nights when we planned to just drive around, we first parked at the Beach or "the Circle" to drink a beer or two. The Beach was dark and no one to bother us, except for an occasional police patrol car. If we were lucky, the weather cooperated for a clear view of the ocean, but normally it was cold and often damp from the fog. The Circle was a round parking lot on the edge of Lake Merced on Lake Merced Boulevard and at the south end of Sunset Boulevard. It was the local make out spot for teenage couples and a beer drinking spot for guys to hang out because it was pitch black with no streetlights around. It could hold over 100 cars, but fortunately it was never that crowded, so there was always enough space between cars so no one could see what we were doing inside. Wherever we parked, we had to keep an eye open for the police. On rare occasions a police car drove slowly through the Circle once or twice with their spotlight shining on each car as they drove by. We always thought they were going to knock on the window, take our names and report us to our parents, which never happened. They never bothered those making out but were mostly looking for kids drinking, so we had to stop drinking until they drove by so they would not see the silhouette of us drinking from a can or bottle. It was also their way to let kids know someone was watching so "cool it." They never caught us drinking when we were parked anywhere, but we had our beer confiscated a couple of times when they saw us drinking while we drove around town. They were good guys about it.

Price of Freedom – a Six Pack

The few times we were stopped by the police, it seemed to carry some weight when we said we went to Riordan. They probably knew that we were not bad kids looking for trouble or causing damage, just out drinking, which was what kids did in those days. The few times we were stopped by the police, they never asked, "Are any of you drinking beer?" It was always "Do you have any beer in the car?" When we told them we did, and they saw no one was drunk, they took the beers and sent us along with a warning. It was a win-win for both of us. We were let go and they got to keep our beer – a small price to pay. We always said what cool cops they were, but the joke was that they probably stopped kids when they needed to stock up their own beer supply. Whether there was any truth to it or not, we could care less knowing we should not have the beer in our possession. More importantly, we were grateful to be let go.

On another occasion, while driving home from a Riordan basketball game, a bunch of us were pulled over by the police. After they asked where we had been and where were we going, the police officers knew we were not looking for trouble and were attending a Catholic school. After confiscating our beer, the officer said, "Let me give you guys some advice. Do not drink beers while going through an intersection," referring to intersections being well lit up where police often parked.

Once in a while after spending some time at the Circle, we checked out the Great Highway and the Ocean Beach. They were just 12 blocks from the Circle and we could start at the south end of the Great Highway and drive the length of it in five minutes. The kids used the 4-lane Great Highway at night to hold drag races, so if we were lucky, we might run across some hot cars drag racing. We never knew who won as there was no room to keep up with them, but we could enjoy the roar of the engines, squealing of rubber skidding on the pavement, and the smell and smoke bellowing from the tires at the start of the races.

Do Not Be Fooled by Appearances

Applebee often borrowed his dad's Chevy pickup truck to go out at night or on dates. His dad was a carpenter and his pickup truck usually was full of tools and material, but the cool thing about the truck was that it had a Corvette engine with dual four-barrel carburetors – a real big thing in those days. It was the hottest engine in any of our classmates' cars. We could tell there was something special under the hood every time he accelerated at a stop sign. He never completely emptied the bed of the truck whenever he went down to the Great Highway to drag. You might call his truck a "sleeper." He sat there at the starting line waiting for the signal to take off. We could see a lot of smirks and hear the chuckles from the bystanders, but that all changed when Tim floored the gas peddle. With ladders on board and paint cans swinging in the wind, he always pulled away and left the other car in the wake of exhaust fumes and tire smoke. For my buddies and me, it was a great laugh because we knew what was coming and the eventual outcome.

Most Memorable Drag Race

The most memorable drag race was the night when two hot rods where gunning their engines, trying to impress the other driver and the small crowd that was watching. The roar of the engines went on for a minute or two until the signal was given to take off. One car jumped out quickly and there was a clatter of metal dragging along the pavement from the other car that slowly rolled forward about 15 feet to a standstill. The car had dropped its transmission. There was nothing more embarrassing to a drag racer than dropping a transmission. He barely got off the starting line, his car falls apart, and he had to face the crowd to his embarrassment, not to mention the hassle of finding a phone booth to get his car towed somewhere late at night.

Cheese It, the Cops!

If there were no drag races, we drove slowly along the Ocean Beach in hopes of spotting a large bonfire out on the sand. If we saw any smoke, we got off the Highway and circled back to park the car across from where we saw the smoke from the fire. We knew people were drinking and possibly playing music and dancing around, so we took a few beers with us, crossed the Highway and joined the crowd. No one cared because whoever started the fire expected strangers to show up. They were seldom expected to be private affairs. It was just meant to be a gathering for anyone interested in having some fun and maybe see others we knew from school or the neighborhood. Because fires on the beach were against the law, we had to keep an eye open for the police. They never made an effort to surprise anyone as the two police officers approached from afar, each with flashlights shining. Sometimes they left the red light on their parked patrol car flashing on the side of the Great Highway. I liked to think the lights were to give us a heads up. Since kids who were there never brought flashlights, it was a pretty good guess that flashlights meant the police, and everyone scattered when the first to spot them yelled "Cops!" I never saw the police ever chase anyone, which meant that their main purpose was to get the fire extinguished. I never stuck around long enough to see if the originators of the fire stuck around to put out the fire or it was left for the police to do it. I suppose it depended on whether the organizers brought so much stuff that they did not have time to gather it all up in time to run for it.

Riding the Running Boards to Sober Up

Whenever Beyma took his car when we drove around the City at night, there was something special about using his car. A couple of us could hang on to each side of his 1939 Plymouth and stand on the running boards, like the Keystone Cops from a 1910s movie, as we sped down the mile and a half stretch of the Great Highway yelling into the wind. If we had a few beers and we needed to sober up a bit, instead of a slap in the face, we could always ride the running boards with the cold salty wind from the ocean blowing in our face. A block or two of that did the trick.

Do Not Piss Off the Hell's Angels

Once at Playland, Applebee and Beyma ran into the Hell's Angels and somehow pissed them off. Beyma jumped into the back of Tim's truck and one of the Hell's Angels threw a K-bar (combat knife) at them and it broke out Tim's rear window. On another occasion one Friday night, one of the Hell's Angels bumped into Beyma's '39 Plymouth rear bumper, and he and Applebee flipped them off (gave them the finger). A chase ensued but they lost the motorcycle gang in Golden Gate Park, which Beyma knew so well.

Cruising the Neighborhood to Pick Up Chicks

There were many Fridays and Saturdays in our junior and senior years when we set out to pick up girls. We drove along a busy street like Ocean Avenue or by a movie theater or sports event that was letting out looking for girls. Sometimes we went to Mel's Drive-In on Geary Street and tried parking next to a car with two or more girls. There were always four to six of us in the car. After the first few months of trying to pick up girls by cruising around, it just got to be the thing to suggest because there was nothing else for us to do while cruising the neighborhoods.

It never struck any of us how ludicrous the whole scene appeared. Why would any girls get in a car with four to six yelling, desperate strangers? However, we did look clean cut so the girls usually smiled and seemed flattered, but they always politely turned us down. We were not smart enough to realize girls would not want to be so outnumbered with five howling, desperate teenagers, and there certainly was no room for more than six in the car. Also, there were always two or more of them, so there was no chance that one was going to leave the others to get in the car. It was not that any of us expected to make a pick up, but it was just a reason to spend some time with our buddies and have a few beers, which was the other thing. The girls probably smelled the beer aroma coming from the car, which was something else none of us thought about. Over a two year period, we were never successful in picking up girls with one exception – two girls got in so we could drive them home, and we did just that – delivered safe and sound.

If we were smarter, we would just go to a dance put on by one of the many all-girls high schools where there were masses of girls to choose from. At the time, there were 14 all-girls Catholic high schools. [69] Like the 1930's bank robber Willie Sutton said when asked why he robbed banks, he so eloquently replied, "Because that's where the money is." Instead of searching for two or three girls walking the streets, we could have found plenty of girls at the dances. The various reasons why it was never suggested including my reason of being shy when I was on my own around girls. I knew I did not do well with one-on-one conversations with girls. Driving around in a group of guys gave me more confidence and anonymity by being in a crowd – little good did that do us. We also might have had better luck driving around in pairs looking for two girls. But Friday and Saturday nights were never about finding girls. It was about spending time with our buddies, laughing a lot, and talking about stuff.

Great Respect From Display of Honesty

We were driving in Ocean Avenue area one night and saw a 24-inch plaster Pakistani male figure sitting with a leg hanging over the ledge of the railing at the top of the front stairs of a house around the corner from the El Rey Theater. It probably was my idea to take the statue and move it a few doors up the block and place it on a similar ledge of a house close enough for the owner to find it in the morning. So one guy got out of the car and stood at the bottom of the staircase ledge with one hand on the statue's leg while another guy quietly went up the stairs and carefully lifted the statue off the ledge so the other guy could grab the statue with both hands and lower it down. As soon as the guy at the top let go of the statue, the weight of the body suspended in the air without any support for just a moment caused the statue to tip, fall and break in two at the knee, and both pieces fell into the flowerbed. Everyone jumped in the car and we sped off. After parking the car to discuss the caper, Lafayette said we should go back and give ourselves up to the owner. At first there was a lot of reluctance because we got away with it, but then we realized it was the right thing to do. We never caused physical damage to property in the past, and we did not want to start then. No one ever expected to damage the statue, but like so many pranks and acts of vandalism, the parties involved

453

never intended to cause any damage and never thought that an accident could happen like this incident. We felt badly for the owner, so we drove back and all of us went up to the door, rang the bell, and told the owner what we did and wanted to get it repaired because Lafayette's dad had a business that specialized in ornamental plaster. **[70]** The owner said if it was repaired, we did not have to pay him anything. That evening's display of honesty by Lafayette by going against the grain of his friends, really impressed me. It was the first time I ever saw someone show that kind of character. I said to myself "I want to be like him." Some of Lafayette rubbed off on me that night. I never realized the good feeling from doing the right thing, and how much it might affect others for the better.

Price for Being Ungrateful

Lafayette went by the next day and picked up the pieces of the statue in the daylight. Because it landed on dirt, there were not that many pieces to pick up. The pieces were put back together and patched as good as new with epoxy cement. The statue needed to be touched up with paint and they left that up to the owner to do. When Lafayette returned the statue to the owner, the guy gave Lafayette a bad time about it not being exactly the same. When Lafayette told us about the owner's response and being so ungrateful, we got ticked off and decided to undo our act of trying to do the right thing and to teach the guy a lesson for being such an ingrate. We felt the guy changed his mind to let us off the hook and wanted us to buy him a new statue after Lafayette's dad did all of that repair work.

So a short time later, we were at a Riordan dance, which was not far from the scene of the crime. We thought this was a good time to knock the statue over again. The plan was that Lafayette would drive his car and someone would jump out, pull the statue over the ledge, jump back in the car and we would speed away. The plan went off without a flaw, and we left with the statue lying in the flowerbed but never checked if it broke again. Lafayette just floored the accelerator and roared off. He thought for sure one of the neighbors might see us and call the cops so he kept the headlights off and drove through the back streets avoiding Ocean Avenue and its bright streetlights while we worked our way back to the dance. We all laughed about it, but at least some of us felt like criminals and our greatest fear was that our parents would find out. It was probably the first time any of us intentionally damaged someone's property, even if it was something that could be replaced for less than $15 or $20. Years later, Lafayette said he was so scared and his heart was pounding like we were robbing a bank, and he still gets nervous just thinking about it.

Prank Led to New Respect for School Administrators

The most memorable night of our carousing was one Friday night when we were driving around, we passed by Riordan. Someone in the car suggested we stop and disturb the brothers as a lark. So we parked the car and quietly gathered in the entry portal to the school. It was dark and no lights were around. The brothers lived over the entry portal. I rang the front doorbell, someone answered over the intercom, and we all just laughed without responding. Then we started yelling to hear the echo in the portal, thinking that no one could see us at night, and by the time anyone came down and opened the front door, we all ran away. We were wrong. The brothers were looking out the windows and calling out "We know who you are." They called out the names of at least a couple of us. That night turned out to be a rude awakening for me.

On Monday I was called into the principal's office. They either saw my face or recognized my voice, but I had no good reason why we did it – "just kidding around." Then Brother Miller explained Riordan had given me a partial scholarship these past years in recognition of my participation on the various sports teams at Riordan. I never knew that. The school had never told me about it. I suspect my folks were delinquent in paying my tuition somewhere along the way. The administration saw that the tuition was a financial strain to them, so they offered to waive some of my tuition each year of my education. That was when my attitude about the principal, the administration and the school completely changed. I no longer thought of them as an institution but as generous human beings that really cared about my parents, me and the other students. From that point on, I tried never to disturb, embarrass or be unappreciative to Riordan and its faculty. My Mom must have asked them not to mention their financial situation to me, and I will always be grateful to the school for being so considerate to my family and preserving their dignity. It led me over the years to make financial contributions to the school to help out other parents and hoping their kids might show appreciation by staying out of trouble and doing well in their endeavors at school.

Where to Find a Date When You Need One

Looking back at high school, I wish I had known girls who were just friends with me. Had I gone to a coeducational school, it probably would have happened. It never crossed my mind to have a girl just as a friend – someone to just talk to, to get advice from, to use as a sounding board, to share experiences with, and to help me to understand girls better. But guys tended to look at girls as just someone to date and make out with. I may have been better at talking to girls if I viewed some of them simply as friends. I would have thought less about their looks and more about their interests, experiences and intelligence.

Finding a date to go to a movie, a dance or a prom was a challenge. There were no girls attending Riordan and I could not call up girls from grammar school because they wanted to date older guys. Actually, I did call up one girl from my St. Paul's days. She must have thought it weird to hear from someone she had not seen in four or five years. That did not go well. She, and her closest friend whom I asked about, supposedly had boyfriends. More than likely, they either did not like me or they did not want to go out with someone their age. I hoped it was the latter. High school girls prided themselves on going out with older boys. High school was a strange period in that regard because age did not seem to be an issue between girls and boys prior to and after high school. I suppose it was one way for girls to feel more grown up during their teens, just as smoking and drinking made guys feel more grown up.

The only other option to finding a date was to go to a Riordan dance, but I only went to the dances to hang out with the guys. Sometimes we just spent 30-60 minutes there to walk around, see who was there, say "Hi" to a few guys, look over the girls and leave. I was so uncomfortable about meeting girls that I rarely stayed the whole evening. It was not worth the agony of being rejected or trying to create small talk simply to find a girl to go to a movie, but it was different when I needed a prom date. In that case, I stayed most of the night at a dance held a month or two before the prom. I did feel more secure going to a Riordan dance than a dance at a girl's high school. It was on my home turf and I could at least recognize the fellas from school. I stopped asking girls in groups of more than three. I figured a girl would be extra discriminating because more of her friends were there to judge her taste. I preferred a group of three, because if a girl accepted, it left two girls to continue talking to each other as opposed to stranding a girl by herself from a group of two. It never crossed my mind to get a buddy to go with me to ask both girls to dance – probably what a couple of girls would prefer. I seemed to have better luck getting a girl to dance just before a prom. Maybe girls knew a prom was coming up, and the guy might ask her to go with him. Girls loved getting all dressed up, getting a corsage, going out to dinner and being able to boast about it the following Monday morning at school.

I never dated a girl more than two or three times in high school. I just had so little to say on dates. I had no skills at small talk. I never felt there was much in my life at that age that anyone was interested in hearing about. I was not a braggart, so I never felt that I could talk about myself. And what would I talk about? Delivering newspapers, going to school, carousing with my buddies? Playing sports was out because it would make me sound conceited. Dating was just uncomfortable for me. I liked being in control and dating was uncontrollable in terms of not being able to carry on prolonged conversations.

Just like kids seldom asked and learned much about their parent's life as a youngster – same thing with dating. I never asked dates about their earlier family or personal life. I only focused on the present days. I never understood that all I had to do in high school was to put the focus on the girl rather than on me – to learn all I could about her by asking about her interests, activities and life. Looking back, I can see where most, if not all of my dates, must have felt that I was not really interested in them. Years later, there was hardly anything I remembered about the girls I dated in high school – only shows how shallow I was at the time.

Small Circle of Dating Destinations

I had a very limited view about dating in that it was for going to a movie, drive-in or prom, and it was only a Friday or Saturday night thing and never a daytime thing, even during the summer. I never considered taking a girl to museums, picnics, sports events, Playland at the Beach, Golden Gate Park, the Zoo or Santa Cruz Amusement Park. That was one of those shoulda, coulda, woulda things. I would sure do things differently if I had the chance to do it over. Taking a date to those places would have been a lot more fun, cheaper in some cases, and would have replaced the need for conversation with the shared experiences.

Since I did not go on that many dates or have a steady girlfriend, dates were something special. If dinner was involved such as prom night or special event, I knew not to go to the big name restaurants at Fisherman's Wharf for tourists. I always went to expensive restaurants. I made good money for a kid delivering newspapers, so money was no object for me. Some of my favorites were Blue Fox, Ernie's, House of Prime Rib, Tonga Room at the Fairmont Hotel, Top of the Mark Hopkins Hotel and Trader Vic's. Each had its own appeal, whether it was the elegance, food, novelty or view. The most fun atmospheres were at the Tonga Room or Trader Vic's in Cosmo Alley where the Mai Tai originated. The most impressive atmosphere was Ernie's Restaurant. The Victorian decor, deep red carpets, red silk brocade walls, crystal chandeliers and the waiters in black ties always intimidated me. I only dated average looking girls, but I wanted them to feel special. I felt she deserved it for wanting to share our time together, which I considered special because it was such a rare occurrence for me to be on a date.

At the end of a date, we often went out for a late night snack – usually to Zim's at 19th and Taraval because many places we went on dates were on the south side of San Francisco. If we spent the evening somewhere on the north side of the City, we went to Mel's Drive-In on Geary Boulevard about five blocks east of 2nd Avenue (at Spruce Street). Although there were other Mel's in the City, this usually was the closest location. We did not have to get out of the car on cold damp nights or search for a parking spot, which was a challenge at Zim's. Mel's had everything a kid would want to order, plus they played music we could hear from our car. The carhops were on roller skates, but no one cared how fast we were served. It was just fun being in the midst of a popular teenager hangout. Coming from a prom all dressed up in such an informal place as Zim's or Mel's made it all the more funky, fun and special. But for everyday eating with my buddies, there was a Mel's Drive-In on Mission Street near Geneva Avenue whenever we were going to the Geneva Drive-In, and Mel's on Lombard Street where a childhood picture of Applebee and his mom hung on the wall, and Mel's on South Van Ness Avenue off 12th Street that was made an icon of the American popular culture in the 1950s and 1960s and memorialized in George Lucas's film *American Graffiti.*

Most Memorable Dating Experiences

The first thing I noticed about my date was her smell. Each of the girls seemed to have a different scent, whether it was the hair shampoo, body lotion, facial cream or something in their clothes. Often it was an unappealing smell and sort of a turnoff but certainly never a deal breaker to having a good time. But I often thought girls should use a little perfume or something that smelled good. Personally, I shaved just before going out on a date and used English Leather aftershave lotion. I liked the scent better than other aftershaves, and it sounded manly. For all I knew, I may have used too much of the lotion and was turning off my dates, but none of them ever mentioned it. Sweet Catholic girls were probably too polite.

Big Boobs and Wanting Sex

One of my most memorable dates was a girl I met at a school dance. All I remember about her was that she had big boobs. I offered to give her a ride home. It turned out, she lived across the Bay in Marin, which did not excite me, but what alternative did I have. When we arrived at her house, I parked the car at the curb. I leaned over to give her a good night kiss, but she had other ideas. Things started to get heated. It finally sank in that she wanted to have sex, but I always had the intention of having sex for the first time on my wedding night. When I slowed her down and said we should cool it, she sat back and said, "Thank you for respecting me. Can we go out again?" I said, "Sure, that would be great." She gave me her phone number with a smile. As I drove away, I thought to myself, *how can I respect her when she was willing to have sex with someone on a first date?* I felt I was not showing respect to her but to the girl I would eventually marry, who would expect me to be a virgin if I expected it of

459

her. It turned out that 11 years later, my wedding night was the first time that I had sex. Saving ourselves for each other was not the main reason we have been married over 50 years, but it was a big reason by starting the marriage on a high note of respect for each other.

Gorgeous Blondes Not Always the Answer

The only time someone tried to fix me up with a date was when Duffy invited me to a small party given by a family he knew in his neighborhood. I dreaded the idea, but he convinced me I would not be sorry. When we arrived I met the parents and brothers – all really nice people. The date turned out to be a gorgeous blonde – one of the prettiest girls I had ever seen – and certainly better looking than any girl I ever dated. I could not believe how warm and friendly she was to me as if we had known each other for ages. I kept telling myself I do not believe this and repeatedly asking myself why would she be interested in me. I struggled through the evening with my difficulty with making small talk, but as I was leaving, she said, "I hope I see you again." It was a blatant invitation to call her and ask her out, which I never did. I do not know why not, but it must have been a case that I felt she was too good for me and I did not deserve her. It was the same stupidity of all those years when I turned down candy being offered to me because I did not want to be beholden to people. In this case, maybe it was for the best. About five years later I ran into her at a party. She was no longer gorgeous. She was actually unattractive as if she had been a real heavy drinker or on dope all that time. She just looked beat up and aged. Who knows what path she might have taken me down if I had started to date her for any length of time, but I doubted she would have wanted me as her only boyfriend anyway.

Bravest Girl Ever Dated

The most famous and bravest girl I ever dated was Shirley O'Neill. Two years later she was swimming off Baker Beach and her boy friend Albert Kogler was attacked by a 15-foot Great White shark about 40-50 yards off shore. Newspapers said that he yelled to her "Go back, go back", but she kept swimming toward him. "I seized his hand, and when I pulled,

460

I could see that his arm was just hanging by a thread." She slipped her arm around him, had a tug of war with the shark to pull Albert away, and swam to the beach. "With a superhuman effort and unbelievable bravery she struggled for 20 minutes to drag him the 40 yards to the shore as the shark attacked and ripped at Albert's body." On the beach, she baptized Albert, who was not a Catholic like her, and had him repeat the words to make an act of contrition to have God forgive his sins. Two hours later, Albert died at the Presidio's Letterman General Hospital. The newspapers referred to as the "Shark Girl," which did not do justice to her heroics. President John F. Kennedy awarded Shirley the Young American Peoples Medal for Bravery for acts of extreme bravery. [71]

Not Going Steady – Significant Game Changer

The fact that I did not have a steady or regular girlfriend throughout high school may have been one of the three most important things in shaping my life, and I was completely unaware of it at the time. Certainly it was not by choice but something that fortunately happened. So many of the guys I knew in school had steady girlfriends in high school and shortly after graduation they were married. Most never went on to college, which was understandable with their responsibilities financially and child rearing. For some, their married lives worked out well, but for others, not so well. Years later I realized that the person we are in high school is different than the person we are in our mid and late twenties. Our interests are different, our goals are different, even some of our values are different. This was particularly true for those who went through college. Early marriages often involved a trade off between raising a family versus personal development. Raising a family for girls at 18 was a high priority at the time. That was not uppermost in the minds of most boys so a lot of guys never had the chance at "being all that they could be," which was true for the girls too.

The other thing I realized years later was that the idea of going steady and committing to dating just one girl was not what most teenagers should do. It was fine to date a girl regularly but not to the exclusion of dating other girls. Shortly after high school, I attended a party at Canas's house. At the time I was going steady with Barry's sister, which meant that I did not go out with other girls. I needed to be faithful to her because I would not want her dating other guys. That was also my feeling about marriage, which I lived by during my married life. Rich's sister Ana, who I knew for years, was at the party. She was one of the prettiest girls I knew. She was a strong person, took no crap from anyone and somewhat of a spitfire – a high-spirited person. Throughout life we all face forks in the road that involve life changing decisions. This was one of those nights. Ana and I got to know each other for the first time, as it was the only time we ever had time together. After everyone had left the party, the Canases were going to bed, but Ana and I chose to stay up to talk, which did not go well due to my shyness. So there were frequent periods of silence, but neither of us minded it. I really wanted to ask her out but kept reminding myself that I was going steady with Barry's sister, and if the shoe was on the other foot and I had been going steady with Ana, she would not want me to date other girls. Also, I was afraid that she would turn me down, but the fact that she was staying up with me must have meant that she liked me. My values won out that night and I never asked Ana out then or later as I continued dating Barry's sister until she broke up with me and I went away to graduate school several years later. I relived that evening many times in my life and each time regretted that I made that decision. If I had asked Ana out and we dated, nothing may have come of it, but who knows? It could have been life changing for both of us. The teenage years should be a period of dating a variety of partners to have a better idea of the kind of person we want to marry in the future.

Making Out and Sex Before Marriage

Unless we were taking a date to a prom dance, most guys took their dates to drive-in theaters with the intent of making out. Other make out spots were Lands End, Twin Peaks, Lake Merced's Circle or a parking spot at the Ocean Beach. A drive-in theater was preferred over a movie theater because it was more private. Whether or not they planned to make out, it was still nice not having strangers sitting next to them, and if they felt like talking, there was no one to tell them to keep quiet. Also, there was no sticky candy on the floor that stuck to the soles of their shoes. For a more romantic setting, guys drove to the top of Twin Peaks where they had a gorgeous view of the City lit up at night. Driving there for the view was the usual line used for going there. If it was overcast, no big deal.

Barry said, "For a lot of dates we would go to the Geneva Drive-In or El Rancho Drive-In. We rolled the window down to hook the sound box on the window and rolled up the window to keep the cold night air out. Anytime we took a date to a drive-in movie, it was automatically assumed that we would make out. Making out consisted of kissing, French kissing if we were lucky."

I never got into the making out scene in theaters and drive-ins because I never dated the same girl more than two or three times and I just did not know how to read a girl's interest in kissing. It was just easier not to try it than to have the girl reject my advances. I never kissed a girl on the first date. I grew up with the belief that I should not kiss a girl goodnight on a first date – a sign of respect for her. I just heard that was the right thing to do, and it made sense to me. It was not until the second or third date before I even tried to kiss a girl goodnight on her doorstep. I figured by then, she must have pretty much liked me. French kissing was becoming popular, but I was always too embarrassed to try it with a girl all through high school. I was always afraid my date would be turned off and get upset, not to mention that I thought it was just weird – sticking a tongue into some stranger's mouth.

Guys did not always have a date for the drive-in, so a movie theater was one place to meet girls. As Barry said, "My friend Mike and I liked to go to the Parkside Theater on Taraval Street because on Saturday nights girls from Abraham Lincoln High School sat in the balcony and waited to be picked up. If there were empty seats on each side of the girls, we sat next to them and slowly put our arm around their shoulders. If they rested their head on our arm the game was on. We began by slowly kissing, which led to deep French kissing, but that was as far as it would go.

My generation had the attitude that one should not have sex before they were married – especially among those of us who were raised as Catholics. One advantage of not dating much or having a steady girlfriend throughout high school was that it reduced the temptations significantly. But there were occasions when the temptation was the greatest. The only girl I ever dated by meeting her at the Parkside Theater was a big-breasted girl who had pretty obvious intentions. When I called for her and met her mother, the mother was pretty disgusted when I told her I met her at the movies. Obviously, it was a pretty common occurrence for her, yet I never thought of it as a "pickup" because we happened to be introduced to each other through a friend. The following Saturday, we went to the park with another couple, without my knowing what they had in mind. It turned out to be a kissing game where a couple went under a blanket together and the other couple held up the blanket like a tent. My date was all over me and as soon as I realized what was going on, I told her I had to go. I thought going down this road with more dates with her, there was going to be problems. It was the last time I saw her.

Dealing With Customers Required a Personality

After my brother was discharged from the service, he went back to the Stonestown Market at the Stonestown Shopping Center and worked as a butcher until he could find a permanent job. He asked me if I wanted to work at the market Saturday to fill in for a guy out sick. The pay was $20 for the day. Mom was against the idea, but Joe said it was easy work – just ask the customer what they wanted, put their order on a piece of wrapping paper, and pass it on to someone else to wrap it up and take payment. The entire day I never felt comfortable with the job. I think it was the dealing with the public for the first time and the constant fear that they would ask me a question I could not answer, like what was the difference between two cuts of meat? I never got any hard questions, did not drop any meat or fish on the floor, and did not irritate any of the customers, but I was never asked back – probably because I showed no personality. I never smiled or engaged in small talk or seemed especially friendly. I would not have invited myself back either.

This was the period when 3-D movies and Cinerama appeared for the first time. The novelty of objects coming out of the screen toward me was a fun and exciting novelty for a while, but later 3-D lost its appeal and no longer important in deciding which movies to attend. Cinerama with the wide wrap around screen impressed me more as I could see more action and panoramic shots of the scenery, but it cost a lot more to see than other movies. Also, the theaters were over on Geary Street and at the Orpheum Theater, and both had bad parking, so I saw very few Cinerama movies.

Downside of Crashing Movies

Occasionally, when we went to the Parkside Theater on a weekend night, in the middle of the movie a side exit door would open and two, three and up to six kids snuck in. It was pretty common for kids to crash the movies by having one buy a ticket, make sure no usher was inside, and then open an exit door to let the others in with the last person closing the door behind him in order to keep the theater dark and make it harder to find the crashers. They always ran in different directions and grabbed any empty seat. I never saw a crasher ever get caught because there was never an usher inside while the movie was on. They were always in the lobby.

One Friday night, a few of my buddies and I tried the same thing. One guy paid to get in, he opened the exit door for us, and we all scattered to the nearest empty seats. The problem was that we had to watch the movie from those seats and we could not sit next to each other, which sort of defeated the purpose of going to the movies with everyone. However, there was a rush of excitement doing something brazen and running the risk of getting caught and possibly turned over to the police. I experienced the prank, got it out of my system, and never did it again. Based on the risk-reward, I figured the risk was too great for the little amount of money involved and it was unfair to the theater owners.

Difference Between a Curious Kid and a Delinquent

Most kids never think they will ever get caught, but many of them were sitting in cells at Juvenile Hall. I always felt that the difference between a kid in jail and other kids was that he got caught. Most kids had done things that could have put them in jail – they just never got caught. In many cases, the difference between a curious kid and a delinquent was that the first tried something once; the latter did it two or more times.

There were rare occasions when you went to the movies by yourself – mainly because your parents disapproved. Barry described one incident: "As a kid I was always attracted to women and particularly curious about naked women as were all boys. I found the epitome of sexuality at the Palace Theater where the 1957 French movie *And God Created Woman* opened. It starred a very sexy actress named Brigitte Bardot. I never knew the movie had been considered too obscene for American audiences and condemned by the Catholic Legion of Decency, so the censors had edited the scenes they considered too revealing and sexy for the puritanical American audience. It did not matter to me. I had never seen in any film any woman who compared to the raw sex appeal of Brigitte Bardot. She was stunning with her long blond hair, full lips, and a body that drove any kid to fantasize about flying to the French Riviera. What I saw probably was a far cry from the original French version, but I saw enough of her suntanned body to understand the real allure of an attractive, sexy lady."

Being a Jerk Was Forgivable, Remaining a Jerk Unforgivable

A bunch of us were going down to the Santa Cruz Amusement Park in my car one Saturday. We were not particularly late or concerned about getting back by a certain time, but I found myself driving like a madman. Never had I driven more than 70-75 mph, but this time I was going over 80 mph in and out of traffic. Someone said maybe I should slow down, but I just shrugged off the suggestion. Thankfully, we got into heavier traffic, forcing me to drive at a safe speed. Looking back, I never figured out what got into me, but it was really stupid. I could have cost a lot of people their lives and for no good reason. There was one time a couple of years earlier, my folks were in the car with me, and I was driving 45 mph in a 35 mph zone – possibly in and out of traffic. Mom asked me to slow down because it was making Dad nervous. I shrugged her off and never slowed down. I always regretted both experiences for being so selfish and uncaring. I learned from both experiences and became a better person by not doing them again. Success often stemmed from making mistakes, learning from them, and not repeating them. Being a jerk was forgivable, remaining a jerk was unforgivable.

No Need to Be Embarrassed Around Strangers

Once we got to Santa Cruz, we went to a secluded part of the beach where there were a lot of large rocks on the edge of the water. There was a walkway about six feet above the water. No one was around and we never went skinny-dipping in the past, so we all took off our trunks and waded in the water. In about 10-15 minutes several older African-American girls came along and some of us scurried to put on their trunks. They got out fast and got dressed. I was slow in reacting, not knowing whether I should get out or hide behind the rocks. I chose to hide but must have misjudged what they could see from above. My privates were hidden but they probably saw my bare butt because they all stopped for a moment, pointed, laughed, made a joke about "not having much to see," then went by still giggling. I was so embarrassed, but learned there was a difference between people I see often and people I will never see again. There was little need to be embarrassed in the latter case.

Near Death Experience

Late one Sunday night, Barry was driving a bunch of us home from a weekend at the Russian River. Barry was the only one awake as the rest of us were really tired and had fallen asleep. About two-thirds of the way home, we almost jumped out of our pants when we heard a loud bang. Barry had dozed off and hit a wood signpost. I was sitting in the front seat and woke up just in time to see the metal sign and broken pole sail over the top of the car. Barry pulled off the highway and saw no damage was done to the top of the car. I often thought later how lucky we were that sign went over the car instead of through the windshield. One or more of us could have been killed. For the rest of the ride home, everyone was wide-awake. There was no need to stop for coffee.

No Pickpocketing on My Watch

A couple of weeks before Christmas, I was riding home on a crowded N-Judah streetcar one afternoon during rush hour. It was a period of time when I always kept an eye open for pickpockets. The newspapers always warned the public about pickpockets, especially around the holidays. Crowded streetcars and buses were a haven for them. On this day, there was a woman with a handbag with the top wide open. This fellow had a raincoat hanging over his arm, which was not suspicious since it had been raining that day. What was suspicious was that I could see him looking directly at the open bag and stared for a while. He looked away and then looked back at the bag. He started to inch his way in her direction. I could see his hand was hidden under the coat so if he picked a wallet, no one would see his hand or the wallet if he got the coat up against the bag. Just as he was inches from the woman, I tapped him on the shoulder and shook my head saying "No." He looked at me somewhat startled and stopped. He then made his way to the front of the streetcar, which was the quickest exit, and got off. The woman never heard about the theft attempt. I never told her. I just pointed to her purse and suggested she close it up in case of pickpockets. She smiled at me and took my suggestion. I adopted the habit of warning women with open handbags from that point forward.

Respect Classmates at All Times

One night at a Riordan basketball game, I had the urge to lead the fans in a cheer. I was always a highly spirited supporter at the Riordan games, whether as a fan or player. I went down from the stands and asked the cheerleaders if I could lead a cheer. They said I definitely could not and only they could lead the cheers. I kept insisting with the head cheerleader and he kept saying "No." Finally, I just ignored him, looked up in the stands and blurted out "Give me an R" and the fans yelled "R". I yelled, "Give me an "I", and they yelled "I". I continued until the cheering section finished spelling out "R-I-O-R-D-A-N." I felt so exhilarated, but the cheerleaders were not smiling. I went back up into the stands and watched the rest of the game. The next morning I realized I was wrong for intruded into their world, and I had no right to do what the cheerleaders worked so hard to do. It was disrespectful. It was as if a guy came out of the stands, stood next to me on the football field, and said, "I'm going to return this kickoff instead of you." I know I would have gotten physical and was lucky the cheerleaders had not decked me. I would have deserved it. It was the only time I ever did anything like that at Riordan events. It was unforgivable.

Going Out on Top With Class

Although the fans did not have a lot to cheer about at our football games due to the history of poor records, our winning basketball team gave us the most to cheer about. Led by All-City, All C.A.L., All-Catholic and All-Metropolitan Ron McGee from our class, the team had a record of 22-9, the most wins ever by a Riordan team since our class came along – nine of the 12 players were seniors. McGee was MVP and Al Martin received the Most Inspirational Award. It was a tribute to Cappy Lavin's first year as head coach and his coaching them since their freshman year. It was also his last year as teacher and coach at Riordan. He went out on top, with a lot of class and all of our respect and admiration. Among Lavin's many accomplishments, he was inducted into the San Francisco Prep Hall of Fame to join others like Sacred Heart's Jim Gentile and St. Ignatius's Fred LaCour from my era.

Canas remembered when the Giants baseball team moved to the City that year: "1958 was an exciting year for West Coast professional baseball. The New York Giants moved to San Francisco and the Brooklyn Dodgers to Los Angeles. Until that moment, most of our buddies had been devout Yankee fans, mainly because we idolized winners. I mean, Mickey, Casey, Yogi, Whitey, and Hank! And a World Series ring in seven of the last 11 World Series. But the mere thought of Willie Mays, who by now I had discovered was not white, playing at Seals Stadium in the middle of the Mission on the same field Riordan played St. Ignatius in a grudge football game the previous year, was mind-boggling. Sure, the Yanks were still the perennial king of baseball and had added more superstars with Mantle, Maris, Berra, Skowron, Turley, Larsen, and Ford to bolster their roster. We were still blown away by them, but our allegiance was starting to wane. A few of us dithered and chose to keep individual heroes instead. Terry Carmody still worshipped Mickey Mantle and Ed Finn revered the new Dodger's pitching phenom, Sandy Koufax, and even subscribed to the *L. A. Times*, something bordering on treason for a City native. I went whichever way the wind blew."

Bragging With a Smirk Was Acceptable, Big-Headedness Was Not

"Interestingly enough, my father, who was not a baseball fan, joined the Giants bandwagon and befriended some of the new Latino players like Orlando Cepeda, Felipe Alou, and pitcher Ramon Monzant. Dad was a 'groupie' and attended the Giant games and practices at Seals Stadium regularly. He also began including them in family gatherings at our home. Monzant even joined them for weekends at the cabin. But I was having nothing to do with it; being a groupie was not cool behavior. But it did not keep me from mentioning to my friends that Giants stars frequented our home, which I said with a smirk. Bragging with a smirk tended to water down criticism of being big-headed, which was also not cool."

When to Choose the Activity With the Most Friends

Baseball season was starting at Riordan and Barry was torn about staying on the varsity in our senior year with the rest of us. As he said, "As a catcher I did not have a very good arm. In fact, I usually bounced the ball to second base on stolen base attempts, so in my senior year I was replaced by junior Angelo Crudo, who eventually was inducted into the Riordan Football Hall of Fame. I don't know why the coach replaced me. I thought I was a better catcher and hitter, but maybe coach decided since I was a senior to give Angelo a chance. In any event I quit the team and turned out for track. I should have stayed with baseball because some of my best friends were on the team, and it turned out I was not very good at track. Riordan had an outstanding reputation in track. Coach Ed Fennelly had assembled teams that won the C.A.L. track and field championships the previous five years (1953-1957). Since I was not superfast he decided to have me run the 440, one of the most difficult races since it required both speed and stamina, which was why Applebee excelled in that event. I never won a race but I did come in third one time." If given the choice of not being good in two different activities, the moral was to choose the one with the most friends. At least companionship and stories could be shared.

Being Replaced Can Be a Blessing

I was on the varsity baseball team in my junior and senior years. I was the starting shortstop for the JVs and backup on the varsity baseball team in my junior year and starting shortstop on the varsity in my senior year. There were a few games that the second-string shortstop started in my place. In all my playing days, I never liked being replaced in a game. No athlete did. Everyone wanted to be on the field. I understood that backup

470

players had to get in the game so coaches could see how they performed in actual game situations, but the rare times when the backup was put in the baseball or football game and I had to sit out, I always viewed it as a "good news, good news" thing. If my replacement got a hit or gained yardage, it worked toward winning the game. If he struck out, made an error or got thrown for a loss, it helped confirm that the coach had made a mistake choosing someone over me and I should have been in the game. Also, temporary replacements could open the crack for more playing time, which could lead to being replaced by a junior if he did well each time, like Connelly did to Baker in football. The important thing was to support all members of the team by my actions and words, but what went on inside me was a reflection of who I really was – a very competitive guy who wanted to win, and if I was the better player, I wanted to be in there. I did not learn until the end of the season that the coach was trying to find someone to play shortstop in order to move me over to second base where I had a better chance of being selected C.A.L. All-League.

A few times I was moved over to second base. It was easier to play because the throw to first was a lot shorter, but making the double play was more awkward. I preferred making the double play from the shortstop side. It was just a smoother and more natural move of running in the same direction as I was throwing the ball to first base. Besides, shortstop saw more action with more ground balls and line drives.

I really liked our baseball hats with the scripted "R" and the scripted "Riordan" across the chest on the jerseys during my junior year. In my senior year, the varsity used the same hats but gave the varsity uniforms to the JV team because they bought new uniforms for the varsity, which only had a large scripted "R" over the left breast on the jersey. These were so ordinary, while the old jerseys looked classy and had more style. Luckily, it did not affect our play.

Size of Glove Did Not Make the Player

I enjoyed playing baseball the most of all the sports, especially at shortstop. I loved the fresh smell of the grass, especially right after it was mowed. I loved the dirt under my feet – a reminder of where I came from and where I will wind up some day. Part of the fun of playing baseball was that I spoke a jargon that was unique to the sport. It was not important that outsiders did not understand, especially since we only had a handful of spectators in the stands. It only mattered that the guys on the team understood the jargon like "throw the ball around the horn," "take two," "protect the plate," "bring him home," "two away," and "can o' corn." On every pitch, I expected the ball to be hit at me. It was disappointing whenever the ball was hit somewhere else. I wanted to be the go-to-guy on every play. With football, there was the excitement of often being the only one back to catch punts and kickoffs, but that only happened a few times during the game. In baseball, I was playing the position the entire game, and there was just me covering the wide hole in between the third baseman, who normally hugged the foul line, and the second baseman, who was on the other side of second base. I do not remember ever making a fielding error or throwing error those three seasons playing for Riordan. What was remarkable about it was I used a glove that was much smaller than those used by my other teammates. Although large gloves increased the chances of catching the ball, I just found them big and awkward.

Throwing Curveballs to First Base

Even if I made one or two throwing errors over three seasons, it was still remarkable because I threw sidearm. That was not intentional. I just never learned or tried to throw overhand like most ballplayers. Throwing sidearm caused a natural curveball and curveballs from shortstop was not a desirable skill for the position, but it got the job done. In order for the ball to wind up in the first baseman's glove, I had to throw the ball to his left side (my right side) to allow for the curve in the throw. If it took a fraction of a second longer to reach the first baseman, no runner ever beat my throw to first as a result.

Decades later sidearm pitchers became very popular, especially at the major league level. Looking back, I wished we had baseball coaches who recognized the pitching advantage of sidearm throwers. I may not have had a good fastball, but my curveball may have been special for a pitcher. I also regretted being one of the fastest kids in school, our coaches did not give me the steal sign more often, preferably the green light to steal at will.

Missing Fine Points of Coaching

Too often coaches who played football in college were asked to coach baseball at Riordan, so it was understandable why we never learned the finer points of playing baseball. This was the case all three years I played for Riordan. They were football guys coaching baseball teams. On the other hand, this year's coach, Al Sanelli was the same guy who asked the students on the first day of his contemporary history class "What was the greatest invention in the history of mankind?" No one knew. He said, "the flush toilet." Everyone burst into laughter. He had served in Korea and had to use a shovel every time he did his business.

Regardless of who coached which sport, I never felt coaches in any of the sports I played taught us the fine points of the game. In football, we were told to run through the line of scrimmage and look around to pick up our blockers, but there were no drills in picking up blockers much less reactions to plugged up holes in the line. There was no advice on open field running, such as lowering our head as if to run through a tackler but run around him at the last second. Or in confronting a tackler, fake running to the left with a little shoulder dip and zig to the left, but do a zag to the right to run around the tackler. Or how do we twirl just before being tackled and run around the tackler? In baseball we never learned how to read pitchers and when to steal on our own. There was no instruction on how to get under the ball to hit home runs. We never practiced hitting to right field in order to bring in a player home from second base. We never learned to leave our feet and dive for groundballs. We needed way more bunting practice. If there was no time at practice for these fine points, homework should have been to go home and practice these things on the weekend with our buddies. I wished the coaches had adopted the credo: Focus – Execute – Improvise. It would have prepared us to think outside the box like running around rather than through a charging tackler in football or stealing a base or bunting on our own in baseball.

Greatest Honor in My Sports Career

I was honored to be picked by the coach to be one of the two captains of our 1958 baseball team. Ed Coleman was the other co-captain. He got it for being the best player on the team. I got it probably because I was the spirit guy. I was constantly chatting up the pitcher. "Hum babe. Hey, batter, batter. No batter. You got 'em. Easy out." Stuff like that. That season our record was 18-3. Ed Coleman recalled "We beat every team in the San Francisco AAA League that we played." We tied Bellarmine for the league championship and had a one game playoff in San Jose. A number of us on our team had faced the Bellarmine pitcher in our sandlot days and knew he was good. A speck of doubt in my mind that we might have trouble hitting him proved true. We lost 1-0. That year I batted .325 and had 11 stolen bases, including a batting average of .333 in league games. Stats during the season meant nothing. Ed pitched his heart out that day, and we did not come through for him. He deserved better.

It was a privilege to be co-captain with Ed Coleman in our senior year. Ed was the best pitcher in the league and best hitter on our team. Without him we would not have been co-champions of our league that year. At season end, Ed received the Most Valuable Player Award and I got the Most Inspirational Player Award – the same year that Barry Sullivan received the same spirit award for football. How ironic and special that two "brothers" had the same attributes to qualify for the same type of award and the chance to display it in two different sports in the same year.

During baseball season, the track coach Fennelly asked our baseball coach if he could borrow me for track meets since Bob Fennell, their fastest sprinter, was out indefinitely with an injury and lots of the meets were expected to be close for the rest of the season. I was excited about the idea, so the coach agreed. In all of the races, Riordan sprint record holder Gary Thiebaut came in first by a yard or so each race and I always took second in the 100-yard dash. I regretted never congratulating him, much less speaking to him. Maybe things would have been different if we practiced together with the team, but I felt a little like an outsider just there to pick up three extra points for the team. I also ran in the C.A.L. track championship finals at Kezar and took second place behind Thiebaut against the leagues best.

Winning at the Expense of Unfairness

After track season was over, Riordan held their award ceremony in the school auditorium one Friday. Athletes who earned their block R were announced and they went up on the stage to get their letter to be worn on their school sweater. I had received a letter for baseball and football already, so I was really looking forward to lettering in track too. It would be special to have lettered in three sports. When they were done calling the names for the track letters, my name was never mentioned. There were names called that included guys who never placed in the top three positions to earn a point for the team. There were runners who often came in last or next to last. It made no sense. I came in second in every race that I ran that season – must be an oversight. On Monday I went to see track coach Fennelly. I asked him if I was supposed to get a letter for track. He said, "Oh, no. You were on the baseball team." I said, "But I finished second every race. There were those who never earned a point, and they got letters." "Yes, but they were at track practice every day. You practiced with the baseball team." I was devastated. It was unfair. Maybe in the past the school never awarded a letter to anyone who participated in two sports at the same time. And maybe I was the first. If so, they could have set a precedence and allowed me to receive a letter in both sports. I made time to go to the meets and participate. I may not have trained with the track team, but I did train by myself running 60 and 100-yard dashes at the Polo Field, which I failed to point out to the coach. I just did not think it would have mattered. I never knew the coach personally, was never in any of his classes, and he never gave me any personal attention or running tips other than how to set up in the starting blocks at the starting line. This was one of the biggest disappointments of my high school years. Lettering in three sports was important to me. In comparison, getting a "D" in chemistry and having to go to summer school the previous year was not that big of a deal to me. I guess the difference was not receiving credit for something I did well was more important than doing poorly at something that I was not good at. The "D" grade was fair; not receiving the letter in track was not fair. Fairness was a virtue I held with great regard all my life. Although experiencing unfair things was part of life, I did not have to accept them, so I turned them into positives as an adult by studying law and sticking up for others. I remembered my own unfair experiences whenever I made decisions that impacted others – the importance of being fair to them.

A more unfair event involving coach Fennelly was at the start of track season in our senior year, when Lafayette and Latour expected to move up from JVs to varsity. They deserved it. But the coach told them he needed them on the JV (130's) team to help them win meets. "What, are you kidding me?" But they both agreed to stay down on JVs while all of their senior classmates moved up to varsity. To this day, Lafayette still thinks of this as his biggest disappointment in high school. Sports should be about what is best for the student, not what is best for the coach, school records and the trophy case. It was like playing in the minors. It was the dream of every kid to make it to the majors. Knowing that their statistics may not be as good as can be compiled by remaining in the minors, the dream was to be able to look back and say I made it to "The Show."

Wrong Righted 60 Years Later

Sixty years later, I contacted Andrew Currier, President of Riordan High School, and explained my story about not receiving a block R for track from 1958. He discussed it with Alumni Relations Director, Paul Cronin, and they decided to send me a block R for track. It was a different time with faculty with different opinions, which I was so grateful. It gave me bragging rights to have lettered in three sports in my senior year – probably the only Riordan student to accomplish it back then. There were others who could have done the same, but I was fortunate to have been given the opportunity to do so. Was it worth my time spent on sports versus academics? For me it was. I accomplished something no one in my class had done. I never could have been unique scholastically no matter how much I studied, but the biggest rewards were the friendships made, experiences shared and character built on the sports teams over the years. Those got balanced out with my studies in college.

Barry admitted later "My youth was the best of times in many ways. My parents gave me a good physical upbringing. We never wanted for food or clothes. We had a comfortable life, and I got to do pretty much what I wanted to do. I will never forget Mom's deathbed confession to me years later, 'I wish I would have been a better mother.' She was the best mother she could have been. She always supported me in all endeavors. But those years were also not so good in some ways. The mental and supportive part of life at home was sometimes lacking. Dad lived through the Depression and if you knew anyone who lived back then, you are well aware of their hardships. *The Grapes of Wrath* by John Steinbeck covered that period sufficiently. I believe it left a scar on Dad's soul that he never could come to grips with. I could never succeed in his eyes, no matter how hard I tried to please him. It was never enough. Nobody suffered as much as Dad. Dad had a secret side of his life that he never talked about, and yet, like the character in F. Scott Fitzgerald's book *The Great Gatsby,* I sometimes wondered if he ever 'killed a man.' He was one tough S.O.B., and he had the good dark looks and broken nose to prove it."

Important Thing Is What We Think of Ourselves

In spite of the harassing Barry endured with the "Tomato" name-calling, he still developed a thick skin to succeed. He was chosen to be our class representative in the discussion of curfew laws with the City Mayor's Committee; he was chairman of the committee to select Athletes of the Month in each sport; he was awarded MVP of the Serra-Riordan homecoming game; he received the Most Inspirational Player Award for football in our senior year for being so active on defense, always hustling, hollering, and urging everyone on. He also received a plaque from the Union 76 Oil Company for his outstanding play. The high energy that Barry showed on the field probably came from his wild child days. More importantly, he was always supporting his family of teammates. I suspect some of that stemmed from not receiving the support from his dad in his youth. He learned not to treat others the same way, and he was not going to let his team down, so he played his heart out. It was not important what others may call us or think of us. It was what we thought of ourselves and how we overcame adversity that was important.

All That Will Remain – "I Did My Best"

High on the wall of the locker room in the Riordan gym was an award board showing the winners of the Most Valuable and Most Inspirational

(Spirited) Player Awards for each sport from year to year. It was the only prominently displayed recognition an athlete received. Having my name added to the board along with Barry and Ed Coleman made me proud of our accomplishments and a nice way to end my four years of high school. Not many years later, the school took down the board, probably because they ran out of space. That is why it would have been nice to have the honor mentioned in the school yearbook so there was a lasting memory of the honor – not just for sports but for the other extracurricular activities. When the board was taken down, it was like our accomplishments were wiped out. The lesson I learned was never to do things with the hope of having my name on anything portable or having something named after me because in 50 years or less, it or my name will be gone – removed or replaced as so often happened, even people's names on buildings. I also realized that in the freshman year, we might not know what we would be good or excel at during high school, just like picking a career. So it was not as important what we chose to do, but to be as good at it as possible, so after all is said and done, we can say "I did my best." We will know, even though no one else will know or care down the road.

Riordan established their Sports Hall of Fame in 1976 and the first class of inductees included Ed Coleman. Applebee was inducted in the second class of inductees in 1981. We all had the pleasure of knowing and walking the hallways with many of those in the Hall of Fame in my senior year. I was honored to play with 14 of 16 of them on the same field:

Baseball: Ed Coleman, '58, Joe Chiamparino '59, Larry Kane '59,
    Ed Preston '59
Basketball: Ron McGee '58, John Galten '59
Football: Rich Horan '58, Angelo Crudo '59, Rich Dixon '59,
    Ray Greggains '59, Tim Moffett '59
Track: Tim Applebee '58, Bob Fennell '58, Rich Kennealy '59,
    Mike Mullany '59, Bill Selmi '59

Our 1958 baseball team had six Riordan Sports Hall of Fame players: Ed Coleman, Joe Chiamparino, Angelo Crudo, Ray Greggains, Larry Kane, and Ed Preston, the most Hall of Famers on any Riordan team at the time and possibly ever.

Ed Coleman made C.A.L. All-League, All-Metropolitan and All-City, and represented Riordan in the *S.F. Examiner* All-Star Game. "He was a

.396 hitter and a very versatile fielder" according to the *Crusader*, not to mention an outstanding pitcher. Ed also was the first Riordan athlete who signed a professional contract. He signed with the Boston Red Sox after graduation. No figures were announced but local Red Sox scout Charlie Wallgren, who lived in the Sunset District's Holy Name parish and signed Ed Coleman and Jim Fregosi, called the contract "substantial" according to the *Crusader*. Ed went on to play in the Class B Carolina League for the Raleigh Capitals, a team with a 78-52 record where Carl Yastrzemski was the league's MVP the following year. Ed had his baseball career cut short before reaching the majors when he injured his leg running through an airport. Talk about unfair. It was that incident that helped change my mind in college about my choice of playing sports or studying. What happened to Ed and the experience of breaking some ribs at football practice in my freshman year in college made me give up sports in college, concentrate on studies, work part time and play blackjack to get through college – best decisions ever.

After the C.A.L. All-League baseball players had been selected, coach Sanelli called me into his office and said, "I would have preferred to play you at second base, but I had no choice," meaning there was no one else who was solid at shortstop. He was implying that I probably would have made the C.A.L. All-League team if I had played second base, not only for my fielding but also for hitting and stolen bases that year. Instead, the All-League selections at shortstop were Ernie Fazio at St. Elizabeth High School and Jim Fregosi at Serra High School. Fazio was later elected to Santa Clara's Baseball Hall of Fame. [72]. Fregosi was later inducted into the Los Angeles Angel's Hall of Fame. I had some regrets but making All-League was less important to me than playing a key position that saw more action and provided a greater contribution to the team's success.

Senior Prom – a Night to Forget

Canas and Carmody double dated to the prom at the St. Francis Yacht Club. As Canas described that evening, "I was elated that my father gave me the keys to his car after telling me I would *never, ever* drive his new '57 Dodge again after getting it in a slight fender bender a year earlier. After the prom, I dropped off my date and we took off for s string of drinking parties. As we got onto Alemany Boulevard from Brotherhood Way, a red '57 Chevy pulled alongside of me and the driver signaled that he wanted to race. Being a total idiot, I floored the Dodge and the race was on...I subsequently 't-boned' (crashed into the side of) the other car. The crash sent Carmody through the front windshield, although he walked away with only a broken nose and a destroyed tuxedo. The rest of us only had a few cuts and bruises. The Dodge died while the red Chevy took off into the dark. When I phoned my father, his silence was deafening. It was not cool. I had nothing to say, and it would have been suicide to tell him that I thought the Dodge was cursed."

Graduation: Chance to Start a New Life

Our graduation ceremony in June 1958 was in the school auditorium. There were 179 graduates that day (12 were omitted from the graduation program) in contrast to the 260 freshmen that enrolled with us four years earlier – a 69% survival rate. Principal Brother Maurice Miller presided. Paul Scannell was our class valedictorian and Bob O'Neill was the class salutatorian. They were two of the smartest kids and received a number of the graduation awards. They did us proud speaking to us and for us. Half the class received Special Good Conduct Diplomas, 22 percent received a variety of Riordan Honors and Awards, and over seven percent received scholarships in comparison to only three percent nationwide. Ten received full college scholarships, two received partial scholarships.

We stood on stage about to leave one sandbox and ready to move on to the biggest sandbox of our life – a world of choices among local and national colleges and jobs. This was what our past prepared us to face – the alternative doors to our future. Out those doors, there would be many forks in the road, the next more important than the last. We would all travel a different journey, but one thing was the same for all of us – the hope that we would some day look back and say, "I enjoyed the trip and am delighted how it turned out."

According to Canas "We were all white Christian young men (if we count five Latinos as members of the Caucasian race), the majority with Irish and Italian surnames. Some of the Holy Name gang and many others were pretty much hung over. We awkwardly marched onto the stage and were on display in staggered bleacher type benches in five rows where we stood through much of the pomp and ceremony of speeches, awards, more speeches, and finally the individual bestowing of diplomas. I knew later that I received one because my father took a host of blurry photographs."

"During the valedictorian speech, a couple of the wise guys on stage had to cut up. Scannell was saying something about shedding our biases, shedding this, shedding that, and Ed Finn, who was standing behind me whispered fairly loudly, 'Alright, everybody strip,' which prompted some in our section to burst out chuckling, which in turn drew the evil eye of Brother Miller. By then we were rummy from standing and the previous night's festivities and we did not much care. I guess we were not ready to *shed* our immaturity just yet."

There were a number of kids on the stage not enjoying the moment and looking back with few fond memories because decades later, some of them said they did not enjoy their high school years. How sad that their most formative years were such miserable experiences. The reasons were an individual thing, but it most likely was a result of their own doing or how other students or parents treated them. Those who were picked on participated in few school extracurricular activities. Those who had few or no friends did not participate in activities. Those who were not good at an activity often did not try a different activity. But like any experiences in life, it got down to how we reacted to the disappointments during and after the experiences. Some remained bitter and others realized our pride would get hurt along the way. It was part of the game. But we needed to learn from it and get back in the game. As I learned at my 8th grade and high school graduations, the degree was not the end, but the beginning of a new life and a much bigger sandbox in which to improve myself.

What Were the Early Years All About?

Barry, Canas and I were standing on the stage, not so much looking to the future as the class valedictorian was suggesting, but reminiscing about our past which experienced the best of times in an era of San Francisco history never to be again and with classmates who would never be as close. But there were other things on our minds too.

Barry was looking at his parents in the audience with mixed memories. "I learned some very good lessons from my parents. I learned the value of hard work, of doing the best I can at whatever job I attempted. I learned to love reading and writing and to have good manners and respect for other people. I learned the value of having a positive attitude from my mother. Yet, I had this image of my mother and father as two gargoyles sitting atop my left and right shoulders. One was very positive and cheerful and the other angry, intimidating, and whispering negative thoughts in my ear, but it was time for me to move on."

I stood there with my two "brothers," not listening to much of the various commencement speeches but thinking about the paths we each took to get here – each overcoming our own personal handicaps and the joy ride we shared along the way. We each started out with different backgrounds, goals, opportunities, determination, motivation, abilities, shortcomings, attitudes, parents, friends, and with some degree of lady luck in our corner.

I thought about my heroes that I met along the way – those who overcame hardships and excelled in their own way. There was Mom who raised me almost single-handedly under trying circumstances. Jim Sullivan, who rose from poverty in the Great Depression to be a major corporation's most successful salesman, was my role model. Jimmy Reidy, the school custodian who inspired my interest and pursuit of education as a college student and educator all my life. Rich Canas who reached the heights of his profession as an immigrant who came to the U.S. as a non-English speaking minority in a white environment. Dennis Beyma who spent his career in the U.S. Marine Corps flying helicopters during the war to save lives. Barry Sullivan who overcame the name-calling and lack of fatherly support to excel on the football field and in college. The "Heroes in the Shadows" who excelled scholastically in spite of the pressures, any name-calling, and their accomplishments going unappreciated and unrecognized. Every kid who faced hardships at home, on the streets, or in school who went on to have success in marriage as a spouse or parent or in their life's occupation or community work.

I also thought about the most influential people in my youth in order of importance: Mom, Dad, the ex-police officer who lent Dad the down payment on their Sunset District house, Doris and Jim Sullivan, the Holy

Name class of 1954, Barry Sullivan, Richard Canas, Jimmy Reidy, Hannah Prendiville, Brother Maurice Miller, Maurice Lafayette, coaches and teachers at Riordan, and Gerry Hipps's dad Manny. It was Mom and Dad who gave me life. I owed everything to them, but it was Mom who almost single handedly raised me through nearly two decades of financial and family hardships. Without the down payment to the house in the Sunset, we most likely would have remained in the Mission District the rest of my youth, and I would have attended a different school instead of Riordan. I would have been denied the opportunities I encountered from my life in the Sunset and at Riordan. The Sullivans were enormous influencers and contributors to those aspects of whom I became that my own parents were not able to provide to me. Being voted Most Likely to Succeed by my 1954 classmates gave me the motivation and confidence to succeed in life. Barry was that best friend that every kid needed to share experiences and good times to make those formative years memorable and a happy part of high school. Canas was the mirror of myself, both coming from humble backgrounds and a constant reminder to each other to be all that we could be. Jimmy Reidy, the family friend who brought joy to our house with every visit and stimulated my interest in mathematics and the importance of an education. Hannah Prendiville gave birth to most of the relatives that gave us so many happy and fun family gatherings, the thing needed to help hold the family together. She taught me charity and kindness to others with the one-dollar bills she slipped me at the end of our visits. Brother Maurice Miller who turned me around from getting into trouble to becoming a student appreciative of the faculty and what Riordan had done for me. Maurice Lafayette who set the example for me to develop character and good virtues. The coaches who allowed me to be a starter on their teams, which gave me motivation and confidence, the qualities necessary for achieving success. The teachers who unselfishly remained dedicated and motivated to do so much for so little in recognition, gratitude and pay. Manny Hipps sending me to jail (Juvenile Hall) overnight taught me not to do anything that would put me in jail again.

But possibly the greatest influence on the person I would become were collectively my buddies in high school, especially the Holy Name gang. As in business, success is more likely if you surround yourself with the best people so the synergy from the whole is greater than the sum of the individual parts. I was lucky to pal around with guys who possessed qualities for us to share, many of which reflected the U.S. Marine Corps 14 Leadership Traits. They all had loyalty, dependability, humility and unselfishness. Individually, there was Applebee (hard work, initiative, judgment), Barry (enthusiasm), Beyma (bearing, courage, decisiveness, patriotism), Canas (perseverance, tact), Carmody (knowledge, patriotism), Hipps (endurance), and Lafayette (integrity, justice). All of these qualities had to have rubbed off on to each one of us to some degree by just being around these guys. These qualities were the invisible influencers that complemented the efforts of our parents, the Riordan teachers, coaches and school administrators to help us become the best versions of ourselves.

Grammar school provided me with a solid foundation for reading, writing and arithmetic. I learned social skills for getting along with others and preparing me for high school, a major life-changing sandbox for my future. Riordan had the goal to mold me into a model student in studies, in sports, and in activities, but they never defined "model." I liked to think it was not just about being successful in grades but about striving to do my best. In that case, I was not a model student in studies. But it was not the school or the teachers' fault that I was a mediocre student. It was entirely my fault. Although I did not think of it at the time, I made many choices along the way – some were good, some bad, most not that important. My biggest handicap, like with so many kids my age, was immaturity. I at times sacrificed too much to pursue my dreams – too much sports and carousing and not enough studying.

On the other hand, there may have been a disproportion of kids like me in my class. Throughout four years of high school, my class always had the fewest outstanding scholars of the four classes. Each year, my class had the fewest students make the school's Honor Roll – usually 8-10 while the other three classes had 20-30. Only 10 in my class in my senior year were among the 58 students who achieved the exceptional grades to be selected as a CSF (California Scholarship Federation) member. But our class was a perfect example of the cliché that the "A" students became the teachers and the "C" students became the major donors – a quality not learned between the covers of a book. Through all the muck and mire, the class of 1958 emerged as one of the three most generous classes in Riordan history for providing financial assistance to the students who followed in our footsteps through the halls of Riordan over the years. Whether through sports or extracurricular activities, we learned pride, loyalty, leadership, appreciation, and generosity – values that helped make a better world for future generations whether in school, work, home or society. Excelling in grades and sports in school were achievements that were washed away with time. The lifetime quality of a man was made up of the intangibles picked up at school – motivation, discipline, respect for others, teamwork, learning from mistakes, and a good heart – for an appreciation only realized over a lifetime of what Riordan gave us and meant to us. Our class's generous school donations over the years was a way of saying, "I like who I became, and I owe a lot of it to Riordan," and why our attitude toward the school was semper fidelis – "always faithful."

We knew that the "A" and "B" students would do just fine, but there would be pressure on them to do well since that was expected of them. For the "A" and "B" students to fail, they would let down their parents, family, friends and colleagues. Some of them had their fill of studying and did not reach their potential after graduation, but many others became the lawyers, doctors, judges, executives, entrepreneurs and profession leaders from our class. On the other hand, "C" students like me had an advantage to succeed in other ways the second time around. There were no particular expectations of us, so there was no pressure to do well. So "C" students often became the risk-takers after graduation. If we failed, we failed. No one expected anything differently, but many of us felt we had something to prove the second time around and we went on to prove it by being the best we could in our careers and family life. [73]

The kids I felt sorry for were the "A" and "B" students who did not meet their parent's lofty expectations. It was like Barry's dad, a grammar school dropout, who rose from poverty to becoming the best and most successful salesman in his company. The bar was set higher than Barry could ever achieve. Since Barry had a higher head start economically and educationally, it was nearly impossible to improve by the same degree. On the other hand, I probably would have been as tough on my kids, which was one reason I believed that I would not have been a good father.

Solving the "Meaning of Life" Riddle

Riordan was a bridge from childhood to adulthood to provide me the opportunity to develop qualities and values that were critical for me to achieve the meaning of my life. At one time or another, most of us have asked ourselves "What is the meaning of life? Why am I here?" I thought about it for decades and came to the conclusion that it was not the same thing for everyone. It was different for each one of us. For those who believed in heaven, the meaning of life was what one envisioned heaven to be like. For some it was reuniting with love ones, for others it was a life of good health, for others it was a job they really enjoyed, and for others it was enough wealth to afford whatever they wanted. I concluded that for me, the meaning of life was the realization that this life was my only chance at my vision of heaven because the other heaven mentioned by the various religions would be a whole lot different than I could imagine. One difference was that this life was never preordained to be fair in spite of everyone going through life complaining about how unfair things were along the way. For example, I was born into a life to be with loved ones, to maintain my good health, to pursue a job I enjoyed, and to accumulate wealth. Some worked at achieving all of them, and others did not work hard enough to achieve them. Each of us was given a fair opportunity to succeed, but the latter group chose otherwise. Unfortunately, some were prevented from achieving what they wanted due to things beyond their control, such as birth defects, fatal or debilitating accidents that were not their fault, or defective genes. That was unfair! What was heaven on earth for me? It was:

• Personal accomplishments
• Contributions to help others
• Provide myself and spouse (family) with what we wanted (some called that happiness)

They would have been my lifetime goals upon graduation, but I never did solve the meaning-of-life-for-me riddle until 30 years later. But based on a childhood of good fortune, perseverance and a lot of luck, I did find my heaven on earth anyway.

So rather than worrying too much about what they want to be, high school graduates should decide whom they want or need to be to achieve their heaven on earth. And rather than rely on luck, they should look at the last four school years to assess their strengths, weaknesses, mistakes and successes to decide what needed to be changed, improved and focused on over the next four to eight years to be the person they want to become. One way or another, they will be a different person by then with different interests, values and goals to direct them along the right paths to achieve their heaven on earth. Graduation is a point in time that gives them a second chance to turn things around in a new sandbox among different people to become someone much better and pointed in a better direction. Part of my heaven was finding the right partner for life. I was determined not to get married before college graduation and to marry someone better than me – someone who could make me a better person. My eventual wife was a University of Southern California graduate with a master's degree, was smarter than me, more cultured than me, and better looking than me. This was a big part of the respect that I held for her all my life. I believed many early marriages ended in divorce by age 30 because one of them outgrew their spouse in some way, making them feel they were "better" than the other, and he or she lost respect for the other as a result.

At graduation, the blackboard of my life was erased so I could face a whole new life – a chance to start all over, having learned from the joys, sorrows, achievements and failures along the way. but the greatest impact on the decisions about my future came from the mistakes made by my parents, kids I knew, and myself. I also learned some critical lessons from Riordan-related contacts after graduation that led to some key decisions.

The event that considerably influenced my future career occurred one or two years after graduation. It was football coaches Fran Hare and Ron Modeste who were the two coached I interviewed as a college assignment to speak to people doing what I was considering doing for a living, which was to be a teacher and coach. They turned me against coaching because they said they did not workout regularly because they were too busy with family and teaching. I was so disillusioned. I never thought about coaches having a family life and not fitting in time to stay in shape, especially working in an athletic environment. I dropped my physical education minor and majored in finance. I never did any coaching but I had a triple career in finance, investments and education all my life.

The best advice I received from Riordan was not from a teacher but from a former classmate. Years after graduation, Mike Duffy told me his then girlfriend's (wife's) father had a real estate investment philosophy based on the fact that he did not have unlimited funds, so he only needed to make one exceptional purchase at a time. For him to get the best deal, he made very low offers on as many properties as necessary before he found that one buyer who accepted his offer. He was in no hurry, as it could take quite a while before he could make a purchase of the best property for the best price. That story stuck with me, and by my 30s, it served me well when I could afford to start buying investment properties in San Francisco. I used aspects of his concept in my investment strategies. I always looked more than 300 properties for sale in the better parts of the City until I found the best property at the best price. I learned along the way that I always found a better property time after time as I searched for the best deal. Although I skipped over many attractive deals, I just knew *this was the one* once I found it. I also realized that I could do this on the side while working full time at my job in the Controller's Department of Bank of America to save up investment capital. When I first interviewed at the Bank, my eventual boss said, "You will never get rich working for the bank." It was obvious, but it served as the single best advice for me to achieve my childhood goal of being rich. I had to find a different path, which I did – real estate investments in San Francisco. I also learned that the secret to making a lot of money in the stock market was not so much what I bought, but when I bought. It was a lot about timing – not being in a hurry and waiting long enough for the best timing while building up capital. Also, it was so much easier to make money once you had money.

Over my 22 years of schooling, I noticed the class leaders, popular kids, leading scholars and best athletes in grammar school did not always achieve the same stature in high school, and most of the high school class leaders, popular kids, scholars and athletes did not achieve the same stature in college. Certainly there were exceptions, but as an academic scholar, I was poor in high school and better in college, and as an athlete, I was better in high school and poorer in college. Some of this was due to a change in interest and effort, but most of it was because the competition was greater. At each new level, there were a lot more outstanding leaders, personalities, scholars and athletes. We may have been a big fish in a small pond, but now we were a small fish in a big pond. I found that insightful cliché in one of the thousands of books I searched through in college in my quest for how to be rich and successful. That included every book related to finance and investments in libraries at three universities that I attended. I used that cliché to determine my career path. I chose to pursue being a big fish in a small pond by being the best in a focused area of specialization. I realized I did not have a degree from Stanford or Harvard to be the best in the business world. The sooner I realized my limitations, the faster I started on the path that would be best for me.

1958 was also momentous for Canas's parents. "My father received his naturalization papers making him and his two children U.S. citizens. Having a U.S. passport and identity as such also meant that he could travel back to El Salvador with some degree of protection when the time came. My mother and father finally returned to their beloved El Salvador. In 1968, Dr. Cañas proudly hung a shingle in front of his new dental office. Teresa enthusiastically organized and managed their new home in the Miramonte District of San Salvador complete with a lush garden, live-in maids, and like-minded friends and neighbors. They lived there the rest of their lives." [74]

Future of Ordinary Kids From Extraordinary Times

What became of the Holy Name gang after high school? I learned that we had five segments to our lives. We are a different person during each segment and we were given a fresh opportunity to change our life at the start of each one. The five segments were: age 0-4 (pre-school), age 5-12 (grammar school), age 13-18 (high school), age 19-25 (college, armed services or entry job), age over 25 (career and family). Graduation from high school meant I was entering the second to last chance for me to turn my life around and start over. My buddies and I learned from our mistakes in high school. It was time to lock and load to refocus our goals, choose the appropriate path, and modify how we would spend our time making that journey.

So the first step on our path down the road was to decide what we were to do regarding the military draft. Our country had a peacetime draft in place since 1940. Men were drafted to maintain our military forces that could not be achieved through voluntary means. Most high school kids approaching graduation thought about it. The options were to volunteer right away so we could select which branch of the services to join; we could enroll in college and ask for deferments until we finished school; or, we could just wait to be drafted, usually into the U.S. Army. Most guys never enlisted and wound up avoiding the draft too. It was an opportunity to put up or shut up – how patriotic were we? We learned a love for our country based on the war movies, respect for the flag in the classroom and at sports events, presence of so many military men walking the streets of the City in their uniform, and the mindset that we should be grateful to a country that had given us and our families so much. We felt it was a small enough price to pay. It was a time when our parents started with so little but were given the opportunity to improve our lives so much, which we did. What better way to show our gratitude than joining another "team" – a concept learned through sports and from the war movies with military platoons and reconnaissance teams acting as one and possibly "taking a bullet" for a buddy. No wonder so many of us volunteered for the armed services right after high school.

I asked Carmody what he was going to do and he said without any hesitation, "Join the U.S. Marines Corps." Years later I asked his brother Tim why he chose the Marines and Tim said, "Because he was influenced by John Wayne who appeared in a lot of USMC war movies." Regardless of the reason, I was so thankful all my life that I followed Carmody's path. I also believed the Marines were special and found out later that you cannot take the Marine out of the boy – talk about a confidence builder. As Marines say "Once a Marine, always a Marine." It was one of the best things I ever did and would recommend to every kid they join the regulars or reserves of some military service. People tended to respect you more out in the workforce. Marines received even more respect.

Carmody and I signed up in March 1958 before we graduated from high school. This meant going to a 3-month boot camp in San Diego upon graduation, followed by active duty in the infantry at Camp Pendleton, CA and a tank battalion at Twentynine Palms, CA. We also finished up serving in the U.S. Marines Corps Reserves in an antiaircraft artillery automatic weapons (howitzer cannon) unit at Treasure Island. We initially went to Boot Camp in June 1958 along with Al Fambrini, another Riordan graduate. I never knew Al in high school as he was in the band all four years and I was in sports – another reason I wished there was a way to get to know those who had different interests in high school, as Al turned out to be one of the nicest guys I ever knew. He went on to a 32-year career with the Petaluma Police Department and retired as a Lieutenant.

Barry Sullivan joined the U.S. Air Force (Security Service) for six years out of high school while Dennis Beyma entered the U.S. Marine Corps after college as an officer. Rich Canas applied for Aviation School in the U.S. Marine Corps but he did not have the required 20/20 vision. We each felt we owed it to our country to serve in the military because we believed it was the least we could do for all that the country gave our families and us. We were all still single, so this was the right time before we created ties to loved ones. My other closest buddies got married and started a family a few years later, which exempted them from the service.

A few of our classmates at Riordan went into the U.S. Army. After getting out of the Army, one of the toughest kids in our class wound up outside a bar down by the City piers with his testicles cut off for calling out the wrong guys – just did not know when to leave his high school ways behind him.

Where did each of the Holy Name gang career paths take us? After his six-year service in the U.S. Air Force, Barry Sullivan graduated from the University of Southern California, wrote movie scripts for Hollywood, pursued acting at San Francisco's American Conservatory Theater, and taught for years in the San Francisco Unified School District. Rich Canas graduated from the University of San Jose, wrote several books [75], served in various law enforcement positions, such as Director of the DEA's U.S. National Drug Intelligence Center, State of New Jersey Director of Homeland Security, and Special Assistant to the President as the Director of Counternarcotics and Counter-terrorism on the National Security Council at the White House. Terry Carmody graduated from the University of San Francisco, spent his entire career with the Santa Clara Police Department and retired as Captain of Detectives. Dennis Beyma graduated from Cal Poly University (California Polytechnic State), then entered the U.S. Marine Corps with the intent to be a fighter pilot, but that choice was denied for being too tall, so he chose a 20-year career of flying helicopter missions in combat, and retired as a decorated Colonel. Tim

Applebee followed in his father's footsteps and passion for working with his hands as Carpenter Foreman for the City of San Francisco overseeing work on the City's historic cable cars, and eventually the Hetch Hetchy project in Tuolumne County as Carpenter Supervisor, when he raised five great kids in Jamestown, CA and was an avid hiker, backpacker, skier, and photographer with his best friend Maurice Lafayette. Gerry Hipps had an illustrious career as a union representative negotiating with union labor leaders and sometimes dealing with mobsters, while being cited often in various books and newspaper articles of his exploits. I received nearly four college degrees (six units shy of a 2nd MBA) including a master's degree in finance from San Francisco State (College) University, which culminated in attending every finance and investment class offered at three colleges. I went on to be the Controller of Information Technology (IT) at Bank of America, studied law at night to receive a degree from LaSalle University, founded the National Association for Bank Cost & Management Accounting for large banks to educate the banking industry, received the first Stanley Price Memorial Lectureship Award for excellence in teaching at Golden Gate University, invested in San Francisco real estate in my spare time, founded the profession of IT Financial Management (ITFM), wrote five books and various articles on ITFM, published a national ITFM magazine, and educated the most professionals in this specialized field personally and through my organization that focused on IT financial management.

I set out at age 7 to be rich. Along the way, I never lost sight of that goal. I realized I could never be the richest guy in the world, so I settled on being rich enough. I realized there was nothing special about merely accumulating money, as there would always be many others with more money than me. After making my first million in my 30s, I set my real career goal to be the leading expert in my field and to educate the most practitioners in that field in the world in order to share knowledge and benefit the career of as many of those as possible in my field. I eventually accomplished my goal to be the best at something by understanding my limitations, setting a realistic goal, finding the right path, using the right resources and getting a lot of help from my colleagues.

Canas said, "Some worked to live, others lived to work. But what was most telling about the character of our Holy Name gang was the fact that their children, albeit spoiled by 1950's standards, grew up principled, patriotic and kind – the only true metrics of success." Two decades had come to an end. A whole generation of kids was blessed to have grown up in the same sandbox, San Francisco at its best, raised by hard working parents with one goal in mind – to do their best to make a better life for their children and lift them out of a simple and humble lifestyle. From the mud – the challenges and obstacles in life – grew our generation of lotus flowers, symbolizing self-regeneration, enlightenment, mental evolution, rebirth and growth.

Bygone Days of Shangri-La and Camelot

My childhood was an extraordinary time to live. San Francisco and the surrounding areas were never better to experience and may never be as perfect again for kids to explore, appreciate and develop. Family life was unique, opportunities were never greater and life was so affordable for kids to have such rich experiences.

There were lots of nearby fun places like Russian River, Marin Town & Country Club, Lake Tahoe and Santa Cruz Boardwalk. San Francisco provided us Playland at the Beach, Golden Gate Park, North Beach, Sutro Baths, Fleishhacker Pool, Mel's Drive-In, Great Highway, movie drive-ins, neighborhood theaters and many long-gone favorite restaurants. Our neighborhoods were safe, clean and free of graffiti and drugs. Local storeowners were known by name and police were kid-friendly. The City had little traffic, lots of street parking and few parking meters. There were organized sports leagues for kids. Playgrounds had director supervision and offered a wide variety of activities, games and sports teams. Schools provided us an affordable and excellent education, taught religious beliefs, enforced discipline, and had dedicated teachers and a plethora of activities. Movies had casts of 1000s along with musical extravaganzas. Local sports heroes played most of their career on our hometown teams.

Home life stemmed from a humble upbringing, taught an appreciation for our few possessions, good manners, tolerance of others, patriotism, and respect for the flag, country, elders and law enforcement. There were special family meals, like Sunday breakfasts, gatherings around the radio at night and holiday meals with the relatives.

Parents did not micromanage and pamper their kids. We could play outside on our own and explore the City on a bicycle. We played games at our friend's houses and traded with them things from our collections. Jobs were available for kids to make our own money. Our life style was cheap with free museum admissions, penny and nickel candy, nine-cent S.F. Seals minor league baseball games, five-cent Coca-Cola, five-cent coffee, nine-cent and 20-cent movies, cheap Chinatown firecrackers, and later, 20-cent gallon of gasoline and reasonable car insurance.

San Francisco in the 1940s and 1950s was a paradise of unmatched beauty with a freedom to explore and face a wide diversity of challenges on my own in order to be all that I could be. It was a period in time that stood for the right values – appreciation, courage, equality, family values, humility, justice, loyalty, optimism, patriotism, and respect. My generation was so blessed with this miraculous window of opportunity.

So much of San Francisco has changed in my lifetime. The City was my Shangri-La and Camelot rolled into one. But like both of them, the memory of the time and place of my youth will go to the grave with my buddies and me, but for future generations, "Don't let it ever be forgot, that moment that begot, no more the time and box of sand, for roots to grow the man, with every chance to do our best, until we're laid to rest." Things were better then in so many ways. It was a period in time that we will cherish and remember for having experienced it rather than a time that was lost forever. The changes to the City for better or worse cannot remove the memories of a by-gone era that made me so happy and proud to have been born there and to have grown up in that exceptional era of San Francisco. It will serve as the model for future generations to strive to regain, and there will be new versions of San Francisco in the future, but there will never be another "Our San Francisco" again. I will always see the City as it was in those glorious days, much like I see my wife today – as the young woman beside me at the alter on our wedding day. And although my Holy Name buddies and I changed over time, we still see each other as we were in our youth. Friendships may fade, the City will change, but memories are forever.

Footnotes

1 At least 275 country houses were deliberately burned down, blown up, or otherwise destroyed by the IRA and most were destroyed during the Irish Civil War in 1922-1923. (Source: "Destruction of Irish Country Houses (1919-1923)," Wikipedia Wiki 2, April 8, 2020. https://wiki2.org/en/Destruction_of_Irish_country_houses_(1919%E2%80%931923).

2 James S. Donnelly Jr., "Big House Burnings in County Cork during the Irish Revolution, 1920-21," National University of Ireland, *Éire-Ireland*, volume 47: 3&4, Fall/Winter 2012. http://www.nuigalway.ie/research/centre_irish_studies/documents/0647.34donnelly.pdf.

3 Tom Doyle, *The Civil War in Kerry*, Cork, Ireland: Mercier Press, 2008, p. 230-232.

4 Chris Carlsson, "Mission." Shaping San Francisco's DigitalArchive@Foundsf. http://www.foundsf.org/index.php?title=category:mission.

5 "He was an Irish playwright, author, Commandant of the 1st Cork Brigade of the IRA and the Lord Mayor of Cork. He died after 74 days on a hunger strike in Brixton Prison, England in 1920. His body lay in Southwark Cathedral in London where tens of thousands of people filed past his coffin. His body was brought straight back to his native Cork by Black and Tans who refused mourners the chance to pay their respects in Dublin." (Source: Chris Keane, "Terence MacSwiney," Irish Volunteers Commemorative Organisation, May 24, 2012. https://irishvolunteers.org/terence-macswiney.)

6 The Crystal Palace Market was a massive 71,000-square-foot shopping bazaar with 65 concessionaires all under a glass-latticed dome. It sold items from nearly 40 countries, everything from produce to sporting goods, from shoe repair to locksmith. (Source: Gail MacGowan, "Crystal Palace Market," Shaping San Francisco's DigitalArchive@Foundsf. http://www.foundsf.org/index.php?title=Crystal_Palace_Market.)

7 Deia de Brito, "17 Reasons Remembered," Shaping San Francisco's DigitalArchive@Foundsf, May 29, 2010. Originally published in *Mission Local*. http://www.foundsf.org/index.php?title=17_Reasons_Remembered.

8 They later discovered that these machines were leaking radiation and were banned due to the leaks and potential harm from frequent use of x-rays on the feet. Foot cancer started appearing among many older people years later. (Source: Eric Limer, "The Insane Cancer Machines That Used to Live in Shoe Stores Everywhere," Gizmodo, July 15, 2013. https://gizmodo.com/the-insane-cancer-machines-that-used-to-live-in-shoe-st-789073694.)

9 Paul McHugh, "Why S.F.'s Ocean Beach is Deadly: Several factors make its riptides among strongest," SFGate, *San Francisco Chronicle*, February 3, 2012. https://www.sfgate.com/news/article/Why-S-F-s-Ocean-Beach-is-Deadly-Several-3002654.php.

10 It originally was built as a church but served as a school seven years later. The entire building was converted into a K-8 school in 1916 when St. Charles Church was built around the corner on South Van Ness Avenue. (Source: "San Francisco Landmark #139: Saint Charles School," NobHill in San Francisco, July 16, 1981. https://noehill.com/sf/landmarks/sf139.asp.)

11 After the 1906 earthquake, the well-to-do built fine homes along Guerrero and Dolores Streets, and along South Van Ness Avenue and Folsom Street between 20th and 26th Streets. Many were large Victorian and richly-ornamented Italianate, Stick Style, and Queen Anne cottages and flats. (Source: Charles Lockwood, "Real Estate Speculation Starts," Shaping San Francisco's DigitalArchive@Foundsf. http://www.foundsf.org/index.php?title=REAL_ESTATE_SPECULATION_STARTS.) Even as a kid, I was impressed by the number of Victorian and Italianate homes and flats there were in the neighborhood – many dating back to the 1860s. They seemed out of place in a low-income neighborhood and I could never understand why they were there. I thought it would be nice if there was a movement to come in and renovate them to bring these homes back to their original elegance. Sure enough it happened – 60 years later.

12 Mukti Jain Campion, "How the World Loved the Swastika – Until Hitler Stole It," *BBC News Magazine*, October 23, 2014. https://www.bbc.com/news/magazine-29644591.

13 "Timeline San Francisco 1930-1959," Timelines of History, *San Francisco Chronicle,* January 31, 2003, p. E4. https://www.timelines.ws/cities/SF_C_1930_1959.html.

14 This may have influenced my interest in collecting Native American crafts and dolls later in life.

15 This was the home of the San Francisco Seals who played in the Pacific Coast League. They were a triple-A team for the Brooklyn Dodgers in 1942-1950, New York Yankees (1951-1955) and Boston Red Sox (1956-1957).

16 The seal had a daily diet of three pounds of food, preferably filet of sole. The team eventually sent the mascot back to the aquarium after realizing they knew nothing about raising a sea lion and keeping an eventual 200-300 pound sea lion. (Source: Michael Clair, "Did you know the San Francisco Seals once had an actual, live seal as their mascot?" CUT4 by MLB.com, January 25, 2018. https://www.mlb.com/cut4/san-francisco-seals-once-had-a-real-seal-mascot-c265309538.)

17 Most of the best players for the Seals were before my time: Frank Crosetti, DiMaggio brothers (Joe, Vince and Dom), Lefty Gomez, Joe Gordon, and Lefty O'Doul.

18 San Francisco Lawn Bowling Club was the oldest municipal lawn bowling club with roots back to 1901 (under a different name) when there were separate clubs for men and women, unlike the merged membership in my youth. It was also the largest lawn bowling club in the U.S. (Source: "America's Oldest Lawn Bowling Club Keeps Game Alive In Golden Gate Park," Hoodline, April 20, 2015. https://hoodline.com/2015/04/america-s-oldest-lawn-bowling-club-keeps-game-alive-in-golden-gate-park.)

19 The S.F. Fly Casting Club is the second oldest casting club in the U.S. and had the largest anglers membership club in the world according to one of its members. The casting pools were 90'x180', 185'x180' and 125'x180'. They contained 2 million gallons of water and were the largest in the world. (Source: "History of Golden Gate Angling & Casting Club," GGACC San Francisco. https://www.ggacc.org/history.)

20 Ron Jones, *Life in the Sunset* (Berkeley: Regent Press. 2015), p. 14.

21 The Merry Go Round is currently at Yerba Buena Gardens between 3rd and 4th Streets, between Archive @ Foundsf Folsom and Mission Streets.

22 "A sailor Edward Tobiaski of Chicago, on leave from the war in the Pacific in 1945, rode the Big Dipper in the rear row of seats with Bernice Bernsten. He repeatedly tried to stand up and when the ride was half completed, his head struck a massive support when he stood up, killing him instantly.
That event likely spawned the local legend about a sailor standing up in a car, losing his head and that head landing in the lap of a girl in a car below. (Source: James. R. Smith, "The Big Dipper at Playland at the Beach," History Smith Tales of California and San Francisco. http://www.historysmith.com/tales_pnatb_dipper_01.html.)

23 I heard stories that did not come from Playland experiences like Basketball Shooting that had rims that were a bit smaller than normal or a little oblong; the backboards were made of a material that caused a harder bounce, making the bank shot harder to sink; balls were over-inflated, giving them more bounce. The secret was to go with a high arc for the swish shot. Throwing baseballs at metal bottles stacked in a pyramid-shape was one of the toughest games to beat as it required a strong arm and extremely accurate throws. The game could be rigged by using one or more bottles that were heavier (as much as 10 pounds) than others and usually placed on the bottom of the stack. The stack could be slightly angled and separated, with the heavier bottle towards the back, making a light toss useless. The solution was to throw a hard fastball at the middle of the bottom row and hope brute force worked. There were other games I stayed away from. Throwing darts at balloons could be rigged by using lighter than normal darts, dull points or under-inflated balloons. Rifle shooting at moving ducks and spinning wheels could have tampered gun sights or air guns with reduced air pressure so BBs bounced off the target.

24 Current Results weather and science facts: San Francisco Temperatures: Averages by Month. https://www.currentresults.com/Weather/California/Places/san-francisco-temperatures-by-month-average.php.

25 The girls, charged with cruelty to animals and petty theft, were lucky to get off with six months probation. (Source: Gary Kamiya, "SF Zoo Monkey Island: Depression jobs and fun for humans, mixed bag for animals," *San Francisco Chronicle*, March 8, 2019. https://www.sfchronicle.com/chronicle_vault/article/SF-Zoo-Monkey-Island-Depression-jobs-and-fun-for-13673722.php.)

26 Jonathan H., "Fleishhacker Pool – A Strange Journey Through S.F. History," Bearings, November 23, 2008. www.terrastories.com/bearings/fleishhacker-pool-san-francisco.

27 On November 20, 1951 San Francisco's firemen voted to end their three-year tradition of decorating the City firehouses for Christmas. The firemen gave lack of money as their reason. Many made up the balance of the yearly decorating costs out of their own pockets, and were not in the mood for such contributions when in that month's election a ballot initiative to increase firefighter pay had been defeated." (Source: Christmas Firehouses 1948-1950," OutsideLands.org, Western Neighborhoods Project. https://www.outsidelands.org/xmas-firehouses.php.)

28 The fireplug was repainted gold every year on April 18th to pay tribute to it being the only source

of water for the 300 neighbors who stopped the advancing inferno that saved the Mission District south of 20th Street and to those who fought the Great Fire described as "hell itself"(2,700-degrees at hottest point) caused by the 1906 earthquake, which destroyed 80% of San Francisco's buildings and rendered over 225,000 of the 400,000 residents homeless. (Source: Mike Aldax, "Fire Hydrant Tradition Steeped in Gold," *San Francisco Examiner*, April 15, 2010.)

29 Many years later, the church was used in the Whoopi Goldberg movie *Sister Act.*

30 We grew up with the term "Negro," which was the accepted norm, until the 1960s when Black American leaders like Malcolm X objected to the word "Negro" and preferred "Black" and "Afro-American." Martin Luther King, Jr. had referred to his race as "Negro" in his famous "I Have a Dream" speech in 1962. (Source: http://e.wikipedia.org/wiki/Negro.) In 1988 Jesse Jackson said that Blacks preferred to be called "African-American." (Source: Ben L. Martin, "From Negro to Black to African American: The Power of Names and Naming" *Political Science Quarterly*, Spring, 1991, Vol. 106, No. 1, pp. 83-107. http://www.jstor.org/stable/2152175.

31 "Timeline San Francisco 1930-1959," Timelines of History, *San Francisco Chronicle,* December 28, 2001, WB p. G7. https://www.timelines.ws/cities/SF_C_1930_1959.HTML.

32 "Success & Discontent (1950-1959)," St. Ignatius College Preparatory. https://www.siprep.org/about-us/our-history/success-discontent-1950-1959

33 The large streetcars were boxy and solidly built from steel, brass, glass, and oak hardwood (plastic was not king at the turn of the century). The electric cars could be piloted on both ends by twin controls to assist in reversing their routes; even the back of the seats could be shifted in opposite directions. Right after World War II, there were over 500 of these steel monsters, vintage 1917 rail cars in service. The streetcars ran on two tracks imbedded into the asphalt street and powered electronically through pull-down poles with rollers running along overhead wires that were strung in various forms of disarray above the streets. Both fronts and backs of each car were adorned with heavy metal guardrails that looked like Hitleresque black mustaches when viewed head-on. Today, such guardrails would be confused with bike racks, but in 1917, they served as bumpers along the busy streets congested with unregulated vintage cars and horse or mule-drawn commercial carriages.

34 He was born in 1872 and attended the Philadelphia Dental College (today known as the Temple University School of Dentistry). At the turn of the century, six weeks after graduating, a frustrated Dr. Parker did not have a single patient. Undaunted, the eccentric Parker decided to take to the streets and advertise. He bought a struggling circus and added an unorthodox twist. He called the spectacle "The Parker Dental Circus." It was a traveling medicine show, complete with a dental chair on a horse-drawn carriage and live band. He advertised *painless* dentistry because of a cocaine solution he concocted to numb pain. Parker the showman quickly prospered. But he also drew the attention and ire of the ADA and was sued for advertising painless dentistry, illegal in some states and unethical everywhere according to the condescending ADA. In brazen defiance, Parker changed his legal name to "Painless Parker." (Source: "Painless Parker," Wikipedia, May 3, 2020. https://en.wikipedia.org/wiki/Painless_Parker.)

35 Rolf G. Behrents, "Dr Edgar R. R. Parker: His time and now," *American Journal of Orthodontics and Dentofacial Orthopedics*, October 2015, Vol 148, Issue 4, p. 522. https://www.ajodo.org/article/S0889-5406(15)00945-2/pdf.

36 Joe Hession, "Fists Fly at Kezar Stadium When 49ers Face Philadelphia Eagles," Levi's Stadium, Artifacts of the Game: 49ers vs. Eagles, September 27, 2014. https://www.levisstadium.com/2014/09/artifact-game-49ers-vs-eagles.

37 "Timeline San Francisco 1930-1959," Timelines of History, *San Francisco Chronicle*, July 8, 2005, p. F6. https://www.timelines.ws/cities/SF_C_1930_1959. html.

38 Richard Ben Cramer, *Joe DiMaggio: The Hero's Life* (New York: Simon & Schuster, 2000), p. 40.

39 kaytisweetlandrasmussen83, "Remembering Leroy," Pachofa-Unfinished, August 2018. https://pachofaunfinished.wordpress.com/2018/05/30/remembering-leroy.

40 Ty Cobb set 90 MLB records including a .366 career batting average, held 12 batting titles, scored 2,246 runs, and stole 892 bases (54 while stealing home). (Source: Kate Feldman, "Ty Cobb, by the numbers," *New York Daily News*, December 18, 2015. https://www.nydailynews.com/sports/baseball/ty-cobb-numbers-article-1.2466507.)

41 Jim Gentile helped lead Sacred Heart High School to the AAA City Championships in 1951 and 1952. The L.A. Dodgers paid the 18-year-old $50,000, their highest bonus at the time. (Source: Brent P. Kelley, *Baseball's Biggest Blunder: The Bonus Rule of 1953-1957*, Lanham, MD: Scarecrow Press, December, 1996, p. 15. https://books.google.com/books/about/Baseball_s_Biggest_Blunder.html?id=HYM22SNJbjIC.)

He never got much of a chance with the Dodgers because he was always playing behind Gil Hodges. His best year in the majors was in 1961 with Baltimore when he hit .302, 46 home runs and 141 runs batted in. He finished third in the MVP voting behind Mickey Mantle and Roger Maris. Unfortunately for him, Maris broke Babe Ruth's record by hitting 61 home runs, Mantle hit 54, and Gentile 46, so many of his exploits have been unnoticed by many baseball fans. Sometimes life throws you a hell of a curveball. He hit six grand slams in his career, more than Babe Ruth and Lou Gehrig, played in six All-Star games, and was inducted in the Baltimore Orioles Hall of Fame.
(Source: Cory Stolzenbach, "Jim Gentile," Society for American Baseball Research. https://sabr.org/bioproj/person/jim-gentile.)

42 Mary Brown, *Sunset District Residential Builders, 1925-1950, Historic Context Statement*, San Francisco City Planning, April 3, 2013, p. 45.

43 ibid., p. 51.

44 St. James High School was established in 1907 by the Marianists and affectionately known as "The Old Brickpile" due to its brick exterior. The school was closed down so the faculty and personnel could staff the newly constructed Riordan High School. (Source: T. William Bolts, *Young Men Dream Dreams, Fifty Years of Archbishop Riordan High School San Francisco 1949-1999*, San Francisco: Archbishop Riordan High School. 2000, p. 18.)

45 Riordan was built on a 400' x 1022' (9½ acre) parcel of the Balboa Reservoir lot, equivalent to three residential blocks (300' bought in 1933 by the Roman Catholic Archbishop of San Francisco and 100' in 1947. The total price was $50,000 ($693,000 now). There was evidence that the City did not willingly want to part with such a large piece of property. In 1952, when the Superintendent of Schools for the Roman Catholic Archdiocese of S.F. requested even more reservoir land, the SFPUC Manager of Utilities declined to sell any more of it and responded: "As you know, we sold you the 400-ft. frontage on Phelan Avenue, although we would have much prefer [sic] to have kept it for reservoir purposes." This suggested the sale was forced on the City by some other agency or individual in City government, which may have been a testament to the influence of the Catholic Church in mid-century San Francisco. (Source: "WAVES, West Campus, and Waterless Basins: the History of the Balboa Reservoir 1945-1983," Sunnyside History Project, February 3, 2018. https://sunnysidehistory.org/2018/02/03/waves-west-campus-and-waterless-basins-the-history-of-the-balboa-reservoir-1945-1983.)

46 African-American population in 1950 was 43,402 (5.7%). (Source: Albert S. Broussard, *Black San Francisco: The Struggle for Racial Equality in the West, 1900-1954*, Lawrence, KS: The University of Kansas Press, 1993, p. 205.)

47 "Timeline San Francisco 1930-1959," Timelines of History, *San Francisco Chronicle*, January 26, 2001, WBb p. 4.

48 Today the annual tuition is $20,000 or more at most Catholic high schools in San Francisco and well worth the money in its own right, under the current job market, economy and environment.

49 "Visco Grgich." Wikipedia, October 5, 2019. https://en.wikipedia.org/wiki/Visco_Grgich.

50 Murray R. Nelson, *Bill Russell: A Biography*, Greenwood Biographies Series, Westport, CT: Greenwood Press, 2005.; and "Remembering Ross Giudice 1924-2017." San Francisco Dons Honor Club, July 20, 2017. https://usfdons.com/news/2017/7/20/dons-honor-club-usf-basketball-great-ross-giudice-passes-away.aspx.

51 James W. Johnson, *The Dandy Dons*. Lincoln, NE: University of Nebraska Press, 2009, pp. 197-8.

52 The Junior Museum was located on a section of San Francisco City College and occupied a former city jailhouse next to the Ingleside Police Station and barn.

53 Robert T. Kiyosaki, *Why "A" Students Work for "C" Students and "B" Students Work for the Government: Rich Dad's Guide to Financial Education for Parents*. Scottsdale, AZ: Plata Publishing, 2012.

54 Edwin Kiester, "11 Secret Habits of Straight-A Students Even Post-Grads Will Want to Steal." *Reader's Digest*, September 21, 2018. https://www.rd.com/list/straight-a-students-secrets.

55 Ross Giudice left Riordan after our junior year, took over as head basketball coach at USF for a year, then chose to focus on running his Brown's Furniture business in the City. (Source: "Remembering Ross Giudice 1924-2017." San Francisco Dons Honor Club, July 20, 2017. https://usfdons.com/news/2017/7/20/dons-honor-club-usf-basketball-great-ross-giudice-passes-away.aspx.)

56 "Timeline San Francisco 1930-1959." Timelines of History, *San Francisco Chronicle*, February 25, 2005, p. F4. https://www.timelines.ws/cities/SF_C_1930_1959.html.

57 Paul Munsey and Cory Suppes,"Kezar Stadium," Stadiums by Munsey & Suppes, About Ballparks.com. http://football.ballparks.com/NFL/SanFrancisco49ers/oldindex.htm.

58 "Kezar Stadium," Fandom, American Football Wiki. https://americanfootball.fandom.com/wiki/Kezar_Stadium.

59 The sports world was shocked that a tiny school from San Francisco and a small conference could be so dominant. They had players Bill Russell, K.C. Jones, Hal Perry, Carl Boldt, Mike Farmer and Gene Brown during that period. The Dons won 60 consecutive games from 1954-56. In 1955 and 1956, All-everything Bill Russell lead them to two consecutive NCAA championships. In the 1955 game, USF won the 17th NCAA basketball championship over LaSalle 77-63. Bill Russell scored 23 and set a 5-game tournament record of 118 points. (Source: "Timeline San Francisco 1930-1959," Timelines of History, San Francisco Chronicle, March 18, 2005, p. F6. https://www.timelines.ws/cities/SF_C_1930_1959. html.)

60 Randy Shaw, "Celebrating Warren Hinckle, Journalist Who Brought Heat to Thousands of SF Tenants," BeyondChron, August 26, 2016. http://beyondchron.org/celebrating-warren-hinckle-journalist-brought-heat-thousands-sf-tenants.

61 Jack Seddon, "Tiger Woods Reveals the Exercise that 'Destroyed' His Body," interview with GolfTV, GolfMagic, May 1, 2020. https://www.golfmagic.com/golf-news/tiger-woods-reveals-exercise-destroyed-his-body.

62 Landmark Designation Report, San Francisco Planning Department, May 10, 2013, pg. 30. https://default.sfplanning.org/Preservation/landmarks_designation/Approved_Doelger_Final_LM_Report.pdf.

63 At the end of WWII, the property was leased to City College of San Francisco to provide housing and classrooms for students including the flood of returning veterans wanting to enroll in college. It became CCSF's West Campus. Fifty-three percent of the students were veterans in 1946. In 1955 the 10-year lease was up with the City's Public Utilities Commission that planned to build a reservoir there, so all the buildings and barracks had to be dismantled or demolished. (Source: Austin White, "Seventy Years of Making Dreams into Reality," City College of San Francisco, 2005, pp. 10-11. https://www.ccsf.edu/en/about-city-college/marketing_publications/history_of_city_college/_jcr_content/contentparsys/documentlink/file.res/History%20of%20City%20College%20of%20San%20Francisco.pdf.)

64 This $5 million reservoir served as a parking lot for Riordan and City College for over 60 years. Riordan students also used it at night as an out of the way dark place for their underage drinking. (Source: "WAVES, West Campus, and Waterless Basins: the History of the Balboa Reservoir 1945-1983," Sunnyside History Project, February 3, 2018 https://sunnysidehistory.org/2018/02/03/waves-west-campus-and-waterless-basins-the-history-of-the-balboa-reservoir-1945-1983.)

65 3,715 out of 13,979 (27%) Sea Cliff residents were Jewish. (Source: Fred Massarik, The Jewish Population of San Francisco, Marin County and The Peninsula 1959 (San Francisco: Jewish Welfare Federation of San Francisco, Marin County & The Peninsula. 1959), p. 7. https://www.bjpa.org/content/upload/bjpa/the_/THE%20JEWISH%20POPULATION%20OF%20SAN%20FRANCISCO%20MARIN%20COUNTY%20AND%20THE%20PENINSULA%201959.pdf.)

66 "A survey of individuals at the level of Executive Vice President of 75 Fortune 500 companies showed that 95% of them played sports in high school. While it might be hard to argue that sports participation could guarantee higher incomes, promotions, and better jobs, the leadership skills and development of teamwork, hard work, and determination might help prepare students to be leaders at work and in their communities later in life." (Source: David Geier, "The Benefits of Playing Sports Aren't Just Physical!" Dr. David Geier. https://www.drdavidgeier.com/benefits-sports.)

67 Herb Caen coined the name "beatnik" in his San Francisco Chronicle column on April 2, 1958 by combining "beat generation" and the Russian "Sputnik" satellite for implying those free spirits may be pro-communists. (Source: Jesse Hamlin, "How Herb Caen Named a Generation," SFGate, San Francisco Chronicle, November 26, 1995. https://www.sfgate.com/entertainment/article/how-herb-caen-named-a-generation-3018725.php.)

68 Reno Taini went on to create the innovative Wilderness School for at-risk teenagers to increase their confidence, to help them stay in school, and to teach them: "Responsibility is the key to success. I want my kids to do something with their ability. Seize an opportunity. Roll up their sleeves and make things happen. Take responsibility for yourself." Reno earned master's and doctorate degrees and taught at Jefferson Union High School in Daly City all his life. He received the San Francisco State University College of Education's Golden Torch Award, was part of NASA's Teacher in Space Program, worked with relief agencies around the world to help young

refugees, and was featured in the TV documentary "Reno's Kids." (Source: Ted DeAdwyler, "Reno Taini, Creator of the Innovative Wilderness School, to Represent SFSU During CSU's Year of Celebrating Teachers," San Francisco State Univ. Public Affairs Press Release, May 24, 1999.
https://www.sfsu.edu/~news/prsrelea/fy98/081.htm.)

69 Frank Dunnigan, "Streetwise: Pleated Skirts and Starched Collars," OutsideLands.org, Western Neighborhoods Project, September 2014.
https://www.outsidelands.org/streetwise_school_uniforms.php.

70 The Lafayette Manufacturing Co. located on Galvez Street in San Francisco did plaster ornamentation on many San Francisco famous buildings such as the major renovation of the Palace of Fine Arts, which included the exterior ornamentation and the interior rotunda ceiling, which Maurice personally worked on. Although the company no longer exists, it is ironic that there is an equestrian statue of Lafayette in the rotunda of the Palace, which will forever link the Lafayette family name to the Palace. The statue by Paul Wayland Bartlett is a replica of the original work that stands in the gardens of the Louvre honoring the French military officer that lead American troops in the American Revolutionary War. (Statue picture: "Fine Arts Rotunda Showing Lafayette Statue," Calisphere, University of California Online Archive.
https://calisphere.org/item/ark:/13030/k64174xd.)

71 "1959/05/07 Albert Kogler - California," Shark Attack Survivors, June 23, 2008.
https://www.sharkattacksurvivors.com/shark_attack/viewtopic.php?t=1093.

72 Following the 1962 NCAA World Series, Ernie Fazio was the first player drafted by the Houston Colt .45's. He played in 141 major league games. His first major league home run was off Hall of Famer Warren Spahn of the Milwaukee (Atlanta) Braves. Coincidently, Fazio was in a trade to the Kansas City Athletics for slugger Jim Gentile [small world!]. (Source: "Ernie Fazio's Meteoric Rise to a Major League Baseball Career," The Baseball Historian, December 4, 2016.
http://baseballhistorian.blogspot.com/2016/12/ernie-fazios-meteoric-rise-to-major.html.)

73 Benjamin Hardy, "10 Reasons Why C Students Are More Successful After Graduation," Observer, February 18, 2016.
https://observer.com/2016/02/10-reasons-why-c-students-are-more-successful-after-graduation.

74 The adventure, exploits, challenges and experiences by Dr. Ricardo and María Teresa Cañas from their years of insurgency in El Salvador to their years in San Francisco and their eventual return to El Salvador are detailed in the recent book by their son, Richard L. Cañas, *Choosing Exile 1930-1950*, Bloomington, IN: Authorhouse Publishing Company, 2020.

75 Among Richard L. Cañas books based on his personal experiences include *Shift - The End of the War on Drugs, The Beginning of the War on Terrorism*, Bloomington, IN: Authorhouse Publishing Company, 2014.

Bibliographies

Articles

Aldax, Mike. "Fire Hydrant Tradition Steeped in Gold." *San Francisco Examiner* April 15, 2010.

America's Oldest Lawn Bowling Club Keeps Game Alive In Golden Gate Park." Hoodline April 20, 2015. https://hoodline.com/2015/04/america-s-oldest-lawn-bowling-club-keeps-game-alive-in-golden-gate-park.

Campion, Mukti Jain. "How the World Loved the Swastika – Until Hitler Stole It." *BBC News Magazine*, October 23, 2014. https://www.bbc.com/news/magazine-29644591.

Carlsson, Chris. "Mission." Shaping San Francisco's Digital Age@Foundsf. http://www.foundsf.org/index.php?title=category:mission.

"Christmas Firehouses 1948-1950." OutsideLands.org, Western Neighborhoods Project. https://www.outsidelands.org/xmas-firehouses.php.

Clair, Michael. "Did you know the San Francisco Seals once had an actual, live seal as their mascot?" CUT4 by MLB.com, January 25, 2018. https://www.mlb.com/cut4/san-francisco-seals-once-had-a-real-seal-mascot-c265309538.

DeAdwyler, Ted, "Reno Taini, Creator of the Innovative Wilderness School, to Represent SFSU During CSU's Year of Celebrating Teachers," San Francisco State University Public Affairs Press Release, May 24, 1999. https://www.sfsu.edu/~news/prsrelea/fy98/081.htm.

de Brito, Deia. "17 Reasons Remembered." Shaping San Francisco's Digital Archive@Foundsf, May 29, 2010. Originally published in *Mission Local*. http:// www.foundsf.org/index.php?title=17_Reasons_Remembered.

"Destruction of Irish Country Houses (1919-1923)." Wikipedia Wiki 2, April 8, 2020. https://wiki2.org/en/Destruction_of_Irish_country_houses_(1919–1923).

Donnelly Jr., James S. "Big House Burnings in County Cork during the Irish Revolution, 1920-21." National University of Ireland, *Éire-Ireland*, volume 47: 3&4, Fall/Winter 2012. http://www.nuigalway.ie/research/centre_irish_studies/documents/0647.34donnelly.pdf.

Dunnigan, Frank. "Streetwise: Pleated Skirts and Starched Collars." Outside Lands.org, Western Neighborhoods Project, September 2014. https:// www.outsidelands.org/streetwise_school_uniforms.php.

"Ernie Fazio's Meteoric Rise to a Major League Baseball Career." The Baseball Historian, December 4, 2016. http://baseballhistorian.blogspot.com/2016/12/ernie-fazios-meteoric-rise-to-major.html.

Feldman, Kate. "Ty Cobb, by the numbers." *New York Daily News*, December 18, 2015. https://www.nydailynews.com/sports/baseball/ty-cobb-numbers-article-1.2466507.

Geier, David. "The Benefits of Playing Sports Aren't Just Physical!" Dr. David Geier. https://www.drdavidgeier.com/benefits-sports.

H., Jonathan. "Fleishhacker Pool – A Strange Journey Through S.F. History." Bearings, November 23, 2008. http://www.terrastories.com/bearings/fleishhacker-pool-san-francisco.

Hamlin, Jesse. "How Herb Caen Named a Generation." SFGate, *San Francisco*

Chronicle, November 26, 1995. https://www.sfgate.com/entertainment/article/how-herb-caen-named-a-generation-3018725.php.

Hardy, Benjamin. "10 Reasons Why C Students Are More Successful After Graduation." Observer, February 18, 2016. https://observer.com/2016/02/10-reasons-why-c-students-are-more-successful-after-graduation.

Hession, Joe. "Fists Fly at Kezar Stadium When 49ers Face Philadelphia Eagles." Levi's Stadium, Artifacts of the Game: 49ers vs. Eagles, September 27, 2014. https://www.levisstadium.com/2014/09/artifact-game-49ers-vs-eagles.

"History of Golden Gate Angling & Casting Club." GGACC San Francisco. https://www.ggacc.org/history.

Kamiya, Gary. "SF Zoo Monkey Island: Depression jobs and fun for humans, mixed bag for animals." *San Francisco Chronicle*, March 8, 2019. https://www.sfchronicle.com/chronicle_vault/article/sf-zoo-monkey-island-depression-jobs-and-fun-for-13673722.php.

kaytisweetlandrasmussen83. "Remembering Leroy." Pachofa-Unfinished, August 2018. https://pachofaunfinished.wordpress.com/2018/05/30/remembering-leroy

Keane, Chris. "Terence MacSwiney." Irish Volunteers Commemorative Organisation, May 24, 2012. https://irishvolunteers.org/terence-macswiney.

"Kezar Stadium." Fandom, American Football Wiki. https://americanfootball.fandom.com/wiki/Kezar_Stadium.

Kiester, Edwin. "11 Secret Habits of Straight-A Students Even Post-Grads Will Want to Steal." *Reader's Digest*, September 21, 2018. https://www.rd.com/list/straight-a-students-secrets.

Limer, Eric. "The Insane Cancer Machines That Used to Live in Shoe Stores Everywhere." Gizmodo, July 15, 2013. https://gizmodo.com/the-insane-cancer-machines-that-used-to-live-in-shoe-st-789073694.

Lookwood, Charles. "Real Estate Speculation Starts." Shaping San Francisco's Digital Age@Foundsf. http://www.foundsf.org/index.php?title=REAL_ESTATE_SPECULATION_STARTS.

MacGowan, Gail. "Crystal Palace Market." Shaping San Francisco's Digital Age @Foundsf. http://www.foundsf.org/index.php?title=Crystal_Palace_Market.

Martin, Ben L., "From Negro to Black to African American: The Power of Names and Naming." *Political Science Quarterly*, Spring, 1991, Vol. 106, No. 1, pp. 83-107. http://www.jstor.org/stable/2152175.

McCloy, Mary. "The Irish in San Francisco." United Irish Societies of San Francisco. 2016. http://uissf.org/history/the-irish-in-san-francisco.

Munsey, Paul and Cory Suppes. "Kezar Stadium." Stadiums by Munsey Suppes, About Ballparks.com. http://football.ballparks.com/NFL/SanFrancisco49ers/oldindex.htm.

"1959/05/07 Albert Kogler - California." Shark Attack Survivors, June 23, 2008, https://www.sharkattacksurvivors.com/shark_attack/viewtopic.php?t=1093.

"Painless Parker." Wikipedia, May 3, 2020. https://en.wikipedia.org/wiki/Painless_Parker.

"Remembering Ross Giudice 1924-2017." San Francisco Dons Honor Club, July 20, 2017. https://usfdons.com/news/2017/7/20/dons-honor-club-usf-basketball-great-ross-giudice-passes-away.aspx.

"San Francisco Landmark #139: Saint Charles School." NobHill in San Francisco July 16, 1981. https://noehill.com/sf/landmarks/sf139.asp.

Seddon, Jack. "Tiger Woods Reveals the Exercise that 'Destroyed' His Body." Interview with GolfTV. GolfMagic, May 1, 2020. https://www.golfmagic. com/golf-news/tiger-woods-reveals-exercise-destroyed-his-body.

Shaw, Randy. "Celebrating Warren Hinckle, Journalist Who Brought Heat to Thousands of SF Tenants." *BeyondChron*, August 26, 2016. http://beyond chron.org/celebrating-warren-hinckle-journalist-brought-heat-thousands-sf-tenants.

Smith, James R. "The Big Dipper at Playland at the Beach." History Smith Tales of California and San Francisco. http://www.historysmith.com/tales_pnatb_dipper_01.html.

Stolzenbach, Cory. "Jim Gentile." Society for American Baseball Research, https://sabr.org/bioproj/person/jim-gentile.

"Visco Grgich." Wikipedia, October 5, 2019. https://en.wikipedia.org/wiki/Visco_Grgich.

White, Austin. "Seventy Years of Making Dreams into Reality." City College of San Francisco, 2005. https://www.ccsf.edu/en/about-city-college/marketing_publications/history_of_city_college/_jcr_content/contentparsys/documentlink/file.res/History%20of%20City%20College%20of%20San%20Francisco.pdf.

Books

Bolts, T. William. *Young Men Dream Dreams, Fifty Years of Archbishop Riordan High School San Francisco 1949-1999*. San Francisco: Archbishop Riordan High School. 2000.

Broussard, Albert S. *Black San Francisco: The Struggle for Racial Equality in the West, 1900-1954*. Lawrence, KS: The University of Kansas Press. 1993.

Cañas, Richard L. *Choosing Exile 1930-1950*. Bloomington, IN: Authorhouse Publishing Company. 2020.

Cañas, Richard L. *Shift - The End of the War on Drugs, The Beginning of the War on Terrorism*. Bloomington, IN: Authorhouse Publishing Company. 2014.

Cramer, Richard Ben. *Joe DiMaggio: The Hero's Life*. New York: Simon & Schuster. 2000.

Dunnigan, Frank. *Growing Up in San Francisco's Western Neighborhoods*. Charleston: The History Press. 2014.

Hannigan, Dave. *Terence MacSwiney: The Hunger Strike that Rocked an Empire*. Dublin: The O'Brien Press. 2010.

Johnson, James W. *The Dandy Dons*. Lincoln, NE: University of Nebraska Press. 2009.

Jones, Ron. *Life in the Sunset*. Berkeley: Regent Press. 2015.

Kiyosaki, Robert T. *Why "A" Students Work for "C" Students and "B" Students Work for the Government: Rich Dad's Guide to Financial Education for Parents*. Scottsdale, AZ: Plata Publishing. 2012.

Massarik, Fred. *The Jewish Population of San Francisco, Marin County and The Peninsula 1959*. San Francisco: Jewish Welfare Federation of San Francisco, Marin County & The Peninsula. 1959, p. 7. https://www.bjpa.org/content/upload/bjpa/the_/THE%20JEWISH%20POPULATION%20OF%20SAN%20FRANCISCO%20MARIN%20COUNTY%20AND%20THE%20PENINSU-LA%201959.pdf.

Nelson, Murray R. *Bill Russell: A Biography*, Greenwood Biographies Series, Westport, CT: Greenwood Press. 2005.

Smith, James R. *San Francisco's Lost Landmarks*. Sanger, CA: Word Dancer Press. 2005.

Newspapers

Crusader, Archbishop Riordan High School, 1954-1959.
San Francisco Chronicle, 1954-1959.
San Francisco Examiner, 1954-1959.

Obituaries

"Tim Applebee, b. 19 June 1940, d. 24 July 2008" obituary. Our Family History: We Lived on the Hill, So. Tuolumne Co. Hist. Society. https://stchsgenealogy.com/p285.htm.

Photographs

"Fine Arts Rotunda Showing Lafayette Statue." Calisphere, University of California Online Archive. https://calisphere.org/item/ark:/13030/k64174xd.

Reports

Brown, Mary. *Sunset District Residential Builders, 1925-1950, Historic Context Statement*. San Francisco City Planning Department, April 3, 2013 pp. 45 and 51. https://commissions.sfplanning.org/hpcpackets/2013.0313U.pdf.

Landmark Designation Report. San Francisco Planning Department, May 10, 2013, pg. 30.https://default.sfplanning.org/Preservation/landmarks_designation/Approved_Doelger_Final_LM_Report.pdf.

Websites

Current Results weather and science facts: San Francisco Temperatures: Averages by Month. https://www.currentresults.com/Weather/California/Places/san-francisco-temperatures-by-month-average.php.

San Francisco Heritage, http://www.sfheritage.org/legacy.

Sproul, Ken. "Growing Up in San Francisco Memories: Boyhood Recollections from the 1940s and 1950s." San Francisco History Boyhood Recollections, April 1910. https://www.sfgenealogy.com/sf/history/hgsproul.htm.

"Timeline San Francisco 1930-1959." Timelines of History, *San Francisco Chronicle*. https://www.timelines.ws/cities/SF_C_1930_1959.html.

Western Neighborhoods Project - San Francisco History, https://www.outside-lands.org.

Yearbooks

Archbishop Riordan High School. *Lance (1955-1958)*. San Francisco: Archbishop Riordan High School. 1955-1958.

Acknowledgement

This book was a collaborative effort thanks to classmates at Holy Name of Jesus Grammar School and Archbishop Riordan High School in the City of San Francisco. The following Riordan 1958 classmates deserve special thanks for their significant contribution to this book:

Terence Quinlan	Arthur Curtis
Richard Canas	Maurice Lafayette
Barry Sullivan	Noel Murray

Our thanks also go out to those who generously shared their stories:

Holy Name Grammar School:

Timothy Carmody ('61)	Nancy Koch ('54)
Michael Chapman ('54)	William Nocetti ('54)
Norma Haller ('54)	Bonnie Pischoff ('54)

Archbishop Riordan High School:

William Andrick ('58)	Richard Kirby ('58)
Dennis Beyma ('58)	Ronald Macaluso ('58)
Raymon Calderaro ('58)	Warren McCausland ('58)
Robert Connelly ('59)	Guido Mori-Prange ('58)
Dennis Creedon ('58)	Paul Scannell ('58)
Thomas Dekker ('58)	David Sereni ('58)
John Galten ('59)	David Shrieve ('59)
Gerald Hipps ('58)	Reno Taini ('59)
Robert Joyce ('59)	Richard Thall ('58)

We are also indebted to Archbishop Riordan High School for the generous access to their archieves, but most importantly, for their discipline, education and opportunities to stumble along the way, to pick ourselves up, to learn from our mistakes, to excel in so many ways in preparing us to do our best on the paths we took down the road. My personal thanks and love to my wife and editor, Susan Quinlan.

General Index

512

514

516

469-470
meals, 191-192, 200
prejudice, dealing with, 187, 193-194, 198, 199-201
pride, 183, 188, 193-194, 400, 446, 469-470
terrorism, fleeing, 185-187, 190, 193, 198, 199, 202, 205-206, 207
sandbox, 5, 11, 12, 14, 33, 62, 68, 84, 85, 163, 287, 288, 365, 374, 383, 385, 480, 481, 484, 487, 492, 494
San Francisco. *See also* pride *under* building character
  attractions, City. *See* Names of Places Index, 407
  attractions, nearby. *See* Names of Places Index
  Bay to Breakers Race, 335
  businesses and stores. *See* Names of Places Index
  Daly City Earthquake (1957), 401-402
  movie theater location, 29, 93, 164, 202, 333-334, 407, 464
  restaurants and bars. *See* Names of Places Index
  safety, 88, 115, 128-129, 160, 168, 205, 493
  schools and churches. *See* Names of Places Index
  Shangri-La and Camelot, 493-494
  street addresses. *See* Street Addresses Index
  street layout, 163-164
  streets and neighborhoods. *See* Names of Places Index
  theaters and drive-ins. *See* Names of Places Index
  traffic, 115, 116, 169, 493
  uniqueness (1940s and 1950s), 493-494
San Francisco Chronicle, 47, 64, 192, 238, 280, 359
  column, "It's News to Me", 238
San Francisco Examiner, 47, 64, 244, 280, 359, 404-405, 444, 478
San Francisco Fire Department, 116, 130, 166, 222-223, 314
  firemen, 116, 222-223
San Francisco 49ers
  "Alley Oop" pass, 332, 438
  fans, rowdy, 239-240
  first home game (1946), 221
  "Million Dollar Backfield", 332
  players. *See also* Names of People Index, 240, 304, 332, 398
  playoffs, 1957 Western Division Conference, 332
San Francisco Municipal Railway (Muni), 16, 164, 192, 315, 426
  fares, 94, 165, 290
  kid-friendly, 71, 290, 316
  N-Judah streetcar, 165, 210, 214, 224-225, 290, 348, 418, 467-468
    maiden voyage, 224
  rush hour, 94, 165, 467

72-Sunset bus, 165, 332
  student car ticket, 71, 165, 290, 316
San Francisco Park & Recreation Department, 132-133, 141
San Francisco Seals, 271, 307, 403, 469-470, 494
  mascot, 89
  stadium, 88-90, 308, 396, 469-470
  smells, 89
self-defense
  benefit of beating, 127
  fistfights, 35, 126-127, 159, 182, 191, 224, 239-240, 316-317, 356, 363, 414
    standards, 354, 388
selfishness, 65, 112, 119, 126, 165, 373, 466, 470
sex
  abstinence, 54, 372, 373, 459-460, 463
  biological changes, 205, 212
  education, 88, 208-209, 463-464
  experiences, 24-25, 62, 131, 159, 205, 231, 264, 350, 352, 431, 459-460, 462-464, 465-466
  nudity attitude, 15, 111, 231, 419, 465, 466-467
  pinups, 169-170, 231, 234, 419
  stories, 264, 352
Sherwood, Don, 180
  "World's Greatest Disc Jockey", 180
shyness, 16, 133, 182, 240, 259, 273, 278, 284, 289, 291, 320, 323, 326, 371, 372, 373, 390, 397, 400, 421, 436, 453, 456, 457, 458, 460, 462, 464
siblings
  admiration, 83, 135, 280, 330, 376
  attitude toward, 18, 27, 112, 113-114, 118, 146, 150-152, 155, 280, 329- 330, 373-374
  experiences shared, 7, 27, 28, 30, 35, 37, 45, 50-51, 53, 69, 83, 88, 102- 103, 110-111, 113, 133, 135, 140-141, 144, 146, 157-158, 170, 186, 188,191, 192, 193, 197, 198, 201, 203, 207, 208, 211, 218, 219, 229, 231, 232-233, 235, 241, 245, 256, 280, 329-330, 348, 364, 387, 464
skid row, 87-88, 128-129
  hobos, 86-87, 128-129, 222
skills, social
  communication, verbal, 44, 130, 146, 250-251, 253, 296-297, 308, 310-311, 321-323, 373, 448, 457, 460, 484
  communication, written, 40-41, 150, 219-220, 239, 296, 305, 308, 310-311, 318, 323-324, 353-354, 390-391
  dances, school, 325, 370-371, 372-373, 392-393, 453, 456-457
  debating, 380, 401
  job-related, 120, 282-286
  speech competition, 380, 401, 448
  speech-making, 44, 250-251, 296-297, 308, 322, 323, 355-356, 429, 480-481
songs. *See* Songs in the Names of Places Index

518

Names of People Index

523

Uris, Leon, 239

Names of Places, Attractions
and Entertainment Index

Street Addresses Index

Sunset District (continued)
Terry Quinlan (2nd home)
3120 Kirkham Street
Tim Applebee
1818 - 35th Avenue

Westwood Park District
Riordan High School
175 (Phelan Ave.) Frida Kahlo Way

Downtown San Francisco
Crystal Palace Market
1175 Market Street
Hirsch & Price Sports Store
41 Sutter Street
McCarthy's Bar
67 - 4th Street
Mel's Drive-In
140 South Van Ness Avenue
O'Connor, Moffat & Co.
101 Stockton Street
Sally Sanford Brothel
1144 Pine Street